Paul Bishop
The Dionysian Self

Monographien und Texte zur Nietzsche-Forschung

Begründet von

Mazzino Montinari · Wolfgang Müller-Lauter
Heinz Wenzel

Herausgegeben von

Ernst Behler · Eckhard Heftrich
Wolfgang Müller-Lauter
Jörg Salaquarda · Josef Simon

Band 30

1995

Walter de Gruyter · Berlin · New York

The Dionysian Self

C. G. Jung's Reception of Friedrich Nietzsche

by

Paul Bishop

1995

Walter de Gruyter · Berlin · New York

Anschriften der Herausgeber:
Prof. Dr. Ernst Behler
Comparative Literature GN-32
University of Washington
Seattle, Washington 98195, U.S.A.
Prof. Dr. Eckhard Heftrich
Germanistisches Institut der Universität Münster
Domplatz 20–22, D–4400 Münster
Prof. Dr. Wolfgang Müller-Lauter
Klopstockstraße 27, D-1000 Berlin 37
Prof. Dr. Jörg Salaquarda (geschäftsführend)
Institut für Systematische Theologie der Universität Wien
Rooseveltplatz 10, A-1090 Wien
Prof. Dr. Josef Simon
Philosophisches Seminar A der Universität Bonn
Am Hof 1, D-53113 Bonn

Library of Congress Cataloging-in-Publication Data

Bishop, Paul, 1967–
The Dionysian self : C. G. Jung's reception of Friedrich Nietzsche by Paul Bishop.
p. cm. – (Monographien und Texte zur Nietzsche-Forschung ; Bd. 30)
Includes bibliographical references and index.
ISBN 3-11-014709-2
1. Jung, C. G. (Carl Gustav), 1875–1961. 2. Nietzsche, Friedrich Wilhelm, 1844–1900–Influence. I. Title. II. Series.
BF109.J8B57 1995
150.19'54'092–dc20 95-32811
CIP

Die Deutsche Bibliothek – Cataloging-in-Publication Data

Bishop, Paul:
The Dionysian self : C. G. Jung's reception of Friedrich Nietzsche / by Paul Bishop. – Berlin ; New York : de Gruyter, 1995
(Monographien und Texte zur Nietzsche-Forschung ; Bd. 30)
Zugl.: Diss.
ISBN 3-11-014709-2
NE: GT

Printed in Germany
Disc conversion and Printing: Arthur Collignon GmbH, Berlin
Binding: Lüderitz & Bauer, Berlin

For
Jenny

Im echten Manne ist ein Kind versteckt: das will spielen [...] Unschuld ist das Kind und Vergessen, ein Neubeginnen, ein Spiel, ein aus sich rollendes Rad, eine erste Bewegung, ein heiliges Ja-sagen.

[*A child is concealed in the true man: it wants to play ... The child is innocence and forgetfulness, a new beginning, a game, a self-propelling wheel, a first motion, a sacred Yes-saying.*]

(Nietzsche, Z I 18/Z I 1)

Im Erwachsenen steckt nämlich ein Kind, ein ewiges Kind, ein immer noch Werdendes, nie Fertiges, das beständiger Pflege, Aufmerksamkeit und Erziehung bedürfte. Das ist der Teil der menschlichen Persönlichkeit, der sich zur Ganzheit entwickeln möchte.

[*For in every adult there lurks a child – an eternal child, something that is always becoming, is never completed, and calls for unceasing care, attention, and education. That is the part of the human personality which wants to develop and become whole.*]

Jung, GW 17 § 286)

Acknowledgements

My greatest debt is to my doctoral supervisor, Dr. Richard Sheppard, who generously spent time on early drafts of my chapters and gave much useful and helpful advice. My thanks are due also to Professor Jeremy Adler and Dr. Ritchie Robertson, who read through an earlier version of the text as a doctoral thesis. And for their contribution to my knowledge of Jung, I should like to acknowledge Dr. Anthony Storr, whose general support and whose advice on Jungian matters were much appreciated; and Dr. Robert Currie, whose lectures first showed me the value of an intellectual-historical approach to Jung.

During the course of my research, I have used various institutions and archives, and in this connection I should like to acknowledge the assistance of the following people and institutions: first and foremost, Ms Jill Hughes, of the Taylorian Institution Library, Oxford, for her invaluable advice and encouragement; Dr. Beat Glaus, Wissenschaftshistorische Sammlungen, E. T. H.-Bibliothek, Zurich; Ms Ellie Stillman and Frau Kopecky, library of the C. G. Jung-Institut, Zurich; Frau Gudrun Seel, library of the Psychologischer Club, Zurich; Dr. Josef Zwicker, Staatsarchiv, Basle; Society of Analytical Psychology, London; Ms Doris Albrecht, Kristine Mann Library, Analytical Psychology Club of New York; International Association for Analytical Psychology, Zurich; Österreichische Nationalbibliothek, Vienna. I am also grateful to have had access to the rich resources of the Widener Library, Harvard University; the British Library, London; and the Bodleian Library, Oxford.

I am very grateful to Herr Franz Jung for giving me access to C. G. Jung's library in Küsnacht and allowing me to transcribe Jung's annotations in his copies of Nietzsche's *Werke*. Dr. Peter Jung and the Erbengemeinschaft C. G. Jung have kindly given me permission to quote from these and other unpublished sources.

In addition, the following people have offered useful information or advice, which I should like to acknowledge here: Mrs. Eveline Bennet; Frau Corniela Brunner-Scharpf; Dr. Liliane Frey-Rohn; Dr. Joseph Henderson; Dr. James Hillman; Frau Manuela Jaeger; the late Frau Aniela Jaffé; Dr. James Jarrett; Mr. William McGuire; Dr. C. A. Meier; Professor Micha Neumann; Dr. Tadeus Reichstein; Mr. Sonu Shamdasani; Dr. Marie-Louise von Franz; and Dr. Joseph and Mrs. Jane Wheelwright.

My research was conducted at Oxford University and Harvard University, for which financial support was provided by the British Academy and by the Lady Julia Henry Fellowship Foundation. In both the Faculty of Medieval and Modern Languages and Literature at Oxford and in the Germanic Department at Harvard I have met congenial company, which stimulated further my interest in my work and eased the task of writing. Research in Zurich was funded by travel grants from the British Academy and from Magdalen College, Oxford. I should like to thank these funding bodies for their support.

Finally, I should like to thank my parents for all their assistance and encouragement. I am particularly grateful to Jennifer Leeder, both for her help with proof-reading various drafts, including the final one, and for her assistance with classical references. Many thanks are also due to the following, for proof-reading, suggestions, help with printing, useful tips and the like: David Cowling; Vicky Lewis; Patrick McGuinness; Kelly Mulroney; Clara Seeger; Leif Wenar; and, above all, David Groiser and Karl Leydecker. The index was prepared with great efficiency by Ms Christine Shuttleworth. Last but not least, it is my pleasure to have completed work on this book amongst my new colleagues in the Department for German Language and Literature and the Centre for Intercultural Germanistics at the University of Glasgow.

In this book, I use material which has earlier appeared in the following articles:

'The Jung/Förster-Nietzsche Correspondence', *German Life and Letters*, 46 (1993);
'The Members of Jung's Seminar on *Zarathustra*', *Spring: A Journal of Archetype and Culture*, 56 (1994);
'Jung's Annotations of Nietzsche's Works: An Analysis', *Nietzsche-Studien*, 24 (1995).

I am grateful to the publishers of these journals for permission to use this material.

March 1995 Paul Bishop

Contents

Acknowledgements IX

Abbreviations XIII

Chapter 1: Introduction 1

Chapter 2: Jung's Early Reception of Nietzsche 21

Chapter 3: Jung's Reception of Nietzsche: The Letters and the Autobiography 43

Chapter 4: Jung's Early Reception of Nietzsche in his Psychoanalytic Writings (1902–1917) 83

Chapter 5: Jung's Reception of Nietzsche in *Psychologische Typen* 124

Chapter 6: Jung's Reception of Nietzsche in his Writings 1922–1934 1: Nietzsche and the Art of Dionysos 156

Chapter 7: Jung's Reception of Nietzsche in his Writings 1922–1934 2: Nietzsche, Freud and Psychology 187

Chapter 8: Jung's Reception of Nietzsche in Three Eranos Lectures: Dionysos and the Alchemical Nietzsche 211

Chapter 9: The Early Seminars (1925–1934) 243

Chapter 10: Jung's Seminar on Nietzsche (1934–1939): Part 1: General Analysis 266

Chapter 11: Jung's Seminar on Nietzsche (1934–1939): Part 2: Later Themes of Jungian Psychology in the Seminar 283

Chapter 12: Jung's Reception of Nietzsche in his Writings 1935–1945: Wotan – the Shadow of Dionysos 298

Chapter 13: The Mystic Dionysos: Nietzsche, Jung, and the Death of God 323

Chapter 14: Conclusion 364

Bibliography 380

Index 397

Abbreviations

Jung

The following abbreviations are used to refer to editions, works, and translations:

GW = *Gesammelte Werke*, edited by Lilly Jung-Merker, Elisabeth Rüf and Leonie Zander, 18 volumes (Olten und Freiburg im Breisgau, 1960–1983). Cited in the text with volume number plus paragraph number.

CW = *Collected Works*, edited by Sir Herbert Read, Michael Fordham, Gerhard Adler and William McGuire, 20 vols (London, 1953–1983). Cited in the text with volume number plus paragraph number.

ZL = *The Zofingia Lectures*, translated by Jan van Heurck (London, 1983). Cited in the text with a paragraph number plus page reference.

B = *Briefe 1906–1961*, edited by Aniela Jaffé, 3 volumes (Olten und Freiburg im Breisgau, 1972–1973). Cited in the text with volume number plus page reference.

L = *Letters*, edited by Gerhard Adler and Aniela Jaffé, 2 volumes (London, 1973–75). Cited in the text with volume number plus page reference.

WSL = *Wandlungen und Symbole der Libido: Beiträge zur Entwicklungsgeschichte des Denkens* (original version of *Symbole der Wandlung*) (Leipzig, 1912). Here quoted with reference to the recent paperback republication (Munich, 1991). Cited in the text with page reference.

PU = *Psychology of the Unconscious: A Study of the Tranformations and Symbolisms of the Libido: A Contribution to the History of the Evolution of Thought*, translated by Beatrice M. Hinkle, introduced by William McGuire (London, 1991). Cited in the text with paragraph number.

SNZ = *Nietzsche's Zarathustra: Notes of the Seminar given in 1934–1939*, edited by James Jarrett, 2 volumes (London, 1989). Cited in the text with volume number plus page reference.

AP = *Analytical Psychology: Notes of the Seminar given in 1925*, edited by William McGuire (London, 1990). Cited in the text with page reference.

DA = *Dream Analysis: Notes of the Seminar given in 1928–1930*, edited by William McGuire (London, 1984). Cited in the text with page reference.

VS = *The Visions Seminars*, selected and edited by Jane A. Pratt and Patricia Berry, 2 vols (Zurich, 1976). Cited in the text with volume number plus page reference.

ETG = *Erinnerungen, Träume, Gedanken von C. G. Jung*, recorded and edited by Aniela Jaffé (Zurich and Stuttgart, 1983). Cited in the text with page reference. The Swiss edition also contains the *VII Sermones ad mortuos.*

MDR = *Memories, Dreams, Reflections*, recorded and edited by Aniela Jaffé, translated by Richard and Clara Winston (London, 1983). Cited in the text with page reference.

FJB = Sigmund Freud/C. G. Jung, *Briefwechsel*, edited by William McGuire and Wolfgang Sauerländer (Frankfurt am Main, 1974). Cited in the text with page reference.

FJL = Sigmund Freud/C. G. Jung, *The Freud/Jung Letters: The Correspondence between Sigmund Freud and C. G. Jung*, edited by William McGuire, translated by Ralph Manheim and R. F. C. Hull (Cambridge, MA, 1988).

Nietzsche

The following abbreviations are used to refer to editions and arrangements of the *Nachlaß*:

N = *Werke in drei Bänden*, edited by Karl Schlechta (Munich, 1966). Cited in the text with volume number plus page reference.

KGW = *Kritische Gesamtausgabe Werke*, edited by Giorgio Colli and Mazzino Montinari, 30 vols (Berlin, 1967 –). Cited in the text with volume number (followed by paragraph reference, where appropriate) plus page reference.

WM = *Wille zur Macht.* Peter Gast's arrangement of the *Nachlaß*, cited in the text with section number.

WP = *The Will to Power*, translated by Walter Kaufmann and R. J. Hollingdale (New York, 1968).

UW = *Die Unschuld des Werdens.* Alfred Baeumler's arrangement of the *Nachlaß*, cited in the text with volume number followed by section number.

The following abbreviations are used to refer to works by Nietzsche in the German original:

GT = *Die Geburt der Tragödie*

UB = *Unzeitgemäße Betrachtungen*

MA = *Menschliches, Allzumenschliches*

MA II VMS = *Vermischte Meinungen und Sprüche*

MA II WS = *Der Wanderer und sein Schatten*

M = *Morgenröte*

FW = *Die fröhliche Wissenschaft*

Z = *Also sprach Zarathustra*

JGB	=	*Jenseits von Gut und Böse*
GM	=	*Zur Genealogie der Moral*
GD	=	*Götzen-Dämmerung*
EH	=	*Ecce Homo* [I= 'Warum ich so weise bin'; II = 'Warum ich so klug bin'; III = 'Warum ich so gute Bücher schreibe'; IV = 'Warum ich ein Schicksal bin']
AC	=	*Der Anti-Christ*
DD	=	*Dionysos-Dithyramben*

The following abbreviations are used to refer to Nietzsche's work in English translation:

BT	=	*The Birth of Tragedy* (translated by Walter Kaufmann, in: *Basic Writings of Nietzsche* (New York, 1968), pp. 1–144).
UM	=	*Untimely Meditations* (translated by R. J. Hollingdale (Cambridge, 1983)).
HA	=	*Human, All Too Human* (translated by R. J. Hollingdale (Cambridge, 1986)).
HA II AOM	=	*Assorted Opinions and Maxims*
HA II WS	=	*The Wanderer and his Shadow*
D	=	*Daybreak* (translated by R. J. Hollingdale (Cambridge, 1982)).
GS	=	*The Gay Science* (translated By Walter Kaufmann (New York, 1974)).
Z	=	*Thus spake Zarathustra* (translated by R. J. Hollingdale (Harmondsworth, 1961)).
BGE	=	*Beyond Good and Evil* (translated by Walter Kaufmann, in: *Basic Writings of Nietzsche* (New York, 1968), pp. 179–435).
GM	=	*On the Genealogy of Morals* (translated by Walter Kaufmann, in: *Basic Writings of Nietzsche* (New York, 1968), pp. 437–599).
TI	=	*Twilight of the Idols* (translated by R. J. Hollingdale (Harmondsworth, 1968)).
EH	=	*Ecce Homo* [I = 'Why I am So Wise'; II = 'Why I am So Clever'; III = 'Why I Write Such Excellent Books'; IV = 'Why I am a Destiny'] (translated by R. J. Hollingdale (Harmondsworth, 1979)).
AC	=	*The Anti-Christ* (translated by R. J. Hollingdale (Harmondsworth, 1968)).
DD	=	*Dithyrambs of Dionysos* (translated by R. J. Hollingdale (London, 1984)).

A note on the translations provided: In this book, all passages in German, including the titles of most books, have been translated into English, placed within square brackets directly after the original quotation. In the case of quotations from Nietzsche, I have used the translations by Walter Kaufmann or R. J. Hollingdale specified above. In the case of texts from the *Nachlaß* which have not been translated by Kaufmann or Hollingdale, they have been translated by me. In the case of quotations from Jung, I have used the translations from the *Collected Works*. Sadly, these translations are often inaccurate to the point of erroneousness. Where translations from the *Collected Works* are good or passable, I have let them stand (in this way, the original and the 'official' translation may be interestingly compared); but where I have felt that they are seriously inaccurate, I have amended them, signalling this by the initials **P. B.** after the quotation except where the amendment is so slight as to be negligible. All other translations are my own.

Where the paragraph number of the same volume of Jung's *Collected Works* is identical with the *Gesammelte Werke*, I have only given the GW reference. When it is different, as is the case with volumes 6 and 14, I have given both the GW and the CW paragraph reference. Volumes 14 and 18 of the *Gesammelte Werke* are published in 2 parts, whereas the corresponding English volumes are not subdivided.

Nietzsche quotations are cited with reference both to the code of abbreviations for titles and section numbers listed above and, for convenience, to the three-volume Schlechta edition of the *Werke*. In this way, reference is made to the most easily available German edition of Nietzsche's works, but quotations may also be located in any other edition or translation as well.

Throughout the book, in quotations and text, spelling and capitalization of key names and concepts have been standardized.

Chapter 1

Introduction

C. G. Jung (1875–1961) is one of the most influential figures in twentieth-century intellectual thought, as well as the founder of a school of psychology which has produced hundreds of trained therapists in its Institutes around the world and which has offered treatment to thousands of patients. Jung himself was extremely modest in his claims to treat his patients or clients successfully,[1] but this book is not about the clinical aspects of his work. Instead, it examines the ideas which inform Jungian therapy and which build the theoretical basis of Analytical Psychology. In doing so, it decisively rejects Jung's repeated but ultimately untenable assertion that there are no philosophical implications to his thought.[2]

More specifically, this book examines Jung's psychology as it developed in response to his reading of Friedrich Nietzsche (1844–1900), to whom he made numerous references throughout his voluminous writings. Although the impact of Nietzsche on Jung has frequently been acknowledged, the extent and nature of this influence have rarely been examined. This book is thus a case-study in reception, examining the affinities between the life and work of Jung and those of Nietzsche. Rather than being an exercise in apologetics, it attempts to return Jung to a tradition of intellectual debate from which, very often thanks to his followers, he has been excluded.

---

[1] 'Ich habe vor Jahren einmal eine Statistik angefertigt über die Resultate meiner Behandlungen. Genau weiß ich die Zahlen nicht mehr, aber vorsichtig gesagt waren ein Drittel wirklich geheilt, ein Drittel weitgehend gebessert und ein Drittel nicht wesentlich beeinflußt' ['Years ago I once drew up statistics on the results of my treatments. I no longer recall the figures exactly; but, on a conservative estimate, a third of my cases were really cured, a third considerably improved, and a third not essentially influenced'] (ETG: p. 148/MDR: p. 165).

[2] One doesn't have to read far in Jung before coming across examples of such a denial, and students of Jung have frequently used them to avoid the metaphysical complexities of his system. But in his autobiography, Jung makes it clear that it was his intellectual labours in general and his study of mythology in particular which brought him to a new view of the psyche, thus enabling him to develop new therapeutic techniques: 'Schon 1909 sah ich ein, daß ich latente Psychosen nicht behandeln kann, wenn ich deren Symbolik nicht verstehe. Damals fing ich an, Mythologie zu studieren' ['As early as 1909 I realized that I could not treat latent psychoses if I did not understand their symbolism. It was then that I began to study mythology'] (ETG: p. 137/MDR: p. 153). And Jung's writings constantly refer to Kant, Schopenhauer – and Nietzsche.

Survey of Previous Research

Due to the inter-disciplinary nature of any study of the intellectual affinities between Nietzsche and Jung, one might expect either an immense overlapping of material from previous research or a dearth of material on a subject which falls between two stools. As far as the psychologists, the writers on Nietzsche, and the intellectual historians and philosophers are concerned, the latter situation is the rule.

For example, none of the three standard introductions to Jung's psychology by Frieda Fordham,[3] Jolande Jacobi,[4] and Edward F. Edinger[5] discusses the relevance of Nietzsche for Jung; nor do the three major books on the history of psychology by James Brown,[6] Paul Roazen[7] and Josef Rattner.[8] As regards the literary critics, the first volume of Bruno Hillebrand's study of the reception of Nietzsche in German literature which covers the period 1873–1963[9] does not mention Jung at all. Of the more overtly psychologically-oriented critics, none of the proponents of so-called 'archetypal criticism' such as Maud Bodkin,[10] Northrop Frye,[11] or even P. W. Martin,[12] actually applies this method to Jung and Nietzsche. Moreover, despite Jung's interest in figures from German literature such as Goethe, Schiller and Hölderlin, as well as Nietzsche, and his own extensive use of imagery and metaphor, there has been no overall study of these literary aspects of his work. Finally, turning to works which are more concerned with the manifestly philosophical aspects of Jung's work and its place in intellectual history, a doctoral dissertation deals precisely with the philosophical aspects of Jung's work by not discussing the Jung-Nietzsche problematic at all![13] A more recent publication on the philosophical issues in the psychology of Jung is also largely silent on the matter.[14]

In contrast, nearly all the published biographies of Jung emphasize the importance which Jung attached to his reading of Nietzsche, be these biographies

---

3 Frieda Fordham, *An Introduction to Jung's Psychology* (Harmondsworth, 1953).

4 Jolande Jacobi, *Komplex/Archetypus/Symbol in der Psychologie C. G. Jungs* (Zurich and Stuttgart, 1957).

5 Edward F. Edinger, *Ego and Archetype: Individuation and the Religious Function of the Psyche* (New York, 1972).

6 J. A. C. Brown, *Freud and the post-Freudians* (Harmondsworth, 1961).

7 Paul Roazen, *Freud and His Followers* (London, 1976).

8 Josef Rattner, *Klassiker der Tiefenpsychologie* (Munich, 1990).

9 Bruno Hillebrand (ed.), *Nietzsche-Rezeption und die deutsche Literatur*, 2 vols (Tübingen, 1978), I.

10 Maud Bodkin, *Archetypal Patterns in Poetry: Psychological Studies of Imagination* (Oxford, 1934).

11 Northrop Frye, *An Anatomy of Criticism: Four Essays* (Princeton, 1957).

12 P. W. Martin, *Experiment in Depth: A Study of the Work of Jung, Eliot and Toynbee* (London, 1955).

13 Dieter Spies, *Philosophische Aspekte der Psychologie C. G. Jungs*, Diss. Ph.D. unpub. (University of Munich, 1975).

14 Marilyn Nagy, *Philosophical Issues in the Psychology of C. G. Jung* (New York, 1991).

of a standard,[15] polemical[16] or hagiographical/'alternative' kind[17] – though their analyses go no further than that. However, in one of the best 'standard' biographies written in English, Vincent Brome adds an appendix on Jung's sources which highlights the particular significance of Nietzsche for him and also refers to Jung's Seminar on Nietzsche's *Also sprach Zarathustra.*[18] Similarly, Barbarah Hannah's biography of Jung, although written by a disciple, distinguishes itself by mentioning the Nietzsche Seminar more than just in passing, relating it both to the political situation in Europe at the time and to the earlier 'Berliner Seminare' of 1933.[19]

In the most recently-published 'standard' biography of Jung, Anthony Stevens suggests the psychological reasons for Jung's interest in Nietzsche, explaining his enthusiasm for such an 'intellectual giant' in the light of Jung's relationship with his father.[20] Likewise, a major example of the hagiographical or 'alternative' kind of biography is also aware of the rôle Nietzsche played in the development of Jung's life and thought, and Colin Wilson attaches great importance to the effect which the reading of Nietzsche had on Jung in the 1890s, in 1902 and in the period when he broke with Freud: 'Jung was far more interested in *supernormal* people, in men like St Augustine and Goethe and Nietzsche – in saints and supermen'.[21]

There are, however, exceptions to the the rule of silence observed by most psychologists, critics of Nietzsche and intellectual historians on the relationship between Nietzsche and Jung. What follows is a survey of the most relevant output of these commentators, who are discussed in the order listed above.

In his introduction to a selection of Jung's writings, the psychologist Anthony Storr discusses the influence of Schopenhauer and Nietzsche, comparing and contrasting Jung with each thinker in both cases. Storr fails to place these

---

15 For example: Gerhard Wehr, *Carl Gustav Jung: Leben, Werk, Wirkung* (Munich, 1985).

16 For example: Paul J. Stern, *C. G. Jung: The Haunted Prophet* (New York, 1976).

17 For example: Laurens van der Post, *Jung and the Story of our Time* (London, 1976).

18 'Philosophically, Nietzsche remained a writer who persistently drew [Jung] back to book after book, partly because Jung saw him as a man with a shadow personality which broke through to shower the reader with fascinating archetypal material straight out of the unconscious' (Vincent Brome, *Jung* (London, 1978), p. 289).

19 'Jung had often reminded us that, although we were fortunately still able to live our ordinary lives, we should never forget the storm clouds hanging over Europe [...] But, as in Berlin, Jung seldom or never mentioned the outer situation directly' (Barbarah Hannah, *Jung: His Life and Work, A Biographical Memoir* (London, 1976). Hannah is referring to the Seminar given from 26 June to 1 July 1933 to the C. G. Jung Gesellschaft at the Harnackhaus in Dahlem, Berlin.

20 Anthony Stevens, *On Jung* (London, 1990), pp. 141–42.

21 Colin Wilson, *Lord of the Underworld* (Wellingborough, 1984), p. 51; and see also p. 101: 'Jung was not fundamentally a scientist; he was a romantic, a man whose deepest feelings had been aroused in the past by Goethe and Schopenhauer and Krafft-Ebing. Jung had turned to science to strengthen his 'reality function', to create a personality capable of meeting the world on its own terms' (p. 51).

writers in a continuous tradition, but his comparisons between Nietzsche and Jung are still valid:

> Jung was also influenced by Nietzsche, who was a passionate individualist; but, whereas Nietzsche stated that God was dead, Jung rediscovered God as the guiding principle of unity within the depths of the individual psyche.[22]

Despite that, in his useful introductory guide to Jung, Storr omits to point out the Nietzschean flavour of a favourite Jungian phrase: 'Jung is fond of phrases like "all-too-human", and to a minor extent may merit the Freudian accusation of regarding sex *per se* as distasteful'.[23] The point here, surely, is that the phrase mentioned is an allusion to Nietzsche, and as such has little to do with the distinction between the Freudian and the Jungian concept of sexuality.

In histories of post-Freudian psychology, Jung is often presented in opposition to Freud. This is certainly the case with Edward Glover,[24] who decides between Freud or Jung in favour of the former but without mentioning how the two thinkers' differing reception of Nietzsche reflects their theoretical differences. The author of a standard Jungian textbook, Liliane Frey-Rohn (see below) decides between Freud or Jung in favour of the latter but goes no further than saying that, for Jung, Nietzsche was 'ein gewichtiger Gewährsmann' ['a source of some importance'].[25] Robert Steele is more fair-minded than both Glover and Frey-Rohn, but also fails to distinguish between the respective relevance of Nietzsche for Freud and Jung. Nevertheless, he does suggest, without arguing his case, that '[Jung's] readings in Nietzsche and spiritism helped Jung develop his arguments against the materialist position that the mind was equal to the brain and that the human spirit did not exist'.[26]

Still on the level of the relationship between the two thinkers, the psychologist Antonio Moreno devoted a chapter of his study on the contemporary significance of Jung by using analytical psychological methods as a tool with which to produce a mini psycho-biography of Nietzsche: 'We have found in the writings of Jung the main ideas and psychological principles we needed for the understanding of Nietzsche's personality'.[27] Moreno neglects, however, to consider whether the usefulness of Jungian thought for an understanding of Nietzsche suggests any affinities between them. And although Peter Homans's

---

22 Anthony Storr (ed.), *Jung: Selected Writings* (London, 1983).

23 Anthony Storr, *Jung* (London, 1973), p. 41.

24 Edward Glover, *Freud or Jung* (London, 1950).

25 Liliane Frey-Rohn, *Von Freud zu Jung: eine vergleichende Studie zur Psychologie des Unbewußten* (Zurich, 1980), p. 231. Frey-Rohn associates Jung's complementarism with Nietzsche but, by referring to an aphorism from the *Nachlaß* (WM/WP 881 = N3: p. 595), misleadingly suggests that he had read the notes for *Der Wille zur Macht*, whereas in fact he found the idea in completely different texts.

26 Robert S. Steele, *Freud and Jung; Conflicts of Interpretation* (London, 1982), p. 42.

27 Antonio Moreno, 'Nietzsche and Jung', in: *Jung, Gods and Modern Man* (London, 1974), p. 216.

study on Jung in the context of modernity mentions that 'Jung was deeply influenced by the thought of Nietzsche',[28] this point is made with reference only to Jung's theory of mass society and is not developed any further.

A similar tendency to look at Nietzsche from a Jungian perspective, but not *vice versa*, is exhibited in a seminal work of Jungian psychology by a former student of C. G. Jung, Liliane Frey-Rohn.[29] Although she does occasionally look at Jung's own remarks specifically on Nietzsche, the general thrust of the work is to provide a depth-psychological analysis of the Nietzschean problematics of Good and Evil, authenticity and the overcoming of Nihilism. Like Moreno, Frey-Rohn fails to question the implications of her own starting-point, namely, the appropriateness of Jungian psychology for dealing with such issues, and ignores the vital question of whether Jungian psychology simply reformulates the same problems in a different language. This book is typical of much Jungian scholarship inasmuch as it disregards the question of intellectual sources, and takes the tenets of Jung's thought for granted.

On the other hand, an article by Ross Woodman in 1986 offers a view of Nietzsche which is explicitly 'contra Jung's'. Woodman not only attributes to Nietzsche a significance in the history of psychology substantially different from the one attributed to him by Jung,[30] but also emphasizes the importance for both Nietzsche and Jung of the 'dark god', Dionysos.[31]

The editor of Jung's Seminar on Nietzsche, James Jarrett, provides an introduction to the two volumes[32] where he outlines the significance of Nietzsche for Jung, and for other twentieth-century thinkers too, in the broadest of terms.[33] Jarrett then goes on to say that Jung 'shared much with Nietzsche' and

---

28 Peter Homans, *Jung in Context: Modernity and the Making of a Psychology* (Chicago, 1979), p. 181.

29 Liliane Frey-Rohn, *Jenseits der Werte seiner Zeit: Friedrich Nietzsche im Spiegel seiner Werke* (Zurich, 1984).

30 'By Nietzsche's releasing soul from its warring enemies and relocating Man in the fictions by which he lives, one might argue that he gave birth to the soul as an object of knowledge, gave birth, that is, to psychology' (Ross Woodman, 'Nietzsche's Madness as Soul-Making: A View contra Jung's', *Spring*, 1986, 101–18 (pp. 103–04).

31 'The *deus absconditus*, the dark Dionysos who is hidden even from himself under the cloak of his own darkness, is everything which appears mindless, causeless, without precedent, unexpected [...] Jung followed Nietzsche in search of the dark God [...] Nietzsche's insanity, which Jung found the "quintessence of horror" [ETG: p. 193/MDR: p. 214], was a stage erected for the soul's performance, the Dionysian theatre in which his soul enacted itself' (ibid., pp. 105–06, 108).

32 C. G. Jung, *Nietzsche's "Zarathustra": Notes of the Seminar given in 1934–1939*, edited by James L. Jarrett, 2 vols (London, 1989).

33 'The written confrontation of giants in intellectual history is always fascinating and often exceedingly illuminating: Plato and Socrates, Aristotle and Plato, Aquinas and Aristotle, and so on down to more recent times: Hegel and Marx, Nietzsche and Schopenhauer, Jung and Freud. Interestingly, Nietzsche seems to have had a particularly magnetic quality for some of the finest intellects of the twentieth century: thus both Karl Jaspers and Martin Heidegger wrote voluminously on this most provocative of thinkers. And then – now – Jung and Nietzsche' (ibid., pp.xvii–xviii).

enumerates about fifteen such affinities, which include a positive attitude towards Dionysos: 'Theirs, alike, was a philosophy of darkness, no less than light, a celebration of the Dionysian spirit'.[34] Although he also mentions two key differences between the two men,[35] he does not distinguish more carefully between Jung's attitude to Dionysos and Nietzsche's, let alone differentiate between the different stages in Jung's evaluation of the Dionysian. Whilst what Jarrett says may be true as far as it goes, he neglects to consider the extent to which the remarkable similarities between the two men may be a direct result of Jung's own reception of Nietzsche. The shift from a general consideration of parallels towards an examination of the genesis of Jung's thought in the light of his reading of Nietzsche remains unmade, and Jarrett fails to suggest what may be at stake in these similarities and differences. A later article by Jarrett on Jung and Nietzsche equally lacks sustained analysis and remains essentially on the level of the anecdotal.[36]

Moving away from a general comparison between the two thinkers, the prominent post-Jungian James Hillman focuses on the common motif of Dionysos to form a link between Jung and Nietzsche. He sketches the Dionysian background of the central Jungian idea of wholeness and integration, and makes the following bold claim: 'There is probably a direct and causal relation between the presence of Nietzsche in Jung's consciousness and the absence of Dionysos, as if the more deeply Jung entered into Nietzsche, the more he was dissuaded from the Dionysian'. Moreover, Hillman distinguishes two stages in Jung's understanding of the Nietzschean Dionysos: 'The first Dionysos of whom Jung writes [...] is neither a figure of antiquity nor a figure in Jung's own life, but one who is vicariously known to Jung through Nietzsche'. The second Dionysos is characterized by his dismemberment, but 'then dismemberment loses the background of Nietzsche and even of the rending by the opposites, and begins to take on a wider archetypal significance'.[37] Before losing himself in the archetypes, Hillman could have related this dual reception of the image of Dionysos

---

34 Ibid., p.xviii, which includes the following summary of their similarities: 'Both – though neither would have put it this way – were in the existentialist tradition of belief that without conflict and suffering, consciousness is doomed to stagnation and regression. Both sought, instead, for a philosophy and psychology [...] whose test is simply but richly this: does it conduce to a life rich in fulfilment, attainment, even transcendence to a realm of integration beyond what is reachable from the comfortable couches of everydayness [...] a celebration of the Dionysian spirit wherein is found the scariness of the unconscious with its alarming dreams which are yet the great source of human creativity'.

35 'The first is that for the one, the aesthetic dimension of life was of primary importance, for the other, the religious, [and the second is that] they differed as to the best path towards a higher level' (ibid., pp.xix–xx).

36 James L. Jarrett, 'Jung and Nietzsche', *Harvest*, 36 (1990), 130–54.

37 James Hillman, 'Dionysus in Jung's Writings', *Spring*, 1972, 191–205 (pp. 194, 197 and 200).

to the radical change which Jung's thought underwent during the period 1913–1919.

Marco Innamorati's recent article on Jung and Nietzsche presents a brief overview of the presence of Nietzsche's Zarathustra in Jung's works to substantiate the claim that 'la prossimità spirituale ed effettiva di Jung allo *Zarathustra*, fu precoce, profonda e costante lungo tutto l'arco della vita del fondatore della psicologia analitica'.[38] Although Innamorati provides a useful conspectus of the affinities between the two men as revealed in the concept of the Shadow and the principles of synchronicity and finalism, his article represents a starting-point for a study of Nietzsche and Jung, rather than coming to any substantive conclusions about the intellectual relationship between them.

In a book which avowedly goes in search of the historical and philosophical context of the enquiries which Jung undertook, John J. Clarke compares the reception of Jung with that of Nietzsche, which in both cases went from vilification and neglect to increasing interest and acceptance, and suggests that Jung's interpretation of *Zarathustra* anticipates other modern re-evaluations, such as those of Walter Kaufmann, Ofelia Schutte and Michel Haar.[39] But Clarke's judgment that 'a heightened awareness, in many respects novel in Western thought, of the irrational forces that lie beneath the rational surface of consciousness' was common to Nietzsche, Jung and, indeed, Schopenhauer patently leaves much both unexplored and unexplained.[40]

Richard Noll's recent book on the Jungian movement performs the valuable service of emphasizing Jung's background in Romantic *Naturphilosophie* as well as, more controversially, claiming that Analytical Psychology is deeply rooted in *völkisch* paganism. However, Noll's argument that, like National Socialism, Analytical Psychology is based on '"Nietzscheanism" in the elitist and pseudoliberational sense astutely identified by [Ferdinand] Tönnies' and that 'the Jung cult and its present day movement is in fact a "Nietzschean religion"'[41] is flawed by his misunderstanding of the rôle that such key concepts as the 'new nobility' and the Superman play in Nietzsche's thought. And although he interestingly identifies the renegade psychoanalyst and Expressionist theorist Otto Gross (1877–1920) as a chief mediator to Jung of certain ideas which allegedly found their source in Nietzsche, Noll fails to take account of the more direct route by which Jung came to Nietzsche, his own reading of Nietzsche's *Werke*.

---

38 Marco Innamorati, 'La presenza dello Zarathustra di Nietzsche nelle opere di Jung', *Giornale storico di psicologia dinimica*, 29 (1991), 73–93.

39 John J. Clarke, *In Search of Jung: Historical and Philosophical Enquiries* (London, 1992), pp. 17–18, 154–55.

40 Ibid., p. 70.

41 Richard Noll, *The Jung Cult: Origins of a Charismatic Religion* (Princeton, 1994, p. 137; see also pp. 263–64.

Turning now to the writers on Nietzsche, one of those mentioned by John Clarke, Walter Kaufmann, acknowledges that 'many of [Nietzsche's] most promising insights were developed after his death by other writers', including Jung, but he gives only one example of how this was done – in a foot-note to a paragraph characterizing Nietzsche's method as that of a 'problem-thinker'.[42] At several points in the section on Jung in his three-volume work *Discovering the Mind*, Kaufmann mentions Jung's interest in Nietzsche, and ultimately sees him as a case-study in *ressentiment* and hence as profoundly un-Nietzschean. However, Kaufmann unhelpfully relates the whole problematic surrounding Jung's alleged *ressentiment* and his attitude to National Socialism to Jung's own notion of the 'Germanic soul', thereby side-stepping one of the most controversial issues surrounding Jung.[43]

Rose Pfeffer correctly identifies Nietzsche's writings as those of a 'disciple of Dionysos', and relates them to a large number of diverse intellectuals, including Nikolai Berdyaev and Paul Tillich, but she does no more than briefly allude to Jung.[44] And whilst Adrian Del Caro's study of Nietzsche's Dionysian aesthetic remarks that Jung's writings 'reveal a deep interest in Nietzsche both as an individual, and as a thinker', this insight remains on the level that 'Jung is able to tell us something about the possible motivations Nietzsche had for writing as he did' and Jung's other comments on Dionysos are ignored.[45] His more recent work again mentions, but does not discuss, Jung as a scholar of Nietzsche.[46]

More interestingly, in an article examining the image of the eagle and the serpent in *Zarathustra*, David Thatcher goes back to the mythic sources of this image and draws a convincing parallel between '"Becoming who one is"' as 'the process to which Nietzsche gave the name "Selbstüberwindung"' and the Jungian concept of 'individuation'.[47] However, Thatcher declines to take one

---

42 Walter Kaufmann, *Nietzsche: Philosopher, Psychologist, Antichrist* (Princeton, 1968), p. 82.

43 'The sickness [which Jung] did not recognize as such was the resentment that kept gnawing at him all his life. Had he really any grasp of Nietzsche, of whom he spoke constantly, emphasizing that he, unlike Freud, had read him, he would have known that *ressentiment* can poison a man's character; also how it can be fought. That he failed to see this is not a minor oversight, rather odd in a man who actually gave seminars on Nietzsche's *Zarathustra*, but a flaw that in 1934 assumed world-historical dimensions. When *ressentiment* exploded in Germany and prepared for mass murder, Jung felt a profound kinship with what happened across the border and coined a phrase that included him too: the Germanic soul' (Walter Kaufmann, *Discovering the Mind*, 3 vols (New York, 1980), III, *Freud versus Adler and Jung*, p. 395).

44 Rose Pfeffer, *Nietzsche: Disciple of Dionysus* (Lewisburg, 1972).

45 Adrian del Caro, *Dionysian Aesthetics: The Role of Destruction and Creation as Reflected in the Life and Works of Friedrich Nietzsche* (Frankfurt am Main, 1981), p. 135.

46 Adrian del Caro, *Nietzsche contra Nietzsche: Creativity and the Anti-Romantic* (Baton Rouge and London, 1991), p. 32.

47 David S. Thatcher, 'Eagle and Serpent in *Zarathustra*', *Nietzsche-Studien*, 6 (1977), 240–60 (p. 256).

further step and suggest Nietzsche as a source for Jung's concept in question. However, in 1958, Anni Carlsson had already suggested that Nietzsche's phenomenology of the Dionysian entitled him to be regarded as an important precursor of depth-psychology and, even more significantly, 'der Vorläufer auch ihrer Verknüpfung von Psychologie und Mythos, will sagen der Usurpation des Mythos durch die Psychologie' ['the precursor also of its combination of psychology and myth, in other words the usurpation of myth by psychology'].[48] As I shall argue in Chapter 13, the turn towards myth for psychological reasons constitutes a major area of common ground between Nietzsche and Jung.

More recently, Graham Parkes has gone beyond the mere recognition of Jungian (and Freudian) ideas as part of the reaches of Nietzsche's psychology, and, alert to the Dionysian undercurrents of *Zarathustra* too, has characterized that text as 'charting the development of a highly complex psyche – a soul composed of many souls – in a network of vivid images woven into a dramatic narrative'.[49] Obviously indebted to Jung, Parkes continues:

> *Thus Spoke Zarathustra* is a play of images constituting a consummate picture of the most comprehensive soul, of psyche in totality. It is possible, and enlightening, to read the entire text as a complex image of a single soul – Zarathustra's – and to understand as the major theme the Dionysiac dissolution of the unitary I through multiple overflowings into a plurality of persons, in the context of a plethora of natural phenomena.[50]

Finally, we turn to the intellectual historians and philosophers. In an article of 1930, William McDougall applied the Nietzschean antinomy of Apollo and Dionysos to the divergence between two dominant traditions in twentieth-century psychology. McDougall argued that Apollonian intellectualism had culminated in the development of Behaviourism, whilst a revival of Dionysian intuition, initiated by Nietzsche, had found expression in the psychologies of Freud and Adler and especially in that of Jung.[51] And in a paper read in 1933 before the Medical Society of Individual Psychology in London, F. G. Crookshank took up Nietzsche's/McDougall's antinomy and fine-tuned it, arguing that 'the bond between Adler and Nietzsche is far closer than that between Nietzsche and Jung', but adding: 'even if some of Jung's principal tenets were [...] anticipated by Nietzsche'.[52]

---

48 Anni Carlsson, 'Der Mythos als Maske Friedrich Nietzsches', *Germanisch-Romanische Monatsschrift*, 39 (1958), 388–401 (p. 391).

49 Graham Parkes, *Composing the Soul: Reaches of Nietzsche's Psychology* (Chicago and London, 1994), p. 6.

50 Ibid., p. 360.

51 William McDougall, 'The Present Chaos in Psychology and the Way Out', *Journal of Philosophical Studies*, 5, no. 19 (July 1930), 353–63.

52 F. G. Crookshank, *Individual Psychology and Nietzsche* (London, 1933). Crookshank further claimed that a passage from the fourth section of Nietzsche's 'Versuch einer Selbstkritik' ['Attempt at a

Two books which deal with the intellectual traditions from which psychology evolved are worthy of particular mention. Although Lancelot Whyte[53] does not link Nietzsche specifically with Jung, his study of the development of the concept of the Unconscious (which includes references to Fichte, Schelling and Schopenhauer as well as Nietzsche) provides useful source material to help place Jung in his intellectual context. The texts from these thinkers anthologized by White would provide the basis for an argument which could demonstrate how both Nietzsche and Jung represent a response to and a continuation of the tradition of German Idealism to which these philosophers belong. However, it is not in the nature of Whyte's study to make these connexions explicit.

The more substantial and immensely detailed study by Henri Ellenberger contains a number of more precise pointers. As well as underlining the importance which Nietzsche had for psychoanalysis in general, Ellenberger draws attention to the fact that Jung interpreted *Also sprach Zarathustra* as the product of a second personality in Nietzsche which had silently developed until, one day, it suddenly broke into the open. Nevertheless, he neglects to draw a parallel here with Jung's own second personality, as he refers to it in his autobiography. Ellenberger also remarks that, early on in his professional career, Jung discovered that an entire paragraph of *Zarathustra* had originated in an article from Justinus Kerner's *Blätter aus Prevorst* and suggested that cryptomnesia could provide an explanation for such occurrences of literary pseudo-plagiarism (see Chapter 4). Moreover, Ellenberger also describes Jung's Seminar on *Zarathustra* as 'the most thorough commentary that has ever been given on Nietzsche's masterpiece'. Overall, Ellenberger's claims for Nietzsche's importance are sweeping: 'More so even than Bachofen, Nietzsche may be considered the common source of Freud, Adler and Jung' (although each of these three responded to Nietzsche in very different ways); and: 'Jung's theories are filled with concepts that can be traced, in more or less modified form, to Nietzsche. Such are Jung's reflections on the problem of evil, on the superior instincts in man, on the unconscious, the old wise man, and many other concepts'.[54] However, because

---

Self-Criticism] – 'Und welche Bedeutung hat dann, physiologisch gefragt, jener Wahnsinn, aus dem die tragische wie die komische Kunst erwuchs, der dionysische Wahnsinn? Wie? Ist Wahnsinn vielleicht nicht notwendig das Symptom der Entartung, des Niedergangs, der überspäten Kultur? Gibt es vielleicht – eine Frage für Irrenärzte – Neurosen der *Gesundheit*? der Volks-Jugend und -Jugendlichkeit?' ['And what, then, is the significance, physiologically speaking, of that madness out of which tragic and comic art developed – the Dionysian madness? How now? Is madness perhaps not necessarily the symptom of degeneration, decline, and the final stage of culture? Are there perhaps – a question for psychiatrists – neuroses of *health*? of the youth and youthfulness of a people?'] (GT/BT Versuch/Attempt § 4; N1: p. 13) – went 'to the very heart of Jung's theory of neurosis' (p. 16).

53 Lancelot L. Whyte, *The Unconscious before Freud* (London, 1960).

54 Henri F. Ellenberger, *The Discovery of the Unconscious: The History and Evolution of Dynamic Psychiatry* (New York, 1970), pp. 169, 170, 722, 276 and 278.

Ellenberger's study is devoted to the whole history of dynamic psychiatry, he cannot pursue the Jung-Nietzsche relationship in any detail. Nevertheless, there is much in what he suggests which a more systematic analysis would both confirm and question.

In his contribution to a volume dealing with the undercurrents of Gnosticism and mysticism in Western philosophy, Tilman Evers points to a connexion between Jung and Nietzsche on both a general and a specific level. First, and more generally, he identifies Nietzsche as a mediator of 'Lebensphilosophie' for Jung's thought;[55] and second, and more specifically, he dubs Nietzsche the most profound philosophical influence on Jung.[56] Because, however, Evers's essay is on Jung and Gnosticism, not Jung and Nietzsche, he goes no further than this.

At the same time, two philosophers in particular have attempted to uncover in a more thorough-going way the affinities between Jung and the German philosophical tradition. In 1953, Rudolf Pannwitz (1881–1969), the radical Nietzschean and follower of Stefan George, discussed Jung's thought with reference to Kant, Husserl and Nietzsche, suggested that Nietzsche's philosophy represented an essential preliminary stage for Jung,[57] and associated Nietzsche's concept of creativity with Jung's concept of individuation.[58]

Similarly, although Friedrich Seifert was primarily concerned to develop the relationship between the Hegelian dialectic and Jungian Analytical Psychology,

---

55 '"Lebensphilosophie" als jener große, auch von Schopenhauer und Nietzsche mitgetragene Strang des Denkens im 19. und im beginnenden 20. Jahrhundert ist vielleicht diejenige philosophische Strömung, die sich am ehesten als Jungs unmittelbare philosophische Herkunft bezeichnen läßt' ['"Lebensphilosophie", the great strain of thought running through the nineteenth and twentieth centuries, represented also by Schopenhauer and Nietzsche, is perhaps the best philosophical trend which can be described as Jung's immediate philosophical background'] (Tilman Evers, 'C. G. Jung – Psychologie und Gnosis', in: *Gnosis und Mystik in der Geschichte der Philosophie*, edited by Peter Koslowski (Zurich and Munich, 1988), pp. 329–351 (p. 332)).

56 'Wollte man *einen* Philosophen nennen, dessen Weltsicht in Jungs Werk immer wieder mitschwingt, so wäre dies Nietzsche, in dessen Verklammerung von Anti-Illusionismus mit Anti-Rationalismus' ['If one had to name *one* philosopher whose view of the world always resonates through Jung's work, it would be Nietzsche, because of the way he embraces anti-illusionism and anti-rationalism'] (ibid., p. 332).

57 'Zu seinen Voraussetzungen gehört die Analyse des historischen Menschen durch Nietzsche, die keiner so tief erkannt und voll genutzt hat' ['His assumptions included Nietzsche's analysis of historical Man, which no-one else has so deeply understood and exploited to the full'] (Rudolf Pannwitz, 'C. G. Jung's Wissenschaft der Seele', *Merkur*, 63 (1953), 418–38 (p. 418)).

58 'Jung erkennt das luziferische Wagnis, das unvermeidlich mit tragischem Schicksal verbunden ist. Dabei ist aufs bestimmte an Nietzsches "Vom Wege des Schaffenden" zu denken' ['Jung recognizes the diabolical risk which is inevitably bound up with tragic fate. Here one cannot but think of Nietzsche's "Of the Way of the Creator"'] (ibid., p. 429). Brief as this analysis is, it says more than one doctoral dissertation on the question of creativity in Jungian psychology, which devotes a chapter to 'Nietzsche und das Schöpferische' where its author discusses the concept of creativity with reference to *Zur Genealogie der Moral* and *Also sprach Zarathustra* but without mentioning what Jung says in this connection! (Verena Kast, *Kreativität in der Psychologie von C. G. Jung*, Diss. Ph.D. unpub. (University of Zurich, 1974)).

he also made two specific references to the relationship between Nietzsche and Jung. He credited the discovery of the two polar types of Apollo and Dionysos (which Jung discussed in detail in *Psychologische Typen* (1921)) to Jung's reading of Nietzsche's *Die Geburt der Tragödie* [*The Birth of Tragedy*] and Bachofen's *Das Mutterrecht* [*Matriliny*], and claimed that the concept of 'Entwicklung' in the Jungian sense had an antecedent in Nietzsche via Dilthey, Simmel, Scheler, Klages, and Heidegger.[59]

Both these writers are considerably more positive about Jung's relation to Nietzsche than was Ernst Bloch (1885–1977), whose book *Das Prinzip Hoffnung* [*The Principle of Hope*] links Jung – whom he calls 'der faschistisch schäumende Psychoanalytiker' ['the fascistically foaming psychoanalyst'] (!) – with Nietzsche in an exceptionally negative manner, seeing the Jungian concept of libido as the 'Bejahung eines Mescalin-Dionysos' ['affirmation of a mescalin Dionysos'].[60] More fruitfully, Christophe Baroni has attempted a synthesis of Nietzschean and Jungian thought. His article on the theological implications of the two thinkers, which rightly sees Jung's work as a reaction and a response to the crisis in religion announced by Nietzsche, draws attention to the points of convergence between the two thinkers.[61] By concentrating on the conceptuality of Nietzsche and Jung, Baroni's thesis, however simplificatory, is more convincing than Gerhard Wehr's book on Nietzsche and Jung, which is purely comparative to the point of simply listing parallels and refuses to acknowledge the implicit debate between these two sets of texts.[62]

In the most recent and, to date, most comprehensive survey of Nietzsche reception in Germany, Steven E. Aschheim places Jung's reading of Nietzsche in the historical context of the Third Reich. Whilst stressing the individuality of Jung's approach, like that of Jaspers or that of Heidegger,[63] at the same time

59 Friedrich Seifert, *Seele und Bewußtsein: Betrachtungen zum Problem der psychischen Realität* (Munich and Basel, 1962), pp. 131, 133.

60 Ernst Bloch, *Das Prinzip Hoffnung*, 3 vols (Frankfurt am Main, 1959), I, p. 65. For further comments regarding Jung, Klages, Prinzhorn and other 'Krypto-Fascisten der Psychologie', see Ernst Bloch, 'Imago aus Schein aus der "Tiefe"', in: *Erbschaft dieser Zeit* (Erweiterte Ausgabe) (Frankfurt am Main, 1985), pp. 344–51.

61 'Après mûre réflexion, nous croyons pouvoir affirmer que malgré des indiscutables différences de langage et de ton, Jung et Nietzsche se retrouvent sur l'essentiel quand ils affirment, chacun à sa manière, qu'il y a en l'homme quelque chose qui le passe infiniment – comme dirait Pascal – et à quoi l'homme a tout intérêt à s'abandonner ou que du moins il doit consulter s'il veut valablement "créer par delà lui-même"' (Christophe Baroni, 'Dieu est-il mort? De Nietzsche à Jung', *Synthèses*, 19, no.224 (January 1965), 328–43 (p. 334)).

62 Gerhard Wehr, *Friedrich Nietzsche als Tiefenpyschologe* (Oberwil b. Zug, 1987).

63 'It was [...] hardly fortuitous that the great minds of the time – especially Jaspers, Jung, and Heidegger – all chose Nietzsche for sustained analyses. If little united their aims, approaches, and conclusions, their use of Nietzsche as a relevant filter and their intense engagement with him was in itself significant. All were complex works inevitably stamped by, and revealing attitudes towards, the novel experience of nazism' (Steven E. Aschheim, *The Nietzsche Legacy in Germany 1890–1990* (Berkeley, 1992), p. 256.

Aschheim emphasizes the relevance to the Seminar on *Zarathustra* of its historico-political background.[64]

There have been only three studies which explicitly tackle the affinities between Jung and Nietzsche. According to Arthur Rudolph, a lecturer in humanities at Arizona State University who went so far as to write to Jung and ask him about Nietzsche's influence (see Chapter 3), Nietzsche had a three-fold significance for Jung 'as a thinker', 'as a personality who embodies the Wotanistic forces of the modern world', and 'as a subject of psychiatric case-study'. However, Rudolph does not investigate more closely the relationship to Nietzsche, 'one of the great fascinations of Carl Gustav Jung'.[65] As the title of Patricia Eileen Dixon's dissertation, soon to be turned into a book, suggests, she sees the fundamental link between them to lie with what she perceives as their common project for 'wholeness through the union of opposites'.[66] But Dixon's study of Jung's reception of Nietzsche is synchronic, ignoring the important shifts in his attitude which I analyse in my chronological survey; and although she recognizes the importance of Dionysos for both thinkers alike, she fails to pursue the implications of Jung's reaction to Nietzsche's Dionysianism for the development of his Analytical Psychology. And while Peggy Nill's article argues that the main conceptual affinity between the two men is the 'schöpferisches Prinzip' ['creative principle'] of 'self-becoming', equating Jung's concept of 'Ethos' with Nietzsche's concept of 'Poiesis', she does not survey the chronological shifts in Jung's reading of Nietzsche.[67]

Having examined the work of these various groups of commentators, we can see that it is no exaggeration to say that the question of Jung's use of Nietzsche has not adequately received the attention which a minority of commentators – albeit a significant one – has both implicitly and explicitly acknowledged that it deserves. There are several reasons for this. First, as Anthony Storr suggests,[68] Jung's contribution to our perception of human nature is still not fully appreciated, and the acceptance by philosophers and cultural critics of

---

64 'The same shaping context, the looming background of nazism, helps to explain the marathon 1934–1939 Zurich seminar Jung held on *Zarathustra*. Jung's remarkable and sustained reflective project – with its deliciously detailed analysis of the inner workings and psychological structure of the Zarathustrian symbolic world – laid bare *Zarathustra* as an example of the creative and demonic gyrations of the collective unconscious. Moreover, it employed Nietzsche and *Zarathustra* as illustrations and affirmations of his own psychological system and sought to uncover some of the deeper, hidden connections between Nietzsche and national socialism' (ibid., p. 258).

65 Arthur Rudolph, 'Jung and Zarathustra', *Philosophy Today*, 18 (Winter 1974), 312–18 (p. 317).

66 Patricia Eileen Dixon, *Nietzsche and Jung: Wholeness through the Union of Opposites*, Diss. Ph.D. unpub. (The American University, Washington D. C.), forthcoming in New York.

67 Peggy Nill, 'Die Versuchung der Psyche: Selbstwerdung als schöpferisches Prinzip bei Nietzsche und C. G. Jung', *Nietzsche-Studien*, 17 (1988), 250–79.

68 Storr, *Jung*, p. 117.

Jung's own ideas has been so slow that the opportunity has not arisen to examine the background to his thought in detail.

Second, the vastness of Jung's output (18 volumes of the *Gesammelte Werke* plus several Seminars, and more seminars to be published)[69] and the seemingly arcane, not to say obscure nature of much of his writing can easily act as a deterrent against studying him in detail.

Third, whilst Jung does not deny the significance of Nietzsche for his thought, he does not always indicate precisely in which areas he is directly or indirectly indebted to Nietzsche. This may have been a question of tactics on Jung's part, as J. Harley Chapman has noted in a different, but similar context.[70]

Fourth, there is a worrying tendency amongst writers, especially if they themselves are Jungians, to refrain from criticism of the master, and an almost total lack of interest in the question of intellectual sources. (It is almost as if they believed that Jungian psychology had fallen straight out of the sky – although Jung's vision of what God did to Basle cathedral should have warned them about what that would mean…). Their immense reluctance to engage with these issues suggests that the Jung-Nietzsche relationship may well be one so problematic that, for psychological reasons on which I do not wish to speculate at this juncture, they refuse to address it.[71]

At the moment, however, there seems to be a turn in the tide of Jung studies towards a more serious examination of the implications of his writings and the aporias in his thought,[72] and this recent work has shown how, in the words of Karin Barnaby and Pellegrino d'Acierno, 'the ideological ways in which Jung has heretofore come to be institutionalized and canonized will be replaced by

---

69 Not all Jung wrote is in the *Gesammelte Werke*: Jung's autobiography (*Erinnerungen, Träume, Gedanken*) was expressly published separately, and the German edition contains the controversial *VII Sermones ad mortuos*. Numerous letters (such as Jung's correspondence while at university with his family) and other documents remain unavailable to scholars. Princeton University Press is planning to publish further seminars by Jung.

70 'Acceptance of metaphysics in the late nineteenth- and early twentieth-century milieu could have jeopardized his scientific undertakings and standing in the scientific community' (J. Harley Chapman, *Jung's Three Theories of Religious Experience* (Lewiston and Queenston, 1988), p. 135).

71 The significance of Nietzsche's thinking for a proper understanding of Jung is, however, not lost on some. On a recent television programme filmed just before his death in 1987, the contemporary Jungian and cultural critic Joseph Campbell showed how it was possible to draw a thread from the story of Gawain and the Green Knight through the temptation of Christ in the wilderness to the way of Buddha and the Nietzschean parable of the three transformations of the spirit (see Helen Oldfield's review of the television series *The Power of Myth* entitled 'The Professor who found True Bliss', *The Guardian*, 16 August 1990).

72 Three particular books exemplify the development of the debate over Jung: *Jung in Modern Perspective*, edited by Renos K. Papadopoulos and Graham Saayman (Hounslow, 1984); *C. G. Jung and the Humanities: Towards a Hermeneutics of Culture*, edited by Karin Barnaby and Pellegrino d'Acierno (London, 1990); and Roger Brooke, *Jung and Phenomenology* (London and New York, 1991).

historiographic and textual analyses that grasp the true dimension of his work'.[73] The recent publication of Jung's Seminar on Nietzsche's *Zarathustra* has aroused interest in Jung in yet more quarters, and the question of Jung's intellectual sources in general and reception of Nietzsche in particular is now on the agenda.

Of all the previous commentators, two writers have come close to anticipating the theme of this book. First, the sociologist Philip Rieff has demonstrated how, 'by resorting to a religious psychology of the Creative Person and collective unconscious, Jung tried to fight off what Nietzsche called "nihilism", the "weirdest of all guests"'.[74] Although Rieff stresses the importance of the 'subterranean God' of Jung's childhood visions, he fails to put a name to this deity – such as Dionysos. And second, the analytical psychologist and biographer, Anthony Stevens, likewise commenting on Jung's famous childhood dream of a giant phallus, has suggested that 'if, with hindsight, we are to give Carl's unnamed phallic god a name, then it must surely be Hermes, messenger of Zeus, god of travellers, conductor of souls'.[75] Because, however, of his failure to note that, for Jung, both Hermes (or Mercurius) and Dionysos are phallic gods,[76] Stevens also ignores the connection between Jung's childhood dreams, his later writings on alchemy, and his reception of Nietzsche.

On a more abstract conceptual level, Karin Barnaby and Pellegrino d'Acierno suggest a parallel between the hermeneutic strategies deployed by Jung and Nietzsche, the importance of whose own contributions to contemporary interpretation theory has been clearly established.[77] According to Barnaby and d'Acierno, 'the Jungian interpretation unfolds as a production – a positing of meanings *in relation to* and not the uncovering of *the meaning*, as in the Freudian interpretation – thereby advancing the genesis of meaning, collaborating in the genesis of the hermeneutic secret', which leads them to the conclusion that 'Jung's "will to interpretation" is much closer to Nietzsche's "progressive" than to Freud's "regressive" hermeneutics'.[78] Their suggestion throws an interesting light on what may also be at stake in the difference between Freud, who claimed never to have read Nietzsche,[79] and Jung, who admitted he had. For, in addition

---

73 Barnaby and d'Acierno, p.xxi.

74 Philip Rieff, *The Triumph of the Therapeutic: Uses of Faith after Freud* (London, 1966), p. 138.

75 Stevens, p. 114.

76 See Jung, GW13 § 246, 278; and WSL: p. 129/PU 211.

77 See Alan D. Schrift, *Nietzsche and the Question of Interpretation: Between Hermeneutics and Deconstruction* (New York and London, 1990).

78 Barnaby and d'Acierno, p.xvii.

79 Freud's reception of Nietzsche has been repeatedly but unsystematically documented. See Rudolf J. Brandt, 'Freud and Nietzsche', *Revue de l'Université d'Ottowa*, 25 (1955), 225–34; Friedrich Tramer, 'Friedrich Nietzsche und Sigmund Freud', *Jahrbuch für Psychologie, Psychotherapie und Anthropologie*, 7 (1960), 325–50; Richard Schmitt, 'Nietzsche's Psychological Theory', *Journal of Existential Psychiatry*, 2 (1961), 71–92; Christo Dimitrov and Assen Jablenski, 'Nietzsche und Freud', *Zeitschrift für psychosomatische Medizin und Psychoanalyse*, 13 (1967), 282–98; Bruce Mazlish,

to the ontological difference between Jung, who had a concept of 'Geist', and Freud, who did not, there is, as Jung liked to point out, a hermeneutic difference between Freud's analytic-reductive method and his own synthetic-constructive method (which corresponds to Paul de Man's 'allegory of reading').[80]

Introductory Remarks on Jung's Reception of Nietzsche

My analysis of Jung's reception of Nietzsche has been supported by the evidence of the marginalia, inscriptions and underlinings in Jung's own copy of Nietzsche's *Werke.*[81] These provide us with much useful information about Jung's reading of Nietzsche. First, they help us to date Jung's acquisition of certain texts; second, they show us which passages Jung read with particular attention; and third, in the case of *Also sprach Zarathustra*, they enable us to look at the same editions from which Jung gave his lectures in his Seminar on Nietzsche. Jung's marginal notes are also a confessional document, revealing not only those passages with which he agreed or disagreed, but also the aporias in his reading. These annotations and my chronological survey help us critically to assess Jung's reception of Nietzsche, instead of dismissing Jung's comments on Nietzsche or exaggerating Jung's debt to him. And that reception is revealed as a process of reaction and response on the part of Jung to a figure he found ceaselessly, but worryingly, fascinating.

This chronological analysis of Jung's reception of Nietzsche structures the book. In Chapter 2, I examine the biographical links which may have stimulated

---

'Freud and Nietzsche', *The Psychoanalytic Review*, 55 (1968), 360–75; Richard Waugamann, 'The Intellectual Relationship between Nietzsche and Freud', *Psychiatry*, 36 (1973), 458–67; Mitchell Ginsberg, 'Nietzschean Psychiatry', in *Nietzsche: A Collection of Critical Essays*, edited by Robert C. Solomon (University of Notre Dame, 1973), pp. 293–315; Jean Granier, 'Le Statut de la philosophie selon Nietzsche et Freud', *Nietzsche-Studien*, 8 (1979), 210–24; Paul Laurent Assoun, *Freud et Nietzsche* (Paris, 1980); Jacob Golomb, 'Freudian Uses and Misuses of Nietzsche', *American Imago*, 37 (1980), 371–85; Lorin Anderson, 'Freud, Nietzsche', *Salmagundi*, No.47–48 (Winter-Spring 1980), 3–29; Rollo May, 'Nietzsches Beiträge zur Psychologie', *Jahrbuch für verstehende Tiefenpsychologie und Kulturanalyse*, 1 (1981), 11–22; Claudia Crawford, 'Nietzsche's Mnemotechnics, the Theory of Ressentiment, and Freud's Topographies of the Psychical Apparatus', *Nietzsche-Studien*, 14 (1985), 281–97; and Jacob Golomb, *Nietzsche's Enticing Psychology of Power* (Ames and Jerusalem, 1989). See also my discussion in Chapter 7 of Jung's remarks about Nietzsche's (apparent) neglect of Freud.

80 See Barnaby and d'Acierno, pp.xviii–xix, and Paul de Man, *Allegories of Reading: Figural Language in Rousseau, Nietzsche, Rilke, and Proust* (New Haven, 1979).

81 Jung owned the 'Kleinoktav-Ausgabe' of Nietzsche's *Gesammelte Werke*, published in 16 volumes by C. G. Naumann and Alfred Kröner between 1899 and 1911. In addition, Jung owned a copy of the English translation by Thomas Common (published in New York but without date of publication nor the publisher's name). For a more detailed discussion of these marginalia and further bibliographical information, see my article 'Jung's Annotations of Nietzsche's Works: An Analysis', *Nietzsche-Studien*, 24 (1995), 271–314.

Jung's interest in Nietzsche, and I look at Jung's earliest, pre-psychoanalytic pronouncements in the Zofingia Lectures. I go on in Chapter 3 to analyse Jung's reception of Nietzsche in his autobiographical sources, showing how Jung's more sophisticated use of Nietzsche in his psychological writings could only happen after he had dissociated himself from Nietzsche on a personal level. The pivotal point in his relationship with Nietzsche turns out to be Jung's breakdown in 1913–1919, traditionally referred to as his period of intense introversion and confrontation with the Unconscious and which I interpret as Jung's own encounter with Dionysos.

Chapters 4, 5, 6, and 7 examine Jung's various uses of Nietzsche in his psychological writings of the early and middle period, whilst Chapter 8 deals with three of Jung's lectures at the Eranos Conferences in Ascona, Switzerland. Three chapters are devoted to Jung's Seminars and his reception of Nietzsche: Chapter 9 looks at Jung's early Seminars up to but not including the Seminar on *Zarathustra* (1934–39), which is instead the focus of Chapters 10 and 11. My chronological survey reaches its conclusion in Chapters 12 and 13 by concentrating on Jung's essays on Nietzsche, National Socialism and the Second World War. Finally, I examine the 'religious' turn in Jung's late writings, which expresses a Romantic yearning for a return to myth. In Jung's case, this is a 'rediscovery' of myth, as opposed to a Nietzschean 'creation' of myth.

Jung's reception of Nietzsche turns out to be more far-reaching, profound and complex than hitherto realized, and his psychology can be understood as a continuing struggle with the implications of the psychological force which Nietzsche called Dionysos and into which, so Jung believed, Nietzsche had gained important insights. The phenomenon of the Dionysian is discussed throughout Jung's writings in various ways – as a manifestation of Jungian (i.e. sexual but also extrasexual) libido (1911–12), as a psychological type (1921), as the source of artistic inspiration (1922/1930–32), as Wotan (1936–1946), and as a component of the Self (1939–1952). The problem of Dionysos is also intimately linked with the question of the Death of God, and Jung's attempt to find a psychological solution to the contemporary crisis in religion. I suggest that Jung's uniquely Nietzschean solution lay in the construction of a Dionysian Self which, through the dialectic of consciousness and the Unconscious, permits the Ego to die and be reborn anew.

Dionysos

Since this book examines the Dionysian as the central point of connection between Jung and Nietzsche, the nature and meaning of Dionysos needs to be addressed. Implicitly I am accepting a certain interpretation of Nietzsche in this book, one which is based on the following three readings. First, Rose Pfeffer emphasizes that 'Nietzsche presents his tragic world view under the symbol of Dionysos and calls himself the "disciple of Dionysos"' and goes so far as to claim that 'without the full recognition that Dionysos, to Nietzsche, is a synthesis of the negative and the positive, a fusion of opposing forces, the most essential aspects of his conception of the tragic, which underlie his whole philosophical thought, cannot be understood'.[82] Second, Karl Löwith relates Dionysos to the key doctrine of Nietzsche's thought as he sees it, the Eternal Recurrence: 'Der radikal vollendete Nihilismus schlägt um in den "klassischen" Positivismus der dionysischen Philosophie der ewigen Wiederkehr des Gleichen' ['Nihilism taken to its radical completion is transformed into the "classical" positivism of the Dionysian philosophy of the Eternal Recurrence of the Same'].[83] And third, particularly in my commentary on Jung's Nietzsche Seminar, I have drawn on Laurence Lampert's interpretation of *Also sprach Zarathustra*, which is itself highly indebted to the approach of Leo Strauss.[84] The significance of Dionysos for post-Nietzschean Western thought in general has been circumscribed by Albert Henrichs,[85] for German romantic literature by Max Baeumer,[86] for Modernism by John Burt Foster, Jr.,[87] and for Nietzsche by M. S. Silk and J. P. Stern.[88] In the course of my work I have referred to two major works of classical scholarship dealing with Dionysos by Károly Kerényi (with whom Jung collaborated) and Walter Otto.[89] I have also referred to Martin Vogel's survey of how the concepts of Apollo and Dionysos have been used by

---

82 Pfeffer, pp. 30–31.

83 Karl Löwith, *Nietzsches Philosophie des ewigen Wiederkehr des Gleichen* (Hamburg, 1978), p. 51.

84 Laurence Lampert, *Nietzsche's Teaching: An Interpretation of Thus Spoke Zarathustra* (New Haven and London, 1986).

85 Albert Henrichs, 'Loss of Self, Suffering, Violence: The Modern View of Dionysus from Nietzsche to Girard', *Harvard Studies in Classical Philology*, 88 (1984), 205–40. See also Henrichs's more recent articles: 'Between Country and City: Cultic Dimensions of Dionysus in Athens and Attica', in: *Cabinet of the Muses: Essays on Classical and Comparative Literature in Honour of Thomas G. Rosenmeyer*, edited by Mark Griffith and Donald Mastronarde (Atlanta, GA, 1990), pp. 257–77; and '"He Has a God in Him": Human and Divine in the Modern Perception of Dionysus', in: *Masks of Dionysus*, edited by Thomas H. Carpenter and Christopher A. Faraone (Ithaca and London, 1993), pp. 13–43.

86 Max L. Baeumer, 'Die romantische Epiphanie des Dionysos', *Monatshefte für deutschen Unterricht, deutsche Sprache und Literatur*, 57 (1965), 225–36; Baeumer, 'Nietzsche and the Tradition of the Dionysian', in *Studies in Nietzsche and the Classical Tradition*, edited by James C. O'Flaherty, Timothy F. Sellner, and Robert M. Helm (North Carolina, 1976); Baeumer, 'Das moderne Phänomen des Dionysischen und seine "Entdeckung" durch Nietzsche', *Nietzsche-Studien*, 6 (1977), 123–53.

87 John Burt Foster, Jr., *Heirs to Dionysus: A Nietzschean Current in Literary Modernism* (Princeton, 1981).

88 M. S. Silk and J. P. Stern, *Nietzsche on Tragedy* (Cambridge, 1981).

89 Károly Kerényi, *Dionysos: Archetypal Image of the Indestructible Life*, translated by Ralph Manheim (Princeton, 1976) and Walter Friedrich Otto, *Dionysos: Mythos und Kultus* (Frankfurt am Main, 1933).

thinkers before and after Nietzsche.[90] For Vogel, the transformation of this polarity is the history of an error; for my purposes, however, his work and that of Manfred Frank[91] serve to show how the Romantic view of the classical world is mediated by nineteenth-century philology via Nietzsche to Jung.

Karl Jaspers has emphasized that Nietzsche is not so much concerned with the details of ancient myth as the symbolic value of Dionysos,[92] and this archetypal significance of Dionysos is well suited to Jungian thought, which concerns itself less with the ontological status of phenomena and more with their *meaning*. Indeed, the discovery of the *symbolic* significance of Dionysos is credited to Nietzsche by Carl Albrecht Bernoulli as his greatest achievement.[93] And Hans Prinzhorn (1866–1933), the German psychiatrist with whose mescalin experiments Jung was familiar, also praised Nietzsche for his prescience in recognizing that the Apollo-Dionysos polarity of Man understood by the Romantics was in danger of disappearing, and for subsequently rescuing it.[94] More recently, the neo-Freudian Norman O. Brown emphasized the importance of 'constructing a Dionysian ego',[95] whilst the neo-Jungian James Hillman takes the figure of Dionysos to represent an act of psychic recuperation of lost powers and potential, now rendered available for use. According to Hillman, to accept Dionysos means:

> to take back into the psyche what has been put upon the body, to take back centuries of misogyny, to take back into consciousness the physical, the feminine and the inferior. This is the redemption of what Jung called [...] 'the earth, darkness, the abysmal side of bodily man with his animal passions and instinctual nature' and [...] 'matter' in general.[96]

In *Jenseits von Gut und Böse* [*Beyond Good and Evil*], Nietzsche's Dionysos expressed the desire to make Man 'stärker, böser, und tiefer; auch schöner' ['stronger, more evil, and more profound; also more beautiful'] (JGB/BGE § 295; N2: p. 756), and in *Zur Genealogie der Moral* [*On the Genealogy of Morals*] Nietzsche called for 'der *erlösende* Mensch der großen Liebe und Verachtung, der schöpferische Geist' ['the *redeeming* Man of great love and contempt, the creative spirit'] (GM II § 24;

---

90 Martin Vogel, *Apollinisch und Dionysisch: Geschichte eines genialen Irrtums* (Studien zur Musikgeschichte des 19. Jahrhunderts, vol. 6) (Regensburg, 1966).

91 Manfred Frank, *Der kommende Gott: Vorlesungen über die Neue Mythologie, I. Teil* (Frankfurt am Main, 1982), and *Gott im Exil: Vorlesungen über die Neue Mythologie, II. Teil* (Frankfurt am Main, 1988).

92 Karl Jaspers, *Nietzsche: Einführung in das Verständnis seines Philosophierens* (Berlin and Leipzig, 1936), pp. 330–31.

93 Carl Albrecht Bernoulli, *Nietzsche in der Schweiz* (Leipzig, 1922).

94 See Hans Prinzhorn, *Nietzsche und das 20. Jahrhundert* (Heidelberg, 1928), p. 35; also 'Nietzsches psychologische Errungenschaften', *Zeitschrift für Menschenkunde*, 2 (1926), 51–58; and 'Der Kampf um Friedrich Nietzsche', *Deutsche Rundschau*, 58 (1932), 117–124. Jung owned a copy of Prinzhorn's *Bildnerei der Geisteskranken* (Berlin, 1922).

95 Norman O. Brown, *Life against Death* (Middletown, 1959), pp. 157–176.

96 James Hillman, 'First Adam, then Eve', *Eranos-Jahrbuch*, 38 (1969), 349–403 (p. 395).

N2: p. 836). Jung's doctrine of the transformations of desire (libido) teaches that this creativity manifests itself in the life of the individual as the overcoming of the Ego and the attainment of the Self as an existential goal. Redemption for both men, then, lies in creation: 'Schaffen – das ist die große Erlösung vom Leiden, und des Lebens Leichtwerden. Aber daß der Schaffende sei, dazu selber tut Leid not und viel Verwandelung' ['Creation – that is the great redemption from suffering, and life's easement. But that the creator may exist, that itself requires suffering and much transformation'] (Z II 2; N2: p. 345). Not only, as I argue in my final chapter, are there deep parallels between the philosophy of Nietzsche and the psychology of Jung, but this should not be surprising, since, as I show in the other chapters, Jung's intellectual development can be read in detail as a reception of Nietzsche's thinking. Jung's statement of 1917 that he was 'von Nietzsche für moderne Psychologie wohlvorbereitet' ['well prepared for modern psychology by Nietzsche'] (GW7 § 199) is also a clue to the philosophical, as opposed to the therapeutic, significance of Analytical Psychology.[97]

[97] Throughout this book, I have taken over Frieda Fordham's (widely adopted) usage (1953, pp. 7 and 84) regarding the designation of the various psychological schools: whilst the term 'psychoanalysis' applies generally to any doctrine of the Unconscious, it is here used contrastively to refer to the work of Freud, and the term 'Analytical Psychology' refers to the work of Jung.

Chapter 2

Jung's Early Reception of Nietzsche

In this chapter, I shall examine the connexions which existed between relatives and personal acquaintances of both Jung and Nietzsche before outlining the pattern of Nietzsche reception at the turn of the century within which Jung's reading of Nietzsche needs to be seen.

Jung and Nietzsche: The Biographical Connexions

Although Jung himself never met Nietzsche, he grew up at a time when the philosopher was still alive in a mental asylum and when, as we shall see, his popularity as a writer was growing. Furthermore, connexions actually existed between Nietzsche and Jung's friends and relatives. For example, Ludwig Binswanger (1881–1966), one of Jung's assistants at the Burghölzli clinic who helped him carry out his experiments on word association, was the nephew of Otto Binswanger (1852–1929), the Professor of Psychiatry and head of the psychiatric clinic at the University of Jena (where he treated Nietzsche after his breakdown in 1889–1890).

More importantly, Jung's parents, Johann Paul Achilles Jung (1842–1896) and Emilie Jung (*née* Preiswerk) (1848–1923), were acquainted with Elisabeth Förster-Nietzsche, Nietzsche's sister and editor (of sorts) of his papers.[1] As Jung records (GW18(i) § 456), he himself corresponded with Frau Förster-Nietzsche because he wanted to establish a connexion between a passage in *Zarathustra* and an episode from Justinus Kerner's *Blätter aus Prevorst*, a book which Nietzsche had read when young.[2] On the death of Nietzsche, Elisabeth included Jung in the list of invitees to the funeral, although there is no evidence to show that Jung either accepted or attended.

Moreover, it has been suggested that Jung's relationship with his father was responsible not only for his intellectual development as a whole, but also, more

[1] According to information provided by Herrn Franz Jung, C. G. Jung's son.

[2] Jung also quotes from her biographical work *Der werdende Nietzsche* (Munich, 1924) with reference to one of Nietzsche's dreams (GW10 § 382).

specifically, for his early interest in Nietzsche. As a child, Jung was sensitive to the crisis of faith that his father, a Protestant minister, went through, and he discusses this in detail in his autobiography. For Marilyn Nagy, 'Jung quite literally took on as his own the unsolved problem of the inner belief of his father and made the *reality of the psyche* the motive of his life'.[3] Anthony Stevens elaborates this point with greater psychological subtlety in his biography of Jung. He reads Jung's intellectual development as a form of 'archetypal compensation' – i.e. as a search for a valid authority to compensate for the lack of authority on the part of Jung's father in matters of religion. Hence, according to Stevens, Jung's fascination with a thinker such as Nietzsche who both heralded the age of radical doubt which troubled Pastor Jung so much and dealt with the contemporary crisis of faith with exemplary openness and honesty. Stevens puts it thus:

> Pastor Jung's powerlessness, his lack of valid authority acquired through confrontation with the truth, meant that those aspects of the father archetype implicated in the *Logos* functions of the masculine principle were only partially activated in the adolescent psyche of Jung. This was his 'unfinished business', and it set him off on a dual quest – for the intellectually courageous father that he lacked and for the initiatory experience that the pastor had failed to provide.[4]

Later on in his life, at university and during his early years as a psychoanalyst, Jung came across three people who had been close to Nietzsche (and who had had, in the first and second cases, a profound intellectual, and in the third case, a profound personal influence upon him). The first of these was Jacob Burckhardt (1818–1897), the Swiss cultural critic and historian who was a professor at Basle from 1858 to 1893.[5] Burckhardt was both a friend and professional colleague of Nietzsche, and he shared the same preoccupations: the question of cultural values, the role of historical study and the need for a spiritual rejuvenation of Europe. The two men came, however, to vastly different conclusions.[6] Jung's

---

[3] Marilyn Nagy, *Philosophical Issues in the Psychology of C. G. Jung* (New York, 1991), p. 12.

[4] Anthony Stevens, *On Jung* (London, 1990), pp. 141–42.

[5] On Nietzsche and Burckhardt, see: Charles Andler, *Nietzsche und Jakob Burckhardt* (Basle and Strasbourg, n.d.); Alfred von Martin, *Nietzsche und Burckhardt* (Munich, 1942); Erich Heller, 'Burckhardt and Nietzsche', in: *The Disinherited Mind* (London, 1952), pp. 59–77; Edgar Salin, *Jakob Burckhardt und Nietzsche* (Basle, 1938) (see note 11). On Jung and Burckhardt, see: Philipp Wolff-Windegg, 'C. G. Jung – Bachofen, Burckhardt, and Basel', *Spring*, 1976, pp. 137–47. A fuller account of intellectual life in late nineteenth-century Basle is provided by Lionel Gossman in *Orpheus philologus: Bachofen versus Mommsen on the Study of Antiquity* (Philadelphia, 1983 [*Transactions of the American Philosophical Society*, vol. 73, pt.5]); 'Basle, Bachofen and the Critique of Modernity in the Second Half of the Nineteenth Century', *Journal of the Warburg and Courtauld Institutes*, 47 (1984), 136–85; and 'Antimodernism in Nineteenth-Century Basle: Franz Overbeck's Antitheology and J. J. Bachofen's Antiphilology', *Interpretation*, 16 (1989), 359–89.

[6] Whereas Burckhardt maintained a paradigmatically logocentric version of history, Nietzsche became increasingly critical of the educational institutions of liberal humanism and launched an attack on Western metaphysics in general and Christianity in particular. See Gary Shapiro, *Nietzschean Narratives* (Bloomington and Indianapolis, 1989), pp. 16–21.

library contains all Burckhardt's major works,[7] and in his autobiographical work *Erinnerungen, Träume, Gedanken* [*Memories, Dreams, Reflections*], Jung mentions that during his time at the Gymnasium he used to see Burckhardt (and Bachofen) on the streets of Basle (ETG: pp. 103, 118–19/MDR: first passage omitted from English version, p. 133). More significantly, Jung quotes Burckhardt as an important authority on Nietzsche by virtue of his personal acquaintance with him, and his critical views were, according to Jung, widespread in university circles at that time:

> Nietzsche wurde damals viel diskutiert, aber meistens abgelehnt, am heftigsten von den "kompetenten" Philosophiestudenten, woraus ich meine Schlüsse auf die in höheren Sphären herrschenden Widerstände zog. Höchste Autorität war natürlich Jacob Burckhardt, von dem verschiedene kritische Äußerungen in bezug auf Nietzsche kolportiert wurden. Zudem gab es einige Leute, die Nietzsche persönlich gekannt hatten und darum imstande waren, allerhand Curiosa nicht gerade sympathischer Art über ihn zu berichten (ETG: p. 108/MDR: p. 122).
>
> [At that time Nietzsche was much discussed, mostly in adverse terms, by the allegedly competent philosophy students, from which I was able to deduce the hostility he aroused in the higher echelons. The supreme authority, of course, was Jacob Burckhardt, whose various critical comments on Nietzsche were bandied about. Moreover, there were some persons at the university who had known Nietzsche personally and were able to recount all sorts of unflattering titbits about him.]

Jung's criticism here is directed not at Burckhardt's sceptical attitude towards Nietzsche, but at those who unthinkingly echo it. And, although the general opinion of Nietzsche expressed by Jung's contemporaries was, apparently, largely negative, it is important to note that this did not hamper Jung's enthusiasm for engaging with his thought (according to his autobiography, his hesitation was due more to personal reasons). There is no evidence that Jung knew Burckhardt personally, but it is likely that Burckhardt's views were mediated by a mutual acquaintance, namely Burckhardt's great nephew, Albert Oeri (1875–1950), a student-colleague and life-long friend of Jung.[8] I have consulted the *Vorlesungsverzeichnisse* in the Staatsarchiv in Basle to establish whether Jung attended any lectures on Nietzsche. From the files examined, it seems that no-one was lecturing on Nietzsche at the time, so that his philosophy had something of an 'alternative' status in relation to 'standard' philosophical thinking. And in fact, although the Danish literary historian Georg Brandes (1842–1927) had given a course of lectures at the University of Copenhagen on the philosophy of his former friend as early as 1888, Nietzsche was first discovered in intellectual circles outside the university system.

---

7 *C. G. Jung-Bibliothek-Katalog* (Küsnacht–Zürich, 1967), p. 14.

8 It may also have been because of Oeri that the early Jungian concept of the 'Urbild' is attributed to Burckhardt. See Werner Kaegi, *Jacob Burckhardt: Eine Biographie*, 7 vols (Basle and Stuttgart, 1947–1982), IV, p. 464, footnote 121).

Although there is less information about Jung's personal contact, if any, with Johann Jakob Bachofen (1815–1887), the historian of law and religion who taught at Basle, he acts as an important link between Nietzsche's interest in ancient Greek culture and Jung's own fascination with Nietzsche and Dionysos. Bachofen was one of Nietzsche's colleagues at Basle, and Nietzsche read his *Gräbersymbolik* whilst he was working on *Die Geburt der Tragödie.* Bachofen's view of the Dionysian is most clearly expounded in *Der Mythus von Orient und Occident* [*The Myth of the East and the West*], in which Dionysos is described as 'der Rätselgott der werdenden Welt, [...] der nicht mit Ordnung und stets gleichbleibendem Ernst, sondern mit Schmerz, Mutwille, Raserei, Ungleichheit sich verbindet, immer täuschend durch den Wechsel der Farben, dem Dualismus eng verwandt, mit seiner Schöpfung dem Tode verfallen und zu Füßen des Delphiers beerdigt' ['the mysterious god of the nascent world ... who is associated, not with order and permanent solemnity, but with pain, mischief, frenzy, dissimilarity, always deceiving by changing colour, closely related to dualism, at his creation destined to die and be buried at the feet of Delphi'].[9] Bachofen's presence at Basle, together with his work on mythology and symbolism and his acquaintance with Nietzsche, provide a telling background to Jung's developing interest in Nietzsche in general and, in his letters to Freud, the Dionysian in particular.

The third person who formed a direct link between Jung and Nietzsche himself was Lou Andreas-Salomé (1861–1937),[10] who became interested in psychoanalysis in the period before the First World War and came to be a prominent member of Freud's circle. Nietzsche had met her through their mutual friend Paul Rée in April 1882 in Rome, and rapidly fell in love with her. Andreas-Salomé and Nietzsche met up several times that year, but their affair ended swiftly and sadly for Nietzsche when she left him for Paul Rée, and Nietzsche's letters to her remain as a testimony of his love and affection for her. In September 1912, Andreas-Salomé introduced herself by letter to Freud and soon became one of his most fervent devotees, regularly attending his Wednesday evening discussions from 30 October 1912 until 2 April 1913. Her posthumously published work *In der Schule bei Freud* [*The Freud Journal*] (Zurich,

---

[9] Johann Jakob Bachofen, *Der Mythus von Orient und Occident: Eine Metaphysik der alten Welt*, edited by Alfred Baeumler (Munich, 1956), pp. 391–92. See also Alfred Bauemler, *Bachofen und Nietzsche* (Zurich, 1929). At the time of writing *Die Geburt der Tragödie,* Nietzsche was a frequent guest at Bachofen's house to dine, and was present at the Bachofens' Christmas Eve party that year (a few days later, *Die Geburt der Tragödie* [*The Birth of Tragedy*] was published). For an account (according to his wife) of Bachofen's inital enthusiasm at the publication of *Die Geburt der Tragödie* and his subsequent disappointment at Nietzsche's later publications, see C. A. Bernoulli, *Johann Jakob Bachofen und das Natursymbol* (Basle, 1924), p. 593).

[10] See Rudolph Binion, *Frau Lou: Nietzsche's Wayward Disciple* (Princeton, 1968); Angela Livingstone, *Lou Andreas-Salomé* (London, 1984); and Cordula Koepcke, *Lou Andreas-Salomé* (Frankfurt am Main, 1986).

1958) provides an interesting first-hand, albeit pro-Freudian account of the discussions and dissensions in the early years of the psychoanalytic movement. Andreas-Salomé was an astute reader of Nietzsche's work, publishing the first serious book on his thought, *Friedrich Nietzsche in seinen Werken* (Vienna, 1894). It is likely that Jung discussed the case of Nietzsche with her, perhaps at the Third International Psychoanalytic Congress in Weimar (1911) or the Fourth International Psychoanalytic Congress in Munich (1913). Certainly, Jung knew her background, for, in a letter to Freud of 2 January 1912, he refers to 'Frau Lou Andreas-Salomé Weimarer Angedenkens' ['of Weimar fame'] in a way which emphasizes her relationship with Nietzsche (FJB: p. 258/FJL: p. 477).

It is hard to gauge the importance of these links for Jung's reception of Nietzsche. Taken singly they do not provide substantial insight, but taken together they suggest that Jung encountered several people who had known Nietzsche personally, and this may well have provided extra impetus to his own desire to engage with his philosophy. The catalogue of Jung's library indicates that Jung also took an interest in the secondary literature on Nietzsche,[11] and in fact, Jung's reading of Nietzsche at university coincided with the first boom in critical commentary on Nietzsche,[12] as is shown by the graph prepared by Herbert Reichert and Karl Schlechta of the number of publications on Nietzsche in various languages from 1870 to 1970.[13] This graph is reproduced as Figure 1.

---

11 Jung's library contains the following works on Nietzsche: Carl Albrecht Bernoulli, *Franz Overbeck und Friedrich Nietzsche: Eine Freundschaft*, 2 vols (Jena, 1908) (this edition contains passages blacked out for legal reasons); F. G. Crookshank, *Individual Psychology and Nietzsche* (London, 1933); Mrs. Havelock Ellis [Edith M. O. Ellis], *Three Modern Seers: Hinton, Nietzsche, Carpenter* (London, 1910); Ernst Horneffer, *Nietzsches Lehre von der ewigen Wiederkunft und deren bisherige Veröffentlichung* (Leipzig, 1900) (inscribed 'Erhalten in Dec 1899 von Frau Dr E Förster-Nietzsche', and this book is probably the gift for which Jung thanked Elisabeth in his letter of 11 December 1899. In his *Gesammelte Werke* Jung makes very little reference to the notion of the Eternal Recurrence, but on the most important occasions when he does (in 1935 and 1939) he also refers to Horneffer (GW14(i) § 148, n.336/ CW14 § 342, n.328 and GW9(i) § 210, n.5; and see SNZ:I: p. 191; II, pp. 1044 and 1263)); Hans Landsberg, *Friedrich Nietzsche und die deutsche Literatur* (Leipzig, 1902); Richard M. Meyer, *Nietzsche: Sein Leben und seine Werke* (Munich, 1913); Paul Julius Möbius, *Über das Pathologische bei Nietzsche* (Wiesbaden, 1902); Edward J. O'Brien, *Son of the Morning: A Portrait of Friedrich Nietzsche* (London, 1932); Edgar Salin, *Jakob Burckhardt und Nietzsche* (Basle, 1938) (Jung's interest in this book must have been great, for his edition as I found it in his personal library contained a letter from Salin of 11 April 1938, replying to a letter of Jung's and apologizing for the late delivery of his book!); Wilhelm Schacht, *Nietzsche: Eine psychiatrisch-philosophische Untersuchung* (Berne, 1901) (the copy is partially uncut); and Franz Unger, *Friedrich Nietzsches Träumen und Sterben* (Munich, 1900) (the copy contains marginal linings).

12 For a general overview of Nietzsche reception, see R. A. Nicholls, 'Beginnings of the Nietzsche Vogue in Germany', *Modern Philology*, 56 (1958/59), 24–37; Bruno Hillebrand (ed.), *Nietzsche und die deutsche Literatur*, 2 vols (Munich, 1978); Alfredo Guzzoni (ed.), *90 Jahre philosophische Nietzsche-Rezeption* (Königstein im Taunus, 1979); and Margot Fleischer, 'Das Spektrum der Nietzsche-Rezeption im geistigen Leben seit der Jahrhundertwende', *Nietzsche-Studien*, 20 (1991), 1–47; and Steven E. Aschheim, *The Nietzsche Legacy in Germany 1890–1990* (Berkeley, 1994).

13 Herbert W. Reichert and Karl Schlechta, *International Nietzsche Bibliography* (revised and expanded) (North Carolina U. P., 1968), graph facing title-page.

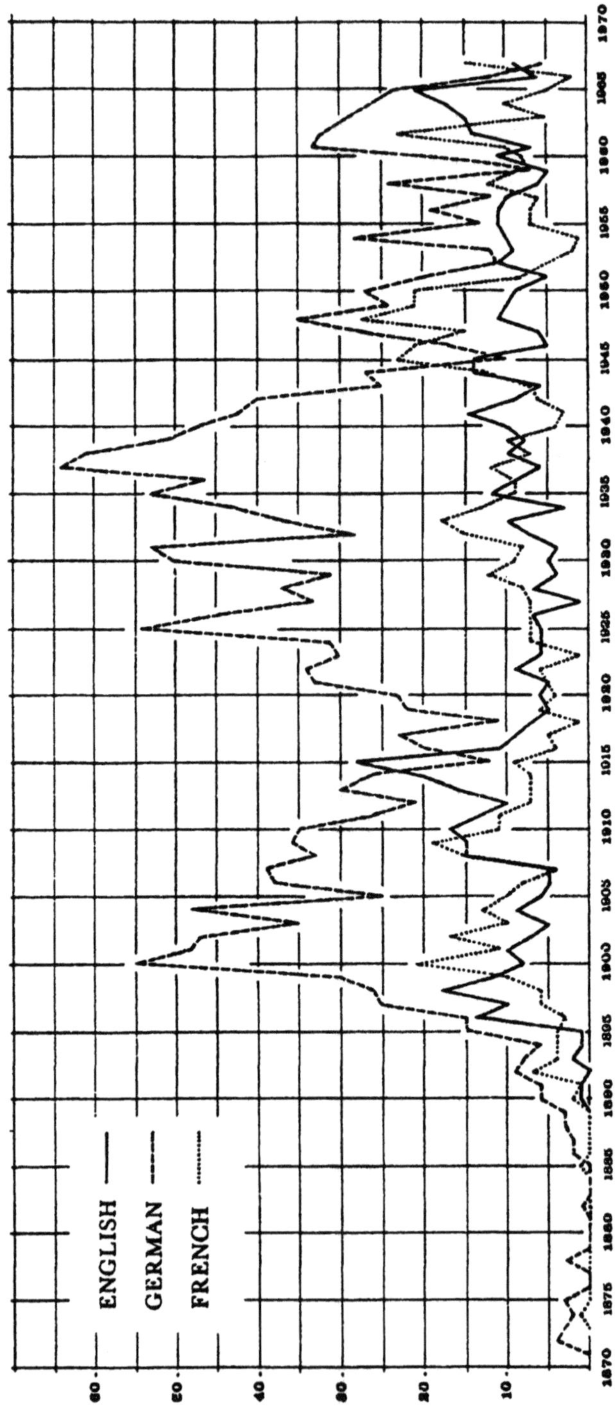

Reprinted from *International Nietzsche Bibliography,* by Herbert W. Reichert and Karl Schlechta. Published for North Carolina Studies in Comparative Literature. Copyright © 1968 by North Carolina Studies in Comparative Literature. Chapel Hill: The University of North Carolina Press. Used by permission of the publisher.

Between 1895 and 1900 – the years when Jung was at the University of Basle – the global number of publications on Nietzsche reached a peak of over 50; and over the same period the number of those written in German nearly quadrupled. As Seth Taylor has observed: 'by 1890, scarcely a year after his own mental collapse, [Nietzsche] was rapidly on his way to becoming nothing short of a cult figure in his homeland'.[14] Another researcher into early Nietzsche reception, the late R. Hinton Thomas, is equally clear about the turning-point in the popularity of Nietzsche: 'The decisive change [in Nietzsche's influence] took place at just about the time when Bismarck's period of office ended [i.e. 20 March 1890]. It happened quickly and it happened dramatically [...] If one had to settle for a single year from which to date this transformation, 1890 would be the one to choose'.[15] According to one source, Duke Carl-August of Sachsen-Weimar is reported to have said to Elisabeth Förster-Nietzsche in the 1890s that it was impossible to open a newspaper without seeing the name of Nietzsche, and that for this reason he had gone to visit the sick philosopher.[16]

The Zofingia Lectures (1896–1899)

On 18 May 1895, Jung became a member of the *Zofingiaverein*, the Swiss student fraternity, and was elected Chairman of the Basle section during the Winter Term of 1897/98. The fraternity had been organized along the lines of the German *Burschenschaften* but was highly conscious of its Swiss identity.[17] Under the motto of 'patriae, amicitiae, litteris', the goals of the club were to discuss, debate – and drink (hence Jung's student nickname, 'Walze' ['barrel'][18]). The Zofingia Lectures – delivered in German but to date published only in English translation[19] – offer an insight into Jung's earliest intellectual preoccupations, those of a medical student who, as he himself admitted, was concerned with 'theological issues' (ZL § 237). We find many of the concerns of Jung's more mature work prefigured here, and Marilyn Nagy has pointed out that these

14 Seth Taylor, *Left-Wing Nietzscheans: The Politics of German Expressionism 1910–1920* (Berlin and New York, 1990) p. 18.

15 Richard Hinton Thomas, *Nietzsche in German Politics and Society 1890–1918* (Manchester, 1983), p. 2.

16 Max Kruse, *Erinnerungen an Elisabeth Förster-Nietzsche*, unpub.ms., Kösen, 7 April 1918; quoted in H. F. Peters, *Zarathustra's Sister: The Case of Elisabeth and Friedrich Nietzsche* (New York, 1977), pp. 169, 238.

17 For more information on the history of the *Zofingiaverein*, see: Werner Kundert, *Abriß der Geschichte des schweizerischen Zofingervereins* (Lausanne, 1961) and Charles Gilliard, *La Société de Zofingue 1819–1919* (Lausanne, 1919).

18 See Albert Oeri, 'Ein paar Erinnerungen', in: *Die kulturelle Bedeutung der komplexen Psychologie* (Berlin, 1935), pp. 524–28.

19 C. G. Jung, *The Zofingia Lectures*, translated by Jan van Heurck (London, 1983).

addresses usefully supplement our understanding of Jung's early intellectual development as depicted in *Erinnerungen, Träume, Gedanken*:

> The publication of the Zofingia Lectures has [...] provided a direct bridge from those late memories of childhood to Jung's actual theoretical formulations as a young man. We can now follow the entire course of Jung's development, from the youth who sought answers in the library of his father and his father's friends, to the student who lectured on philosophy to his comrades, to the physician who invented a terminology of his own to express what he understood of human experience [...] Jung's earliest convictions were also his last ones.[20]

Nagy's last comment in the quotation above is particularly apt, since the defence of metaphysics in general and religion in particular mounted by Jung in these lectures against the attacks of materialism anticipate his defence in his later writings of the 'God-concept' in the light of the Nietzschean 'Death of God'. Because some of these lectures pre-date Jung's first reading at university of Nietzsche, his post-1900 work stands in the shadow of Nietzsche to an extent that these lectures, as will become clear, do not.

According to *Erinnerungen, Träume, Gedanken*, Jung found that Kant was the answer to the problem posed by Schopenhauer's pessimism. However, by examining the number of times which Jung cited Kant, Schopenhauer, Nietzsche, and Eduard von Hartmann in the Zofingia Lectures, a slightly different picture of Jung's opinions and his early reaction to Nietzsche emerges. In his first lecture, 'The Border Zones of Exact Science' (delivered in November 1896), Jung quoted twice from Kant, on both occasions from his *Träume eines Geistersehers, erläutert durch Träume der Metaphysik* [*Dreams of a Spirit-Seer elucidated by Dreams of Metaphysics*] (1766). Jung made no specific reference to Nietzsche, although there is a throwaway line about 'superhuman energy'. In his second lecture, entitled 'Some Thoughts on Psychology' (May 1897), Jung quoted directly from Kant on no less than thirteen occasions (from *Träume eines Geistersehers* and from his *Vorlesungen über Psychologie* [*Lectures on Psychology*])[21] and twice made further references to him, whilst he quoted half as many times from Schopenhauer's *Die Welt als Wille und Vorstellung* [*The World as Will and Representation*] and his *Parerga und Paralipomena.*

Jung's third talk, his brief 'Inaugural Address Upon Assuming the Chairmanship of the Zofingia Club' (Winter Term 1897/98), which made several allusions to such political events as the War between Greece and Turkey of 1897, contained almost no philosophical references, in keeping with the tone of the address. However, Jung concluded with a humorous but significant reference to

---

20 Marilyn Nagy, *Philosophical Issues in the Psychology of C. G. Jung* (New York, 1991), p. 12.

21 Jung is probably referring to *Immanuel Kants Vorlesungen über Psychologie mit einer Einleitung, Kants mystische Weltanschauung*, edited by Carl du Prel (Leipzig, 1889).

Nietzsche: 'We should always do our duty. For, Nietzsche notwithstanding, there is something to morality after all' (ZL § 161). Nietzsche's supposed 'anti-morality' was a commonplace of early Nietzsche reception; and Jung's comment here suggests that he was aware of this. The fourth lecture, 'Thoughts on the Nature and Value of Speculative Enquiry' (Summer 1898), contained only one direct quotation from Kant's *Allgemeine Naturgeschichte und Theorie des Himmels* [*Universal Natural History and Theory of the Heavens*] (1755), and referred to him on only five further occasions (mainly to ideas typical of the *Kritik der reinen Vernunft* [*Critique of Pure Reason*] (1791)). There are, however, three direct quotations from *Die Welt als Wille und Vorstellung*, and Jung made a further five references to Schopenhauer. Moreover, Jung mentioned Eduard von Hartmann (1842–1906) on six occasions (including one passage making a detailed comparison between him and Schopenhauer (ZL § 199)), and gave one direct quotation (from his *Philosophie des Unbewußten* [*Philosophy of the Unconscious*] (1869)). There are even two references to Schelling, and one quotation is attributed to him. The fifth and final Zofingia Lecture, entitled 'Thoughts on the Interpretation of Christianity, with Reference to the Theory of Albrecht Ritschl' (January 1899), opens with a quotation from the *Unzeitgemäße Betrachtungen* [*Untimely Meditations*] and later on mentions the 'revaluation of all values' and the 'untimeliness' of Nietzsche. Here, Jung referred only four times to Kant or Kantianism (always negatively), twice to Schopenhauer, and once to Eduard von Hartmann, from whom he did, however, quote directly on a further two occasions.

It is clear from this analysis that between 1896 and 1899, Jung became very interested in Kant, particularly his pre-critical philosophy, but subsequently moved away from him. Jung not only refers to and quotes from Kant less often, but his earlier, mainly positive references to him become references which are highly negative. Indeed, by his third lecture, it seems that Jung was more interested in comparing Schopenhauer's conception of the Will with Hartmann's notion of the Unconscious than seriously tackling the epistemology of Kant's *Kritik der reinen Vernunft* – as if the conception of the 'Ding an sich' was proving to be too worrying and problematic for him, even though he tried to define it away. And although his interest in Nietzsche was clearly developing, Jung drew mainly on material from the early writings (e.g. *Menschliches, Allzumenschliches* [*Human, All Too Human*] and the *Unzeitgemäße Betrachtungen*). This bears out what Jung wrote in his letters and in his autobiography about which works of Nietzsche he read at university. Thus, the background to Jung's interest in Nietzsche is clearly his involvement with Kantian and post-Kantian philosophy. Between 1896 and 1898, i.e. in the period from the first to the last of the lectures, Jung moved from a pro-Kantian position to one which denied the basic tenets of his critical philosophy and even rejected the critical project as a whole. However, Jung's would-be Kantianism was highly unconventional.

In his first lecture, 'The Border Zones of Exact Science', Jung discusses what he sees as a 'collision between reality and reason' (ZL § 43, 50). At the very beginning, Jung appeals to Kant with two quotations from his *Traüme eines Geistersehers* (1766). In this essay, Kant took up in a highly equivocal manner the claims of Emanuel Swedenborg (1688–1772) to have seen the Stockholm fire of 1756,[22] and ends by defining metaphysics as 'eine Wissenschaft von den *Grenzen der menschlichen Vernunft*' ['a science of the *limits of human reason*'].[23] Jung, however, refers to this text at the outset of an argument whose conclusion is a denial of this definition. Examining the puzzle represented (then, as now) by gravity and other physical phenomena, Jung claims that any material or scientific explanation of them inevitably leads to the postulation of an immaterial or metaphysical realm (ZL § 57). Referring to the debate between mechanism and vitalism which was not only going on at the time but also informed the development of Jung's own thought, Jung discerned in the 'insoluble contradiction between reality and the claim of reason' a modern antinomy of reason, i.e. 'the most violent collision between two claims, both of which are consistent with reason' (ZL § 55). As might be expected, he clearly has sympathies with the vitalist position (ZL § 58), concluding: 'The position of contemporary sceptical materialist opinion constitutes, simply, intellectual death' (ZL § 63). The last sentence – 'What we want is to allow the immaterial to retain its immaterial properties' (ZL § 66) – suggests that it would be possible to open up metaphysical questions to scientific exploration which would not deny them their non-physical status. Such a task could well be said to be the task of psychology as Jung came to understand it.

His second lecture, 'Some Thoughts on Psychology', begins and ends with the question of morality. Again claiming to take a Kantian standpoint, Jung argues that 'we must institute a "revolution from above" by *forcing* morality on science and its exponents through certain transcendental truths' (ZL § 138). In this way, Jung seeks to impose a limit on knowledge in the name of morality – 'no truth obtained by unethical means has the moral right to exist' (ibid.) – rather than by appealing to any transcendental arguments. Jung defines his own position vis-à-vis Kant as follows: 'Kant's epistemology endures unaltered, but his dogmatic teachings have undergone changes as must occur with every dogmatic system' (ZL § 104). However, Jung is no conventional neo-Kantian either, and in this lecture (which contains the largest number of Kantian references of

[22] Throughout his later writings, Jung made repeated reference to this incident in the context of his discussion of the Leibniz/Geulincx problem. See his letters to Hans Bender of 12 February, 6 March and 10 April 1958 (B3: pp. 154–56, 160–62, 169–71/L2: pp. 414–16, 420–21, 428–30) and his essay on synchronicity (GW8 § 927–38).

[23] Immanuel Kant, *Träume eines Geistersehers, erläutert durch Träume der Metaphysik* (1766) (Erlangen, 1988), p. 115.

the five), Kant appears in some rather unusual company such as Carl du Prel (1839–1899),[24] Johann Zöllner (1834–1882),[25] Gustav Fechner (1801–1887)[26] and other assorted spiritualists such as Alexander Aksakov (1833–1903)[27] and William Crookes (1832–1919).[28] The conundrums posed by recent scientific discoveries during the nineteenth century for the Cartesian/Newtonian world view and its anthropocentric assumptions[29] was a genuine one, and spiritualism was, at that time, a subject of serious investigation,[30] a fact which explains why Jung attributes so much importance to such apparently occult topics. However, there is no excuse for his complete misreading of Kant's *Träume eines Geistersehers*, which, according to Jung, 'tested the validity of Swedenborg's claims amd gave them a thorough and unbiased reading' (ZL § 105). Jung completely overlooks the sarcastic tone of this tract, ignores its description of Swedenborg as the 'Kandidaten des Hospitals', and he even goes so far as to agree with the view, attributed to Carl du Prel, that 'if Kant were alive today, he would undoubtedly be a spiritualist'! The target of Jung's invective is again materialism (ZL § 109), and in his description of two kinds of psychology, Jung clearly wants to propose what he would later call 'eine "Psychologie mit Seele"' ['a "psychology with "soul"'].[31] Jung divides psychology into rational psychology (based on what he

---

24 Baron Karl Ludwig August Friedrich Maximilien Alfred DuPrel, famous spiritualist; see his *Das Rätsel des Menschen* (Leipzig, 1892).

25 Johann Karl Friedrich Zöllner, author of *Wissenschaftliche Abhandlungen*, 3 vols (Leipzig, 1878–1879); vol. 3 is entitled *Die transzendentale Physik und die sogennante Philosophie.*

26 Gustav Theodor Fechner, the founder of psychophysics, whose basic tenets were, first, panpyschism (the doctrine that all objects in the universe – not just animal but also vegetable and mineral – possess a soul), and second, psycho-physical parallelism. See *Nana oder über das Seelenleben von Pflanzen* (Leipzig, 1848), *Zend-Avesta oder über die Dinge des Himmels und das Jenseits*, 3 vols (Leipzig, 1851) and *Elemente der Psychophysik* (Leipzig, 1860). Freud was also interested in Fechner, as he stated in his autobiography: 'Ich war immer für die Ideen G. Th. *Fechners* zugänglich und habe mich auch in wichtigen Punkten an diesen Denker angelehnt' ['I always had time for the ideas of G. T. Fechner and in important points I have also followed this thinker'] (*Gesammelte Werke*, 18 vols (Frankfurt am Main, 1968–1978), XIV, p. 86.

27 Alexander Nicolaevic Aksakow, *Animismus und Spiritismus: Versuch einer kritischen Prüfung der medizinischen Phänomene mit besonderer Berücksichtigung der Hypothesen der Halluzinationen und des Unbewußten* (Leipzig, 1890).

28 Sir William Crookes, an English spiritualist whose scientific work led to the discovery of cathode rays.

29 See Fritjof Capra, *The Turning Point* (New York, 1982).

30 For a closer study of the link between the study of 'Geist' and the study of 'Geister', see 'Anhang: Das "Parapsychische", Okkultismus, Spiritismus, Theosophie' in: Traugott Oesterreich, *Die deutsche Philosophie des XIX. Jahrhunderts und der Gegenwart: IV. Teil von Friedrich Überwegs Grundriß der Geschichte der Philosophie*, 11 edition (Berlin, 1916), pp. 412–14; and Hans von Noorden, 'Das Rätsel des Hellsehens: Probleme von Kant bis C. G. Jung', *Schopenhauer-Jahrbuch*, 52 (1971), 19–39. Jung's choice of a female subject was not unusual; see Alex Owen, *The Darkened Room* (London, 1989).

31 See his lecture originally entitled 'Die Entschleierung der Seele' ['The Unveiling of the Soul'] given in Vienna in 1931 ('Das Grundproblem der gegenwärtigen Psychologie', GW8 649–88). According to Herbert Schnädelbach (*Philosophie in Deutschland 1831–1933* (Frankfurt am Main,

calls the 'category of causality') and empirical psychology (based on 'documentary evidence' which rehearses the case for telekinetic, telepathic and prophetic phenomena).

Jung's so-called rational psychology is essentially a defence of vitalism, and he identifies this 'vital principle' with the Will to Life (ZL § 86) or a 'life force' (ZL § 95): 'Thus it appears that the *principium vitae* constitutes, so to speak, the scaffolding on which matter is built up' (ZL § 89). On Jung's account, this vital principle extends beyond consciousness, and by this he means that it is purely instinctual, i.e. unconscious: 'it also maintains the vegetative functions of our body which [...] are not under our conscious control' (ZL § 96). Claiming to base himself on Schopenhauer, Jung argues that both conscious and unconscious functions are common to a transcendental subject, which Jung terms the 'soul'.

Jung's view here of the soul directly anticipates his statements about the psyche in 'Über die Energetik der Seele' ['On Psychic Energy'] (whose German title preserves the vocabulary of 'soul')[32] and 'Theoretische Überlegungen zum Wesen des Psychischen' ['On the Nature of the Psyche'].[33] According to Jung in 1897, the 'soul' has two important characteristics. First, it is intelligent, by which Jung appears to imply that some kind of an entelechy is at work: 'The criterion of intelligence is the purposefulness of its acts [and] undeniably our bodies impress us as highly purposeful' (ZL § 97). Although Jung disavows the concept of teleology in his discussion of the 'energic' or final point of view in 'Über die Energetik der Seele' (GW8 § 3, n.4), and in 'Theoretische Überlegungen' explicitly dissociates himself from Hans Driesch's (1867–1941) concept

1983), p. 298, note 235), the expression 'Psychologie ohne Seele' was coined by Friedrich Albert Lange (1828–1875) (*Geschichte des Materialismus und Kritik seiner Bedeutung in der Gegenwart* [*History of Materialism and Critique of its Meaning in the Present Day*], 2 vols, edited by Alfred Schmidt (Frankfurt am Main, 1974), II, p. 823). Nietzsche read Lange in his early years and described him as 'einen höchst aufgeklärten Kantianer und Naturforscher' ['a highly enlightened Kantian and natural scientist'] (letter to Carl von Gersdorff of August 1866 (N3: p. 970), declaring *Die Geschichte des Materialismus* to be 'ein Buch, das unendlich mehr gibt als der Titel verspricht und das man als einen wahren Schatz wieder und wieder anschauen und durchlesen mag' ['a book which delivers much more than the title promises and which, as a real treasure, one wants to look at and read through again and again'] (letter to Gersdorff of 16 February 1868 (N3: p. 991)). The idea was that psychology could be a 'science of the soul' was expressly rejected by Wilhelm Wundt in his *Grundriß der Psychologie* (Leipzig, 1896). For this reason, Jung has a highly negative view of Wundt both here and elsewhere (ZL § 108, 248). By 1911/12, Jung was, however, more positively disposed to Wundt (WSL: pp. 27, 33 and 133; PU § 23, 29, n.18, 219, n.4.)

32 'Über die Energetik der Seele' (GW8 § 1–130) was published in 1928, although Jung started work on the paper in about 1912, soon after the publication of *Wandlungen und Symbole der Libido* [*Psychology of the Unconscious*].

33 The first version of 'Theoretische Überlegungen zum Wesen des Psychischen' appeared in 1946 and it was republished in 1954 (GW8 § 343–442).

of a psychoid entelechy (GW8 § 368),[34] he nonetheless concedes the notion of a goal or *telos* (whilst simultaneously denying the possibility of ever attaining it) in the latter work when he writes that the psychic wholeness comprehended in the unity of consciousness is an ideal goal that has never yet been reached (GW8 § 366). Second, Jung claims in 1897 that the soul is independent of space and time (and therefore in this sense *beyond* them): whilst recognizing that space and time are only categories of the understanding (more properly, they are the forms or conditions of sensory intuition), Jung then equates the soul with the 'Ding an sich' (ZL § 98). Going beyond the limits of the *Kritik der reinen Vernunft*, where Kant's transcendental dialectic merely posits the unity of the thinking subject, i.e. transcendental apperception, Jung here identifies the transcendental subject with the 'Ding an sich'. Jung follows the Kantian distinction between substance and subject, however, when he argues that 'the soul does not represent a force in a material form, and thus there can be no judgment concerning it' (ZL § 99).[35]

It is clear from these similarities that, even *before* he had read Nietzsche, in 1897 Jung's understanding of the transcendental subject (which he then called the soul) is identical with his view in the Thirties and Forties (i.e. after he was saturated in Nietzsche's work) of the transcendental subject (which he now called the psyche).[36] Indeed, this reworking of the notion of transcendental subjectivity shows that it remained unaffected by Nietzsche's deconstruction of the subject, and Jung may well have held on to this view all the more determinedly for having read Nietzsche. In general, however, Jung was distracted from Nietzsche's (anti-) epistemology by a deeper interest in the concept of the Dionysian. By failing to appreciate to what extent Nietzsche's philosophy was a post-Kantian, indeed an anti-Kantian philosophy, Jung may also have missed the chance to examine more carefully his own precarious use of Kant.

The title of Jung's fourth lecture, 'Thoughts on the Nature and the Value of Speculative Enquiry', is more obviously neo-Kantian in flavour. In his second lecture, Jung had drawn a contrast between Kant – 'this greatest of all sages ever born on German soil' – and 'his puerile epigones' (ZL § 105); and in 1898

---

[34] According to Jung, Driesch's notion of the psychoid in his *Philosophie des Organischen*, 2 vols (Leipzig, 1909), is indeed an entelechy. Jung is at pains to distinguish his use of 'psychoid' (for him an adjective, not a noun) from either Driesch's entelechy or Eugen Bleuler's concept of 'die Psychoide' in *Die Psychoide als Prinzip der organischen Entwicklung* (Berlin, 1925) (GW8 § 368).

[35] Finally, Jung comes to the more conventionally Kantian conclusion that the soul must be postulated as being immortal.

[36] In his letter to H. J. Barrett (originally written in English) of 12 October 1956, Jung writes: 'the psyche is capable of functioning unhampered by the categories of time and space. *Ergo* it is in itself an equally transcendental being and therefore relatively [!] non-spatial and "eternal"'. Characteristically, Jung goes on to say: 'This does not mean that I hold any kind of convictions as to the transcendental nature of the psyche. It may be anything' (B3: p. 61/L2: p. 333). Jung did not bother with this kind of disclaimer in his earlier philosophical sallies.

he referred again to 'the epigones of Kant'. This is, of course, a jibe at the title of Otto Liebmann's *Kant und die Epigonen* (1865) which marked the beginning of the Kantian renaissance in Europe. Indeed, Jung is sceptical about post-Kantian thought in general, and criticizes Fichte, Schelling and Hegel for their 'lapses' (ZL § 175). But rather than quoting Kant or Schopenhauer, Jung instead makes references to Nietzsche and Eduard von Hartmann. Hartmann enjoyed immense popularity in the late nineteenth and early twentieth century: *Philosophie des Unbewußten*, first published in 1868, was in its eleventh edition by 1904. Jung's library contains the edition of 1872.[37] Although Hartmann himself described his work as 'eine Synthese Hegel's und Schopenhauer's unter einem entscheidenden Uebergewicht des ersteren, vollzogen nach Anleitung der Principienlehre aus Schelling's positiver Philosophie und des Begriffs des Unbewußten aus Schelling's erstem System' ['a synthesis of Hegel and Schopenhauer with the decisive predominance of the former, performed under the guidance of the doctrine of principles from Schelling's positive philosophy and the concept of the Unconscious from Schelling's first system'],[38] it is not so much his roots in German Idealism as his emphasis on the concept of the Unconscious which made his thought attractive to Jung. At the start of his lecture, Jung points out that the 'extraordinarily productive [...] secularization of human interests' has been achieved at the expense of Man's relation with instinct and Nature.[39] However, this link with Nature is said to be preserved – in the Unconscious.[40] This alienation from Nature and overcommitment to materialist values is, according to Jung, responsible for Man's 'unhappiness', for Jung locates the source of happiness not in the external world or Man's relation to it, but in 'the unfathomable depths of our own being' (ZL § 171).

Jung seeks to describe the source of this happiness with two phrases from Kant's vocabulary: 'It is the gratification of two a priori requirements – the categorical imperative and the category of causality – that [...] makes a person happy' (ZL § 172). Jung begins his elaboration of these ideas by defining the categorical imperative:

> It is the irrepressible demand to do what we regard as good, and refrain from doing what we regard as morally evil. It gives us a feeling of pleasure to act in accordance

---

[37] Jung's library also contains Hartmann's *Die deutsche Ästhetik seit Kant* (Leipzig, 1886) and two later works, *Die moderne Psychologie* (Leipzig, 1901) and *Die Weltanschauung der modernen Physik* (Baad Sachse, 1909).

[38] Eduard von Hartmann, *Philosophie des Unbewußten* (Leipzig, 1923), 'Vorwort zur zwölften Auflage', p. xiv – xv.

[39] This is the first version of a view of the history of Western civilization which Jung was often to rehearse in his writings. For example, see GW5 § 102 – 13, GW8 § 649 – 51.

[40] 'The process of perfecting external relations has torn Man away from his bond with nature, but only from the conscious bond, not from the unconscious' (ZL § 170).

with the requirements of the categorical imperative, just as the gratification of any instinct brings with it a certain quantity of pleasure (ZL § 171).

However, this account runs counter to Kant's own assertion in the *Kritik der praktischen Vernunft* [*Critique of Practical Reason*] that the objective of practical reason is the greatest good and *not* the happiness of the doer. In Kant's view, happiness is connected with virtue only through two of the postulates of practical reason: the existence of God and the immortality of the soul.[41] Jung then moves on to the category of causality, a term whose usage is, in this lecture, even more problematic. In her introduction to the Zofingia Lectures, Marie-Louise von Franz interprets the 'causal instinct' as 'an individual urge to *understand* outer and inner reality' (ZL: p.xx), and Marilyn Nagy takes it to connote a 'teleological world-view'.[42] However, when Jung first introduces the term (ZL § 171), he plainly means causality as a category, one of the twelve pure concepts of the understanding. In a garbled version of Schopenhauer's *Über die vierfache Wurzel des Satzes vom zureichenden Grunde* [*On the Fourfold Root of the Principle of Sufficient Reason*] (1813), Jung talks about the reduction of the number of categories from twelve to three: time, space, and causality. However, time and space are not, strictly speaking, categories for either Kant or Schopenhauer. In fact, because both space and time determine each other reciprocally but non-causally, they are inseparable, constituting together the *a priori* form of sense perception (elucidated in the Transcendental Aesthetic of Kant and called the *principium individuationis* by Schopenhauer). Later in his lecture, Jung claims that 'the category of causality' can be designated an 'instinct' and attributes this position to the physicist Hermann von Helmholtz (1821 – 1894),[43] apparently also assigning *a priori* status to what he calls the 'causal instinct' (ZL § 178). Amongst this semi-Kantian language, Jung slips in a far more Fichtean terminology of purposiveness[44] and striving;[45] and when, even further on, he says that 'in every

---

41 Marilyn Nagy interprets the categorical imperative (as used here by Jung) to refer to the third postulate of practical reason, i.e. the 'conviction of inner freedom' (p. 21).

42 Nagy, p. 89.

43 Hermann von Helmholtz was heavily influenced by Kant and undertook major empirical work on sense perception, in his *Handbuch der physiologischen Optik* (Leipzig, 1856 – 1866). See Nagy, pp. 64 – 67.

44 'According to the principle of sufficient reason, a notion of purpose must exist prior to every action intended to have a purposeful character' (ZL § 176). Again, the imprecision of Jung's language obscures what appears to be a reference to the principle of *agendi* (motivation).

45 Jung uses the idea of striving in a manner reminiscent of Fichte on three occasions. First, he says that: 'In the final analysis the striving for happiness can be described as the motivation for every human act' (ZL § 174). Second, Jung discusses physical phenomena in terms of a striving to achieve absolute inertia and a striving towards unlimited change and ceaseless activity (ZL § 208 – 15). Third, he identifies 'the true root of our nature' as 'unconditional activity' (ZL § 225). The extent of Jung's knowledge of Fichte is unknown, and his library contains none of Fichte's works, even though Jung at one point refers to him by name (ZL § 175). Equally, there are a number of statements in this lecture which invite comparison with Schelling. However,

healthy, reflective person the simple need to satisfy the principle of causality develops into a metaphysical longing, into religion' (ZL § 181), it becomes necessary for us to consider von Franz's and Nagy's definitions and ask just what kind of a causality Jung is discussing...

Jung's argument involves a consideration of the nature of 'instinct', and he notes that 'instinctive actions' were the subject of much interest for such earlier nineteenth-century thinkers as Schelling, Darwin, Schopenhauer and von Hartmann. However, in order to consider this unconscious (as opposed to rational) phenomenon, Jung has to abandon the Kantian terminology (which he has been using with only limited success) and appeal to – Nietzsche: 'As Nietzsche says, our philosophy should, first and foremost, be a philosophy of what lies nearest to hand' (ZL § 175).[46] According to Jung, both external and intrapsychic reality deserve to be given an equal ontological footing and grounded, not in reason, but in experience:

> Our philosophy should consist in drawing inferences about the unknown, in accordance with the principle of sufficient reason, on the basis of *real experience*, and not in drawing inferences about the inner world on the basis of the outer, or denying external reality by affirming only the inner world (ZL § 175).

Jung defines an instinct in teleological – or, to use his later terminology, final[47] – terms: 'An instinctive action is an action whose cause can be material, i.e., tangible, but whose true motivation is a purposeful idea which is unknown to us' (ZL § 177). Earlier in his lecture, Jung had argued that although reason could not discern what the purpose external to ourselves actually was, it was nevertheless possible to demonstrate that there was indeed a purpose (ZL § 175). Now he suggests, however, that 'causality' (whatever he means by that) leads ultimately to the postulation of a transcendental (i.e. transcendent) 'Ding an sich' which guarantees the continuity between the world of perception and the realm of transcendence:

> Causality leads us to a *Ding an sich* for which we cannot account further, to a cause whose nature is transcendental. In this sense the category of causality must be interpreted as a totally wondrous a priori reference to causes of a transcendental nature,

---

Jung's library does contain Schelling's *Philosophie der Mythologie*, *Sämtliche Werke*, 2/1 and 2/2 (Stuttgart and Augsburg, 1856–57) and *Über die Gottheiten von Samothrace* (Stuttgart, 1815). The copy of Schelling's *Philosophie der Mythologie* contains marginal markings in Jung's hand, and he refers to Schelling in 1911/12 (WSL: p. 44, n.43; PU § 50, n.37).

[46] This is probably an allusion to a line from *Menschliches, Allzumenschliches*: 'Wir müssen wieder *gute Nachbarn der nächsten Dinge* werden' ['We must again become *good neighbours to the closest things*'] (MA/HA WS § 16; N1: p. 882).

[47] See my comment in the text about Jung's careful avoidance of the term 'teleology' – but the distinction seems very fine, particularly since Jung here admits that there is a goal, albeit an unknown one. One suggestion as to why Jung prefers to use 'final' instead of 'teleological' is because he wishes to preserve the notion that the goal can never actually be reached.

> i.e., to a world of the invisible and incomprehensible, a continuation of material nature into the incalculable, the immeasurable, and the inscrutable (ZL § 184).

And from this, Jung concludes that if 'causality has purpose', then 'science, philosophy, and religion also have a use – a transcendental [i.e. transcendent] use' (ZL § 185). In contradiction to the Third Critique then, which admits only of a critique of teleological *judgment* ('Urteilskraft'), Jung is erecting in this lecture a metaphysic of purpose,[48] a desire which anticipates his later insistence that, against all the odds, life does indeed have meaning.[49]

In endorsement of this view, Jung quotes two further passages which he attributes to Nietzsche – a highly ironic move given that the deconstruction of the notion of causality lies at the heart of Nietzsche's mature philosophy. From here, it is only a short step to an attack on the concept of the *Ding an sich*, but Jung does not do this in the same way in which Nietzsche did (cf. WM/WP 557 = N3: pp. 502–03).[50] From the definition that 'the *Ding an sich* includes everything that eludes our perception, everything of which we have no tangible image', Jung goes on to suggest that the concept of the *Ding an sich* is indeed a limiting one, but only temporarily so: 'If we do not yet possess a graphic image of the cause of a phenomenon, we create a so-called principle, i.e. we postulate the existence of a *Ding an sich* that cannot be explained with the means now at our disposal' (ZL § 196).

Having disputed the status of the *Ding an sich*, Jung reviews two other post-Kantian solutions of this epistemological problem: first, Schopenhauer's notion of the Will,[51] and second, von Hartmann's concept of the Unconscious.[52] According to Jung, a basic dualism is common to their respective interpretations of the *Ding an sich* (which in both cases is a suffering *Ding an sich*); and Jung detects the existence of opposites in a further five thinkers: the author of Ecclesiasticus (a book in the Old Testament Apocrypha), the German mystical philosopher Jakob Böhme (1575–1624), Wundt, Schelling and the Greek pre-Socratic philosopher Empedocles. The underlying thought here is the concept

48 Cf. Stephan Körner, *Kant* (Harmondsworth, 1955), p. 209.

49 'Das Leben ist Sinn und Unsinn, oder es hat Sinn und Unsinn. Ich habe die ängstliche Hoffnung, der Sinn werde überwiegen und die Schlacht gewinnen' ['Life is – or has – meaning and meaninglessness. I cherish the anxious hope that meaning will preponderate and win the battle'] (ETG: p. 360/MDR: pp. 391–92).

50 Jung never really came to terms with Nietzsche's attack on causality and, because Nietzsche's position is most clearly explained in his notes for *Der Wille zur Macht* and other *Nachlaß* writings, it is probable that Jung never fully realized this.

51 In *Wandlungen und Symbole der Libido*, Jung identifies Schopenhauer's Will with his revised concept of Freudian libido (WSL: p. 130/PU § 212).

52 In a letter to A. Vetter of 8 April 1932, Jung appears to identify the Collective Unconscious with the *Ding an sich* (B1: p. 124/L1: p. 91).

of polarity (ZL § 218–22).[53] In fact, Jung goes so far as to suggest that everything in the world bears witness to this struggle between opposites for superiority, and casts this idea in the following highly Nietzschean way: 'If we contemplate nature with objectivity, are we not compelled to think: Two radically different powers are here engaged in a furious struggle for domination?' (ZL § 205).[54] According to Jung, even current scientific views understand natural phenomena in terms of two different kinds of striving (one towards stasis, another towards ceaseless activity), echoing the similar dualism of the principles of attraction and repulsion which Jung found in Kant's *Allgemeine Naturgeschichte und Theorie des Himmels*.[55] Jung turns to the German chemist Friedlieb Ferdinand Runge (1795–1867) and Faust's 'Zwei Seelen wohnen, ach! in meiner Brust' ['Alas, there dwell two souls in my breast'] for evidence to support his contention that there is dualism in the realm of organic nature as well: 'Man's inner dualism is the direct continuation of the dualism of inorganic nature' (ZL § 224). Indeed, in his first recorded psychological interpretation of Goethe, Jung reads Faust's exclamation as 'the internal reflection of this struggle, in the form of a feeling of psychic schism' (ZL § 223).[56]

From all these (largely anti-Kantian) reflections, Jung draws five main conclusions. First, we must 'reject the secularization of human interests' (ZL § 227), so that our goals must henceforth no longer be material but 'transcendental' (i.e. transcendent). Second, as a result (and the Nietzschean overtones are unmistakeable), 'we will affirm the will to personality, to individuality' (ZL § 227). Third, we must accept that 'no diversity can develop without the existence of an opposite', and this is Jung's justification for suffering. Fourth, bearing in mind the painful condition of living in a world of opposites, Jung rejects optimism and advocates a pessimistic view of the world (a Schopenhauerian suggestion supported with a quotation from *Die Welt als Wille und Vorstellung*) (ZL § 229).

---

[53] Polarity is a key concept in Schelling's 'Naturphilosophie', in which dynamic polarities are said to structure all natural phenomena (Schelling, *Von der Weltseele* [*Of the World Soul*] (1798), in: *Ausgewählte Werke*, 10 vols (Darmstadt, 1975–1976), VI, p. 444). The notion of polarity is also important in the later thought of Jung (GW13 § 18, 40; GW7 § 115) and is intimately related to the problem of the opposites. See also William Willeford, 'Jung's Polaristic Thought in its Historical Setting', *Analytische Psychologie*, 6 (1975), 218–39.

[54] Cf. 'Nur, wo Leben ist, da ist auch Wille: aber nicht Wille zum Leben, sondern [...] Wille zur Macht!' ['Only where life is, there is also will: not will to life, but "Will to Power!"'] (Z II 12; N2: p. 372); 'Wir haben zwei "Willen zur Macht" im Kampfe gesehn' ['We have seen two "wills to power" in battle'] (WM/WP 401 = N3: p. 739). However, Jung assigns this conflict to a principle which is more Schopenhauerian than Nietzschean: 'So striking is the impression of antagonistic aims in nature, that this strife was even admitted into science in the form of a biological principle: the struggle for existence' (ZL § 206).

[55] Basing itself on the Newtonian theory of attraction, this pre-critical work deals mainly with theories of astronomy.

[56] Compare with Jung's comments about his own personality split, where he refers to the same line from *Faust I* (L./112) (ETG: p. 238/MDR: p. 261).

Fifth, and most importantly from the perspective of his later work, Jung not only claims that both reason and Christianity point towards pessimism, but that, in the language of theology, the world is 'evil' (ZL § 232).

In other words, right at the beginning of Jung's intellectual biography, we find the embryo of an idea that, in the shape of the concept of the Pleroma, would play a part in his *VII Sermones ad mortuos* (1916) and which he developed further in his last extensive work, *Mysterium Coniunctionis* (1955/56): the idea of the *unus mundus*. Jung's statement here is clearly a denial of the basic Kantian position, but in terms of post-Kantian philosophy, it echoes the chief tenet of Schelling's 'Identitätsphilosophie': 'Alles, was ist, ist an sich Eines' ['Everything that is, is in itself one'].[57] It is hard to tell whether Jung realized how close he was to Schelling in this respect, or whether he would have been surprised to see to what extent he was still caught up within a philosophical tradition from which he had tried to find a psychological exit. And Jung's later attitude to the question of Good and Evil is already anticipated here in his highly Manichaean assertion that there is such a thing as Evil – rather than merely an absence of Good.[58]

It seems strange that, after all his efforts to fill in the worrying lacunae of Kantian epistemology and to erect a metaphysics of purpose, Jung should have concluded his lecture by preaching an attitude of pessimism and asserting that 'the whole cosmos is grounded in Evil'. However, his final words are given over to two further quotations from Nietzsche, and perhaps Jung was already aware that his confidence and certainties were going to be shaken – and that he would have to go much further in rejecting the language of Kantian philosophy before he could translate what he thought and believed into the vocabulary of Analytical Psychology. In fact, it was not until Jung had undergone his own experience of the Dionysian that he was able to put both Kant and Nietzsche into psychological perspective.

Jung's fifth lecture is his most overtly theological, as he admits in his opening words (ZL § 237). The lecture is a rejection of the 'Systematic Theology' of Albrecht Ritschl (1822–1889),[59] and its whole tone, including its criticism of

---

57 This is a quotation from *Darstellung meines Systems der Philosophie (1801)* [*Statement of My System of Philosophy*]; see Schelling, VIII, p. 15. Schelling's concept of the Absolute (the identity of Mind and Nature) belongs in a tradition which stretches back, through Spinoza's notion of substance in his *Ethica* (1677) and Giordano Bruno's *Della causa, principio ed uno* (1584), to the Parmenidean notion of pure, indeterminate being (the identity of thinking and being).

58 The question of Evil, examined by Hume in his *Dialogues Concerning Natural Religion* (1779), provoked the further discussion by Kant in *Die Religion innerhalb der Grenzen der bloßen Vernunft* [*Religion within the Bounds of Reason Alone*] (1793), and in *Über das Wesen der menschlichen Freiheit* [*On the Nature of Human Freedom*] (1809), Schelling also conceded the actuality of Evil within the world. There is another important philosophico-theological tradition behind Jung's thought here.

59 See Marilyn Nagy, 'Self and Freedom in Jung's Lecture on Ritschl', *Journal of Analytical Psychology*, 35 (1990), 443–57.

Ritschl's style, is reminiscent of Nietzsche's attack of David Friedrich Strauss in the first of the *Unzeitgemäße Betrachtungen* (1873). Where Nietzsche had poured scorn on Strauss for his supposedly 'philistine' and 'barbaric' reinterpretation of Christianity, Jung upbraided Ritschl for his rejection of philosophical Idealism and mystical experience.[60] Indeed, Jung opens his lecture with an impassioned plea for justice from Nietzsche's essay on 'Schopenhauer als Erzieher' ['Schopenhauer as Educator'] (ZL: p. 93). The praise in the following paragraph for 'alien, almost supramundane beings who relate to the historical conditions just enough to be understood, but who essentially represent a new species of Man' (ZL § 243) recalls Nietzsche's encomium in the *Unzeitgemäße Betrachtungen* of the great men of the past and the brave philosophers of genius.

Jung takes a highly negative view of Kant on all four occasions on which he refers to him in the fifth lecture, and there are equally hard words for Wundt and von Hartmann (ZL § 248), although von Hartmann is used much more positively at a later stage (ZL § 287). Jung questions Kant's religious integrity in the face of the 'purely negative limiting concept of the *Ding an sich*' (ZL § 248). He castigates Ritschl's alleged 'artful epistemology which, in genuine Kantian fashion, is calibrated wholly with reference to the normal man' (ZL § 251) and its supposed 'ominous taint of Kantian subjectivism' (ZL § 270), complaining that 'the normal man in Kant's critique of pure reason has little taste for the element of mystery in religion' (ZL § 282). This leads to the crux of Jung's difficulty with Ritschl's theology (and, implicitly, Kant's rationalistic approach to religion too).

Jung's objection to Ritschl's theology is threefold. First, he claims that Ritschl 'rejects any illuministic or subjective knowledge' (ZL § 257). Second, as a result, Jung argues that because 'Ritschl develops his foundation of ethics within the sphere of discursive reason and sensory perceptibility [...] he sees no other way to acquire motivations with respect to value, than the way of conscious sensation' (ZL § 259, 264). Third, 'Ritschl's theory of the relationship of Man with God and Christ derives from this epistemological necessity' (ZL § 264). Jung understands Ritschl to mean that there can be no direct revelation from God to Man and no *unio mystica* (ZL § 254–55), and so he expresses outrage and despair over the absence from Ritschl's system of what he considers to be a key religious category – mystery (ZL § 283, 288). Instead of the historical Jesus

---

60 Albrecht Ritschl studied theology in Tübingen, amongst other places, and he was Professor of Theology at Bonn from 1859 to 1864 and at Göttingen from 1864 until his death. In his lectures on Systematic Theology, Ritschl argued against the reduction of religion to experience and insisted that faith rested, not on the intellect, but in the creation of 'Werturteile'. Accordingly, the Incarnation is not an historical fact but the expression of the 'Offenbarungswert' ['revelatory value'] of God. Ritschl's followers stressed the importance of community ethics and diminished the importance of metaphysics and religious experience (see *The Oxford Dictionary of the Christian Church*, edited by F. L. Cross (Oxford, 1974), p. 1189).

offered by Ritschl, Jung wants to cling onto Christ as 'a metaphysical figure with whom we are bound in a mystical union which raises us up out of the sensory world' (ZL § 289). To Ritschl's historical Christ Jung opposes the mysticism of Heinrich Seuse (Suso) (1300–1366) and Jakob Böhme.

Ritschl's systematic theology did indeed, like Kant's philosophy, repudiate both metaphysics and religious experience as a basis for religion, and Jung takes his stand on a radical subjectivism directly opposed to this position. Bearing in mind his intense interest in spiritualism at this time, his deeply emotional reaction to his father's crisis of faith, and his own traumatic psychological experiences as a child, the adoption of such a 'fundamentalist' position is perhaps not surprising. However, there is also a deeper and more fundamental problem with which Jung's lecture is trying to come to terms. According to Ritschl, true faith is based not on intellectual understanding but on the perception of value in what happens, i.e. the making of 'Werturteile' ['judgments of value']. Jung talks about 'value' almost twenty times during his lecture, and perhaps his greatest discomfort with Ritschl's theology derives from its suggestion that the value of the content of religious dogmas is relative, not absolute.

At one point, Jung refers to Nietzsche using the recognizable phrase 'the "untimely" non-philosopher', and the lecture's penultimate paragraph mentions an idea from Nietzsche's critique of asceticism without really exploring its implications:

> Anyone who wishes to hold fast to the metaphysical reality of the elements of Christian faith must realize these dangers and difficulties [of mysticism] and must never lose sight of the fact that Christianity represents nothing less than the break with an entire world, a dehumanization of Man, a "revaluation of all values" (Nietzsche) (ZL § 290).

The defence of Christianity which Jung mounts here strongly suggests either that he was not yet familiar with Nietzsche's critique or that he was reacting against it. Walter Kaufmann has suggested that it was probably reading Nietzsche that 'put an end to Jung's Christianity – or drove it underground – and made him ready to embrace Freud'.[61] And according to his autobiography, Jung's relationship to Nietzsche was characterized by a considerable degree of ambivalence.

The critic who wishes to establish the significance of the references to Nietzsche in the Zofingia Lectures encounters problems similar to those mentioned by, amongst others, Nicholls, Hinton Thomas and Aschheim,[62] for, as

---

[61] Walter Kaufmann, *Freud, Adler, and Jung* (New York, 1980), p. 426.

[62] 'Nietzsche became a measure by which men analysed their own inadequacy, or he was the hope of escape from the despair of decadence [...] Serious scholarly investigation of Nietzsche as a philosopher limped far behind' (R. A. Nicholls, p. 37).

these lectures reveal, Jung's relation during his time at university to the figure of Nietzsche was at once highly personal and, at this stage, intellectually very indirect. However, by looking at his comments on Nietzsche in the light of his philosophical and, indeed, theological concerns in general and his reading of Kant in particular, the Zofingia Lectures anticipate Jung's mature work in at least seven important and interrelated ways. First, they propose a science of metaphysics and religion which does not deny their non-physical status. Second, they reject materialism and propose 'eine "Psychologie mit Seele"'. Third, they transfer the notion of transcendental subjectivity implicit in the concept of the soul to the concept of the psyche. Fourth, they consider more closely the psychological significance of 'instinct'. Fifth, they give central significance to the problems of dualism (the opposites in general and polarity in particular). Sixth, they attempt to unite the opposites via a form of psycho-philosophical monism (called, in the language of Gnosticism, the Pleroma, and in the language of alchemy, the *unus mundus*). And seventh, they take seriously the problem of Evil and the question which it raises about the possibility of any morality 'beyond Good and Evil'. But until his own encounter with Dionysos, Jung's dissatisfaction with philosophy had not yet been pushed to its furthest limit. And only then would Jung's psychology become an 'Auseinandersetzung' with Nietzsche to a much greater extent than it had been with Kant.

Having provided the context of Jung's reception of Nietzsche, I shall now turn to Jung's autobiography and, in the light of evidence from other sources and statements, show that a clear pattern emerges between Jung's personal feelings (as he recorded them) about Nietzsche and his actual use of Nietzsche in his writings, which I shall then examine in chronological order.

Chapter 3

Jung's Reception of Nietzsche: The Letters and the Autobiography

Our four main sources of information concerning what Jung himself thought about his relation to Nietzsche are his letters, his interviews, his autobiography, and his Seminars. Each of these four sources is in some way problematic: Jung's interviewers never sought to elicit really detailed information;[1] the existing edition of Jung's *Briefe* is by no means complete;[2] Jung's 'autobiography', *Erinnerungen, Träume, Gedanken* [*Memories, Dreams, Reflections*] was compiled by his secretary, Aniela Jaffé, and so its authorship is not entirely Jung's;[3] and records of the Seminars are based on notes taken by those present. Nevertheless, these four sources usefully complement Jung's professional reception of Nietzsche by giving us at least glimpses of his more personal response. The Seminars are discussed in Chapters 9, 10 and 11, and in this chapter I shall deal with his interviews, letters and autobiography.

Interviews and Letters

Jung did not mention Nietzsche in his interviews, and this reflects his tendency simply to respond to the questions which he was asked, often on issues of the

[1] *C. G. Jung Speaking*, edited by William McGuire and R. F. C. Hull (Princeton, 1977); hereafter cited in the text as JS followed by a page reference. See also Richard I. Evans, *Jung on Elementary Psychology* (London, 1979).

[2] C. G. Jung, *Briefe*, edited by Aniela Jaffé, 3 vols (Olten und Freiburg im Breisgau, 1972–73); hereafter cited in the text as B followed by a volume number and page reference. Because some of Jung's letters were originally written in English, I have quoted where appropriate from: C. G. Jung, *Letters*, edited by Gerhard Adler and Aniela Jaffé, 2 vols (London, 1973–1975); hereafter cited in the text as L plus a volume number and a page reference. I also refer to Sigmund Freud/C. G. Jung, *Briefwechsel*, edited by William McGuire and Wolfgang Sauerländer (Frankfurt am Main, 1974); hereafter cited in the text as FJB followed by a page reference. For the English version, I have used the translations by Ralph Manheim and R. F. C. Hull in *The Freud/Jung Letters* (Cambridge, MA, 1974); hereafter cited in the text as FJL followed by a page reference. Jung's letters from his time at university remain inaccessible in family archives. According to Herr Franz Jung, they make no reference to Nietzsche.

[3] *Erinnerungen, Träume, Gedanken von C. G. Jung: Aufgezeichnet und herausgegeben von Aniela Jaffé* (Olten und Freiburg im Breisgau, 1971); translated by Richard and Clara Winston, *Memories, Dreams,*

day and largely trivial, rather than setting his own agenda. On those occasions when the issue of Nietzsche was brought up, Jung usually but not always acclaimed him as an important influence on Analytical Psychology, suggesting an underlying ambiguity in his relationship to him and a reluctance to be perspicuous about his intellectual sources.

In *Autobiography of a Spy*, Jung's follower and a member of the Seminar on *Zarathustra*, Mary Bancroft, relates how she interviewed Jung on the occasion of his seventy-fifth birthday in 1945 and records his following remark about Nietzsche: '"I thought him a poet, but a morbid poet! And I thought him a marvellous psychologist!"'.[4] In 1952, during a discussion between Ira Progoff and Jung, taken down by Ximena de Angulo (JS: pp. 205–18), Jung admitted the influence of Burckhardt and Nietzsche but characterized them as 'indirect, "side influences"' (JS: p. 207). Nevertheless, looking back with the undoubted benefit of hindsight, Jung apparently appreciated Nietzsche 'as a great psychological critic' who had allegedly foreseen the wars to come in the twentieth century. However, according to Progoff, the 'deepest impression' that Nietzsche had made on Jung had been 'as a phenomenon': '[Jung] saw the non-ego at work in [Nietzsche]; Nietzsche was in a fever, a passion that "gripped" Jung'. Progoff further reported Jung as saying: '"In 1888 [in fact, 1889] he went mad. That was a tremendous event; it made a deep impression on me"'. In 1957 Jung gave a film interview to Richard Evans (JS: pp. 276–352), where he was emphatic about Nietzsche's importance for him (JS: p. 280).

On all such occasions, Jung's statements went unchallenged and unqueried. For example, how much did Jung know about Nietzsche's mental collapse? Was there a connection between Jung's interest in Nietzsche's madness and his own mental breakdown in 1913 to 1919? And if Nietzsche's psychology was built upon the power drive, what was the nature of the drive in Jung's own system?

In his letters (mostly written in German, although some are in English), Jung's references to Nietzsche are also infrequent, considering the importance he allegedly attached to Nietzsche. However, the period from 1929 to 1943 when Jung didn't mention him at all roughly coincides with Jung's Seminar on *Zarathustra* (1934–1939), where Nietzsche was under intensive discussion. Of the sixteen times in the published correspondence where Jung refers to Nietzsche,[5] the most important are the letter to Freud of 25/31 December 1909

Reflections: Recorded and edited by Aniela Jaffé (London, 1963). Referred to respectively in the text as ETG and MDR, followed by a page reference.

[4] Mary Bancroft, *Autobiography of a Spy* (New York, 1983), p. 252.

[5] Jung mentions Nietzsche in his published correspondence on the following sixteen occasions: (1) letter to Freud of 25 November 1907, where Nietzsche is mentioned in the context of Otto Gross's views on sexuality; (2) letter to Freud of 25/31 December 1909; (3) letter to Freud of 2 January 1912, where reference is made to Lou Andreas-Salomé's relationship with Nietzsche; (4) letter to Freud of 3 March 1912; (5) letter to Hermann Graf Keyserling of 2

(see below), the two letters to Keyserling of 2 January and 12 May 1928 (to which we will also return later), and two letters written towards the end of his life dated 27 April 1959 and 5 January 1961, where Jung replied to a specific question about the philosophical influences on his thought. In the other letters, Nietzsche is mentioned only in passing or Jung repeats what he has said more clearly elsewhere.

In the last two letters mentioned above, Jung dealt with his correspondents' enquiries in a tantalizingly imprecise manner, acknowledging the influence of Nietzsche but declining to go into details. For example, on 27 April 1959, in reply to a question from Dr. Joseph F. Rychlak about the possible influence of Hegel on his thought, Jung wrote: 'The philosophical influence that has prevailed in my education dates from Plato, Kant, Schopenhauer, Ed[uard] v[on] Hartmann, and Nietzsche' (B3: pp. 246–47/L2: pp. 500–01). Jung then went on in the same letter to launch a bitter attack on Hegel – 'who in my very incompetent opinion is not even a proper philosopher but a misfired psychologist' – and to deny any traces at all of dialectical thought in his work.[6] Nor did

January 1928; (6) letter to Hermann Graf Keyserling of 12 May 1928; (7) letter to Walter Robert Corti of 30 April 1929; (8) letter to Arnold Künzli of 28 February 1943; (9) letter to Arnold Künzli of 16 March 1943; (10) letter to Miss Piloo Nanavutty of 11 November 1948; (11) letter to Dr. Willi Bremi of 11 December 1953; (12) letter to Professor Ernst Hanhart of 2 March 1957; (13) letter to Dr. Herbert E. Bowman of 18 June 1958; (14) letter to Joseph F. Rychlak of 27 April 1959; (15) letter to Margaret Sittler of 29 March 1960; (16) letter to Rev. Arthur W. Rudolph of 5 January 1961. In addition, one further unpublished source has come to light. In his letter to Jung of July 1948, Dr. Piroja Bahadurji asked him about a remark in his Seminar of 1934 concerning the 'primitive age' to which Zarathustra (the Persian prophet) belonged. In a hitherto unpublished letter to Bahadurji of 30 September 1948, Jung replied: 'My remark about Zarathustra in my seminar about Nietzche's Zarathustra doesn't mean a belittling of this very great prophet. It was only a sidelight thrown on him in comparison with Nietzsche's Zarathustra. I have studied his life and his religion and it has filled me with admiration. I only wanted to emphasize the enormous age and the remoteness of old Zarathustra over against Nietzsche's figure of Zarathustra'. (I am grateful to Mr. Sonu Shamdasani for drawing this part of the Jung-Bahadurji correspondence to my attention).

6 In the same letter, Jung admitted (and it will come as no surprise) that he had 'never studied Hegel properly'. Nevertheless, Jung still felt qualified to describe Hegel as 'un psychologue raté' and still claimed that there was 'a remarkable coincidence between certain tenets of Hegelian philosophy and my findings concerning the Collective Unconscious' (B3: p. 247/L2: p. 502) (cf. the judgment of Rudolf Haym on the *Phänomenologie* as 'eine *durch die Geschichte und Unordnung gebrachte Psychologie und eine durch die Psychologie in Zerrüttung gebrachte Geschichte*' (*Hegel und seine Zeit: Vorlesungen über Entstehung und Entwicklung, Wesen und Werth der Hegel'schen Philosophie* (Berlin, 1857), p. 243)). In 'Theoretische Überlegungen zum Wesen des Psychischen' ['On the Nature of the Psyche'] (1947/1954), Jung wrote: 'Hegel [war] ein verkappter Psychologe [...] und [projizierte] große Wahrheiten aus dem Bereich des Subjekts in einen selbstgeschaffenen Kosmos hinaus' ['Hegel was a psychologist in disguise who projected great truths out of the subjective sphere into a cosmos he himself had created'] (GW8 § 358). For further discussion of Jung and Hegel, see Friedrich Seifert, *Seele und Bewußtsein* (Munich and Basle, 1962); Barbara Eckman, 'Jung, Hegel, and the Subjective Universe', *Spring*, 1986, 88–99; Wolfgang Giegerich, 'The Rescue of the World: Jung, Hegel, and the Subjective Universe', *Spring*, 1987, 107–14; and Hester Solo-

Jung give much away in a letter of 5 January 1961 (almost exactly six months before his death) to the Rev. Arthur W. Rudolph, in reply to the more specific question of the influence of Nietzsche. Whilst confirming the legitimacy of the enquiry, Jung wrote: 'It would be too ambitious a task to give you a detailed account of the influence of Nietzsche's thoughts on my own development' (B3: p. 370/L2: p. 621). This was not much for the addressee to go on, who still proceeded to write a dissertation which included a study of the influence of Nietzsche on Jung's work and later contributed an article on the same subject.[7] But the implication is that Nietzsche's influence was substantial, and in the same letter he went on to place his discovery of Nietzsche in the context of his university years: 'As a matter of fact, living in the same town where Nietzsche spent his life as a professor of philosophy [*sic*], I grew up in an atmosphere still vibrating from the impact of his teachings, although it was chiefly resistance which met his onslaught' (B3: p. 370/L2: pp. 621–22).

Jung is referring here of course to the University of Basle where Nietzsche had taught (as a philologist) from 1869 to 1879, and where Jung had studied in the medical faculty from the 'Sommersemester' of 1895 to the 'Wintersemester' of 1900/1901. What Jung says here confirms the general cultural significance of Nietzsche at that time in Basle. Moreover, Jung also described in this letter the strong impression that Nietzsche had made on him personally at that time:

> I could not help being deeply impressed by his indubitable inspiration ("Ergriffenheit"). He was sincere, which cannot be said of so many academic teachers to whom career and vanity mean infinitely more than the truth (B3: p. 370–71/L2: p. 622).

Jung's use of the word 'Ergriffenheit' suggests the unconscious nature of Nietzsche's inspiration, an issue which arose in his letters to Förster-Nietzsche and is repeatedly mentioned in his *Gesammelte Werke*, particularly with reference to the archetype of Wotan/Dionysos. Moreover, like Nietzsche, Jung felt that he had to leave his academic career in order to progress in life (Nietzsche after two years of illness in 1879, Jung in 1913 at the start of a period of mental illness or intense preoccupation with images of the Unconscious). Furthermore, in the same letter, Jung also hierarchized his reading of Nietzsche's texts, privileging *Zarathustra*, the critique of religion and the essays of 'untimely' cultural criticism over his work on the genealogy of morals or the doctrine of the Eternal Recurrence (both of which belong to the later period of Nietzsche's writing). In short, Jung implicitly suggests in this letter that he preferred the early to the late Nietzsche:

---

mon, 'The Transcendent Function and Hegel's Dialectical Vision', *Journal of Analytical Psychology*, 39 (1994), 77–100.

7 Arthur William Rudolph, *Superhistorical Individuality in Nietzsche's Thought*, Diss. Ph. D. unpub. (University of Southern California, 1963). See also his 'Jung and Zarathustra', *Philosophy Today*, 18 (Winter 1974), 312–18.

> The fact that impressed me the most was his encounter with Zarathustra and then his "religious" critique, which gives a legitimate place in philosophy to passion as the very real motive of philosophizing. The *Unzeitgemäße Betrachtungen* were to me an eye-opener, less so the *Genealogy of Morals* or his idea of the "Eternal Return" of all things. His all-pervading psychological penetration has given me a deep understanding of what psychology is able to do (B3: p. 371/L2: p. 622).

There are three further points to note in respect of these remarks. First, although Jung claims that the *Unzeitgemäße Betrachtungen* [*Untimely Meditations*] were more important for him than *Zur Genealogie der Moral* [*On the Genealogy of Morals*], in fact only the copy of the latter work in Jung's edition of Nietzsche's *Werke* contains any annotations. However, these annotations probably date from a later period than his university days.[8] Second, the emphasis which Jung places on the primacy of passion in Nietzsche sounds like a coded reference to the importance of Dionysos, as well as recalling Nietzsche's own formulation of the return to the affects and the emotions in the notes for *Der Wille zur Macht* [*The Will to Power*]: 'Das Recht auf den großen *Affekt* – für den Erkennenden wieder zurückzugewinnen!' ['To win back for the man of knowledge the right to great affects!'] (WM/WP 612 = N3: p. 532). And third, Jung appreciates Nietzsche's texts themselves as examples of psychological analysis. *In fine*, Jung summed up Nietzsche's considerable influence on him as follows: 'All in all Nietzsche was to me the only man of that time who gave some adequate answers to certain urgent questions which then were more felt than thought' (B3: p. 371/L2: p. 622). The nature of these questions, and the extent to which Jung did or did not find his answers adequate, are discussed in this chapter.

Although this is as far as Jung was ever prepared to go in his letters over the question of direct influence, it contains much which confirms what he had to say about his reception of Nietzsche in *Erinnerungen, Träume, Gedanken* (1962), the text which will provide much of the ground for our later discussion of the intellectual affinities between the two men. Bearing in mind the main emphases of the letter of 5 January 1961 – Nietzsche's profound effect on the university atmosphere in Basle; the authenticity and intensity of Nietzsche's experiences; the significance for Nietzsche of (Dionysian) passion; Nietzsche's works as models of psychological investigation; and the relevance of Nietzsche's fundamental questions to the contemporary situation as perceived by Jung – let us now see how Jung presents these concerns in his autobiography.

---

[8] I am grateful to Herr Franz Jung for permission to transcribe Jung's underlinings and annotations in his edition of Nietzsche's *Werke* in his personal library at Küsnacht. The dating of Jung's marginalia is discussed in my article 'Jung's Annotations of Nietzsche's Works: An Analysis', *Nietzsche-Studien*, 24 (1995), 271–314.

Erinnerungen, Träume, Gedanken

It must be remembered that Jung's autobiography is questionable as an exact historical source.[9] Bearing this in mind, we need to read *Erinnerungen, Träume, Gedanken* for its gaps and silences, for what it fails to say as much as for what it does. Reviewing the book in 1964, the paediatrician and psychoanalyst Donald Winnicott claimed that its publication provided analysts 'with a chance, perhaps the last chance they will have, to come to terms with Jung'.[10] The psychoanalyst Erich Fromm argued that 'by revealing the man', the autobiography 'shows that Jung's emphasis on the Collective Unconscious and his opposition to Freud's personal Unconscious had the function of protecting him from becoming aware of his own repressed experiences by making his Unconscious part of a mythical entity that rules all men alike and knows no good or evil'.[11] And, rightly, the sociologist Philip Rieff has described the book as 'at once [Jung's] religious testament and his science, stated in terms of a personal confession'.[12]

As Aniela Jaffé's introduction indicates, Jung began work on the book in 1957 with Jaffé herself, his former secretary, as chief collaborator; and it includes passages where it is evident that the line between remembering and vague reminiscing is a thin one. As befits a man for whom the psyche was a profound reality (ETG: p. 3/MDR: p. 9), Jung says that he can understand himself only in the light of the inner happenings of life: 'Mein Leben ist die Geschichte einer Selbstverwirklichung des Unbewußten' ['My life is a story of the self-realization of the Unconscious'] (ETG: p. 10/MDR: p. 17). In fact, Jung had so little regard for his memoirs as a scientific work that he was content practically to attribute their authorship to Aniela Jaffé and expressly excluded them from the *Gesammelte Werke*. He nonetheless granted permission to publish *Erinnerungen, Träume, Gedanken*, thus spreading his message and a carefully cultivated image of himself whilst attempting to preserve some sort of scientific reputation. Despite the atmosphere of mystery which surrounds the book and its pretence to give us the 'authentic' Jung, there are three good reasons for studying, albeit critically, what *Erinnerungen, Träume, Gedanken* says.

---

[9] See Ake Tilander, 'C. G. Jung's Autobiography: An Evaluation of C. G. Jung's Autobiography as a Source of Information on his Psychohistory', *Journal of Personality and Clinical Studies*, 6 (1990), 25–34; and Naomi R. Goldenberg, 'Looking at Jung Looking at Himself: A Psychoanalytic Rereading of *Memories, Dreams, Reflections*', in: *Returning Words to Flesh: Feminism, Psychoanalysis, and the Resurrection of the Body* (Boston, 1990), pp. 116–45.

[10] Donald Winnicott, book-review of Jung's *Memories, Dreams, Reflections*, *International Journal of Psychoanalysis*, 45 (1964), 450–55. Winnicott also drew attention to the problems of mistranslation in the English version which 'could queer the pitch for further games of Jung-analysis', and they have in fact done so.

[11] Erich Fromm, 'C. G. Jung: Prophet of the Unconscious', *Scientific American*, vol.209, no.3 (September 1963), 283–90 (p. 283).

[12] Philip Rieff, *The Triumph of the Therapeutic: Uses of Faith after Freud* (London, 1966), p. 139.

First and foremost, Jung's memoirs tell us what he wanted us to think about his relationship to Nietzsche's philosophy, and in so doing, they confirm the significance which Nietzsche had for him – even if they do not necessarily indicate (directly) the precise extent or nature of that significance. Second, by comparing what Jung says in his memoirs about his reception of Nietzsche with his letters and the texts in the *Gesammelte Werke*, we can evolve a firm factual basis on which to discuss more theoretical issues. We notice, for example, that the order in which he says he started reading Nietzsche corroborates what he wrote to Rudolph on 5 January 1961. Third, and more importantly, we realize that whilst the references to Nietzsche in Jung's published works become *more and more* detailed and substantial over time, he himself became *less and less* inclined to discuss this aspect of his work in his autobiography. Even after establishing the importance of Nietzsche for him during his student and childhood years, Jung fails to mention the Seminar on *Zarathustra* which took place over a period of 5 years! But a comparison of Jung's autobiography with his *Werke* very clearly suggests that we can see his thought as a developing response to the problem of the Dionysian, which Nietzsche had posed but been unable to answer this side of insanity.

In fact, the problem of the Dionysian is the guiding thread through Jung's (labyrinthine) reception of Nietzsche. In a letter to Freud of 11 February 1910, he discussed openly the problem of Dionysos – 'den weissagenden Gott der Rebe' ['the soothsaying god of the vine'] – and analysis of his autobiography and correspondence reveals the following pattern. When the problem of the Dionysian is most acute for Jung, he claims to identify with Nietzsche. However, after finding a 'solution' for his own psychic experiences during the years 1913–19, Jung moved away from Nietzsche and was thus in a better position to develop his ideas on Nietzsche from this critical distance.

So, as far as Jung's relationship to Nietzsche is concerned, we can see three parallel movements running through the development of his thought. First, there is a move away from Nietzsche on the personal level. Second, this is accompanied by an increasingly sophisticated approach to Nietzsche's texts in his psychological writings. Third, at the same time, Jung becomes increasingly aware of the significance of the problem of Dionysos. From its definition in the letter to Freud of 11 February 1910 to the explicit exposition in the essay 'Wotan' of 1936 (GW10 § 371–99), the Dionysian problematic takes on both ethical and political dimensions. The correlation of these three trends is too precise to be a coincidence. Moreover, it makes psychological sense to say that Jung could best understand those problems which he had solved for himself. Jung's psychiatric practice was based on his own self-therapy, and he was one of the first psychoanalysts to insist that the analyst himself should undergo analysis.[13] Just

[13] See Anthony Storr, *Freud* (Oxford, 1989), p. 41.

as Nietzsche's philosophy tells the story of his own self-overcomings and is written, *à la* Zarathustra, in his own blood (MA/HA II Vorrede/Prologue § 1; N1: p. 737; cf. Z I 7; N2: p. 305), so Jung's work represents in many respects his own overcoming of Nietzsche and a coming-to-terms with what Nietzsche called 'das Dionysische'.

Early visions

Before looking at Jung's first direct reference to Nietzsche in his autobiography, we must briefly consider two of his childhood visions which suggest that, very early on in his life, Jung had intimations of forces corresponding to the experience of the dark underside of life which Nietzsche called Dionysos. First, there was Jung's dream of an underground temple containing a giant ritual phallus. Jung calls the phallus 'ein unterirdischer und nicht zu erwähnender Gott' ['a subterranean god not to be named'] (ETG: p. 19/MDR: p. 28). Seen in its cultural context, Jung's subterranean god represents 'the great phallus of Lord Jesus, whom nineteenth-century pietism had castrated', i.e. 'the suppressed aspects of divinity'.[14] In fact, Jung himself calls the phallus God's subterreanean counterpart – 'seinen unterirdischen Gegenspieler' ['his underground counterpart'].

Commenting on this dream, Jung attaches immense importance to it, and regards it as a kind of initiation: 'Durch diesen Kindertraum wurde ich in die Geheimnisse der Erde eingeweiht [...] Es war eine Art Initiation in das Reich des Dunkeln' ['Through this childhood dream I was initiated into the secrets of the earth ... It was an initiation into the realm of darkness'] (ETG: p. 21/MDR: p. 30). Detecting in this vision the activity of an unknown Other, Jung suggests that his later thought in particular is intimately connected with the message of this dream, and he even goes so far as to date his intellectual work as a whole right back to this dream – 'Damals hat mein geistiges Leben seinen unbewußten Anfang genommen' ['My intellectual life had its unconscious beginnings at that time']:

> Wer stellte das Oben und das Unten zusammen und legte damit den Grund zu all dem, was die ganze zweite Hälfte meines Lebens mit Stürmen leidenschaftlichster Natur erfüllte? [...] Wer anders als der fremde Gast, der von Oben und von Unten kam? (ETG: p. 21/MDR: p. 30).
>
> [Who brought the Above and Below together, and laid the foundations for everything that was to fill the second half of my life with stormiest passion? ... Who but that alien guest who came both from Above and from Below?]

---

[14] See Anthony Stevens, *On Jung* (Harmondsworth, 1991), p. 103; Rieff, p. 110; and Daniel C. Noel, 'Veiled Kabir: C. G. Jung's Phallic Self-Image', *Spring* 1974, 224–42.

In Jung's work, the phallus as a symbol nearly always has religious rather than sexual implications. In the early text *Wandlungen und Symbole der Libido* [*Psychology of the Unconscious*] (1911/12), he wrote: '*Der Phallus ist die Quelle von Leben und Libido, der große Schöpfer und Wundertäter*' ['*The phallus is the source of life and libido, the great creator and worker of miracles*'] (WSL: p. 100/PU § 164), and pointed out that Dionysos is a phallic god. In his post-war writings on alchemy, Jung paid particular attention to Mercurius, who is associated both with Hermes (another phallic god) and with Dionysos. Anthony Stevens has commented on the significance of Jung's vision of the phallus and related it to the core thinking of Analytical Psychology as follows:

> That first dream determined [Jung's] fate. Henceforth the main focus of his interest would be underground, his destiny being a lifelong struggle to redeem the *numen* interred in this subterranean vault [...] Most important of all, the sperm generated by the dream phallus resulted, after thirty years' gestation, in the birth of one tremendous idea: *the hypothesis of the collective Unconscious.*[15]

The ritual phallus – the subterranean god – does not just compensate for the suppressed aspects of the divinity, but also fuses with it. In his autobiography, Jung repeatedly stresses the horror of his childhood discovery that God could be 'etwas Furchtbares' ['something terrible'] (ETG: p. 46/MDR: p. 57) and that, contrary to His Christian image, He was full of 'Dunkelheiten' ['dark aspects'] (ETG: p. 63/MDR: p. 76). Nor could Jung accept that the universe was the ordered and harmonic whole that Christianity pretended it was: 'Wenn Gott das "höchste Gut" ist, warum ist Seine Welt, Sein Geschöpf so unvollkommen, so verdorben, so erbarmungswürdig?' ['If God is the highest Good, why is the world, His Creation, so imperfect, so corrupt, so pitiable?'] (ETG: p. 64/MDR: p. 77). As Philip Rieff points out: 'Lord Jesus himself became dark, identical with the phallus'.[16]

Second, the message of the ambivalence of God was conveyed to Jung during his later childhood (c.1886) in the vision of God, sitting on His heavenly throne, and dropping an enormous turd on the roof of Basle Cathedral, thereby destroying it. Jung thus conceived of God as being both creative and destructive, good and evil, 'ein verheerendes Feuer und eine unbeschreibliche Gnade' ['annihilating fire and an indescribable grace'] (ETG: p. 61/MDR: p. 74). Together with the dream of the phallus, this vision led to a profound religious crisis. The early collapse of his belief in a logocentric, ordered cosmos in general and the myth of Christianity in particular, spurred Jung on to invent (or rediscover) an

---

15 Stevens, p. 115.
16 Rieff, p. 111.

alternative myth and reinstate through Dionysos the lost numinosity of religion.[17]

In his autobiography, Jung emphasized the immense significance of these visions – 'Das waren die entscheidenden Ereignisse meines Lebens' ['These were the crucial experiences of my life'] – but he failed to give any more details about the nature of the deity thus revealed to him. He refers to the God of his childhood simply as the Other: 'Die Gespräche mit jenem "Anderen" waren meine tiefsten Erlebnisse: einesteils blutiger Kampf, andererseits höchstes Entzücken' ['These talks with the "Other" were my profoundest experiences: on the one hand a bloody struggle, on the other supreme ecstasy'] (ETG: p. 53/MDR: p. 65). Bearing in mind Jung's interest in Nietzsche which would soon develop, however, I suggest that these visions represent an early intuition of the Dionysian.

Gymnasialzeit (1881–1895)

Paradoxically, the first mention of Nietzsche in Jung's autobiography refers to his not being mentioned at all. Jung began attending the Gymnasium in Basle in 1886, when he was eleven years old, and he lunched regularly in the household of his uncle, who was the Pastor of St. Alban's church in Basle. Jung writes that he found himself alienated from the bourgeois complacency of his uncle's family's world view, and implies that he had encountered Nietzsche's name elsewhere during his school years – i.e. very early on in his intellectual development (ETG: p. 79/MDR: p. 92). Whilst Jung grew up in a learnèd and intellectual climate (and his works are rich in Patristic and Scholastic references), he was nevertheless intensely dissatisfied with it. Not for the first time, Jung associates Nietzsche with Jacob Burckhardt (1818–97), the Swiss 'Kulturkritiker' who had been a colleague and friend of the philosopher. Despite the lack of intellectual stimulation in his conversations with his friends and relatives, which contributed to making Jung a very lonely child, the period of his school years saw him reading an impressively wide range of material. Indeed, he refers to this period of his life – extending from his seventeenth year up to the end of his medical studies – as his 'philosophische Entwicklung' ['philosophical development'] (ETG: p. 75/MDR: p. 89). Jung describes how he began, between the ages of sixteen

[17] 'By rendering the suppressed underground emotions conscious and acceptable, Jung legitimates the demonic and destructive as having rights of their own on the strength of their therapeutic potential [...] Thus Jung found his way out of the religious impasse [...] in an integrative personal symbolism, in a meta-religion, revealed originally to himself alone, which he then translated, without disclosing its divine source, into a psychotherapy which could be useful in the revitalization of any and all religious contents' (Rieff, p. 111–13).

and nineteen, to pursue systematically those questions which he had been consciously framing (and unconsciously sensing). In so doing, he turned initially to the pre-Socratics – Heraclitus (to whom Jung later often refers), Pythagoras, Empedocles – and to Plato, as well as to such medieval schoolmen as Thomas Aquinas. Apart from Meister Eckhart, however, all these authors apparently left him unsatisfied, and eighteenth-century philosophy (presumably of the Enlightenment) and Hegel are given very short shrift indeed. In other words, Jung was familiar with the philosophical tradition which had preceded Nietzsche, but was also highly critical of it.

Jung also maintained that his two great discoveries in this period were two important intellectual predecessors of Nietzsche – Schopenhauer[18] and Kant.[19] In his autobiography, Jung talks about Schopenhauer in a highly positive manner: 'Der große Fund meiner Nachforschung [...] war Schopenhauer. Er war der erste, der vom Leiden der Welt sprach, welches uns sichtbar und aufdringlich umgibt, von Verwirrung, Leidenschaft, Bösem, das alle anderen kaum zu beachten schienen und immer in Harmonie und Verständlichkeit auflösen wollten' ['The great find resulting from my researches was Schopenhauer. He was the first to speak of the suffering of the world, which visibly and glaringly surrounds us, and of confusion, passion, Evil – all those things which the others hardly seemed to notice and always tried to resolve into all-embracing harmony and comprehensibility'] (ETG: p. 74/MDR: p. 88). As well as praising Schopenhauer, in a manner reminiscent of Nietzsche's third *Unzeitgemäße Betrachtung*, 'Schopenhauer als Erzieher' ['Schopenhauer as Educator'] (1874), for his intellectual honesty and for rejecting all blithe optimism, Jung's acclamation sounds an almost Gnostic note in its emphasis on the flawed nature of the world, and hints at a key theme in Jung's psychological writings – the problem of Evil. However, Jung tempered his encomium with the following reservations: 'Schopenhauers düsteres Gemälde der Welt fand meinen ungeteilten Beifall, nicht aber seine Problemlösung' ['Schopenhauer's sombre picture of the world had my undivided

---

18 For further discussion of Jung and Schopenhauer, see: Henry Walter Braun, 'C. G. Jung und Schopenhauer', *Schopenhauer-Jahrbuch*, 46 (1965), 76–87; and James L. Jarrett, 'Schopenhauer and Jung', *Spring*, 1981, 193–204.

19 For further discussion of Jung and Kant, see: Eugen Bär, 'Archetypes and Ideas: Jung and Kant', *Philosophy Today*, 20 (1976), 114–23; Stephanie de Voogd, 'C. G. Jung: Psychologist of the Future, 'Philosopher' of the Past', *Spring*, 1977, 175–82; David Pugmire, 'Understanding the Psyche: Some Philosophical Roots and Affinities of Analytical Psychology', *Harvest*, 27 (1981), 90–102; and Stephanie de Voogd, 'Fantasy versus Fiction: Jung's Kantianism Appraised', in *Jung in Modern Perspective*, edited by Renos K. Papadopoulos and Graham S. Saayman (Hounslow, 1984), pp. 204–28. Mary Bancroft reports Jung as saying: '"Of course, [...] the real basis of my philosophical education was Kant. Anyone who doesn't understand Kant and Kant's theory of cognition cannot understand my psychology. Such people mix up psychology and metaphysics. They think that when I say 'God,' I mean God, rather than the *idea* of God."' (Mary Bancroft, *Autobiography of a Spy* (New York, 1983), p. 253).

approval, but not his solution of the problem'] (ETG: p. 75/MDR: p. 88). Jung could not accept Schopenhauer's implicit equation of the Will with a blind God, and was puzzled by his idea that the Will could turn and deny itself. In a similar vein, although Nietzsche accepted much of Schopenhauer's analysis of the problem of existence, he, like Jung, rejected the Schopenhauerian solution of the denial of the Will and replaced it with the affirmation of life which was, in his words, synonymous with the Will to Power.

At the same time, Jung's reasons for rejecting Schopenhauer's solution to the problem of existence were very different from Nietzsche's, and for him the antidote to Schopenhauer was at that time Kant. In effect going back to Schopenhauer's own sources, Jung not only believed that he had discovered a fundamental flaw in Schopenhauer's system, he also, as the following quotation clearly shows, thought that he had been able to overcome Schopenhauer's pessimism using Kant's epistemology: '[Schopenhauer] hatte die Todsünde begangen, eine metaphysische Aussage zu machen, nämlich ein bloßes nooumenon [*sic*], ein "Ding an sich" zu hypostasieren und zu qualifizieren' ['Schopenhauer had committed the deadly sin of making a metaphysical statement, by hypostatizing a mere noumenon, a *Ding an sich*, and by qualifying it' (P. B.)] (ETG: p. 75/MDR: p. 89). Of course, saying that his fatal mistake was to have made a metaphysical statement is more an indication of Jung's distrust of the discourse of metaphysics and philosophical terminology than a substantial critique of Schopenhauer. At any rate, even before he actually looked at Nietzsche's writings properly, Jung was well acquainted with Enlightenment and post-Enlightenment thought – the background to Nietzsche's philosophy.

At a later stage in his autobiography, Jung makes a profoundly important comment about himself and his relationship to contemporary history when he was still at the Gymnasium. He writes: 'Von diesem Zeitgeist wurde ich in jungen Jahren (etwa 1893) unbewußt gefangen und hatte keine Mittel, mich ihm zu entziehen' ['In my youth (around 1893) I was unconsciously caught up by this spirit of the age, and had no methods at hand for extricating myself from it'] (ETG: pp. 238–39/MDR: p. 262). Jung characterized this 'Zeitgeist' in terms of the music of Wagner (reviving old archetypes of German mythology) and of the Dionysian experience of Nietzsche. Jung associates Nietzsche with an era whose dominant archetype was that of Dionysos – or, more accurately, the closely-linked figure of Wotan (who, on Jung's account, was most clearly evident during the Second World War).[20] According to Jung, the consequences of the events of 1871 (the coronation of Kaiser Wilhelm I at Versailles) could still be felt in the 1890s, and led ultimately to the disaster of the First World War. Both

[20] In Chapter 8, I discuss a likely confusion/conflation in Jung's autobiography of World Wars One and Two, and the possible reasons for this.

the cultural and the political tendencies of the time are subsumed by Jung under the mythological figure of Dionysos:

> Jacob Burckhardt [rief] beim Eintreffen der Nachricht von der Kaiserkrönung in Versailles aus: "Das ist der Untergang Deutschlands". Schon pochten die Archetypen Wagners an die Tore, und mit ihnen kam das dionysische Erlebnis Nietzsches, das man besser dem Rauschgott Wotan zuschreibt (ETG: p. 238/MDR: p. 262).
>
> [When the news arrived of the crowning of Kaiser Wilhelm I at Versailles, Jacob Burckhardt exclaimed, "That is the doom of Germany". The archetypes of Wagner were already knocking at the gates, and along with them came the Dionysian experience of Nietzsche – which might better be ascribed to the god of ecstasy, Wotan.]

Typically, it is unclear whether by 'das dionysische Erlebnis Nietzsches' Jung is referring to *Die Geburt die Tragödie* [*The Birth of Tragedy*] (1872), which argued for the union of Apollo and Dionysos in tragedy as a remedy for a time of historical tension, or to a putative experience in Nietzsche's biography. As on many occasions, Jung appears to conflate Nietzsche's life and work – perhaps because life and work were so closely related in his own case.

University (1895–1900)

Jung felt himself to be linked to Nietzsche by more than just the 'Zeitgeist' during his time at university. As we saw in Chapter 2, Nietzsche was very much 'in the air' at the time, and Jung says that he was able to receive personal testimony in Basle about the behaviour of Nietzsche from people who had known him while he was teaching there, in particular from the 'höchste Autorität' ['supreme authority'] Jacob Burckhardt, 'von dem verschiedene kritische Äußerungen in bezug auf Nietzsche kolportiert wurden' ['whose various critical comments on Nietzsche were bandied about'] (ETG: p. 108/MDR: p. 122). In his Seminar on *Zarathustra*, Jung gave more details about this local reception of Nietzsche. However, as we also saw in Chapter 2, Jung's use of Nietzsche in his Zofingia Lectures is remarkably tentative, and takes place against his growing disaffection with Kant.

Despite the popularity of Nietzsche at the time and the mediation of his presence through Jacob Burckhardt, and despite the lack of self-consciousness with which Jung had read other philosophers during his years at school, he wrote in his autobiography that he had hesitated when it came to Nietzsche: 'Nietzsche hatte schon für einige Zeit auf dem Programm gestanden, aber ich zögerte mit der Lektüre, da ich mich ungenügend vorbereitet fühlte' ['Nietzsche had been on my programme for some time, but I hesitated to begin reading him because I felt I was insufficiently prepared'] (ETG: p. 108/MDR: p. 122). If Jung could cope with Kant and Schopenhauer, yet hesitated over Nietzsche, then there was clearly a problem here of a more intimate and personal rather than simply intellectual nature, as Jung himself was prepared to admit.

What was this problem? According to Jung, he was afraid of discovering that he was in some sense identical with Nietzsche: 'Ich fürchtete mich vor der möglichen Erkenntnis, daß ich wie Nietzsche "Auch Einer" war' ['I feared I might be forced to recognize that I too, like Nietzsche, was "another one in the same mould"' (P. B.)] (ETG: p. 109/MDR: p. 122).[21] Jung maintains that, at that time, he was acutely aware of some fundamental similarity with Nietzsche: 'es war eine geheime Angst, ich könnte ihm vielleicht ähnlich sein, wenigstens in dem Punkte des "Geheimnisses", das ihn in seiner Umwelt isolierte' ['I was held back by a secret fear that I might perhaps be like him, at least in regard to the "secret" which had isolated him from his environment']. Indeed, there is a basic similarity between the psychologist and the philosopher in two main respects.

First, there is the question of Jung's 'secret'. As he wrote: 'der Einzelne [bedarf] auf seinem einsamen Pfade eines Geheimnisses, das man aus irgendwelchen Gründen nicht preisgeben darf oder kann' ['the individual on his lonely path needs a secret which for various reasons he may not or cannot reveal'] (ETG: p. 346/MDR: p. 376), and this idea runs like a leitmotif throughout his autobiography. In Jung's case, the secret is associated with the disturbing visions which the young Carl Gustav had experienced in the course of his childhood years (his dream of the ritual phallus and the vision of God defecating on the roof of Basle cathedral): powerful intuitions of the Dionysian. According to Jung: 'Der Traum vom ithyphallischen Gotte war mein erstes großes Geheimnis' ['the dream of the ithyphallic god was my first great secret'] (ETG: p. 33/MDR: p. 42); and the totality of these visions and experiences constituted that 'secret' which was a crucial part of his early life: 'Dieser Besitz an Geheimnis hat mich damals stark geprägt [...] Meine ganze Jugend kann unter dem Begriff des Geheimnisses verstanden werden' ['This possession of a secret had a very powerful formative influence on my character ... My entire youth can be understood in terms of this secret'] (ETG: pp. 28, 47/MDR: pp. 37, 58). The 'secret' similarity

[21] A reference to the humorous novel *Auch Einer* (1879) by Friedrich Theodor Vischer (1807–1887) (Jung's library contains the 1902 edition). It is no coincidence that Jung refers to this novel, which contains an episode where the main character starts to flog a carter who is maltreating his horse and is fatally wounded by the knife wielded by the carter. There is a clear and obvious parallel here with Nietzsche's collapse in Turin as a result of embracing a horse being viciously whipped. In Gottfried Benn's poem 'Turin', which refers to this event, there are in fact *two* horses being whipped – and in a dream which Jung revealed to Freud, the same motif occurs (see note 26 below). For an empirically-oriented discussion of Nietzsche, Vischer and the horse, see Reinhold Grimm, 'Embracing Two Horses: Tragedy, Humor, and Inwardness; or, Nietzsche, Vischer, and Julius Bahnsen', *Nietzsche-Studien*, 18 (1989), 203–20; for a philosophical meditation on how to embrace the horse, see David L. Miller, 'Nietzsche's Horse and other Tracings of the Gods', *Stanford Italian Review*, 6 (1986), 159–70.

between Jung and Nietzsche thus lies in the link between Nietzsche's thought and Jung's early childhood visions: the common problematic of the Dionysian.

And second, there was Jung's sensation (which can be dated back to roughly 1886) that he was actually two different persons: 'Persönlichkeit Nr. 1' – the school-child growing up in Klein-Hüningen near Basle at the end of the nineteenth century – and 'Persönlichkeit Nr. 2' – a timeless, eternal counterpart, his own 'Other' (ETG: p. 50/MDR: p. 62). According to his autobiography, Jung used to sit on a stone and contemplate this internalized *sub specie aeternitatis*: 'Ich war die Summe meiner Emotionen und ein Anderes in mir war der zeitlose Stein' ['I was the sum of my emotions and the "Other" in me was the timeless, imperishable stone'] (ETG: p. 48/MDR: p. 59).[22]

Jung came to believe that Nietzsche, like him, had possessed a dual personality which came into the open when he wrote *Zarathustra*. Jung recorded in his autobiography that it was when he read *Zarathustra* while a student that he came to see how his Personality Number Two corresponded to Nietzsche's number two – i.e. Zarathustra – which in turn corresponded to Goethe's number two – i.e. Faust. Thus, in his reading of *Zarathustra* (and indeed of *Faust*), Jung felt personally involved: 'Das war, wie Goethes "Faust", ein stärkstes Erlebnis. Zarathustra war der Faust Nietzsches, und Nr. 2 war mein Zarathustra' ['This, like Goethe's *Faust*, was a tremendous experience for me. Zarathustra was Nietzsche's Faust, his No. 2, and my No. 2 now corresponded to Zarathustra'] (ETG: p. 109/MDR: p. 123). According to Jung, the story of Faust mirrored the existential tensions of his youth – 'Zwei Seelen wohnen, ach! in meiner Brust' ['Alas, there dwell two souls in my breast'] – which lay right at the heart of his psychological problem: '"Faust" hatte in mir eine Saite zum Erklingen gebracht [...] Meine inneren Gegensätze erschienen hier dramatisiert' ['*Faust* struck a chord in me ... My own inner contradictions appeared here in dramatized form'] (ETG: p. 239/MDR: p. 262).[23]

Whilst Jung may have felt that his dilemma was very similar to Nietzsche's, he also regarded Nietzsche's fate very much in the sense of 'there but for the grace of God go I'. Although Jung shared with Nietzsche a sense of double identity, there was a highly significant difference. Whereas, in Jung's view, Nietzsche's dual personality had only come to the fore in *Zarathustra* (i.e. only

[22] In his essay 'Über den Granit' ['On Granite'] (1784), Goethe recounts sitting on a lump of granite on the top of a mountain and reflects on how the rock connects him to the deepest strata of the earth (Goethe, *Werke* (*Hamburger Ausgabe*), 14 vols (Munich, 1981), XIII, pp. 253–58). See Keiji Nishitani, *The Self-Overcoming of Nihilism* (Albany, 1990), pp. 91–92; and Graham Parkes, *Composing the Soul: Reaches of Nietzsche's Psychology* (Chicago and London, 1994), p. 135. Jung introjects this Goethean topos, identifying the unchanging geological substance with the eternal structures of the Unconscious.

[23] As we shall see, Jung often discusses Nietzsche with reference to Goethe's *Faust*, which is a common intertext for both writers.

when it was too late), Jung felt that he had been able to identify and deal with the same problem from an early age and, as a direct result of reading Nietzsche, had escaped the fate which had befallen the philosopher. This is how Jung describes Nietzsche's mistake: 'Das also, dachte ich, war sein krankhaftes Mißverständnis: daß er Nr. 2 ungescheut und ahnungslos herausließ auf eine Welt, die von dergleichen Dingen nichts wußte und nichts verstand' ['That, I thought, was his morbid misunderstanding: that he fearlessly and unsuspectingly let his No. 2 loose upon a world that knew and understood nothing about such things'] (ETG: p. 110/MDR: p. 123).

Jung pointed to Nietzsche's sense of mission as one of the consequences of this error, and claimed that Nietzsche's sense of frustration and his inevitable failure (ending in madness) could account for the rhetorical exaggeration of his language. At the risk of underrating, to the point of ignoring, the extent to which Nietzsche developed an argued position, Jung here focused on one single aspect of Nietzsche's project, the Revaluation of All Values, and emphasized the personal consequences of this project for its thinker: 'Er war von der kindischen Hoffnung beseelt, Menschen zu finden, die seine Ekstase mitfühlen und die "Umwertung aller Werte" verstehen könnten' ['He was moved by the childish hope of finding people who would be able to share his ecstasies and could grasp his "Revaluation of All Values"'] (ETG: p. 110/MDR: p. 123). Alluding to the 'Possenreißer' scene in the first part of *Zarathustra*, Jung says that Nietzsche's project led ultimately to his own destruction: 'Und er fiel – dieser Seiltänzer – sogar noch über sich selbst hinaus' ['And he fell – tightrope-walker that he proclaimed himself to be – into depths far beyond himself'] (ETG: p. 110/MDR: p. 124).

Furthermore, Jung thought that the consequences of Nietzsche's teaching were dangerous, not just for Nietzsche himself but also for the world which at first ignored his message and then, whilst misunderstanding Nietzsche, committed itself to that misunderstanding. Two of Jung's friends, both homosexual, so the autobiography tells us, fell foul of the teaching of Nietzsche: one committed suicide, the other ran to seed. Only he, Jung, had been able to analyze Nietzsche's tragic demise, understand its causes, and thus avoid the same fate.[24]

Jung's first reading of *Zarathustra* was thus a dead end: 'Wie mir der "Faust" eine Türe öffnete, so schlug mir "Zarathustra" eine zu, und dies gründlich und auf lange Zeit hinaus' ['Just as *Faust* had opened a door for me, *Zarathustra* slammed one shut, and it remained shut for a long time to come'] (ETG: p. 110/MDR: p. 124). A dead end, that is, in terms of intellectual response, but not in

[24] The identity of these friends cannot be ascertained, and the significance of their homosexuality remains unexplained by Jung. Is it a reference to Nietzsche's alleged homosexuality, or a reflection of Jung's sexual conservatism?

terms of therapeutic benefits, as Jung suggested in his Seminar on *Zarathustra*. Whilst his autobiography stresses the generally negative consequences of reading Nietzsche, Jung here emphasised its positive usefulness:

> When I read *Zarathustra* for the first time as a student of twenty-three, of course I did not understand it all, but I got a tremendous impression. I could not say it was this or that, though the poetical beauty of some of the chapters impressed me, but particularly the strange *thought* got hold of me. He helped me in many respects, as many other people have been helped by him (SNZ:I: p. 544).

In this way, Jung expresses a deep sense of equivocation with regard to his reading of Nietzsche. Both a danger and, for that very reason, a solution to this sense of threat, Nietzsche represented not just an intellectual but also a highly personal challenge to Jung. Just such a mixture of personal and intellectual investment was also a key ingredient in his relationship with Sigmund Freud.

Freud and Jung

Jung first made contact with Freud in March or early April 1906, when he sent him a copy of *Diagnostische Assoziationsstudien* [*Diagnostic Association Studies*] which contained work by himself and his Burghölzli colleagues. This letter inaugurated a correspondence which was to last a decade, and which represents an important source of information on the growth of psychoanalysis and clarifies the reasons why Jung moved away from Freud.[25] In December 1906 and January 1907, shortly before Jung's first meeting with Freud in Vienna in March of that year, they discussed in their correspondence a dream which Jung had published in *Über die Psychologie der Dementia praecox* [*The Psychology of Dementia praecox*] (1907, foreword dated July 1906) and had attributed to a friend.[26] But in his letter of 29 December 1906, Jung revealed to Freud that the dream was in fact his own: 'Der Träumer ist mir genau bekannt: ich bin es selber' ['I know the dreamer intimately: he is myself'] (FJB: p. 15/FJL: p. 14). As Herbert Lehmann has convincingly demonstrated, this dream also relates to Jung's attitude towards

---

[25] See P. J. van der Leeuw, 'The Impact of the Freud-Jung Correspondence on the history of ideas', *International Review of Psycho-Analysis*, 4 (1977), 349–62; Daniel Dervin, 'A Crux in the Jung/Freud letters', *Bulletin of the Menninger Clinic*, 41 (1977), 131–44; Edwin R. Wallace, 'A Commentary on the Freud-Jung letters', *Psychoanalytic Review*, 67 (1980), 111–37. For further discussion, see George B. Hogenson, *Jung's Struggle with Freud* (Notre Dame and London, 1983).

[26] In this dream, Jung saw horses being hoisted in the air by thick cables. As he was looking at one of the horses in particular, the cable broke and the horse fell to the ground. It leapt up and galloped away, dragging a log. Then he saw another horse beside the first one, trying to slow it down, and the runaway horse was finally stopped when a cab drove in front of it (see GW3 § 123–33).

Nietzsche at this time.[27] A comparison between this dream and the parable of the tightrope-walker in the 'Vorreden' of *Zarathustra* (Z Vorrede/Prologue § 6; N2: pp. 285–86) shows a number of parallels in terms of ideas and images. Clearly, this dream was very significant for Jung, for he not only sent the book which contained it to Freud, but also revealed several personal details necessary for its interpretation. Lehmann's article provides evidence that Jung may have been influenced by Nietzsche on a deeply unconscious level at this stage in his life and that, as a result, he may have identified with Nietzsche even more than he admitted or more than he even consciously knew. Lehmann goes so far as to suggest that Jung's identification with Nietzsche puts a new perspective on the affair with Sabina Spielrein,[28] arguing that Jung may have wanted to recreate in his relationship with her Nietzsche's relationship with Lou Andreas-Salomé. On Lehmann's account, it is also conceivable that Jung's unconscious identification with Nietzsche led him to re-stage with Freud the friendship between Nietzsche and Wagner and, inevitably, the eventual break between the two men. Just as Nietzsche's 'Vorwort an Richard Wagner' in *Die Geburt der Tragödie* pays extravagant tribute to Wagner, Jung's preface to *Über die Psychologie der Dementia praecox* eulogizes 'die genialen Konzeptionen Freuds' ['the brilliant discoveries of Freud'] (GW3: Vorwort/Foreword, p. 3). As we shall see in Chapter 4, *Wandlungen und Symbole der Libido* implicitly recalls the Nietzsche-Wagner split.

According to *Erinnerungen, Träume, Gedanken*, Jung met Freud for a second time in Vienna in 1910 (ETG: pp. 154, 157/MDR: pp. 173, 176). There is no documentation of such a visit, and Jung was probably thinking of his visit with his wife from 25 to 30 March 1909, following his resignation from the Burghölzli Clinic. Jung's remarks in his autobiography about a conversation during this meeting throw light on his attitude not just towards Nietzsche but also towards Freud (and Alfred Adler). However, the correspondence between Jung and Freud provides a more reliable documentation of what was at stake in their disagreement.

Jung's letters of the period between 1909 and 1910 clearly reflect his growing interest in mythological motifs in general and the god Dionysos in particular. In a letter of 14 October 1909, we find Jung toying with the idea of writing a comprehensive mythology: 'Die Archäologie, resp. die Mythengeschichte hat

---

[27] Herbert Lehmann, 'Jung contra Freud/Nietzsche contra Wagner', *International Review of Psycho-Analysis*, 13 (1986), 201–09. Lehmann argues: 'The dream indicates that Jung had some concerns about losing control, and that because of his identification with Nietzsche this had some ominous meaning for him in regard to his mental stability' (p. 201).

[28] Aldo Carotenuto, *A Secret Symmetry: Sabina Spielrein between Jung and Freud* (New York, 1982) documents Jung's love-affair with one of his patients, who later wrote on psychoanalysis (Sabina Spielrein, *Sämtliche Schriften* (Freiburg, 1988)). The most recent study of Spielrein's relation to Jung is John Kerr, *A Most Dangerous Method: The Story of Jung, Freud, and Sabina Spielrein* (London, 1994), especially pp. 111–13.

mich nämlich sehr gefaßt' ['Archaeology or rather mythology has got me in its grip'] (FJB: p. 157/FJL: pp. 251–52). Freud's response to this enthusiasm was to offer a few words of encouragement, but it was no more: 'Es freut mich, daß Sie meine Überzeugung teilen, die Mythologie müßte ganz von uns erobert werden' ['I am glad you share my belief that we must conquer the whole field of mythology'] (letter of 17 October 1909) (FJB: p. 280/FJL: p. 255). In his letter of 8 November 1909, Jung excitedly told Freud how his studies of the history of symbolism, particularly Friedrich Creuzer's *Symbolik und Mythologie der alten Völker, besonders bei den Griechen* [*Symbolism and Mythology of the Ancient Peoples, Particularly the Greeks*] (1810–23) and Richard Payne Knight's *A Discourse on the Worship of Priapus and its Connection with the Mystic Theology of the Ancients* (London, 1865[2]), had revived his interest in archaeology, and he raised his eyebrows at the prudery of Herodotus: 'Jammerschade ist es, daß die Prüderie schon bei Herodot ihre wunderlichsten Blüten treibt; vieles verschweigt er zugegebenermaßen aus "Anstandsgründen". Woher die Griechen schon so früh das gelernt haben?' ['It's a crying shame that already with Herodotus prudery puts forth its quaint blossoms: on his own admission he covers up a lot of things "for reasons of decency". Where did the Greeks learn that from so early?'] (FJB: p. 284/FJL: p. 258). It is unlikely that Freud suspected where Jung's mythological investigations would lead his 'Kronprinz' nor that Dionysos's feet would soon dance to a different tune from Freud's sexual theory. As far as Freud was concerned, the 'nuclear complex of neurosis' was the incest fantasy, a key aspect of the sexual theory of libido; but Jung's letters later in 1909 started to link his reading of mythology with Freud's incest theories in a less literal and more symbolic way which presaged the final break between the two men.

Above all, Jung's attention in 1909 became fixed on the image of the god who dies and is reborn, and in a letter of 15 November 1909 Jung explictly associated Dionysos with the Egyptian god Osiris and other (phallic) deities:

> Reden wir von besserm! d. h. von der Mythologie [...] Der sterbende und wiedererwachende Gott (Orpheusmysterien, Thammuz, Osiris [Dionysos], Adonis etc.) ist überall phallisch. (Beim Dionysosfest in Ägypten ziehen die Weiber den Phallus an einer Schnur auf und nieder: "der sterbende und wiedererwachende Gott.") (FJB: pp. 289–90/FJL: p. 263; the square brackets round 'Dionysos' are Jung's).

> [Now to better things – mythology ... The dying and resurgent god (Orphic mysteries, Thammuz, Osiris [Dionysos], Adonis, etc.) is everywhere phallic. At the Dionysos festival in Egypt the women pulled the phallus up and down on a string: "the dying and resurgent god".]

And Jung foregrounded the problem of the Dionysian with even greater transparency a few weeks later in his long letter of 25/31 December 1909. Here, Jung agrees with Freud that the incest taboo is highly significant, but suggests that the importance of the Dionysian elements in previous cultures had not been sufficiently appreciated, claiming that 'Das Letzte der Neurose und Psychose werden wir ohne Mythologie und Kulturgeschichte nicht lösen' ['We shall not solve the ultimate secrets of neurosis and psychosis without mythology and the history of civilization']:

> Ich wälze mich mit dem Problem der Antike um und um. Es ist ein schweres Stück! [...] Von Dionysos möchte ich Ihnen gerne vieles sagen, wenn es für einen Brief nicht zuviel wäre. Nietzsche scheint davon sehr viel geahnt zu haben. Mir kommt es vor, als ob das Dionysische eine in ihrer historischen Bedeutung nicht genügend gewürdigte Rückschlagwelle der Sexualität gewesen sei, von der wesentliche Elemente ins Christentum hinüberflossen, aber in einer andern Kompromißverwendung (FJB: pp. 307–08/FJL: pp. 279–80).
>
> [I am turning over and over in my mind the problem of antiquity. It's a hard nut! ... I'd like to tell you many things about Dionysos were it not too much for a letter. Nietzsche seems to have intuited a great deal of it. I have an idea that the Dionysian frenzy was a backwash of sexuality, a backwash whose historical significance has been insufficiently appreciated, essential elements of which overflowed into Christianity but in another compromise formation.]

Not only does Jung make a clear link between Nietzsche and the Dionysian, but he says that Nietzsche has an 'intuition' of this phenomenon, although he suggests by this that Nietzsche had not grasped its full implications.[29] There is a clear reluctance on Jung's part to discuss all this in the letter, not just because he is deviating from the classic Freudian position stressing sexuality as the unique origin of neurotic disorders, but perhaps also because Jung had still not fully dissociated himself on a personal level from the figure of Nietzsche.

In a letter written less than a month afterwards on 11 February 1910, Jung attempted to define the programme of psychoanalysis (which Freud and Jung referred to in their correspondence by means of the two Greek letters 'psi' [Ψ] and 'alpha' [α]) in terms of the Dionysian. The context of the letter was a discussion of an organization called the 'Internationaler Orden für Ethik und Kultur' ['International Fraternity for Ethics and Culture'], founded by Alfred Knapp, but Jung rejected the idea of such an association and instead outlined a programme to found a genuinely psychoanalytical – and Dionysian – ethics.

At the beginning of this letter, he refers to his state of mind with a Nietzschean metaphor: 'Gegenwärtig stehe ich überhaupt so ganz in der Mitte des Waagebalkens zwischen dionysisch and apollinisch' ['At present I am sitting so precariously on the fence between the Dionysian and the Apollonian']), an intertextual nod in the direction of *Die Geburt der Tragödie.* Owing to this confusion of mind, he wonders whether the old 'Kulturdummheiten' ['cultural stupidi-

[29] Jung himself at this stage is still working towards the position which he adopts in *Wandlungen und Symbole der Libido* (1911/12), namely that the incest-taboo is responsible for the canalization of libido and the creation of self-consciousness.

ties'] such as monasteries might not be worthwhile reintroducing, but, having advocated this Apollonian approach, he ponders the uses of Evil – 'das Böse, das wir ja doch lieben müssen, um von der Tugendobsession etwas loszukommen, die uns krank macht und die Existenzfreude verbietet?' ['must we not love Evil if we are to break away from the obsession with virtue that makes us sick and forbids us the joys of life?'] (FJB: p. 323/FJL: p. 293). Moral relativism, the association of virtue with sickness, and the desire to promote the sheer joy of life give a Nietzschean tone to this extraordinary statement.

According to Jung, any ethics must be based, not on artifice ('künstlich') but on the primacy of instinct, of which – so he says – race is the bearer ('von den tiefen Instinkten der Rasse unterfüttert'). Denying that the need for religion can be overcome, Jung looks for a new saviour, not in coalitions and fraternities, nor in any form of rationality, but in myth. The emphasis on the necessity of myth was to become a perennial theme in Jungian thought:

> Religion kann nur durch Religion ersetzt werden. Ist im International Orden etwa ein neuer Heiland? Was für einen neuen Mythos gibt er uns, um darin zu leben? Aus purem Vernunftübermut sind nur Weise ethisch, die übrigen bedürfen des ewig wahren Mythos (FJB: pp. 323–24/FJL: p. 294).

> [Religion can be replaced only by religion. Is there perchance a new saviour in the International Fraternity? What sort of new myth does it hand out for us to live by? Only the wise are ethical from sheer intellectual presumption, the rest of us need the eternal truth of myth.]

The same letter goes on to a discussion of 'das ethische Problem der Sexualfreiheit' ['the ethical problem of sexual freedom'] and Jung's insistence that Christianity must be replaced with something equivalent. In contrast to the impotence of the ideological vacuum at the heart of any ethical fraternity, he argues that only religion can tap into the immense vital forces of instinct: 'Ich denke mir für die Ψα eine weit schönere und umfänglichere Aufgabe als ein Einmünden in einen ethischen Orden' ['I imagine a far finer and more comprehensive task for Ψα than alliance with an ethical fraternity'] (FJB: p. 324/FJL: p. 294).

Instead of committing the intellectual presumption of relying entirely on rationality, Jung proposes to revive religion and, in a passage which equates Christ with Dionysos, he argues that it should be the task of psychoanalysis to create a new Dionysian myth:

> Ich denke, man müsse der Ψα noch Zeit lassen, von vielen Zentren aus die Völker zu infiltrieren, beim Intellektuellen den Sinn fürs Symbolische und Mythische wiederzubeleben, den Christum sachte in den weissagenden Gott der Rebe, der er war, zurückzuverwandeln, und so jene ekstatischen Triebkräfte des Christentums aufzusaugen, alles zu dem *einen* Ende, den Kultus und den heiligen Mythos zu dem zu machen, was sie waren, nämlich zum trunkenen Freudenfeste, wo der Mensch in Ethos und Heiligkeit Tier sein darf. Das war ja die große Schönheit und Zweck-

mäßigkeit antiker Religion, die aus Gott weiß was für temporären biologischen Bedürfnissen zum Jammerinstitut geworden ist (FJB: p. 324/FJL: p. 294).

[I think we must give Ψα time to infiltrate into people from many centres, to revivify among intellectuals a feeling for symbol and myth, ever so gently to transform Christ back into the soothsaying god of the vine, which he was, and in this way absorb those ecstatic instinctual forces of Christianity for the *one* purpose of making the cult and the sacred myth what they once were – a drunken feast of joy where Man regained the ethos and holiness of an animal. That was the beauty and purpose of classical religion, which from God knows what temporary biological needs has turned into a Misery Institute.]

Rather than aiming like an ethical fraternity to hem in and control Man's most basic instincts, Jung proposes that the goal of psychoanalysis should be, in the manner of the religions of antiquity, to provide Man with a means of making use of these libidinal resources.

In place of the Nietzschean opposition 'Dionysos gegen den Gekreuzigten' ['Dionysos against the Crucified'] (EH IV § 9; N2: p. 1159), Jung evolves a programme which will transform the Crucified back into the god of the grape, thereby releasing hitherto inhibited powers of vitality. Jung's last phrase in the passage quoted above is reminiscent of the remark in *Zur Genealogie der Moral*: 'Die Erde war zu lange schon ein Irrenhaus!' ['Too long, the earth has been a madhouse!'] (GM II § 22; N2: p. 834), and his argument for the liberation of the animal energies in Man and the revival of the psychological values of old mythological structures bring this programme close to the gospel of Zarathustra. Jung summed up his new vision of the project of psychoanalysis as follows:

Eine echte und rechte ethische Entwicklung kann das Christentum nicht lassen, sondern muß in ihm emporwachsen, muß seinen Hymnus der Liebe, den Schmerz und das Entzücken über den sterbenden und wiedererstehenden Gott, die mystische Kraft des Weines und die anthropophagischen Schauer des Abendmahles zur Vollendung führen – nur *diese* ethische Entwicklung macht sich die Lebenskräfte der Religion dienstbar (FJB: p. 324/FJL: p. 294).

[A genuine and proper ethical development cannot abandon Christianity but must grow up within it, must bring to fruition its hymn of love, the agony and ecstasy over the dying and resurgent god, the mystic power of the wine, the awesome anthropophagy of the Last Supper – only *this* ethical development can serve the vital forces of religion.]

Thus Christianity should not be abandoned but instead should be advanced and returned to the rôle of organizing and making available Man's instinctual forces. The function of religion, Jung implicitly suggests, is to advance the state of culture. More poetically in *Zarathustra*, Nietzsche gives us the following vision: 'Wollust: für die freien Herzen unschuldig und frei, das Garten-Glück der Erde, aller Zukunft Dankes-Überschwang an das Jetzt [...] Wollust: das große Gleichnis-Glück für höheres Glück und höchste Hoffnung' ['Sensual pleasure:

innocent and free to free hearts, the earth's garden-joy, an overflowing of thanks to the present from all the future ... Sensual pleasure: the great symbolic happiness of a higher happiness and highest hope'] (Z III 10 § 2; N2: p. 436). For Nietzsche and for Jung, the goal is to maintain the primacy of instinct, and to invent a religion which will enhance and cultivate it.

Jung's letters show how his foregrounding of Dionysos as a regenerative power formed part of his move away from Freud. Indeed, Freud's response to the above letter was terse and contained the curt remark: 'An Ersatz für die Religion denke ich nicht; dies Bedürfnis muß sublimiert werden' ['I am not thinking of a substitute for religion: this need must be sublimated'] (letter of 13 February 1910) (FJB: p. 326/FJL: p. 295). The conflict with Freud sharpened over the next few months and culminated eventually in a complete break, whose consequences were profound both for Jung personally and also for his understanding of Nietzsche.

These reflexions on the nature of the Dionysian took Jung further and further away from Freud's position. Despite Freud's positive pre-war attitude to Eros, the central difficulty was Jung's more generous and less purely sex-oriented concept of libido which was expounded in *Wandlungen und Symbole der Libido*. From the Jung/Freud correspondence, it seems that Jung's intense personal interest in mythology was connected with his attempts to revise the concept of libido. In a letter to Freud of 8 May 1911 (in which he both proclaimed his opposition to occultism and announced an interest in astrology!), Jung described his investigations of mythology in (highly mythical) terms of a sojourn in a dark, sweet-scented land of magic:

> In diesen dunkeln Ländern gibt es wunderseltsame Sachen. Lassen Sie mich bitte ohne Besorgnis in diesen Unendlichkeiten herumschweifen. Ich werde reiche Beute für die Erkenntnis der menschlichen Seele heimbringen. Ich muß mich eine Zeitlang an magischen Düften berauschen, um ganz verstehen zu können, was für Geheimnisse das Unbewußte in seinen Abgründen birgt (FJB: p. 465/FJL: p. 421).

> [There are strange and wondrous things in these lands of darkness. Please don't worry about my wanderings in these infinitudes. I shall return laden with rich booty for our knowledge of the human psyche. For a while longer I must intoxicate myself on magic perfumes in order to fathom the secrets that lie hidden in the abysses of the Unconscious.]

By 23 June 1911, it was clear that, as far as Jung was concerned, the symbolism of the incest fantasy had less to do with what happened between Oedipus and Jocasta, i.e. real sexual desire, than with the meaning of the mysterious Mothers whom Faust encounters in the celebrated scene in Part II of Goethe's dramatic play (ll.6287–90):

> Die unbewußte Phantasie ist eine unglaubliche Hexenküche:
> "Gestaltung, Umgestaltung,
> Des ewigen Sinnes ewige Unterhaltung,
> Umschwebt von Bildern aller Kreatur.
> Sie sehn dich nicht, denn Schemen sehn sie nur."

Hier ist die Gebärmutter des Geistes, wie der Herr Urgroßvater richtig erkannt hat (FJB: pp. 475–76/FJL: p. 431).[30]

[Unconscious fantasy is an amazing witches' cauldron:
"Formation, transformation,
Eternal mind's eternal recreation,
Thronged round with images of things to be,
They see you not, shadows are all they see".
This is the matrix of the mind, as the little great-grandfather correctly saw.]

Later in his autobiography, Jung speaks of those who are driven by a daemon and refers to precisely the same scene from *Faust II* (ll.6222–23) as he had quoted in his letter to Freud of 23 June 1911:

Wer also, veranlaßt durch seinen Daemon, den Schritt über die Grenze der Zwischenstufe hinaus wagt, kommt recht eigentlich in das "Unbetretene, nicht zu Betretende", wo keine sicheren Wege ihn führen und kein Gehäuse ein schützendes Dach über ihn breitet (ETG: p. 347/MDR: p. 377).

[The man, therefore, who, driven by his daemon, steps beyond the limits of the intermediary stage, truly enters the "untrodden, untreadable regions", where there are no charted ways and no shelter spreads a protecting roof over his head.]

The evidence from Jung's correspondence with Freud is that his mythological readings amounted to an intellectual descent to the realm of the mysterious Mothers. The psychological equivalent was soon to follow, in the form of a psychotic collapse. Later on, in a letter of 29 August 1911 (FJB: p. 484/FJL: p. 439), Jung compared the results of Freudian psychoanalysis with the Gnostic search for 'σοψία' (= Wisdom) – surely a compliment designed to annoy Freud! Finally, in a letter of 25 February 1912, Jung returned to the image of the Goethean Mothers and actually spoke of his research in terms of a descent to the underworld (or 'katabasis'):

Es handelt sich im wesentlichen um eine Elaboration aller Probleme, die aus der Inzestlibido zur Mutter, aus der libidobesetzten Mutterimago hervorgehen. Diesmal ist es die Mutter, an die ich mich gewagt habe. Was mich also versteckt, das ist die κατάβασις in das Reich der Mütter, wo bekanntlich Theseus und Peirithoos sitzengeblieben sind, am Felsen angewachsen (FJB: p. 540/FJL: p. 487).

[Essentially, it is an elaboration of all the problems that arise out of the mother-incest libido, or rather, the libido-cathected mother-imago. This time I have ventured to tackle the mother. So what is keeping me hidden is the κατάβασις to the realm of

[30] In his autobiography, Jung refers to a family legend according to which his grandfather was a natural son of Goethe. Whilst Aniela Jaffé, the editor (and probably more than just that) of Jung's autobiography, claims that Jung was annoyed by this story, it is nonetheless mentioned twice in *Erinnerungen, Träume, Gedanken*, confirming thereby his personal investment in this legendary kinship. This supposedly illegitimate relation to Goethe symbolizes Jung's repeated appropriation of *Faust* to his own analytical psychological ends.

the Mothers, where, as we know, Theseus and Peirithoos remained stuck, grown fast to the rocks.]

What Freud had seen in mythology as the expression of an ancient incest-taboo had now effectively been completely reinterpreted by Jung as a return to a non-sexual Mother, symbolizing the Unconscious, and this was the message of *Wandlungen und Symbole der Libido*.

Less than a year before the final break with Freud in January 1913, Jung quoted a lengthy passage from *Zarathustra* in a letter of 3 March 1912. The passage comes from the final section of 'Von der schenkenden Tugend' ['Of the Bestowing Virtue'] and, bearing in mind Jung's concern with Nietzsche and the Dionysian, it was highly appropriate that he should have presaged the break with Freud in this way:

> Ich lasse 'Zarathustra' für mich reden:
> "Man vergilt einem Lehrer schlecht, wenn man immer nur der Schüler bleibt. Und warum wollt ihr nicht an meinem Kranze rupfen? Ihr verehrt mich; aber wie, wenn eure Verehrung eines Tages umfällt! Hütet euch, daß euch nicht eine Bildsäule erschlage.
> Ihr hattet euch noch nicht gesucht: da fandet ihr mich. So tun alle Gläubigen –. Nun heiße ich euch, mich verlieren und euch finden; und erst, wenn ihr mich alle verleugnet habe, will ich euch wiederkehren".
> Solches haben Sie mir durch die Ψα gelehrt. Als einer, der Ihnen wirklich folgt, muß ich wohl tapfer [sein], nicht zum mindesten Ihnen gegenüber (FJB: pp. 544–45/FJL: pp. 491–92).

> [Let Zarathustra speak for me:
> "One repays a teacher badly if one remains only a pupil. And why, then, should you not pluck at my laurels? You respect me; but how if one day your respect should tumble? Take care that a falling statue does not strike you dead!
> You had not yet sought yourselves when you found me. Thus do all believers –. Now I bid you lose me and find yourselves; and only when you have all denied me will I return to you".
> This is what you have taught me through Ψα. As one who is truly your follower, I must be stout-hearted, not least towards you.]

However, the final, inevitable break with Freud was followed by Jung's own personal 'katabasis', and this time not simply in the form of intellectual delvings into dusty old tomes on mythology. In his autobiography, Jung relates that, after his break with Freud, he experienced a dream in which frost transformed a leaf-bearing tree – his tree of life – into sweet grapes, full of healing juices, which he plucked and offered to a waiting crowd (ETG: p. 179/MDR: p. 200). According to the psychoanalyst John Gedo,[31] the conclusion of this dream symbolizes

[31] John E. Gedo, *Magna est vis veritatis tuae et praevalebit: Comments on the Freud-Jung Correspondence* (unpublished m.s., 1974); quoted by Peter Homans in *Jung in Context: Modernity and the Making of a Psychology* (Chicago and London, 1979), p. 79.

Jung's desire to fit the rôle which he had earlier assigned to Freud and psychoanalysis and become 'der weissagende Gott der Rebe' ['the soothsaying god of the vine'] – his own transformation into Dionysos.

Confrontation with the Unconscious (1913–1919)

During the period 1913–1919, Jung underwent a series of remarkable experiences which make up what is often described as a period of intense introversion or confrontation with the Unconscious. (In his autobiography, Jung talks about his 'Auseinandersetzung mit dem Unbewußten'). I interpret Jung's psychotic breakdown as his encounter with Dionysos, the psychological counterpart to his study of the myth of Dionysos.

On the level of foreign affairs, Europe was slowly moving towards war. On 28 June 1914, Archduke Ferdinand was assassinated in Sarajevo; on 1 August, Germany declared war on Russia, and on 3 August against France. Switzerland was suddenly surrounded by international conflict. On the level of Jung's personal and professional life, there were profound changes taking place as well during the same period. 1913 saw the final break with Freud, precipitated by the publication in 1911 and 1912 of *Wandlungen und Symbole der Libido*, and in the same year Jung resigned his lectureship at Zurich University. In 1914, he resigned as president of the International Psychoanalytic Association, and apparently he was also experiencing problems with his marriage in the wake of his affair with Sabina Spielrein.

In 1912, Jung began to experience a series of fantasies and, as he put it: 'ich überließ mich bewußt den Impulsen des Unbewußten' ['I consciously submitted myself to the impulses of the Unconscious'] (ETG: p. 177/MDR: p. 197). By way of therapy, he began to play with stones and blocks as he had done when a child: 'so blieb mir nichts anderes übrig, als wieder dorthin zurückzukehren und das Kind mit seinen kindlichen Spielen auf gut Glück wieder aufzunehmen' ['I had no choice but to return to it and take up once more that child's life with his childish games'] (ETG: p. 177/MDR: pp. 197–98). One day, having constructed a miniature church, Jung searched along the shore for a stone to act as an altar. One stone in particular which he found in the gravel was not only the right shape for the altar but reminded him of his earlier vision of the phallus: 'So setzte ich [den Stein] in die Mitte unter die Kuppel, und während ich das tat, fiel mir der unterirdische Phallus aus meinem Kindertraum ein. Dieser Zusammenhang erweckte in mir ein Gefühl der Befriedigung' ['I placed the stone in the middle under the dome, and as I did so, I recalled the underground phallus of my childhood dream. This connection gave me a feeling of satisfaction'] (ETG: p. 178/MDR: p. 198). More 'subterreanean' experiences were to follow.

Jung himself saw in the worsening political situation in Europe a parallel to his own tensions.[32] In the autumn of 1913 and the spring of 1914, Jung experienced a series of visions of mass destruction. Jung says in his autobiography that when the war actually broke out, he felt that his task was now to explore his own psyche and that of Mankind in general (ETG: p. 180/MDR: p. 200). Jung relates the visions and vivid dreams he experienced in 1913 and 1914 to two key figures of German literature, Hölderlin and Nietzsche. In other words, Jung understood himself as the survivor of experiences which had destroyed both Hölderlin and Nietzsche, both of whom were concerned with understanding those primal forces subsumed under the name of Dionysos. In his Nietzsche Seminar of 21 November 1934, Jung referred to this time as the beginning of his first serious engagement with Nietzsche's key text, *Zarathustra*:

> I read *Zarathustra* for the first time with consciousness in the first year of the war, in November 1914, twenty years ago; then suddenly the spirit seized me and carried me to a desert country in which I read *Zarathustra* (SNZ:I:p. 259).

Although Jung claimed that his second reading was more 'conscious' than the first at university had been, he nonetheless described it in ecstatic terms which suggest an emotional as well as an intellectual experience. (It is interesting to note that, at about the same time (1916), and also in his thirties, the German theologian Paul Tillich (1886–1965) had his own 'Zarathustra-Erlebnis' which is reported in his biography in very similar terms.[33] There is no evidence that Jung had ever heard of this account, which is a remarkable example of what he would have called 'synchronicity', and which by any standard represents an extremely close biographical parallel).

In his autobiography, Jung used the metaphor of the subterraneous to describe these experiences: 'Unter der Schwelle des Bewußtseins war alles lebendig' ['Below the threshold of consciousness everything was seething with life'] (ETG: p. 181/MDR: p. 202); and: 'Um die Phantasien, die mich unterirdisch bewegten, zu fassen, mußte ich mich sozusagen in sie hinunterfallen lassen' ['In order to

---

32 'Gegen Herbst 1913 schien sich der Druck, den ich bisher in mir gefühlt hatte, nach außen zu verlegen, so als läge etwas in der Luft; tatsächlich erschien sie mir dunkler als zuvor. Es war, als ginge es nicht mehr um eine psychische Situation, sondern um konkrete Wirklichkeit. Dieser Eindruck verstärkte sich mehr und mehr' ['Towards the autumn of 1913 the pressure which I had felt was in *me* seemed to be moving outwards, as though there were something in the air. The atmosphere actually seemed to me darker than it had been. It was as though the sense of oppression no longer sprang exclusively from a psychic situation, but from concrete reality. This feeling grew more and more intense'] (ETG: p. 178/MDR: p. 199).

33 See Wilhelm and Marjon Pauck, *Paul Tillich: Sein Leben und Denken*, 2 vols (Stuttgart and Frankfurt am Main, 1977), I, pp. 63–64. In her autobiography, Hannah Tillich mentions the importance of Nietzsche for her husband (*From Time to Time* (New York, 1973), p. 101).

grasp the fantasies which were stirring in me "underground", I knew that I had to let myself plummet down into them, as it were'] (ETG: p. 182/MDR: p. 202). The image of falling is also the one he used to describe the most intense of these experiences: 'dann ließ ich mich fallen' ['Then I let myself drop']. According to Jung, the ensuing vision contained the same imagery of the solar mythology which he had analysed in *Wandlungen und Symbole der Libido*: 'ein Helden- und Sonnenmythus, ein Drama von Tod und Wiedererneuerung' ['a hero and solar myth, a drama of death and renewal'] (ETG: p. 183/MDR: p. 203). And on yet another occasion, Jung uses the same metaphor of descent: 'Um die Phantasien zu fassen, stellte ich mir oft einen Abstieg vor. Einmal bedurfte es sogar mehrerer Versuche, um in die Tiefe zu gelangen' ['In order to seize hold of the fantasies, I frequently imagined a steep descent. Once it even needed several attempts to get to the very bottom' (P.B.)] (ETG: p. 184/MDR: p. 205). In these visions, Jung encountered a number of figures which often formed pairs, such as Philemon and Ka ('der geistige Aspekt' ['the spiritual aspect'] and 'der Naturgeist' ['the spirit of Nature']), or Elijah and Salome, whom Jung reluctantly interprets as 'Verkörperungen von Logos und Eros' ['personifications of Logos and Eros'], preferring to call them 'Verdeutlichungen unbewußter Hintergrundsvorgänge' ['clarifications of unconscious underlying processes' (P. B.)] (ETG: pp. 185–86/MDR: pp. 205–07).

There are numerous parallels in literature to what Jung experienced.[34] First, there is Odysseus's visit to the Sojourn of the Dead (the 'nekyia'), which, according to Gerhard Wehr, was read to Jung by his friend Albert Oeri during a four day long cruise on Lake Zurich shortly before his own descent to the underworld.[35] Second, there is Leo Frobenius's discussion of the story of the 'Nachtmeerfahrt', a variant of the archetypal motif of the 'nekyia' or night sea-journey, in *Das Zeitalter des Sonnengottes* [*The Age of the Sun-God*] (Berlin, 1914) (which Jung quoted extensively in *Wandlungen und Symbole der Libido*).

Third, as Edward F. Edinger has pointed out, Jung's decision to plummet and let himself drop – 'dann ließ ich mich fallen' – closely corresponds to the scene in *Faust II* when, in order to enter the realm of the Mothers, Faust stamps his foot and disappears.[36] And just as Jung encountered the images of Elijah and Salomé, Faust brought up the images of Paris and Helen. In his autobiography, Jung wrote that the Daemonic in *Faust* stood in an important relation to the mystery of the Mothers: 'Das eigentliche Problem [in *Faust*] sah ich bei Mephisto, dessen Gestalt mir haften blieb und von dem ich unklar eine Beziehung zum Muttermysterium ahnte' ['The real problem, it seemed to me, lay with

[34] See Stevens, p. 178; and see Chapter 6, pp. 175–76.

[35] Gerhard Wehr, *Carl Gustav Jung: Leben, Werk, Wirkung* (Munich, 1985), p. 160.

[36] Edward F. Edinger, *Goethe's Faust: Notes for a Jungian Commentary* (Toronto, 1990), p. 57.

Mephistopheles, whose whole figure made the deepest impression on me, and who, I vaguely sensed, had a relationship to the mystery of the Mothers'] (ETG: pp. 65–66/MDR: p. 78). And Jung's descent to the Mothers also involved a daemonic element; he described Ka, one of the fantastic figures whom he encountered, as 'etwas Dämonisches, man könnte auch sagen: Mephistophelisches' ['something daemonic – one might also say, Mephistophelic'] (ETG: p. 188/ MDR: p. 209).

Fourth, Nietzsche also uses the topos of the descent to Hades in two important aphorisms in *Menschliches, Allzumenschliches* [*Human, All Too Human*]. In 'Im Hades lassen' ['Leaving in Hades'], Nietzsche suggested: 'Viele Dinge muß man im Hades halbbewußten Fühlens lassen und nicht aus ihrem Schatten-Dasein erlösen wollen, sonst werden sie, als Gedanke und Wort, unsere dämonischen Herren und verlangen grausam nach unserem Blut' ['There are many things we must leave in the Hades of half-conscious feeling, and not desire to redeem them out of their shadow existence, otherwise they will, as thoughts and words, become our daemonic masters and cruelly demand our blood of us'] (MA/HA VMS/AOM § 374; N1: p. 863). However, Jung's psychic explorations redeemed his shadowy intuitions of the Dionysian precisely by confronting them, thus effectively reversing the strategy which Nietzsche here advocates. And in a longer aphorism entitled 'Die Hadesfahrt' ['Descent into Hades'], Nietzsche returned to the same motif in a more elaborate, yet playful manner:

> Auch ich bin in der Unterwelt gewesen, wie Odysseus, und werde es noch öfter sein; und nicht nur Hammel habe ich geopfert, um mit einigen Toten reden zu können, sondern des eignen Blutes nicht geschont. Vier Paare waren es, welche sich mir, dem Opfernden nicht versagten: Epikur und Montaigne, Goethe und Spinoza, Plato und Rousseau, Pascal und Schopenhauer [...] Was ich auch nur sage, beschließe, für mich und andere ausdenke: auf jene acht hefte ich die Augen und sehe die ihrigen auf mich geheftet. – [...] (MA/HA VMS/AOM § 408).

> [I too have been in the underworld, like Odysseus, and will often be there again; and I have not sacrificed only rams to be able to talk with the dead, but have not spared my own blood as well. There have been four pairs who did not refuse themselves to me, the sacrificer: Epicurus and Montaigne, Goethe and Spinoza, Plato and Rousseau, Pascal and Schopenhauer ... Whatever I say, resolve, cogitate for myself and others: upon these eight I fix my eyes and see theirs fixed upon me.]

Finally, there are parallels between Jung's experiences and Nietzsche's account of Dionysos in *Die Geburt der Tragödie*. Stressing how the roots of Jungian theory are to be found in his own personal experience, Jung wrote in his autobiography:

> [Mein selbständiger Weg] begann damit, daß ich mich mit den Bildern meines eigenen Unbewußten beschäftigte. Diese Zeit dauerte von 1913 bis 1917, dann flaute der Strom der Phantasien ab. Erst als es ruhiger geworden und ich nicht mehr im Zauberberg gefangen war, konnte ich mich objektiv dazu einstellen und anfangen, darüber nachzudenken (ETG: p. 210/MDR: p. 233).

> [My own way had a starting point in my intense preoccupation with the images of my own Unconscious. This period lasted from 1913 to 1917; then the stream of fantasies ebbed away. Not until it had subsided and I was no longer held captive inside the magic mountain was I able to take an objective view of that whole experience and begin to reflect upon it.]

The term 'Zauberberg' is precisely that which Nietzsche famously used in *Die Geburt der Tragödie* in connexion with the Dionysian experience: 'Jetzt öffnet sich uns gleichsam der olympische Zauberberg und zeigt uns seine Wurzeln' ['Now the Olympian magic mountain opens before us and reveals its roots to us'] (GT/BT § 3; N1: p. 30). Not only are the 'Wurzeln' of the 'olympische Zauberberg' common to both Nietzsche and Jung, but Jung also adopts the idea that, behind everything, there is one creative source, which Nietzsche called the 'Ur-mutter' ['primordial mother'] (GT/BT § 16; N1: p. 93).[37] This notion lies at the heart of Jung's theories concerning the creativity of the Unconscious. As far as Jung is concerned, 'die psychische Objektivität, die "Wirklichkeit der Seele"' ['psychic objectivity, the reality of the soul'] (ETG: p. 186/MDR: p. 208) is the source of libidinal energy which transcends the individual. In Analytical Psychology, the aim of therapy is to 'tap' into this collective Unconscious by understanding, and even welcoming, its influence on the individual psyche.

Unfortunately, the documents which contain Jung's visionary experiences, although preserved, remain inaccessible to scholars.[38] However, a flavour of Jung's thinking at this time is given by the *VII Sermones ad mortuos*,[39] written in 1916 when Jung was just beginning to recover from his psychic turmoil. An apostate in relation to Freudian psychoanalysis, Jung imitated the language of early Christian heresy to write a new Gnostic scripture, whose contents adumbrated in quasi-poetic, mystic language those ideas he would later express in

---

37 Rose Pfeffer has emphasized those elements of transcendence in Nietzsche's thought which are often overlooked, and related them to Goethe: 'While violently attacking Platonic-Christian transcendent metaphysics, Nietzsche remains deeply rooted in its tradition. And in spite of the fact that, by a reversal of Platonism, he creates a new metaphysics of change and becoming, a longing to shatter the *principium individuationis* and penetrate behind phenomena is never absent in the complexity of Nietzsche's thought. He abolishes the Kantian distinction between the noumenal and the phenomenal, and denies the existence of the "thing in itself" as a metaphysical foundation, and yet he continues to refer to the "Ur-Eine", the mystical ground and "womb of being". And Goethe, too, longs with Faust to enter the "realm of mothers" and "see what binds the world together in its innermost essence" (*Nietzsche: Disciple of Dionysus* (Lewisburg, 1972), pp. 232–33).

38 See Mike Bygrave, 'Jung: the Key that's Hidden at 228 Seestrasse', *The Independent*, 28 March 1992, p. 29, for a report of another recent attempt to gain access to the so-called 'Red Book' which failed.

39 See ETG: pp. 389–98; in English, *VII Sermones ad mortuos: The Seven Sermons to the Dead written by Basilides*, translated by H. G. Baynes (London, 1967). For more detailed information on the publishing history of this text, see Stephen A. Hoeller, *The Gnostic Jung and the Seven Sermons to the Dead* (Wheaton, 1982), pp. 219–20.

more scientific form in the vocabulary of Analytical Psychology: 'So bildeten die Gespräche mit den Toten, die "Septem Sermones", eine Art Vorspiel zu dem, was ich der Welt über das Unbewußte mitzuteilen hatte: eine Art von Ordnungsschema und Deutung der allgemeinen Inhalte des Unbewußten' ['These conversations with the dead formed a kind of prelude to what I had to communicate to the world about the Unconscious: a kind of pattern of order and interpretation of its general contents'] (ETG: p. 195/MDR: p. 217). Jung also used Gnostic language in his discussion of the Collective Unconscious in a letter of 10 January 1929 to Dr. Kurt Plachte, according to which the 'Pleroma' (i.e. the Collective Unconscious) is the source of those reconciling symbols which, by mediating consciousness and the Unconscious, permit us to grow beyond our Ego and become a more fully integrated Self.[40]

Jung's study of Gnostic literature is also important because, together with his own personal experiences, it led him to an entirely new understanding of Goethe's *Faust* and Nietzsche's *Zarathustra*. According to his autobiography, Jung concluded that he could resituate both these works within the matrix of the mythopoeic imagination which, in his view, had disappeared in the modern age of rationality. Both *Faust* and *Zarathustra* could be subsumed in the Golden (or Homeric) Chain, the alchemical term for the series of great wise men, starting with Hermes Trismegistus, which links heaven and earth:

> Faust II ist jedoch mehr als ein literarischer Versuch. Er ist ein Glied in der Aurea Catena, welche, von den Anfängen der philosophischen Alchemie und des Gnostizismus bis zu Nietzsches Zarathustra – meist unpopulär, zweideutig und gefährlich – eine Entdeckungsreise zum andern Pol der Welt darstellt (ETG: p. 192–93/MDR: pp. 213–14).
>
> [The second part of *Faust*, too, is more than a literary exercise. It is a link in the *Aurea Catena* which has existed from the beginnings of philosophical alchemy and Gnosticism down to Nietzsche's *Zarathustra*. Unpopular, ambiguous, and dangerous, it is a voyage of discovery to the other pole of the world.]

This other 'pole' is the Unconscious, and Jung was to explore the 'alchemical' undertones in Nietzsche in his Eranos lectures of 1933 and 1936 on psychology and alchemy. Thus, his reading of Nietzsche was intimately bound up with those areas of interest – Gnosticism, mysticism, alchemy – which moved to the forefront of Jung's intellectual preoccupations from 1916 onwards.

Reflecting on his survival of this experience of what he called 'introversion', Jung was eager to emphasize less the similarities between himself and Nietzsche (in contrast to earlier in his autobiography) and more the personal differences

---

[40] 'Ich nenne [...] die Sphäre paradoxer Existenz, eben das instinktive Unbewußte: *Pleroma*, in Anlehnung an die Gnosis' ['I call the sphere of paradoxical existence, i.e. the instinctive Unconscious, the Pleroma, a term borrowed from Gnosticism'] (B1: pp. 87–88/L1: p. 61).

between them. After all, Jung's confrontation with the Unconscious did not lead to permanent insanity, as had Nietzsche's encounter with Dionysos. Jung suggests in his autobiography that his psychic stability had been guaranteed partly by the presence of his family and partly by the routine of his psychiatric practice, whereas the lonely and nomadic Nietzsche had had nothing to anchor him in reality. Jung claims that this loss of contact with the outer world of reality was in part responsible for Nietzsche's identification with the inner world of his thoughts:

> Nietzsche hatte den Boden unter den Füßen verloren, weil er nichts anderes besaß als die innere Welt seiner Gedanken – die überdies ihn mehr besaß als er sie. Er war entwurzelt und schwebte über der Erde, und deshalb verfiel er der Übertreibung und der Unwirklichkeit (ETG: p. 193/MDR: p. 214).

> [Nietzsche had lost the ground under his feet because he possessed nothing more than the inner world of his thoughts – which incidentally possessed him more than he it. He was uprooted and hovered above the earth, and therefore he succumbed to exaggeration and irreality.]

This phase thus formed the transitional period in Jung's personal attitude towards Nietzsche. On the evidence of his autobiography, by this stage, Jung was beginning to realize how his personal situation differed from Nietzsche's, and this marks the start of his dissociation from Nietzsche. On the basis of what he says in his Seminar, this period also marked a more thorough and detailed 'Auseinandersetzung' with the text of *Zarathustra*. Jung's most important literary and artistic productions of this period sadly remain under lock and key, but from his published writings and seminars after his breakdown it is clear that his understanding of Nietzsche's writings had become much deeper and correspondingly more innovative.

Bollingen

The most important of Jung's psychological writings after his breakdown is *Psychologische Typen* [*Psychological Types*] (GW6), published in 1921 although work on it had begun after 1916. After his engagement with the Unconscious, Jung was concerned with defining more precisely the differences between his approach to the problems of psychology and those of Freud and Adler. In *Psychologische Typen*, Nietzsche was categorized typologically (although there is some confusion as to whether he was an introverted intuitive type (GW6 § 225/CW6 § 242) or an introverted thinking type (GW6 § 704/CW6 § 632)). Thus by this stage Jung's earlier feeling of close association with the identity of Nietzsche had diminished to the extent that Nietzsche could be labelled as a particular type and left at a distance. Although Jung devoted an entire chapter of *Psycholo-*

gische Typen to detailed analysis of 'das Apollinische und das Dionysische' (GW6 § 206–25/CW6 § 223–42), his discussion of the work in his autobiography merely mentions Nietzsche's name in passing (ETG: p. 211/MDR: p. 233).

Whilst developing the tenets of Analytical Psychology on paper (*Psychologische Typen* contains an important appendix where Jung tries to define his new terminology), he also felt the need to express his ideas in a different and more tangible medium. In 1922 he acquired a piece of land in Bollingen (by Lake Zurich) from Linda and Hans Fierz-David (who later attended the Seminar on *Zarathustra*). The first part of the 'Tower' which Jung constructed there – 'ein Bekenntnis in Stein' ['a confession of faith in stone'] as he called it (ETG: p. 227/MDR: p. 250) – was completed in the Winter of 1923–1924, and in the following years he gradually added to it until it became 'ein Symbol der psychischen Ganzheit' ['a symbol of psychic wholeness'] (ETG: p. 229/MDR: p. 252).[41] Jung's relation to this building was particularly intense, and in his autobiography he writes about the sensations of timelessness and spacelessness which he experienced in it: 'In Bollingen bin ich in meinem eigentlichsten Wesen, in dem, was mir entspricht. Hier bin ich sozusagen der "uralte Sohn der Mutter"' ['At Bollingen I am in the midst of my true life, I am most deeply myself. Here I am, as it were, the "age-old son of the mother"'] (ETG: p. 229/MDR: p. 252). Over the years, Jung carved a number of inscriptions into the building, including the following, at first placed over the gate of the Tower and later moved to the entrance of the second tower:

Philemonis Sacrum
Fausti Poenitentia.

[Shrine of Philemon
Repentance of Faust]

The Philemon referred to is the old man in *Faust II*, who, along with his wife Baucis, is murdered at the command of Faust. For Jung, *Faust* reflected the collective fate of the Germans: 'Goethes seltsamer Heldenmythus [war] kollektiv [...] und [nahm] deutsches Schicksal prophetisch voraus' ['Goethe's strange heroic myth was a collective experience and prophetically anticipated the fate of

41 According to Jung, the Tower was an architectural representation of the matrix of Being: 'ein Mutterschoß, oder eine mütterliche Gestalt, in der ich wieder sein konnte, wie ich bin, war und sein werde' ['a maternal womb or a maternal figure in which I could become what I was, what I am and will be'] (ETG: p. 229/MDR: p. 252). Curiously enough, the opening of Nietzsche's autobiographical work *Ecce Homo* also suggests an identification with the Mother: 'Das Glück meines Daseins, seine Einzigkeit vielleicht, liegt in seinem Verhängnis: ich bin, um es in Rätselform auszudrücken, als mein Vater bereits gestorben, als meine Mutter lebe ich noch und werde alt' ['The fortunateness of my existence, its uniqueness perhaps, lies in its fatality: to express it in the form of a riddle, as my father I have already died, as my mother I still live and grow old'] (EH I § 1; N2: p. 1070).

the Germans'] (ETG: p. 238/MDR: p. 261). In his autobiography, Jung casts his own work as an attempt to compensate for what is missing in Faust's character, and, implicitly, as a reparation for two world wars: 'Später knüpfte ich in meinem Werk bewußt an das an, was Faust übergangen hatte: die Respektierung der ewigen Menschenrechte, die Anerkennung des Alten und die Kontinuität der Kultur und der Geistesgeschichte' ['Later I consciously linked my work to what Faust had passed over: respect for the eternal rights of Man, recognition of "the ancient", and the continuity of culture and intellectual history'] (ETG: p. 239/ MDR: p. 262).

Clearly then, Jung wants to present his work as an act of recuperation situated in the humanistic tradition, and this perspective also governs his attitude towards Nietzsche. On the one hand, Jung's reaction to his own individual psychological difficulties was also a response to the collective problems – political and religious – of his time, and a defence of those humanistic values which Faust rejects and which, in his philosophy, Nietzsche tried to deconstruct. On the other hand, Nietzsche and Jung clearly *do* share a certain number of concerns, and Jung's own summary of his aims and goals contains an allusion to *Zarathustra*:

> Je weniger wir verstehen, wonach unsere Väter und Vorväter gesucht haben, desto weniger verstehen wir uns selbst, und helfen mit allen Kräften, die Instinkt- und Wurzellosigkeit des Einzelmenschen zu vermehren, so daß er als Massenpartikel nur noch dem "Geist der Schwere" folgt (ETG: p. 240/MDR: p. 263).
>
> [The less we understand of what our fathers and forefathers sought, the less we understand ourselves, and thus we help with all our might to rob the individual of his roots and his guiding instincts, so that he becomes a particle in the mass, ruled only by what Nietzsche called the Spirit of Gravity.]

Despite the imprecision of that particular reference, Jung's comments on *Faust* in his autobiography and in his psychological writings, and above all the inscription I have mentioned on the Tower at Bollingen, are clearly linked with Jung's sense of equivocation in his dealings with Nietzsche. This connection comes to the fore quite explicitly in a letter to Hermann Graf Keyserling of 2 January 1928:

> Ich habe Nietzsches amor fati verehren müssen, bis es mir zu dick kam; dann baute ich ein kleines Haus weit draußen in der Nähe der Berge und setzte, in Stein gemeißelt, eine kleine Inschrift in die Mauer: Philemonis sacrum Fausti poenitentia, und "des-identifizierte" mich von dem lieben Gott. Diese gewiß sehr unheilige Handlungsweise habe ich nie bereut (B1: p. 72/L1: p. 49).
>
> [I was compelled to respect Nietzsche's *amor fati* until I had my fill of it, then I built a little house way out in the country near the mountains and carved an inscription on the wall: *Philemonis sacrum – Fausti poenitentia*, and "dis-identified" myself with the god. I have never regretted this doubtless very unholy act.]

This only apparently obscure statement supports my argument that Jung tried to distance himself considerably from Nietzsche in the Twenties and that his reading of Nietzsche and his reading of Goethe were very closely related.

Journeys round the world (1924–1926)

Although 1925 saw another surge in German publications on Nietzsche (as Reichert and Schlechta's graph, reproduced in Chapter 2, indicates), Jung was out of Europe for the greater part of 1924–1926. In December 1923 he made a trip to the United States and in January 1924 he visited the Pueblo Indians in New Mexico as well as New Orleans and New York; and in 1925 he travelled on safari to Kenya, Uganda and the Nile, and visited the Elgonyi on Mount Elgon in Africa.

These excursions round the globe formed the external correlative of his inward journeyings, and Jung underwent experiences of a similar intensity. Having found confirmation of his idea of the Collective Unconscious in the tribal rites and mythologies of these different countries, Jung was also able in his autobiography to relate Nietzsche to these experiences, too. Just as he placed Nietzsche's *Zarathustra* in an alchemical context, so he could situate Nietzsche's experiences within a world-mythological vision. Accordingly, Jung suggests there is a basic similarity between Nietzsche's 'revelation' of the doctrine of the Eternal Recurrence in the Engadine as recounted in *Ecce Homo* (EH Z § 1; N2: p. 1128) and Moses's encounter with God on Mount Sinai in the Old Testament and the rituals of the Pueblo Indian mountain religion (ETG: p. 256/MDR: p. 281).

Jung's accounts of his visits are not so much the chapters of a travelogue as a series of what Roger Brooke has called 'ontological visions',[42] analogues to Nietzsche's inspirational experience in the Engadine in 1881[43] and akin to the mystical sense of unity which Nietzsche described as the effect of the Dionysian in *Die Geburt der Tragödie.* Two such 'ontological transformations' (Brooke) are his account of the sunrise on Mount Elgon (ETG: pp. 271–72/MDR: p. 297–98) and of an experience in a village on the way from Lake Albert to Rejâf in the Sudan, when he participated in a negro tribal dance of truly Dionysian intensity (ETG: p. 274/MDR: p. 300). The significance of these experiences is summed up by Jung as follows: 'In der lebendigen psychischen Struktur geschieht nichts auf bloß mechanische Weise, sondern in der Ökonomie des Gan-

[42] Roger Brooke, *Jung and Phenomenology* (London and New York, 1991), pp. 52–62.
[43] In fact, in his account of his visit to Nairobi, Jung explicitly compares the light of tropical Africa to the sunlight of the Engadine (ETG: p. 258/MDR: p. 283).

zen, bezogen aufs Ganze: es ist zweckhaft und hat Sinn' ['In the living psychic structure, nothing takes place in a merely mechanical fashion; everything fits into the economy of the whole, relates to the whole. That is to say, it is all purposeful and has meaning'] (ETG: p. 249/MDR: p. 274).

By this stage, such visions no longer terrified Jung, and the stability of his personal identity is reflected in his complete dissociation from Nietzsche. In fact, three letters of 1928 and 1929 contain highly negative comments about Nietzsche. First, in a letter of 12 May 1928 to Hermann Graf Keyserling, Jung somewhat tartly rejected the humour of Keyserling's book *Das Spektrum Europas* [translated as *Europe*] (1928), and made the following sceptical observation about the laughter of Nietzsche which is ultimately, according to Jung, not funny: 'Ich glaube nicht, daß der "letzte Mensch" "herzlich" lacht, auch nicht "homerisch", sondern, mit Verlaub zu sagen, etwa wie Nietzsche [...] Auch bei Nietzsche kann man nie lachen. Das Gelächter der Entfremdung steckt nicht an' ['I don't believe the "Last Man" laughs "heartily", nor "like a homeric hero", but, if I may say so, rather like Nietzsche ... Nor can one laugh when reading Nietzsche. The laughter of alienation is not infectious'] (B1: p. 74/L1: pp. 51–52).

Second, in a letter of 30 April 1929 to Walter Robert Corti, Jung criticized the over-development of the intuitive side of Nietzsche's intellectual faculty. Interestingly, Jung does not exempt himself from this fault; however, his recognition of this flaw indicates a certain distance from Nietzsche (whilst at the same time allowing him to place himself in distinguished philosophical company!): '"Überentwicklung der intellektuellen Intuition" ist eine Diagnose, die ich auch von Schopenhauer und Nietzsche und vielen andern machen würde. Ich selber bin einseitig in dieser Hinsicht' ['"Hypertrophy of intellectual intuition" is a diagnosis I would apply also to Nietzsche and Schopenhauer and many others. I myself am one-sided in this respect'] (B1: p. 91/L1: p. 64). He went on to criticize the discrepancy between the inner and the outer life in men of ideas in general and Nietzsche in particular and, recalling a line from *Menschliches, Allzumenschliches*, said that he would attribute Nietzsche's eventual demise to his world-negating life, if he did not know about its biological or physiological causes. This is a rare admission on the part of Jung that Nietzsche's insanity can be explained physiologically rather than psychologically:

> Oh, ihr Träger der Idee, warum könnt Ihr nicht anders, als Eure Idee durch ein möglichst närrisches äußeres Leben zu verhanswursten? Nietzsche predigte: "Ihr sollt wieder Freunde der nächsten Dinge werden". Ich würde sein weltfernes Leben dafür zur Verantwortung ziehen, wenn ich nicht wüßte, daß die Syphilis in ihm stak und die Paralyse als Damoklesschwert über ihm hing (B1: p. 92/L1: p. 65; cf. MA/HA WS § 16; N1: p. 882).
>
> [O you carriers of ideas, why do you have to make buffoons of them by the idiotic life you lead? Nietzsche preached: "You should make friends with the nearest

things". I would hold his world-negating life responsible for this did I not know that syphilis lurked in him and that paralysis hung over him like the sword of Damocles.]

And third, in a much later letter of 28 February 1943 to Arnold Künzli, an attack on Heidegger opened out into a vituperative attempt to delineate a 'psychopathology of the philosophers', including Nietzsche:

> Ein Kapitel einer zukünftigen kritischen Philosophie wird betitelt sein: "Die Psychopathologie der Philosophie". Hegel zerbirst von Anmaßung und Eitelkeit, Nietzsche trieft von geschändeter Sexualität usw. Es gibt kein Denken an sich [...] *Die Neurose dementiert jeden Philosophen*, denn er ist uneins mit sich selber. Seine Philosophie ist dann nichts als die systematisierte Bekämpfung der eigenen Unsicherheit (B1: p. 410/ L1: p. 332).

> [In the critical philosophy of the future there will be a chapter on "The Psychology of Philosophy". Hegel is fit to burst with presumption and vanity, Nietzsche drips with outraged sexuality, and so on. There is no thinking *qua* thinking ... Neurosis addles the brains of every philosopher because he is at odds with himself. His philosophy is then nothing but a systematized struggle with his own uncertainty.]

Just as the neurosis of the philosopher is said to act as a means of compensating for his own imbalances, so Nietzsche himself might be said to have acted as a compensatory device for the imbalances in Jung's character – imbalances which Jung had by now long overcome after his period of coming to terms with his own Unconscious (1913–1919). As a result, Jung was able to put an increasingly large distance between himself and Nietzsche. This distance was probably necessary for Jung to explore his own identity as fully as he did in Africa. Jung felt that he had been able, albeit with difficulty, to integrate his experiences of the ontological unity of Being into his personality – unlike Nietzsche and his intuition of the Dionysian. However, in his next letter to Künzli of 16 March 1943, Jung was also kinder to Nietzsche. Here he imagined a 'healthy' Nietzsche, one who would not have fallen prey to syphilis and neurosis: Nietzsche as Goethe. Again, Jung failed clearly to distinguish between the physiological and psychological levels of the possible cause of Nietzsche's demise:

> Nietzsches syphilitische Infektion hatte zweifellos einen stark neurotisierenden Einfluß auf sein Leben. Man könnte sich aber einen *gesunden* Nietzsche denken mit Schöpferkraft ohne Überspanntheit – etwa wie Goethe. Er hätte etwa Ähnliches geschrieben, weniger laut, weniger grell – d. h. weniger deutsch – etwas gehemmter, etwas verantwortlicher – etwas verständiger und ehrfürchtiger. Jacob Burckhardt hätte ihm Freund sein können... (B1: pp. 411–12/L1: p. 333).

> [Nietzsche's syphilitic infection undoubtedly exerted a strongly neuroticizing influence on his life. But one could imagine a *sound* Nietzsche possessed of creative power without hypertension – something like Goethe. He would have written much the same as he did, but less strident, less shrill – i.e., less German – more restrained, more responsible, more reasonable and reverent. Jacob Burckhardt might have been a friend to him...]

Even on this account, however, Nietzsche amounts to no more than a failure to reach personally that level of integration which he himself so much admired in Goethe (GD 9 § 49; N2: p. 1024–25), and which, at the end of his autobiography, it is hinted that Jung himself had achieved (ETG: pp. 360–61/MDR: pp. 391–92).

Jung and Dionysos

There is a large gap in Jung's autobiography, between the account of his trip to visit the Pueblo Indians and his description of his final years, where Nietzsche is not mentioned at all. Nor do the references in his letters of this time amount to much, with the exception of the letter of 5 January 1961 to Arthur W. Rudolph. In a letter to Professor Ernst Hanhart of 2 March 1957, Jung uses Nietzsche and Wagner as a typological pair which he sets beside Freud and Adler and the Dionysian and the Apollonian (B3: p. 78/L2: p. 349), and in a letter to Dr. Herbert E. Bowman of 18 June 1958, he once again refers to Goethe's *Faust* and Nietzsche's *Zarathustra* as literary representations of the (failed) attempt to discover the Self by uniting the opposites (B3: p. 195/L2: p. 453).

The last time that Jung mentioned Nietzsche in his autobiography occurs towards the end of the penultimate chapter. In the context of what amounts to a summary of the existential project which he had undertaken in his life and work, Jung says that his psychology represents an answer to the 'problem' of Faust and the 'problem' of Nietzsche, and the solution to 'die überpersönliche Lebensaufgabe, die ich nur mit Mühe realisiere' ['the suprapersonal life task, which I accomplish only by effort and with difficulty']:

> Bin ich vielleicht darum beeindruckt von der Tatsache, daß der Schluß von Faust keine Lösung enthält? Oder von dem Problem, an dem Nietzsche gescheitert ist: dem dionysischen Erlebnis, das dem christlichen Menschen entgangen zu sein scheint? Oder ist es der unruhvolle Wotan-Hermes meiner alemannischen und fränkischen Ahnen, der mir herausfordernde Fragen stellt? (ETG: p. 321/MDR: p. 350).
>
> [Could that be why I am so impressed by the fact that the conclusion of *Faust* contains no solution? Or by the problem on which Nietzsche foundered: the Dionysian side of life, to which the Christian seems to have lost the way? Or is it the restless Wotan-Hermes of my Alemannic and Frankish ancestors who poses challenging riddles?]

The passage above confirms what I have suggested in my survey of Jung's letters and autobiography – the problem of the Dionysian is the guiding thread through Jung's reception of Nietzsche. Implicit, too, in the above quotation is

Jung's overcoming of the Dionysian problematic. Whereas the conclusion of *Faust* contains no solution and Nietzsche succumbs to the Dionysian experience, Jung offers Analytical Psychology as a means of understanding these questions intellectually and, through therapy, dealing with them on the personal level.

Jung's own solution to the problem of the Dionysian, which he had discussed in the letter to Freud of 11 February 1910 as the problem of creating a new ethical order and of the transformation of Christ back into Dionysos, is referred to again in symbolic terms in the chapter of *Erinnerungen, Träume, Gedanken* called 'Der Turm'. In this passage Jung describes his own coat of arms, consisting of a blue cross in the upper right of the shield and, in the lower left, blue grapes in a field of gold, separated by a blue bar with a gold star:

> Mein Wappen enthält [...] oben rechts ein blaues Kreuz und unten links eine blaue Traube in goldenem Feld, dazwischen in blauem Balken einen goldenen Stern. Diese aufdringliche Symbolik ist freimaurerisch, beziehungsweise rosenkreuzerisch. Wie Kreuz und Rose die rosenkreuzerische Gegensatzproblematik ("per crucem ad rosam") darstellen, nämlich das Christliche und das Dionysische, so auch Kreuz und Traube, als Symbole des himmlischen und chthonischen Geistes. Das vereinigende Symbol ist durch den goldenen Stern dargestellt, das Aurum Philosophorum (ETG: p. 236/MDR: p. 259).

> [My coat of arms contains a cross azure in chief dexter and in base sinister a blue bunch of grapes in a field d'or; separating these is an etoile d'or in a fess azure. The symbolism of these arms is Masonic, or Rosicrucian. Just as cross and rose represent the Rosicrucian problem of the opposites ("*per crucem ad rosam*"), that is, the Christian and Dionysian elements, so cross and grapes are symbols of the heavenly and chthonic spirit. The uniting symbol is the gold star, the *aurum philosophorum*.]

In this device, the Jungian answer to Dionysos is made clear: Dionysos, the creative power of the Unconscious, must be integrated into the conscious life of the psyche. In the face of all opposites (and, in the struggle with Freud, in the face of all psychoanalytical opposition), Jung declares the *conjunctio oppositorum*, the union of the opposites. According to *Die Geburt der Tragödie*, the union of Dionysos and Apollo was achieved 'durch einen metaphysischen Wunderakt des hellenischen "Willens"' ['by a metaphysical miracle of Hellenic "will"'] (GT/BT § 1; N1: p. 21) – and the union of consciousness and the Unconscious is just as miraculous. The uniting symbol of Dionysos and Christ in Jung's coat of arms is the gold star. And as both Jung and Nietzsche knew, 'gold star' is the meaning of the name – Zarathustra.[44]

Throughout his writings, Jung uses Nietzsche in different ways to help unite the various opposites: to unite the sexual and non-sexual aspects of libido in a theory of psychic energy; to unite different psychological approaches through a reconciling symbol; to unite discipline and passion in the production of art; and

---

[44] See Chapter 10, n.47 (p. 282).

to unite the psychological concepts of God and the Self in the notion of the 'Gottmensch'. Furthermore, the specifically Nietzschean problematic of Dionysos is addressed in works such as 'Wotan' (1936) and 'Nach der Katastrophe' ['After the Catastrophe'] (1945), and much of Jung's later writing on theology is concerned to reply to the statement that 'Gott ist tot!' by the reinstatement of the 'subterranean' force which he had encountered in his childhood visions. And finally, Jung's theory of the quaternity of the Self reveals a complementarity of morals which is indeed 'jenseits von Gut und Böse'. His notion of the Self is founded on a Dionysian process of life, death and rebirth – it is thus a Dionysian Self.

A chronological survey of the development and increasing sophistication of Jung's reception of Nietzsche in his psychological writings forms a necessary counterpart to the examination of the change in Jung's response to Nietzsche on a personal level that we have undertaken in this chapter, and will provide the context for a detailed analysis of the Seminar on *Zarathustra* (1934–39). Accordingly, in Chapter 4, I discuss Jung's early psychoanalytic writings and the text which marks the break with Freud, *Wandlungen und Symbole der Libido.*

Chapter 4

Jung's Early Reception of Nietzsche in his Psychoanalytic Writings (1902–1917)

In this chapter, I shall examine Jung's use of Nietzsche in his theoretical writings from the publication of his doctoral dissertation in 1902 up to the texts written or revised when Jung was coming out of a period of emotional and intellectual turmoil (1913–1919). I shall argue that, in the early phase of his writings, there are already indications of the increasingly complex understanding of Nietzsche which Jung was to develop in his later life.

1902–10: A Case of Cryptomnesia

In *Zur Psychologie und Pathologie sogenannter occulter Phänomene* [*On the Psychology and Pathology of So-Called Occult Phenomena*], his MD Dissertation at the University of Zurich (1902) (GW1 § 1–150), Jung drew attention to an aspect of Nietzsche's *Zarathustra* to which he was to refer again in at least four other publications later on in his career (in 'Kryptomnesie' ['Cryptomnesia'] (1905) (GW1 § 166–86), an expanded version of his medical dissertation; twice in his Seminar on *Zarathustra* (SNZ:II:pp. 1217–18, 1383); and finally in his last piece of writing, 'Approaching the Unconscious' (GW18(i) § 416–607), an essay written in English for the book *Man and his Symbols* (1964)).

In his dissertation, Jung pointed out that there was a remarkable similarity between a passage in 'Von großen Ereignissen' ['Of Great Events'] in Part Two of *Also sprach Zarathustra* and the account of an incident which was originally reported in a ship's log for 1686 and reprinted in *Blätter aus Prevorst* (1831–37), a collection of reports of occult and unexplained phenomena put together by the Swabian physician and Romantic writer Justinus Kerner (1786–1862). Jung was so struck by the similarity of these passages that he maintained that Nietzsche must have read this account and then reproduced it almost word for word many years later, without knowing that he was doing so. Jung argued that this was a classic case of cryptomnesia, that is to say, a case of unconsciously remembering something which one believes one has forgotten.[1] As he relates

[1] For definitions of cryptomnesia, see GW1 § 138 and GW1 § 180.

in his dissertation, he even went so far as to contact Nietzsche's sister, Elisabeth Förster-Nietzsche, asking her if she could provide any explanation for this coincidence.[2] In her reply of 24 November 1899, Elisabeth told Jung that her brother knew the book by Kerner and, moreover, that she and her brother had read the book together when he was 11 years old. She also sent him a copy of Ernst Horneffer's *Nietzsches Lehre der ewigen Wiederkunft und deren bisherige Veröffentlichung* [*Nietzsche's Doctrine of the Eternal Recurrence and its Publication Hitherto*] (Leipzig, 1900) which is in Jung's library and which is inscribed 'Erhalten in Dec 1899 von Frau Dr E Förster-Nietzsche'.

The Jung/Förster-Nietzsche correspondence reveals to what extent Elisabeth Förster-Nietzsche influenced Jung's interpretation of this case of cryptomnesia in his dissertation. On the merely verbal level, there is a distinct echo of Elisabeth's letter in response to his enquiry (and a misreading of the town where Nietzsche's grandfather lived).[3] On the conceptual level, we see in Jung's first letter how he takes over part of the image of Nietzsche which was created and propagated by Elisabeth during the years of her brother's madness: Friedrich Nietzsche as the 'inspired' man of 'genius'. Jung suggests in his dissertation that the cause of this case of cryptomnesia is to be found in the inspired creative mood in which Nietzsche wrote *Zarathustra*.[4] Similarly, in his dissertation Jung speaks of Nietzsche's 'poetic ecstasy' when writing *Zarathustra*,[5] and in a footnote, he refers to Nietzsche's own account in *Ecce Homo* of the inspirational mood in which he wrote *Zarathustra* (GW1 § 139, n.121). However, although *Ecce Homo* was written down in 1888, this work was not published until 1908, and then in a limited edition, and a generally available edition did not appear until 1911. Thus, there are two likely sources for Jung's detailed knowledge of *Ecce Homo* at such an early date (1902). First, Elisabeth Förster-Nietzsche's *Das Leben Friedrich Nietzsche's* (Leipzig 1895, reprinted 1897), for in a passage which is contained in Jung's draft (but not in the letter which he actually sent), Jung mentioned that he was familiar with Elisabeth's biography of Nietzsche, by

---

2 See GW1: § 141. For the texts of the letters between Jung and Nietzsche's sister, see my article 'The Jung/Förster-Nietzsche Correspondence', *German Life and Letters*, 46 (1993), 319–30.

3 'Nietzsche [hat], zwischen dem zwölften und fünfzehnten Jahr, bei seinem Großvater in Pobler [*sic*] sich lebhaft mit Just[inus] Kerner beschäftigt und später sicher nicht mehr' ['Nietzsche had taken a lively interest in Kerner when staying with his grandfather, Pastor Oehler, in Pobles, between the ages of 12 and 15, but certainly not later;] (GW1 § 141); cf. 'Mit Justinus Kerner hat sich m[ein] Br[uder] in seinen Kinderjahren im Alter von 12–15 Jahren lebhaft beschäftigt, später allerdings nie mehr' ['My brother had taken a lively interest in Justinus Kerner in his childhood years between the ages of 12 and 15'].

4 'Der psychologische Grund zu dieser äusserst frappanten, unbewussten Reminiscenz scheint in der göttlichen Begeisterung ("Inspiration"), aus welcher "Zarathustra" geboren ward, zu liegen' ['The psychological reason for this extremely remarkable unconscious memory seems to lie in the divine enthusiasm ("inspiration") out of which *Zarathustra* was born'].

5 See GW1 § 142.

which he almost certainly meant the above work.[6] And second, the same section from *Ecce Homo* is also quoted in 'Die Entstehung von "Also sprach Zarathustra"' (written in 1899), Elisabeth's contribution to the *Nachberichte* in the 1901 edition of *Also sprach Zarathustra* which, according to an inscription inside the copy in Jung's library, he obtained in October of that year. There Elisabeth refers to Nietzsche's 'entzückten Zustand' ['enraptured condition'] and quotes *in extenso* one passage in particular from the 'autobiographischen Skizzen', *Ecce Homo*, which begins with Nietzsche's rhetorical question '– Hat Jemand, Ende des neunzehnten Jahrhunderts, einen deutlichen Begriff davon, was Dichter starker Zeitalter *Inspiration* nannten?' ['Has anyone at the end of the nineteenth century a distinct conception of what poets of strong ages called *inspiration*?'].[7] This passage is marked with pencil in the margins of Jung's own edition, and Jung quotes it at similar length in the footnotes to his doctoral dissertation.[8]

Jung's doctoral dissertation is a controversial work, based as it is on experimental observation of his fifteen-and-a-half-year-old cousin, Hélène ('Helly') Preiswerk, a reputed medium.[9] We know from his autobiography (ETG: p. 113/MDR: p. 127) and the dissertation (GW1 § 37) that his experiments with his cousin followed his own personal experiences of occult phenomena but also that he had started reading Nietzsche by the time he was conducting these experiments – i.e. in the Summer and Autumn of 1898. And in her book which examines the background to Jung's investigations of the occult,[10] Stefanie Zumstein-Preiswerk draws attention to the sittings where, through the young medium, Jung's grandfather, Samuel Preiswerk (1799–1871), is supposed to have delivered warnings with great urgency about the errors of Nietzsche's philosophy in respect of the existence of God.[11] According to Zumstein-Preis-

---

6 In her biography, Elisabeth quotes the account of 'die unvergleichliche Stimmung, in welcher der Zarathustra geschaffen wurde' ['the incomparable mood in which *Zarathustra* was composed'] from Nietzsche's 'Lebenserinnerungen', later published in *Ecce Homo* (Elisabeth Förster-Nietzsche, *Das Leben Friedrich Nietzsche's*, 2 vols (Leipzig 1895–1904), II, p. 426).

7 Friedrich Nietzsche, *Also sprach Zarathustra*, Leipzig 1901, p. 482 (volume 6 of Nietzsche, *Werke* ('Kleinoktav-Ausgabe'), 16 vols (Leipzig 1898–1911)). This is the edition which Jung owned. Cf. EH Z 3; N2: p. 1131.

8 In 'Kryptomnesie' (1905), Jung incorporated the quotations from *Ecce Homo* into the text.

9 It is likely that Jung found a model for these experiments in the work of Théodore Flournoy (1854–1920), a Swiss psychologist and disciple of the German psychologist and philosopher Wilhelm Wundt (1832–1920) (see Henri Ellenberger, *The Discovery of the Unconscious* (New York, 1970), pp. 315–17).

10 Stefanie Zumstein-Preiswerk, *C. G. Jungs Medium: Die Geschichte der Helly Preiswerk* (Munich, 1975). For a review of this book, see James Hillman, 'Some early background to Jung's ideas: notes on *C. G. Jung's Medium* by Stefanie Zumstein-Preiswerk', *Spring* (1976), 123–36; and for a detailed discussion of the evasions and repressions in Jung's analysis of Helly, see William B. Goodheart, 'C. G. Jung's First "Patient": On the Seminal Emergence of Jung's Thought', *Journal of Analytical Psychology*, 29 (1984), 1–34. The most recent discussion is in F. X. Charet, *Spiritualism and the Foundations of C. G. Jung's Psychology* (New York, 1993), pp. 149–68.

11 In Jung's dissertation, the relevant passages are in GW1 § 49 and § 51.

werk's sources, these warnings were also directed at Jung, and she interprets the whole affair as an indication of how closely Hélène Preiswerk had become acquainted with the intellectual preoccupations of her older cousin.[12]

Sceptics will rejoice when they learn, as Jung's dissertation points out, that Samuel Preiswerk had died too early to have read a word of Nietzsche. (If Jung's grandfather was indeed speaking from the Beyond, then it might be assumed that this problem could be ignored, of course). But what this incident clearly suggests is that, during the time he was working on his dissertation in Zurich (i.e. 1900–1902), Jung was intensely concerned with questions of religion and that he (or others close to him, such as Hélène) projected this concern into his work. As we have seen, Jung's attitude to Nietzsche during his time at Basle was thoroughly equivocal. Thus, taken together with his remarks in his autobiography and his continuing interest in religious and theological matters, the incidents recorded in his dissertation and his references to Nietzsche and Kerner suggest that, during his time as a clinical assistant in Zurich from 1899 to 1902, Jung found that he could deal with Nietzsche only at a distance. Or in other words, his use of Nietzsche as a case of cryptomnesia allowed him to maintain his interest in Nietzsche whilst minimizing the risk of that personal identification with him which, according to his autobiography, he strongly felt.

Furthermore, Jung's early interest in occult phenomena and cryptomnesia, which are clearly intertwined with his interest in Nietzsche, prefigures the way in which he would later regard Nietzsche in the light of his theory of the archetypes. Whereas the early Jung discussed Nietzsche's state of 'Ergriffenheit' ['gripped by emotion'] when composing *Zarathustra*, the later Jung, particularly in his Seminar on *Zarathustra*, claimed that Nietzsche had been 'possessed' by various archetypes, notably the archetypes of the Wise Old Man and of the Anima.[13] Moreover, there is a clear line of development from Jung's emphasis in his doctoral dissertation and his article 'Kryptomnesie' on the power and autonomy of the Unconscious – 'der Dämon des Unbewußten' ['the daemon of the Unconscious'][14] – to his later notion of the archetypes, described in 1952 in their multiplicity as 'spontane Phänomene, die unserer Willkür entzogen sind, und man ist daher berechtigt, ihnen eine gewisse Autonomie zuzuschreiben' ['spontaneous phenomena which are not subject to our will, and we are therefore justified in ascribing to them a certain autonomy'] (GW11 § 557).

---

12 Zumstein-Preiswerk, p. 82.

13 For example, see Jung's seminars on Nietzsche of 7 November 1934 (SNZ:I:p. 220) and 4 December 1935 (SNZ:I:p. 731).

14 'Niemand hat den Zustand des Bewußtseins unter dem Einfluß eines unbewußten automatischen Komplexes besser beschrieben als Nietzsche selbst' ['No one has descried the state of consciousness when under the influence of an automatic complex better than Nietzsche himself'] (GW1 § 184).

For Jung, this example of cryptomnesia and, indeed, the ultimate fate of Nietzsche were a powerful demonstration of 'die Ohnmacht des Bewußtseins gegenüber der Gewalt des aus dem Unbewußten auftauchenden Automatismus' ['the impotence of consciousness in face of the tremendous automatism driving up from the Unconscious'] (GW1 § 184). In this way, Jung's early reading of Nietzsche laid the foundation for one of the most influential concepts of his psychological theory: the archetype, with its emphasis on the power of the Unconscious as the source of the creative impulse.

Jung's Break with Freud: the Background

Jung's break with Freud is the all-important background of his developing reception of Nietzsche during the early psychoanalytic years. The theoretical exchanges between Freud and Jung in their letters of 1909–11 provide an elegant exposition of the issues at stake. As we saw in the previous chapter, Jung had, by 1910, developed a clear and distinctly different view from that of Freud as to the purpose of psychoanalysis, and this was set out programmatically in his letter of 11 February 1910 (FJB: pp. 323–25/FJL: pp. 293–94). In that letter (quoted in Chapter 3), Jung characterized the task of psychoanalysis as follows: first, to reinstate elements of symbolism and mythology in intellectual discourse; second, to transform Christ back into Dionysos; and third, to create an ethical space for the animal component of human nature.

In a letter to Freud of 30 January 1910, Jung referred to a lecture on 'Symbolik' which he had recently delivered to groups of students (FJB: pp. 317–19/ FJL: pp. 288–90). According to Jung, he had tried in these lectures to understand symbolism in psychogenetic terms – 'nämlich zu zeigen, daß an der Individualphantasie das primum movens der Individualkonflikt, Stoff oder Form (wie man lieber will) aber mythisch ist, oder mythologisch typisch' ['i.e., to show that in the individual fantasy the *primum movens*, the individual conflict, material or form (whichever you prefer), is mythic, or mythologically typical']. Although, in this letter, Jung also expressed the wish that Freud would look at and comment on his material, it appears that he did not actually send anything to Freud at that juncture. The lecture referred to in the letter of 30 January was probably the same lecture which Jung gave in May 1910 to the Schweizerische Psychiaterversammlung in Herisau and whose content he characterized as 'Mythologisches, was größten Beifall fand' ['mythological stuff that aroused great applause'] in a letter to Freud of 24 May 1910 (FJB: p. 352/FJL: p. 319). Then, in a letter to Freud of 2 June 1910, Jung discussed the incest-taboo with reference to ancient Persian mythology (see below) and promised Freud that he would soon send him material relating to this question.

Jung must have sent some of his material to Freud around this time, because an undated fragment from c. 22 June 1910 which is published in the Freud-Jung correspondence as a supplement to Freud's letter to Jung of 19 June 1910 (FJB: pp. 367–70/FJL: pp. 332–35) gives us an idea of Freud's reaction to what appears to be the lecture in question.[15] Although the lecture itself is lost, it is likely that Jung used material from it for his book *Wandlungen und Symbole der Libido* [*Psychology of the Unconscious*]. The phrase which most struck Freud was apparently Jung's formulation regarding the self-destructiveness of the sexual drive: 'Bei dem Satz "Die Sexualität geht an sich selber zugrunde" erfolgt ein energisches Schütteln des Kopfes. Solcher Tiefsinn ist vielleicht nicht klar genug für mythologisches Denken' ['The sentence, "sexuality destroys itself", provokes a vigorous shaking of the head. Such profundity is perhaps not clear enough for mythological thinking'] (FJB: pp. 368–69/FJL: p. 334). In a letter of 26 June 1910 replying to Freud's criticisms (which suggests that Jung *was* the recipient of the undated fragment), Jung admitted that the phrase 'Die Sexualität geht an sich selber zugrunde' was 'eine höchst paradoxe Formulierung' ['an extremely paradoxical formulation'] and one with which he was not totally satisfied (FJB: p. 370/FJL: p. 335).

From the undated fragment containing Freud's criticisms, Jung's letter of 26 June 1910 and sections of *Wandlungen und Symbole*, we may assume that Jung had based his ideas about the self-destructiveness of the sexual drive (which presupposes an inner antinomy in that drive) on an interpretation of the cult of Mithras, a Persian religious cult that flourished in the late Roman Empire and rivalled Christianity in the second century. The central image of Mithraic iconography depicts the god (Mithras) in the act of sacrificing a bull. In his response of c. 22 June 1910 to Jung's lecture on 'Symbolik', Freud had interpreted this sacrifice as a symbol of repression – the (conscious) Ego sacrificing the (unconscious) libidinal drives in a '*mythologische[r] Projektion der Verdrängung* [...] Im Grunde ein Stück des Kastrationskomplexes' ['*mythological projection of repression* ... Basically, a part of the castration complex'] (FJB: p. 369/FJL: p. 334).

Jung's reading of the symbolical sacrifice of the bull in his letter of 26 June 1910 is profoundly different. He draws attention to the fact that a symbol of fecundity (the bull) is being sacrificed by another sexual symbol (Mithras himself). Jung then drew a parallel with Christian mythology and saw a darker, more necessary purpose in the symbol: 'Das Selbstopfer ist freiwillig und unfreiwillig (derselbe Konflikt im Christustod). Es ist eine böse Notwendigkeit darin' ['The self-sacrifice is voluntary and involuntary at once (the same conflict as in the death of Christ). There is an evil necessity in it'] (FJB: p. 370/FJL: p. 336). Concentrating on what he diagnosed as the immanent conflict within the libidi-

[15] This document exists only in photocopied form; the original has not yet been found.

nal economy, Jung suggested that the rôle of the incest-taboo was of fundamental significance as an expression of this inner antinomy:

> Es dürfte sich um einen *Konflikt im Innern der Sexualität* handeln: Die einzig mögliche Grundlage dieses Konflikts scheint das *Inzestverbot* zu sein, das die Ursexualität ins Mark getroffen hat. Man könnte also etwa sagen: Das Inzestverbot vertritt der Libido den nächsten und bequemsten Weg, macht daher die Libido überhaupt schlecht. Aus dieser Verdrängung muß sie sich befreien, da sie zu ihrer Fortpflanzungsbestimmung gelangen muß (FJB: pp. 370–71/FJL: p. 336).

> [What it boils down to is a *conflict at the heart of sexuality itself.* The only possible reason for this conflict seems to be the *incest prohibition* which struck at the root of primitive sexuality. You could also say: the incest prohibition blocks the nearest and most convenient outlet for the libido and makes it altogether bad. Somehow the libido has to free itself from this repression since it must reach its propagative goal.]

Although Jung does not go so far as to say that the libido is in fact non-sexual (or more than purely sexual) in nature, the all-important move towards this later conclusion is made with the notion that libido can be diverted (or canalized) into non-propagatory activities. As Jung later formulated the idea: 'es handelt sich um einen innern Widerstand, indem *Wollen* gegen *Wollen*, *Libido* gegen *Libido* tritt [...] Der psychologische Zwang zur Libidoüberleitung beruht auf einer ursprünglichen Uneinigkeit des Wollens' ['it is a question of an internal resistance; will opposes will; libido opposes libido ... The psychological compulsion for the transformation of the libido is based on an original diversion of the will'] (WSL: p. 159/PU § 249).

According to Jung's letter of 26 June 1910, the struggle which is immanent within the libido was symbolically represented by two mythologems. First, in the Persian Song of Tishtriya, by the fight between two horses, one white (Tishtriya) and one black (Apaosha);[16] and second, in the ancient Iranian astral myth. He had already referred to both these myths in his letter to Freud of 2 June 1910 in the context of a discussion of the incest-taboo. There, he had related the antinomy between libidinal satisfaction and propagation brought about by the incest-taboo to the astral myth (the 'death' of the sun in winter and its 'rebirth' in spring) and the struggle between the two horses for a water-lake, and concluded that the message of Mithraism was the promise of fecun-

[16] 'Tishtryia = nach Betätigung strebende Libido, Apaosha = Libido im Widerstand (inzestuöse Libido). Mit der Figur des Mithras kommt zuerst folgende Neuigkeit: Tishtryia und Apaosha sind jetzt zwei dem Mithras hingegebene Symbole (Schlange und Pferd = Bruder und Schwester des Chiwantopel, d. h. der Mensch mit der tätigen und der im Widerstand befindlichen Libido (Stier und Schlange)' ['Tishtriya = active libido, Apaosha = resistant (incestuous) libido. The figure of Mithras brings a new development: Tishtriya and Apaosha now symbolize the dual aspect of Mithras as Man's active and resistant libido (bull and serpent), just as horse and serpent = brother and sister of Chiwantopel'] (FJB: p. 371/FJL: p. 336).

dity.[17] In his letter of 26 June 1910, Jung argued that Mithraic symbolism used the imagery of the natural cycle of solar death and rebirth, as a metaphor for fecundity,[18] drawing attention for the first time to the significance in myth of the hero-figure – 'der nämlich *das freiwillig zu tun versteht*, was die Verdrängung will, nämlich temporärer oder dauernder Verzicht auf Fruchtbarkeit [...], zunächst zur Erreichung eines sittlichen Ideals der Triebbeherrschung' ['who *understands how to accomplish of his own free will* what the repression is after – namely, temporary or permanent renunciation of fruitfulness ... in order to realize the ethical ideal of the subjugation of instinct'] (FJB: p. 371/FJL: p. 336). An analysis of the hero-motif would occupy most of the second part of *Wandlungen und Symbole der Libido.* Finally, according to Jung in his letter of 26 June, the mastery of the libidinal drives created the space for ethical life and initiated the painful process of 'domestication': 'Die Leiden der Menschheit bei den verschiedenen Anläufen zur "Domestikation" müssen beträchtliche gewesen sein' ['The sufferings of humanity must have been immense during the various attempts at "domestication"'] (FJB: p. 371/FJL: p. 336; cf. WSL: p. 78/PU § 123).

It is odd that Freud, who was later to evolve the idea that the Unconscious is characterized by an internal struggle between Eros and Thanatos, should have objected to what Jung himself called his 'paradoxer Satz von der an sich selbst zugrunde gehenden Sexualität' ['paradoxical dictum about sexuality destroying itself'] (FJB: p. 372/FJL: p. 337). At this stage, however, Freud still believed in the creative nature of the de-repressed Eros, whereas Jung wanted to see a dialectic of life and death within the sexual drive itself, thereby taking the first step towards an understanding of the libido as a more than purely sexual drive. Within Nietzsche's philosophy, Dionysos is characterized by a similarly dual nature, destroying the unity of the individual but thereby restoring the primordial

17 'Der "Kernkomplex" scheint die durch das Inzestverbot verursachte tiefgreifende Störung zwischen Libidobefriedigung und Fortpflanzung zu sein. Der Astralmythus ist nach den Regeln der Traumdeutung aufzulösen' ['The "nuclear complex" seems to be the profound disturbance – caused by the incest prohibition – between libidinal gratification and propagation. The astral myth can be solved in accordance with the rules of dream interpretation'] (FJB: pp. 360–61/FJL: p. 326). Jung uses this example a third time in *Wandlungen und Symbole der Libido* as 'ein *Symbol der Libido im Widerstand*' ['a symbol of the *libido in opposition*']: 'In diesem Liede sieht man in der Symbolwahl sehr schön, wie Libido gegen Libido gesetzt ist, Wollen gegen Wollen' ['In this song one sees very beautifully in the choice of symbol how libido is opposed to libido, will against will'] (WSL: pp. 256–57/PU § 398). Jung's use of the astral myth in *Wandlungen und Symbole der Libido* is much more extensive (cf. WSL: pp. 119, 175, 285, 335/PU § 200, 282, 459, 566) and is conflated not only with Frobenius's motif of the 'Nachtmeerfahrt' (WSL: pp. 211–13/PU § 324–25) but also with imagery from Nietzsche's *Zarathustra* (WSL: pp. 362–63/PU § 615).

18 'So wie die Sonne oder die Fruchtbarkeit der Natur auch lange unter der Macht des Winters leidet und schließlich doch zur Herrschaft gelangt, so wirst du dich befreien' ['just as the sun or the fruitfulness of Nature languishes in the grip of winter and yet finally triumphs, so will you wrench yourself free and blossom with fruitfulness'] (FJB: p. 371/FJL: p. 336).

unity. Furthermore, Jung's view that civilization (or domestication) can be bought only at the price of libidinal repression is highly reminiscent of Nietzsche's *Zur Genealogie der Moral* [*On the Genealogy of Morals*], particularly section 16 of Part II (N2: pp. 824–26). Here, Nietzsche suggested that, in the course of societal development, the radical re-direction of Man's drives was effected, and that this process was accompanied by pain. Indeed, Nietzsche used the term 'Verinnerlichung des Menschen' ['internalization of Man'], and in *Wandlungen und Symbole der Libido*, Jung discusses 'die Libido, die nach innen, ins Subjekt gewendet ist' ['the libido, which is turned inward into the subject'] (WSL: p. 94/PU § 152). It was only some twenty years later, in *Das Unbehagen in der Kultur* [*Civilization and its Discontents*] (1930), that Freud was to express a similar view about the consequences of societal development. Jung's statement in his letter of 5 January 1961 (B3: pp. 370–71/L2: pp. 621–22) that *Zur Genealogie der Moral* had been less important for him than *Unzeitgemäße Betrachtungen* [*Untimely Meditations*] by no means precludes the influence of the aforementioned work by Nietzsche on Jung's thinking at this stage. The marginal lines against the key passages of section 16 of the 'Zweite Abhandlung' in Jung's copy of *Zur Genealogie der Moral* were probably made in 1910, and there is clear evidence that, by 1911, Jung had read at least the 'Vorrede' to *Jenseits von Gut und Böse* [*Beyond Good and Evil*], for the first part of *Wandlungen und Symbole der Libido* makes reference to a remark, attributed to Nietzsche, about the 'prachtvolle Spannung' ['magnificent tension'] of the German mind in the Middle Ages (WSL: p. 33/PU § 30; cf. JGB/BGE Vorrede/Preface; N2: p. 566). It was not for nothing that Jung made a point of mentioning Nietzsche in his correspondence with Freud.

The intricacy of the debate concerning the incest-taboo, accompanied by Jung's interest in works on mythology such as Friedrich Creuzer's *Symbolik und Mythologie der alten Völker* [*Symbolism and Mythology of the Ancient Peoples*] (1810–23) (FJB: p. 284/FJL: p. 258), disguises the fact that Jung's move away from Freud was also a move towards Nietzsche. However, rather than claiming Nietzsche as a conceptual source in *Wandlungen und Symbole der Libido*, Jung quarries Nietzsche's texts for examples of imagery to support his own ideas. Above all, Jung's key mythologem is already in place by 1910: his interpretation of the astral myth anticipates his later use of motifs of death and rebirth, of the phallic pattern of erection and detumescence, and of the descent of the sun and its subsequent ascent, which he associates with Dionysos.

Having drawn attention to the conflict which is intrinsic to the libido, the stage was set for a full-scale revision of Jung's view both of the basic nature of sexuality and of the incest-taboo. Following his letter to Freud of 3 March 1912 in which he made his 'Declaration of Independence', as Freud later termed it (FJB: p. 554/FJL: p. 500) by quoting Zarathustra's dictum 'Man vergilt einem Lehrer schlecht, wenn man immer nur der Schüler bleibt' ['One repays a teacher badly if one remains only a pupil'] (FJB: pp. 544/FJL: p. 491; cf. Z I 22 § 3; N2: p. 339), Jung presented his revised view of the incest-taboo in four letters to Freud of 27 April, 8 and 17 May[19] and 2 August 1912. In successive steps, Jung distanced himself further and further from the idea that the incest-taboo relates to any literal sexual desire for the mother – the classic Freudian view – and instituted, in place of the figure of the forbidden maternal object, the figure of the mythical Mother. On 2 August 1912 Jung wrote to Freud: 'Das Tatsächliche am Inzest ist doch nur die Regressivbewegung der Libido und nicht die Mutter [...] Das Phantasie *heißt* unter Umständen, in der Regel meistens, *Mutter*' ['The salient fact is simply the regressive movement of libido and not the mother ... In certain circumstances, indeed as a general rule, the fantasy object is *called* "mother" '] (FJB: p. 567/FJL: p. 512). In other words, by August 1912, Jung had clearly stated that, in his view, the object of incestual desire was not the flesh-and-blood mother, but a phantastic or archetypal Mother in a sense more akin to the Mothers of Goethe's *Faust* and the Primal Mother(s) ('Urmutter'/'Mütter des Seins') of Nietzsche's *Die Geburt der Tragödie*, two works which function as important intertexts of *Wandlungen und Symbole der Libido*. Jung's revision of his view on the incest-taboo led, *mutatis mutandis*, to a revision of his view on the basic nature of sexuality.

By this time relations between Jung and Freud had considerably deteriorated – in less than five months their correspondence would practically cease – but there was no need for Jung to write to Freud about his view of the basic nature of sexuality. In early September 1912, the *Jahrbuch für psychoanalytische und psychopathologische Forschungen*, III. Band, 1 Hälfte (Januar 1912) appeared. Jung had left for a trip to America on 7 September and his wife sent a copy to Freud on 10 September 1912. The issue in question contained the second part of *Wandlungen und Symbole der Libido* and, in particular, a new definition of the term 'Libido':

> Man kann sagen, daß dem Libidobegriff, wie er sich in den neuen Arbeiten Freuds und seiner Schule entwickelt hat, im biologischen Gebiete funktionell dieselbe Bedeutung zukommt wie dem Begriff der *Energie* auf physikalischem Gebiete seit Robert Mayer (WSL: p. 132/PU § 218).
>
> [It can be said that the conception of libido as developed in the new work of Freud and of his school has functionally the same significance in the biological territory as has the conception of energy since the time of Robert Mayer in the physical realm.]

In Jung's view, the repression of sexual desire dictated by the incest-taboo was in actual fact '*der Zwang zur Kultur*' ['*the compulsion towards culture*' (P. B.)] (FJB:

[19] In his letter to Freud of 8 May 1912, Jung argued that the incest-taboo could never really have been necessary (FJB: p. 557/FJL: p. 503), and in his letter to Freud of 17 May 1912, Jung claimed that the incest-taboo had as much to do with preventing sexual relations within the family as the animal cult had to do with actual sodomy (FJB: pp. 560–61/FJL: p. 506).

p. 372/FJL: p. 337; cf. WSL: p. 265/PU § 419), and this abandonment of the purely sexual interpretation of the incest-taboo led him to reject the idea of the purely sexual nature of libido. And if the incest-taboo was not to be understood literally, then this cast doubt on the nature and meaning of the 'Oedipus complex', the corner-stone of Freudian theory. The break between Freud and Jung was therefore inevitable.

Wandlungen und Symbole der Libido

Wandlungen und Symbole der Libido [literally, 'Transformations and Symbols of the Libido'] is often said to be Jung's most important book. Vincent Brome assesses its importance thus: 'In a different category altogether, [it] not only made the break with Freud inevitable, but also developed [Jung's] reputation as an original thinker in psychoanalysis'.[20] And Peter Homans summarizes the scope of the work in the following way: 'In writing *Symbols of Transformation*, Jung narcissistically and grandiosely attempted to fuse his own fantasies with the great myths of the past and, at the same time, repudiated traditional Christianity by interpreting it by the libido theory'.[21] More recently, John Kerr has summed up *Wandlungen und Symbole der Libido* thus: 'The central motif was clearly Faustian: casting aside the constraints of Christianity, Jung meant to make a descent into the depths of the soul, there to find the roots of Man's being in the symbols of the libido which had been handed down from ancient times, and so to find redemption despite his own genial psychoanalytic pact with the devil'.[22] Looking back on his book in his preface to the revised edition of 1950, Jung himself claimed: 'So wurde dieses Buch ein Markstein, gesetzt an der Stelle, wo sich zwei Wege trennten' ['Thus this book became a landmark, set up on the spot where two ways divided'] (WSL: p. 9/CW5: p.xxiv).[23]

The work's central thesis concerning the return of the libido to an unconscious source of new psychological life (a process which Jung called 'introversion') revives in psychological form many notions of the classical Mysteries of

---

20 Vincent Brome, *Jung: Man and Myth* (London, 1980), p. 155.

21 Peter Homans, *Jung in Context* (Chicago and London, 1979), p. 129.

22 John Kerr, *A Most Dangerous Method: The Story of Jung, Freud, and Sabina Spielrein* (London, 1994), p. 326.

23 The revisions undertaken in the 1950 edition which is republished in the *Gesammelte Werke* substantially alter the structure and tone of the book, and references here are made to the recent reissue of the original text of 1911/1912, for many years unavailable: C. G. Jung, *Wandlungen und Symbole der Libido: Beiträge zur Entwicklungsgeschichte des Denkens* (Munich, 1991) (cited in the text as WSL plus page reference). The English translation used is *Psychology of the Unconscious*, translated by Beatrice Hinkle (New York and London, 1916), recently reissued under the same title with an introduction by William McGuire (London, 1991) (cited in the text as PU followed by a paragraph number).

Dionysos, in which the god was ripped apart and reconstituted. This preoccupation with Dionysos and antiquity was not peculiar to Jung and can be read as continuing an important topos of Romantic literature, the hope for what Hölderlin called 'den kommenden Gott' ['the coming god'].[24] Bearing in mind Jung's equation of libido with Dionysos and the symbol of the phallus (see below), this Romantic designation of Dionysos is highly appropriate! But whereas the mythologem of the dying and rising god underpins *Wandlungen und Symbole der Libido* in an obvious way, Nietzsche's Dionysos is present in the margins of the text – or, more accurately, at the centre of the elaborate labyrinth of symbolic parallels to which, according to Jung's preface of 1950, Miss Miller's fantasies provided the (somewhat tangled) thread of Ariadne (WSL: p. 10/CW5: p.xxv). Although the thread leading from Nietzsche to Jung, interwoven as it is with the debate with Freud on the nature of the libido and his neo-Romantic use of ideas and imagery from the cult of Dionysos, is equally knotted, it can be untangled to show the relevance of Nietzsche for the ideas of this pioneering work.

(i) Libido

As I suggested above, *Wandlungen und Symbole* marked a dual move: away from Freud and towards Nietzsche. Jung mentions Nietzsche as many as 34 times, i.e. more frequently than any other source apart from Freud. The book itself is presented as a detailed commentary on the visions of Frank Miller, originally published by Théodore Flournoy in 1906,[25] and the relationship between this original text and Jung's commentary is comparable to that between the aphorism from *Zarathustra* and the third essay of *Zur Genealogie der Moral* which interprets it. Furthermore, just as Nietzsche proposes a '*genealogical*' approach to morality, so Jung offers what he calls a '*genetic*' theory of libido (WSL: pp. 137, 142/PU § 222, 230). The title of Jung's work – Symbols and Transformations of the Libido – thus has a double meaning: first, it refers to Jung's idea that the regression (transformation) of the libido has a positive meaning and function; and second, it refers to precisely this transformation of the concept of the libido undertaken by Jung's revision of Freudian psychoanalysis. By examining Jung's

---

[24] Friedrich Hölderlin, 'Brod und Wein', in: *Sämtliche Werke*, 6 vols (Stuttgart, 1944–1962), II, pp. 94–99 (p. 96). See also Manfred Frank, *Der kommende Gott: Vorlesungen über die Neue Mythologie, I. Teil* (Frankfurt am Main, 1982).

[25] Théodore Flournoy, 'Quelques faits d'imagination créatrice subconsciente', *Archives de psychologie*, 5 (1906), 36–51. For further information on this case, see Sonu Shamdasani, 'A Woman called Frank', *Spring*, 50 (1990), pp. 26–56.

concept of libido we can see how Jung addresses himself to issues which are both Freudian and Nietzschean.

Jung's account of the symbols and transformation of the libido – the symbolic transformation of the libido and the symbols of libidinal transformation – uses a central notion from the cult of Dionysos and other mystery cults, and one primary image: the phallus. His account of the libido operates both on the ontogenetic and on the phylogenetic level.

Jung characterized his revised (transformed) concept of libido in the following seven ways: first, in the physical terminology of energy (see above); second, in Schelling's psychological terminology as 'das Vorbewußte' ['the Preconscious'] (WSL: p. 44, n.43/PU § 50, n.37); and third, in the metaphysical terminology of the Will, particularly Schopenhauer's notion of the Will: '[der] Begriff [der Libido ist] weit genug [...], um alle die unerhört mannigfaltigen Manifestationen des Willens im Schopenhauerschen Sinne zu decken' ['the concept of the libido is wide enough to cover all the unknown and countless manifestations of the Will in the sense of Schopenhauer'] (WSL: p. 130, cf. pp. 138–39/PU § 212, cf.223). However, Jung also made a connection between the libido and the concept of the Will in *Also sprach Zarathustra* (which he fails to distinguish from Schopenhauer's): 'Es gibt nichts anderes, als daß der Mensch mit diesem Willen zusammengehe, was uns Nietzsches Zarathustra eindringlich lehrt' ['Nothing remains for Mankind but to work in harmony with this Will. Nietzsche's Zarathustra teaches us this impressively'] (WSL: p. 72/PU § 111). Fourth, he assigned a cosmological status to the libido: 'Das Ur- und Allwesen, dessen Begriff sich, ins Psychologische zurückübersetzt, mit dem Libidobegriff deckt' ['The primal and omniscient being, the idea of whom, translated back into psychology, is comprehended in the conception of libido' (P. B.)] (WSL: p. 161, n.28/PU § 251, n. 29). Fifth, he used theological terms to define libido: 'Die Libido ist Gott und Teufel' ['The libido is God and Devil'] (WSL: p. 113/ PU § 195). And for Jung, even God is a psychological concept: 'Dieser Gott wohnt im Herzen, im Unbewußten, im Reich der Metapsychologie' ['This God lives in the heart, in the Unconscious, in the realm of metapsychology'] (WSL: p. 71/PU § 111). Conflating psychology and theology yet further, Jung described this libidinal god as both a creator and a destroyer: 'Gott ist [...] die segenspendende, fruchtbare Natur – die unbezähmbare Wildheit und Schrankenlosigkeit der Natur – und die überwältigende Gefahr der entfesselten Gewalt [...] seine andere Seite, die man Teufel nennt' ['God is the fruitful Nature giving forth abundance, – the untamable wildness and boundlessness of Nature, – and the overwhelming danger of the unchained power ... his other side which Man calls the Devil'] (WSL: p. 71/PU § 110–11). According to Jung, the libido (or power, or energy) is the true content of the category of the divine, although not its form: 'Wie leicht verständlich, ist das Wirksame an der Gottesidee nicht die

Form, sondern die Kraft, die Libido' ['As is easily understood, that which is valuable in the God-creating idea is not the form but the power, the libido'] (WSL: p. 72/PU § 111). Sixth, Jung defines the essence of the libido as both 'Nützliches und Schädliches, Gutes und Böses' ['what is useful and what is injurious, Good and Evil' (P. B.)] (WSL: pp. 123–24/PU § 201). And seventh, through the symbol of the phallus, Jung explicitly linked his notion of the libido with Dionysos. These characterizations add up to a concept of libido which is not as close to Schopenhauer's Will to Life as it is to Nietzsche's Will to Power, creative and destructive, beyond Good and Evil (albeit with a more overtly theological echo).

(ii) Dionysos and the phallus

Jung's statements in *Wandlungen und Symbole der Libido* on the psychological meaning of the phallus are often overlooked and are deliberately underplayed by the Jungian School.[26] By referring to the phallus rather than the penis, Jung makes it clear that his concept is not biological but symbolic. (Indeed, Jung is reported to have once said: the penis is a phallic symbol). In his letter to Freud of 15 November 1909, Jung had expressed his interest in ancient phallic ceremonies and syncretically assimilated them to the single mythologem of 'der sterbende und wiedererwachende Gott' ['the dying and resurgent god'] (FJB: pp. 289–90/ FJL: p. 263).[27] Here, Jung associates Dionysos with such gods as Phales and Hermes: 'Der Gefährte des Dionysos war Phales, eine aus der phallischen Herme des Dionysos hervorgegangene Personifikation des Phallus [...] Nun ist Dionysos unter verschiedenen Aspekten ein *phallischer Gott*' ['The companion of Dionysos was Phales, a personification of the phallus proceeding from the phallic Herme of Dionysos ... Now, under various aspects, Dionysos is a phallic god'] (WSL: pp. 41, 129/PU § 45, 211). The phallic significance of Dionysos in antiquity had been known to Nietzsche as well, as is suggested by his reference to sexual symbolism, procreation, pregnancy and birth in the context of 'that wonderful phenomenon' of Dionysos. In a section of *Götzen-Dämmerung* [*Twilight of the Idols*] marked by Jung in his copy with a marginal line, Nietzsche had

---

[26] None of the secondary literature on Jung discusses these passages in *Wandlungen und Symbole der Libido.* This is mainly due to the suppression of the original form of the text and its replacement with the later (heavily revised) version of 1950, but it also reflects a tendency on the part of commentators, especially those in the Jungian tradition, to ignore his earlier theoretical formulations.

[27] Of course, Jung was not the first to seek to reduce various religious cults to one single structural principle; for example, in his *Philosophie der Offenbarung* (1840–1841), Schelling had tried to do the same: 'So ist Alles Dionysos' ['Thus everything is Dionysos'] (F. W. J. Schelling, *Philosophie der Offenbarung 1841/42*, edited by Manfred Frank (Frankfurt am Main, 1977), p. 237).

pointed out the importance of sexual symbolism for the Greeks: 'Den Griechen war [...] das *geschlechtliche* Symbol das ehrwürdige Symbol an sich, der eigentliche Tiefsinn innerhalb der ganzen antiken Frömmigkeit' ['the *sexual* symbol was to the Greeks the symbol venerable as such, the intrinsic profound meaning of all antique piety'] (GD/TI 10 § 4; N2: p. 1031).[28] Just as, for Nietzsche, the doctrines of the Dionysian mystery cult taught that there was a higher symbolism in the process of procreation, so, for Jung, the phallus is not a symbol of sexual difference, but symbolizes a process of psychological revitalization. Not surprisingly, therefore, he even stresses that genital differentiation is irrelevant in the symbolic representations of the libido: 'die Geschlechtsunterschiede sind im Grunde genommen sekundärer Natur und spielen psychologisch nicht die Rolle, wie man etwa bei oberflächlicher Betrachtung vermuten könnte' ['differences of sex are basically of secondary nature and psychologically do not play the part which superficial observation might lead one to expect' (P. B.)] (WSL: p. 403/PU § 691). (When considering Jung's concept of the phallus as a symbol, it is useful to remember the dream of the phallus which he had when a child, whose significance he saw not as sexual, but rather as religious, as 'ein unterirdischer und nicht zu erwähnender Gott' ['a subterranean god not to be named'] (ETG: p. 19/MDR: p. 28)). Indeed, Jung sees the phallus as a unique symbol of the libido, the creative drive:

> *Der Phallus ist die Quelle von Leben und Libido, der große Schöpfer und Wundertäter* [...] Der Phallus ist das Wesen, das sich ohne Glieder bewegt, das sieht ohne Augen, das die Zukunft weiß; und als symbolischen Repräsentanten der überall verbreiteten Schöpferkraft ist ihm Unsterblichkeit vindiziert (WSL: pp. 100, 127/PU § 164, 209).

> [*The phallus is the source of life and libido, the great creator and worker of miracles* ... The phallus is the being, which moves without limbs, which sees without eyes, which knows the future; and as a symbolic representative of the universal creative power existent everywhere immortality is vindicated in it.]

---

[28] 'Dionysos selbst wurde niemals phallisch dargestellt, doch seine Gefolgsleute, die Silenen und Satyrn, und der ihm nahestehende, der Gärten schützende Priapos waren Ithyphallen' ['Dionysos himself was never depicted phallically, but his followers, the sileni and satyrs and Priapus, who was related to him and protected the gardens, were ithyphalli'] (Martin Persson Nilsson, *Geschichte der griechischen Religion* (*Handbuch der Altertumswissenschaft*, 5. Abteilung, 2. Teil), 2 vols (Munich, 1941–1950), I, p. 552). More generally on the history of phallic worship and its Dionysian origins, see Richard Payne Knight, *A Discourse on the Worship of Priapus and its Connection with the Mystic Theology of the Ancients* (London, 1786), and Thomas Wright, *The Worship of the Generative Powers During the Middle Ages of Western Europe* (London, 1866). Jung owned Knight's book in the 1865 edition and referred to it in his letter to Freud of 8 November 1909 (FJB: p. 284/FJL: p. 258). Freud later purchased a copy. Hans Herter suggested that the cult of the phallus was of fundamental importance in the Dionysian rites (*Vom dionysischen Tanz zum komischen Spiel: Die Anfänge der attischen Komödie* (Iserlohn, 1947), p. 27). Jung's library contains a copy of Herter's *De Priapo* (Giessen, 1932).

According to Jung, the libido stands in a particular relationship to its ultimate source, the Unconscious. It not only springs from it, but it can flow back into it. To convey his notion of a return to the Unconscious, Jung turns to the astral myth for images of ascent (congruent with the image of the rising phallus), representing the libido striving towards consciousness, and descent (congruent with the image of the phallus resuming flaccidity), representing the return of the libido to the Unconscious. The astral myth symbolizes the transformation of the (phallic) libido: Jung observes that '"urtümliche" Libidosymbolik' ['primitive libido symbolism'] shows 'wie unmittelbar die Beziehung zwischen phallischer Libido und Licht ist' ['how immediate the connection is between phallic libido and light'] (WSL: p. 220/PU § 335). Using a schema adapted from Otto Rank's *Der Mythus von der Geburt des Helden* (1909), Jung takes the symbolical figure of the hero to represent a personification of the libido in this process of transformation (WSL: p. 206/PU § 317). Furthermore, the hero can also be represented by Dionysos (WSL: p. 187, n.15/PU § 297, n.14). In this respect both Dionysos and Christ can be assimilated into the same figure:

> Dionysos steht in einem innigen Zusammenhang mit der Psychologie des vorderasiatischen, sterbenden und auferstehenden Gottheilandes, dessen mannigfache Abwandlungen sich in der Figur des Christos zu einem die Jahrtausende überdauernden festen Gebilde verdichtet haben (WSL: p. 130/PU § 212).

> [Dionysos stands in an intimate relation with the psychology of the early Asiatic god who died and rose again from the dead and whose manifold manifestations have been brought together in the figure of Christ into a firm personality enduring for centuries.]

Jung termed the return of the libido to the Unconscious 'introversion', and used other images for the same process, such as the night sea-journey ('Nachtmeerfahrt') of Leo Frobenius (WSL: p. 211/PU § 324–25), and the 'katabasis' which he had mentioned in his letter to Freud of 25 February 1912 (FJB: p. 540/FJL: pp. 487–88). Indeed, Jung's own subterranean psychic voyages which he experienced after the break with Freud are a perfect example of the process of introversion. The natural cycle of life, death and rebirth, and its physiological and cosmological analogues – the erection, detumescence, and rearousal of the phallus, the rising and setting sun which rises again – are psychologized by Jung into an intrapsychic, archetypal pattern which applies to every individual on the ontogenetic level. Thus, the paradox of 'die an sich selber zugrunde gehende Sexualität' had become elevated into a principle of individual development:

> Am Morgen des Lebens reißt sich der Mensch schmerzvoll los von der Mutter, dem heimatlichen Herde, um kämpfend zu seiner Höhe emporzusteigen, seinen schlimmsten Feind nicht vor sich sehend, sondern in sich tragend, jene tödliche Sehnsucht nach dem eigenen Abgrund, nach dem Ertrinken in der eigenen Quelle, nach der

Verschlingung in die Mutter. Sein Leben ist ein beständiges Ringen mit dem Tode, eine gewaltsame und vorübergehende Befreiung von der stets lauernden Nacht (WSL: p. 335/PU § 566).

[In the morning of life Man painfully tears himself loose from the mother, from the domestic hearth, to rise through battle to his heights. Not seeing his worst enemy in front of him, but bearing him within himself as a deadly longing for the depths within, for drowning in his own source, for becoming absorbed into the Mother, his life is a constant struggle with death, a violent and transitory delivery from the always lurking night.]

As this passage and others make clear, the internal antinomy of the libido dictates that it seek not only its own propagation but also its own demise – 'den *Abstieg und das Ende wollend*' ['willing the descent and the end'] (WSL: p. 362/PU § 614). Thus the libido might not just be like Schopenhauer's concept of the Will to Life, as Jung recognizes, but in its self-destructiveness similar to Nietzsche's Will to Power, a connection Jung does not make.[29]

Jung explicitly associates the nexus of images and symbols used to describe the introversion of the libido with three literary examples: Goethe's *Faust*, the poetry of Hölderlin and the poetry of Nietzsche. First, the descent of Faust to the Mothers is taken by Jung as a symbol of the desire of the individual to return to the Mother, but, in accordance with his revised sense of the incest-taboo, that return is not construed biologically but as a return to the Unconscious.[30] The realm of the Mothers is said by Jung to represent the Unconscious, the realm of imagination or phantasy (WSL: p. 366, n.208/PU § 629, n.1). Elsewhere, the Mother is understood by Jung as a symbol of the source of the libido (WSL: p. 385/PU § 658), and he attributes archetypal qualities to the figure of the Mother, speaking of 'das "große, urtümliche Bild" der Mutter, die uns erstmals einzige Welt bedeutete und nachmals zum Symbol von aller Welt wurde' ['the "great primitive image" of the Mother who, in the first place, meant to us our individual world and afterwards became the symbol of all worlds' (P. B.)] (WSL: p. 248/PU § 381). Although Jung introduces the Mother archetype via the Faustian Mothers, the cult of the Great Mother has a direct association with the cult of Dionysos, as Schelling pointed out in *Die Weltalter* [*The Ages of the*

[29] 'Es ist nicht nur so, daß die Libido ein unaufhaltsames Vorwärtsstreben, ein endloses Leben und Aufbauenwollen wäre, als welches Schopenhauer seinen Weltwillen formuliert hat, wobei der Tod und jegliches Ende eine von außen herantretende Tücke oder Fatalität ist; sondern die Libido will, dem Sonnengleichnis entsprechend, auch den Untergang ihrer Bildung' ['It is not only as if the libido might be an irresistible striving forward, an endless life and will for construction, such as Schopenhauer has formulated in his world will, death and every end being some malignancy or fatality coming from without, but the libido, corresponding to the sun, also wills the destruction of its creation'] (WSL: p. 408/PU § 696).

[30] The link between the Faustian Mothers and Jung's archetypes of the Collective Unconscious is made by Ulrich Wesche, 'The Spirits' Chorus in *Faust*: A Jungian Reading', *Germanic Notes*, 14, no.4 (1983), pp. 49–51.

World] (1811–13),[31] and the same motif of the 'Müttern des Seins' ['Mothers of Being'] is used by Nietzsche in *Die Geburt der Tragödie* (GT/BT § 20; N1: p. 113).

Jung also refers to the moment when Mephistopheles gives Faust a glowing key to gain entrance to the realm of the Mothers: 'Er wächst in meiner Hand, er leuchtet, blitzt!' ['It grows, it shines, increases in my hand!'] (WSL: p. 220/ PU § 335; cf. *Faust II*, l.6261). On Jung's account, this key is not just a phallic symbol, but also 'ein phallisches Symbol *der Libido*' (my emphasis), i.e. a symbol of phallic libido, or a symbol of the libidinal phallus. Jung also illustrates his point that the relationship between consciousness and the Unconscious is a dialectical one which determines the pattern of life with reference to *Faust*. Jung presents Faust's dilemma as follows: Faust – who is subject to desire ('Sehnsucht'), passion ('Leidenschaft'), the libidinal drive ('Drang der Libido') – is caught between two realms (the 'Jenseitigen' and the 'Diesseits'), both of which lead to death: 'Was soll der Ausweg sein, zwischen der Scylla der Weltverneinung und der Charybdis der Weltbejahung?' ['What is to be the way out between the Scylla of renunciation of the world and the Charybdis of the acceptance of the world?'] (WSL: pp. 87, 89/PU § 136, 141). To use Jung's later terminology, Faust is clearly a victim of the opposites, and Jung repeatedly presents Man's main psychological problem in terms of libidinal conflict: 'Wollen gegen Wollen, Libido gegen Libido' (WSL: pp. 159, 177, 256, 284/PU § 249, 284, 398, 457). According to Jung, Faust's descent to the realm of the Mothers is an attempt to resolve this crisis by readjusting the balance between unconscious libidinal desire and consciousness (WSL: p. 328/PU § 549). If advance in the 'Diesseits', i.e. the realm of consciousness, is not possible, then the libido returns to its unconscious source, i.e. introverts (WSL: p. 284/PU § 458). Jung stresses that the process of introversion is a dangerous one, and Faust's wager is thus a psychological gamble for high existential stakes: in entering the realm of the Unconscious, he must risk loss of consciousness – i.e. death – to gain greater consciousness – i.e. new life.

Second, and analogously, Jung finds symbols of the introversion of the libido in various poetic texts of Hölderlin (WSL: p. 371/PU § 637). Referring in particular to the poem 'Patmos' (the 1802 version), Jung claims: 'In ihm leuchten die uralten Gedanken des Mythos wieder auf, die in Symbole gekleidete Ahnung

[31] F. W. J. Schelling, *Die Weltalter*, edited by Manfred Schröter (Munich, 1946), pp. 42–43. According to Bachofen, Dionysos was closely related to the Earth-Mother deities ('der Frauen Gott'), even if he was a masculine god (*Der Mythus von Orient und Occident*, edited by Manfred Schröter and introduced by Alfred Baeumler (Munich, 1965), p. 357. In his *Dionysisch und Apollinisch* (Regensburg, 1966), Martin Vogel explains that 'Dionysos war mit dem Kult der "Großen Mutter" eng verbunden' ['Dionysos was closely connected with the cult of the "Great Mother"'] (p. 56).

des sonnenhaften Sterbens und Wiedererstehens des Lebens' ['In it the primitive thoughts of the myth, the suggestions clad in symbols, of the sun-like death and resurrection of life, again burst forth'] (WSL: p. 380/PU § 650). Indeed, he elides its opening lines with a reference to *Faust*: 'Diese Worte zeigen an, daß die Libido nun auf den tiefsten Grund gelangt ist, wo "die Gefahr groß" ist. Dort ist "der Gott nahe"' ['These words mean that the libido has now sunk to the lowest depths, where "the danger is great". There "the God is near"'] (WSL: p. 381/PU § 652; cf. *Faust* II: l.6291). The location of Mount Etna in the poem 'Empedokles' (1797), the figure of Thetis in 'Achill' (1798) and the landscapes in 'Patmos' (1802) are all read by Jung as symbols of that unconscious libidinal source which he elsewhere subsumes under the symbol of the Mother. However, the choice of texts by Hölderlin also serves another function, namely to introduce further Dionysian overtones into Jung's text. Jung himself points out the 'dionysische Anspielung' ['Dionysian allusion'] in the poem 'Der Mensch' (1798) (WSL: p. 374/PU § 642), but the identification of Christ with Dionysos is said to structure both Hölderlin's classical odes and his hymns, such as 'Patmos', thus echoing Jung's own project to turn Christ back into Dionysos.[32]

Third, Jung claims, for reasons similar to those for quoting Hölderlin, that it is in Nietzsche that one can best find both the intuition and the poetic expression of those same mythologems which Jungian psychology seeks to reinvest with meaning:

> Was bei Nietzsche wie dichterische Redefigur anmutet, ist eigentlich uralter Mythus. Es ist, wie wenn dem Dichter noch die Ahnung oder die Fähigkeit gegeben wäre, unter den Worten unserer heutigen Sprache und in den Bildern, die sich seiner Phantasie aufdrängten, jene unvergänglichen Schatten längst vergangener Geisteswelten zu fühlen und wieder wirklich zu machen (WSL: p. 293/PU § 471).
>
> [That which in Nietzsche appears as a poetical figure of speech is really a primitive myth. It is as if the poet still possessed a dim idea or capacity to feel and reactivate those imperishable phantoms of long-past worlds of thought in the words of our present-day and in the images which crowd themselves into his phantasy.]

Jung uses Nietzsche's works in five different ways, concentrating in particular on his (often neglected) lyric output. First, he takes an important image of introversion from Nietzsche's poetry: 'Die Libido sinkt in ihre "eigene Tiefe" (ein bekanntes Gleichnis Nietzsches)' ['The libido sinks into its "own depths" (a well-known comparison of Nietzsche's'] (WSL: p. 284/PU § 458). Second, Jung interprets the symbolism in the vision of the Shepherd and the Snake

---

32 For more information on the use of Dionysian motifs in Hölderlin's lyric and the connection with Nietzsche, see: Gunter Martens, 'Hölderlin-Rezeption in der Nachfolge Nietzsches – Stationen der Aneignung eines Dichters', *Hölderlin-Jahrbuch*, 23 (1982/83), 54–78; and Helmut Pfotenhauer, 'Dionysos: Heinse – Hölderlin – Nietzsche', *Hölderlin-Jahrbuch*, 26 (1988/89), 38–59.

(Z III 2 §; N2: p. 410) in terms of the dialectic of life and death involved in the process of introversion: 'Die Schlange repräsentiert die sich introvertierende Libido. Durch die Introversion wird man vom Gotte befruchtet, begeistert, wieder erzeugt und wieder geboren' ['The snake represents the introverting libido. Through introversion one is fertilized, inspired, regenerated and reborn from the god'] (WSL: pp. 354–55/PU § 596). Over and above that, he relates this imagery back to an incident from Nietzsche's biography.[33] Third, Jung finds what he calls 'den rettenden Gedanken' ['the saving thought'], the psychological redemption of introversion, expressed in two other passages from *Zarathustra*. Conflating two excerpts from 'Vom freien Tode' ['Of Voluntary Death'] and 'Von der schenkenden Tugend' ['Of the Bestowing Virtue'] (Z I 21, 22; N2: pp. 334, 340), Jung reads Nietzsche's image of the 'Großer Mittag' in terms of the astral myth, interpreting it as the psychological moment of introversion (WSL: p. 362/PU § 614). Fourth, Jung equates this archetypal cycle with the Eternal Return, again psychologizing Nietzsche's thought (WSL: p. 382/PU § 655; cf. Z III 16 § 4; N2: p. 475). And fifth, Jung quotes extensive passages from Nietzsche's late cycle of poems, the *Dionysos-Dithyramben* (written 1882–1888) and interprets them as symbols of the libido and introversion. For example, he interprets the flame and the snake of 'Das Feuerzeichen' ['The Fire-Signal'] (DD 5; N2: p. 1253) in the light of the iconography of antiquity as symbols of the libido.[34] He reads the images of 'Zwischen Raubvögeln' ['Amid Birds of Prey'] (DD 4; N2: p. 1250) as symbols of intrapsychic conflict and of introversion.[35] He interprets 'Klage der Ariadne' ['Ariadne's Complaint'] (DD 7; N2: p. 1256) as an expression of the psychological pain experienced in the process of introversion,[36] and glosses 'Ruhm und Ewigkeit' ['Fame and Eternity'] as another image of introversion, with the poisonous basilisk representing death,

[33] The incident is reported in Carl Albrecht Bernoulli, *Franz Overbeck und Friedrich Nietzsche*, 2 vols (Jena, 1908), I, p. 72. See WSL: p. 48, n.1/PU § 58, n.1. For further commentary on this dream, see Chapter 9, p. 255.

[34] See WSL: pp. 99–100, 102 /PU § 162–64, 171. For another (quasi-Jungian) reading of 'Das Feuerzeichen', see Adrian Del Caro, 'The Immolation of Zarathustra: A Look at "The Fire Beacon"', *Colloquia Germanica*, 17 (1984), 252–56.

[35] 'Es ist ein phallischer Akt der Vereinigung mit sich selbst, eine Art Selbstbefruchtung (Introversion), auch eine Selbstvergewaltigung, ein Selbstmord, daher sich Zarathustra als Selbsthenker bezeichnen kann, wie Odin, der sich selber dem Odin opfert' ['It is a phallic act of union with one's self, a sort of self-fertilization (introversion); also a self-violation, a self-murder; therefore, Zarathustra may call himself his own hangman, like Odin, who sacrifices himself to Odin'] (WSL: pp. 284/PU § 457; cf. WSL: p. 292/PU § 470).

[36] 'Es bedarf keiner langatmigen Erklärung, um in diesem Gleichnis das alte, universelle Bild des gemarterten Gottesopfers zu erkennen, dem wir bereits begegneten bei den mexikanischen Kreuzopfern und dem Odinsopfer' ['No long-drawn-out explanation is necessary to enable us to recognize in this comparison the old, universal idea of the martyred sacrifice of god, which we have met previously in the Mexican sacrifice of the cross and in the sacrifice of Odin'] (WSL: p. 282–83/PU § 455).

and the egg, life.[37] He finds in the poems 'Von der Armut des Reichsten' ['Of the Poverty of the Richest Man'] (DD 9; N2: p. 1265–66), 'Die Sonne sinkt' ['The Sun Sinks'] (DD 6; N2: p. 1254) and sections 111 and 113 of the 'Bruchstücke zu den Dionysos-Dithyramben (Lieder Zarathustras)' ['Fragments from the Dionysos-Dithyrambs'][38] another storehouse of archetypal imagery which elaborates the previous texts: 'Wiederum bei Nietzsche belebt sich das alte, anscheinend längst erstorbene Bild' ['In Nietzsche the old, apparently long extinct idea is again revived'] (WSL: p. 357/PU § 601). And 'Die Wüste wächst: weh dem, der Wüsten birgt...' ['The Desert Grows: Woe to Him Who Harbours Deserts...'] (DD 2; N2: p. 1244–47) provides Jung with yet another symbolic representation of the introversion of the libido, announcing the mysterious but wonderful transformation of death into life:

> Auch Nietzsche spricht dieses Geheimnis aus [...] Alle diese Symbole stellen das Zurückholen der Libido aus der inzestuösen Bindung dar, woraus neues Leben gewonnen wird. Die Zurückholung geschieht unter Symbolen, welche die Betätigung des Inzestwunsches darstellen (WSL: pp. 359–60/PU § 607–08).
>
> [Nietzsche, too, gives expression to this mystery ... All these symbols represent the liberation of the libido from the incestuous fixation through which new life is attained. The liberation is accomplished under symbols, which represent the activity of the incest wish.]

The imagery of Nietzche's poetry is thus invested by Jung with psychological importance and treated as a series of variations on a single symbolic theme: the introversion of the libido as represented by the descent of the hero (Dionysos) to the libidinal depths (the Mother).

(iii) A Theory of Culture and Religion

So far we have followed Jung's argument as it applies to the ontogenetic, i.e. individual, level. However, Jung's revised theory of the libido also enabled him to offer a theory of cultural development and to link this with the turn-of-the-century crisis in morality and religion. The starting-point of Jung's account is

[37] 'Der Held, der die Erneuerung der Welt, die Besiegung des Todes zu leisten hat, ist die Libido, die, sich selber in der Introversion bebrütend, als Schlange das eigene Ei umschlingend, anscheinend mit giftigem Biß das Leben bedroht, um es in den Tod zu führen, und aus jener Nacht, sich selber überwindend, wieder gebiert. Nietzsche kennt dieses Bild' ['The hero, who is to accomplish the rejuvenation of the world and the conquest of death, is the libido, which, brooding upon itself in introversion, coiling as a snake around its own egg, apparently threatens life with a poisonous bite, in order to lead it to death, and from that darkness, conquering itself, gives birth to itself again. Nietzsche knows this conception'] (WSL: p. 356/PU § 600).

[38] 'Reden, Geheimnisse und Bilder (1882–1888)', in: *Bruchstücke zu den Dionysos-Dithyramben (Lieder Zarathustras) 1882–1888* ('Kleinoktav-Ausgabe', VIII, p. 393).

the transformative capacity of the libido: 'das Geheimnis der Kulturentwicklung ist die *Beweglichkeit und Verlagerungsfähigkeit der Libido*' ['the secret of the development of culture lies in the *mobility of the libido*, and in its capacity for transference'] (WSL: p. 31/PU § 25). Taking up his argument (as that was stated in the debate over the incest-taboo in his correspondence with Freud) with all its Nietzschean overtones, Jung defined the historical function of the incest-taboo as the impulse to domestication – the reorganization (through introversion) of animal libido to make it available for the purposes of culture.[39]

The underlying mechanism by which libido is introverted is, according to Jung, the symbol-making process.[40] The ability of Man to find symbols by means of analogy allows libido to adapt itself to goals beyond those of biology and permits the development of culture. Thus, for Jung, the development of culture is virtually synonymous with the creation of metaphor: 'dem Wörtchen "gleichwie" [muß] eine ganz unerhörte Wichtigkeit für die Entwicklungsgeschichte des Denkens zugestanden werden' ['an absolutely overweening importance must be granted to the little phrase "even as" in the history of the development of thought'] (WSL: p. 146/PU § 236).[41] Arguing that all symbols are 'Libidogleichnisse' ['libidinal allegories'], Jung rejects the Freudian interpretation of symbols as anatomical emblems. Instead, he suggests that the difference of individual objects belies the fundamental libidinal unity which they represent: 'Die feste Bedeutung der Dinge hat in diesem Reich ein Ende. Einzige Realität ist dort die Libido; ihr ist: "Alles Vergängliche nur ein Gleichnis"' ['In this realm there is no fixed significance of things. The only reality here is the libido, for which "all that is perishable is merely a symbol"'] (WSL: p. 221/PU § 339; cf. *Faust II*, ll.12104–05).

---

[39] 'Vielmehr muß man wahrscheinlich das in letzter Linie und ursprünglich als "Inzestverbot" sich ausdrückende Gesetz als den *Zwang zur Domestikation* auffassen und das Religionssystem als Institution bezeichnen, welche die den Kulturzwecken nicht unmittelbar dienenden Triebkräfte animalischer Natur zunächst aufnimmt, organisiert und allmählich zu sublimierter Anwendung fähig macht' ['Rather one must understand the law which is ultimately expressed as "incest prohibition" as coercion to domestication, and consider the religious systems as institutions which first receive, then organize and gradually sublimate, the motor forces of the animal nature not immediately available for cultural purposes'] (WSL: p. 265/PU § 419).

[40] This argument is extended in GW8 § 88–113.

[41] According to the notes in Nietzsche's *Nachlaß*, the world produced by language is one of infinite transposition of images, i.e. metaphor: 'es *gibt* nichts, es *ist* nichts, alles wird, d.h. ist Vorstellung [...] alles Vorhandene ist in *doppelter* Weise *Vorstellung*: einmal als *Bild*, dann als *Bild des Bildes* ['there *is* nothing, it *is* nothing, everything becomes, i.e. is representation ... all presence is in a two-fold way *representation*: first as *image*, then as the *image* of the *image*'] Friedrich Nietzsche, *Nachgelassene Fragmente: Herbst 1869 bis Herbst 1872*, in: *Werke: Kritische Gesamtausgabe*, edited by Giorgio Colli and Mazzino Montinari (Berlin and New York, 1978), III 3, pp. 224 (7[203]) and 216 (7[175]).

According to Jung's account of human progess, the libido is made available for higher cultural goals by the formation of religious symbols.[42] The truth of the symbol is, on Jung's account, a preeminently psychological one:

> Der religiöse Mythus tritt uns aber hier als eine der größten und bedeutsamsten menschlichen Institutionen entgegen [...] Das Symbol, vom Standpunkt des real Wahren aus betrachtet, ist zwar täuschend, aber es ist *psychologisch* wahr, denn es war und ist die Brücke zu allen größten Errungenschaften der Menschheit (WSL: p. 230–31/PU § 353).
>
> The religious myth meets us here as one of the greatest and most significant human institutions ... The symbol, considered from the standpoint of actual truth, is misleading, indeed, but it is *psychologically true*, because it was and is the bridge to all the greatest achievements of humanity.]

Jung then goes on to define the function of the symbol as to provide complete moral autonomy, construed as the mediation of the freedom of the individual and the predetermination of psychological necessity, i.e. '*wenn der Mensch ohne Zwang das wollen könnte, was er doch tun muß*' ['*where Man could without compulsion wish that which he must do*'], but without recourse to religious symbolism and, presumably, theology (WSL: p. 231/PU § 354). An important predecessor and a probable source of Jung's account of the essential characteristics of the symbol is Friedrich Creuzer's *Symbolik und Mythologie der alten Völker* (1810–23), where the symbol is defined as an expression of 'das *Momentane*, das *Totale*, das *Unergründliche ihres Ursprungs*, das *Nothwendige*' ['presence, totality, the unfathomable in origin, necessity'].[43]

Jung argues that, historically, Mithraism – and Christianity – provided the means not just to repress the libido but also to rechannel it into the projects and purposes of civilization, and he defines the function of Christianity and Mithraism as the 'moralische Bändigung animalischer Triebe' ['moral restraint of animal impulses'] (WSL: p. 79/PU § 124).[44] Thus, Jung describes the historical

---

[42] 'Den Weg, wie der Mensch seine inzestuös gebundene Libido doch zur Betätigung bringen kann, scheinen die religiös-mythologischen Symbole gewiesen zu haben' ['The path by which Man may manifest his incestuously fixed libido seems to have been pointed out by the religious mythological symbols'] (WSL: p. 225/PU § 345).

[43] Friedrich Creuzer, *Symbolik und Mythologie der alten Völker, besonders der Griechen*, 4 vols (Leipzig and Darmstadt 1810–1823, repub. Darmstadt, 1973), IV, p. 535.

[44] 'Die christliche Erziehung hat durch die säkulare Übung der naiven Projektion, die, wie wir gesehen haben, nichts anderes als eine verhüllte oder mittelbare Realübertragung (durchs Geistige, durch den logos) ist, eine weitgehende Schwächung des Animalischen zustande gebracht, so daß ein großer Betrag an Triebkräften für die Arbeit sozialer Erhaltung und Fruchtbarkeit frei werden konnte' ['By means of the secular practice of the naïve projection which is, as we have seen, nothing else than a veiled or indirect real-transference (through the spiritual, through the logos), Christian training has produced a widespread weakening of the animal nature so that a great part of the strength of the impulses could be set free for the work of social preservation and fruitfulness'] (WSL: pp. 81–82/PU § 127).

function of Christianity in both negative and positive terms just as Nietzsche, in *Zur Genealogie der Moral*, criticises the ascetic priest for his nay-saying denial of the Will, but points out that the Will itself is nevertheless thereby saved: 'lieber will noch der Mensch *das Nichts* wollen, als *nicht* wollen' ['Man would rather will *nothingness* than *not* will'] (GM III § 28; N2: p. 900)). First, and negatively, Jung claims that '*Das Christentum mit seiner Verdrängung des manifest Sexuellen ist das Negativ des antiken Sexualkultus*' ['*Christianity, with its repression of the manifest sexual, is the negative of the ancient sexual cult*'] (WSL: p. 227/PU § 347). Second, and positively, Christianity also represents the founding moment of science and technology: 'So trat der Mensch in ein neues und unabhängiges Verhältnis zur Natur, womit der Grund zu Naturwissenschaft und Technik gelegt wurde' ['Thus Man entered into a new and independent relation to Nature whereby the foundation was laid for natural science and technology' (P. B.)] (WSL: p. 83/PU § 130).

Sketching out an argument which he would pursue in greater detail in his writings of the 1940s, Jung presents this moment of technological advance in terms of a 'dialectic of enlightenment' which rebounds upon the psyche of Man: 'Die Welt ist nicht nur entgöttert [...] sondern auch etwas entseelt' ['The world has not only lost its God ... but also to some extent has lost its soul as well'] (WSL: p. 83/PU § 130). At the same time, Jung is conscious that Christianity is in decline and that he lives 'in einer Zeit, wo ein großer Teil der Menschheit anfängt, das Christentum wegzulegen' ['at a time, when a large part of Mankind is beginning to discard Christianity'] (WSL: p. 228/PU § 349). Conscious of the benefits which religion in general and Christianity in particular have allegedly brought to civilization, the consequences are, for Jung, disturbing. Alarmed by what he calls 'die antike Raserei' ['the ancient frenzy of ecstasy' (P. B.)] and 'das antike Problem der Ausgelassenheit' ['the ancient problem of licentiousness'], Jung warns against 'ein Rausch der Entsittlichung' ['a frenzy of depravation' (P. B.)] (WSL: pp. 228–29/PU § 349). In other words, Jung is frightened of precisely those forces which Nietzsche placed under the sign of Dionysos – that same libidinal energy which he, Jung, would also attribute to Dionysos in 'Neue Bahnen der Psychologie' ['New Paths in Psychology'] (1912). In an age where faith in the efficacy of Christian myth and symbols is in decline, Jung defines the dilemma facing religion in the following programmatic terms: 'Die Klippe ist die *unglückselige Verquickung* von *Religion* und *Moral*. Das ist zu überwinden' ['The stumbling block is the *unhappy combination of religion and morality*. That must be overcome'] (WSL: p. 84/PU § 130).

Jung's solution to the problem of the relation between religion and morality needs to be examined in terms of Kant's solution of almost a century before – which Jung inverts. In the Introduction to the Second Edition of the *Kritik der reinen Vernunft* [*Critique of Pure Reason*] (1787), Kant claimed that he had had to abolish knowledge in order to make room for belief: 'Ich mußte also das *Wissen* aufheben, um zum *Glauben* Platz zu bekommen'.[45] In Kantian terms, this means that limitation of reason imposed in that work is followed by the declaration of the categorical imperative in the *Critique of Practical Reason*, which replaces both the dictates of theology (in Kant's system, we can understand God only as an idea, or regulative principle) and the dogmatism of metaphysics as the source of morality. But Jung reverses Kant's formula, proposing instead to abolish belief and replace it with knowledge – knowledge of the symbol. This constitutes, in Jung's terms, the redemption in psychological terms of both faith and non-belief:

> Ich denke, *der Glaube sollte durch das Verstehen ersetzt werden*, so behalten wir die Schönheit des Symbols und sind doch frei von den niederdrückenden Folgen der Unterwerfung im Glauben. Dieses wäre wohl die psychoanalytische Heilung des Glaubens und des Unglaubens (WSL: p. 232/PU § 356).
>
> [I think *belief should be replaced by understanding*; then we would keep the beauty of the symbol, but still remain free from the depressing results of submission to belief. This would be the psychoanalytic cure for belief and disbelief.]

As early as 1912, then, Jung had set his post-Nietzschean agenda for the transformation of faith into a secular, psychological religion.

There are two further uses of Nietzsche in *Wandlungen und Symbole der Libido* which indicate his importance for Jung in ways which were to become explicit later on. First, although Jung had not yet fully defined the concept of the archetype by 1912, he associated its precursor – the idea of 'archaic images' – with two passages ('Traum und Kultur' ['Dream and Culture'] and 'Logik des Traumes' ['Logic of the Dream']) from Nietzsche's *Menschliches, Allzumenschliches* [*Human, All Too Human*]: 'im Schlaf und Traum machen wir das Pensum früheren Menschtums durch [...] Wie jetzt noch der Mensch im Traume schließt, schloß die Menschheit auch im Wachen viele Jahrtausende hindurch' ['In our sleep and in our dreams we pass through the whole thought of earlier humanity ... in the same way that Man reasons in his dreams, he reasoned when in the waking state many thousands of years'] (WSL: pp. 37–38/PU § 37; cf. MA/HA I § 12, 13; N1: pp. 454–55).[46] Much of Jung's understanding of the importance of dreams can also be read as a gloss on this passage. Immediately after quoting this extract from *Menschliches, Allzumenschliches*, Jung develops Freud's notion of the archaic nature of dreams as that is set out in 'Der Dichter

45 Immanuel Kant, *Die Kritik der reinen Vernunft*, edited by Raymund Schmidt (Hamburg, 1990), p. 28 ('Vorrede zur zweiten Auflage', B xxx).

46 In a passage on regression in dreams added to *Die Traumdeutung* in 1919 (*Gesammelte Werke*, II/III, p. 554) Freud referred to exactly the same passage from Nietzsche. Freud's notion of the 'archaische Erbschaft des Menschen' ['archaic inheritance of humanity'] moves him close to the Jungian notion of the Collective Unconscious, and Freud's later work in general is more in line with Jung's historical-cultural project, although neither man ever acknowledged this.

und das Phantasieren' ['Creative Writers and Day-Dreaming'] (1909) into the claim that myths are 'traumähnliche Gebilden' ['dreamlike images']. Later on, he describes the Mother as 'das "große, urtümliche Bild"' ['the "great, primitive image"'] (WSL: p. 248/PU § 381), apparently borrowing the expression from Jacob Burckhardt (WSL: p. 47, n.48/PU § 56, n.42), alhough he could also have found the term in *Die Geburt der Tragödie*, where Nietzsche talks about 'das Verhältnis des griechischen Künstlers zu seinen Urbildern' ['the relation of the Greek artist to his archetypes'] (GT/BT § 2; N1: p. 26), or elsewhere in that work (see below). It was out of these ideas that Jung's notions of the Collective Unconscious and the archetypes would eventually develop.

Second, Jung returns to *Menschliches, Allzumenschliches* in his discussion of the archetypal image of the Mother. Revealing an archetypal fullness and exhibiting a positive-negative polarity, the image of the Mother is, according to Jung, one manifestation of the immense (and hence dangerous) energic powers of the Unconscious. In his 'Vorrede' to the first volume of *Menschliches, Allzumenschliches*, Nietzsche discusses his feelings of isolation using metaphors of strangulation and the image of the '*mater saeva cupidinum*' (the savage mother of desires): 'Die Einsamkeit umringt und umringelt ihn, immer drohender, würgender, herz-zuschnürender, jene furchtbare Göttin und *mater saeva cupidinum* [...]' ['Solitude encircles and embraces him, ever more threatening, suffocating, heart-tightening, that terrible goddess and *mater saeva cupidinum*'] (MA/HA Vorrede/Preface § 3; N1: p. 440). Jung interprets this as an image of uncoordinated libidinal energy, represented imagistically in the transformation of the Mother into a threatening serpent.[47] He also describes this image as an unparalleled image of the liberation ('Loslösung') from the libidinal desires of childhood,[48] even though the original context in which Nietzsche had used the image was his 'große Loslösung' from Romanticism, *Sturm und Drang* and Wagner. Here Nietzsche also speaks of: 'Ein plötzlicher Schrecken und Argwohn gegen das, was [die junge Seele] liebte, [...] ein Haß auf die Liebe, vielleicht ein tempelschänderischer Griff und Blick *rückwärts*, dorthin, wo sie bis dahin anbetete und liebte' ['A sudden terror and suspicion of what the youthful soul loved ... a hatred of love, perhaps a dese-

---

[47] 'Die von der Mutter zurückgenommene Libido, welche nur widerstrebend zurückkommt, wird bedrohend wie eine Schlange, das Symbol des Todes, denn die Beziehung zur Mutter hat aufzuhören, zu *sterben*, woran man *selber fast stirbt*' ['The libido taken away from the mother, who is abandoned only reluctantly, becomes threatening as a serpent, the symbol of death, for the relation to the mother must cease, *must die*, which itself *almost causes Man's death*'] (WSL: p. 299/ PU § 480).

[48] 'In "Mater saeva cupidinum" erreicht das Bild eine seltene, fast bewußte Vollendung. Es kommt mir nicht zu, versuchen zu wollen, mit besseren Worten die Psychologie der Loslösung von der Kindheit zu schildern, als dies Nietzsche getan hat' ['In "Mater saeva cupidinum" the idea attains rare, almost conscious, perfection. I do not presume to try to paint in better words than has Nietzsche the psychology of the wrench from childhood'] (WSL: p. 299/PU § 480–81).

crating blow and glance *backwards* to where it formerly loved and worshipped'] (MA/HA Vorrede/Preface § 3; N1: pp. 439–40). Although this highly metaphoric passage refers in the first place to Nietzsche's break with Wagner, it could equally well be applied to the turmoil caused by Jung's break with Freud. Jung's abandonment of Freud's purely sexual interpretation of the incest-taboo in favour of the view that incest wishes symbolized deeper tendencies can well be seen as 'ein tempelschänderischer Griff rückwärts', and indeed, Jung glosses this phrase as signifying incest, not in the literal sense, however, but in the sense of a libidinal investment in the Mother:

> Der "tempelschänderische Griff rückwärts", von dem Nietzsche spricht, entpuppt sich, seiner Inzesthülle verkleidet, als ein ursprünglich passives Steckenbleiben der Libido in den ersten Kindheitsobjekten [...] Diese gefährliche, dem primitiven Menschen vor allen andern zukommende Leidenschaft ist es, die unter der bedenklichen Maske der Inzestsymbole erscheint, von der uns die Inzestangst wegzutreiben hat, und die unter dem Bilde der "furchtbaren Mutter" vor allem zu überwinden ist (WSL: p. 178/PU § 284–85).

> [The "sacrilegious backward grasp" of which Nietzsche speaks reveals itself, stripped of its incest covering, as an original passive arrest of the libido in its first object of childhood ... This dangerous passion, belonging above all others to primitive Man, appears under the hazardous mask of the incest symbol, from which the incest fear must drive us away, and which must be conquered, in the first place, under the image of the "Terrible Mother".]

Thus, Jung pursues his anti-Freudian argument with what we can now see as a highly tendentious use of Nietzschean references which operates on two levels: overtly, there is the theoretical question of the non-sexual interpretation of libido, and covertly, there is the debate between Jung and Freud which was conducted over precisely this issue and led to their break. By referring simultaneously to an incestuous act symbolizing a confrontation with the archetypal powers of the Unconscious, and to Nietzsche's/Jung's break with Wagner/Freud, the highly complex metaphor 'ein tempelschänderischer Griff rückwärts' conflates these two levels.

The main Nietzsche texts which Jung used in *Wandlungen und Symbole der Libido* were *Menschliches, Allzumenschliches, Also sprach Zarathustra* and the *Dionysos-Dithyramben*. Despite his obvious interest in Dionysos and the references to Schopenhauer's metaphysics of the Will, Jung made no explicit reference to *Die Geburt der Tragödie*. This is odd since, in his letter to Freud of 25/31 December 1909, Jung had connected Nietzsche with the problem of the Dionysian (FJB: p. 308/FJL: p. 280) and Nietzsche's work on tragedy most obviously expounds his Dionysian metaphysics.

Moreover, there are at least ten passages in *Wandlungen und Symbole der Libido* which echo, on the verbal or the conceptual level or both, passages from *Die*

Geburt der Tragödie.[49] All these passages are marked in the margin of Jung's copy, although it is difficult to tell when precisely they were made. First, Nietzsche describes the effect of the Dionysian as a reunion of all objects from the individuated world in the collectivity of Nature, the Primal Mother(s) ('Urmutter'/ 'Mütter des Seins'). Jung uses a similar idea to present his conception of the libido in a phrase which expresses his characteristic yearning for totality:

> [Die Libido] ist unser Unsterbliches, indem sie jenes Band darstellt, durch welches wir uns als nie erlöschend, in der Rasse fühlen. Sie ist Leben vom Leben der Menschheit. Ihre aus den Tiefen des Unbewußten emporströmenden Quellen kommen, wie unser Leben überhaupt, aus dem Stamme der ganzen Menschheit, indem wir ja nur ein von der Mutter abgebrochener und verpflanzter Zweig sind (WSL: pp. 202–03/ PU § 315).

> [The libido is that part of us which is immortal, since it represents that bond through which we feel that in the race we are never extinguished. It is life from the life of Mankind. Its springs, which well up from the depths of the Unconscious, come, as does our life in general, from the root of the whole of humanity, since we are indeed only a twig broken off from the Mother and transplanted.]

Second, Nietzsche calls the satyr in tragic drama 'das Urbild des Menschen' ['the archetype of Man'] (GT/BT § 8; N1: p. 49). Similarly, Jung uses Jacob Burckhardt's concept of 'ein großes, urtümliches Bild', and refers to the Mother as 'das Urobjekt' ['the primordial object'] (WSL: p. 392/PU § 672). Third, Nietzsche discusses Oedipus with relation to the problem of incest and the story of the Sphinx (GT/BT § 9; N1: pp. 56–57). Jung also discusses the story of Oedipus and the Sphinx, but without relating it to Freud's reading (WSL: pp. 182–84/ PU § 292).[50]

Fourth, Nietzsche identifies Prometheus, Oedipus and other dramatic figures in Greek tragedy with Dionysos, who is said to be the typical/archetypal hero of tragic drama and to possess the 'typische "Idealität" jener berühmten Figuren' ['the typical "ideality" of these famous figures'] (GT/BT § 10; N1: p. 61). Jung likewise concentrates on the rôle in myth of the hero (see Chapter 6 of Part II, entitled 'Die unbewußte Entstehung des Heros' ['The Unconscious Origin of the Hero']), and in an art-historical footnote he cites the head of Dionysos at Leiden as an example of the hero as an image of the libido (WSL: p. 187, n.15/PU § 296, n.14). Fifth, Nietzsche draws attention to the underlying

---

[49] Beyond the textual similarities, it is interesting to note that Nietzsche too knew about the Mithras cult. For an account of Nietzsche's reflections on the Mithras grotto on the island of Capri, see Joachim Köhler, *Zarathustras Geheimnis: Friedrich Nietzsche und seine verschlüsselte Botschaft* (Reinbek bei Hamburg, 1992), pp. 192–96), as well as Friedrich Nietzsche, *Sämtliche Werke: Kritische Studienausgabe*, edited by Giorgio Colli and Mazzino Montinari (Munich and Berlin, 1980), VIII, pp. 506–09.

[50] In the revised version of 1952, this section is expanded, and Jung relates the figure of the sphinx to the Mother archetype (GW5 § 264).

meaning of the Dionysos-Zagreus: individuation as the source of all suffering, and envisions the cult of Dionysos and later tragedy as a means of coping with that suffering.[51] Jung associates the creation of the individual with the advent of sin and the fear of death, and hence a suffering which only the symbolism of religion could express: 'Ganze Religionen wurden gebaut, um der Größe dieses Konfliktes Worte zu leihen' ['Entire religions were constructed in order to give words to the immensity of this conflict'] (WSL: p. 265/PU § 419).

Sixth, in an important passage, Nietzsche describes the decay of religions in terms of the disappearance of their mythical content: 'Denn dies ist die Art, wie Religionen abzusterben pflegen: [...] wenn also das Gefühl für den Mythus abstirbt und an seine Stelle der Anspruch der Religion auf historische Grundlagen tritt' ['For this is the way in which religions are wont to die out: ... the feeling for myth perishes, and its place is taken by the claim of religion to historical foundations'] (GT/BT § 10; N1: p. 63). Jung, too, had identified the historicization of Christianity as the beginning of its demise in his Zofingia lecture on Albrecht Ritschl in 1899, and in *Wandlungen und Symbole der Libido* he addresses the problem of the decline of religion by transforming religious belief into psychological knowledge (WSL: p. 232/PU § 356) and instituting the creation of a secular, personal myth. In 1950, looking back on the first edition, he wrote: 'Ich fand mich gedrängt, mich allen Ernstes zu fragen: "Was ist der Mythus, den du lebst?"' ['I was driven to ask myself in all seriousness: "What is the myth you are living?"'] (WSL: p. 9/CW5: p.xxiv). Jung's intense concern with myth places him in the tradition of Romantic seekers for what Hegel called 'das gesicherte Asyl' ['the secure sanctuary'].[52] Seventh, Nietzsche defines instinct as 'die schöpferisch-affirmative Kraft' ['the creative-affirmative force'] (GT/BT § 13; N1: p. 77). Similarly, Jung's concept of libido integrates the creativity of instinctuality with the creative and destructive capacities of an energically-conceived Will to Power.

Eighth, Nietzsche himself uses Goethe's *Faust* as an intertext in describing the effect of the Dionysian: 'während unter dem mystischen Jubelruf des Dionysos der Bann der Individuation zersprengt wird und der Weg zu den Müttern des Seins, zu dem innersten Kern der Dinge offenliegt' ['by the mystical triumphant cry of Dionysos the spell of individuation is broken, and the way lies open to the Mothers of Being, to the innermost heart of things'] (GT/BT § 16;

[51] '[...] daß diese Zerstückelung, das eigentlich dionysische *Leiden*, gleich einer Umwandlung in Luft, Wasser, Erde und Feuer sei, daß wir also den Zustand der Individuation als den Quell und Urgrund alles Leidens, als etwas an sich Verwerfliches, zu betrachten hätten' ['this dismemberment, the properly Dionysian *suffering*, is like a transformation into air, water, earth, and fire ... we are therefore to regard the state of individuation as the origin and primal cause of all suffering, as something objectionable in itself'] (GT/BT § 10; N1: p. 61).

[52] G. W. F. Hegel, *Ästhetik*, edited by F. Bassenge (Berlin, 1955), p. 1084.

N1: p. 88).[53] Analogously, as we have seen, Jung's references to *Faust II* are frequent and extensive, and he quotes at length from the Mothers' Scene which, he says, reveals 'die tiefsten Wurzeln faustischer Sehnsucht' ['the deepest roots of Faustian longings'] (WSL: p. 206/PU § 317). Ninth, Nietzsche refers to the notion of the 'Urwesen' ['primorial being'] (GT/BT § 17; N1: p. 93), and, in a similar vein, Jung identifies 'das Ur- und Allwesen' with the libido (WSL: p. 161, n.28/PU § 251, n.29).

Tenth, Nietzsche describes the effect of the Dionysian as the moment 'wo wir gleichsam mit der unermeßlichen Urlust am Dasein eins geworden sind' ['when we have become, as it were, one with the infinite primordial joy in existence'] (GT/BT § 17; N1: p. 93). Similarly, Jung describes the desire of the mythic hero as the myth of our own Unconscious, 'jene ungestillte und selten stillbare Sehnsucht nach allen tiefsten Quellen seines eignen Seins, nach dem Leibe der Mutter und in ihm nach der Gemeinschaft mit dem unendlichen Leben in den unzähligen Formen des Daseins' ['an unquenchable longing for all the deepest sources of our own being, for the body of the mother, and through it for communion with infinite life in the countless forms of existence'] (WSL: p. 206/PU § 317).

In addition, one passage from Nietzsche's *Die Geburt der Tragödie*, which is not marked by Jung, nonetheless reads like a summary of Jung's text by transposing Myth itself into the rôle of the tragic hero:

> Durch die Tragödie kommt der Mythus zu seinem tiefsten Inhalt, seiner ausdrucksvollsten Form; noch einmal erhebt er sich, wie ein verwundeter Held, und der ganze Überschuß von Kraft, samt der weisheitsvollen Ruhe des Sterbenden, brennt in seinem Auge mit letztem, mächtigem Leuchten (GT/BT § 10; N1: p. 63).
>
> [Through tragedy the myth attains its most profound content, its most expressive form; it rises once more like a wounded hero, and its whole excess of strength, together with the philosophic calm of the dying, burns in its eyes with a last powerful gleam.]

In *Wandlungen und Symbole der Libido*, the dramatic mediation of myth in the form of tragedy is replaced by a psychologization of the symbolic content of myth. However, Jung's system preserves the dialectic of life and death suggested by Nietzsche in *Die Geburt der Tragödie*: 'zum Kampfe des Lebens ist alle Libido

[53] Rose Pfeffer sees the ontological similarities between *Die Geburt der Tragödie* and Goethe's *Faust* as evidence of a 'yearning for the eternal and universal' on the part of Nietzsche as follows: '[Nietzsche] abolishes the Kantian distinction between the noumenal and the phenomenal, and denies the existence of the "thing in itself" as a metaphysical foundation, and yet he continues to refer to the "Ur-Eine", the mystical ground and the "womb of being". And Goethe, too, longs with Faust to enter the "realm of mothers" and "see what binds the world together in its innermost essence"' (Rose Pfeffer, *Nietzsche: Disciple of Dionysus* (Lewisburg, 1972), pp. 81 and 233).

benötigt, und es darf keine zurückbleiben [...] Dieser Schritt zum neuen Leben bedeutet aber zugleich den Tod des vergangenen Lebens' ['the entire libido is demanded for the battle of life, and there can be no remaining behind ... This step towards a new life means, at the same time, the death of the past life'] (WSL: p. 294/PU § 473). This is the message of the mythic descent to the underworld: 'Diese Unterweltsfahrt war ein Jungbrunnen für [die Libido] gewesen, und aus ihrem scheinbaren Tode erwacht neue Fruchtbarkeit' ['This journey to the underworld has been a fountain of youth for the libido, and new fertility springs from its apparent death' (P. B.)] (WSL: p. 285/PU § 459). Psychologically speaking, Jung regards creativity as inextricably linked with death: 'Daß der höchste Gipfel des Lebens durch die Symbolik des Todes ausgedrückt wird, ist eine bekannte Tatsache, denn das Schaffen über sich selber hinaus bedeutet den eigenen Tod' ['That the highest summit of life is expressed through the symbolism of death is a well-known fact; for creation beyond one's self means personal death'] (WSL: pp. 276–77/PU § 441).

The number of parallels suggests that Jung did have some knowledge of *Die Geburt der Tragödie* before or during the composition of *Wandlungen und Symbole der Libido.* Nietzsche's work is most noticeable in Jung's text by the surprising absence of any direct reference to it, however, even though he made extensive use of Nietzsche's other writings, particularly the *Dionysos-Dithyramben.* Whereas the direct references to Nietzsche are more illustrative and anecdotal than substantive, *Wandlungen und Symbole der Libido* is saturated with the thinking behind *Die Geburt der Tragödie* and shares many of its intellectual sources (Schelling, Schopenhauer, Creuzer). Even though Jung had been open in his letters to Freud about his interest in Nietzsche, it seems that Jung wished – consciously or unconsciously – to suppress the major Nietzschean influence of his first major work. As a result, the presence of Nietzsche's Dionysos in *Wandlungen und Symbole der Libido* is hidden by the wealth of learned allusions and obscure references, but it is still a presence which cannot be ignored.

'Neue Bahnen der Psychologie' (1912)

In 'Neue Bahnen der Psychologie' ['New Paths in Psychology'] (the first version of *Über die Psychologie des Unbewußten* [*On the Psychology of the Unconscious*] (1942)), published in *Raschers Jahrbuch für Schweizer Art und Kunst* (Zurich, 1912),[54] Jung

[54] John Kerr has suggested that the title and place of publication of this paper may be significant. According to Kerr, Jung's paper took its title from an Austrian *Provinzkunst* novel called *Neue Bahnen*, 'one of a series of novels in the "blood and soil" tradition [...] which glorified the folkways of the peasant and condemned the corrupting influence of the modern city' (Kerr, pp. 386–87). Kerr is probably referring to *Die neue Bahn* by Peter Rosegger (1843–1918), a

examined the significance of the Dionysian in the general development of human culture more explicitly than he had done in *Wandlungen und Symbole der Libido.* His initial premise in this work is even more clearly allied to that behind *Zur Genealogie der Moral*: 'Bekanntlich besteht der Kulturprozeß in einer fortschreitenden Bändigung des Animalischen im Menschen; es ist ein Domestikationsprozeß' ['The growth of culture consists, as we know, in a progressive subjugation of the animal in Man'] (GW7 § 426). On this account, however, a breakdown can occur in the process of adaptation to the demands of the 'Kulturzwang' ['the compulsion towards culture'], with the result that Mankind gives in to the experience of 'Rausch' ['frenzy']. According to Jung, this has happened on two occasions. On the first, antiquity was deluged by a wave of Dionysian orgies and absorbed these impulses (GW7 § 426). Here, like Nietzsche in *Die Geburt der Tragödie*, Jung is drawing attention to the Dionysian roots of ancient Greek culture, and also suggesting that the asceticism of Stoicism, Mithraism and Christianity represented a reaction to this overflow of animal instincts. On the second occasion, the Renaissance, 'eine zweite Welle dionysischen Freiheitsrausches ging [...] durch die abendländische Menschheit' ['a second wave of Dionysian licentiousness swept over the West'] (GW7 § 427). In his later writings, Jung became aware (as early as 1918, so he claimed in retrospect) of a third return of Dionysos, this time incarnated as Wotan. Although Jung left a question-mark in 1912 over the state of contemporary society, remarking 'Es ist schwer, die eigene Zeit zu berurteilen' ['It is difficult to gauge the spirit of one's own time'], it is clear that he believed it to suffer from a problem which is closely connected with sexuality:

> [...] so finden wir im langen Register unserer gegenwärtigen sozialen Fragen nicht zuletzt die "sexuelle Frage", die getragen ist von Menschen, welche an der bestehenden Sexualmoral rütteln und die Last moralischer Schuld, welche vergangene Jahrhunderte auf den Eros gehäuft haben, abwerfen möchten (GW7 § 426).
>
> [we shall find that in the long catalogue of our present social questions by no means the last is the so-called "sexual question". This is discussed by men and women who challenge the existing sexual morality and who seek to throw off the burden of moral guilt which past centuries have heaped upon Eros.]

But according to Jung, the 'sexuelle Frage' is just one example, albeit acute, of an overarching problem: the collapse of morality in general and of the religious

---

prolific writer in the *Heimatliteratur* tradition. But *Die neue Bahn* was not published (posthumously in Berlin) until 1924, whereas Jung's paper, 'Neue Bahnen in der Psychologie', was published in 1912. There is no evidence that Jung ever read any novels by Rosegger. By contrast, Jung's title might have far more liberal echoes. *Neue Bahnen* was the name of the periodical edited by Louise Otto-Peters (1819–1895), the founder (in 1865) of the *Allgemeine Deutsche Frauenverein*, an early feminist organization. It would have suited Jung's sexual conservatism to echo Peters, who argued for women's equality primarily in the socio-economic realm, whereas her femininst opponent, Luise Aston (1814–1871), demanded sexual equality.

notions which had underpinned it. Indeed, Jung diagnoses contemporary society as being fundamentally neurotic (GW7 § 428). The thinking behind this diagnosis is very close to Nietzsche's classic analysis of the dialectic between religion and morality as found in, for example, *Zur Genealogie der Moral* and *Der Antichrist* (written 1888, published 1895): after the 'Death of God', so Nietzsche argued, morality had lost any firm foundation, although he also claimed that religion, and particularly Christianity, were only ever a product and a justification of the morality of 'ressentiment' anyway.

After this discussion in 'Neue Bahnen der Psychologie' (which occurs roughly in the middle of the work), Jung did not develop his thoughts about the Dionysian any further; nor did he make any further reference to Nietzsche. In line with my argument in Chapter 3, this is probably because, in 1912, Jung had still not yet gained sufficient distance from Nietzsche to give the philosopher a clear and distinct place in his theories. As I showed above, even *Wandlungen und Symbole der Libido* uses a number of Nietzschean *topoi*, without mentioning their source – if indeed Jung himself was clear about that source. However, when Jung came to revise the original paper in 1916 for republication as *Die Psychologie der unbewußten Prozesse* [*The Psychology of Unconscious Processes*, translated in revised form as *On the Psychology of the Unconscious*] (1917), he added several new chapters, including one devoted entirely to Nietzsche and entitled 'Der andere Gesichtspunkt: Der Wille zur Macht' ['The Other Point of View: The Will to Power'], to which I shall return later in this chapter.

VII Sermones ad mortuos

In Chapter 3, I listed the salient features of Jung's mental breakdown which took place between 1913 and 1919, a period described by Anthony Storr as one of introversion[55] and by Jung himself as 'Die Auseinandersetzung mit dem Unbewußten' ['Confrontation with the Unconscious'] (ETG: p. 174/MDR: p. 194). The fruits of the intense psychic activity which took place during this period can be seen in several works (not all of them published), the first of which are the imaginative fantasies which Jung wrote down between 1913 and 1916 in the so-called 'Schwarzes Buch' ['Black Book'] and later transferred, embellished with drawings, to the 'Rotes Buch' ['Red Book']. Unfortunately, both manuscripts are unpublished and remain unavailable for inspection, access being forbidden by Jung's family and literary executors.[56] However, according

[55] Anthony Storr, *Jung: Selected Writings* (London, 1983), p. 407.

[56] Some extracts from the 'Red Book' are however reproduced in Gerhard Wehr, *An Illustrated Biography of C. G. Jung*, translated by Michael Kohn (Boston, 1989), pp. 42, 46, 55, 140–41.

to Jung himself, the 'Rotes Buch' contains his attempts at painting mandalas (ETG: pp. 191–92, 199/MDR: pp. 212–13, 220–21), magic circles which, in Jungian psychology, symbolize the central goal or the Self as a psychic totality. Thus, in all probability, Jung's mandalas represented an attempt to work out a new sense of identity in visual terms, and in his autobiography, he defined the mandala and the Self in terms borrowed from Goethe's *Faust II*: 'Nur allmählich kam ich darauf, was das Mandala eigentlich ist: "Gestaltung – Umgestaltung, des ewigen Sinnes ewige Unterhaltung"' ['Only gradually did I discover what the mandala really is: "Formation, Transformation, Eternal Mind's eternal recreation"'] (ETG: p. 199/MDR: p. 221).

Although Jung himself does not say so, this project of fashioning a self is profoundly Nietzschean in spirit. In *Die Geburt der Tragödie*, Nietzsche maintained that life and the world are justified only aesthetically, describing art as 'die eigentlich *metaphysische* Tätigkeit' ['the truly *metaphysical* activity'] (GT/BT Versuch/Attempt § 5; N1: p. 14). Under the effect of the Dionysian, he added: 'der Mensch ist nicht mehr Künstler, er ist Kunstwerk geworden' ['Man is no longer an artist, he has become a work of art'] (BT/GT § 1; N1: p. 25). According to Alexander Nehamas,[57] Nietzsche's whole *oeuvre* constitutes an invitation to transform onself into a work of art and hence create for oneself a new identity. The concept of the Self was later developed in Jung's thinking, and I shall discuss it with reference to its Nietzschean source in Chapter 13.

The second important text is the *VII Sermones ad mortuos*, which was written in 1916 and has a long and complicated history of publication.[58] The similarity of intent and execution between Nietzsche's *Zarathustra* and Jung's mock-epic also reveals the differences between them. Whereas Nietzsche turned to the diction of Luther and disguised his discreet use of classical symbolism under heavily overdetermined imagery in order to discover a new poetic language,[59] Jung went back to one of the sources of Christianity – Gnosticism – and deployed an alarming austerity of style. And whereas Nietzsche's use of rhetoric is both deliberate and ironic, and his jokes are in earnest, Jung's very seriousness borders unintentionally on the parodic. At one point, an explicitly Nietzschean theme is taken up in the Second Sermon when the 'spirits of the dead' ask: 'Von Gott wollen wir wissen. wo ist Gott? ist Gott tot?' ['We want to know about God. where is God? is God dead?'] (ETG: p. 391). According to the Sermons, however, God *is* still alive and is defined in terms of the Gnostic

---

57 Alexander Nehamas, *Nietzsche: Life as Literature* (Cambridge, MA, 1986). See FW/GS § 361; N2: pp. 234–35.

58 See Stephen A. Hoeller, *The Gnostic Jung and the Seven Sermons to the Dead* (Madras and London, 1982), pp. 219–20.

59 For a more detailed account of Nietzsche's attempt in *Zarathustra* to create a 'private language', see Gary Shapiro, *Nietzschean Narratives* (Bloomington and Indianapolis, 1989), pp. 71–96.

concepts of the Pleroma (interpreted by various commentators as the archetype of the Self, or the Collective Unconscious, or Kant's realm of the *noumenon*) and the Creatura (an imaginative prototype of the Jungian Ego, or the libido understood as a principle extended to all creatures needing internal opposition to exist as individuals, or to the phenomenal world):[60]

> Gott ist nicht tot, er ist so lebendig wie je. Gott ist Creatur, denn er ist etwas bestimmtes und darum vom Pleroma unterschieden. Gott ist eigenschaft des Pleroma, und alles, was ich von der Creatur sagte, gilt auch von ihm (ETG: p. 391).
>
> [God is not dead, he is just as alive as ever. God is Creatura, for he is something definite and therefore differentiated from the Pleroma. God is a quality of the Pleroma, and everything that I say about the Creatura is also true of him.]

Thus, Jung explicitly rejected Nietzsche's notion of the 'Death of God' inasmuch as this is a metaphysical statement. However, Jung's translation of metaphysics into psychology leaves a question-mark over his concept of God, and the ontological status of the divinity continues to be problematic throughout Jung's writings up to and including his *Antwort auf Hiob* [*Answer to Job*] (1952) (GW11 § 553–758).

Referring to the psychological condition in which these phantasies – and fantastic texts – were produced, Jung wrote in his autobiography that he conceived of his visions in terms of the result of a descent. The most intense of these experiences is dated by Jung as 12 December 1913: 'dann ließ ich mich fallen' ['Then I let myself drop'] (ETG: p. 182/MDR: p. 203). His confrontation with the archetypes of the Collective Unconscious is presented in *Erinnerungen, Träume, Gedanken* as a journey to the psychological 'underworld', the Jungian equivalent of the experience of the Dionysian. In his later writings on the psychological interpretation of art, Jung would again use the model of a descent to the Unconscious, echoing several passages from *Die Geburt der Tragödie* (see Chapter 6).

As I suggested in Chapter 3, there are clear and important points of correlation between Nietzsche's experience of the Dionysian, Jungian psychology and Jung's own psychological development in the period before, during and after the break with Freud. Jung's interest in Nietzsche seems to have been stimulated not least by the fact that he was unconsciously following a Nietzschean programme of self-discovery or, more accurately, self-creation. This would explain why the references to Nietzsche become more frequent and more complex from now on, culminating in the great psychological reckoning with Nietzsche in the form of the Seminar on *Zarathustra* (1934–1939).

---

60 See Nandor Fodor, 'Jung's Sermons to the Dead', *The Psychoanalytic Review*, 51 (1964), 74–78; James W. Heisig, 'The *VII Sermones*: Play and Theory', *Spring*, 1972, 206–18; Hoeller, 1982; Judith Hubback, 'VII Sermones ad mortuos', *Journal of Analytical Psychology*, 11 (1986), 95–112;

Dionysos and the Self-Regulating Psyche

As we have seen, 1916 formed a 'Schlüsseljahr' in terms of Jung's psychological development, and in December of that year he completed his revision of 'Neue Bahnen der Psychologie' (1912), which was published in 1917 as *Die Psychologie der unbewußten Prozesse.* Also in 1916 Jung wrote the text 'Die transzendente Funktion' ['The Transcendent Function'], the manuscript of which lay in Jung's files until 1953 and which was first published only in 1957 (GW8 § 131–93). Both texts illuminate each other, and in addition to casting the ideas of *Wandlungen und Symbole der Libido* into more systematic form, both contain much that is new in respect of Jung's reception of Nietzsche in general and *Zarathustra* in particular.

The theoretical background which both these texts provide to Jung's reading of Nietzsche is the concept of the self-regulating psyche. By analogy with the idea of the self-regulatory, homeostatic organism in the physiological sphere, Jung claimed that there was an empirically demonstrable compensatory function at work in psychological processes which balances any tendency towards one-sidedness ('Einseitigkeit') on the part of the consciousness. In other words, whilst consciousness in itself is fine, too much of it is a bad thing, and the Unconscious (the instinctual life) should not be neglected, for if it is, it will assert its influence in unpredictable ways.[61] However, civilisation has led Western Man to overprivilege the conscious mind and neglect the Unconscious, with disastrous results.[62] In 'Die transzendente Funktion', Jung sees Nietzsche's *Zarathustra* as an example of the suppression of the unconscious regulating influence. According to Jung, the discovery in *Zarathustra* of 'der höhere Mensch' ['the Higher Man'] and 'der häßlichste Mensch' ['the Ugliest Man'] expresses this regulating influence:

> die "höheren" Menschen wollen Zarathustra in die Sphäre der Durchschnittsmenschheit, wie sie von jeher war, herunterziehen, und der "häßlichste" Mensch ist sogar die Personifikation der Gegenwirkung selber (GW8 § 162).

E. M. Brenner, 'Gnosticism and Psychology: Jung's *Septem Sermones ad Mortuos*', *Journal of Analytical Psychology*, 35 (1990), 397–419; and Christine Maillard, *Les Sept sermons aux morts de Carl Gustav Jung* (Nancy, 1993).

[61] 'Da die Psyche ein selbstregulierender Apparat wie der lebende Körper ist, so bereitet sich im Unbewußten jeweils die regulierende Gegenwirkung vor' ['Since the psyche is a self-regulatory system, just as the body is, the regulatory counteraction will always develop in the Unconscious'] (GW8 § 159, 158). Jung's model constitutes his version of the Freudian warning against the 'return of the repressed'.

[62] Compare with Schiller's argument in *Über die ästhetische Erziehung des Menschen in einer Reihe von Briefen* [*On the Aesthetic Education of Man in a Series of Letters* (1795), discussed in further detail in Chapter 5.

> [the "Higher" Men want to drag Zarathustra down to the collective sphere of average humanity as it always has been, while the "Ugliest" Man is actually the personification of the counteraction.]

However, the moral conviction of Zarathustra is said to suppress this regulating influence:

> Aber der "moralische Löwe" Zarathustras "brüllt" alle diese Einflüsse, vor allem aber das Mitleid, wieder in die Höhle des Unbewußten zurück. Damit ist der regulierende Einfluß unterdrückt (GW8 § 162).
>
> [But the roaring lion of Zarathustra's moral conviction forces all these influences, above all the feeling of pity, back again into the cave of the Unconscious. Thus the regulating influence is suppressed.]

'Die Wüste wächst: weh Dem, der Wüsten birgt!', sung by Zarathustra's Shadow, refers to a lion, which is exhorted to 'moralisch brüllen!': 'Als moralischer Löwe/ Vor den Töchtern der Wüste brüllen!' ['roar like a moral lion before the daughters of the desert!'] (Z IV 16 § 2; N2: p. 544), and the song can be read as a frustrated renunciation of sensuality.[63] Later on, in the final chapter of Part IV, Zarathustra's lion chases away the Higher Men by roaring loudly at them (Z IV 20; N2: p. 560). But what kind of morality does the lion represent? And can one so easily equate Zarathusta's cave with the Unconscious?

A clue which enables us to deal with these difficulties is provided by Jung's marginal annotations on the last page of his edition of *Zarathustra*. There he writes: 'Moral} Der Löwe schreckt das Menschliche wieder weg' ['Moral: the lion frightens the human away again'] and adds:

> Eigentlich um nun die gewonnene Einsicht in die menschliche Natur wirklich zu leben und nicht bloß zu denken. Daraus würde ein Kampf mit dem Löwen entstehen und aus seiner Überwindung würde der puer aeternus, eben das Kind entstehen. Das fällt aber schon in die Krankheit.
>
> [In fact, the insight gained into human nature must now be really experienced and not merely thought. Out of that a struggle with the lion would arise and out of its overcoming the puer aeternus, precisely the child, will arise. That however is already falling into the sickness.]

Difficult as these pencillings are to interpret, they seem to suggest three things. First, that in Jung's eyes, Nietzsche's struggle with his own human nature kept separate those antinomies of existence ('leben'/'denken') which the Jungian union of opposites would overcome. And second, that since the concomitant

---

[63] For further analysis of this poem, see C. A. Miller, 'Nietzsche's "Daughters of the Desert": A Reconsideration', *Nietzsche-Studien*, 2 (1973), 157–95; and Philip Grundlehner, *The Poetry of Friedrich Nietzsche* (New York and Oxford, 1986), pp. 230–51. For a discussion of a source of the lion motif, see William Musgrave Calder III, 'The Lion Laughed', *Nietzsche-Studien*, 14 (1985), 357–59.

psychological rebirth (symbolized by the archetype of the 'puer aeternus', or the eternal child) was excluded as a possibility, then Nietzsche's madness ('die Krankheit') was inevitable. And third, Jung was attempting to relate his own archetypal framework to the main iconographical features (the lion, the child) of Nietzsche's text.

In 'Die transzendente Funktion', the focus then shifts away from internal events in *Zarathustra* towards the working-out of Nietzsche's psychological tensions in his other writings. The effects of the suppression of the unconscious regulatory influence, Jung continues, becomes evident in Nietzsche's other texts in the form of 'die geheime Wirkung des Unbewußten' ['the secret action of the Unconscious']. Jung gives two examples: first, Nietzsche's move away from Wagner, and second, his attitude towards St. Paul, whose own psychology was in turn, Jung argues, similar to Nietzsche's (GW8 § 162). This secret counteraction of the Unconscious is said to have finally broken through to the surface in Nietzsche's psychotic self-identification with the crucified Christ and the dismembered Dionysos-Zagreus:

> Wie bekannt, brachte ihm die Psychose zuallererst die Identifikation mit dem "Gekreuzigten" und dem zerrissenen Zagreus. Diese Gegenwirkung hatte mit dieser Katastrophe die Oberfläche erreicht (GW8 § 162).
>
> [As is well known, Nietzsche's psychosis first produced an identification with the "Crucified Christ" and then with the dismembered Dionysos. With this catastrophe the counteraction at last broke through the surface.]

At the same time, the real nature of the underlying problem is revealed and given a name: Dionysos. Expressed like this, Nietzsche's situation must have been all too close to Jung's own for comfort. Like Nietzsche, Jung had just abandoned his erstwhile intellectual mentor, and, like Nietzsche, Jung was suffering a mental breakdown. Unlike Nietzsche, however, he was able to cure himself. In *Psychologische Typen*, Jung would not only link 'Einseitigkeit' with the problem of barbarism, but also discuss in more detail the work of the transcendent function: the mediation of the opposites – expressed in the Nietzschean antinomy of the Dionysian and the Apollonian – through the symbol.

Jung says much the same thing about Nietzsche's fate and the symbolism of *Zarathustra* in *Die Psychologie der unbewußten Prozesse*, but he approaches the subject in a different context. Jung opens the third chapter by claiming that Freud's major achievement was the revelation of the 'shadow side' of Man, i.e. the animal, instinct-driven aspect of his nature. According to Jung, this frightening discovery shows a 'daemonic dynamic' at work in humanity.[64] In effect, this is

[64] 'Es hat eben etwas Furchtbares an sich, daß der Mensch auch eine Schattenseite hat, welche nicht nur etwa aus kleinen Schwächen und Schönheitsfehlern besteht, sondern aus einer geradezu dämonischen Dynamik' ['And indeed it is a frightening thought that Man also has a

a plea to take the Dionysian aspect of human nature seriously. For Jung, the body is the concrete expression of this animal aspect, whose instinct-driven nature he once again emphasizes, so that the acceptance of the shadow-side of human nature is also the acceptance of these immensely powerful drives (or, in Nietzschean terms, the Dionysian) (GW7 § 37). The task of integrating the Dionysian instincts – or the Shadow – is difficult, and the process of confronting the Shadow is an important practical aspect of Jungian analysis.[65] In his later writings on the Second World War, Jung would identify the Shadow with one particular manifestation of Dionysos: Wotan.

Jung then shifts the discussion to a consideration of the classically Nietzschean problematic of affirming the 'Tiernatur des Menschen' ['Man's animal nature'], asking: 'Hat man es sich klargemacht, was das heißt: zum Triebe ja zu sagen?' ['Has anyone made it clear to himself what that means – a yea-saying to instinct?'] (GW7 § 36). Concentrating on the implications of Nietzsche's 'Yea-saying' attitude to life and the Dionysian, Jung argues that the idea of the Superman involves obedience to one's instinctual drives and self-transcendence ('die Idee des Menschen, der, seinem Trieb gehorchend, auch noch über sich selbst hinausgeht' ['the idea of the man who through obedience to instinct transcends himself']). Jung compares this theory with the praxis of Nietzsche's life, switching from textual analysis to biography. He sees a prefiguration of Nietzsche's own fate and mental collapse in the fall of the tight-rope walker in Part I of *Zarathustra*: 'Deine Seele wird noch schneller tot sein als dein Leib' ['Your soul will be dead even before your body'] (Z Vorrede/Prologue § 6; N2: p. 286) and in the words of the dwarf in Part III: 'O Zarathustra, du Stein der Weisheit [...]! Dich selber warfst du so hoch, – aber jeder geworfene Stein – muß fallen! Verurteilt zu dir selber und zur eignen Steinigung: o Zarathustra, weit warfst du ja den Stein, – aber auf *dich* wird er zurückfallen!' ['O Zarathustra, you stone of wisdom! ... You have thrown yourself thus high, but every stone that is thrown – must fall! Condemned by yourself and to your own stone-throwing: O Zarathustra, far indeed have you thrown your stone' but it will fall back upon *you*!'] (Z III 2 § 1; N2: p. 407).

On the evidence of this reading, it seems that the basis of Jung's allegorical interpretation in his Seminar (1934–1939), which assumed that the various figures of *Zarathustra* represent literary projections of aspects of Nietzsche's psyche, was in place as early as 1917. Jung's conclusion in the same year that: 'Nietzsche war, unbeschadet seiner Größe und Bedeutung, eine krankhafte Persönlichkeit' ['For all his greatness and importance, Nietzsche's was a pathological personal-

---

shadow-side to him, consisting not just of little weaknesses and foibles, but of a positively daemonic dynamism'] (GW7 § 35).

65 For Jung's definition of the process of 'coming to terms with the Shadow' or the 'Realisierung des Schattens', see GW8 § 409.

ity'] (GW7 § 37), represents his most critical judgment up to this point. Nevertheless, despite the severity of his tone, Jung's analysis here of Nietzsche is more substantial than any hitherto. Distance from Nietzsche has not lent enchantment to the view but, more importantly, added critical depth.

Conclusion

The crossroads between Jung and Nietzsche is marked in *Die Psychologie der unbewußten Prozesse* by its references to Heraclitus, whom Jung judged to be 'wirklich ein großer Weiser' ['indeed a very great sage'] (GW7 § 111), and the principle of constant flux.[66] In Jung's terms, the dissociation of personality involved in the process of introversion is the moment of 'enantiodromia',[67] the effects of which are comparable to the dismemberment of Dionysos: 'Die Enantiodromie ist das Auseinandergerissensein in die Gegensatzpaare [...] das Auseinandergerissensein des Zagreus, das auch Nietzsche zu Beginn seiner Geisteskrankheit erfuhr' ['Enantiodromia means being torn asunder into pairs of opposites ... being torn asunder like Zagreus. This was what Nietzsche experienced at the onset of his malady'] (GW7 § 113). The task of Jungian psychology is thus to mediate this opposition by means of the transcendent function, and Jung casts this idea in the Nietzschean terms of 'value'. Implicitly, Jung rejects a simple revaluation ('Umwertung') of values and aims to preserve one set of (conscious) values whilst also acquiring another (unconscious) set:

> Es ist natürlich ein Grundirrtum zu glauben, wenn wir den Unwert in einem Wert oder die Unwahrheit in einer Wahrheit einsehen, daß dann der Wert oder die Wahrheit aufgehoben sei. Sie sind nur *relativ* geworden. *Alles Menschliche ist relativ, weil alles auf innerer Gegensätzlichkeit beruht, denn alles ist energetisches Phänomen* [...] Nicht um eine

---

[66] For Nietzsche's discussions of Heraclitus, see 'Uber das Pathos der Wahrheit' ['On the Pathos of Truth'] and *Die Philosophie im tragischen Zeitalter der Griechen* [*Philosophy in the Tragic Age of the Greeks*] (N3: pp. 269–71, 369–84); GD III § 2 (N2: pp. 957–58); and EH GT/BT § 3 (N2: p. 1111). For further discussion of Nietzsche's relation to Heraclitus, see Jackson P. Hershbell and Stephen A. Nimis, 'Nietzsche and Heraclitus', *Nietzsche-Studien*, 8 (1979), 17–38; and Sarah Kofman, 'Nietzsche and the Obscurity of Heraclitus', *Diacritics*, 17, no.3 (Fall 1987), 39–55; and for a further discussion of Jung's relation to Heraclitus, see: Garfield Tourney, 'Empedocles and Freud, Heraclitus and Jung', *Bulletin of the History of Medicine*, 30 (1956), 109–23; and R. C. Bodlander, 'Heraklit und Jung', *Analytische Psychologie*, 21, no.2 (June, 1990), 142–49.

[67] The concept of 'enantiodromia' derives from Heraclitus and refers to a moment of reversal when something changes into its opposite (see *Die Vorsokratiker*, translated and edited by Jaap Mansfeld, 2 vols (Stuttgart, 1983), I, pp. 257 and 265 (fragments 45 and 67). In *Psychologische Typen* (1921), Jung defines enantiodromia as 'das Hervortreten des unbewußten Gegensatzes, namentlich in der zeitlichen Folge [...] Ein gutes Beispiel für Enantiodromia ist [...] die Christusidentifikation des erkrankten Nietzsche' ['the emergence of the unconscious opposite in the course of time ... A good example of enantiodromia is the self-identification of Nietzsche with Christ'] (GW6 § 793–98/CW6 708–09).

Konversion ins Gegenteil, sondern um eine *Erhaltung der früheren Werte zusammen mit einer Anerkennung ihres Gegenteils*, darum handelt es sich (GW7 § 115–16).

[It is of course a fundamental mistake to imagine that when we see the non-value in a value or the untruth in a truth, the value or the truth ceases to exist. It has only become *relative*. Everything human is relative, because everything rests on an inner polarity; for everything is a phenomenon of energy ... The point is not conversion into the opposite but conservation of previous values together with recognition of their opposites.]

In Jungian psychology, the values must be revalued not just once, but ceaselessly; the opposites must be overcome over and over again; and the dialectic between consciousness and the Unconscious is a life's work. The god must be born, die and be reborn, again and again.

At the end of *Die Psychologie der unbewußten Prozesse*, Jung acknowledged his debt to Nietzsche: 'ich kam von der Psychiatrie her, von Nietzsche für moderne Psychologie wohlvorbereitet' ['I approached from the side of psychiatry, well prepared for modern psychology by Nietzsche'] (GW7 § 199). The point of that remark is to put as much distance as possible between him and Freud, whereas the Freud/Jung correspondence reveals that, in reality, Jung had been one of Freud's closest followers until he had started to drift away from him as a result of his study of mythology and his reading of Nietzsche. However, as I have shown above, Jung did not just derive several key concepts from Nietzsche and then exemplify these from his life and biography, but he also envisaged Analytical Psychology as an antidote to Nietzsche's collapse (mental and theoretical). Central to Jung's interest in Nietzsche was his concern with Dionysos, and he was driven to take a more than just intellectual interest in the problem of the Dionysian after his own personal experiences between 1913 and 1919. Although *Wandlungen und Symbole der Libido* (1911/12) is partly written within a framework derived from *Die Geburt der Tragödie*, it was not until 1921, in his next major work, *Psychologische Typen*, that he provided an explicit psychological reading of the rôles of both Apollo and Dionysos in Nietzsche's account of tragedy. It is to that work that I shall turn in the next chapter.

Chapter 5

Jung's Reception of Nietzsche in *Psychologische Typen*

'Zur Frage der Psychologischen Typen' (1913)

Typology plays a key rôle in Jungian psychology, and Jung developed the idea of different psychological types whilst he was engaged in defining the difference between his own approach to psychology and those of Freud and Adler.[1] The division of types into introverted and extraverted and of psychic processes into the four functions of Thinking, Feeling, Sensation and Intuition was far more sophisticated than any simple racial distinctions that Jung was tempted to make in articles like 'Über das Unbewußte' ['On the Rôle of the Unconscious']. Although Jung wrote his definitive text on the problem of typology in 1921, in an earlier paper called 'Zur Frage der Psychologischen Typen' ['A Contribution to the Study of Psychological Types'] (GW6 § 931 – 50/CW6 § 858 – 82), given at the Psychoanalytic Congress in Munich in September 1913, he devoted a whole paragraph to Nietzsche and sketched out certain ideas which he would take up, expand and in some cases change in *Psychologische Typen* [*Psychological Types*] (1921).

In the 1913 paper, Jung discussed the difference between the introverted and extraverted types in terms of a distinction which was to be found in the work of six other writers: first, in Schiller's distinction between the 'naive' and 'sentimental' types of poet; second, in Nietzsche's opposition between the Apollonian and the Dionysian in *Die Geburt der Tragödie* [*The Birth of Tragedy*]; third, in Otto Gross's two forms of inferiority, 'einen Typus mit verflacht-verbreitertem Bewußtsein und einen Typus mit verengt-vertieftem Bewußtsein' ['a type with a diffuse and shallow consciousness, and another with a contracted and deep consciousness'] (GW6 § 948/CW6 § 879); fourth, in Wilhelm Ostwald's division of the character of the genius into romantic and classical; fifth, in William

[1] 'Die sexuelle Interpretation einerseits und die Machtabsichten des "Dogmas" andererseits führten mich im Laufe der Jahre zum typologischen Problem, sowie zur Polarität und Energetik der Seele' ['What with the sexual interpretation on the one hand and the power drive of dogma on the other I was led, over the years, to a consideration of the problem of typology'] (ETG: p. 159/MDR: p. 178). If *Wandlungen und Symbole der Libido* had cost Jung his friendship with Freud, then *Psychologische Typen* was necessary for understanding *inter alia* why that relationship had failed.

James's division between 'tender-minded' and 'tough-minded'; and sixth, in Wilhelm Worringer's distinction between the 'Einfühlungsdrang' ['empathy'] and the 'Abstraktionsdrang' ['abstraction']. It is, however, the typologies of Schiller and Nietzsche which concern us here, not least because, as I shall argue below, Jung's understanding of their respective typologies changed between 1913 and 1921, becoming more circumspect vis-à-vis Schiller and reversing his understanding of Nietzsche's concept of the Dionysian.

In 'Zur Frage der Psychologischen Typen', Jung introduces Nietzsche's pair of opposites as a parallel to the opposition between introversion and extraversion (GW6 § 946/CW6 § 876). He describes their typological significance in the following manner, noting that to each of the opposing elements there corresponds a psychological condition: 'Traum' ['dream'] (Apollo) and 'Rausch' ['ecstasy, intoxication'] (Dionysos). Jung defines the conditions of dreaming and ecstasy in the following way: 'Der Traum ist das innerste aller psychischen Erlebnisse, der Rausch das am meisten selbstvergessene, von sich selber befreite Streben nach der Vielheit der Objekte' ['In a dream the individual is shut up in himself, it is the most intimate of all psychic experiences; in intoxication, he is liberated from himself, and, utterly self-forgetful, plunges into the multiplicity of the objective world']. Jung then goes on to discuss Apollo, taking over Nietzsche's citation from Schopenhauer of the image of a lonely man in a boat out on the sea (the world) with only the *principium individuationis* (related to Apollo) for support, and he concludes: 'Das Apollinische ist daher, wie Nietzsche es auffaßt, das auf sich selber Zurückgezogensein, die Introversion' ['The Apollonian state, therefore, as Nietzsche conceives it, is a withdrawal into oneself, or introversion'] (GW6 § 946/CW6 § 877). Finally, Jung defines the Dionysian (in contrast to the Apollonian) as 'das entfesselte Hinausströmen der Libido in die Dinge' ['the unleashing of a torrent of libido into things'], and quotes the passage from *Die Geburt der Tragödie* where the Dionysian is described as the 'Evangelium der Weltenharmonie [...] als ob der Schleier der Maya zerrissen wäre und nur noch in Fetzen vor dem geheimnisvollen Ur-Einen herumflattere' ['the gospel of universal harmony ... as if the veil of *maya* had been torn aside and were now merely fluttering in tatters before the mysterious primordial unity'] (GT/BT § 1; N1: p. 25).

Although Jung concluded that 'diese Auffassung bedarf keines weiteren Kommentars' ['any commentary on this passage would be superfluous'], he was wrong, for, as these passages stand, there is a clear contradiction between the meaning which they have in their original context and what Jung wants them to mean. Where Jung equated the Dionysian with the striving for a multiplicity of objects, the passage from *Die Geburt der Tragödie* quoted above actually says the opposite: namely, that a mystic unity is revealed to the ecstatic reveller. Furthermore, Jung failed to appreciate the polemical nature of Nietzsche's equation of

Apollo with the Schopenhauerian *principium individuationis.* Although *Die Geburt der Tragödie* can be read as a strategic inversion of Schopenhauer's *Die Welt als Wille und Vorstellung* [*The World as Will and Representation*], Jung does not seem to have noticed this. However, in his more mature work on typology in 1921, Jung's reading of Nietzsche's opposition of Dionysos and Apollo was more detailed and less simplified than had been the case in his lecture of 1913.

Nietzsche on barbarism

The word 'Barbar' ['barbarian'] occurs frequently in Nietzsche's works and serves as a terminus for his reflexions on the 'höhere Menschen' ['Higher Men'] who, so he hoped, would arise. In the fifth section of *Menschliches, Allzumenschliches* [*Human, All Too Human*] entitled 'Anzeichen höherer und niederer Kultur' ['Tokens of Higher and Lower Culture'], Nietzsche criticized contemporary society for falling into the second category, and claimed in the aphorism 'Die moderne Unruhe' ['Modern restlessness'] that 'Aus Mangel an Ruhe läuft unsere Zivilisation in eine neue Barbarei aus' ['From lack of repose our civilization is turning into a new barbarism'] (MA/HA I § 285; N1: p. 620). Whilst the use of the term here is wholly negative, it recurs in *Morgenröte* with a more ambiguous significance for, in the section entitled 'Das Streben nach Auszeichnung' ['The Striving for Distinction'], Nietzsche contrasts the ascetic, who internalizes and himself suffers pain, with 'sein Gegenbild auf der ersten Sprosse der Leiter, der *Barbar*' ['his counterpart on the first step of the ladder, the *barbarian*'], who causes the same pain to others (M/D § 113; N1: p. 1086). Further on in the same text, Nietzsche juxtaposes 'Barbarei' with 'Erkenntnis', and laments the domination of the latter over the former with all its grievous consequences.[2]

In Nietzsche's later writings, however, and in particular the notes which would appear as *Der Wille zur Macht,* the sense of the term 'Barbarei' is almost wholly positive. According to these notes and sketches, there are two kinds of barbarians: those who have previously been sought 'in der Tiefe' ['in the depths'], and 'eine *andere Art Barbaren,* die kommen aus der Höhe' ['another type of barbarian, who comes from the heights'], who are 'eine Art von erobernden und herrschenden Naturen, welche nach einem Stoffe suchen, die sie gestalten

[2] 'Warum fürchten und hassen wir eine mögliche Rückkehr zur Barbarei? Weil sie die Menschen unglücklicher machen würde, als sie es sind? Ach nein! Die Barbaren aller Zeiten hatten *mehr* Glück: täuschen wir uns nicht! [...] Ja, wir hassen die Barbarei – wir wollen alle lieber den Untergang der Menschheit als den Rückgang der Erkenntnis!' ['Why do we fear and hate a possible reversion to barbarism? Because it would make people unhappier than they are? Oh no! The barbarians of every age were *happier*: let us not deceive ourselves! ... Yes, we hate barbarism – we would all prefer the destruction of Mankind to a regression of knowledge!'] (M/D § 429; N1: pp. 1223–24).

können' ['a species of conquering and ruling natures in search of material to mould'] (WM/WP 900 = N3: p. 846). These barbarians, exemplified for Nietzsche by Prometheus, are described elsewhere as 'die Zyniker, die Versucher, die Eroberer' ['cynics, experimenters, conquerors'], who have in common the 'Vereinigung der geistigen Überlegenheit mit Wohlbefinden und Überschuß an Kräften' ['union of spiritual superiority with well-being and an excess of strength'] (WM/WP 899 = N3: p. 449). Such 'neue *Barbaren*' ['new *barbarians*'] are close in conception to the Superman.

Jung probably picked up the theme of 'Barbarei' from reading the discussion in the earlier *Die Geburt der Tragödie*. Indeed, his own discussion of the problem of barbarism contains something of the ambiguity of Nietzsche's use of the term, in that (like Nietzsche) he sets up two different senses of 'Barbarei', only (unlike Nietzsche) both equally negative.

In *Die Geburt der Tragödie*, Nietzsche contrasts the Apollinian world of 'das Individuum, d. h. die Einhaltung der Grenzen des Individuums, das *Maß* im hellenischen Sinne' ['the individual, i.e., the delimiting of the boundaries of the individual, *measure* in the Hellenic sense'] with the 'titanenhaft' ['titanic'] and 'barbarisch' ['barbaric'] world of the Dionysian, with its concomitant '*Übermaß*' ['*excess*'], for which the fate of Prometheus ('von den Geiern zerrissen' ['torn to pieces by the vultures']), due to his 'titanenhaften Liebe zu den Menschen' ['because of his titanic love for Man'], serves as an example (GT/BT § 4; N1: pp. 33–34). On Nietzsche's account, these two worlds of Apollo and Dionysos are nonetheless equally dependent on each other.[3] Nietzsche's description of the effects of the Dionysian is also worthy of note, as it anticipates a later image, namely that of the 'blonde Bestie' ['blond beast']. This animal, or at any rate an ancestor of it, first makes its appearance in *Die Geburt der Tragödie* when, discussing the Dionysian rites, Nietzsche says that they released 'gerade die wildesten Bestien der Natur' ['precisely the wildest beasts of nature']. For Nietzsche, therefore, the question of bar-

[3] '"Titanenhaft" und "barbarisch" dünkte dem apollinischen Griechen auch die Wirkung, die das *Dionysische* erregte: ohne dabei sich verhehlen zu können, daß er selbst doch zugleich auch innerlich mit jenen gestürzten Titanen und Heroen verwandt sei. Ja er mußte noch mehr empfinden: sein ganzes Dasein, mit aller Schönheit und Mäßigung, ruhte auf einem verhüllten Untergrunde des Leidens und der Erkenntnis, der ihm wieder durch jenes Dionysische aufgedeckt wurde. Und siehe! Apollo konnte nicht ohne Dionysos leben! Das "Titanische" und das "Barbarische" war zuletzt eine eben solche Notwendigkeit wie das Apollinische!' ['The effects wrought by the *Dionysian* also seemed "titanic" and "barbaric" to the Apollonian Greek; while at the same time he could not conceal from himself that he, too, was inwardly related to these overthrown Titans and heroes. Indeed, he had to recognize even more than this: despite all its beauty and moderation, his entire existence rested on a hidden substratum of suffering and of knowledge, revealed to him by the Dionysian. And behold! Apollo could not live without Dionysos! The "titanic" and the "barbaric" were in the last analysis as necessary as the Apollonian'] (GT/BT § 4; N1: p. 34).

barism is closely linked to the image of the blond beast and all that it implies in the context of *Zur Genealogie der Moral* [*On the Genealogy of Morals*].

Nevertheless, Nietzsche is careful to distinguish between Dionysian *Greeks* and Dionysian *barbarians* (GT/BT § 2; N1: p. 26). Although both are said to participate in those primal energies released in the Dionysian orgy, the Dionysian barbarians allegedly merely regressed to the condition of animals, whereas something much more important was achieved in the Greeks' synthesis of Dionysos with Apollo: '[wir erkennen], im Vergleiche mit jenen babylonischen Sakäen und ihrem Rückschritte des Menschen zum Tiger und Affen, in den dionysischen Orgien der Griechen die Bedeutung von Welterlösungsfesten und Verklärungstagen' ['we shall now recognize in the Dionysian orgies of the Greeks, as compared with the Babylonian Sacaea with their reversion of Man to the tiger and the ape, the significance of festivals of world redemption and days of transfiguration'] (GT/BT § 2; N1: p. 27). As we shall see, this all-important distinction between the Dionysian Greek (or artist) and the barbarian gets lost in Jung's discussion of Apollo and Dionysos. But first we need to look at Jung's discussion of the problem of barbarism and its possible solution which lie at the heart of *Psychologische Typen* (1921).

The Beast Stirs?

Jung's essay 'Über das Unbewußte', published in 1918 in two sections of the periodical *Schweizerland: Monatshefte für Schweizer Art und Kunst*, contains one particular passage which was to become highly significant – or so Jung claimed – in the Thirties. Here, Jung described the Christianization of the Germanic barbarians in terms of a repressive domestication:

> Das Christentum zerteilte den germanischen Barbaren in seine untere und obere Hälfte, und so gelang es ihm – nämlich durch Verdrängung der dunklen Seite – die helle Seite zu domestizieren und für die Kultur geschickt zu machen. Die untere Hälfte aber harrt der Erlösung und einer zweiten Domestikation [...] Je mehr die unbedingte Autorität der christlichen Weltanschauung sich verliert, desto vernehmlicher wird sich die "blonde Bestie" in ihrem unterirdischen Gefängnis umdrehen und uns mit einem Ausbruch mit verheerenden Folgen bedrohen. Diese Erscheinung findet als psychologische Revolution statt, wie sie auch als soziales Phänomen auftreten kann (GW10 § 17).

> [Christianity split the Germanic barbarian into an upper and a lower half, and enabled him, by repressing the dark side, to domesticate the brighter half and fit it for civilization. But the lower, darker half still awaits redemption and a second spell of domestication ... As the Christian view of the world loses its authority, the more menacingly will the "blond beast" be heard prowling about in its underground prison, ready at any moment to burst out with devastating consequences. When this happens in the individual it brings about a psychological revolution, but it can also take a social form.]

At first sight, Jung is repeating what he had said in *Wandlungen und Symbole der Libido* [*Psychology of the Unconscious*] and *Die Psychologie der unbewußten Prozesse* [translated as *On the Psychology of the Unconscious*] about the problematic conditions in which cultural development takes place. Moreover, the language is highly reminiscent of Nietzsche: indeed, the whole passage sounds as if it could be a conflation of two extracts from Nietzsche's *Zur Genealogie der Moral.* First: 'Alle Instinkte, welche sich nicht nach außen entladen, *wenden sich nach innen* – dies ist das, was ich die *Verinnerlichung* des Menschen nenne' ['All instincts that do not discharge themselves outwardly *turn inward* – this is what I call the *internalization of Man*'] (GM II § 16; N2: p. 825). And second: 'Auf dem Grunde aller dieser vornehmen Rassen ist das Raubtier, die prachtvolle nach Beute und Sieg lüstern schweifende *blonde Bestie* nicht zu verkennen; es bedarf für diesen verborgenen Grund von Zeit zu Zeit der Entladung, das Tier muß wieder heraus, muß wieder in die Wildnis zurück' ['One cannot fail to see at the bottom of all these noble races the beast of prey, the splendid *blond beast* prowling about avidly in search of spoil and victory; this hidden core needs to erupt from time to time, the animal has to get out again and go back to the wilderness'] (GM I § 11; N2: p. 786). Indeed, Jung highlighted the first passage in the margin of his personal edition of Nietzsche, and noted, in the back of his copy, the page reference to the 'blonde Bestie'.[4]

In later years, Jung was to attach particular importance to the passage from 'Über das Unbewußte' quoted above, both during his Tavistock Lectures of 1935 (GW18(i) § 371), and in a talk on the BBC's Third Programme of 3 November 1946 called 'The Fight with the Shadow' (GW10 § 447), where he claimed that, in this passage, he was warning about the National Socialists' rise to power in Germany and the Second World War. However, given the original date of publication of 'Über das Unbewußte', its first readers must have taken it as a reference to the First World War rather than a statement of things to come.

Jung's attitude to National Socialism is not unrelated to his reception of Nietzsche and the notion of the Dionysian, especially given the way in which the Nazis appropriated Nietzsche to support their doctrines. Indeed, as Andrew Samuels and Aniela Jaffé (amongst others) have noted, Jung's relationship to National Socialism was an uncomfortable albeit distant one.[5] And although,

---

[4] In fact, two out of the three references by Nietzsche to the 'blonde Bestie' occur in *Zur Genealogie der Moral.* Nietzsche's use of this image is very sparing; it is however his most notorious image, and likely, for this reason, to have caught Jung's attention.

[5] See the essays collected in *Lingering Shadows: Jungians, Freudians, and Anti-Semitism*, edited by Aryeh Maidenbaum and Stephen A. Martin (Boston and London, 1991). The main accusations against Jung have been summarized by S. Grossman under the following headings. First: Jung's alleged anti-Semitism and support for a Germanic (racial) psychotherapy; second, his ambivalent comments on Hitler and the Nazi régime; and third, his ties with the 'gleichgeschaltete' *Allgemeine*

more recently, Micha Neumann has again voiced the view that anti-Semitism was part of the shadow-side of Jung's personality,[6] there is no evidence, despite his brief correspondence with Elisabeth Förster-Nietzsche, that Jung was ever involved with her politically suspect misuse of Nietzsche.[7]

As early as 1918 in 'Über das Unbewußte', Jung had drawn a distinction between the psychology of the Aryan European and that of the Jew (GW10 § 18), and had then gone on tendentiously to locate the root of his theoretical differences with Freud and Adler in race:

> Der Jude lebt in der Regel in freundlicher Nachbarschaft des Irdischen, ohne jedoch die Macht des Erdhaften zu empfinden [...] ich begreife vollkommen, daß Freuds und Adlers Reduktionen auf primitive Sexualwünsche und auf primitive Machtabsichten für den Juden etwas Wohltätiges und Befriedigendes, weil Vereinfachendes an sich haben, weshalb sich Freud mit einer gewissen Berechtigung meinen Einwänden gegenüber verschließt. Für die germanische Mentalität sind aber diese spezifisch jüdischen Doktrinen durchaus unbefriedigend, denn wir Germanen haben noch einen echten Barbaren in uns, der nicht mit sich spassen läßt und dessen Erscheinen für uns keine Erleichterung und keinen angenehmen Zeitvertreib bedeutet (GW10 § 19).

> [As a rule, the Jew lives in amicable relationship with the earth, but without feeling the power of the chthonic ... I can understand very well that Freud's and Adler's reduction of everything psychic to primitive sexual wishes and power-drives has something about it that is beneficial and satisfying to the Jew, because it is a form of simplification. For this reason, Freud is perhaps right to close his eyes to my objections. But these specifically Jewish doctrines are thoroughly unsatisfying to the Germanic mentality; we still have a genuine barbarian in us who is not to be trifled with, and whose manifestation is no comfort for us and not a pleasant way of passing the time.]

The argument here is quite clear: it is explicitly racist, implicitly anti-Semitic, and Jung's mixture of pride and embarrassment when he talks about 'einen echten Barbaren in uns [Germanen]' tells us a lot about his own personal psychology. The tone may again be due in part to Nietzsche, who had singled

---

Ärztliche Gesellschaft für Psychotherapie (S. Grossman, 'C. G. Jung and National Socialism', *Journal of European Studies*, 9 (1979), 231–59 (p. 231). The renegade Hungaro-American psychologist Thomas Szasz comments on this aspect of the Freud/Jung dispute in the following words: 'Freud and the Freudians have deprived Jung of many of his best ideas and, to boot, have defamed him as an anti-Semite. Actually, Jung was far more candid and correct than Freud in identifying psychotherapy as an ethical rather than technical enterprise; and Freud was far more anti-Christian than Jung was anti-Semitic' (*Heresies* (New York, 1976), p. 139).

6 'In Jungscher Terminologie würde ich behaupten, daß Antisemitismus ein Bestandteil von Jungs Schatten gewesen ist' ['To use Jungian terminology, I would say that antisemitism was a component of Jung's Shadow'] (Micha Neumann, 'Die Beziehungen zwischen Erich Neumann und C. G. Jung und die Frage des Antisemitismus', *Analytische Psychologie*, 23 (1992), 3–23 (p. 22).

7 This misuse is documented in H. F. Peters, *Zarathustra's Sister: The Case of Elisabeth and Friedrich Nietzsche* (New York, 1977) and Ben Macintyre, *Forgotten Fatherland: The Search for Elisabeth Nietzsche* (London, 1992).

out the Jews as a special race in *Jenseits von Gut und Böse* [*Beyond Good and Evil*] and *Zur Genealogie der Moral*, and whose remarks, despite his avowed opposition to anti-Semitism,[8] were to be used by the National Socialists as anti-Semitic ammunition in their propaganda campaigns. However, the key word in this paragraph is the term 'Barbar', which Jung defines as 'den Barbaren von vorgestern, nämlich ein Wesen, dem die Sache in unangenehmster Weise plötzlich *ernst* wird' ['the barbarian of yesterday, a being for whom matters suddenly become *serious* in the most unpleasant way']. Jung then continues by associating this experience of barbarism with Nietzsche:

> Diese ärgerliche Eigentümlichkeit des Barbaren ist auch Nietzsche aufgefallen, wohl aus eigenster Erfahrung – darum schätzte er die jüdische Mentalität, und darum predigte er das Tanzen und Fliegen und Nichternstnehmen. Er übersah dabei, daß es nicht der Barbar ist, der ernst nimmt, sondern *es* nimmt *ihn* ernst. Das böse Wesen faßt ihn. Und wen hat es ernster genommen als eben gerade Nietzsche selbst? (GW10 § 19)
>
> [This annoying peculiarity of the barbarian was apparent also to Nietzsche – no doubt from personal experience – which is why he thought highly of the Jewish mentality and preached about dancing and flying and not taking things seriously. But he overlooked the fact that it is not the barbarian in us who takes things seriously – they become serious for him. He is gripped by the daemon. And who took things more seriously than Nietzsche himself?]

Although Jung here acknowledges Nietzsche's special interest in the Jews, two more important points should be noted. First, Jung describes barbarism as a condition which robs the barbarian of his autonomy and individuality. And second, Jung says that Nietzsche himself had personal experience of this condition and refers to Nietzsche's emphasis on dancing, flying and light-heartedness (all three of which constantly recur as images in *Also sprach Zarathustra*). More importantly still, Jung describes the barbarian condition here using exactly the same kind of language which he employs to describe his understanding of Nietzsche's experience of the Dionysian.

In other words, we are seeing here the next shift in Jung's reception of Nietzsche: the exploration of the social implications of the psychology of the Dionysian which would be taken further during Jung's reflections on psychological types. Furthermore, it is necessary to place Jung's attitude to Fascism in the context of his concern, in the years immediately following the First World War, with the problem of 'das Barbarische', and this is closely bound up with his interpretation of the Dionysian in his *Psychologische Typen*.

---

[8] Cf. Nietzsche's last letter to Jacob Burckhardt of 6 January 1889, which proclaimed: 'Wilhelm Bismarck und alle Antisemiten abgeschafft' ['Wilhelm Bismarck and all antisemites abolished'] (N3: p. 1352).

Jung's Discussion of Barbarism

As I have suggested above, there are two types of barbarism which need to be distinguished in Jung's account of this problem in *Psychologische Typen*. On the one hand, there is a barbarism born of the overdevelopment of a differentiated psychological function – this is the barbarism of 'Einseitigkeit' ['one-sidedness']: 'Es ist eben das Zeichen des barbarischen Zustandes, daß der Wille einseitig durch die eine Funktion bestimmt ist' ['It is truly a sign of the barbarian state that the will is determined unilaterally by one function'] (GW6 § 169/CW6 § 178). More precisely, barbarism is said here to be a condition of unconscious one-sidedness, as opposed to conscious, controlled 'Einseitigkeit': 'Die bewußte Fähigkeit zur Einseitigkeit ist ein Zeichen höchster Kultur. Die unwillkürliche Einseitigkeit aber, d. h. das Nichtanderskönnen als Einseitigsein, ist ein Zeichen von Barbarei' ['A conscious capacity for one-sidedness is a sign of the highest culture, but involuntary one-sidedness, i.e. the inability to be anything but one-sided, is a sign of barbarism'] (GW6 § 376/CW6 § 346). This 'Einseitigkeit' is thus a double barbarism:[9] first, because, according to Jung, Man's psychology overprizes one function and allows itself to be swept away by it 'in barbarischer Weise' ['in a barbaric manner'] – and second, because, the spontaneous release of Man's repressed functions causes an explosion of energy which is also barbaric.[10]

On the face of it, this barbarism of one-sidedness – a kind of super-Apollonian barbarism – could be overcome by allowing the (unconscious) repressed functions to return. However, Jung, puts a question mark over such simple de-repression on the grounds that it would result in an outburst of untamed energy as the force of the repressed is unleashed: 'Es ist eine Katastrophe der Kultur, so wie wir sie heute noch verstehen, wenn die barbarische Seite des Europäers sich zum Worte meldet' ['For culture, as we understand it today, it is certainly a catastrophe when the barbarian side of the European comes uppermost'] (GW6 § 164/CW6 § 172). In other words, Jung's argument is that de-repression merely results in a loss of (moral) values, and if we set this passage against another one

[9] 'Ob sich nun aber das Ungezähmte, Maßlose und Disproportionierte in der Sinnlichkeit – in abiectissimo loco – oder in der höchst entwickelten Funktion als Überschätzung oder Deifikation derselben zeigt, es ist im Grunde genommen dasselbe, nämlich *Barbarei*' ['Whether the untamed, extravagent, disproportionate energy shows itself in sensuality – in *abjectissimo loco* – or in an overestimation and deification of the most highly developed function, it is at bottom the same: barbarism'] (GW6 § 154/CW6 § 160).

[10] Jung's double use of the term 'Barbarei' can be compared with Hegel's two uses of 'Barbarei' in his *Aufsätze aus dem Kritischen Journal der Philosophie* (1802–03), where he distinguishes between 'natürliche Barbarei' ['natural barbarism'] and 'die Barbarei der Kultur' ['the barbarism of culture'] (G. W. F. Hegel, *Werke*, 20 vols (Frankfurt am Main, 1986), II, *Jenaer Schriften 1801–1807*, p. 271).

from a later chapter which continues this discussion, we can see that, as far as Jung is concerned, contemporary Man is caught in a double bind. For, whilst one-sidedness and its concomitant repression causes barbarism, the de-repression involved in counteracting this one-sidedness is equally likely to bring about a state of barbarism:

> Wir sind eben immer noch so unerzogen, daß wir Gesetze von außen brauchen und einen Zuchtmeister, resp. Vater darüber, damit wir wissen, was gut ist, und das Rechte tun können. Und weil wir noch so barbarisch sind, so kommt uns das Vertrauen in die Gesetze der menschlichen Natur und des menschlichen Pfades als ein gefährlicher und unethischer Naturalismus vor. Warum? Weil bei dem Barbaren unter der dünnen Kulturhaut gleich die Bestie kommt, und davor hat er mit Recht Angst. Aber das Tier wird nicht überwunden dadurch, daß es in einen Käfig gesperrt wird (GW6 § 400/CW6 § 357).
>
> [We are still so uneducated that we actually need laws from without, and a task-master or Father above, to show us what is good and the right thing to do. And because we are still such barbarians, any trust in the laws of human nature seems to us a dangerous and unethical naturalism. Why is this? Because under the barbarian's thin veneer of culture the wild beast lurks in readiness, amply justifying his fear. But the beast is not tamed by locking it up in a cage.]

Once again, this image is very reminiscent of Nietzsche's *Zur Genealogie der Moral* when he mentions 'das Raubtier, das prachtvolle nach Beute und Sieg lüstern schweifende *blonde Bestie*' ['the beast of prey, the splendid *blond beast* prowling about avidly in search of spoil and victory'] (GM I § 11; N2: p. 786), although there is less enthusiasm in Jung's tone here than there had been in 'Über das Unbewußte' of three years previously.

Jung seeks to find a way out of this double bind – the barbarism of repressive morality and the barbarism of de-repressed (amoral) freedom – by locating the source of a liberating morality not in any external authority, but rather within the individual:

> *Es gibt keine Sittlichkeit ohne Freiheit.* Wenn ein Barbar seine Bestie losläßt, so ist das keine Freiheit, sondern eine Unfreiheit. Um frei sein zu können, muß zuvor die Barbarei überwunden werden. Dies geschieht im Prinzip dadurch, daß Grund und Motivkraft der Sittlichkeit vom Individuum als Bestandteile seiner eigenen Natur empfunden und wahrgenommen werden, und nicht als äußere Beschränkungen (GW6 § 400/CW6 § 357).
>
> [*There is no morality without freedom.* When the barbarian lets loose the beast within him, that is not freedom but bondage. Barbarism must first be vanquished before freedom can be won. This happens, in principle, when the basic root and driving force of morality are felt by the individual as constituents of his own nature and not as external restrictions.]

This notion of a moral imperative that is immanent in human nature is very close to Nietzsche's discussion of morality in *Jenseits von Gut und Böse*, where he suggests that the revalued values of the new morality are the product of the self, and that the most outstanding type of human being is the one who can determine his own values: '*Die eigentlichen Philosophen aber sind Befehlende und Gesetzgeber*' ['*Genuine philosophers, however, are commanders and legislators*'] (JGB/BGE § 211; N2: p. 676). At the same time, however, Jung distances his position from Nietzsche's by giving his argument a Kantian twist. Although, Jung argues, the individual must understand the moral code as his own, it must also involve a universal quality. As he said in *Die Psychologie der unbewußten Prozesse*: 'Die Moral wird nicht von außen aufgenötigt – man hat sie schließlich a priori in sich selbst' ['Morality is not imposed from outside; we have it in ourselves from the start'] (GW7 § 30). To the next question – 'Wie aber kann der Mensch [...] zu dieser Empfindung und Einsicht gelangen?' ['How is Man to attain this realization?'] – Jung answers in a less Kantian way that there is only one way: 'durch den Konflikt der Gegensätze' ['through the conflict of opposites'] (GW6 § 400/CW6 § 357). The problem of opposites – the fundamental problem of all Jung's writing – is approached in *Psychologische Typen* through Jung's Schillerian critique of Western society, his rejection of Schiller's solution, and his proposal – over and above what Nietzsche says about Apollo and Dionysos in *Die Geburt der Tragödie* – of the reconciling symbol as the means to his own solution.

Schiller's Social Critique

The second chapter of *Psychologische Typen* consists of a critical account of the consequences of Western cultural development, and here Jung uses Schiller's analysis of contemporary society as that is set out in *Über die ästhetische Erziehung des Menschen in einer Reihe von Briefen* [*On the Aesthetic Education of Man in a Series of Letters*] (1975) as a basis for his own critique.[11] Reading Schiller's text as a study of the psychological dilemma of modern Man written from the perspective of an introverted thinking type (GW6 § 99/CW6 § 104), Jung claims that the problem of Man's disharmony with himself lies at the core of Schiller's discussion.[12] As Jung puts it: 'mit sicherem Griffe hebt [Schiller] als Grundmotiv die Differenzierung der Individuen heraus' ['with sure instinct Schiller hits on the differentiation of the individual as the basic motive'] (GW6 § 100/CW6 § 105), and he

---

11 Friedrich Schiller, *On the Aesthetic Education of Man in a Series of Letters*, edited and translated by Elizabeth M. Wilkinson and L. A. Willoughby (Oxford, 1967). Henceforth referred to as 'AE' (*Ästhetische Erziehung*) followed by a page reference.

12 For an analysis of the way that Schiller anticipates the basic concepts of Jung's Analytical Psychology, see: Karin Barnaby, 'A Poet's Intuition of C. G. Jung's Psychology in "Über naive und sentimentalische Dichtung"', in *Friedrich von Schiller and the Drama of Human Existence*, edited by Alexander Ugrinsky (New York, 1988), pp. 119–28).

quotes from the Sixth Letter where Schiller had written: 'Die Kultur selbst war es, welche der neuern Menschheit diese Wunde schlug' ['It was culture itself which inflicted this wound upon modern Man'] (AE: p. 32). Jung also takes up this image of the wound of modern Man by linking it with the wound of Amfortas in Wagner's *Parsifal*;[13] and the notion of the wound that must be healed becomes in itself a leitmotiv in the developing dramaturgy of *Psychologische Typen*.

According to Jung, Christianity represented an advance over classical civilization by proclaiming the value of the individual (GW6 § 105/CW6 § 108), but the price of this is said to be the transposition into the individual subject of the early social differentiation between superior and inferior. Or, to put it another way, this social differentiation became psychically internalized:

> Damit wurde psychologisch die äußere soziale Form der antiken Kultur ins Subjekt verlegt, wodurch im Einzelnen ein innerer Zustand erzeugt wurde, der in der Antike ein äußerer Zustand gewesen war, nämlich eine herrschende bevorzugte Funktion, die auf Kosten einer minderwertigen Mehrheit sich entwickelte und differenzierte (GW6 § 105/CW6 § 108).
>
> [Psychologically this meant that the external form of society in classical civilization was transferred into the subject, so that a condition was produced within the individual which in the ancient world had been external, namely a dominating, privileged function which was developed and differentiated at the expense of an inferior minority.]

By means of this psychological process, Jung argues, a democratic, egalitarian collective culture came into being, which was, however, based psychologically upon a 'subjektive Sklavenkultur' ['subjective slave culture']. This sounds like a Nietzschean formulation, and indeed, Jung does share Nietzsche's concern with the triumph of the collective over the individual, for he describes the internalization of functional differentiation as 'eine Verlegung der antiken Mehrheitsversklavung ins Psychologische, wodurch zwar die Kollektivkultur erhöht, die Individualkultur aber erniedrigt wird' ['a transfer of the old mass enslavement into the psychological sphere, with the result that, while collective culture was enhanced, individual culture was degraded'] (GW6 § 105/CW6 § 108).

Again, Jung's analysis is close to Nietzsche's *Zur Genealogie der Moral* on two counts. First, Jung pits the collective against the individual; and second, he fears that the process of socialization produces a harmful effect – i.e. a 'wound' –

---

[13] 'Die Auflösung des harmonischen Zusammenwirkens der seelischen Kräfte im instinktiven Leben ist wie eine stets offene und nie verheilende Wunde, eine wahre Amfortaswunde' ['The breakdown of the harmonious cooperation of psychic forces in instinctive life is like an ever open and never healing wound, a veritable Amfortas' wound'] (GW6 § 100/CW6 § 105). Jung used this image again eight years later in 1929 in his 'Kommentar zu "Das Geheimnis der Goldenen Blüte"' ['Commentary on "The Secret of the Golden Flower"']: 'Noch sind die Amfortaswunde und die faustische Zerrissenheit des germanischen Menschen nicht geheilt' ['The Amfortas wound and the Faustian split in the Germanic Man are still not healed'] (GW13 § 70).

in the individual (GW6 § 105/CW6 § 108). The image of a 'verstümmelte' ['mutilated'] human nature is also to be found in Schiller's Sixth Letter (AE: p. 42), and Jung claims that Schiller was not only aware of this inner conflict but also 'daß aus eben diesem Widerstreit in ihm die Sehnsucht entsprungen ist, jene Einheitlichkeit oder Gleichförmigkeit zu finden, welche auch den unterdrückten und im Sklavendienste schmachtenden Funktionen die Erlösung bringen sollte und damit die Wiederherstellung eines harmonischen Lebens' ['it was just this antagonism in himself that generated a longing for the coherence or homogeneity which should bring deliverance to the suppressed functions languishing in servitude and a restoration of harmonious living'] (GW6 § 111/CW6 § 114). Again, in the same paragraph, Jung links Schiller's project, even more explicitly, with Wagner's *Parsifal*: 'Dieser Gedanke bewegte auch Wagner in seinem *Parsifal*, und er verlieh ihm symbolischen Ausdruck in der Wiederbringung des verlorenen Speeres und der Heilung der Wunde. Was Wagner im künstlerischen symbolischen Ausdruck zu sagen versuchte, das bemüht sich Schiller in philosophischer Überlegung klar zu machen' ['This idea is also the *leit-motif* of Wagner's *Parsifal*, and it is given symbolic expression in the restoration of the missing spear and the healing of the wound. What Wagner tried to say in artistic and symbolic terms Schiller laboured to make clear in his philosophical reflections' (P. B.)].

How could the wound be healed? Schiller's answer in the Sixth Letter runs as follows: 'so muß es bei uns stehen, diese Totalität in unsrer Natur, welche die Kunst zerstört hat, durch eine höhere Kunst wiederherzustellen' ['it must be open to us to restore by means of a higher Art the totality of our nature which the arts themselves have destroyed'] (AE: p. 42), but Jung regards this as a nostalgic desire to turn the clock back to a particular historical period – classical Greece: 'Er sagt es nicht laut, aber implicite deutlich genug, daß sein Problem um ein *Wiederaufnehmen antiker Lebensart und Lebensauffassung* geht' ['Although it is nowhere openly stated, the implication is clear enough that his problem revolved round the resumption of a classical mode of life and view of the world'] (GW6 § 111/CW6 § 114). As Jung points out, the inhabitant of Schiller's classical Greece is very close to Rousseau's *l'homme naturel*: 'Gemeinsam [...] ist beiden die *retrospektive Orientierung* und, damit unzertrennlich verknüpft, die Idealisierung und Überschätzung der Vergangenheit' ['This retrospective orientation is common to both and is inextricably bound up with an idealization and overvaluation of the past'] (GW6 § 121/CW6 § 122).

As far as Schiller was concerned, the problem of modern Man could be reduced to the antinomy between the 'Stofftrieb' (the impulse to absorb the world's sensuous reality) and the 'Formtrieb' (the impulse to order our experience). The way out of the conflict between these two impulses was, Schiller then contended, to be found in a third, mediating drive whose existence he first denied (AE: p. 84) but then defined in the Fourteenth Letter as the 'Spieltrieb', the ludic drive. For Schiller: 'der Mensch spielt nur, wo er in voller Bedeutung des Worts Mensch ist, und *er ist nur da ganz Mensch, wo er spielt*' ['Man only plays when he is in the fullest sense of the word a human being, and *he is only fully a human being when he plays*'] (AE: p. 106). Jung, however, much to the later irritation of Herbert Marcuse,[14] saw great danger in this psychological strategy of simple de-repression, which, in his view, ran the risk of unleashing precisely the barbaric side of Man:

> Es war Schiller eigentlich bewußt, was es heißen könnte, den "Spieltrieb" gewissermaßen an oberste Stelle zu setzen. Wie wir bereits sahen, bewirkt die Aufhebung der Verdrängung ein Aufeinanderprallen der Gegensätze und eine Ausgleichung, die notwendig mit einer Heruntersetzung der bisher höchsten Werte endet [...] wer bürgt dafür, daß der Mensch dieser Art, wenn er zu spielen anfängt, sich gerade die ästhetische Stimmung und den Genuß echter Schönheit zum Ziel setzen wird? (GW6 § 164/CW6 § 172).

> [Schiller was in fact aware what it might mean to give first place to the play instinct. As we have seen, the release of repression brings a collision between the opposites, causing an equalization that necessarily results in a lowering of the value that was highest ... who can guarantee that such a man, when he begins to play, will make the aesthetic temper and the enjoyment of genuine beauty his goal?]

The basis of Jung's objection is that the release of the ludic drive gives no guarantee of moral order, with the result that the double bind of civilization – the barbarism of the over-Apollonian Man or the barbarism of the Dionysian Man – persists. Jung's way out of this aporia is found only via his examination of Nietzsche's critique of Schiller, which is then, in turn, subjected to a critique on its own terms.

Goethe, Wagner, Nietzsche

Psychologische Typen contains several further examples of ways in which Jung had used Nietzsche in his earlier texts. First, Jung refers to Nietzsche in passing without attaching much significance to the quotation cited; e.g. in Chapter Six, Jung throws in a reference to Nietzsche's poem 'Der Wanderer' ['The Wanderer'] from '"Scherz, List und Rache"' ['"Joke, Cunning, and Revenge"'], the twenty-seventh of 63 poems which preface *Die fröhliche Wissenschaft* [*The Gay Science*]: 'Verloren bist Du, glaubst Du – an Gefahr' ['you are lost if you believe in danger'] (GW6 § 543/CW6 § 475; cf. N2: p. 23). Second, Jung takes Nietzsche's

[14] See Herbert Marcuse, *Eros and Civilization* (London, 1956), p. 192: 'The idealistic and aesthetic sublimations which prevail in Schiller's work do not vitiate its radical implications. Jung recognized these implications and was duly frightened by them'.

poetry as an example of a psychological state by referring to the poem 'Der du mit dem Flammenspeere' ['You who with a flaming spear'] which opens the fourth book of *Die fröhliche Wissenschaft* (GW6 § 394/CW6 § 353; cf. N2: p. 161). And third, Jung uses Nietzsche himself both as an example of a psychological type (the introverted intuitive) (GW6 § 225, 704, 845/CW6 § 242, 632, 699), and as an example of the phenomenon of enantiodromia, comparing him to St. Paul, Raymond Lull and Swedenborg (GW6 § 798/CW6 § 709). However, Nietzsche plays a much more central rôle in *Psychologische Typen* as an aspect of Jung's critique of Schiller.

> Das von Schiller empfundene und teilweise bearbeitete Problem wurde in neuer und eigenartiger Weise von Nietzsche wieder aufgenommen in seiner von 1871 datierten Schrift *Die Geburt der Tragödie.* Dieses Jugendwerk bezieht sich zwar nicht auf Schiller, sondern weit mehr auf Schopenhauer und Goethe. Es hat aber, wenigstens anscheinend, mit Schiller den Ästhetismus und den Griechenglauben, mit Schopenhauer den Pessimismus und das Erlösungsmotiv, und unendlich vieles mit Goethes *Faust* gemeinsam (GW6 § 206/CW6 § 223).

> [The problem discerned and partially worked out by Schiller was taken up again in a new and original way by Nietzsche in his book *The Birth of Tragedy* (1871). This early work is more nearly related to Schopenhauer and Goethe than to Schiller. But it at least appears to share Schiller's aestheticism {or 'aesthetism' – see below} and Hellenism, while having pessimism and the motif of deliverance in common with Schopenhauer and unlimited points of contact with Goethe's *Faust.*]

This paragraph suggests that Nietzsche forms part of what Jung perceives to be a continuous tradition within German literature and philosophy, a kind of psychological *philosophia perennis* which runs through German Romanticism and German Idealism.

As a psychological type (see below), Nietzsche is contrasted with Wagner in the chapter on 'Das Typenproblem in der Dichtkunst' ['The Type Problem in Poetry']. Here, Jung emphasizes the importance which these two men had for the contemporary generation and, by implication, for him too: 'Es ist nun meines Erachtens für unsere Psychologie bezeichnend, daß an der Schwelle der neuesten Zeit zwei Geister stehen, denen ein gewaltiger Einfluß auf die Herzen und die Köpfe der jungen Generation vorbehalten war: Wagner und Nietzsche' ['It is, I think, characteristic of our psychology that we find on the threshold of the new age two figures who were destined to exert an immense influence on the hearts and minds of the younger generation: Wagner and Nietzsche'] (GW6 § 453/CW6 § 408). As in *Die Psychologie der unbewußten Prozesse*, Nietzsche is associated with the Will to Power, whilst Wagner is placed under the sign of Eros (GW7 § 43). However, unlike in his previous writings, Jung makes no attempt to associate these psychological stances with Freud (Eros) and Adler (Power). Instead, Jung identifies love as the main theme in Wagner's operas from *Tristan*, through the *Ring* cycle, to *Parsifal*: Wagner is said to be 'ein Anwalt der Liebe, der in seiner Musik die ganze Skala der Gefühlstöne von Tristan hinunter bis zur blutschänderischen Leidenschaft und von Tristan hinauf bis zur höchsten Geistigkeit des Grals erklingen läßt' ['the prophet of love, whose music runs the whole gamut of feeling from Tristan down to incestuous passion, then up again from Tristan to the sublime spirituality of Parsifal'] (GW6 § 453/CW6 § 408). Moreover, Jung compares Wagner's choice of the Grail legend for *Parsifal* with Goethe's use of Dante's *Divina Commedia* for the end of *Faust II*, and draws attention to the aristocratic quality of Nietzsche's imagery: 'Wagner knüpft in seinem höchsten und letzten Ausdruck an die Gralslegende an, wie Goethe an Dante, Nietzsche aber an das Bild einer Herrenkaste und einer Herrenmoral, wie das Mittelalter es mehr als einmal verwirklichte in vielen heroischen und ritterlichen Gestalten mit blondem Haar' ['Wagner, in his last and loftiest utterance, harked back to the Grail legend, as Goethe did to Dante, but Nietzsche seized on the idea of a master caste and a master morality, an idea embodied in many a fair-haired hero and knight of the Middle Ages'] (GW6 § 453/CW6 § 408).

Thus, according to Jung, at one level the common link between Goethe, Wagner and Nietzsche is their interest in the Middle Ages. But at another level, Jung suspects that an even deeper common problem underlies the medieval motifs: 'Daß drei der größten deutschen Geister in ihren größten Werken an die frühmittelalterliche Psychologie anknüpfen, scheint mir zu beweisen, daß eben jene Zeit eine Frage übrig gelassen hat, die seither nicht beantwortet worden ist' ['The fact that three of the greatest minds of Germany should fasten on early medieval psychology in their most important works is proof, it seems to me, that that age has left behind a question which still remains to be answered'] (GW6 § 454/CW6 § 409). This problem is the reconciliation of the opposites, one such pair being Apollo and Dionysos.

Dionysos and Apollo

Dionysos and Apollo are one in a series of pairs of opposites mentioned by Jung refers in *Psychologische Typen*, the Introduction to which opens with an extract from *Zur Geschichte der Religion und Philosophie in Deutschland* [*On the History of Religion and Philosophy in Germany*] (1834–35) where Heine contrasts Plato with Aristotle:

> Plato and Aristoteles! Das sind nicht bloß die zwei Systeme, sondern auch die Typen zweier verschiedener Menschennaturen, die sich seit undenklicher Zeit, unter allen Kostümen, mehr oder weniger feindselig entgegenstehen (GW6: p. 1/CW6: p. 2).[15]

[15] Heinrich Heine, *Sämtliche Werke*, 10 vols (Leipzig, 1910–1920), VII, p. 253. See also Goethe's discussion of Plato and Aristoteles as 'getrennte Repräsentanten herrlicher, nicht leicht zu ver-

[Plato and Aristotle! These are not merely two systems, they are types of two distinct human natures, which from time immemorial, under every sort of disguise, stand more or less inimically opposed.]

Jung takes over this opposition between Plato and Aristotle, turning it into that between the introverted and the extraverted. By so doing, he not only makes a distinction between two types but also renders this polarity internal to the personality (GW6/CW6 § 1–4). According to Jung, the existence of these two distinct types is 'eine eigentlich schon längst bekannte Tatsache' ['a fact that has long been known'], and he cites as an example Goethe's notion of the all-embracing principles of 'systole' and 'diastole'.[16]

A similar typological division underlies in Jung's view the Gnostic distinction between thinking, feeling and sensation; the contrast between the two Patristic thinkers Tertullian and Origen; the medieval controversy between Nominalism and Realism; Schiller's poetic antinomy of the 'naive' and the 'sentimental'; and Nietzsche's artistic antinomy between Apollo and Dionysos. Nietzsche himself pointed out that his concept of Apollo corresponded to Schiller's concept of the 'naive' (GT/BT § 3; N1: p. 31); and Jung follows Nietzsche in further comparing these two 'Triebe' to the two corresponding psychological (as Jung would say) and physiological (as Nietzsche put it) states of dreaming ('Traum') and frenzy or intoxication ('Rausch'). Although, as he had done in 'Zur Frage der psychologischen Typen' (1913), Jung accepts Nietzsche's equation of Apollo with the *principium individuationis*, his understanding of the Dionysian has undergone a radical change since his essay of 1913. In the 1913 essay, Jung had defined the Dionysian as the investment of libido in as many objects in the world outside the self as possible, or 'das [...] von sich selber befreite Streben nach der Vielheit der Objekte' ['plunging into the multiplicity of the objective world'] (GW6 § 946/CW6 § 876). By 1921, however, Jung had seen that the destruction of the *principium individuationis* did not mean just the destruction of the individual but, more importantly, the abolition of individuation. On Jung's revised account of the Nietzschean Dionysian, the multiplicity of single individ-

---

einender Eigenschaften' *Materialien zur Geschichte der Farbenlehre* (1805–10) (Johann Wolfgang von Goethe, *Werke* (*Hamburger Ausgabe*), 14 vols (Munich, 1981), XIV, p. 54).

[16] The terms 'systole' and 'diastole' occur at various points in Goethe's scientific writings, and are explicated most fully in *Zur Farbenlehre* (*On the Theory of Colours*], in the section entitled 'Nachbarliche Verhältnisse' ['Neighbouring Relations'] (Goethe, *Werke*, XIII, p. 488). F. W. J. Schelling accepted a similar set of principles (*Die Weltalter*, in: *Werke*, 6 vols (Munich, 1958–1959), IV, p. 696. Jung in effect turns what for Goethe and Schelling are cosmological principles into psychological mechanisms whereby the individual subject deals with the objectivity (of the outside world) and his own subjectivity. The process of diastole is associated with the extraverted standpoint, which subordinates the subject to the object (GW6/CW6 § 5). According to Jung, these two mechanisms, or attitudes, oppose each other (GW6/CW6 § 6). It is Goethe's terminology employed in this sense that Jung uses to discuss the psychological attributes of Apollo and Dionysos.

uals gives way to the unity of the individuated one and, *mutatis mutandis*, the individual merges with the collective and hence with the unity of Being:

> Das Dionysische [...] ist das Grauen über die Zerbrechung des Individuationsprinzips, und zugleich die "wonnevolle Verzückung" darüber, daß es zerbrochen ist. Das Dionysische ist daher vergleichbar dem Rausch, der das Individuelle auflöst in die kollektiven Triebe und Inhalte, eine Zersprengung des abgeschlossenen Ich durch die Welt (GW6 § 210/CW6 § 227).

> [The Dionysian is the horror of the annihilation of the *principium individuationis* and at the same time "rapturous delight" in its destruction. It is therefore comparable to intoxication, which dissolves the individual into his collective instincts and components – an explosion of the isolated Ego through the world.]

With Dionysos, there are no individuals, no individuality: 'Seine Individualität muß daher gänzlich aufgehoben sein' ['His individuality is entirely obliterated']. In Goethean terms, Nietzsche's Dionysos is the diastole, i.e. 'eine Entfaltung [...] ein Herauf- und Hinausströmenlassen [...] eine die Welt umfassende Bewegung' ['an unfolding, a streaming outwards and upwards, a motion embracing the whole world'] as represented in Schiller's 'An die Freude' ['Ode to Joy'] (1786) (GW6 § 216/CW6 § 234; cf. GT/BT 1; N1: pp. 24–25).

However, Jung is no longer content, as he had been in 1913, to associate the Dionysian with the attitude of extraversion and, concomitantly, Apollo with introversion. Instead, he sets up a new pair of categories in order to accommodate the Apollo/Dionysos antinomy. Now he claims that it is necessary to go beyond the distinction between introversion and extraversion and consider a new set which is beyond 'logisch-rationale Bearbeitung' ['logical and rational elaboration'], the so-called 'aesthetic' functions (in the Kantian sense of the first Critique).[17] Jung claims to have derived these psychological functions directly from Nietzsche, whereas it is, in fact, more likely that the comparative approach to Schiller and Nietzsche forced Jung to consider a set of functions beyond his original pair (Thinking and Feeling):

> Nietzsches Begriffe führen uns somit zu den Prinzipien eines dritten und vierten psychologischen Typus, die man als ästhetische Typen gegenüber den rationalen Typen (Denk- und Fühltypen) bezeichnen könnte (GW6 § 223/CW6 § 240).

> [Nietzsche's concepts thus lead us to the principles of a third and fourth psychological type, which one might call "aesthetic" types as opposed to rational types (Thinking and Feeling).]

---

[17] The so-called aesthetic (or 'irrational') functions – 'Intuition' or Intuition (inner perception, i.e. the perception of ideas) and 'Empfindung' or Sensation ('entwickelt die Sinne, den Instinkt, die Affizierbarkeit' ['develops the senses, instinct, affectivity']) are of fundamental importance for Jung's theory of psychological types and the operation of the consciousness, and he suggests even that the rational functions of Thinking and Feeling may be derived from the irrational ones of Intuition and Sensation (GW6 § 222/CW6 § 239).

The two categories of 'Intuition' (Intuition) and 'Empfindung' (Sensation) are associated with Apollo and Dionysos respectively: 'Das Apollinische ist eine innere Wahrnehmung, eine Intuition der Ideenwelt' ['The Apollonian mode is an inner perception, and intuition of the world of ideas'], and 'Das dionysische Gefühl hat den durchaus archaischen Charakter der affektiven Empfindung' ['Dionysian feeling has the thoroughly archaic character of affective sensation'] (GW6 § 221/CW6 § 238).

However, Jung's discussion of Nietzsche's 'fundamentales Gegensatzpaar' ['fundamental pair of opposites'] also continues and sustains his critique of 'Barbarei' in 'Über das Unbewußte' (1918), and questions further the possibility of reconciling the opposites in a religious symbol. Jung believed that Nietzsche had gone beyond Schiller and discovered a richer set of antinomies, subsumed under the opposition of Dionysos and Apollo, which nonetheless gave Jung hope that the opposites could indeed be reconciled.

Nietzsche contra Schiller

Jung is sceptical of Nietzsche's claim that, under the influence of the Dionysian, 'Der Mensch [...] ist Kunstwerk geworden' ['Man has become a work of art'] (GT/BT § 1; N1: p. 25), for he sees the Dionysian instead as a symptom of 'Barbarei'. Indeed, Jung argues that Dionysian Man is only a work of art to the extent that he represents an expression of the instinctive libido: 'die schöpferische Dynamis, die Libido in der Form des Triebes, bemächtigt sich des Individuums als eines Objektes und gebraucht es als Werkzeug oder Ausdruck' ['the creative dynamism, libido in instinctive form, takes possession of the individual as though he were an object and uses him as a tool or as an expression of itself'] (GW6 § 210/CW6 § 227). Rather than being a work of art, Man in the Dionysian state is said to be a piece of raw Nature, and beyond even animal inhibitions, 'nichts als bloße Natur, nicht einmal ein auf sich und sein Wesen beschränktes Tier, ungezügelt, in jeder Hinsicht ein Wildbach' ['nothing but sheer Nature, unbridled, a raging torrent, not even an animal that is restricted to itself and the laws of its being'].[18] Clearly, Jung has overlooked Nietzsche's distinction between the Dionysian Greek and the Dionysian barbarian.

---

18 It is Dionysian Man's loss of individuality and over-identification with the Unconscious which qualifies him, in Jung's eyes, as a barbarian (GW6 § 212/CW6 § 230). Jung regards Man in the Dionysian state as a barbarian, because he is one-sided – and with such a massive over-balance on the side of the Unconscious that the individual Unconscious disappears along with the conscious mind, and the individual is entirely swallowed up in the Collective Unconscious (what Jung later called 'Inflation').

Nevertheless, Jung believed that Nietzsche represents an advance on Schiller, claiming that his antinomies, whilst superficially similar to Schiller's, contain elements not to be found in Schiller. Jung contrasts Nietzsche's allegedly deeper vision with Schiller's by means of images of light and colour:

> Und in dem Maße, als Schiller sozusagen zaghaft und mit blassen Farben anfängt, Licht und Schatten zu malen, und den in der eigenen Seele empfundenen Gegensatz als "naiv" gegen "sentimentalisch" zu begreifen, unter Ausschließung alles Hintergründigen und Abgründigen menschlicher Natur, greift Nietzsches Auffassung tiefer und spannt einen Gegensatz, der in seinem einen Teile der strahlenden Schönheit der Schillerschen Vision in nichts nachsteht, aber in seinem andern Teile unendlich dunklere Töne findet, welche zwar die Kraft des Lichtes erhöhen, aber eine noch tiefere Nacht hinter sich ahnen lassen (GW6 § 206/CW6 § 224).
>
> [Whereas Schiller begins to paint light and shade almost timorously and in pallid hues, apprehending the conflict in his own psyche as "naïve" versus "sentimental", and excluding everything that belongs to the background and abysmal depths of human nature, Nietzsche has a profounder grasp and spans an opposition which, in one aspect, is no whit inferior to the dazzling beauty of Schiller's vision, whilst its other aspect reveals infinitely darker tones that certainly enhance the effect of the light but also allow still blacker depths to be divined.]

In Jung's view, Schiller's formula in the *Elfter Brief* of the *Ästhetische Erziehung* – 'um [...] nicht bloß Welt zu sein, muß [der Mensch] der Materie Form erteilen; [...] er soll alles Innre veräußern und alles Äußere formen' ['in order not to be mere world, Man must impart form to matter ... he is to externalize all that is within him, and give form to all that is outside him'] (AE: p. 76) – is too simple. Although this formula is, in Jung's view, typical of the introverted thinking type, its danger is said to lie in the way that the introvert seeks to subordinate the object to his own subjectivity, and, in so doing, de-represses without control, unleashing the inferior functions of the psyche – i.e. the irrational, Dionysian instincts:[19]

> Es müßte denn sein, daß Schiller es darauf ankommen ließe, dem Objekt Gewalt anzutun. Damit würde er aber der archaischen minderwertigen Funktion ein uneingeschränktes Existenzrecht einräumen, was bekanntlich Nietzsche dann – wenigstens theoretisch – getan hat (GW6 § 142/CW6 § 149).
>
> [One is forced to conclude that Schiller would let it go so far that violence was done to the object. But that would be to concede to the archaic, inferior function an unlimited right to existence, which as we know Nietzsche, at least in theory, actually did.]

In other words, according to Jung, Schiller deliberately chose to ignore Dionysos – hence his happy view of ancient Greece – and was in this respect typical of

[19] As far as Jung is concerned, such naïveté on the part of Schiller shows that he was not part of that age whose beginning was marked by Nietzsche – the age of 'psychological criticism' (GW6 § 142/CW6 § 149).

his times (GW6 § 142/CW6 § 149). Although Jung quotes the sixteenth strophe of Schiller's ballad 'Der Taucher' ['The Diver'] (1798), which speaks of the horror of the underworld – 'Da unten aber ist's fürchterlich' ['In that nether world is terror'] – Schiller does not, in Jung's view, deal seriously with 'die Abgründe menschlichen Wesens' ['the abysses of human nature'] (GW6 § 143/CW6 § 150). Conversely, according to Jung, it was Nietzsche's achievement to uncover, in *Die Geburt der Tragödie*, the Dionysian impulses behind the serenity of the Apollonian surface of Greek culture and to remind modern Man of the reality of Dionysos in his *Zarathustra*. In an allusion to the passage where Nietzsche speaks of Dionysian magic tearing the Apollonian veil of Maya into shreds (GT/BT § 1; N1: p. 25), Jung says that Nietzsche pointed the way to a great struggle, or psychological crisis, which lay ahead:

> Als Schiller lebte, war eben die Zeit der Auseinandersetzung mit dem Unteren noch nicht gekommen. Nietzsche stand dieser Zeit auch innerlich viel näher, daher es ihm gewiß war, daß wir uns einer Epoche größten Kampfes nähern. Darum zerriß er auch, als der einzige wahre Schüler Schopenhauers, den Schleier der Naivität und holte in seinem *Zarathustra* einiges davon herauf, was zum lebendigsten Inhalt einer kommenden Zeit bestimmt war (GW6 § 144/CW6 § 151).
>
> [When Schiller lived, the time for dealing with that nether world had not yet come. Nietzsche at heart was much nearer to it; to him it was certain that we were approaching an epoch of unprecedented struggle. He it was, the only true pupil of Schopenhauer, who tore through the veil of naïveté and in his *Zarathustra* conjured up from the nether region ideas that were destined to be the most vital content of the coming age.]

In this way, Jung draws attention to the substantial difference between Schiller and Nietzsche in their attitude towards classical Greece: Nietzsche is said to look into precisely those Dionysian depths which Schiller preferred to ignore. As far as Jung is concerned, the conceptual inadequacy of Schiller's notion in the Twenty-Second Letter of the mediatory state of 'die ästhetische Stimmung des Gemüts' ['the aesthetic mode of the psyche'] (AE: p. 150) becomes evident from the absence of ugliness in his understanding of beauty: 'Damit ist auch die vermittelnde Funktion ihrer Wirksamkeit beraubt, indem sie als Schönheit ohne Weiteres die Häßlichkeit, um die es sich doch auch handelt, zu kurz kommen läßt' ['From the very outset, therefore, the edge is taken off the mediating function, since beauty immediately prevails over ugliness, whereas it is equally a question of ugliness'] (GW6 § 190/CW6 § 206). According to Jung, there is a fundamental deficiency in Schiller's view of human nature:

> Schiller definiert als "ästhetische Beschaffenheit" einer Sache, daß sie sich "auf das Ganze unserer verschiedenen Kräfte" bezieht. Dementsprechend kann also "schön" und "ästhetisch" nicht zusammenfallen, denn unsere verschiedenen Kräfte sind auch ästhetisch verschieden, schön und häßlich, und nur ein unverbesserlicher Idealist

> und Optimist könnte das "Ganze" der menschlichen Natur als schlechthin "schön" erdichten (GW6 § 190/CW6 § 206).
>
> [Schiller defines a thing's "aesthetic character" as its relation to "the totality of our various functions". Consequently "beauty" cannot coincide with "aesthetic", since our various faculties also vary aesthetically: some are beautiful, some are ugly, and only an incorrigible idealist and optimist could conceive the "totality" of human nature as simply "beautiful".]

Jung expresses this conceptual deficiency in the image of a repeated encounter between Schiller and a figure whom he never recognizes: the Ugliest Man:

> [Schiller] ist hier an einer Grenze seiner selbst und seiner Zeit angelangt, die ihm zu überschreiten unmöglich war, denn überall stieß er an den unsichtbaren "häßlichsten Menschen", dessen Entdeckung unserem Zeitalter und Nietzsche vorbehalten war (GW6 § 192/CW6 § 208).
>
> [Here Schiller comes up against a barrier common both to himself and his time which it was impossible for him to overstep, for everywhere he encountered the invisible "Ugliest Man", whose discovery was reserved for our age and Nietzsche.]

The figure of the Ugliest Man is to be found in Part Four of *Also sprach Zarathustra* (Z IV § 7; N2: pp. 501–05), where 'der häßlichste Mensch' declares himself to be God's murderer. However, within Jung's psychology, the figure acquires a rather different significance. The Ugliest Man had made his first appearance in Jung's writings in the essay on 'Die transzendente Funktion' ['The Transcendent Function'] (1916), where Jung had described him as a personification of the compensatory counteraction of the unconscious regulatory influence within the psychic economy of Zarathustra (GW8 § 162). By 1921, however, the figure of the Ugliest Man had achieved greater prominence in Jung's thought and is mentioned four times in *Psychologische Typen*. In this work he is described as the Shadow-side of the personality ('bei Nietzsche entdeckt Zarathustra seinen Schatten im "häßlichsten Menschen"' ['In Nietzsche, Zarathustra discovered his Shadow in the "Ugliest Man"']) (GW6 § 810/CW6 § 706); as the suppressed dark side of Man ('In *Zarathustra* finden wir gegen den Schluß ein treffliches Beispiel für die Unterdrückung der Antithese in der Gestalt des "häßlichsten Menschen"' ['In *Zarathustra* we find an excellent example of the suppressed antithesis in the "Ugliest Man"']) (GW6 § 908/CW6 § 829); and as an expression of the Collective Unconscious of the time, inasmuch as in *Zarathustra* we are meant to see 'die ikonoklastische Empörung gegen die herkömmliche Moralatmosphäre und das Aufnehmen des "häßlichsten" Menschen' ['iconoclastic revolt against the conventional moral atmosphere, and acceptance of the "Ugliest Man"'] (GW6 § 318/CW6 § 322). However much we may try to suppress it, Jung argues, the Shadow or the Ugliest Man is an essential component of our psychological make-up, and hence Schiller's understanding of the human personality is bound to founder if this aspect of psychic constitution is ignored.

Critique of Aesthetism

Jung points out that Nietzsche can also fall prey to the same 'aesthetic fallacy' as Schiller – in other words, that he inclines to ascribe to art alone the mediating rôle between consciousness and the Unconscious: 'Nietzsche [hat] gleich wie Schiller die ausgesprochene Tendenz [...], der Kunst die vermittelnde und erlösende Rolle zuzuschreiben' ['Nietzsche, like Schiller, had a pronounced tendency to credit art with a mediating and redeeming rôle'] (GW6 § 212/CW6 § 230). This tendency to ascribe priority to the artistic is termed by Jung 'Ästhetismus' or, in English, 'Aesthetism' (and this peculiar usage is retained here to avoid confusion with the notion of 'Aestheticism'). But equally, says Jung, there are also times when, so to speak, Nietzsche himself draws aside this aesthetic covering (an image reminiscent of the Dionysian destruction of the Apollonian veil of Maya): 'aus gewissen Gründen hat Nietzsche diese Hervorhebung [i.e. the barbaric nature of the Dionysian] unterlassen und dadurch einen trügerischen ästhetischen Schleier über das Problem ausgebreitet, den er allerdings an einigen Stellen unwillkürlich lüften muß' ['for some reason Nietzsche has ommitted to make it clear, and has consequently shed a deceptive aesthetic veil over the problem, which at times he himself has involuntarily to draw aside'] (GW6 § 210/CW6 § 227).

However barbaric the manifestations of Dionysos may have been, Jung detects in the opposition between Apollo and Dionysos an essentially religious conflict:

> [Nietzsche] vergißt [...] völlig, daß es sich beim Kampfe Apollos gegen Dionysos und ihrer schließlichen Versöhnung für die Griechen niemals um ein ästhetisches Problem handelte, sondern um eine *religiöse Frage* (GW6 § 213/CW6 § 231).

> [Nietzsche quite forgets that in the struggle between Apollo and Dionysos and in their ultimate reconciliation the problem for the Greeks was never an aesthetic one, but was essentially religious.]

To show the religious origin of the Apollo/Dionysos conflict, Jung traces the Dionysian satyr-feasts back to the totem-feast and points out that 'der Dionysoskult hatte vielerorts einen mystisch-spekulativen Einschlag und hat jedenfalls einen sehr starken, religiös erregenden Einfluß ausgeübt' ['the cult of Dionysos had in many places a mystical and speculative streak, and in any case exercised a very strong religious influence'] (GW6 § 213/CW6 § 231). Jung also draws an analogy between the origin of Western theatre in the medieval passion-play and the development of Greek tragedy from religious (Dionysian) ceremonies. According to Jung, the modern perspective of Aesthetism overlooks the religious dimension to these problems and so fails to tackle the real issues at stake:

> Der Ästhetismus ist eine moderne Brille, durch welche die psychologischen Geheimnisse des Dionysoskultes in einem Lichte gesehen werden, in dem sie die Alten

> sicherlich nie sahen und erlebten. Wie bei Schiller, so wird auch bei Nietzsche der religiöse Gesichtspunkt völlig übersehen und durch die ästhetische Betrachtung ersetzt [...] So ist mit der Auffassung, der Kampf zwischen Apollo und Dionysos sei eine Frage gegensätzlicher Kunsttriebe, das Problem in einer historisch und materiell ungerechtfertigten Weise auf das ästhetische Gebiet verschoben, womit es einer Teilbetrachtung unterworfen wird, die niemals imstande ist, seinem wirklichen Inhalt gerecht zu werden (GW6 § 213/CW6 § 231).
>
> [Aesthetism is a modern bias that shows the psychological mysteries of the Dionysos cult in a light in which they were assuredly never seen or experienced by the ancients. With Nietzsche as with Schiller the religious viewpoint is entirely overlooked and is replaced by the aesthetic ... In adopting the view that the antagonism between Apollo and Dionysos is purely a question of conflicting artistic impulses, the problem is shifted to the aesthetic sphere in a way that is both historically and materially unjustified, and is subjected to a partial approach which can never do justice to its real content.]

Jung casts further doubt on Nietzsche's aesthetic leanings when he identifies what he perceives to be the weak spot in Nietzsche's claims regarding the basis of classical Greek civilization in general and the origin of tragedy in particular. In *Die Geburt der Tragödie*, Nietzsche had suggested that Greek culture managed to combine the Apollonian with the Dionysian, or, as Jung paraphrases it: 'Nietzsche betrachtet die Versöhnung des delphischen Apollo mit Dionysos als ein Symbol der Versöhnung dieser Gegensätze in der Brust des zivilisierten Griechen' ['Nietzsche considers the reconciliation of the Delphic Apollo with Dionysos a symbol of the reconciliation of these opposites in the breast of the civilized Greek'] (GW6 § 211/CW6 § 228). However, according to Jung, Nietzsche's own 'kompensatorische Formel' ['compensatory formula'] deconstructs such an easy reconciliation, and shows this union to be merely the object of desire:

> Er vergißt aber dabei seine eigene kompensatorische Formel, nach der die Götter des Olymp ihr Licht der Dunkelheit der griechischen Seele verdanken: danach wäre die Versöhnung Apollos mit Dionysos ein schöner Schein [cf. GT/BT 1; N1: p. 22], ein Desideratum, hervorgerufen durch die Not, die die zivilisierte Hälfte des Griechen empfand im Kampfe mit seiner barbarischen Seite, die sich eben gerade im dionysischen Zustand hemmungslos Bahn brach (GW6 § 211/CW6 § 228).
>
> [But here he forgets his own compensatory formula, according to which the gods of Olympus owe their splendour to the darkness of the Greek psyche. By this token, the reconciliation of Apollo and Dionysos would be a beautiful illusion, a desideratum evoked by the need of the civilized Greek in his struggle with his own barbarian side, the very element that broke out unchecked in the Dionysian rout.]

Here Jung is suggesting that Apollo never quite got the better of Dionysos; or, in other words, that the reconciliation of Apollo with Dionysos represents a goal to be striven for, and not an actual state of past or present culture. For Jung, Nietzsche's vision of a reconciliation between Apollo and Dionysos is itself just another Apollonian illusion – 'ein schöner Schein' – and, according to Jung, this can be explained by another rule of compensation, i.e. 'zwischen der Religion eines Volkes und seinem wirklichen Lebenswandel besteht immer eine kompensatorische Beziehung' ['between the religion of a people and its actual mode of life there is always a compensatory relation'] (GW6 § 211/CW6 § 229). With this move, it becomes clear that Jung's agenda is, unlike Nietzsche's, not an aesthetic, but a religious one.

Jung's Yearning for Religious Reconciliation

As we have seen, Jung has doubts not only about Nietzsche's account of the Greek resolution between Apollo and Dionysos, but also about Schiller's resolution of the conflict between the 'Formtrieb' and the 'Stofftrieb' by means of the 'Spieltrieb', which Jung equates with his own notion of 'Phantasietätigkeit' ['phantasy activity'] (GW6 § 163/CW6 § 171). Nevertheless, it is this latter concept which, in Jung's view, points the way towards a solution. For, according to Jung, the reconciliation of the opposites is essentially an non-rational or irrational matter – 'Gegensätze lassen sich nur praktisch als Kompromiß vereinigen oder *irrational*, indem zwischen ihnen ein *Novum* entsteht, das von beiden verschieden ist und doch geeignet, ihre Energien gleichermaßen aufzunehmen als ein Ausdruck beider und keines von beiden' ['In practice, opposites can be united only in the form of a compromise, or *irrationally*, some new thing arising between them which, although different from both, yet has the power to take up their energies in equal measure as an expression of both and of neither'] – and such a reconciliation cannot be thought, but must, rather, be lived: 'Dergleichen ist nicht zu ersinnen, sondern kann allein durch das Leben geschaffen werden' ['Such an expression cannot be contrived by reason, it can only be created through living'] (GW6 § 161/CW6 § 169).

In Jung's terminology, the mediating agent in this process is directly analogous to the 'Spieltrieb', namely the 'lebende Gestalt', defined by Jung as a symbol:[20]

> Der Gegenstand der vermittelnden Funktion heißt nun nach Schiller "lebende Gestalt", welche eben das Symbol wäre, in welchem sich die Gegensätze einigen, "ein Begriff, der allen ästhetischen Beschaffenheiten der Erscheinungen, und mit einem Worte dem, was man in weitester Bedeutung Schönheit nennt, zur Bezeichnung dient" [...] Dieser Inhalt müßte, nach Schillers Definition, ein *symbolischer* sein, denn nur dem Symbol kann die vermittelnde Stellung zwischen den Gegensätzen zukommen (GW6 § 162, 169/CW6 § 171, 178 [cf. Fifteenth Letter, AE: p. 100]).

[20] Jung had first discussed the nature of the symbol in *Wandlungen und Symbole der Libido* (WSL: pp. 230–31/PU § 353–54).

[The object of the mediating function, therefore, according to Schiller, is "living form", for this would be precisely a symbol in which the opposites are united; "a concept serving to designate all the aesthetic qualities of phenomena and, in a word, what in the widest sense of the term we call beauty" ... According to Schiller, this must be a *symbolic* content, since the mediating position, between the opposites can be reached only by the symbol.]

Jung also calls the 'Phantasietätigkeit' which unites the opposites in the symbol the 'Transcendent Function' (GW6 § 174/CW6 § 184). In *Die Psychologie der unbewußten Prozesse* (1917), Jung had already suggested that Goethe's *Faust II* can be read as an example of the work of the Transcendent Function (GW7 § 121), but it was only in *Psychologische Typen* of 1921 that he went into details. And here he argues that *Faust II* shows how the symbol exists to direct the flow of the libido and promote the cause of life:

Goethe läßt dem Dreifuß der Mütter die Götterbilder von Paris und Helena entschweben, das verjüngte Elternpaar einerseits, anderseits aber das Symbol eines inneren Vereinigungsprozesses, den Faust leidenschaftlich für sich begehrt als höchste innere Versöhnung, wie die nachfolgende Szene deutlich zeigt, und wie aus dem weiteren Verlauf des zweiten Teiles ebenso deutlich hervorgeht. Wie wir gerade an dem Beispiele des Faust sehen können, bedeutet die Vision des Symbols einen Hinweis auf den weiteren Weg des Lebens, eine Anlockung der Libido zu einem annoch fernen Ziel, das aber von da an unauslöschlich in ihm wirkt, so daß sein Leben, entfacht wie eine Flamme, stetig weiter schreitet zu fernen Zielen (GW6 § 188/CW6 § 202).

[Goethe makes the divine images of Paris and Helen float up from the tripod of the Mothers – on the one hand the rejuvenated pair, on the other the symbol of a process of inner union, which is precisely what Faust passionately craves for himself as the supreme inner atonement. This is clearly shown in the ensuing scene as also from the further course of the drama. As we can see from the example of Faust, the vision of the symbol is a pointer to the onward course of life, beckoning the libido towards a still distant goal – but a goal that henceforth will burn unquenchably within him, so that his life, kindled as by a flame, moves steadily towards the far-off beacon.]

Jung also adds at this juncture that Goethe's scene reveals the essentially religious nature of the symbol, and indeed, at this stage, Jung equates religion with the acceptance of the reality of the symbol:

Durch das Tatsächlichnehmen des Symbols kam die Menschheit zu ihren Göttern, d. h. zur *Tatsächlichkeit des Gedankens*, welcher den Menschen zum Herrn der Erde gemacht hat. Die Andacht ist, wie sie auch Schiller richtig auffaßt, eine regressive Bewegung der Libido zum Ursprünglichen, ein Hinuntertauchen in die Quelle des Anfangs. Daraus erhebt sich als ein Bild der beginnenden Progressivbewegung das *Symbol*, welches eine zusammenfassende Resultante aller unbewußten Faktoren darstellt, die "lebende Gestalt", wie Schiller das Symbol nennt, ein Gottesbild, wie die Geschichte es zeigt [...]. Das ist auch die spezifisch lebenfördernde Bedeutung des Symbols. Das ist auch der Wert und Sinn des religiösen Symbols (GW6 § 188/CW6 § 202).

> [Humanity came to its gods by accepting the reality of the symbol, that is, it came to the *reality of thought*, which had made Man lord of the earth. Devotion, as Schiller correctly conceived it, is a regressive movement of the libido towards the primordial, a diving down into the source of the first beginnings. Out of this there arises, as an image of the incipient progressive movement, the symbol, which is a condensation of all the operative unconscious factors – "living form", as Schiller says, and a God-image, as history proves ... This is the specific life-promoting significance of the symbol, and such, too, is the meaning and value of religious symbols.]

Clearly, this has immense implications for both Jungian aesthetics (see Chapter 6) and Jung's attitude towards religion (see Chapter 13). But it is also closely related to our study of Jung and Nietzsche, because it indicates the framework within which Jung read not just Goethe, Wagner and Schopenhauer, but also Nietzsche's *Zarathustra*. As Jung himself put it in *Psychologische Typen*: 'Die Problemlösung im *Faust*, im *Parzival* von Wagner, bei Schopenhauer, selbst bei Nietzsches *Zarathustra* ist *religiös*' ['The solution of the problem in *Faust*, in Wagner's *Parsifal*, in Schopenhauer, and even in Nietzsche's *Zarathustra*, is *religious*'] (GW6 § 320/CW6 § 324).

On Jung's account, religion, so understood, stands in an essentially compensatory relation to reality (see above) – 'sonst hätte ja die Religion gar keinen praktischen Sinn' ['otherwise religion would have no practical significance at all'] (GW6 § 211/CW6 § 229). Thus, the reconciliation between Apollo and Dionysos proposed by Nietzsche as existing in substance as the basis of Greek civilization bears witness, then as later, to the desire for such a reconciliation:

> Darum dürfen wir auch gerade aus dem Symbol der delphischen Versöhnung auf einen besonders heftigen Zwiespalt im griechischen Wesen schließen. Daraus würde sich die Erlösungssehnsucht erklären, welche den Mysterien jene gewaltige Bedeutung für das griechische Volksleben gab, und welche von den früheren Griechenschwärmern gänzlich übersehen wurde. Man begnügte sich damit, an den Griechen naiv alles zu sehen, was einem selber fehlte (GW6 § 211/CW6 § 229).

> [We may therefore infer from the symbol of the Delphic reconciliation an especially violent split in the Greek character. This would also explain the longing for deliverance which gave the mysteries their immense significance for the social life of Greece, and which was completely overlooked by the early admirers of the Greek world. They were content with naïvely attributing to the Greeks everything they themselves lacked.]

Jung seeks to resist the aesthetist pull of Nietzsche's text and, by focusing his attention on a key phrase describing the reconciliation between the Apollonian and the Dionysian, bring out the psychological insight contained there which Nietzsche had intuited ('Trotz der ästhetischen Auffassung aber hat Nietzsche doch damals schon die Ahnung der wirklichen Lösung des Problems gehabt' ['But even at that time, in spite of his Aesthetism, Nietzche had an inkling of the real solution'] (GW6 § 215/CW6 § 233)).

Accordingly, when Nietzsche writes that the antagonism between Apollo and Dionysos was bridged 'durch einen metaphysischen Akt des hellenischen "Willens"' ['by a metaphysical miracle of the Hellenic "Will"'] (GT/BT § 1; N1: p. 21), Jung interprets the Will here in what he calls the Schopenhauerian sense. As for the word 'metaphysisch', Jung takes it to mean, in psychological terms, 'unconscious'.[21] Thus, as far as Jung is concerned, the reconciliation of Dionysos and Apollo is a *psychological act*, an intuition of the union of the opposites and the mediation between consciousness and the Unconscious which lies at the heart of his psychological system:

> Wenn wir also "metaphysisch" in Nietzsches Formel durch "unbewußt" ersetzen, dann wäre der gesuchte Schlüssel dieses Problems ein unbewußter "Wunderakt". Ein "Wunder" ist irrational, also ist der Akt ein unbewußtes irrationales Geschehen, eine Bildung aus sich ohne Dazutun der Vernunft und der zielbewußten Absicht; es ergibt sich, es wird, als ein Wachstumsphänomen der schaffenden Natur und nicht aus Erklügelung menschlichen Witzes, eine Geburt aus sehnsüchtiger Erwartung, aus Glauben und Hoffnung (GW6 § 215/CW6 § 233).

> [If, then, we replace "metaphysical" in Nietzsche's formula by "unconscious", the desired key to the problem would be an unconscious "miracle". A "miracle" is irrational, hence the act is an unconscious irrational happening, shaping itself without the assistance of reason and conscious purpose. It happens of itself, it just grows, like a phenomenon of creative Nature, and not from any clever trick of human wit; it is the fruit of yearning expectation, of faith and hope.]

Given that the vocabulary of that final phrase clearly shifts the discussion into the religious sphere, we have moved from the birth of tragedy *à la* Nietzsche to a spiritual rebirth *à la* Jung. For Jung, *Die Geburt der Tragödie* points to the creative power of the Unconscious, and for him, this alone can provide the solution to the double-edged problem of 'Barbarei' – i.e. the repression or release of Dionysos.

Psycho-biographical postscript: Nietzsche as a psychological type

Jung also draws attention to Nietzsche's personal psycho-biography in *Psychologische Typen*, making a distinction between the Nietzsche of 1871–1872 who wrote the main text of *Die Geburt der Tragödie* and the Nietzsche of 1883–1886 who wrote *Zarathustra* and the 'Versuch einer Selbstkritik' ['Attempt at Self-Criticism']. Where the earlier Nietzsche is the aesthetic Nietzsche (GW6 § 214/

[21] This equation between the metaphysical and the psychological is made again in Jung's 1938 Eranos lecture 'Die psychologischen Aspekte des Mutterarchetypus' ['Psychological Aspects of the Mother Archetype'] (GW9 (i) § 148–198) where Kant's transcendental logic is understood as a set of psychic functions (GW9(i) § 150).

CW6 § 232), the later is the Dionysian – 'der *Eingeweihte und Jünger seines Gottes*' ['the *initiate and disciple of his god*'], as Nietzsche himself puts it (GT/BT § Versuch/Attempt 5; N1: p. 12). Jung claims that although Nietzsche tries to protect himself from Dionysos by means of his 'Aesthetism' (the treatment of the Dionysian as an aesthetic, rather than religious, or psychological problem), he was already so close to Dionysos that his later experience of the Dionysian should come as no surprise:

> Die besondere Tiefe, mit der Nietzsche das Problem trotz ästhetischer Selbstsicherung erfaßt hat, war der Wirklichkeit schon so nahe, daß sein späteres dionysisches Erleben beinahe als unvermeidliche Konsequenz erscheint (GW6 § 215/CW6 § 233).
>
> [Nietzsche's profound grasp of the problem in spite of his aesthetic defences was already so close to the real thing that his later Dionysian experience seems almost an inevitable consequence.]

Again, Jung relentlessly links the Dionysos of Nietzsche's texts with his own version of Nietzsche's biography. As Jung succinctly phrases it: 'Dionysos scheint sich aber an Nietzsche gerächt zu haben' ['Dionysos, however, seems to have taken his revenge on Nietzsche'] (GW6 § 214/CW6 § 232).

Jung attributes the discovery of the fundamental Jungian categories of 'Empfindung' and 'Intuition' to his reading of Nietzsche, and claims that, by bringing into relief the psychological functions of Intuition and Sensation, Nietzsche gives us an important clue to his own psychological make-up:

> Die Tatsache, daß Nietzsche gerade die psychologische Funktion der Intuition einerseits und die der Empfindung und des Triebes anderseits hervorhebt, dürfte kennzeichnend sein für seine eigene, persönliche Psychologie (GW6 § 225/CW6 § 242).
>
> [The fact that it is just the psychological functions of intuition on the one hand and sensation and instinct on the other that Nietzsche emphasizes must be characteristic of his own personal psychology.]

Jung deduces that Nietzsche himself was an introverted intuitive type ('Er ist wohl dem intuitiven Typus zuzurechnen mit Neigung nach der introvierten Seite' ['He must surely be reckoned an intuitive with leanings towards introversion']) and finds evidence of this in the broad range of Nietzsche's *oeuvre*, from *Die Geburt der Tragödie* and *Also sprach Zarathustra* (characteristic of his intuitive character) to his aphoristic writings (expressive of his introverted intellectual side). Given Nietzsche's psychological make-up, Jung argues that it is not surprising that his very first work (i.e. *Die Geburt der Tragödie*) should have foregrounded his own psychological attitudes, by means of which Nietzsche was able to gain insight into the Dionysian aspects of his own Unconscious:

> Es ist bei dieser Sachlage nicht erstaunlich, daß er in seinem Anfangswerk die Tatsachen seiner persönlichen Psychologie unbewußt in den Vordergrund stellt [...] Mittels dieser Einstellung gewann er auch die tiefe Einsicht in die dionysischen Qua-

litäten seines Unbewußten, deren rohe Form allerdings, soweit wir wissen, erst beim Ausbruch seiner Krankheit die Oberfläche des Bewußtseins erreichte, nachdem sie sich in mannigfachen erotischen Andeutungen in seinen Schriften schon vorher verraten hatte (GW6 § 225/CW6 § 242).

[Under these circumstances it is not surprising that in his early work he unwittingly sets the facts of his personal psychology in the foreground ... By means of this attitude he also gained deep insight into the Dionysian qualities of his Unconscious, the crude forms of which, so far as we know, reached the surface of his consciousness only after the outbreak of his illness, although they had previously revealed their presence in various erotic allusions.]

Later on, Jung argues that his 'Intuitionismus' enabled Nietzsche to transcend purely intellectual philosophy and enter the realm of artistic creation.[22] As a result, he calls *Zarathustra* the best example of the 'intuitive Methode' of which Schopenhauer and Hegel are said to be precursors (though in what way is not made clear).[23] Furthermore, Jung claims that the creativity which Nietzsche proposes opens the way for a new kind of thinking.[24]

Jung's achievement by this stage vis-à-vis his relation to Nietzsche was apparently to have overcome his earlier fear that he might somehow share his fate and to be able to put Nietzsche firmly in a distinct psychological category. Or could he? Jung causes some confusion when, at a later point, he refers to Nietzsche as an example of an introverted thinking type (GW6 § 704/CW6 § 632). In view of the fact that Jung classified himself as an introverted thinker,[25] this comment later on in the book might represent an unconscious slip on Jung's part and suggests that there was still some residual identification with Nietzsche. Nevertheless, Jung had clearly moved away from Nietzsche on the conscious level and he in effect deconstructs *Die Geburt der Tragödie* in order to show that whilst it represented an advance on Schiller, its insights were, in his view, still not as superior as his own.

---

22 'In unvergleichlich höherem Maße hat Nietzsche die intuitive Quelle genützt und sich damit vom bloßen Intellekt in seiner philosophischen Anschauungsbildung befreit' ['Nietzsche made far greater use of the intuitive source and in so doing he freed himself from the bonds of the intellect in shaping his philosophical ideas'] (GW6 § 605/CW6 § 540).

23 'Wenn man also von einer "intuitiven Methode" überhaupt sprechen darf, so hat meines Erachtens Nietzsches *Zarathustra* dafür das beste Exempel gegeben und zugleich die Möglichkeit nicht-intellektualistischer und doch philosophischer Problemerfassung schlagend dargetan. Als Vorläufer des Nietzscheschen Intuitionismus erscheinen mir Schopenhauer und Hegel' ['If one may speak of an intuitive method at all, *Zarathustra* is in my view the best example of it, and at the same time a vivid illustration of how the problem can be grasped in a non-intellectual and yet philosophical way. As forerunners of Nietzsche's intuitive approach I would mention Schopenhauer and Hegel'] (GW6 § 605/CW6 § 540).

24 See GW6 § 606/CW6 § 541.

25 See Anthony Storr, *Jung* (London, 1973), pp. 78–79; and *C. G Jung Speaking*, edited by William McGuire and R. F. C. Hull (Princeton, 1977), p. 256.

Conclusion

Psychologische Typen thus represents an advance in the complexity and sophistication of Jung's use of Nietzsche in seven major respects. First, Jung's concern with the negative effects of de-repressed unconscious forces is linked to Nietzsche through his identification of one kind of barbarian with the Dionysian Man – and the question of how society is to cope with Dionysos is a problem which was to remain with Jung right up to his Seminar on *Zarathustra*. At the same time, we have seen how this identification of barbarism with Dionysos rests upon a misreading of *Die Geburt der Tragödie*. Second, and by contrast, Jung has corrected his earlier misreading of the Dionysian as a desire for multiplicity and now correctly interprets Dionysos as a drive towards a more fundamental unity. Third, the thesis of *Psychologische Typen* can be read as a psychological account of Nietzsche's perspectivism. As Jung wrote in his autobiography, 'Das Typenbuch brachte die Erkenntnis, daß jedes Urteil eines Menschen durch seinen Typus beschränkt und jede Betrachungsweise eine relative ist' ['The book on types yielded the insight that every judgment made by an individual is conditioned by his personality type and that every point of view is necessarily relative'] (ETG: p. 211/MDR: p. 234). However, as Jung went on to explain, this relativism (or perspectivism) raised the issue of combining these views, which are seen not so much to contradict as to complement: 'Damit erhob sich die Frage nach der Einheit, die diese Vielheit kompensiert' ['This raised the question of the unity which must compensate this diversity']. On this level, then, Jung's psychological writings after 1921 are motivated by a Dionysian drive to create, amongst diversity, a higher unity or totality. Fourth, whilst Jung uses Nietzsche to deconstruct Schiller's *Ästhetische Erziehung*, he regards *Die Geburt der Tragödie* as a text whose own 'compensatory formula' (no Apollo without Dionysos) deconstructs Nietzsche's vision (allegedly itself Apollonian) of a union between Apollo and Dionysos. Fifth, Jung derives two key psychological categories – 'Intuition' and 'Empfindung' – from his reading of Nietzsche's *Die Geburt der Tragödie*, and his system of typology is now mature enough to assign Nietzsche a position within it (probably as an introverted intuitive type). In fact, in 1923, Jung was able to refer jokingly to Dionysos to make a point about typological complementarism.[26] Sixth, Jung's concept of Dionysos has become more complex: whilst a simple release of Dionysian energy is shown to be retrograde (a point with which Nietzsche would have agreed), the integration of unconscious energy into conscious life is shown to be the psychological aspect of the problem of opposites which Jung is keen, even desperate, to solve. This changing view of

[26] See the lecture 'Psychologische Typen' delivered in 1923 and published in 1925 (GW6 § 972, 974/CW6 § 908, 910).

Dionysos may be connected with Jung's experience of the First World War, which Jung anticipated in a series of visions (ETG: pp. 178–80/MDR: pp. 199–201). What for the individual is a psychic conflict is for society a war or revolution – and just as traumatic.[27] The same compensatory functions apply to society as to the individual. Seventh, and finally, there are signs that Jung can conceive of an answer to this social problem only in religious, i.e. psychological terms. In this respect, the Jungian concept of the symbol is of immense importance, especially for his theory of art, which, as the next chapter shows, is also deeply indebted to the aesthetics of *Die Geburt der Tragödie*.

[27] See Jung's letter of 10 October 1933 to Albert Oppenheimer (B1: p. 170/L1: pp. 128–29).

Chapter 6

Jung's Reception of Nietzsche in his Writings 1922–1934: I

Nietzsche and the Art of Dionysos

In this chapter I shall examine Jung's use of Nietzsche in his psychological theory of art as this developed in his theoretical writings of the Twenties and Thirties.[1] Not only is this use of Nietzsche relevant to Jung's concern with the soteriological rôle of art discussed in the previous chapter, but it also shows Jung's positive understanding of the Dionysian as the essentially creative force behind art. The view of art which Jung developed is particularly appropriate for understanding Modernist literature and painting, and Jung commented in particular on works by Joyce and Picasso. Moreover, in the essays and lectures of this period, Jung laid the foundations for his analysis of Nietzsche in his Seminar (1934–1939) on *Also sprach Zarathustra.*

'Über die Beziehungen der analytischen Psychologie zum dichterischen Kunstwerk' (1922)

In *Psychologische Typen*, Jung had assigned prime importance to the psychic act of 'Phantasie' ['phantasy'], which he described as a 'Lebensprozeß' ['vital process'] and a 'beständiger Schöpferakt' ['continually creative act'] (GW6 § 73/CW6 § 78). According to Jung, 'Phantasie' is the power which both integrates the psychological functions of the individual and constitutes the psychological reality of the world: 'Die Phantasie ist ebenso sehr Gefühl wie Gedanke, sie ist ebenso intuitiv wie empfindend [...] Die Psyche erschafft täglich die Wirklichkeit' ['Phantasy is just as much feeling as thinking; as much intuition as sensation ... The psyche creates reality every day'] (GW6 § 73/CW6 § 78). Moreover, Jung explains that 'Phantasie' works both causally as a symptom of a physiological condition, and purposively ('finally'), as the symbol of future psychological development (GW6 § 867/CW6 § 720). According to Jung's view of art, the importance of the artist resides in his ability to develop such symbols in his works,

---

[1] For an overview of various theories of creativity, see Anthony Storr, *The Dynamics of Creation* (London, 1972), and *Creativity*, edited by P. E. Vernon (Harmondsworth, 1972).

and inasmuch as he creates the symbols which point the way to the future, the artist is said not merely to represent, but also to educate:

> Weil die aktive Phantasie das hauptsächliche Merkmal der künstlerischen Geistestätigkeit ist, so ist der Künstler nicht bloß ein *Darsteller*, sondern ein *Schöpfer* und darum ein *Erzieher*, denn seine Werke haben den Wert von Symbolen, welche künftige Entwicklungslinien vorzeichnen (GW6 § 867/CW6 § 720).
>
> [Because active phantasy is the chief mark of the artistic mentality, the artist is not just a *reproducer* of appearances but a *creator* and *educator*, for his works have the value symbols that adumbrate lines of future development.]

The concept of the symbol-creating function of 'Phantasie' provides the connecting link from *Psychologische Typen*; Jung's views on the rôle of the artist are set out in his 1922 lecture 'Über die Beziehungen der Analytischen Psychologie zum dichterischen Kunstwerk' ['On the Relation of Analytical Psychology to Poetry'] (GW15 § 97–132) and his 1930 contribution to Emil Ermatinger's *Philosophie der Literaturwissenschaft* entitled 'Psychologie und Dichtung' ['Psychology and Literature'] (GW15 § 133–62) (also originally delivered as a lecture, probably in 1930). In both essays, Nietzsche's fundamental opposition between Apollo and Dionysos lies behind all the distinctions in Jung's artistic typology, even though those have been ostensibly borrowed from Schiller's *Über naive und sentimentalische Dichtung* [*On Naïve and Sentimental Poetry*]. The difference between Jung's two statements of his psychological approach to art lies in their emphases. Where, in the 1922 lecture, Jung had stressed the psychological and indeed sociological importance he ascribed to art and had cited Nietzsche's work as an example of these functions, the 1930 essay is more clearly informed by Nietzsche's conception of Dionysos in *Die Geburt der Tragödie* [*The Birth of Tragedy*].

Although Jung opens his 1922 lecture by strictly delimiting the scope of his enquiry, by the time of its conclusion, he is using mythology to link art with the project of Analytical Psychology. In this lecture, Jung argues that artistic practice is a legitimate object of investigation for the psychologist because art is a psychological activity. But at the same time, he also states that psychological study can deal only with the actual process of artistic creation, and not with what he calls 'das eigentliche Wesen der Kunst' ['the essential nature of art']. 'Die Frage, was Kunst in sich selbst sei' ['The question of what art is in itself'] can be answered only by aesthetics, not psychology (GW15 § 97). Despite that caveat, Jung does in effect develop an aesthetics of Analytical Psychology in this lecture, and his caveat should not blind us to his underlying intent.

In the 1922 lecture, Jung rejects theoretical reflections which seek to reduce art to the product of a more elementary psychological state. Thus, for Jung, Freudian readings of works of art which understand them in terms of the secondary process are unsatisfactory because of their reductionism. At the time of

Jung's writing, Freud had already produced a substantial corpus of art criticism,[2] whose fundamental tenet is summarized in the concluding paragraph of the twenty-third Introductory Lecture on Psychoanalysis: 'Der Künstler ist im Ansatze auch ein Introvertierter, der es nicht weit zur Neurose hat' ['The artist is basically an introvert, who is not far from being neurotic'].[3] Jung explicitly opposes this view, criticizing its implicit equation between a work of art and a neurosis and the explanation of the former in terms of the latter, so that, as he put it, 'der Dichter wird zum klinischen Fall, eventuell zum soundsovielten Beispiel der psychopathia sexualis' ['the poet becomes a clinical case and, very likely, yet another addition to the curiosa of *psychopathia sexualis*'] (GW15 § 100–01). Furthermore, Jung also rejected Freud's 'reduktive Methode' because, in his view, it closes its eyes to what is unique in a work of art and because it both misunderstands and misrepresents art.

As an example of where Freud's reductive method might go wrong, Jung takes Nietzsche. In a rare passage actually acknowledging the physiological reasons for Nietzsche's mental breakdown,[4] Jung writes:

> Eine solche Sektion ist gewiß sehr interessant und vielleicht von ebensoviel wissenschaftlichem Wert wie die Obduktion des Gehirns von Nietzsche, die nur zeigen könnte, an welcher atypischen Form von Paralyse er gestorben ist. Hat dies aber mit "Zarathustra" etwas zu tun? Was immer seine Hinter- und Untergründe gewesen sein mögen, ist er nicht ganz und *eine* Welt, jenseits von menschlicher, allzumenschlicher Unzulänglichkeit, jenseits von Migräne und Gehirnzellenatrophie? (GW15 § 103).

> [The results are no doubt very interesting and may perhaps have the same kind of scientific value as, for instance, a post-mortem exhibition of the brain of Nietzsche, which might conceivably show us the particular atypical form of paralysis from which he died. But what would this have to do with *Zarathustra*? Whatever its subterranean background may have been, is it not a whole world in itself, beyond the human, all-too-human imperfections, beyond the world of migraine and cerebral atrophy?]

Jung does not mention the most likely cause of Nietzsche's collapse and paralysis – tertiary syphilis – but then he is not interested in such physiological details. Rather, his argument rests on his claim that the world of *Also sprach Zarathustra* is a poetic universe *sui generis* which cannot be understood merely by examining its physiological, biological or medical origins. For Jung, the poet's vision cuts off

---

2 This includes: 'Der Wahn und die Träume in W. Jensens "Gradiva"' ['Delusions and Dreams in Jensen's *Gradiva*'] (1907), 'Der Dichter und das Phantasieren' ['Creative Writers and Day-Dreaming'] (1908), 'Eine Kindheitserinnerung des Leonardo da Vinci' ['Leonardo da Vinci and a Memory of his Childhood'] (1910) and 'Der Moses des Michelangelo' ['The Moses of Michelangelo'] (1914).

3 Sigmund Freud, *Gesammelte Werke*, 18 vols (Frankfurt am Main, 1968–1978), XI, p. 390. See also Richard Wollheim, 'Freud and the Understanding of Art', in *On Art and the Mind* (London, 1973), pp. 202–19).

4 For a detailed medical discussion of Nietzsche's mental illness, see Pia Daniela Volz, *Nietzsche im Labyrinth seiner Krankheit: Eine medizinisch-biographische Untersuchung* (Würzburg, 1990).

the work of art from the material world and makes of it a coherent intellectual/ imaginative whole which deserves to be understood on its own terms.

Behind this approach lies Jung's distinction between the causal and the final points of view as explained in his essay 'Über die Energetik der Seele' ['On Psychic Energy'] (begun 1912 but not published until 1928) (GW8 § 1–5). There Jung had written: 'Was der kausalen Betrachtung *Tatsache* ist, ist der finalen *Symbol*' ['What to the causal view is *fact* to the final view is *symbol*'], adding 'und umgekehrt' ['and vice versa'] (GW8 § 45). And in *Psychologische Typen*, he had explained the symbol in terms of its relation to the Transcendent Function which was said to mediate between consciousness and the Unconscious.[5] In 'Über die Beziehung der analytischen Psychologie zum dichterischen Kunstwerk', Jung repeats these previous distinctions between his understanding of Freud's concept of the symbol ('*Zeichen* oder *Symptome* von Hintergrundsvorgängen' ['*signs* or *symptoms* of the subliminal processes']) and the symbol as he, Jung, now understands it ('ein Ausdruck [...] für eine noch nicht anders oder besser zu fassende Anschauung' ['an expression of an intuitive idea that cannot yet be formulated in any other or better way']) (GW15 § 105).

By 1922, then, Jung's more generous understanding of the symbol is linked to the intuitive and hence to the inexpressible, and this has two important consequences for Jung's understanding of art. First, the work of art is said to express concerns beyond the purely individual and personal ones of its creator: 'Die Einstellung aufs Persönliche, welche durch die Frage nach der persönlichen Kausalität veranlaßt wird, ist dem Kunstwerk gegenüber insofern ganz inadäquat, als das Kunstwerk kein Mensch, sondern überpersönlich ist' ['The personal orientation which is needed when dealing with personal aetiology is quite inadequate when dealing with a work of art, since a work of art is not a human being, but is something supra-personal' (P. B.)] (GW15 § 107). Second, the extent to which the universal prevails over the particular becomes the criterion according to which, on Jung's account, any work of art should be judged: 'Das echte Kunstwerk hat sogar seinen besonderen Sinn darin, daß es ihm gelingt, sich aus den Beengungen und Sackgassen des Persönlichen zu befreien und all die Vergänglichkeit und Kurzatmigkeit des Nur-Persönlichen weit unter sich zu lassen' ['The special significance of a true work of art resides in the fact that it has

[5] 'Der von Thesis und Antithesis bearbeitete Rohstoff, der in seinem Formungsprozeß die Gegensätze vereinigt, ist das lebendige Symbol. In seinem für eine lange Epoche nicht aufzulösenden Rohstoff liegt sein Ahnungsreiches, und in der Gestalt, die sein Rohstoff durch die Einwirkung der Gegensätze empfängt, liegt seine Wirkung auf alle psychischen Funktionen' ['The raw material shaped by thesis and antithesis, and in the shaping of which the opposites are united, is the living symbol. Its profundity of meaning is inherent in the raw material itself, the very stuff of the psyche, transcending time and dissolution; and its configuration by the opposites ensures its sovereign power over all the psychic functions'] (GW6 § 908/CW6 § 828).

escaped from the limitations and impasses of the personal and left behind the transitoriness and panting feebleness of what is merely personal' (P. B.)] (ibid.).

This conception of art is underpinned by an imagery of organic growth,[6] and Jung relentlessly repeats these organic metaphors: the plant in the soil (GW15 § 107–08), the tree in the earth (GW15 § 115), and the child in the womb (GW15 § 122). Each of these three key images serves to reinforce the central point: the autonomy of the process of artistic creation, which, in Jung's view, guarantees the significance of the work of art:

> Das Kunstwerk aber ist nicht nur Hergekommenes und Abgeleitetes, sondern es ist eine schöpferische Neugestaltung eben jener Bedingungen, aus denen eine kausalistische Psychologie es gültig ableiten wollte. Die Pflanze ist nicht ein bloßes Produkt des Bodens, sondern ein in sich selbst ruhender, lebendiger, schöpferischer Prozeß, dessen Wesenheit mit der Beschaffenheit des Bodens nichts zu tun hat. So will das Kunstwerk betrachtet sein als eine alle Vorbedingungen frei ergreifende, schöpferische Gestaltung. Sein Sinn und seine ihm eigentümliche Art ruhen in ihm selber und nicht in seinen äußeren Vorbedingungen (GW15 § 108).

> [But a work of art is not transmitted or derived – it is a creative reorganization of those very conditions to which a causalistic psychology must always reduce it. The plant is not a mere product of the soil; it is a living, self-contained process which in essence has nothing to do with the character of the soil. In the same way, the meaning and individual quality of a work of art inhere within it and not in its extrinsic determinants.]

In order to understand a work of art, then, it is necessary to detach oneself from the creative process which has produced it and look at it from an external position. This gives access to its 'meaning': 'Zum Erkennen [...] müssen wir [...] den schöpferischen Prozeß [...] von außen ansehen, und dann erst wird er zum Bilde, welches Bedeutungen ausspricht. Dann dürfen wir nicht nur, sondern müssen sogar von Sinn sprechen' ['For the purpose of cognitive understanding we must look at the creative process from the outside; only then does it become an image that expresses significance. At the point we may not only but are indeed bound to speak of meaning' (P. B.)] (GW15 § 121).

This insistence on the autonomy of art is the key tenet of Jung's aesthetics, and he tries to use that concept to set up a typology of art and artists based on Schiller's categories of the 'Sentimental' and the 'Naive' (the Introverted and the Extraverted as Jung had reinterpreted them in *Psychologische Typen* one year previously). Behind this typology, however, there lies a distinctly Nietzschean perspective on art. The first category, that of the 'Naive'/Introverted, includes those works of art where the material is governed by the conscious intention of

---

6 This trope is a distinctly Romantic one. For example, Coleridge's terminology for the imagination is couched in biological terms (see M. H. Abrams, *The Mirror and the Lamp* (Oxford, 1953), p. 124).

the artist, and, in Jung's view, a good example of this category would be provided by Schiller. However, since, in *Die Geburt der Tragödie*, Nietzsche identifies the 'Naive' with Apollo (GT/BT § 3; N1: p. 31), the emphasis on form and control proper to Schiller's 'Naive' and Jung's Introverted is thoroughly Apollonian in the Nietzschean sense. The second category, that of the 'Sentimental'/Extraverted, includes those works of art where the reverse is the case, and Jung places Nietzsche's *Zarathustra* and Goethe's *Faust II* in this category:

> Diese Werke drängen sich dem Autor förmlich auf, seine Hand ist gewissermaßen ergriffen, seine Feder schreibt Dinge, deren sein Geist mit Erstaunen gewahr wird. Das Werk bringt seine Form mit [...] Er kann nur gehorchen und dem anscheinend fremden Impulse folgen, fühlend, daß sein Werk größer ist als er und darum eine Gewalt über ihn hat, der er nichts vorschreiben kann. Er ist nicht identisch mit dem Prozeß der schöpferischen Gestaltung; er ist sich dessen bewußt, daß er unterhalb seines Werkes steht oder zum mindesten daneben, gleichsam wie eine zweite Person, die in den Bannkreis eines fremden Willens geraten ist (GW15 § 110).

> [These works positively force themselves upon the author; his hand is as it were seized, his pen writes things that his mind contemplates with amazement. The work brings with it its own form ... He can only obey the apparently alien impulse within him and follow where it leads, sensing that his work is greater than himself, and wields a power which is not his and which he cannot command. Here the artist is not identical with the process of creation; he is aware that he is subordinate to his work or stands outside it, as though he were a second person, who had fallen within the magic circle of an alien will. (P. B.)]

This description of the control of the individual artist by the unconscious powers of creation harks back to 'Kryptomnesie' and Jung's account there, drawing on Nietsche's *Ecce Homo*, of the composition of *Zarathustra*. Furthermore, in 'Wotan' Jung describes the effect of the Wotan/Dionysos archetype as a state of 'Ergriffenheit' ['being gripped by emotion'], a Dionysian emphasis which would become more pronounced, albeit more elusively articulated, in his writings of the Thirties. Of *Faust II*,[7] Jung says: 'Hier zeichnet sich der Stoff durch hartnäckige Widersetzlichkeit aus' ['here the material is distinguished by its persistent obstreperousness' (P. B.)] (GW15 § 111), and in his view, *Zarathustra* is an even better example of this extraverted attitude. To support his notion that in extraverted works the subject-matter escapes the artist's control, Jung refers to Nietzsche's poem 'Sils-Maria' from the 'Lieder des Prinzen Vogelfrei' ['Songs

---

[7] Jung is of course wrong to include Goethe's *Faust II* (or even *Faust I*!) in the class of those works 'die mehr oder weniger als Ganzes und Fertiges dem Autor in die Feder fließen' ['which flow, more or less complete and finished, into the pen of the author'] (GW15 § 110). A section of Act III of *Faust II* was written in 1800, and most of the rest of *Faust II* was done between 1826 and 1832. As for Nietzsche's *Zarathustra*, its composition was spread over the years 1883 to 1885. Jung's comments make most sense when interpreted as referring not literally to the chronological genesis of a work of art but rather to the effect of unified poetic conception proper to the work as a whole.

of Prince Vogelfrei'] in *Die fröhliche Wissensschaft* [*The Gay Science*] (N2: p. 271), interpreting the line 'Da [...] wurde eins zu zwei' ['Then one turned into two'] in a purely biographical way – something which he would do repeatedly twelve years later in the Seminar on *Zarathustra*.

Within the above, dualistic typology, Jung allows that the work of the same artist may involve differing psychological attitudes. For example, he compares Schiller's (introverted) plays with his (extraverted) philosophical texts, and Goethe's (introverted) poetry with the (extraverted) drama *Faust II*. He also sees a similar dichotomy in Nietzsche's writings, contrasting his (introverted) aphorisms with the (extraverted) 'zusammenhängenden Strom des "Zarathustra"' ['coherent stream of *Zarathustra*' (P. B.)] (GW15 § 117). Moreover, according to Jung's dualistic scheme, a work of art comes into being either in accordance with or in total disregard of the wishes of the individual artist. In both cases, however, the same force is said to be at work, and, in line with his organic imagery, Jung links this force to Nature: 'Das ungeborene Werk in der Seele des Künstlers ist eine Naturkraft, die entweder mit tyrannischer Gewalt oder mit jener subtilen List des Naturzweckes sich durchsetzt, unbekümmert um das persönliche Wohl und Wehe des Menschen, welcher der Träger des Schöpferischen ist' ['The unborn work in the psyche of the artist is a force of Nature that achieves its end either with tyrannical might or with the subtle cunning of Nature herself, uncaring about the personal fate of the man who is the vehicle of the creative force' (P. B.)] (GW15 § 115). Just as Hegel's Universal Spirit accomplishes its world-historical purposes through 'die List der Vernunft' ['the cunning of reason'], so Jung's work of art might be said to achieve self-expression by equally duplicitous means. Indeed, Jung even goes so far as to suggest that the creative process behind a work of art is autonomous in the same way that a psychological complex is. By this stage in Jung's writings, the psychological complex shares all the characteristics of an archetype (a mode of autonomy which Jung had discussed as early as 1905 in 'Kryptomnesie'). And in his 1930 essay on literature, Jung would hint that this natural force is none other than the Dionysian.

Unfortunately, the final result of Jung's emphasis on the autonomy of the forces at work in a work of art brings about the collapse of his dualistic typological schema. For it may be, he argues, that the conscious control of the 'Naive'/ Introverted artist over his work is, ultimately, no more than apparent. As a result, even the introverted work of art may say more than the artist thinks it does: 'so hätte auch sein Werk jene symbolischen, ins Unbestimmte reichenden und das zeitgenössische Bewußtsein übersteigenden Eigenschaften' ['thus his work would have those symbolic qualities which reach into what is beyond certainty and transcend contemporary consciousness' (P. B.)] (GW15 § 118). As the Seminar on *Zarathustra* would show, Jung was all too prepared to make liberal use of the latitude of interpretation for which this notion allows. More intriguingly, Jung's concept of artistic autonomy also means that any given work of art may say more than its contemporary readers are aware of: '[diese Eigenschaften] wären nur versteckter, weil auch der Leser nicht über die durch den Zeitgeist festgelegten Grenzen des Bewußtseins des Autors hinausreichte' ['these qualities would be all the more hidden, because the reader as well could not get beyond the limits of the author's consciousness which are established by the spirit of the age' (P. B.)] (ibid.). In particular, Jung suggests that the symbolic qualities of a work of art will often be misunderstood or, because of their unconscious origins, be ignored: 'Symbol aber würde heißen: Möglichkeit und Andeutung eines noch weiteren, höheren Sinnes jenseits unseres derzeitigen Fassungsvermögens' ['A symbol would be the possibility and intimation of a wider, higher meaning beyond the limits of our present comprehension' (P. B.)] (ibid.).

Because it shows more transparently the workings of the Unconscious, Jung is more interested in art at the overtly 'Sentimental'/Extraverted end of the spectrum, i.e. in those works for which he establishes the following criteria:

> Fremdartigkeit von Bild und Form [...], Gedanken, die nur ahnungsweise zu erfassen wären, eine bedeutungsschwangere Sprache, deren Ausdrücke den Wert echter Symbole hätten, weil sie bestmöglich noch Unbekanntes ausdrücken und Brücken sind, zu einem unsichtbaren Ufer hinübergeschlagen (GW15 § 116).

> [Strangeness of image and form, thoughts which could only be comprehended intuitively, a language pregnant with meanings, whose expressions have the value of real symbols because they express in the best way possible things which are still unknown and are bridges extended towards an invisible shore. (P. B.)]

This notion of the prospective meaning of a work of art – a bridge extended towards an unseen shore, in Jung's highly Nietzschean phrase (cf. Z Vorrede/ Prologue 4; N2: p. 281) – accords well with the Jungian principle of finalism. Because they contain symbols which will be understood only in the future, artistic works can prefigure the line of future developments in social and religious psychology (as Jung had already suggested in *Psychologische Typen*). It also explains Jung's confident insistence in his Seminar that Nietzsche's *Zarathustra* was a book uniquely relevant to his contemporary society (SNZ:II:pp. 893, 1037).

The 1922 essay provides us with the background to Jung's general approach to the interpretation of texts, as exemplified in his *Zarathustra* Seminar in particular. For a work to contain symbols which point to the future, its source must, in a sense, be timeless, and the only way to understand the symbol is to look back to the past. For, in Jungian terms, the source of all great art is the Collective Unconscious and the meaning of the symbol is archetypal.[8] Indeed, in his essay

---

[8] Jung first introduced the highly contentious notion of the Collective Unconscious in 1917 in *Die Psychologie der unbewußten Prozesse* [translated as *On the Psychology of the Unconscious*] (GW7

of 1930, Jung would go on to suggest that the confrontation with the Unconscious which lies at the source of the work of art is in fact an encounter with Dionysos.

In effect, Jung's 1922 essay adds another dimension to the Freudian approach to art, while not, of course, accepting that art is merely sublimation. Instead of examining the work of art in terms of the writer's personal Unconscious, he suggests that the source of symbolic art is the Collective Unconscious: 'jener Sphäre unbewußter Mythologie, deren urtümliche Bilder Gemeingut der Menschheit sind' ['that sphere of unconscious mythology whose primordial images are the common heritage of Mankind'] (GW15 § 125). Jung quotes Gerhart Hauptmann's remark that 'Dichten heißt, hinter Worten das Urwort erklingen lassen' ['Poetry evokes out of words the resonance of the primordial word'] and suggests that this insight could be used to generate the following question as a methodological guide for interpretative purposes: 'Auf welches urtümliche Bild des kollektiven Unbewußten kann das im Kunstwerk entwickelte Bild zurückgeführt werden?' ['To which primordial image of the Collective Unconscious can the image developed in the work of art be traced back?'] (GW15 § 124).

In the 1922 lecture, Jung's definition of primordial images is characteristically woolly and confused, for he refers to them as 'mnemische Bilder' ['mnemonic images'], 'angeborene Möglichkeiten von Vorstellungen' ['inborn possibilities of representations'], 'Kategorien der Phantasietätigkeit' ['categories of phantasy activity'] and 'Ideen a priori' ['*a priori* ideas'] (with a good many 'sozusagen's and 'gewissermaßen's scattered in amongst them). Nevertheless, the important point is Jung's claim that immediate perception of these various forms of 'das urtümliche Bild oder der Archetypus' ['the primordial image or archetype'] is impossible:

> Sie erscheinen nur im gestalteten Stoff als regulative Prinzipien seiner Gestaltung, das heißt nur durch den Rückschluß aus dem vollendeten Kunstwerk vermögen wir die primitive Vorlage des urtümlichen Bildes zu rekonstruieren (GW15 § 126).
>
> [They appear only in the shaped material of art as the regulative principles that shape it; that is to say, only by inferences drawn from the finished work of art can we reconstruct the age-old original of the primordial image.]

In other words, Jung is claiming that the universal (the archetype itself) must be sought in the particular (the archetypal image in the work of art). Moreover, he is also arguing that the reader must penetrate a formal literary surface before reaching the archetypal material. However, it must also be said that, in practice, Jung's sensitivity towards surface form is particularly weak, and that he tends

§ 1–201, especially 97–120), but the concept already informed Jung's conclusions in *Wandlungen und Symbole der Libido* [*Psychology of the Unconscious*] (1911/12).

to turn quickly to the more overtly archetypal aspects of symbolic works of art, i.e. their mythological resonances. And in his 1922 lecture, the link between the archetypal and myth was made explicit.[9]

If the first step in the process of interpretation consists in the identification of mythical/archetypal figures or situations, the second is their translation into conceptual form. This demands a conceptually appropriate language, and Jung drops a heavy hint that only that provided by Analytical Psychology will be equal to the task:

> Aber auch die mythologischen Gestalten sind für sich selbst schon Elaborate schöpferischer Phantasie, und sie harren noch ihrer Übersetzung in eine begriffliche Sprache, wovon erst mühsame Anfänge existieren (GW15 § 127).
>
> [But the mythological figures are also in themselves concoctions of the creative phantasy and still await their translation into a conceptual language, of which only the arduous beginnings exist. (P. B.)]

Or, to put it another way, Jung is implying that the project of Analytical Psychology can provide a universal interpretation of art, irrespective of the period or culture of its origin:

> Die zum größten Teil noch zu schaffenden Begriffe könnten uns eine abstrakte, wissenschaftliche Erkenntnis der unbewußten Prozesse vermitteln, welche die Wurzeln der urtümlichen Bilder sind (GW15 § 127).
>
> [Those concepts, which for the most part still have to be created, could provide us with an abstract scientific knowledge of the unconscious processes which lie at the roots of the primordial images. (P. B.)]

The scope of Jung's argument has widened considerably since the cautious beginning of his lecture, and in its final paragraphs, Jung examines the sociological implications of the mythological background of certain works of art. According to Jung, it is the archetypal quality of art which explains its peculiar emotional appeal, enabling it to speak not to our individual, but to our collective memory: 'Der Moment, wo die mythologische Situation eintritt, ist immer gekennzeichnet durch eine besondere emotionale Intensität [...] Wir sind in solchen Momenten nicht mehr Einzelwesen, sondern Gattung, die Stimme der ganzen Menschheit erhebt sich in uns' ['The moment when the mythological situation occurs is always characterized by a peculiar emotional intensity ... At such moments we are no longer individual beings, but the species, the voice of all Mankind arises within us' (P. B.)] (GW15 § 128). This overcoming of the principle of individuation and concomitant sense of universal union is not only mentioned by Nietzsche in *Die Geburt der Tragödie* but also attributed to the presence of Dio-

---

[9] 'Das urtümliche Bild oder der Archetypus ist [...] in erster Linie mythologische Figur' ['The primordial image or archetype is essentially a mythological figure'] (GW15 § 127).

nysos: '[jeder] fühlt sich [...] mit seinem Nächsten nicht nur vereinigt, versöhnt, verschmolzen, sondern eins' ['each one feels himself not only united, reconciled, and fused with his neighbour, but as one with him'] (GT/BT § 1; N1: p. 25). Thus, both Jung's and Nietzsche's accounts of the origin of art attribute the highest importance to Dionysos, with Jung's argument applying those ideas which Nietzsche had formulated with regard to the origin of tragedy more generally to (extraverted) art. These Nietzschean echoes become increasingly audible in 1930.

With this transition from the individual to the collective, Jung claims that fresh possibilities for humanity arise inasmuch as the archetypal energies invoked by the work of art provide new solutions to the problems of mankind. First, it can compensate for the one-sidedness of the age in which it is produced (and here Jung is returning to his concern with the problem of barbarism which he had identified in *Psychologische Typen* as 'Einseitigkeit' ['one-sidedness']). And second, it can teach us about precisely those things which are lacking from contemporary culture (and here Jung is returning to his definition of the artist as 'Erzieher' (GW6 § 867/CW6 § 720)):

> Darin liegt die soziale Bedeutsamkeit der Kunst: sie arbeitet stets an der Erziehung des Zeitgeistes, denn sie führt jene Gestalten herauf, die dem Zeitgeist am meisten mangelten (GW15 § 130).
>
> [Therein lies the social significance of art: it is constantly at work educating the spirit of the age, conjuring up the forms in which the age is most lacking.]

Thus, in the quest for the archetypal universal in art, Jung's argument has shifted from psychological aesthetics to soteriology:

> Wer mit Urbildern spricht, spricht wie mit tausend Stimmen, er ergreift und überwältigt, zugleich erhebt er das, was er bezeichnet, aus dem Einmaligen und Vergänglichen in die Sphäre des immer Seienden [...], und dadurch löst er auch in uns alle jene hilfreichen Kräfte, die es der Menschheit je und je ermöglicht haben, sich aus aller Fährnis zu retten und auch die längste Nacht zu überdauern (GW15 § 129).
>
> [Whoever speaks in primordial images, speaks as if with a thousand voices, he grips emotionally and overpowers, while at the same time he raises up what he expresses out of the occasional and the transitory into the sphere of the eternal, and thereby he releases in us all those beneficent forces, which ever and anon have enabled Mankind to find a refuge from every peril and to outlive the longest night.(P. B.)]

There are very strong echoes here of *Die Geburt der Tragödie*, where Nietzsche claims that theatrical art enables mankind to withstand the tragic implications of Dionysian insight (GT/BT § 5; N1: p. 40). Just as, for Nietzsche, art was essentially a survival mechanism, so too, for Jung, art essentially aids the development of humanity. Ultimately, with its emphasis on the Dionysian inspiration and the saving power of art, Jung's 1922 lecture on art and psychology could be described as a reworking of Nietzsche's *Die Geburt der Tragödie.*

I have rehearsed Jung's early views on art in such detail because they are indispensable for an understanding of Jung's approach to Nietzsche in his Seminar on *Zarathustra*, with the following four ideas outlined in the 1922 lecture being of particular importance for the later work. First, Jung's insistence on the conceptual unity and autonomy of the work of art is a consequence of his rejection of the reductive reading method of Freud. Because the work of art is not simply a pathological symptom of the neurotic condition of the artist, *Zarathustra* is not just the work of a madman. But second, as Freud would also argue, the work of art nonetheless stands in a compensatory relation both to the artist and to his society. Accordingly, in his Seminar, Jung attempts to place *Zarathustra* in its historical, intellectual and cultural context since, for Jung, Nietzsche's encounter with Dionysos was of significance not just for Nietzsche himself but also for his society and, by extension, for Jung's as well. Third, Jung's notion that the work of art has a relation to the future is reflected in his understanding of *Zarathustra* as a proleptic text, anticipating key developments in the twentieth century. Although these developments were primarily of a psychological order (e.g. the reactivation of the Dionysos/Wotan archetype), they also had definite concrete, historical consequences (i.e. the rise of National Socialism). Fourth, because Jung also argues that to understand what the work of art says about the future, we must look for its references to the past, Jung could undertake a thorough investigation of the mythological motifs and archetypal symbols which are contained in *Zarathustra* on the assumption that its message is relevant not only to the present but for all time.

Much of Nietzsche's thinking in *Die Geburt der Tragödie* about Dionysos which implicitly informed Jung's thinking on art in 1922 was made more explicit in his lecture of 1930, to which we will now turn.

'Psychologie und Dichtung' (1930)

Jung's views on art in general and literature in particular as expressed in 'Psychologie und Dichtung' (1930 and revised in 1950), are in substance identical with those voiced more circumspectly in 1922. However, the emphasis on the Dionysian origin of art is much greater and much more clearly foregrounded in the later article. Furthermore, Jung's view of the Dionysian in 1930 is an inversion of the view which he had elaborated in *Psychologische Typen*. Whereas, in 1921, Jung had put Dionysos under a negative sign, now, in 1930, he puts him under a positive sign. This dual shift can be explained through Jung's increasing interest in the Dionysian as reflected in the seminars which he gave between 1925 and 1936.

As always, Jung emphasizes the ineluctability of the creative forces at work in art:

> Alle psychischen Abläufe innerhalb des Bewußtseins mögen kausal erklärbar sein; das Schöpferische aber, das in der Unabsehbarkeit des Unbewußten wurzelt, wird sich menschlicher Erkenntnis auf ewig verschließen. Es wird sich immer nur in seinem Erscheinen beschreiben, und es wird sich ahnen, aber nicht greifen lassen (GW15 § 135).
>
> [All conscious psychic processes may well be causally explicable; but the creative act, being rooted in the immensity of the Unconscious, will forever elude our attempts at understanding. It describes itself only in its manifestations; it can be guessed at, but never wholly grasped.]

Since the inner meaning of art is said to resist conceptual expression and to be comprehensible only intuitively, Jung's approach to art is necessarily limited to a psychological, i.e. archetypal, phenomenology. However, Jung does, as we shall see, go some way to analysing what he calls 'das Schöpferische', which he then identifies with Dionysos.

In his 1930 lecture, Jung abandons his categorization of art into introverted and extraverted types, and he sets up instead an opposition between 'die *psychologische*' and 'die *visionäre* Art des Schaffens' ['the *psychological* and the *visionary* mode of creation'] (GW15 § 139). As Jung's English translators pointed out, this is an unfortunate choice of terminology since the 'visionary' mode of artistic creation expresses equally 'psychological' material.[10] Jung's dualistic typology is thus set to collapse right from the beginning.

Jung still emphasizes that the collectivity, just as much as the individual, stands in need of compensation by means of the Unconscious: 'Eine Zeitepoche ist wie die Seele eines Einzelnen, sie hat ihre besondere, spezifisch beschränkte Bewußtseinslage und bedarf daher einer Kompensation' ['An epoch is like the soul of an individual, it has its own particular, specifically limited conscious outlook and therefore requires compensation' (P. B.)] (GW15 § 153). And within his aesthetic soteriology, the artist is still a key figure:

> [die Kompensation wird] durch das kollektive Unbewußte auf solche Weise geleistet [...], daß ein Dichter oder ein Seher dem Unausgesprochenen der Zeitlage Ausdruck verleiht und in Bild oder Tat das heraufführt, was das unverstandene Bedürfnis aller erwartete, sei es nun im Guten oder im Bösen, zur Heilung einer Epoche oder zu deren Zerstörung (GW15 § 153).
>
> [This compensation is effected by the Collective Unconscious when a poet or seer lends expression to the unspoken desire of his times and shows the way, by word

[10] 'The designation "psychological" is somewhat confusing in this context because, as the subsequent discussion makes clear, the "visionary" mode deals equally with "psychological" material. Moreover, "psychological" is used in still another sense in paragraphs 136–37, where the "psychological novel" is contrasted with the "non-psychological novel"' (CW15, p. 89, n.2).

> or deed, to its fulfilment – regardless whether this blind collective need results in Good or Evil, in the salvation of an epoch or its destruction.]

According to Jung, the specific problem which the Collective Unconscious strives to solve is that of one-sidedness ('Einseitigkeit'), which Jung had earlier identified as 'barbarism':

> Verirrt sich aber das Bewußtsein in eine einseitige und darum falsche Einstellung, so werden diese "Instinkte" belebt und senden ihre Bilder in die Träume der Einzelnen und die Gesichte der Künstler und Seher, um damit das seelische Gleichgewicht wieder herzustellen (GW15 § 160).
>
> [If consciousness strays however into a one-sided and therefore false attitude, these "instincts" are animated and send their images into the dreams of the individual and the visions of artists and seers, in order to restore the psychic balance. (P. B.)]

In his 1922 lecture, Jung had not made it totally clear which collectivity defined the collective psyche, even though his vocabulary suggested that he was thinking along the lines of national divisions. By 1930, however, this emphasis on the national characteristics of certain works of art had become much clearer, and to illustrate this point, Jung uses Nietzsche. According to Jung, Nietzsche's *Zarathustra*, like Goethe's *Faust*, are works of art which reflect in some profound (but unstated) way their Teutonic origin: 'Ist es denkbar, daß ein Nichtdeutscher einen "*Faust*" oder "*Also sprach Zarathustra*" geschrieben hätte?' ['Could we conceive of anyone but a German writing *Faust* or *Thus spoke Zarathustra*?'] (GW15 § 159). Jung does not explain the nature of this connection between Nietzsche, Goethe and the German mind, and substantiates his case only by means of a simple appeal to Jacob Burckhardt's comment in a letter to Albert Brenner on the archetypal nature of *Faust*.[11] In the case of both *Zarathustra* and *Faust*, the dominant archetype behind the work is said to be that of the Old Wise Man with all his attendant ambiguities: 'Beide spielen wohl auf dasselbe an, auf etwas, was in der deutschen Seele vibriert [...] die Figur eines Arztes und Lehrers einerseits und des düsteren Zauberers andererseits; der Archetypus einesteils des Weisen, Hilfreichen und Erlösenden, anderenteils des Magiers, Blenders, Verführers und Teufels' ['Both of them appeal to the same thing, striking a chord that vibrates in the German psyche ... on the one hand the figure of a healer or teacher, and on the other the dark and forbidding image of a magician; on the one hand the archetype of the Old Wise Man, the helper and redeemer, on the other hand the wizard, deceiver, tempter and devil' (P. B.)] (GW15 § 159). The significance of Zarathustra as the archetype of the Old Wise Man would be discussed at greater length in the Nietzsche Seminar.

---

[11] See 'Briefe Jakob Burckhardts an Albert Brenner. Mit Einleitung und Anmerkungen von Hans Brenner', *Basler Jahrbuch 1901* (Basle, 1901), 87–110.

In the 1930 lecture, Jung associates two further key aspects of his theory of art with Nietzsche *inter alios*: first, the authenticity of the artist's original vision, and second, the archetypal nature of the imagery used to express that vision. According to Jung, the foundation of all those works of art which concern him is to be found in what he terms the 'Urvision' or the 'Urerlebnis', a primordial experience which he describes in terms that are remarkably similar to Nietzsche's account of the Dionysian in *Die Geburt der Tragödie*, and which is, moreover, explicitly linked with Nietzsche:

> Der Wert und die Wucht liegen auf der Ungeheuerlichkeit des Erlebnisses, das fremd und kalt oder bedeutend und erhaben aus zeitlosen Tiefen auftaucht, einerseits von schillernder, dämonisch-grotesker Art, menschliche Werte und schöne Formen zersprengend, ein schreckenerregender Knäuel des ewigen Chaos oder ein "crimen laesae majestatis humanae", um mit Nietzsche zu reden, andererseits eine Offenbarung, deren Höhen und Tiefen zu ergründen menschliche Ahnung kaum genügt, oder eine Schönheit, welche zu erfassen Worte sich vergeblich mühen (GW15 § 141).
>
> [The value and the impact derive from the dreadfulness of the experience, which arises, alien and cold or meaningful and sublime from timeless depths; on the one hand enigmatic and daemonically-grotesque, exploding human values and beautiful forms, a terrifying muddle of eternal chaos or a "crimen laesae majestatis humanae", as Nietzsche puts it, and on the other hand a revelation whose heights and depths are beyond our human intuition to fathom, or a beauty, which words vainly struggle to grasp. (P. B.)]

In the case of Nietzsche, Jung gives a name to this experience: it is his 'dionysisches Erlebnis' (GW15 § 142). As so often, Jung links Nietzsche with Goethe, and here he equates the experience of the Dionysian with the Mothers Scene in *Faust II*, the timeless, spaceless world of 'Gestaltung, Umgestaltung, / Des ewigen Sinnes ewige Unterhaltung' ['Formation, transformation, / Eternal Mind's eternal recreation'] (GW15 § 141). We see here again the spatial metaphor of descent and ascent which is common to the Goethean and Nietzschean intertexts and which Jung had used in *Psychologische Typen* to describe the descent of the libido to the primordial source of all beginnings and its symbol-bearing upward journey: 'eine regressive Bewegung der Libido zum Ursprünglichen, ein Hinuntertauchen in die Quelle des Anfangs. Daraus erhebt sich als ein Bild der beginnenden Progressivbewegung das *Symbol*' ['a regressive movement of libido towards the primordial, a diving down into the source of the first beginnings. Out of this there rises, as an image of the incipient progressive movement, the symbol'] (GW6 § 188/CW6 § 202).

In 'Psychologie und Dichtung', Jung refers a second time to the 'Mothers Scene' when he characterizes the unconscious source of Being from which the creative process arises as feminine – the creative Mother: 'Die Psychologie des Schöpferischen ist eigentlich weibliche Psychologie, denn das schöpferische Werk wächst aus unbewußten Tiefen empor, recht eigentlich aus dem Reiche der Mütter' ['The psychology of creativity is in fact female psychology, for the creative work arises from unconscious depths, indeed from the realm of the Mothers'] (GW15 § 159). Similarly, in *Psychologische Typen*, Jung had drawn attention to the way in which Paris and Helen in *Faust II* float up out of the tripod of the Mothers (GW6 § 188/CW6 § 202).

This notion of the descent to the creative Mother may well have been mediated from Goethe to Jung by Nietzsche, given the following parallels. First, in *Die Geburt der Tragödie*, Nietzsche says that Dionysian art reveals Nature as the eternally creative Mother: 'In der dionysischen Kunst und in deren tragischer Symbolik redet uns dieselbe Natur mit ihrer wahren, unverstellten Stimme an: "Seid wie ich bin! Unter dem unaufhörlichen Wechsel der Erscheinungen die ewig schöpferische, ewig zum Dasein zwingende, an diesem Erscheinungswechsel sich ewig befriedigende Urmutter!"' ['In Dionysian art and in its tragic symbolism the same nature cries out to us with its true, undissembled voice: "Be as I am! Amid the ceaseless flux of phenomena I am the eternally creative primordial mother, eternally impelling to existence, eternally finding satisfaction in this change of phenomena!"'] (GT/BT § 16; N1: p. 93). Second, Jung emphasizes that the terror inspired by the primordial vision is so great that man tries to hide himself from it by means of a naive belief in universal order whose purpose is to cover over the chaos at the heart of Being: 'Der Kosmos ist sein Tagglauben, der ihn vor der Nachtangst des Chaos bewahren soll' ['The ordered cosmos he believes in by day is meant to protect him from the fear of chaos that besets him by night'] (GW15 § 148). Similarly, in *Die Geburt der Tragödie*, Nietzsche says that the Dionysian recognition of 'die Schrecken und Entsetzlichkeiten des Daseins' ['the terror and horror of existence'] (GT/BT § 3; N1: p. 30) can be coped with only thanks to Apollinian illusion. Third, Jung makes clear the unconscious nature of this primordial experience: 'Das Erlebnis menschlicher Leidenschaft steht innerhalb der Grenzen des Bewußtseins, der Gegenstand der Vision aber jenseits' ['Human passion falls within the sphere of conscious experiences, while the object of the vision lies beyond it'] (GW15 § 148). Similarly, in *Die Geburt der Tragödie*, Nietzsche speaks of the 'instinktiv unbewußte dionysische Weisheit' ['instinctive unconscious Dionysian wisdom'] (GT/BT § 16; N1: p. 92). Finally, Jung argues at the end of his article that in order to understand the meaning of such works of art, we must not only grasp the Dionysian nature of the primordial experience which has inspired it, but also participate in that unconscious, unindividuated experience itself:

> Um [den] Sinn [des Kunstwerks] zu verstehen, muß man sich von ihm gestalten lassen, wie es den Dichter gestaltet hat. Und dann verstehen wir auch, was sein Urerlebnis war: er hat jene heilsame und erlösende seelische Tiefe berührt, wo noch kein Einzelner zur Einsamkeit des Bewußtseins sich abgesondert hat, um einen leidensvollen Irrweg einzuschlagen; wo noch alle in derselben Schwingung begriffen

sind, und darum Empfinden und Handeln des Einzelnen noch in alle Menschheit hinausreicht (GW15 § 161).

[To grasp the work of art's meaning, we must allow it to shape us as it shaped him. Then we also understand the nature of his primordial experience. He has plunged into the healing and redeeming depths of the collective psyche, where no-one is not lost in the isolation of consciousness and its errors and sufferings, but where everyone is caught in a common rhythm which allows the individual to communicate his feelings and strivings to Mankind as a whole.]

Similarly, in *Die Geburt der Tragödie*, Nietzsche writes that Dionysian art affirms the union between the individual and his neighbour, reconciles Nature with Man, overcomes the alienation which derives from the *principium individuationis* and reveals the primal unity – 'als ob der Schleier der Maja zerrissen wäre und nur noch in Fetzen vor dem geheimnisvollen Ur-Einen herumflattere' ['as if the veil of maya had been torn aside and were now merely fluttering in tatters before the mysterious primordial unity'] (GT/BT § 1; N1: p. 25).[12] Since the Dionysian 'Urerlebnis' is ineffable – 'wort- und bildlos' ['wordless and imageless'] (GW15 § 151) – the only artistic form in which to cast it is, in Jung's view, mythological imagery. This accounts for what Jung characterizes as Nietzsche's hieratic style in *Also sprach Zarathustra*: 'Nietzsche greift auf den sakralen Stil, den Dithyrambus und den sagenhaften Seher der Vorzeit zurück' ['Nietzsche goes back to the sacral style, the dithyramb and the legendary seer of dim and distant times' (P. B.)]. This rare characterization by Jung of Nietzsche's style represents an attempt to situate Nietzsche in a tradition of archetypal writing. Jung is arguing that although, formally, Nietzsche's texts belong to the past, their content looks forward to the future: 'Jeder dieser Dichter spricht mit der Stimme von Tausenden und Zehntausenden, Wandlungen im Zeitbewußtsein vorausverkündend' ['Each of these poets speaks with the voice of thousands and tens of thousands, foretelling changes in the conscious outlook of his time'] (GW15 § 154). According to Jung, works like the *Hypnerotomachia Poliphili* attributed to the Dominican monk Francesco Colonna, Goethe's *Faust* and Spitteler's *Prometheus*, all, like Nietzsche's *Zarathustra*, symbolize the tensions between different historical periods, the old and the new. Although the scheme by which Jung relates all these works (GW15 § 154) is not entirely clear, the general pattern seems to be that each work represents a psychological response to the changes in Western Man's relation to the divine or to the Anima. In Nietzsche's case, Man's relation to the divine is abruptly ended – the Death of God is announced – and the psychological response is equally extreme – the Superman is proclaimed: 'Nietzsche verkündet den Gottestod [...] bemächtigte

[12] Jung also uses Gnostic vocabulary to refer to the Dionysian 'Urvision', equating the 'Pleroma' (a Gnostic expression for the Ground of Being he used in the *VII Sermones ad mortuos*) with the world of the primordial vision, i.e. the Unconscious (GW15 § 149).

sich wiederum des Übermenschen, und dieser mußte sich noch in sein eigenes Verderben stürzen' ['Nietzsche proclaims the Death of God and seizes hold of the Superman, who in turn must bring disaster upon himself' (P. B.)] (GW15 § 154).

Although Jung's explicit discussion of Nietzsche in 'Psychologie und Dichtung' is flawed by its brevity and incoherence, the clear parallels between Jung's view of art and Nietzsche's views in *Die Geburt der Tragödie* demonstrate that Jung had assimilated Nietzsche's ideas to a greater extent than he was prepared to admit, or even than he himself might have realized. But, more importantly still, by 1930, Jung has radically altered his view of the artist as that was set out in *Psychologische Typen*.

In *Die Geburt der Tragödie*, Nietzsche writes that under the influence of Dionysos: 'Der Mensch ist nicht mehr Künstler, er ist Kunstwerk geworden' ['Man is no longer an artist, he has become a work of art'] (GT/BT § 1; N1: p. 25). In *Psychologische Typen*, Jung had explicitly rejected this view and, although he made the connection between Dionysos, the Unconscious and Nature, he had identified the Dionysian with the barbaric: 'Im dionysischen Zustand wurde also der Grieche keineswegs zunächst zum Kunstwerk, sondern er wurde von seinem eigenen barbarischen Wesen ergriffen, seiner Individualität beraubt, in alle seine kollektiven Bestandteile aufgelöst, eins gemacht mit dem kollektiven Unbewußten (unter Aufgabe seiner individuellen Ziele), eins mit "dem Genius der Gattung, ja der Natur"' ['Thus in the Dionysian state the Greek was anything but a "work of art"; on the contrary, he was gripped by his own barbarian nature, robbed of his individuality, dissolved into the Collective Unconscious (through the surrender of his individual aims), and one with "the genius of the race, even with Nature herself"'] (GW6 § 212/CW6 § 230; cf. GT/BT 2; N1: p. 28 [and FW/GS 354; N2: p. 219]).

In 'Psychologie und Dichtung', however, Jung clearly states, following Nietzsche, that in the course of artistic activity, the artist himself disappears into his work: 'als Künstler ist er sein Werk und kein Mensch' ['as an artist he is nothing but his work, and not a human being'] (GW15 § 156). Concomitantly, Jung's later view of the Dionysian employs a vocabulary of artistic volition, for just as Nietzsche speaks of Dionysos and Apollo as 'Kunsttriebe' (GT/BT § 2; N1: p. 26), so Jung writes that 'die Kunst ist [dem Künstler] eingeboren wie ein Trieb, der ihn erfaßt und zum Instrument macht. Das in letzter Linie in ihm Wollende ist nicht er, der persönliche Mensch, sondern das Kunstwerk' ['Art is innate to the artist like a drive which seizes him and makes him its instrument. What ultimately wills in him is not the personal man but the work of art' (P. B.)] (GW15 § 157). Furthermore, just as Nietzsche says that, under the spell of Dionysos, '[jeder] fühlt sich [...] mit seinem Nächsten nicht nur vereinigt, versöhnt, verschmolzen, sondern eins' ['each one feels himself not only united, reconciled, and fused with his neighbour, but as one with him'] (GT/BT § 1; N1: p. 25), so Jung writes that, in the grip of the creative drive, the artist is 'in höherem Sinne "Mensch", er ist *Kollektivmensch*' ['"Man" in a higher sense, he is Collective Man'] (GW15 § 157). By means of artistic production, the creative individual is said by Jung to transcend the limits of his own subjectivity:

> Jeder schöpferische Mensch ist eine Dualität oder eine Synthese paradoxer Eigenschaften. *Einerseits ist er menschlich-persönlich, andererseits aber unpersönlicher, schöpferischer Prozeß* (GW15 § 157).
>
> [Every creative person is a duality or synthesis of paradoxical qualities. *On the one hand he is human and personal, on the hand he is an impersonal, creative process.* (P. B.)]

Nietzsche also reminds us that the whole point of tragedy was the identification of Dionysos both as the victim *and* as the chief murderer, and that participation in the tragic moment allowed the artistic genius to transcend the divide between subject and object:

> Nur soweit der Genius im Aktus der künstlerischen Zeugung mit jenem Urkünstler der Welt verschmilzt, weiß er etwas über das ewige Wesen der Kunst; denn in jenem Zustande ist er, wunderbarerweise, dem unheimlichen Bild des Märchens gleich, das die Augen drehn umd sich selber anschaun kann; jetzt ist er zugleich Subjekt und Objekt, zugleich Dichter, Schauspieler und Zuschauer (GT/BT § 5; N1: p. 40).
>
> [Only insofar as the genius in the act of artistic creation coalesces with this primordial artist of the world, does he know anything of the eternal essence of art; for in this state he is, in a marvellous manner, like the weird image of the fairy tale which can turn its eyes at will and behold itself; he is at once subject and object, at once poet, actor, and spectator.]

Jung's view of the artist in 1930 is essentially different from his 1921/22 views because of his greater confidence in the autonomy of the psyche and the constructive potential of de-repressed Dionysian energies. Jung's view of the Dionysian in 1930 is also much more positive than that which he had held in *Psychologische Typen*. Indeed, it amounts to an inversion of that earlier view. This shift has taken place mainly because of the change of context in which Jung discusses Dionysos. In 'Über das Unbewußte' ['On the Rôle of the Unconscious'] (1918), Jung had characterized the psychological problem of the age in terms of the Nietzschean image of the 'blonde Bestie' ['blond beast'] which threatens to break out. In *Psychologische Typen*, the barbaric aspect of man had been identified with the Dionysian, and the division of Man which his cultural domestication entails had been identified with the Schillerian notion of a debilitating blow to mankind. Both religious devotion as conceived by Schiller (as *Psychologische Typen* reminds us) and the return to the primordial experience in the process of artistic creativity (as discussed in the two essays on psychology and art of 1922 and 1930) represent a return to Dionysos, as Jung speaks of them in identical terms:

as a descent into the Collective Unconscious – 'das Wiedereintauchen in den Urzustand der "participation mystique"' ['this re-immersion in the primordial state of "participation mystique"'] (GW15 § 162) – and the ascent of the archetypal image, the symbol – 'daraus erhebt sich als ein Bild der beginnenden Progressivbewegung das *Symbol*, welches eine zusammenfassende Resultante aller unbewußten Faktoren darstellt' ['out of this there arises, as an image of the incipient progressive movement, the symbol, which is a condensation of all the operative unconscious factors'] (GW6 § 188/CW6 § 202).

It is therefore not inappropriate to speak of Jung trying to drive out the Devil with Beelzebub: Dionysos, as the source of artistic creativity, against Dionysos, the one-sidedness of barbarism (as defined in *Psychologische Typen*). Yet these two different understandings of Dionysos are, in Jungian thought, not so much pitted against each other as reciprocal. In tragedy, according to Nietzsche, Dionysos was both the victim and the murderer. In Jung, Dionysos is both the danger (a repressed archetype returning, as Jung saw in the late Thirties and early Forties, in negative form as Wotan) and the 'saving thought' (archetypal inspiration from the Collective Unconscious). Jung's optimism about a Religion of Art (my phrase, not his) was however shaken in the years which followed, when Jung's concern about a barbaric outburst of Dionysos was proved right – or so he thought – in the form of the eruption of Dionysos/Wotan and, as he had predicted – or so he claimed – the blond beast stalked Europe and especially Germany in the guise of National Socialism. Thereafter, the return of the god Dionysos began to be considered in a more overtly theological sense.

In addition to the two theoretical papers on psychology and art discussed above, another important source for Jungian aesthetics is two articles, one dealing with a writer and the other with an artist, which Jung wrote in 1932. Both Joyce and Picasso exemplify a style of writing/art that may be classified as Modernism; and the mythologem of Dionysos (as Nietzsche used it), which played such a large part in Jung's theoretical treatises on art, is a recurring motif in many other Modernist writers, too.

Dionysian Modernism

As Evans Lansing Smith has pointed out,[13] the notion of the descent into the Dionysian underworld was the underlying mythic idea for many of the Modernist writers who wrote during Jung's lifetime, for example, Joseph Conrad (in

[13] 'The descent to the underworld (*nekyia*) is the single most important myth for the modernist authors who wrote during C. G. Jung's lifetime [...]' (Evans Lansing Smith, 'Descent to the Underworld: Jung and His Brothers', in *C. G. Jung and the Humanities: Towards a Hermeneutics of Culture*, edited by Karin Barnaby and Pellegrino d'Acierno (London, 1990), pp. 250–64).

Heart of Darkness (1902)), T. S. Eliot's *The Waste Land* (1922), or Thomas Mann, whose combination of 'myth plus psychology'[14] in *Tod in Venedig* (1912) represents a thoroughly Dionysian encounter, and whose *Joseph und seine Brüder* involves a Gnostic-style cosmological descent.[15] Indeed, much modern literature can also be read in terms of the myth of another deity closely related to Dionysos, Orpheus.[16] According to Walter Strauss: 'All descents into darkness require a process of self-destruction, self-abnegation, so that the new being can be born – this is the psychoanalytical, ontological, and theological meaning of the Orphic descent in modern times',[17] and he has shown how texts as diverse as Novalis's *Hymnen an die Nacht* (written 1799), Gérard de Nerval's *Aurélia* (1855), Mallarmé's sonnets (e.g. the Orphic descent or *katábasis* in 'Ses purs ongles' and the *anábasis* in 'Quand l'ombre menaça') and his *Igitur* (written c.1869)), Rimbaud's poem 'Une Saison en enfer' (1873) and Hermann Broch's *Der Tod des Vergil* (1945) (one of Jung's favourite books) can be read as re-enactments of a central myth of descent and return. The *locus classicus* for the *nekyia* is the descent to Hades in Homer's *The Odyssey* (Book 11), which, in his autobiography, Jung remembers was read to him by his friend Albert Oeri on a boating expedition during his student days in the translation by Voss (ETG: p. 103).[18] Furthermore, Jung's own Dionysian experience of the Unconscious fits into this pattern, with reference to both his biography and his psychological writings.[19] First, as we saw in Chapter 3, Jung regarded his own breakdown and period of intense introversion (which constituted his own personal encounter with Dionysos) as a descent to the underworld through which he moved in order to find shape and significance in his life and work. Second, as we saw in Chapter 4, Jung's key work, *Wandlungen und Symbole der Libido* (1911/12), is primarily about the descent of the hero into the primordial Mother – i.e. the regression of libido into the depths of the Unconscious.

---

14 See André von Gronicka, '"Myth plus Psychology": A Style Analysis of *Death in Venice*', *Germanic Review*, 31 (1956), 191–205.

15 See also my article '*Jung-Joseph*: Analytical Psychology in Thomas Mann's "Joseph" Tetralogy', *The Modern Language Review*, March 1996.

16 For further discussion of the relation between Dionysos and Orpheus, see F. M. Cornford, *From Religion to Philosophy* (London, 1912), p. 195; Jane Harrison, *Prolegomena to the Study of Greek Religion* (London, 1935), p. 455; Eva Kushner, *Le Mythe d'Orphée dans la littérature française contemporaine* (Paris, 1961), p. 55; and Robert McGrahey, *The Orphic Moment: Shaman to Poet-Thinker in Plato, Nietzsche, and Mallarmé* (New York, 1994).

17 Walter A. Strauss, *Descent and Return: The Orphic Theme in Modern Literature* (Cambridge, MA, 1971), p. 86.

18 Strangely, this highly significant incident is omitted from the English translation.

19 For further discussion of this point, see Robert W. Brockway, 'Religion and "Creative Illness" in Jung's Night Journey into the Psychic Depth', *Journal of Dharma*, 14, no.3 (July–September 1989), 277–86.

In other words, Modernism is not so much concerned with the necessity of the descent into the underworld as a precondition for the production of art as it is concerned to foreground this descent and re-enact the encounter with Dionysos.[20] To a certain extent, perhaps more unconsciously than consciously, Jung, too, understood this, and two other essays from the Thirties in which he examined a major European novel, Joyce's *Ulysses*, and the output of a major European painter, Picasso, further elaborate his notion of the Dionysian influence in art as a positive, or at any rate creative, phenomenon.[21] The stimulus for these artistic analyses is not hard to find: Jung had analysed Joyce's daughter, Lucia, in 1918, and at the time had taken a dim view of her own and her father's literary output (in this respect, Jung's highly ambivalent article on *Ulysses* represents both a repetition and a revision of his earlier lack of enthusiasm); and in 1932, the Zurich Kunsthaus exhibited 460 works by Picasso. In both essays, Jung was concerned to show the relevance of Analytical Psychology to an understanding of major currents in European Modernism, and since they stand as rare examples in the *Gesammelte Werke* of the pure application of Jungian literary and artistic theory, it is to these that we shall now turn.

Jung on Joyce

'"Ulysses": Ein Monolog' ['"Ulysses": A Monologue'] was first published in the *Europäische Revue* in 1932, but an earlier version had been written in 1930, shortly after 'Psychologie und Dichtung' had been delivered. In his headnote to the reprinted version of his essay on Joyce in *Wirklichkeit der Seele*,[22] Jung wrote that he wanted both to demonstrate the contemporary relevance of *Ulysses* as 'ein wesentliches und für unsere Zeit kennzeichnendes document humain' ['an important "document humain" very characteristic of our time'] and to show 'Ideen, die in meinen Werken eine nicht unbeträchtliche Rolle spielen, in praktischer Anwendung auf einen konkreten Stoff' ['how ideas that play a considerable rôle in my work can be applied to material in practice'] (GW15: p. 121/CW15: p. 109). In other words, Jung's article on Joyce is to be taken as an example of how to use Analytical Psychology in literary interpretation.[23]

---

20 See John Burt Foster jr., *Heirs to Dionysos: A Nietzschean Current in Literary Modernism* (Princeton, 1981).

21 '"Ulysses": Ein Monolog' (GW15 § 163–203) and 'Picasso' (GW15 § 204–14).

22 C. G. Jung, *Wirklichkeit der Seele* (Zurich, 1934).

23 Despite the overtly mythical overtones of Joyce's works, few literary critics have examined his works from the point of view of Analytical Psychology – perhaps wisely, in the light of the sense of disappointment which Jung's own essay arouses. For a highly negative commentary on Jung's interpretation, see Jean-Louis Houdebine, 'Jung et Joyce', *Tel Quel*, 81 (Autumn 1979), 63–65. However, there have been two more constructive attempts to read Joyce in the light of

Jung's panegyric judgment with which his essay concludes modifies the vituperative criticism expressed earlier on in the article, and Jung makes the claim that *Ulysses* represents an important advance in the consciousness of modern man:

> O "*Ulysses*" du bist ein wahrhaftes Andachtsbuch für den objektgläubigen, objektverfluchten weißhäutigen Menschen! Du bist ein Exercitium, eine Askesis, ein qualvolles Ritual, eine magische Prozedur, achtzehn hintereinander geschaltete alchymische Retorten, in denen mit Säuren, Giftdämpfen, Kälten und Hitzen der Homunkulus eines neuen Weltbewußtseins herausdestilliert wird! (GW15 § 201).
>
> [O *Ulysses*, you are truly a devotional book for the object-besotted, object-ridden white Man! You are a spiritual exercise, an ascetic discipline, an agonizing ritual, an arcane procedure, eighteen alchemical alembics piled on top of one another, where amid acids, poisonous fumes, and fire and ice, the homunculus of a new, universal consciousness is distilled!]

Although the article does not establish an obvious connection between the two authors, it is clear that Nietzsche provides Jung with a conceptual framework for the discussion of Joyce's work, given that, at five points in the essay, Jung compares Joyce's novel with Nietzsche's writings and ideas. First, as far as Jung is concerned, Modernist texts give expression to those same Dionysian forces ('das nicht zu Bändigende, das nicht Einzufangende' ['forces beyond control or capture']) which overwhelmed Nietzsche (GW15 § 178). Indeed, according to Jung, Goethe (in *Faust*), Hölderlin and Nietzsche (in *Zarathustra*) are all forerunners of Modernism, the chief characteristic of which is said to lie in its destruction of old ideals and in its rebarbative tone:[24]

> Selbst die dunkelsten Phasen des "*Faust*", 2.Teil, "*Zarathustra*", ja "*Ecce Homo*" noch, wollten sich der Welt so oder so empfehlen. Aber erst die Modernen haben es erreicht, die Kunst der Rückenseite, oder die Rückseite der Kunst zu erschaffen, das heißt jene Kunst, die sich nicht mehr, weder laut noch leise, empfiehlt, die endlich laut sagt, was es denn ist, das nicht mehr mittun will, die nun mit jenem widerspenstigen Gegenwillen spricht, der bei allen Vorläufern der Moderne (Hölderlin nicht zu vergessen!) sich zwar zaghaft, aber doch merklich störend dazwischen drängte und alte Ideale zum Abbröckeln brachte (GW15 § 178).

Jungian psychology. First, in *Joyce between Freud and Jung* (New York, 1980), Sheldon R. Brivic uses both Freudian psychoanalysis and Jungian psychology as tools to interpret Joyce's *oeuvre* as a 'sweeping movement from bitterness and rejection to good humour and acceptance'. And second, in *Joyce's Book of the Dark: Finnegans Wake* (Madison, 1986), John Bishop suggests that the descent into the underworld of dream and myth of its main character, Finnegan-HCE, is based on the Egyptian *Book of the Dead*.

24 Jung's overall attitude to Modernism is highly ambivalent: in 'Nach der Katastrophe' ['After the Catastrophe'] he showed his less progressive side by attacking modern literature, atonalism and Cubism, with shades of the Nazi discourse of 'Entartete Kunst' in his use of a medical vocabulary to discuss art (GW10 § 430). This trope can be traced back to Nietzsche, or even Goethe, who both classified art into categories of sickness and health.

[Even the darkest passages in the second part of *Faust*, even *Zarathustra* and, indeed, *Ecce Homo*, try in one way or another to recommend themselves to the public. But it is only the Moderns who have succeeded in creating an art in reverse, a backside of art that makes no attempt to be ingratiating, that tells us just where we get off, speaking with the same rebellious contrariness that had made itself disturbing in those precursors of the Moderns (not forgetting Hölderlin) who had already started to topple the old ideals.]

Having situated Joyce within the tradition of Dionysian Modernism, Jung proceeds, in the rest of his article, to show why he considers Joyce to represent an advance on Goethe and Nietzsche.

Second, Jung examines *Ulysses* in the light of a previously-cited phrase from Nietzsche's *Menschliches, Allzumenschliches* [*Human, All Too Human*]: 'Der "*Ulysses*" zeigt es, wie man Nietzsches "tempelschänderischen Griff rückwärts" machen muß' ['*Ulysses* shows how one should execute Nietzsche's "sacrilegious backward grasp"'] (GW15 § 182, cf.MA/HA I Vorrede/Preface 3; N1: p. 440).[25] According to Jung, *Ulysses*, adopts an 'appropriate attitude' to deal with 'die Schattenseite der Welt' ['the shadow-side of the world'] and, in doing so, releases the forces of negative emotion ('Einzig dadurch wird das Spiel negativer emotionaler Kräfte ausgelöst' ['Only in this way can the forces of negative emotion be mobilized']). As a result, Joyce is said to depict the dark-side of life even more successfully than Nietzsche: '[*Ulysses*] macht [den tempelschänderischen Griff rückwärts] vor, kalt und sachlich, dermaßen "entgöttert", wie selbst Nietzsche es nie träumte' ['Joyce sets about the sacrilegious backward grasp coldly and objectively, and shows himself more "bereft of gods" than Nietzsche had ever dreamed of being'] (GW15 § 182).

Third, Jung claims that this encounter with the dark and destructive side of life has a positive outcome. Because it reveals the illusory system of prejudices which emasculates life and makes impossible demands, Jung argues that *Ulysses* is a liberating experience – which Jung then discusses in Nietzschean terms: '"Sklavenaufstand in der Moral" wäre ein Nietzschesches Motto für den "*Ulysses*"' ['Nietzsche's "slave-uprising in morals" would be a good motto for *Ulysses*'] (GW15 § 182). In *Zur Genealogie der Moral* [*On the Genealogy of Morals*], Nietzsche had argued that the slave-uprising embodied in the morals of Christianity represented a Revaluation of all Values (cf. GM I 7, 8; N2: pp. 780–81). Similarly, the idea of liberation in the moral sphere lies behind Jung's claim that Joyce's novel shows that 'Wenn auch das Böse und Zerstörerische überwiegt, so lebt es

25 See *Wandlungen und Symbole der Libido*: 'Der "tempelschänderische Griff rückwärts", von dem Nietzsche spricht, entpuppt sich, seiner Inzesthülle entkleidet, als ein ursprünglich passives Steckenbleiben in der Libido bei den ersten Kindheitsobjekten' ['The "sacrilegious backward grasp" of which Nietzsche speaks reveals itself, stripped of its incest covering, as an original passive arrest of the libido in its first object of childhood'] (WSL: p. 178/PU § 284) (see Chapter 4, p. 109).

doch am Lichte neben oder sogar vielleicht über dem "Guten"' ['Even though what is evil and destructive predominates, it is nontheless close to the light or even to what is "good"' (P. B.)] (GW15 § 182).

Fourth, Jung compares the symbolism of *Ulysses* with that of *Zarathustra* and *Faust II*. Although it is said to contain symbolism and be set against an archetypal background, *Ulysses* is, on Jung's account, neither a dream nor a revelation of the Unconscious: 'Es ist sogar von stärkerer Absichtlichkeit und ausschließlicherer Tendenz als Nietzsches "*Zarathustra*" oder Goethes "*Faust*"', 2.Teil' ['Compared with *Zarathustra* or the second part of *Faust*, it shows an even stronger purposiveness and sense of direction'] (GW15 § 185). For Jung, Joyce's novel is too dispassionate to be fully 'symbolic', whereas the more direct and less mediated symbolism of *Zarathustra* makes that, psychologically speaking, a more important work.

Finally, Jung suggests that, like *Zarathustra*, *Ulysses* creates an autotelic world, representing nobody's travels other than its own, and that Joyce's novel is, at the same time, his own 'homecoming':

> Ulysses ist der Schöpfergott in Joyce, ein wahrhafter Demiurg, dem es gelungen ist, sich von der Verwicklung in seine Welt geistiger wie physischer Natur zu befreien und sie mit losgelöstem Bewußtsein zu betrachten. Zum Menschen Joyce verhält sich Ulysses wie Faust zu Goethe, wie Zarathustra zu Nietzsche. Ulysses ist das höhere Selbst, das aus blinder Weltverwicklung zur göttlichen Heimat zurückkehrt. Im ganzen Buch tritt kein Ulysses auf, das Buch selber ist Ulysses, ein Mikrokosmos in Joyce, die Welt des Selbst und das Selbst einer Welt in einem (GW15 § 192).
>
> [Ulysses is the creator-god in Joyce, a true demi-urge who has freed himself from entanglement in the physical and mental world and contemplates them with detached consciousness. He is for Joyce what Faust was for Goethe, or Zarathustra for Nietzsche. He is the higher Self who returns to his divine home after blind entanglement in *samsara*. In the whole book no Ulysses appears; the book itself is Ulysses, a microcosm of James Joyce, the world of the Self and the Self of the world in one.]

Similarly, in his Nietzsche Seminar, Jung would argue that the world of *Zarathustra* is a microcosm of Nietzsche and an exploration of the Self (i.e. 'die Welt des Selbst und das Selbst einer Welt in einem').

Taken together with his two essays on art of 1922 and 1930, the passages comparing *Ulysses* with *Zarathustra* in the essay on Joyce show that, by the early 1930s, Jung had developed his own distinctively psychological interpretative approach to Nietzsche in general and to *Zarathustra* in particular. And it was this interpretative framework which, in 1934, encouraged him to initiate his Seminar which dealt, not as previously, with dreams and psychiatric cases, but with a literary-philosophical text. On one level a confession of its own maturity, Analytical Psychology's 'Auseinandersetzung' with Nietzsche at the same time represents a return to its major intellectual source.

Jung on Picasso

The second of Jung's essays on specific artists, 'Picasso', was first published in the *Neue Zürcher Zeitung* of 13 November 1932, shortly after the publication of his essay on Joyce. In it, Jung's dualistic categorization of art and artists reappears in an analogous clinical categorization of patients: neurotics and schizophrenics (GW15 § 208). The art of the second group, into which Picasso falls, is said to be characterized by the contradictory and fragmentary nature of its form. Since both 'Über die Beziehung der Analytischen Psychologie zum dichterischen Kunstwerk' and 'Psychologie und Dichtung' had included *Zarathustra* in this second category, Jung's following comments can also be read with implicit reference to Nietzsche:

> Rein formal herrscht der Charakter der *Zerrissenheit* vor, der sich in den sogenannten Bruchlinien ausdrückt, das heißt einer Art psychischer Verwerfungsspalten, die sich durch das Bild ziehen. Das Bild läßt kalt oder wirkt erschreckend wegen seiner paradoxen, gefühlstörenden, schauerlichen oder grotesken Rücksichtslosigkeit auf den Betrachtenden. Picasso gehört zu dieser Gruppe (GW15 § 208).
>
> [From a purely formal point of view, the main characteristic is one of fragmentation, which expresses itself in the so-called "lines of fracture" – that is, a series of psychic "fault-lines" which runs right through the picture. The picture leaves one cold, or disturbs one by its paradoxical, emotionally disturbing, eerie or grotesque lack of concern for the beholder. Picasso belongs to this group. (P. B.)]

The link with Dionysos here lies in the notion of 'Zerrissenheit' ['fragmentation'] since Dionysos-Zagreus was, as Jung knew, ripped to pieces. Furthermore, Nietzsche himself cultivated an aesthetic of the fragment, and *Zarathustra* contains many 'grotesque' and 'uncanny' passages. Jung draws a further distinction between the neurotic and the schizophrenic in their respective relationship to the symbolic. Whereas the neurotic searches for and presents the meaning of the symbolic content to the spectator, the schizophrenic seems 'als ob er das Opfer dieses Sinnes sei' ['as if he were a victim of this meaning'] (GW15 § 209). Jung would develop this idea in his Seminar on *Zarathustra*, where he argued that Nietzsche was a victim of the archetypes.

Jung dedicates the rest of his article on Picasso to an examination of the symbol of the *nekyia* or night sea-journey: 'der Hadesfahrt, dem Abstieg ins Unbewußte und dem Abschied von der Oberwelt' ['the journey to Hades, the descent into the Collective Unconscious, and the leave-taking from the upper world'] (GW15 § 210). According to Jung, works from Picasso's so-called 'Blue Period' (roughly between 1901 and 1904) demonstrate that Picasso was undergoing the visionary 'Urerlebnis':

> Wenn ich sage "er", so meine ich damit jene Persönlichkeit in Picasso, welche das Unterweltsschicksal erleidet, jenen Menschen, der nicht in die Tagwelt, sondern

> schicksalhaft ins Dunkle sich wendet, nicht dem Ideal des anerkannt Schönen und Guten folgend, sondern der dämonischen Anziehungskraft des Häßlichen und Bösen, das im modernen Menschen antichristlich und luziferisch emporschwillt und Weltuntergangsstimmung erzeugt, eben diese helle Tagwelt mit Hadesnebeln umschleiert, mit tödlicher Zersetzung ansteckt und schließlich wie ein Erdbebengebiet in Fragmente, Bruchlinien, Überbleibsel, Schutt, Fetzen und anorganische Einheiten auflöst (GW15 § 210).
>
> [When I say "he", I mean that personality in Picasso which suffers the underworld fate – the man in him who does not turn towards the day-world, but is fatefully drawn into the dark; who follows not the accepted ideals of goodness and beauty, but the daemonic attraction of ugliness and Evil. It is these antichristian and Luciferian forces that well up in modern Man and engender an all-pervading sense of doom, veiling the bright world of day with the mists of Hades, infecting it with deadly decay, and finally, like an earthquake, dissolving it into fragments, fractures, discarded remnants, debris, shreds, and disorganized units.]

This passage can clearly be read in Nietzschean terms. The descent into the Unconscious corresponds to the victory of Dionysos over Apollo and the concomitant destruction of the form-sustaining *principium individuationis*, represented by the swirl of the satyr-chorus.

Jung provides further examples of the artistic encounter with the Unconscious in the form of an encounter with a dark female figure, which Jung assimilates to the Anima archetype in works of Wagner and Goethe (GW15 § 211). In the case of Wagner, Parsifal encounters Kundry, who is said to be 'von schauerlich-grotesker, vorweltlicher Häßlichkeit oder infernalischer Schönheit' ['of horribly grotesque, primeval ugliness or else of infernal beauty']. And in the case of Goethe, Jung detects a correspondence between the four female figures of *Faust* (Gretchen, Helen, Maria, and 'das Ewig-Weibliche' ['the Eternal Feminine']) and the four female figures of the Gnostic underworld (Eva, Helena, Maria and Sophia).[26] According to Jung, the metamorphoses of Faust find a parallel in Picasso's art in the 'Unterweltsform des tragischen *Harlekin*' ['underworld form of the tragic Harlequin'], for, as Jung remarks, 'Harlekin ist [...] ein alter chthonischer Gott' ['Harlequin is an ancient chthonic god'], a god of the underworld. Jung emphasizes the Dionysian moment in the descent into the Unconscious as represented in Goethe's *Faust* on the one hand and in Picasso's

---

[26] In *Die Psychologie der Übertragung* [*The Psychology of the Transference*] (1946), Jung identified in these figures four stages of the 'heterosexuellen Eros, resp. des Animabildes' ['the heterosexual Eros or anima-figure'] and, correspondingly, four stages of the Eros cult: from the biological stage (Eve, or Gretchen), through the aesthetic/romantic (Helen) and the religious (Mary) stages, to the spiritual (Sophia, or the Eternal Feminine) (GW16 § 361). Jung also referred to Helena-Maria-Sophia as a 'gnostische Reihe' ['Gnostic sequence'] in a letter of 22 March 1939 which gave a more detailed psychological account of *Faust* (B1: pp. 333–35; L1: pp. 264–66). Jung's point with regard to Picasso is that this shift from the realm of 'Natur' to that of 'Geist' is complemented by the emergence of a chthonic figure (Harlequin or Dionysos).

art on the other by comparing them with his clinical experiences, referring to the tendency of his patients to return to ancient times and revel in 'Evokationen antiker Dionysismen' ['evocations of Dionysian orgies'] (GW15 § 212). Furthermore, Jung once more identifies the descent into the unconscious underworld with the Mothers Scene in *Faust II*. On Jung's account, the goal of that descent is the attainment of primordial totality, i.e. Nietzsche's Dionysian experience:[27]

> Die Fahrt durch die Seelengeschichte der Menschheit hat den Zweck, den Menschen als Ganzes wiederherzustellen, indem sie die Erinnerung des Blutes wachruft. Der Abstieg zu den Müttern dient Faust dazu, den sündhaft ganzen Menschen heraufzuholen, Paris und Helena – jenen Menschen, der, ob der Verirrung ins Einseitige der jeweiligen Gegenwart, in Vergessenheit geriet (GW15 § 213).

> [The journey through the psychic history of Mankind has as its object the restoration of the whole Man, by awakening the memories in the blood. The descent to the Mothers enabled Faust to raise up the sinfully whole human being – Paris united with Helena – that *homo totus* who was forgotten when contemporary Man lost himself in one-sidedness.]

The peculiar phrase 'die Erinnerung des Blutes' refers to the reactivation of the archetypes in the psyche, and once more, Jung sees the awakening of the Unconscious as a necessary compensation for the one-sidedness of modern society. Jung emphasizes, however, that the descent into the unconscious realm of Dionysos, the journey through the psychic history of Mankind, is fraught with danger: 'dieses Abenteuer des Innern ist eine gefährliche Sache, die auf jeder Stufe zum Stillstand oder zur katastrophalen Zersprengung der zusammengespannten Gegensätze führen kann' ['this inner adventure is a hazardous affair and can lead at any moment to a standstill or to a catastrophic bursting asunder of the opposites'] (GW15 § 214). For Jung, the figure of Harlequin, who is said to be 'von tragischer Zweideutigkeit' ['tragically ambiguous'], points to the perils of the confrontation with the Unconscious, with Dionysos and the underworld: '[Harlekin] ist ja der Held, der die Fährnisse des Hades durchschreiten soll; aber wird es ihm gelingen?' ['Harlequin is indeed the hero who must pass through the perils of Hades, but will he succeed?'] (GW15 § 214). Why should Jung put this question-mark over the Dionysian 'Urerlebnis', the confrontation with the Unconscious? There seem to be two main reasons. First, although Jung himself had successfully recovered from a similar experience dur-

[27] The link between the realm of the Goethean Mothers or the primal Mother, and the creative (unconscious) source is made again in the Nietzsche Seminar: 'there is a beautiful verse in *Faust* about the kingdom of the mothers where everything is in a continuous state of self-renewal, a continuous rearrangement. And this kingdom of the mothers is the abyss of the deity [...] we have a peculiar sphere in our unconscious which corresponds to such concepts, and we call that "God", the creative or the creating god' (SNZ:I:p. 54). As part of these associations there is the idea that creation also involves destruction, as indeed the artist's consciousness is destroyed and recreated by the *nekyia* into the Dionysian, collective Unconscious.

ing his breakdown following his break with Freud, the trauma of this encounter had left him with no doubt as to the perils of such psychic processes. Second, Jung was only too familiar with a case where the encounter with Dionysos knew no such happy ending: that of Nietzsche. Indeed, in the Picasso essay, Jung explicitly associates the figure of Harlequin with the 'Possenreißer' ['buffoon'] from the 'Vorreden' of *Zarathustra* (Z Vorrede/Prologue § 8; N2: pp. 287–88), whose words Jung reads as a prophetic announcement of the outcome of Nietzsche's attempt to confront the Dionysian, as the concluding words of his article make clear:

> Harlekin ist mir unheimlich. Zu sehr erinnert er mich an jenen "bunten Gesellen, einem Possenreißer gleich" in Nietzsches "*Zarathustra*", der über den nichts ahnenden Seiltänzer (die Parallele zu Bajazzo) wegsprang und ihn dadurch tötete. Dort spricht Zarathustra die für Nietzsche sich grauenhaft erfüllenden Worte: "Deine Seele wird noch schneller todt als dein Leib: fürchte nun Nichts mehr!" Wer der "Possenreißer" ist, das sagen seine Worte, die er dem Seiltänzer, seinem schwächeren alter ego, zuruft: "einem Bessern, als du bist, sperrst du die freie Bahn!" Er ist der Größere, der die Schale sprengt, und diese Schale ist manchmal – das Gehirn (GW15 § 214).

> [Harlequin gives me the creeps – he is too reminiscent of that "motley fellow, like a buffoon" in *Zarathustra*, who jumped over the unsuspecting rope-dancer (another Pagliacci) and thereby brought about his death. Zarathustra then spoke the words that were to prove so horrifyingly true of Nietzsche himself: "Your soul will be dead even sooner than your body: fear nothing more!" Who the buffoon is, is made plain as he cries out to the rope-dancer, his weaker *alto ego*: "To one better than yourself you bar the way!" He is the greater personality who bursts the shell, and this shell is sometimes – the brain.]

Who then is this unknown figure, who tears apart the shell of outer appearance ('Schale') and brings about the demise of Nietzsche? There can be no doubt that here, yet again, Jung is very much concerned with the figure of Dionysos. Jung's ambivalence towards Dionysos, expressed earlier in *Psychologische Typen*, returns here in modified form. As James Wyly has pointed out, Jung comes close to predicting that Picasso would, like Nietzsche, go mad: 'In Jung's view Picasso must either integrate the whole of the psychic material he has encountered into a "living" unity of the "greater personality", or fragment into psychosis'. Pointing to Picasso's over 91 years of painting and meditation, Wyly justifiably concludes that '[Picasso's] life is a compelling demonstration of the power of the psyche to heal itself, once access to its depths is gained and – understood'.[28] If this is the case, then Picasso stands along with those other Modernist artists, including Jung himself, who looked on Dionysos and lived.

---

[28] James Wyly, 'Jung and Picasso', *Quadrant*, 19 (1986), 7–21 (pp. 8, 18). For an alternative, less constructive reading of Jung's essay, see Jean-Louis Houdebine, 'Jung et Picasso: le déni de l'exception', *Tel Quel*, 90 (Winter 1981), 45–55.

Conclusion

Both Jung's theory of art and his interpretative praxis reveal upon examination a large number of difficulties. Restricting ourselves here to the theoretical level, we may well want to enquire about the following four aporias in Jung's thinking about art.[29] First, Jung's view, not just Freud's, involves the risk of reductionism. Whilst rejecting Freudian psychological criticism because of its alleged reductionism, Jung's own approach threatens to reduce art and literature to a series of archetypal manifestations, irrespective of the author's intentions and any notion of textuality. By stressing the work's autonomous archetypal content and playing down its formal negotiations within a particular set of traditions, the status of the work of art is reduced from that of a self-conscious product to that of an unconscious object, its signification open only to interpretation by the analytical psychologist. Second, there is the problem of methodology. By what criteria can we establish the presence of an archetypal motif in a work? Indeed, how could we determine the presence of one archetype as opposed to another? Then again, searching for archetypes presupposes their presence in the first place, and so works of art fall into two simple categories: those which are open to archetypal interpretation and those which are not. Third, Jung says the following of the artist's condition:

> Er bewegt sich innerhalb der Grenzen des zeitgenössischen Bewußtseins und hätte keinerlei Möglichkeit, sich eines archimedischen Punktes außerhalb seiner Welt zu bemächtigen, mittels dessen er imstande wäre, sein zeitgenössisches Bewußtsein aus den Angeln zu heben (GW15 § 118).
>
> [He works within the limitations of contemporary consciousness and has no possibility of gaining hold of an Archimedean point outside his world by means of which he would be able to lift his contemporary consciousness off its hinges. (P. B.)]

But if this *is* the case, how does the analytical psychologist or the literary critic using archetypal methods get round this same problem? Surely his interpretation will be just as circumscribed by the presuppositions and limitations of the age as the artist was by the presuppositions and limitations of his own?[30] Finally,

---

29 For a more detailed discussion of these difficulties and their solutions at the hands of Ernst Cassirer, Maud Bodkin and Northrop Frye, see James Baird, 'Jungian Psychology in Criticism: Theoretical Problems', in: *Literary Criticism and Psychology*, edited by J. P. Strelka (*Yearbook of Comparative Criticism*, VII) (Pennsylvania University, 1976), pp. 3–30. For Jung's influence on at least one Marxist critic, see Robert Currie, 'Christopher Caudwell: Marxist Illusion, Jungian Reality', *The British Journal of Aesthetics*, vol. 18, no. 4 (Autumn 1978), 291–99. More generally, see Morris H. Philipson, *An Outline of Jungian Aesthetics* (Boston, 1994[2]).

30 This problem is endemic to Jungian thought and represents an aporia at the very heart of Analytical Psychology, as Jung himself frequently recognized; see 'Grundfragen der Psychotherapie' ['Fundamental Questions of Psychotherapy'] (1951): 'Ich bilde mir nicht ein, über oder jenseits der Psyche zu stehen, so daß ich sie gewissermaßen von einem transzendentalen archimedischen Punkt aus zu beurteilen vermöchte' ['I do not imagine for a moment that I can

the major danger which Jung's theory poses is the immense interpretative licence that it sanctions. Caution laid aside, artistic interpretation can become self-fulfilling prophecy, justified only by the invocation of the archetype. Just how serious these difficulties are will be seen when we look in more detail at the Nietzsche Seminar. Nevertheless, a large body of Jungian interpretation has built up over the years and much of it proves very useful for the interpretation of literary texts.[31]

Significantly, there is no question for Jung that a purely physiological explanation of Nietzsche's madness would be sufficient to explain its real cause – or rather, more precisely and in more Jungian terms, its real significance. As far as Jung is concerned, those creative forces of the Collective Unconscious, the sources of the creative imagination and the experiences of the primordial vision, can be subsumed, as they were by Nietzsche, under the figure of Dionysos. In essence, Jung's aesthetics and analytical psychological literary theory are in fact based, albeit in unacknowledged form, on Nietzsche's *Die Geburt der Tragödie.*

stand above or beyond the psyche, so that it would be possible to judge it, as it were, from some transcendental Archimedean point "outside"] (GW16 § 254).

[31] See Jos van Meurs, *Jungian Literary Criticism, 1920–1980: An Annotated, Critical Bibliography of Works in English* (Metuchen, NJ, 1988). The most recent example of archetypal criticism is Camille Paglia's *Sexual Personae* (Yale, 1990), which draws heavily on Jungian notions.

Chapter 7

Jung's Reception of Nietzsche in his Writings 1922–1934: II

Nietzsche, Freud, and Psychology

In his article 'Der Gegensatz Freud und Jung' ['Freud and Jung: Contrasts'], first published in the *Kölnische Zeitung* of 7 May 1929 (GW4 § 768–84), Jung claimed that the basis of the division between himself and Freud lay in the alleged 'Verschiedenheit der prinzipiellen Voraussetzungen' ['essential differences in our basic assumptions'] (GW4 § 784), and significantly, this was one occasion on which Jung did not strive to 'unite the opposites'. Several of Jung's essays and articles in the Thirties explored the above difference of opinion from Jung's own perspective. But whilst Jung assigned to Nietzsche an important place in the history of psychology, he never precisely defined Nietzsche's historical rôle. Nietzsche's contribution to the history of psychology in general has been sketched out elsewhere,[1] and in this chapter, I shall discuss both the substance of the claims which Jung made between 1925 and 1934 about Nietzsche's position in the history of psychology and the extent to which they are true for Analytical Psychology.

'Psychologie mit und ohne Seele'

Ever since Aristotle's *De anima*, the discipline of psychology had been subsumed under that of philosophy.[2] Kant, for example, made room in his critical philosophy for rational psychology, not as a doctrine but as a discipline which would impose immovable limits on speculative reason, and thereby avoided the twin dangers of 'seelenloser Materialism' ['soulless materialism'] and 'grundloser Spiritualism' ['groundless spiritualism'].[3] The background to Jung's thinking on the

---

[1] See Henri Ellenberger, *The Discovery of the Unconscious: The History and Evolution of Dynamic Psychiatry* (New York, 1970), pp. 271–78; Walter Kaufmann, 'Nietzsche als der erste große Psychologe', *Nietzsche-Studien*, 7 (1978), 261–75; Rollo May, 'Nietzsches Beiträge zur Psychologie', *Jahrbuch für Verstehende Tiefenpsychologie und Kulturanalyse*, 1 (1981), 11–22;

[2] See Herbert Schnädelbach, *Philosophie in Deutschland 1831–1933* (Frankfurt am Main, 1983), p. 309.

[3] Immanuel Kant, *Kritik der reinen Vernunft*, edited by Raymund Schmidt (Hamburg, 1990), B 421, pp. 413b–14b.

methodology and object of psychology was the 'seelenloser Materialism' of which Kant had warned, and as a reaction against which Jung moved to the brink (and perhaps further) of 'grundloser Spiritualism'. For the dominant trend in nineteenth-century German intellectual life was a return to Kantian critical philosophy and the debates surrounding the scientific status of psychology and its methodology clearly informed Jung's *Zofingia Lectures.*[4] Thus, to understand Analytical Psychology in terms of the influence of Nietzsche involves situating Jung within the debates and traditions of the nineteenth century in general and the so-called 'struggle for the soul' in particular.

In his *Neue Kritik der Vernunft* [*New Critique of Reason*] (1807), Jakob Friedrich Fries (1773–1843) had tried to establish Kant's *a priori* forms of perception not by any transcendental method but by psychological investigation. Arguing that all knowledge was a psychic function, Fries claimed that psychology was the fundamental discipline on which all others, even philosophy, were based ('psychische Anthropologie'). The claim that the basis of philosophy is provided not by the method of logical critique but by the psychological analysis of consciousness may be described as 'psychologism'. It is a position from which Jung theoretically distanced himself, disavowing that his statements about psychology represented transcendental claims. Nevertheless, in practice, Jung came very close to adopting a 'psychologistic' stance.

The famous 'Materialismusstreit' at the Convention of Natural Scientists at Göttingen of September 1854 centred on the question as to whether consciousness (or spirit) was a function of the body or independent of it.[5] At stake in the so-called 'struggle for the soul' were not just Fries's claim that psychology was the basis of all other disciplines, but the very notion of a non-material 'Geist', which was attacked by out-and-out materalists such as Ludwig Büchner (1824–1899), whose *Kraft und Stoff* [*Energy and Matter*] (1855) enjoyed immense popularity (cf. ZL § 109, 136, 287), and Jacob Moleschott (1822–1893), the author of *Der Kreislauf des Lebens* [*The Cycle of Life*] (1852) who had also taught physiology in Zurich. The development of psychology in the wake of this dispute followed two related but distinct paths.

---

4 For further information, see: Traugott Oesterreich, *Die deutsche Philosophie des XIX. Jahrhunderts und der Gegenwart: IV. Teil von Friedrich Überwegs Grundriß der Geschichte der Philosophie* (Berlin, 1916[11]).

5 'The materialism debate, despite its frequent philosophical inanities, performed an important service in calling attention to the limitations of science and in exposing the banality of popular scientism. Immanuel Kant, who had abolished dogmatic metaphysics of a different kind, was invoked in the antimaterialist cause [...] Kant's concept of pure reason was singularly appropriate for the antimaterialists because it preserved the autonomy of consciousness, while neither making ungrounded metaphysical claims for its powers nor denying the indispensability of experience' (Thomas E. Willey, *Back to Kant* (Detroit, 1978), p. 96).

On the one hand, there was the 'spiritualist' path, represented by Gustav Theodor Fechner (1801–1887) and Rudolf Hermann Lotze (1817–1881), whose fundamental assumption was the existence of a non-physical, non-material psyche. According to Fechner, the founder of 'psychophysics', the material world is a manifestation of a higher, psychic reality, and he posited an exact correspondence between material and psychic reality – a physio-psychic parallelism.[6] Similar claims, if less startlingly expressed, were made in Lotze's *Medizinische Psychologie* (1852). Although the book is subtitled *Physiologie der Seele*, Lotze also posits the body-soul relationship in dualistic terms, and his later *System der Philosophie* also suggested, against the claims of 'psychologism', that metaphysics was the basis of psychology, and not *vice versa*.[7]

On the other hand, there was the 'materialist' path, represented by Friedrich Albert Lange (1828–1875) and Wilhelm Wundt (1832–1920), which emphasized the status of psychology as a rigorous, scientific discipline. It was Lange who coined the phrase 'Psychologie ohne Seele', and although by no means a crude materialist, Lange equated the transcendental method of Kant with the psychological analysis of the mind[8] but denied any noumenal status to the soul, holding strictly to the definition of the 'Ding-an-sich' as a 'Grenzbegriff'.[9] For Lange, as for other thinkers in this category, 'Kant's theory of knowledge had great relevance for intellectuals who were seeking to comprehend the possibility of scientific knowledge without yielding to the simplicities of metaphysical materialism'.[10] Wundt, for his part, took up the claims of Fechnerian psychophysics and tried to build them into a larger, experimental psychology. As well as adopting a psychologistic position,[11] his actualistic, voluntaristic psychology was also

---

6 'Jede höhere Individualität ist das Band der niederen Individualitäten [...] Wie ich Bilder und Gedanken emporwerfe im Gehirn [...], so wirft die Erde ihre lebendigen Seelen und deren Geschicke empor' ['Each higher individuality connects the lower individualities ... Just as I call up images and thoughts in my brain ... so the earth calls up its living souls and their fates'] (Gustav Theodor Fechner, *Zend-Avesta oder über die Dinge des Himmels und des Jenseits*, 3 vols (Leipzig, 1851), cited from third edition, 2 vols (Leipzig, 1906), I, p. 40). Jung owned a copy of the 1901 edition.

7 'Nicht Psychologie kann Grundlage der Metaphysik, sondern nur diese die Grundlage sein' ['Psychology cannot be the foundation of metaphysics, but rather only the latter can be the foundation'] (R. H. Lotze, *System der Philosophie*, 2 vols (Leipzig, 1874–1879), cited from the second, revised edition, 2 vols (Leipzig 1912), II, p. 17.

8 F. A. Lange, *Geschichte des Materialismus und Kritik seiner Bedeutung in der Gegenwart*, edited by Alfred Schmidt, 2 vols (Frankfurt am Main, 1974), II, p. 864.

9 F. A. Lange, II, pp. 621 and 867.

10 Willey, ibid., p. 96.

11 'Es gibt [...] keine einzige Naturerscheinung, die nicht auch unter einem veränderten Gesichtspunkte Gegenstand psychologischer Untersuchung sein könnte' ['There is no single natural phenomenon which could not also from a different point of view be the object of psychological investigation'] (Wilhelm Wundt, *Grundzüge der physiologischen Psychologie* (Leipzig, 1911[6]), p. 2).

'without a soul'.[12] Within the terms of this debate, Jungian psychology can be seen as an attempt to contruct a psychology 'with a soul', or more precisely, 'with a psyche', but without explicitly engaging in metaphysics.[13] Inevitably though, as Jung once said, 'das Ganze der Seele kann vom Intellekt allein nie erfaßt werden' ['the totality of the psyche can never be grasped by intellect alone'] (GW7 § 201), and he believed that the truth of the psyche ultimately eluded conceptual judgment.

In his introduction to W. M. Kranefeldt's introductory text on psychoanalysis *Die Psychoanalyse: Psychoanalytische Psychologie* [translated as *Secret Ways of the Mind*] (1930) (GW4 § 745–67), as in his 'Allgemeines zur Komplextheorie' ['A Review of the Complex Theory'] (1934) (GW8 § 194–219), Jung reserved a place for Nietzsche in the history of psychology, but on neither occasion did he offer a justification of this claim. In what way can Nietzsche be said to prophesy 'eine Entdeckung der Seele als einer neuen Tatsache' ['the discovery of the psyche as a new fact']? After all, according to Zarathustra: 'der Erwachte, der Wissende sagt: Leib bin ich ganz und gar, und nichts außerdem; und Seele ist nur ein Wort für ein Etwas am Leibe' ['the awakened, the enlightened man says: I am body entirely, and nothing beside; and soul is only a word for something in the body'] (Z I 4; N2: p. 300). Furthermore, there is evidence that Nietzsche's materialistic view of psychology had been influenced by such nineteenth-century thinkers as F. A. Lange.[14] Jung, on the other hand, was in many ways concerned with reversing the Enlightenment project, rather than, like Nietzsche, completing and thereby superseding it.[15] However, consideration of Jung's and Nietzsche's attitude towards the task of psychology shows a clear convergence between the two thinkers. To a surprisingly large extent, Jung shared Nietzsche's vision of what the task of psychology should be. Moreover, Jung came to formulate his view of psychology on a Nietzschean basis as an anti-Freudian strategy. Jung's appropriation of Nietzschean psychology was based above all on a close reading of *Jenseits von Gut und Böse* [*Beyond Good and Evil*], a text which he heavily

---

12 'Seine Psychologie ist durchaus Psychologie ohne Seele' ['His psychology is entirely a psychology without soul'] (Oesterreich, p. 313).

13 See 'Das Grundproblem der gegenwärtigen Psychologie' ['Basic Postulates of Analytical Psychology'] (given as a lecture in Vienna and first published as 'Die Entschleierung der Seele' in 1931, and republished under the present title in 1934 (GW8 § 649–688).

14 See Jörg Salaquarda, 'Nietzsche und Lange', *Nietzsche-Studien*, 7 (1978), 236–53, and 'Der Standpunkt des Ideals bei Lange und Nietzsche', *Studi Tedeschi*, 22, no.1 (1979), 133–60; G. J. Stack, *Lange und Nietzsche* (Berlin and New York, 1983); and K. J. Ansell-Pearson, 'The Question of F. A. Lange's Influence on Nietzsche', *Nietzsche-Studien*, 17 (1988), 539–54.

15 In order to defend Analytical Psychology – a psychology *with* a psyche – against the claims of psychoanalysis and psychobiology, Jung turned to pre-Enlightenment sources and developed a programme for a psychology which would go beyond modern ones to unveil that aspect of the psyche which had been left uncovered – not the biological, but the spiritual aspect (GW8 § 688).

annotated in his own copy but only once referred to in his published work (GW9(i) § 61).

In 'Die psychologischen Aspekte des Mutterarchetypus' ['The Psychological Aspects of the Mother Archetype'] (1934), Jung claimed that after Kant's *Kritik der reinen Vernunft* the activities of understanding and reason should no longer be understood as processes subject to the laws of logic, but rather as psychic functions corresponding to the personality.[16] In other words: 'die Persönlichkeit Kants [war] eine nicht unwesentliche Voraussetzung der "*Kritik der reinen Vernunft*"' ['Kant's personality was a decisive conditioning factor of his *Critique of Pure Reason*'] (GW9(i) § 150). Jung's argument here is distinctly Nietzschean, for he took it from *Jenseits von Gut und Böse*, as his marginal annotations to that work show. There Nietzsche, too, had argued that philosophy could take the form of a psychological critique of personal outlooks and attitudes disguised as philosophy:

> Allmählich hat sich mir herausgestellt, was jede große Philosophie bisher war: nämlich das Selbstbekenntnis ihres Urhebers und eine Art ungewollter und unvermerkter *mémoires* (JGB/BGE § 6, cf. § 3; N2: p. 571, cf.p. 569).

> [Gradually it has become clear to me what every great philosophy so far has been: namely, the personal confession of its author and a kind of involuntary and unconscious memoir.]

Moreover, Nietzsche had been prepared to admit that this was the truth of his own philosophy: 'Meine Schriften reden *nur* von meinen Überwindungen' ['My writings speak only of my overcomings'] (MA/HA II Vorrede/Prologue § 1; N1: p. 737), and his view that the nature of truth is essentially subjective is emphasized by his (ironic) use of subtitles like 'Wir Gelehrten' ['We Scholars'] and 'Unsere Tugenden' ['Our Virtues']. Equally, Jung's work on typology had

---

[16] 'Bezeichnenderweise ist es gerade Kants Kategorienlehre, welche einerseits jeden Versuch einer Metaphysik im alten Sinne im Keime erstickt, andererseits aber eine Wiedergeburt Platonischen Geistes vorbereitet [...] In den anderthalben Jahrhunderten, die seit der "*Kritik der reinen Vernunft*" verstrichen sind, hat sich allmählich die Einsicht Bahn gebrochen, daß Denken, Vernunft, Verstand usw. keine für sich existierenden, von aller subjektiven Bedingtheit befreiten und nur den ewigen Gesetzen der Logik dienstbaren Vorgänge sind, sondern psychische Funktionen, welche einer Persönlichkeit zu- und untergeordnet werden. Die Frage lautet nicht mehr: Ist es gesehen, gehört, mit Händen betastet, gewogen, gezählt, gedacht und logisch befunden worden? sondern sie lautet: *Wer* sieht, *wer* hört, *wer* hat gedacht?' ['Significantly enough, it is Kant's doctrine of categories, more than anything else, that destroys in embryo every attempt to revive metaphysics in the old sense of the word, but at the same time paves the way for a rebirth of the Platonic spirit [...] During the century and a half that have elapsed since the appearance of the *Critique of Pure Reason*, the conviction has gradually gained ground that thinking, understanding, and reasoning cannot be regarded as independent processes subject only to the eternal laws of logic, but that they are *psychic functions* co-ordinated with the personality and subordinate to it. We no longer ask, "Has this or that been seen, heard, handled, weighed, counted, thought, and found to be logical?" We ask instead, "*Who* saw, heard, or thought?"'] (GW9(i) § 150).

suggested that different individuals worked with different psychic economies, and in *Erinnerungen, Träume, Gedanken* [*Memories, Dreams, Reflections*] Jung emphasized the subjective impulses behind his own work:

> Meine Werke können als Stationen meines Lebens angesehen werden, sie sind Ausdruck meiner inneren Entwicklung [...] Alle meine Schriften sind sozusagen Aufträge von innen her; sie entstanden unter einem schicksalhaften Zwang. Was ich schrieb, hat mich von innen überfallen (ETG: p. 225/MDR: p. 249).

> [My works can be regarded as stations along my life's way, they are the expression of my inner development ... All my writings may be considered tasks imposed from within; their source was a fateful compulsion. What I wrote were things that assailed me from within myself (P. B.).]

Or, as Nietzsche put it in his account of the composition of *Zarathustra*: 'ich habe nie eine Wahl gehabt' ['I never had any choice'] (EH Z § 3; N2: p. 1131).

Furthermore, where psychology had hitherto been subordinated to philosophy, this state of affairs would now be reversed, as Jung claims that Nietzsche had foreseen: 'Bis vor kurzem noch war die Psychologie ein besonderer Teil der Philosophie, aber jetzt nähert sich, wie Nietzsche es vorausgesagt hat, ein Aufstieg der Psychologie, der die Philosophie zu verschlucken droht' ['Until recently psychology was a special branch of philosophy, but now we are coming to something which Nietzsche foresaw – the rise of psychology in its own right, so much so that it is even threatening to swallow philosophy'] (GW8 § 659). Jung was very probably thinking here of another section of *Jenseits von Gut und Böse*, also underlined in Jung's copy, where Nietzsche proclaimed psychology as the 'Herrin der Wissenschaften' ['queen of the sciences'] (JGB/BGE § 23; N2: pp. 586–87). And although Jung had his doubts about the Superman as a fit goal for human striving, his own *telos* of complementarism appears in Nietzsche's descriptions of the 'komplementärer Mensch' ['complementary Man'] from *Jenseits von Gut und Böse* in whom existence is said to justify itself (JGB/BGE § 207; N2: p. 669). In another section of *Jenseits von Gut und Böse* which Jung marked in his copy, Nietzsche dispensed the following advice to psychologists: study the philosophy of the 'norm' in its fight against the exemption, and vivisect yourselves! (JGB/BGE § 218; N2: p. 683). To the extent that *Erinnerungen, Träume, Gedanken* reveals Jung's psychology as a therapeutic solution to his own problems, derived from the successful resolution of his encounter with Dionysos in the form of psychotic breakdown, Analytical Psychology itself can be read as a product of Jung's dissection of his own personality.

In other words, Jung had at least two reasons to refer to Nietzsche as a predecessor of Analytical Psychology. First, Nietzsche had claimed that all philosophy hitherto had been merely the expression of the prejudices of the philosophers, and Jung treats philosophical statements as indicative of psychological attitudes. Second, both Nietzsche and Jung agree on the preeminence of psychology, whatever the difference in their psychological outlooks. In addition, Nietzschean imagery also influenced the characterizations of two Jungian archetypes: the Old Wise Man and the Anima (see below). Finally, Jung's appeal to Nietzsche has an additional, highly polemical purpose. For, keen as he was at this stage to emphasize the uniqueness of Analytical Psychology, Jung's words of praise for Nietzsche's intuitive insights in the field of psychology served as a means of attacking Freudian psychoanalysis.

Nietzsche and Freud

In his four accounts of Freudian psychoanalysis from the Twenties and Thirties, Jung was at pains to stress its allegedly materialist basis and to distinguish his own Analytical Psychology from it, using Nietzsche as part of this critique. At the same time as Jung's attitude to Freud became increasingly hostile, however, he began to perceive in Nietzsche the same limitations which he disliked in Freud. In the end, he came to take the view that, like Freud, Nietzsche had been too much a product of his times to overcome the materialism which had characterized them. But Jung also came to see that Nietzsche's spectacular failure to negotiate with Dionysos pointed the way to his, Jung's, more successful accommodation with the Dionysian Unconscious. This shift in Jung's view of the relationship between Freud and Nietzsche, and his increasingly ambiguous stance towards Nietzsche, is evident in the four major discussions of Freud published between 1927 and 1939.

First, in his lecture 'Analytische Psychologie und Weltanschauung' ['Analytical Psychology and "Weltanschauung"'] (GW8 § 689–741), delivered in 1927 and first published in extended form in 1931, Jung placed Freud firmly in the nineteenth century: 'Es ist der wohlbekannte rationalistische Materialismus des ausgehenden 19. Jahrhunderts, der als führende Idee über der Deutungspsychologie der Freudschen Psychoanalyse steht' ['It is the well-known rationalistic materialism of the late nineteenth century, which is the guiding principle of the interpretative psychology underlying Freud's psychoanalysis'] (GW8 § 705). Second, however, in 1930, in his preface to Kranefeldt's *Die Psychoanalyse*, Jung was still prepared to place Freud in a much broader intellectual tradition which, in his view, stretched back to the Reformation and finally manifested itself in a manner foreseen by Nietzsche – as psychology (GW4 § 748).

Third, in 'Sigmund Freud als kulturhistorische Erscheinung' ['Sigmund Freud in his Historical Setting'] (GW15 § 44–59), first published in 1932 in the journal *Charakter: Eine Vierteljahresschrift für psychodiagnostische Studien und verwandte Gebiete* [*Character: A Quarterly for Psychodiagnostic Studies and Related Subjects*] (which Jung co-edited), Jung wrote a more critical account of Freud's historical importance and its limitations as he saw them. Jung's criticisms of Freud here help to clarify his own theoretical intentions and delineate his own therapeutic aims more clearly. According to Jung, Freud represented a reaction against the moral and intellectual climate of his time, and in this respect he is compared to Nietzsche as 'eine Antwort auf die Krankheit des 19. Jahrhunderts' ['an answer to the sickness of the nineteenth century'] (GW15 § 52). The emphasis on the fundamentally reactive nature of Freud's work is reflected by Jung's decision to place him in the category of 'ressentiment' discussed by Nietzsche, here labelled as 'sein größerer geistiger Zeitgenosse' ['his greater intellectual contemporary']. Jung further emphasized the essentially destructive rather than constructive nature of the work of both men by alluding to the subtitle of *Götzen-Dämmerung*, 'Wie man mit dem Hammer philosophiert' [*Twilight of the Idols*, 'How to Philosophize with a Hammer'] – 'es war die Zeit der geistigen "Leisetreterei", die schließlich einen Nietzsche gebar, der sich eines Hammers zum Philosophieren bediente' ['it was an age of mental "pussyfooting" that finally gave birth to Nietzsche, who was driven to philosophize with a hammer'] (GW15 § 48) – and by qualifying Freud in the following terms: 'Er ist ein großer Zerstörer, der die Fesseln der Vergangenheit zersprengt' ['He is a great destroyer who breaks the fetters of the past'] (GW15 § 49). Jung then went on to attack what he perceived as Freud's destructiveness and negativity on two levels: his methodology, and its consequences for psychoanalysis. He concluded that Freud offered no prospect for the future: 'Freud [bedeutet] kein Programm' (GW15 § 54, cf. § 59). Whereas Freud's greatness resembled that of 'ein alttestamentlicher Prophet' ['an Old Testament prophet'], Jung's view suggests that there was a need for a new gospel.

Indeed, Jung made it clear that, as far he was concerned, the ultimate agenda of psychoanalysis was not a scientific one: 'Die psychoanalytische Theorie hat aber geheimerweise gar nicht die Absicht, als wissenschaftliche Wahrheit zu gelten, sondern sie strebt nach Wirkung auf ein breites Publikum' ['Secretly, psychoanalytic theory has no intention of passing as a strict scientific truth; it aims rather at influencing a wider public'] (GW15 § 56). Here, Jung imputes to Freudian psychoanalysis precisely that kind of programme which he himself had devised for it in his letter of 11 February 1910. By the same token, however, Jung's own analytical psychological goals were not very different, particularly if we are to believe a document which is purportedly Jung's address at the founding of the Psychological Club, Zurich in 1916.[17] But implicitly, and increasingly in

[17] This typed paper in the English language, with corrections possibly in Jung's handwriting, is reprinted, with slight changes, by Richard Noll in *The Jung Cult: Origins of a Charismatic Movement* (Princeton, 1994), pp. 250–54. The document was found in the Fanny Bowditch Katz papers in the C. G. Jung Oral History Archive at the Francis A. Countway Library of Medicine of Harvard University. Jung, or whoever the author of this address is, draws on imagery from Goethe's projected religious epic poem 'Die Geheimnisse' ['The Mysteries'] (written 1783–84).

the wake of his later research, Jung's programme was fast becoming a quasi-religious one, anyway. His startlingly bold rejection – as late as in the Thirties – of the claims to scientific status of Freudian psychoanalysis should not deceive us into thinking that Jung had in any way abandoned his own ethical and religious ambitions as outlined in his letter to Freud of 11 February 1910.

Fourth, in 'Sigmund Freud: Ein Nachruf' ['In Memory of Sigmund Freud'] (GW15 § 60–73), published in the *Sonntagsblatt der Basler Nachrichten* of 1 October 1939, a week after Freud's death, Jung's criticisms were, uncharitably, even more acute. Moreover, this attitude evinced a clear shift in Jung's attitude with regard to Nietzsche, who appears in a much more negative light than in 1932. Jung took Freud's claims that he, Freud, had never read Nietzsche, as evidence of the lack of philosophical depth in his work (GW15 § 61). Whether Freud did actually tell Jung personally that he had never read Nietzsche is impossible to know. At any rate, it accords with what Freud wrote in 'Zur Geschichte der psychoanalytischen Bewegung' ['On the History of the Psycho-Analytic Movement'] (1914), where he nevertheless admitted that Nietzsche's 'intuitive insights' did anticipate the results of psychoanalytic research.[18] Just over a decade later, Freud repeated this claim in his 'Selbstdarstellung' ['An Autobiographical Study'] of 1925.[19]

These statements have puzzled many critics, among them Henri Ellenberger and Michel Foucault,[20] since the affinities between Nietzsche and Freud are so apparent. At university, Freud was a member of the Reading Society of the German Students of Vienna where Nietzsche was discussed.[21] Furthermore, Nietzsche was frequently talked about in meetings of the Vienna Psychoanalytic Society, as the Minutes of the Society reveal; and on 28 October 1908, Freud diagnosed Nietzsche as a 'rätselhafte Persönlichkeit' ['enigmatic personality'] and possibly sexually abnormal.[22] And he also knew Lou Andreas-Salomé, arguably Nietzsche's closest friend and perhaps even lover, much better than Jung did, and she became a member of Viennese psychoanalytic circles. In fact, Lorin Anderson has convincingly demonstrated that Freud was nothing less than a

18 Freud, 'Zur Geschichte der psychoanalytischen Bewegung', in: *Gesammelte Werke*, 18 vols (Frankfurt am Main, 1968–1978), X, p. 53.

19 Freud, 'Selbstdarstellung', in: *Gesammelte Werke*, XIV, p. 86.

20 Michel Foucault, 'Nietzsche, Freud, Marx', in: *Nietzsche* (Cahiers de Royaumont, Philosophie, no.VI) (Paris, 1967), p. 198; Ellenberger, pp. 276–78.

21 Anthony Storr, *Freud* (Oxford, 1989), p. 120.

22 *Protokolle der Wiener Psychoanalytische Vereinigung*, edited by Herman Nunberg and Ernst Federn, 4 vols (Frankfurt am Main, 1976–1981), II, pp. 22–27 (cf. I, pp. 334–39). Curiously, Freud attributed to Jung the allegation that Nietzsche had infected himself with syphilis in a male brothel but saw no significance in this claim: 'Jung will erfahren haben, daß [Nietzsche] sich die Lues in einem homosexuellen Bordell geholt habe. Das spiele jedoch gar keine Rolle' ['Jung claims to have discovered that Nietzsche caught his syphilis in a homosexual brothel. But that doesn't concern us at all'] (p. 27).

'secret disciple' of Nietzsche.[23] It is therefore highly ironic that Jung should have criticized Freud for his ignorance of Nietzsche, when all the evidence suggests that, despite his disclaimers, he was an avid reader of the German philosopher. Freud's declared distance from Nietzsche, and his remark about wanting to 'retain his impartiality', make sense, however, in the light of Jung's earlier haste to link his own cause with that of Nietzsche. Even though Freud had disputed any Nietzschean influence during the meetings of the Vienna Psychoanalytic Society, Jung's quotation from *Zarathustra* in his letter to Freud of 3 March 1912 (FJB: p. 544/FJL: p. 491), when he signalled his imminent departure from the sexual theory of libido, had effectively placed the philosopher between the two psychoanalysts. However, it is strange that Jung should have remained impervious to the Nietzschean elements in Freud's thought, given that both his *Wandlungen und Symbole der Libido* [*Psychology of the Unconscious*] and Freud's *Das Unbehagen in der Kultur* [*Civilization and its Discontents*] have much in common with *Zur Genealogie der Moral* [*On the Genealogy of Morals*], and that his whole psychology can be read as a reaction and response to Nietzsche. This omission, together with his persistent reluctance to point to any specific features of Nietzsche's psychological thought, shows Jung deliberately underplaying the extent of his own theoretical debt to Nietzsche in very much the same way that Freud had done.

In his obituary of Freud, Jung applied precisely the same epithet to him which he had earlier applied to Nietzsche: 'ein "Ergriffener" ' ['a man possessed'] (GW15 § 71).[24] Moreover, Jung's critique of Freud is not just a repetition of what he had written in 1932, for this criticism is now also applied to Nietzsche. Jung's move away from Nietzsche suggests on the surface that his more detailed involvement with the philosopher in his Seminar (1934–39) was leading him to take a more detached and sceptical view. Whereas, in 1932, Jung had held Nietzsche to be superior to Freud, in 1939 he suggested that Nietzsche, too, needed to be superseded. The diminution of Jung's enthusiasm for Nietzsche is marked by a return to a previous concern, the question of value ('Wert'):

> Freud war ein großer Zerstörer, aber die Zeit der Jahrhundertwende bot so viel Gelegenheit zum Einreißen, daß auch ein Nietzsche nicht genügt hat [...] Freud war kein Prophet, aber er ist eine prophetische Figur. In ihm wie in Nietzsche kündigt sich die Gigantomachie unsrer Tage an, wo es sich zeigen wird und muß, ob unsere höchsten Werte so wirklich sind, daß ihr Glanz nicht in der acherontischen Flut erlischt (GW15 § 69).

---

[23] Lorin Anderson, 'Freud, Nietzsche', *Salmagundi*, no. 47–48 (Winter-Spring 1980), 3–29. For further bibliographical information, see my note to Chapter 1 above, and Joachim Köhler's account of 'Freuds Abwehrschlacht' with Nietzsche in *Zarathustra Geheimnis: Friedrich Nietzsche und seine verschlüsselte Botschaft* (Reinbek bei Hamburg, 1992), pp. 347–61.

[24] According to Jung, the victim of 'Ergriffenheit' can never escape until he understands by what he is possessed (GW15 § 72).

[Freud was a great destroyer, but the turn of the century offered so many opportunities for debunking that even Nietzsche was not enough ... Freud was no prophet, but he is a prophetic figure. Like Nietzsche, he heralds the battle of the earthborn giants of our day, where time will tell – and must tell – whether our highest values are so real that their glitter is not extinguished in the Acherontian flood (P. B.).]

Jung argued that Freud's methodology, based on the premises of nineteenth-century scientific materialism (GW15 § 70), could not but miss the inner value of its psychological subject-matter and fail to see the good in what it studied. The project of Analytical Psychology could therefore be summarized as the revaluation of everything that Freud had devalued and as a demand instead for creativity (GW15 § 69). Using a dental metaphor ('Man hat Freud schon öfters mit dem Zahnarzt verglichen' ['Freud has often been compared to a dentist']), Jung says that psychoanalysis cannot offer any fillings: 'Die Freudsche Psychologie offriert keinen Ersatz für verlorengegangene Substanz' ['Freudian psychology does not fill the gap'] (GW15 § 69). Adopting this metaphor, we can say that Jung wanted to provide a metaphysical replacement to fill up the value-gap in modern life: 'Geist'.[25]

By using the term 'Geist' in this context, the nature of the 'values' which Jung thought the modern world had lost becomes clear.[26] Rather than referring to any simple moral code, the values for which Jung is searching are those whose loss Nietzsche had described as 'der *Nihilismus* als *psychologischer Zustand*' ['Nihilism as a psychological condition'] (WM/WP 12 = N3: pp. 676–78), and these are clearly also metaphysical values.[27] For Jung, as for Nietzsche, the question of value ('Wert') is thus closely related to the question of meaning ('Sinn').[28] Despite his ambiguous stance vis-à-vis Nietzsche on the surface, Jung's response to the problem of meaning is articulated under a profoundly

---

25 The fundamental difference between the views of Freud and Jung on the nature of the psyche is thus revealed. For Freud, the psyche is split into various factions which contest for power, whereas for Jung, however, there is always the possibility of mediation between these contesting forces and uniting the opposites.

26 Jung compares Freud's negative attitude to 'Geist' with that of Ludwig Klages in *Der Geist als Widersacher der Seele* (1929–1932), where 'Geist' is conceived of as an invading element inimical to life. According to Jung, Freud reduced the psychological agency of 'Geist' to a mere formula (GW15 § 72). Freud's explanations, Jung argues, fail to understand the vital and energic content of psychological problems (GW15 § 73). Jung rejects this reductionism, and emphasizes the therapeutic efficacy of 'Geist': 'In Wirklichkeit besiegt nur der *Geist* die "Geister"' ['in reality only the spirit can cast out the "spirits"'] (GW15 § 73).

27 Schnädelbach, p. 203.

28 'Die moderne Frage nach dem "Sinn" – ein Wort, das erst durch Nietzsche seine uns geläufige Bedeutungsschwere gewonnen hat – ist im Grunde die Frage nach dem Guten, formuliert im Zustand ontologischer Ratlosigkeit' ['The modern problem of "meaning" – a word which first gained through Nietzsche the weight of significance to which we have become accustomed – is basically the problem of what is good, formulated in a condition of ontological perplexity'] (Helmut Kuhn, 'Das Gute', in: *Handbuch philosophischer Grundbegriffe*, edited by Hermann Krings et al. (Munich, 1973), p. 672.

Nietzschean influence. This response, formulated in his archetypal theory and the notion of 'Geist', is indebted to Nietzsche, not overtly on the conceptual level, but on the more literary level of image. Jung came to see in the figure of Zarathustra an example of the archetype of the Old Wise Man and began to consider the work itself as a manifestation of 'Geist'. Moreover, as the following section makes clear, Jung's description of the Anima also owes much to passages from Nietzsche's *Also sprach Zarathustra* from which he has appropriated imagery for his own purposes.

The Spirit and the Anima

In his 1926 lecture 'Geist und Leben' ['Spirit and Life'] (GW8 § 601–648), Jung had discussed the etymology of the term and the uses of the concept,[29] and referred to Nietzsche's *Zarathustra* as an example of a manifestation of 'Geist' (GW8 § 643). In 'Über die Archetypen des kollektiven Unbewußten' ['Archetypes of the Collective Unconscious'], first published in the *Eranos-Jahrbuch 1934* (GW9(i) § 1–110), Jung read Zarathustra's encounter with the old man in the forest (Z Vorrede/Prologue § 2; N2: pp. 278–79) in the same terms as the pastor's dream he is analysing, i.e. as an image of the crisis in contemporary religion – the descent of the Spirit to the realm of Nature (GW9(i) § 36). According to the pre-Socratic philosopher Heraclitus, 'fire' was associated with rationality, and, although 'cold' and 'warm', 'damp' and 'dry' were perpetually transforming themselves into each other, the wise soul was 'dry'.[30] Adapting these cosmic categories for his psychological argument, Jung suggested that the descent of the spirit and its change from fire into water meant a return to the instincts (GW9(i) § 41).

Just as Jung argued that the claims of the instinctual life (the 'Sympathikus') demand to be taken more seriously, so Nietzsche had acclaimed the superiority of instinct: 'Das Genie sitzt im Instinkt; die Güte ebenfalls. Man handelt nur vollkommen, sofern man instinktiv handelt' ['Genius resides in instincts; so does goodness. One only acts with perfection inasmuch as one acts instinctively'] (WM/WP 440 = N3: pp. 824–25). Furthermore, Jung defined the 'world of water' (the Collective Unconscious) in terms identical to Nietzsche's vision of

[29] 'Wie "lebendiges Wesen" ein Inbegriff des Lebens im Körper ist, so ist "Geist" ein Inbegriff des seelischen Wesens, wie ja auch oft der Begriff Geist vermischt mit dem Begriff Seele gebraucht wird' ['Just as the "living body" is the quintessence of life in the body, so "spirit" is the quintessence of the life in the mind; indeed, the concept of "spirit" is often used interchangeably with the concept "mind"'] (GW8 § 621; cf. GW8 § 626, 648).

[30] *Die Vorsokratiker*, translated and edited by Jaap Mansfeld, 2 vols (Stuttgart, 1983), I, pp. 263–71 (fragments 64, 65 and 88).

the Dionysian realm beyond the *principium individuationis* where subjectivity and objectivity are dissolved in an all-embracing unity,[31] the womb of Being which Jung further associates (as he did in 'Psychologie und Dichtung' ['Psychology and Literature'] (GW15 § 149)) with the Gnostic concept of the *pleroma*:

> Es ist die Welt des Wassers, in der alles Lebendige suspendiert schwebt, wo das Reich des "Sympathikus", der Seele alles Lebendigen, beginnt, wo ich untrennbar dieses und jenes bin, wo ich den anderen in mir erlebe und der andere als Ich mich erlebt [...] Kaum berührt einen nämlich das Unbewußte, so ist man es schon, indem man seiner selber unbewußt wird. Das ist die Urgefahr, die den primitiven Menschen, der ja selber noch so nahe diesem Pleroma steht, instinktmäßig bekannt und ein Gegenstand des Schreckens ist (GW9(i) § 45–47).

> [It is the world of water, where all life floats in suspension; where the realm of the sympathetic system, the soul of everything living, begins; where I am indivisibly this *and* that; where I experience the Other in myself and the Other-than-myself experiences me ... The Unconscious no sooner touches us than we *are* it – we become unconscious of ourselves. That is the age-old danger, instinctively known and feared by primitive Man, who himself stands so very close to this pleroma.]

For Jung, the need for this vital new impulse of spirit constitutes the fundamental 'Problematik' of modern civilization. On the one hand, the decay of religion is said to have led to the development of psychology (which can only understand the 'gods' – the archetypes – at the price of no longer believing in their divinity), and to have wrought an immense change in the psyche: 'Seitdem die Sterne vom Himmel gefallen und unsere höchsten Symbole verblaßt sind, herrscht geheimes Leben im Unbewußten. Deshalb haben wir heutzutage eine Psychologie, und deshalb reden wir vom Unbewußten' ['Since the stars have fallen from heaven and our highest symbols have paled, a secret life holds sway in the Unconscious. That is why we have a psychology today, and why we speak of the Unconscious'] (GW9(i) § 50). The desymbolized modern world is, according to Jung, a logical consequence of a tendency which originated in Protestantism and culminated in Nietzsche:

> Die entsymbolisierte Welt des Protestanten hat zunächst eine ungesunde Sentimentalität hervorgebracht und sodann eine Verschärfung des moralischen Konfliktes, der logischerweise zum Nietzscheschen "Jenseits von Gut und Böse" führt, und zwar lediglich infolge seiner Unerträglichkeit (GW9(i) § 61).

> [The desymbolized world of the Protestant produced first an unhealthy sentimentality and then a sharpening of the moral conflict, which, because it was so unbearable, led logically to Nietzsche's "beyond Good and Evil".]

---

[31] As Bruce Detwiler has pointed out, Dionysos is associated in classical mythology with water (*Nietzsche and the Politics of Aristocratic Radicalism* (Chicago, 1990), p. 162), and, in 'Die Philosophie im tragischen Zeitalter der Griechen' ['Philosophy in the Tragic Age of the Greeks'](1873), Nietzsche noted that the notion of water as the most basic element had been the beginning of Greek philosophy (N3: p. 361).

And on the other hand, this change – i.e. the return of Spirit to Nature, the encounter of consciousness with the Unconscious – prefigures a new possibility: 'Unser Unbewußtes aber birgt belebtes Wasser, das heißt naturhaft gewordenen Geist, um dessentwillen es aufgestört ist' ['Our Unconscious, on the other hand, hides living water, spirit that has become nature, and that is why it is disturbed'] (GW9(i) § 50). This fresh opportunity is represented, mediated through a reference to *The Poetic Edda*,[32] in Dionysian terms:

> Der Himmel ist uns physikalischer Weltraum geworden, und das göttliche Empyreum eine schöne Erinnerung, wie es einstmals war. Unser "Herz aber glüht", und geheime Unruhe benagt die Wurzeln unseres Seins. Mit der *Völuspâ* können wir fragen:
>
> Was murmelt noch Wodan mit Mimes Haupte?
> Schon kocht es im Quell –.
>
> (GW9(i) § 50).

> [Heaven has become for us the cosmic space of the physicists, and the divine empyrean a fair memory of things that once were. But "the heart glows", and a secret unrest gnaws at the roots of our being. In the words of the *Völuspa* we may ask:
> What murmurs Wotan over Mimir's head?
> Already the spring boils...]

At this juncture, no more is said about Wotan/Dionysos, but Jung would return to this particular manifestation of Dionysos just two years later in 'Wotan' (1936). Instead, Jung developed the idea that the way out of the modern psychological impasse is *via* the archetypes, and in particular that of the Anima.

Playing with etymology, Jung equates 'Anima' (the Latin word for 'soul') with the soul ('die Seele') and further Gothic and Greek roots (GW9(i) § 55). It is hard to define this rich and ambiguous Jungian category, but it is said, *inter alia*, to be, like life, beyond moral norms or, *à la* Nietzsche, beyond Good and Evil: 'das Leben an sich [ist] kein nur Gutes [...]; es ist auch böse. Indem die Anima das Leben will, will sie Gutes und Böses. Im elfischen Lebensbereich gibt es diese Kategorien nicht' ['life in itself is not good only, it is also evil. Because the Anima wants life, she wants both Good and Evil. These categories do not exist in the elfin realm'] (GW9(i) § 59). The following three characteristics are the most important. First, Jung defines the Anima as a daemon: 'Seele zu haben, ist das Wagnis des Lebens, denn die Seele ist ein lebenspendender Dämon, der sein elfisches Spiel unterhalb und oberhalb der menschlichen Existenz spielt' ['But to have soul is the whole venture of life, for soul is the life-giving daemon who plays his elfin game above and below human existence'] (GW9(i) § 56). Second, the Anima is essentially irra-

---

[32] The *Völuspâ* (= the words of the prophetess) is the first poem of the *Great Edda* (attributed to Sigmund the Sage), dating from the 7th to the 13th centuries. At the bidding of Odin, the prophetess (*volva*) describes the creation of the world, the world-tree Yggdrasil, the twilight of the gods and the beginning of Time.

tional: 'keine dogmatische Seele, keine anima rationalis, welche ein philosophischer Begriff ist, sondern ein natürlicher Archetypus' ['not the soul in the dogmatic sense, not an *anima rationalis*, which is a philosophical conception, but a natural archetype'] (GW9(i) § 57). And third, in Goethe's *Faust*, the Anima is a psychopomp (from the Greek: a conductor of souls), like Hermes: 'dieselbe Anima kann auch als ein Engel des Lichts, als Psychopompos erscheinen und zum höchsten Sinne führen, wie der "*Faust*" aufweist' ['the Anima can also appear as an angel of light, a psychopomp who points the way to the highest meaning, as we know from *Faust*'] (GW9(i) § 60).

Kathleen Higgins has argued that the Jungian concept of the Anima is useful in understanding Nietzsche's attitude towards Cosima Wagner and Lou Andreas-Salomé, and pointed out that the figure of Ariadne in Nietzsche's writing embodies the key features of the Jungian Anima.[33] If Cosima Wagner and Lou Andreas-Salomé were Nietzsche's Ariadne/Anima figures, then it could be said that 'Helly' Preiswerk, Sabina Spielrein and the dream fantasies of Miss Frank Miller represent Jung's encounter with Ariadne. The figure of Ariadne forms a mysterious complement to the god Dionysos, to whose return and to whose union *Also sprach Zarathustra* persistently alludes.[34] Commenting on 'Das Nachtlied' ['The Night Song'] as a Dionysian dithyramb, expressing Dionysos's longing for Ariadne, Nietzsche remarked: 'Wer weiß außer mir, was *Ariadne* ist!...' ['Who knows except me what *Ariadne* is!...'] (EH Z § 8; N2: pp. 1136–38). Although Robin Alice Roth has rejected Higgins's interpretation of Ariadne as the Jungian Anima,[35] her critique fails to take into account the formative influence of Nietzsche on the development of Jung's archetype.

Jung's assertion in *Aion* (1951) that the Anima is closely related to the image of the Mother and that 'jede Mutter und jede Geliebte [ist] die Trägerin und

[33] 'The Jungian anima's many correspondences with the mythological Ariadne [...] suggest the possible relevance of that concept to Nietzsche's Ariadne. Jung's account of the psychologically odd behaviour caused by a man's inability to come to terms with the anima [...] matches behaviour attributed to Nietzsche in connection with his relationship to Lou Salomé [...] Jung's account of the anima, and particularly his discussion of the dangers of anima projection, provides a means for interpreting Nietzsche's fascination with Cosima Wagner' (Kathleen Higgins, 'The Night Song's Answer', *International Studies in Philosophy*, 17/II (1985), 33–50 (pp. 36–38)).

[34] Laurence Lampert, *Nietzsche's Teaching: An Interpretation of Thus Spake Zarathustra* (New Haven and London, 1986), pp. 8–9. For further discussion of Nietzsche and Ariadne, see: Karl Reinhardt, *Nietzsches Klage der Ariadne* (Frankfurt am Main, 1936); Károly Kerényi, 'Nietzsche und Ariadne: Gedanken über die Zukunft des Humanismus', *Neue Schweizer Rundschau*, 7, November 1944, 402–12; Erich F. Podach, *Ein Blick in Notizbücher Nietzsches: Eine schaffensanalytische Studie* (Heidelberg, 1963), pp. 115–28; and Lampert, p. 346.

[35] 'Arguing that Nietzsche's "Ariadne" resembles a Jungian anima is dangerous because Nietzsche never read Jung and therefore could not himself have intended any Jungian notions' (Robin Alice Roth, 'Answer to "The Night Song's Answer"', *International Studies in Philosophy*, 17/II (1985), 51–54 (p. 51)).

Verwirklicherin dieser gefährlichen Spiegelung [...], welche dem Wesen des Mannes zutiefst eignet' ['every mother and beloved is the carrier and embodiment of this dangerous mirage, which corresponds to the deepest reality in a man'] (GW9(ii) § 24) apparently echoes an observation from Nietzsche's *Menschliches, Allzumenschliches* [*Human, All Too Human*]: 'Jedermann trägt ein Bild des Weibes von der Mutter her in sich' ['Everyone bears within him a picture of woman derived from his mother'] (MA/HA I § 380; N1: p. 647). Jung, however, did not annotate this aphorism. But close reading of 'Über die Archetypen des kollektiven Unbewußten' reveals that Jung's description of the Anima as early as 1934 has its literary counterpart in another part of Nietzsche. For example, in 'Von der großen Sehnsucht' ['Of the Great Longing'] (Z III 14; N2: pp. 467–69), Zarathustra apostrophizes his soul ('O meine Seele ...'). However, more importantly, Jung's archetype of the Anima (the soul) takes form on the basis of deeper influence from the figure of Life in 'Das Tanzlied' ['The Dance Song'] and 'Das andere Tanzlied' ['The Second Dance Song'] (Z II 10, Z III 15; N2: pp. 364–66, 470–73). Nietzschean imagery and Jungian psychology are thus brought together to produce the archetype of the Anima.

Specifically, the following seven major characteristics are common to both Nietzsche's and Jung's quasi-allegorical figures. First, and most obviously, Jung's Anima is feminine in gender, and appears in a bewildering variety of forms:

> Das, was nicht Ich, nämlich männlich, ist, ist höchst wahrscheinlich weiblich, und weil das Nicht-Ich als dem Ich nicht zugehörig und darum als außerhalb empfunden wird, so ist das Animabild in der Regel auch immer auf Frauen projiziert [...] Dem antiken Menschen erscheint die Anima als Göttin oder als Hexe; der mittelalterliche Mensch dagegen hat die Göttin durch die Himmelskönigin und durch die Mutter Kirche ersetzt (GW9(i) § 58, 61).
>
> [What is Not-I, not masculine, is most probably feminine, and because the Not-I is felt as not belonging to me and therefore as outside me, the Anima-image is usually projected upon women ... To the men of antiquity the Anima appeared as a goddess or a witch, while for medieval Man the goddess was replaced by the Queen of Heaven and Mother Church.]

Correspondingly, in 'Das Tanzlied', Zarathustra addresses Life in the following way:

> Aber veränderlich bin ich nur und wild und in allem ein Weib, und kein tugendhaftes:
> Ob ich schon euch Männern ›die Tiefe‹ heiße oder ›die Treue‹, ›die Ewige‹, die ›Geheimnisvolle‹ (Z II 10; N2: p. 365)
>
> [But I am merely changeable and untamed and in everything a woman, and no virtuous one:
> Although you men call me "profound" or "faithful", "eternal", "mysterious".]

Second, both the Anima ('die Seele') and Life are fundamentally ambiguous and ambivalent figures. According to Jung, the Anima is a cunning temptress:

> Die Seele verführt die nicht lebenwollende Trägheit des Stoffes mit List und spielerischer Täuschung zum Leben. Sie überzeugt von unglaubwürdigen Dingen, damit das Leben gelebt werde. Sie ist voll von Fallstricken und Fußangeln, damit der Mensch zu Fall komme, die Erde erreiche, sich dort verwickle und daran hängenbleibe, damit das Leben gelebt werde (GW9(i) § 56).

> [With her cunning play of illusions the soul lures into life the inertness of matter that does not want to live. She makes us believe incredible things, that life may be lived. She is full of snares and traps, in order than Man should fall, should reach the earth, entangle himself there, and stay caught, so that life should be lived.]

Correspondingly, in 'Das andere Tanzlied', Zarathustra addresses Life as a dangerous temptress:

> – wer haßte dich nicht, dich große Binderin, Umwinderin, Versucherin, Sucherin, Finderin! Wer liebte dich nicht, dich unschuldige, ungeduldige, windseilige, kindsäugige Sünderin!
>
> Wohin ziehst du mich jetzt, du Ausbund und Unband? Und jetzt fliehst du mich wieder, du süßer Wildfang und Undank! (Z III 15; N2: p. 470).

> [who would not hate you, great woman who binds us, enwinds us, seduces us, seeks us, finds us! Who would not love you, you innocent, impatient, wind-swift, child-eyed sinner!
>
> Where now do you take me, you unruly paragon! And again you forsake me, you sweet, ungrateful tomboy!]

Third, the encounter with the Anima or with Life is essentially conflictual. According to Jung, 'seit Anbeginn [steht] der erdgeborene Mensch mit seinem heilsamen Tierinstinkt im Kampfe mit seiner Seele und deren Dämonie' ['since the beginning of time, Man, with his wholesome animal instinct, has been engaged in combat with his soul and its daemonism'] (GW9(i) § 60). Correspondingly, 'Das andere Tanzlied' describes a great hunt in deadly earnest, as Zarathustra cracks his whip and tries to give chase.

Fourth, according to Jung, 'indem die Anima das Leben will, will sie Gutes und Böses' ['because the Anima wants life, she wants both Good and Evil'] (GW9(i) § 59). Correspondingly, Life calls to Zarathustra: 'Wir sind beide zwei rechte Tunichtgute und Tunichtböse. Jenseits von Gut und Böse fanden wir unser Eiland und unsre grüne Wiese' ['We are both proper ne'er-do-wells and ne'er-do-ills. Beyond Good and Evil did we discover our island and our green meadow'] (Z III 15; N2: p. 471).

Fifth, according to Jung, the Anima is 'die Schlange im Paradies des harmlosen Menschen voll guter Vorsätze und Absichten' ['the serpent in the paradise of the harmless man with good resolutions and intentions' (P. B.)] (GW9(i) § 59). Correspondingly, in 'Das andere Tanzlied', Life is accompanied by snakes, and Zarathustra calls her 'diese verfluchte flinke gelenke Schlange' ['this accursed, nimble, supple snake'] (Z III 15; N2: p. 471).

Sixth, Jung repeatedly emphasizes that the Anima can be like a witch (GW9(i) § 54, 61). Correspondingly, Zarathustra calls Life a 'Hexe' ['witch'] and a 'Schlupf-Hexe' ['slippery witch'] (Z III 15; N2: p. 471). And seventh, according to Jung, 'Weisheit und Narrheit erscheinen im elfischen Wesen nicht nur als eines und dasselbe, sondern *sind* eines und dasselbe, solange sie durch die Anima dargestellt werden. Das Leben ist närrisch *und* bedeutend' ['In elfin nature wisdom and folly appear as one and the same; and they *are* one and the same as long as they are acted out by the Anima. Life is crazy and meaningful at once'] (GW9(i) § 65). Correspondingly, in 'Das andere Tanzlied' Life uses an almost identical oxymoronic expression to describe another female figure, Zarathustra's Wisdom: 'Ah, diese tolle alte Närrin von Weisheit!' ['Ah, this crazy old fool, Wisdom!'] (Z III 15; N2: p. 472). And in his copy of *Zarathustra*, Jung wrote the word 'Anima' twice in the margin of this chapter.

Beyond these correspondences of vocabulary lies an important but unspoken conceptual affinity. For 'Das andere Tanzlied' (which simultaneously complements and 'takes back' the first 'Tanzlied') sings, albeit enigmatically, of the return of Dionysos which had been hinted at in 'Von der großen Sehnsucht'.[36] As pointed out above, Jung drew on an image borrowed from the ancient Nordic Edda, the *Völuspâ*, to describe the new force which was breaking through the psychological stalemate of modern life: Wotan. Underlying Jung's notion of the Anima, then, is a complex nexus of image and concept: Anima/Life/Dionysos.

Excursus: Jung, Nietzsche and the Concept of Meaning

This affinity of thought between Nietzsche and Jung goes even deeper than verbal and imagistic similarity in yet another respect. According to Jung, just as the Anima is the *'Archetypus des Lebens'* [*'archetype of life'*], so there is an *'Archetypus des Sinnes'* [*'archetype of meaning'*] (GW9(i) § 66). Why do we need the archetype of meaning? Jung argued that meaning ('Sinn') is not inherent in life – 'Im Grunde genommen bedeutet nichts etwas' ['Basically nothing means anything' (P. B.)] – because meaning relies on a spectator to perceive this meaning: 'als es noch keine denkenden Menschen gab, war niemand da, der die Erscheinungen deutete' ['when there were no thinking people, there was nobody there to interpret phenomena' (P. B.)] (GW9(i) § 65). In other words, just as Sartre held that existence precedes essence, so Jung wants to argue that life is prior to meaning, and that meaning, rather than being immanent, is actually the result of interpretation ('Sinngebung'). According to Jung, life appears to be prior to meaning ('Sinn'):

[36] See Lampert, pp. 234–40.

'Die Formen unserer Sinngebung sind historische Kategorien' ['The forms we use for assigning meaning are historical categories'] (GW9(i) § 67). Thus, life and the Anima are essentially meaningless, to the extent that meaning is not an immanent category. Nevertheless, according to Jung, that does not mean that there is no structure to existence:

> So sind die Anima und damit das Leben insofern bedeutungslos, als sie keine Deutung anbieten. Sie haben aber ein deutbares Wesen, denn in allem Chaos ist Kosmos und in aller Unordnung geheime Ordnung, in aller Willkür stetiges Gesetz, denn alles Wirkende beruht auf dem Gegensatz. Um dies zu erkennen, bedarf es des diskriminierenden Menschenverstandes, der alles in antinomische Urteile auflöst [...] Man ist in ziellosem Erleben verstrickt und verwirrt, und das Urteil mit allen seinen Kategorien erweist sich als machtlos (GW9(i) § 66).
>
> [Thus the Anima and life itself are meaningless insofar as they offer no interpretation. Yet they have a nature which can be interpreted, for in all chaos there is a cosmos, in all disorder a secret order, in all caprice a fixed law, for everything that has an effect is predicated on its opposite. It takes Man's discriminating understanding, which breaks everything down into antinomial judgments, to recognize this ... We are caught and entangled in meaningless experience, and the judging intellect with its categories proves itself powerless. (P. B.)]

The way out of such logical antinomies and existential aporias lies for Jung in apprehending the structures of existence, which he calls the archetypes, and in understanding Being as 'cosmos' (the Greek term for the world as an ordered unity, as opposed to chaos). Understanding of this fact relies on language, which Jung thought was one way back to these existential structures: 'Die Sinngebung bedient sich gewisser sprachlicher Matrizen, die ihrerseits wieder von urtümlichen Bildern abstammen [...] überall geraten wir in die Sprach- und Motivgeschichte, die immer stracks in die primitive Wunderwelt zurückführt' ['Interpretations make use of certain linguistic matrices that are themselves derived from primordial images ... everywhere we find ourselves confronted with the history of language, with images and motifs that lead straight back to the primitive wonder-world'] (GW9(i) § 67). Thus, for Jung, meaning is the result of an existential hermeneutic which reveals to us an archetypal reality.

Nietzsche's answer to what he calls 'the Schopenhauerian question' – '*hat denn das Dasein überhaupt einen Sinn?*' ['*Has existence any meaning at all?*'] (FW/GS § 357; N2: p. 228) – is equally complex. For Nietzsche, too, meaning ('Sinn') exists only as a product of interpretation. According to Nietzsche's notes in his *Nachlaß*, there is no meaning in itself or 'Sinn an sich' (WM/WP 556, 590 = N3: pp. 487, 503). Throughout his work, Nietzsche apparently denies any notion of cosmic order and, in *Die fröhliche Wissenschaft* [*The Gay Science*], he argues that the world is in fact nothing but chaos: 'Der Gesamtcharakter der Welt ist dagegen in alle Ewigkeit Chaos, nicht im Sinne der fehlenden Notwendigkeit, sondern der fehlenden Ordnung, Gliederung, Form, Schönheit, Weisheit, und wie alle unsere ästhetischen Menschlichkeiten heißen' ['The total character of the world, however, is in all eternity chaos – in the sense not of a lack of necessity but of a lack of order, arrangement, form, beauty, wisdom, and whatever other names there are for our aesthetic anthropomorphisms'] (FW/GS § 109; N2: p. 115). In this passage, however, Nietzsche specifically makes the point that chaos can coexist with necessity ('Notwendigkeit'), and so leaves open the possibility of organization through necessity. In fact, whilst Nietzsche denies the existence of an immanent meaning in life, his whole philosophy is an invitation to *create* such meaning, and a celebration of the man who does so with his Dionysian wisdom – the Superman. This 'Notwendigkeit' takes the form of the Eternal Recurrence, and the Dionysian Superman *is* in fact the 'meaning' of the earth: 'Der Übermensch ist der Sinn der Erde' ['The Superman is the meaning of the earth'] (Z Vorrede/Prologue § 3; N2: p. 280). For Nietzsche, interpretation (as the creation of meaning) and meaning itself are both synonymous with the Will to Power: 'Aller Sinn ist Wille zur Macht [...] das Interpretieren selbst als eine Form des Willens zur Macht' ['All meaning is Will to Power ... the interpretation itself is a form of the Will to Power'] (WM/WP 590, 556 = N3: pp. 503, 487). Indeed, Jean Granier has described Nietzsche's existential hermeneutic as 'l'essence de l'Etre comme Etre-interprété'.[37]

Thus, whilst one side of the Nietzschean coin is Nihilism, the other side is, in the words of R. J. Hollingdale, 'non-metaphysical transcendence'.[38] As Nietzsche put it in his unpublished notes for *Der Wille zur Macht*, 'ein Ziel ist immer noch ein Sinn' ['any goal at least constitutes some meaning'] (WM/WP 12 = N3: p. 677). The structures which underpin the Nietzschean universe are certainly not static Jungian archetypes; instead, Nietzsche collapses all interpretation and meaning into an expression of the Will to Power. Furthermore, existence is organized through the expression of the Will to Power in time, i.e. the Eternal Recurrence, which structures existence through repetition. Chaos and Eternal Recurrence are not mutually contradictory, for, as Nietzsche argues in a note from the *Nachlaß*: 'Das "Chaos des Alls" als Ausschluß jeder Zweckthätigkeit steht *nicht* im Widerspruch zum Gedanken des Kreislaufes: letzterer ist eben eine *unvernünftige Nothwendigkeit*' ['The "chaos of the universe" as the exclusion of all purposeful activity does *not* stand in contradiction to the thought of the cycle: the latter is precisely an *irrational necessity*'].[39] The imposition of structure (and hence of meaning) onto the meaningless world of ceaseless Becoming, is the challenge which Nietzsche invites us to accept. Clearly, 'meaning' in such a universe is beyond any logico-rational categories, and indeed is intended by

---

37 Jean Granier, *Le Problème de la vérité dans la philosophie de Nietzsche* (Paris, 1966), p. 463.

38 See *A Nietzsche Reader*, edited by R. J. Hollingdale (Harmondsworth, 1977), p. 11.

39 Nietzsche, *Kritische Gesamtausgabe Werke*, edited by G. Colli and M. Montinari, 30 vols (Berlin, 1976 –), V 2, 11 [225], p. 426.

Nietzsche to be the affair of the individual. As Ophelia Schutte has argued, the Will to Power is 'the self-given designation for that which resists being assimilated into discursive thought'.[40]

Nietzsche's discussion of the Will to Power also reveals an important similarity with Jung's principle of the opposites: 'alles Wirkende beruht auf dem Gegensatz' ['everything that has an effect is predicated on its opposite'] (GW9(i) § 66). According to Nietzsche, 'Der Wille zur Macht [ist] nicht ein Sein, nicht ein Werden, sondern ein *Pathos*' ['The Will to Power is not a Being, not a Becoming, but a *pathos*'], in the sense of a disposition or tendency of fields of force, i.e. structures of power: 'dynamische Quanta, in einem Spannungsverhältnis zu allen anderen Quanten, deren Wesen [...] in ihrem "Wirken" auf dieselben [besteht]' ['dynamic quanta, in a relation of tension to all other dynamic quanta, whose essence lies in their "effect" upon all other quanta'] (WM/WP 635 = N3: p. 778). The predication of these dynamic quanta on opposition constitutes what Nietzsche calls '*den Gegensatz-Charakter des Daseins*' ['*the antithetical character of existence*'] (WM/WP 881 = N3: p. 595). Furthermore, just as Jung seeks to find the underlying unity in all opposition, so Nietzsche's opposites are not absolute but relative, and subsumed by the greater unity of the Will to Power: 'Ruhe – Bewegung, fest – locker: alles Gegensätze, die nicht an sich existieren und mit denen tatsächlich nur *Gradverschiedenheiten* ausgedrückt werden [...] Es gibt keine Gegensätze: nur von denen der Logik her haben wir den Begriff des Gegensatzes – und von da aus fälschlich in die Dinge übertragen' ['rest – motion, firm – loose: opposites that do not exist in themselves and that actually express only variations in degree ... There are no opposites: only from those of logic do we derive the concept of opposites – and falsely transfer it to things'] (WM/WP 552; N3: p. 541; cf. WM/WP 516, 530, 693; N3: pp. 537–58, 886, 778; JGB/BGE § 2; N2: p. 568).

In other words, Nietzsche's view that 'reality' is constituted by the constantly changing disposition of the Will to Power has much in common with Jung's view that 'reality' is constituted by the (archetypal) psychic images within us and, more importantly, the changes which they bring about in us. However, the chief difference between Jung and Nietzsche lies in the question of what it is that it is said to structure existence. In Jung's psychic monism, the archetypes function as categories of the imagination, canalizing the libido and, by giving it shape and form, endowing life with meaning. Apart from the temporal structuring of the Eternal Recurrence, Nietzsche's 'volitionary' monism by contrast knows no such structures, and the ceaseless flux of Becoming – the perpetual struggle of the Will to Power – resists attempts to exercise conceptual mastery over it.[41]

---

[40] Ofelia Schutte, *Beyond Nihilism: Nietzsche without Masks* (Chicago and London, 1984), p. 50.

[41] In *Heidegger and Jaspers on Nietzsche* (The Hague, 1973), Richard Lowell Howey has argued that Nietzsche transforms the dualism of Being and Becoming into a 'dialectical monism' – a

Zarathustra as Archetype

Towards the end of his essay 'Über die Archetypen des kollektiven Unbewußten' and following his discussion of the Anima, Jung makes a further reference to *Zarathustra* in which he claims to detect the presence of another, related archetype – the Old Wise Man. This archetype manifests itself in a manner distinctively different from the Anima, but its function is similar: 'Er ist, wie die Anima, ein unsterblicher Dämon, welcher die chaotischen Dunkelheiten des bloßen Lebens mit dem Lichte des Sinnes durchdringt' ['He is, like the Anima, an immortal daemon that pierces the chaotic darkness of brute life with the light of meaning'] (GW9(i) § 77). According to Jung, this archetype is at work in the figure of Zarathustra, the mouthpiece of Dionysian wisdom:

> Er ist der Erleuchtende, der Lehrer und Meister, ein Psychopompos (Führer der Seelen), dessen Personifikation selbst der "Zertrümmerer der Tafeln", Nietzsche, nicht entgehen konnte, hat er doch dessen Inkarnation in Zarathustra, dem überlegenen Geiste eines beinahe homerischen Zeitalters, zum Träger und Verkünder seiner eigenen "dionysischen" Erleuchtung und Entzückung aufgerufen. Gott war ihm zwar tot, aber der Dämon der Weisheit wurde ihm zum sozusagen leibhaftigen Zweiten, wie er sagt:
>
> Da, plötzlich, Freundin! wurde Eins zu Zwei –
> Und Zarathustra ging an mir vorbei...
>
> (GW9(i) § 77).
>
> [He is the enlightener, the master and teacher, a psychopomp whose personification even Nietzsche, that breaker of tablets, could not escape – for he had called up his reincarnation in Zarathustra, the lofty spirit of an almost Homeric age, as the carrier and mouthpiece of his own "Dionysian" enlightenment and ecstasy. For him God

---

synthesis of Heraclitus and Parmenides – or a 'volitionary' monism (p. 49); cf. 'Dem Werden den Charakter des Seins *aufzuprägen* – das ist der *höchste Wille zur Macht* [...] *Daß alles wiederkehrt*, ist die extremste *Annäherung einer Welt des Werdens an die des Seins* – *Gipfel der Betrachtung*' ['To impose upon Becoming the character of Being – that is the supreme Will to Power ... That *everything recurs* is the closest *approximation of a world of Becoming to a world of Being*. – high point of the meditation'] (WM/WP 617 = N3: p. 895); 'Gesetzt endlich, daß es gelänge, unser gesamtes Triebleben als die Ausgestaltung und Verzweigung *einer* Grundform des Willens zu erklären – nämlich des Willens zur Macht, wie es *mein* Satz ist –; gesetzt, daß man alle organischen Funktionen auf diesen Willen zur Macht zurückführen könnte und in ihm auch die Lösung des Problems der Zeugung und Ernährung – es ist *ein* Problem – fände, so hätte man damit sich das Recht verschafft, *alle* wirkende Kraft eindeutig zu bestimmen als: *Wille zur Macht*. Die Welt von innen gesehen, die Welt auf ihren "intelligiblen Charakter" hin bestimmt und bezeichnet – sie wäre eben "Wille zur Macht" und nichts außerdem' ['Suppose, finally, we succeeded in explaining our entire instinctive life as the development and ramification of *one* basic form of the will – namely, the Will to Power, as *my* proposition has it; suppose all organic functions could be traced back to this Will to Power and one could also find in it the solution of the problem of procreation and nourishment – it is *one* problem – then one would have gained the right to determine *all* efficient force univocally as – *Will to Power*. The world viewed from inside, the world defined and determined according to its "intelligible character" – it would be "Will to Power" and nothing else'] (JGB/BGE § 36; N2: p. 601).

was dead, but the driving daemon of wisdom became as it were his bodily double. He himself says:

Then, suddenly, friend, one turned into two –
And Zarathustra walked into my view.]

Here, Jung sees Zarathustra not just as a figure of Nietzsche's poetic imagination, but as an autonomous *Gestalt*, i.e. an archetype. And because the arrival of Zarathustra was preceded by the death of God, the archetype is said to herald the arrival of a new source of life out of darkness and the absence of meaning:

> Zarathustra ist für Nietzsche mehr als poetische Figur, er ist ein unwillkürliches Bekenntnis. Auch er hatte sich in den Dunkelheiten eines gottabgewandten, entchristlichten Lebens verirrt, und darum trat zu ihm der Offenbarende und Erleuchtende, als redender Quell seiner Seele. Daher stammt die hieratische Sprache des "*Zarathustra*", denn das ist der Stil dieses Archetypus (GW9(i) § 77).

> [Zarathustra is more for Nietzsche than a poetic figure; he is an involuntary confession, a testament. Nietzsche too had lost his way in the darkness of a life that turned its back upon God and Christianity, and that is why there came to him the revealer and enlightener, the speaking fountainhead of his soul. Here is the source of the hieratic language of *Zarathustra*, for that is the style of this archetype.]

Because Jung sensed that *Zarathustra* represented an advance in the consciousness of the reality of the archetypes, his choice of Nietzsche's epic work for his Seminar from 1934 to 1939 was natural in the light of his previous intellectual development. Thus Nietzsche was a 'psycho-logist' for Jung in yet another sense: through him – in *Zarathustra* – Jung believed that the *psyche* had become word ('logos') and archetypal image.

By 1934, the year when he began his Seminar on Nietzsche, we can see that Jung's attitude to Nietzsche had altered in the following four respects. First, whilst Jung regarded Nietzsche, as he did Freud, as a product of his times, he nonetheless believed that Nietzsche pointed the way beyond Freud. He not only appreciated Nietzsche's emphasis on the importance of psychology but, more importantly, Jung was beginning to think that *Also sprach Zarathustra* contained precisely the sort of archetypal revelation which he believed contained 'der rettende Gedanke' ['the saving thought'] from the Unconscious. Second, two of Jung's key archetypes took form on the basis of deep Nietzschean influence: his description of the Anima contains a very large number of parallels with Nietzsche's description of the figure of Life, and in Zarathustra himself Jung saw the 'Gestalt' of the Old Wise Man. This fact suggests that Jung was already well-acquainted with *Zarathustra* before the Seminar began, and had incorporated Nietzschean ideas and images possibly even more than he was aware. In his Seminar on Nietzsche, Jung dated his reading of *Zarathustra* back to 1898, but claimed that he returned to the book in November 1914 and only then began annotating his copy (SNZ:I:p. 259). Third, Jung had by 1934 developed a model of the psyche which, despite its Kantian elements, was in fact much more indebted to Nietzsche, in that his own psychic monism (everything is Psyche) corresponded in several key respects to Nietzsche's volitionary monism (everything is Will to Power). And fourth, Jung was beginning to see the influence of the archetypes in the political and social events around him, in particular that of the Dionysos/Wotan archetype.

Chapter 8

Jung's Reception of Nietzsche in Three Eranos Lectures: Dionysos and the Alchemical Nietzsche

Early in the Twenties, Olga Fröbe-Kapteyn (1881–1962), the daughter of Dutch parents, had a villa called Casa Gabriella built in the grounds of her property by Lake Maggiore near Ascona in Switzerland.[1] She used her contacts to set up an international seminar dedicated to bringing together Eastern and Western philosophy. Included among the lecturers whom she invited was C. G. Jung, and his presence ensured that the concepts of Analytical Psychology provided the dominant intellectual framework for the Eranos Conferences.[2] The name of the meetings – 'eranos', a Greek word, meaning a meal to which everyone contributed – was suggested by the theologian and philosopher of religion Rudolf Otto (1869–1937), and the list of contributors over the years includes Martin Buber (1878–1965), Gershom Scholem (1897–1982), Mircea Éliade (1907–1986), and Daisetz Teitaro Suzuki (1870–1966). Furthermore, two Nietzsche scholars – Ernst Benz (b.1907) and Karl Löwith (1897–1973) – and two classical scholars whose work included special studies on Dionysos – Károly Kerényi (1897–1973) and Walter Friedrich Otto (1874–1958) – also lectured at Eranos.[3]

---

1 For an account of the vigorous intellectual activity in the twentieth century in this small Swiss-lake village, see Martin Green, *Mountain of Truth: The Counterculture begins: Ascona, 1900–1920* (Hanover and London, 1986).

2 For more information on the Eranos Conferences, see Vincent Brome, *Jung* (London, 1978), pp. 212–16, and William McGuire, *Bollingen: An Adventure in Collecting the Past* (Princeton, 1982), pp. 117–81. According to Brome, Casa Gabriella was also the site of some latter-day libations to Dionysos: 'The night came, famous now in the memories of Eranos, when what Jaffé described as a "nocturnal celebration on the terrace ..." developed into a party where "merrymaking resounded far over the lake". Such a pitch did the party reach that neighbours "far and wide" sent in complaints to Mrs Froebe who, herself lost in the spirit of the moment, simply ignored them. As for Jung, like everyone else he grew tipsy on wine, and moved among the throng encouraging those who hesitated to dig deeper into Dionysos. "It was", as one woman present said, "the nearest I ever came to wicked abandonment in my life." And Aniela Jaffé later recorded: "Jung was here, there and everywhere, bubbling over with wit, mockery and drunken spirit. Only a poet could describe this gay and abandoned 'night-sea journey'."'

3 Even though Ernst Benz, author of *Nietzsches Ideen zur Geschichte des Christentums wider der Kirche* (Leiden, 1956), Karl Löwith, author of *Kierkegaard and Nietzsche* (Frankfurt am Main, 1933) and *Nietzsches Philosophie der ewigen Wiederkunft des Gleichen* (Berlin, 1935), Károly Kerényi, author of *Dionysos und das Tragische in der Antigone* (Frankfurt am Main, 1935) and *Die Herkunft der Dionysos-*

Between 1931 and 1951, Jung himself delivered 14 lectures *in toto* to the Eranos Conferences, and many of his most important theoretical texts were first offered as papers here. In this chapter I shall concentrate on three papers, starting with 'Traumsymbole des Individuationsprozesses' ['Dream Symbols of the Process of Individuation'] (1935), which contains a discussion of the Dionysian and what it meant for Nietzsche. Then I shall look at two further papers, 'Zur Empirie des Individuationsprozesses' ['A Study in the Process of Individuation'] (1933) and 'Die Erlösungsvorstellungen in der Alchemie' ['The Idea of Redemption in Alchemy'] (1936), where Jung discussed Nietzsche in the light of his recently-acquired interest in alchemy, showing why he believed that *Zarathustra* represented a substantial psychological advance on Goethe's *Faust*. As well as both reflecting and complementing Jung's treatment of Nietzsche in his *Zarathustra* Seminar, which he was concurrently delivering in Zurich (1934–1939), the claims of both papers and Jung's discussion of Faust and Zarathustra anticipate his later analysis of the Second World War and the psychological roots of German Fascism.

'Was hat Dionysos Nietzsche bedeutet!'

'Traumsymbole des Individuationsprozesses' represents Jung's first systematic attempt to link the medieval tradition of alchemy with the fundamental concepts of Analytical Psychology. First delivered as a lecture to the Eranos Conference held from 12 to 22 August 1935[4] and later published in an expanded version in *Psychologie und Alchemie* [*Psychology and Alchemy*] (1944), this paper, like the earlier 'Zur Empirie des Individuationsprozesses' (1933) (see below), analyses a series of dreams produced by one of Jung's patients. In it, Jung repeatedly draws attention to the importance of Dionysos, emphasizing the rôle of the instincts (associated here with the earth) in the psychic economy. In *Wandlungen und Symbole der Libido* [*Psychology of the Unconscious*] (1911/12), Jung had interpreted the visions of Miss Frank Miller as various stages in her individuation process, and had provided side-illustrations from Nietzsche. Now he moved the importance of the Dionysian to centre-stage, and the rites of Dionysos are held to be the

religion (Cologne, 1956), and Walter F. Otto, author of *Dionysos: Mythos und Kultus* (Frankfurt am Main, 1933) did not lecture at Eranos until the Forties and Fifties (except Otto, who lectured on 'Der Sinn der eleusinischen Mysterien' in 1939), Jung's post-war thinking about Nietzsche and the Dionysian may well have been influenced by these contacts; and Jung himself played an important part in creating a forum for such distinguished international scholarship.

4 'Traumsymbole des Individuationsprozesses: Ein Beitrag zur Kenntnis der in den Träumen sich kundgebenden Vorgänge des Unbewußten', *Eranos-Jahrbuch*, 3 (1935), pp. 13–133. The alterations made in the version published in GW12 § 44–331 are essentially minor, and so I quote from the version in the *Gesammelte Werke*.

most impressive example of the psychological process of renewal.[5] His remarks on Nietzsche are made in the context of the analysis of his patient's dreams.

In his commentary on Dream 18 (in the first series of dreams), Jung referred to Zarathustra's command in 'Von den Freuden- und Leidenschaften' ['Of Joys and Passions'] not to give names to one's virtues (Z I 5; N2: p. 302).[6] Approving of this refusal to shape and name, which disintegrates the psyche into discrete units and yields to the 'Banalität des äußeren Aspektes' ['banality of the outward aspect'], Jung claimed that psychic being can be divided into different aspects only because it is from its origins a plurality, lacking that integrated unity which he predicated of the 'Self':

> Auf Seelisches angewendet, wäre es das, was Nietzsche im "*Zarathustra*" verwirft: nämlich den Tugenden Namen zu geben. Durch Formung und Benennung wird das seelische Wesen in gemünzte und bewertete Einheiten aufgelöst. Dies ist aber nur darum möglich, weil es auch ein angeborenes Vielerlei, eine Zusammenhäufung von nicht integrierten Erbeinheiten ist. Der natürliche Mensch ist kein Selbst, sondern Massenpartikel und Masse, ein Kollektivum bis zu dem Grade, daß er seines Ich nicht einmal sicher ist (GW12 § 104).

> [Applied psychologically, this is just what Nietzsche refuses to do in his *Zarathustra*: to give names to the virtues. By being shaped and named, psychic life is broken down into coined and valued units. But this is possible only because it is intrinsically a great variety of things, an accumulation of unintegrated hereditary parts. Natural

---

[5] The main sources of Jung's knowledge about Dionysos were: Friedrich Creuzer, *Symbolik und Mythologie der alten Völker, besonders der Griechen*, 2 vols (Darmstadt and Leipzig, 1810–1821); Pierre Nicolas Rolle's *Recherches sur le culte de Bacchus, symbole de la force reproductive de la nature*, 2 vols (Paris, 1824); Ludwig Preller, *Griechische Mythologie*, 2 vols (Berlin, 1860); Jacob Burckhardt's *Griechische Kulturgeschichte*, 4 vols (1898–1902), and Erwin Rohde's *Psyche: Seelencult und Unsterblichkeit der Griechen* (Tübingen, 1907⁴) – all owned by Jung and contained in his library – and, of course, Nietzsche's *Die Geburt der Tragödie* (1872), which relied on these sources and played a rôle in mediating them to Jung.

[6] The relevant part of Nietzsche's text is as follows:

Mein Bruder, wenn du eine Tugend hast, und es deine Tugend ist, so hast du sie mit niemamdem gemeinsam.

Freilich, du willst sie beim Namen nennen und liebkosen, du willst sie am Ohre zupfen und Kurzweil mit ihr treiben.

Und siehe! Nun hast du ihren Namen mit dem Volke gemeinsam und bist Volk und Herde geworden mit deiner Tugend!

Besser tätest du, zu sagen: "Unaussprechbar ist und namenlos, was meiner Seele Qual und Süße macht und auch noch der Hunger meiner Eingeweide ist". (Z I 5; N2: p. 302).

[My brother, if you have a virtue, and it is your own virtue, you have it in common with no one.

To be sure, you want to call it by a name and caress it; you want to pull its ears and amuse yourself with it.

And behold! Now you have its name in common with the people and have become of the people and the herd with your virtue!

You would do better to say: "Unutterable and nameless is that which torments and delights my soul and is also the hunger of my belly".]

See also Jung's comments in his Nietzsche lectures of 6 and 13 March 1935 (SNZ:I:pp. 424–54).

> Man is not a "Self" – he is the mass and a particle in the mass, collective to such a degree that he is not even sure of his Ego.]

Jung's reference is a clue to the Nietzschean origin of his concept of the Self. In the preceding section of *Zarathustra* entitled 'Von den Verächtern des Leibes' ['Of the Despisers of the Body'], Nietzsche questions the supremacy of the conscious Ego and suggests that behind (or beyond) it lies the Self ('das Selbst'). As Nietzsche put it in *Jenseits von Gut und Böse* [*Beyond Good and Evil*], the 'Ich' is a 'synthetic' concept (JGB/BGE § 19; N2: p. 582; cf. WM/WP 371 = N3: p. 850), and subjectivity a mere superstition, the 'Subjekt- und Ich-Aberglaube' (JGB/BGE Vorrede/Prologue; N2: p. 565). Indeed, in his notes for *Der Wille zur Macht*, Nietzsche put the multiplicity of the Self at the head of the list of 'his' hypotheses (WM/WP 490 = N3: p. 473). Moreover, Nietzsche's notion of the Self implies the possibility of the creation of an integrated whole, as is clear from the association made in *Menschliches, Allzumenschliches* [*Human, All Too Human*] between the Self and the Will: 'Die tätigen, erfolgreichen Naturen handeln nicht nach dem Spruche "kenne dich selbst", sondern wie als ob ihnen der Befehl vorschwebe: *wolle* ein Selbst, so *wirst* du ein Selbst' ['Active, successful natures act, not according to the dictum "know thyself", but as if there hovered before them the commandment: *will* a self and thou shalt *become* a self'] (MA/HA VMS/AOM § 366; N1: p. 862). The links between the Nietzschean and Jungian Self are discussed in more detail in Chapter 13.

On Jung's account, natural (i.e. primitive) Man has no 'self' inasmuch as he is not sufficiently individuated to be sure of his own subjectivity as opposed to the collective identity of the mass. Jung argued that the function of the primitive mysteries of transformation is to support the construction of the Ego and oppose the force of the collective (or animal) psyche:

> Darum bedarf [der Mensch] schon seit uralten Zeiten der Wandlungsmysterien, die ihn zu "etwas" machen und damit der tierähnlichen Kollektivpsyche, die ein bloßes Vielerlei ist, entreißen (GW12 § 104).

> [That is why since time immemorial Man has needed the transformation mysteries to turn him into something, and to rescue him from the animal collective psyche, which is nothing but a *variété*.]

According to Jung, the psychic goal to be reached (the telos of history as well as the aim of the Individuation Process) is not just life in and for itself, but life plus consciousness: 'Nicht daß Leben an und für sich geschieht, sondern daß es auch gewußt werde, das ist wirkliches Leben' ['Life that just happens in and for itself is not real life; it is real only when it is *known*']. But only a unified personality, not the multiplicity of the unintegrated human being, is able to experience life in its many diverse aspects: 'Nur die geeinte Persönlichkeit kann Leben erfahren, nicht aber jenes in Teilaspekte aufgespaltene Ereignis, das sich auch Mensch nennt' ['Only a unified personality can experience life, not that personality which is split up into partial aspects, that bundle of odds and ends which also calls itself "Man"'] (GW12 § 105). In particular, Jung identified the mystery rites from which tragedy evolved as the most significant rites through which such a synthetic unity could be achieved. Implicitly referring to *Die Geburt der Tragödie* [*The Birth of Tragedy*], Jung suggested that the function of tragedy was to provide a link back with the primordial unity:

> Das Bocksspiel wird zur "Tragödie". Das Satyrspiel ist nach aller Analogie eine Mysterienhandlung, von der man wohl annehmen darf, daß ihr Zweck, wie überall, die Rückverbindung des Menschen mit der natürlichen Ahnenreihe und so mit der Lebensquelle war (GW12 § 105).
>
> [The "play of goats" will develop into a "tragedy". According to all the analogies, the satyr play was a mystery performance, from which we may assume that its purpose, as everywhere, was to re-establish Man's connection with his natural ancestry and thus with the source of life.]

In *Psychologischen Typen* [*Psychological Types*] (1921), Jung had referred to the satyr as simultaneously representing the divine and the animal aspects of Man (GW6 § 210/CW6 § 227), and he took up this symbolism in 'Traumsymbole des Individuationsprozesses'. In his analysis of Dream 22, Jung defined the tragic implication of the satyr-play in terms of a two-way transformation: that of the divine into the animal on the one hand ('die blutige Zerreißung des Tier gewordenen Gottes' ['the bloody dismemberment of the god who has become an animal']) and that of the animal into the divine on the other ('die tierhafte Göttlichkeit der uranfänglichen Seele' ['the animal divinity of the primordial psyche']) (GW12 § 118). According to Jung, what Antiquity knew about the strange and paradoxical nature of Man had been revived for the modern age by Nietzsche. And once again, Jung insisted that Nietzsche's experience of the Dionysian had been a personal one, seeing in Nietzsche's madness and premature death a fate identical to that of Dionysos-Zagreus:

> Und was hat ihm [= Nietzsche] Dionysos bedeutet! Man muß wohl ernst nehmen, was er selber darüber sagt – noch mehr: was ihm selber zustieß. Unzweifelhaft wußte er im Prodromalstadium seiner fatalen Krankheit, daß ihm das düstere Schicksal des Zagreus beschieden war (GW12 § 118).
>
> [But what did Dionysos mean to Nietzsche? What he says about it must be taken seriously; what it did to him still more so. There can be no doubt that he knew, in the preliminary stages of his fatal illness, that the dismal fate of Zagreus was reserved for him.]

Jung argued that knowledge of the Dionysian had been repressed in the course of civilization, but he thought that it still threatened to break out. What appear to be political and social factors are, in Jung's view, symptoms of a deeper underlying cause: Dionysos. In the following passage, Jung expressed his full ambivalence towards what he called a 'blessed and terrible' experience:

> Dionysos bedeutet den Abgrund der leidenschaftlichen Auflösung aller menschlichen Besonderung in die tierhafte Göttlichkeit der uranfänglichen Seele – ein segensreiches und furchtbares Erlebnis, dem eine wohlumhegte Kulturmenschheit entronnen zu sein glaubt, bis es ihr wieder gelingt, einen neuen Blutrausch zu entfesseln, worüber sich dann alle Wohlgesinnten verwundern, um das Großkapital, die Rüstungsindustrie, die Juden und die Freimaurer dafür anzuklagen (GW12 § 118).
>
> [Dionysos is the abyss of impassioned dissolution, where all human distinctions are merged in the animal divinity of the primordial psyche – a blissful and terrible experience. Humanity, huddling behind the walls of its culture, believes it has escaped this experience, until it succeeds in letting loose another orgy of bloodshed. All well-meaning people are amazed when this happens and blame high finance, the armaments industry, the Jews or the freemasons.]

Jung's argument is not unique in terms of psychoanalytic forays into sociology. Five years earlier in 1930, Freud had uttered a very similar warning in *Das Unbehagen in der Kultur* [*Civilization and its Discontents*], attributing social and political 'discontent' in civilization to the unavoidable repression/sublimation of instinct and libidinal energies in the construction of culture.[7] But whereas Freud divided the repressed forces of the psyche into two major drives of Eros (the life-instinct) and Thanatos (the death-instinct), Jung subsumed instinctual life as a whole under a single emblem: Dionysos.

In his analysis of Dream 6 (of the second series), Jung discovered further Dionysian imagery in his patient's dreams and commented on it in detail. The Dionysian mysteries are said to be an example of the 'leftward way' – that is, a psychological approach which lays stress not on the conscious but the unconscious aspects of human awareness. In Jung's characterization, the 'leftward way' is the path downwards to the Unconscious: 'nicht ins Reich der Götter und ewigen Ideen hinauf, sondern hinunter in die Naturgeschichte, in die tierische Instinktgrundlage des menschlichen Wesens' ['not upwards to the kingdom of the gods and eternal ideas, but down into natural history, into the bestial instinctive foundations of human existence'] (GW12 § 169). The 'animal instincts' are explicitly identified with Dionysos: 'Es handelt sich also um ein – antik

[7] 'Die Triebsublimierung ist ein besonders hervorstechender Zug der Kulturentwicklung, sie macht es möglich, daß höhere psychische Tätigkeiten, wissenschaftliche, künstlerische, ideologische, eine so bedeutsame Rolle im Kulturleben spielen [...] [Es ist] unmöglich zu übersehen, in welchem Ausmaß die Kultur auf Triebverzicht aufgebaut ist, wie sehr sie gerade die Nichtbefriedigung [...] von mächtigen Trieben zur Voraussetzung hat' ['Sublimation of the drives is a particularly striking feature of cultural development – it enables higher psychic activities (of a scientific, artistic, or ideological kind) to play such an important part in cultural life. It is impossible to overlook the extent to which culture is based on the renunciation of drives and presupposes precisely the non-satisfaction of powerful drives'] (Sigmund Freud, *Gesammelte Werke* (Frankfurt am Main, 1968–1978), XIV, p. 457).

ausgedrückt – dionysisches Mysterium' ['we are therefore dealing, to put it in classical language, with a Dionysian mystery'] (ibid.). On Jung's interpretation of the psychological significance of the Dionysian rites, the consecration to the god and the sleep of incubation (a ritual death) represent the integration of the Unconscious side into the individual's psyche, and thus a stage in the return to the source of life itself:

> Die Rückidentifikation mit den menschlichen und tierischen Ahnen bedeutet psychologisch eine Integration des Unbewußten, recht eigentlich ein Erneuerungsbad in der Lebensquelle [...] das heißt unbewußt wie im Schlafe, in der Trunkenheit und im Tode; daher der Inkubationsschlaf, die dionysische Weihe und der rituelle Tod in der Initiation (GW12 § 171).
>
> [This atavistic identification with human and animal ancestors can be interpreted psychologically as an integration of the Unconscious, a veritable bath of renewal in the life-source ... unconscious as in sleep, intoxication, and death. Hence the sleep of incubation, the Dionysian orgy, and the ritual death in initiation.]

Whilst admitting that the conceptions of mystery religions could easily be understood in terms of infantile regressions (as classical Freudian theory had argued), Jung pointed out that such an interpretation missed the deeper significance of ritual practices. For according to Jung, the goal of Dionysian regression is of the greatest significance: through it, the separation of consciousness and the Unconscious is overcome, and Man is united once more with his instinctual life:

> Die Symbolik der Erneuerungsriten, wenn ernst genommen, weist über das bloß Infantile und Archaische hinaus auf jene angeborene psychische Disposition, welche das Resultat und Depositum aller Ahnenleben zurück bis zur Tierheit ist [...] Es handelt sich um Versuche, die Abtrennung des Bewußtseins vom Unbewußten, welches die eigentliche Lebensquelle ist, aufzuheben und eine Wiedervereinigung des Individuums mit dem Mutterboden der vererbten, instinktiven Disposition herbeizuführen (GW12 § 174).
>
> [The symbolism of the rites of renewal, if taken seriously, points far beyond the merely archaic and infantile to Man's innate psychic disposition, which is the result and deposit of all ancestral life right down to the animal level ... The rites are attempts to abolish the separation between the conscious mind and the Unconscious, the real source of life, and to bring about a reunion of the individual with the native soil of his inherited, instinctive make-up.]

Whilst acknowledging the right of consciousness to its own place in the psychic economy of the individual and granting it its own autonomy, Jung nonetheless argued that the price of an increase in consciousness is an increasing alienation from the life of the instincts. And for Jung, this 'Instinktfremdheit' and 'Instinktlosigkeit' explains Man's current psychological straits, together with his sense that he has somehow lost his way. This claim sounds an existential note in Jung's project: 'Instinktlosigkeit aber ist die Quelle endloser Irrungen und

Wirrungen' ['Loss of instinct is the source of endless error and confusion'] (GW12 § 174).

In at least six ways throughout this lecture, Jung stressed the need, as he saw it, to return to the instincts. First, by virtue of its own inner structures, 'unreasoning' instinct is said not so much to rebel against order as actually to found it. Or in other words, Jung wanted to prioritize the instincts over the Ego: 'Nicht daß der vernunftlose Instinkt eo ipso gegen festgefügte Ordnung rebellierte – ist er doch selber durch seine innere Gesetzmäßigkeit das festgefügteste Gebilde, und ist er doch überdies der schöpferische Urgrund aller gebundenen Ordnung' ['Not that unreasoning instinct rebels of itself against firmly established order; by the strict logic of its own inner laws it is itself of the finest structure imaginable and, in addition, the creative foundation of all binding order'] (GW12 § 93). Similarly, in Nietzsche's view, the realm of Dionysos is ontologically prior to that of Apollo, and consciousness is a mere manifestation of an unconscious drive which he called the Will to Power. Jung continued: 'Das Geheimnis ist, daß nur *das* Leben hat, was sich auch selber wiederum aufheben kann' ['The secret is that only that which can destroy itself is truly alive'], recalling the secret which the allegorical figure of Life whispers in the ear of Zarathustra: 'ich bin das, *was sich immer selber überwinden muß*' ['I am that *which must overcome itself again and again*'] (Z II 12; N2: p. 371; cf. Z II 7; N2: p. 358), whereupon Zarathustra proclaims all life to be Will to Power.

Second, this return to the instincts, the creative source of life, is, in Jung's account, described as a downward journey to the Dionysian mysteries: 'ein sozusagen systematischer Abstieg "ad inferos", eine psychologische nekyia' ['a kind of systematic descent *ad inferos*, a psychological *nekyia*'] (GW12 § 178). Third, part of the return to the world of instinct involves the acceptance of its concrete expression, that is to say, the body. In the case which he was studying, Jung showed that the dreamer must decide to accept and act upon 'den Körper und die Instinktwelt, die Wirklichkeit des Liebes- und Lebensproblems' ['the body and the world of instinct, the reality of the problems posed by love and life'] (GW12 § 163). For his part, Nietzsche's Zarathustra taught that the needs of the spirit were determined by the purposes of the body: 'Der schaffende Leib schuf sich den Geist als eine Hand seines Willens' ['The creative body created spirit for itself, as a hand of its will'] (Z I 4; N2: p. 301).

Fourth, Jung used the image of the earth in his discussion of the instinctual life, contrasting the 'airiness' of certain attitudes with the more solid, 'down to earth' approach which he advocated:

> Man soll nicht mit "geistigen" Intuitionen sich über die "Erde", das heißt über die harte Wirklichkeit, erheben und ihr damit davonlaufen [...] Nur Götter gehen über die Regenbogenbrücke; die Sterblichen aber wandeln auf der Erde und sind deren Gesetzen unterworfen (GW12 § 148).

[We should not rise above the earth with aid of "spiritual" intuitions and run away from hard reality ... Only the gods can pass over the rainbow bridge; mortal men must stick to the earth and are subject to its laws.]

Less fatalistically perhaps, but no less emphatically, Zarathustra's first command bids men: '*bleibt der Erde treu*' ['*remain true to the earth*'] (Z Vorrede/Prologue § 3; N2: p. 280). And in 'Das Eselsfest' ['The Ass Festival'], Zarathustra points to the heavens and declares: 'Aber wir wollen auch gar nicht ins Himmelreich: Männer sind wir geworden, – *so wollen wir das Erdenreich*' ['But we certainly do not want to enter the kingdom of heaven: we have become men, *so we want the kingdom of earth*'] (Z IV 18 § 2; N2: p. 550). For Jung, the earth represents the realm of the instincts, i.e. the Unconscious: 'Das Unbewußte ist [...] der Erdenrest, welcher menschlicher Natur anhaftet und ihre ersehnte Kristallklarheit schmerzlich trübt' ['The Unconscious is the earthiness that clings to our human nature and sadly clouds the crystal clarity we long for'] (GW12 § 207).[8] Similarly, for Nietzsche, the acceptance of the earth as opposed to any nebulous higher realm is also an invitation to use the dark soil into which, in order to grow, the tree's roots must reach down (Z I 8; N2: p. 307) (cf. GW8 § 148).

Fifth, Jung discussed the rôle of the instincts in terms of the contrast between dark and light: '"Dunkel" ist chthonisch, das heißt irdisch-wirklich' ['"Dark" means chthonic, i.e. concrete and earthy'] (GW12 § 240), and in his analysis, Jung diagnosed that the dreamer had to accept the 'dark side' of his

---

[8] Jung had emphasized the importance of 'the earth' in 'Seele und Erde' ['Mind and Earth'] (GW10 § 49–103) (first given as a lecture under the title 'Die Erdbedingtheit der Psyche' ['The Determination of the Psyche by the Earth'] to the *Gesellschaft für freie Philosophie* (also known as the *Schule der Weisheit*) in Darmstadt in 1927 and published in the same year in the collection of essays *Mensch und Erde*, edited by Hermann Graf Keyserling (1880–1946, the founder of the school) (Darmstadt, 1927), pp. 83–138): '[...] wer aber bei seiner Erde bleibt, hat *Dauer*. Entfernung vom Unbewußten und damit von historischer Bedingtheit bedeutet *Wurzellosigkeit*. Das ist die Gefahr für den Eroberer fremden Bodens; das ist aber auch die Gefahr für den Einzelnen, wenn er durch Einseitigkeit in irgendeinem -ismus den Zusammenhang mit dem dunkeln, mütterlichen, erdhaften Urgrund seines Wesens verliert' ['he who is rooted in the soil endures. Alienation from the Unconscious and from its historical conditions spells rootlessness. That is the danger that lies in wait for the conqueror of foreign lands, and for every individual who, through one-sided allegiance to any kind of -ism, loses touch with the dark, maternal, earthy ground of his being'] (GW10 § 103). Some of Jung's remarks in this paper bring him close to such Far Right ideological themes as the mystique of the soil of Maurice Barrès (1862–1923), the notion of the 'métèque' of Charles Maurras (1868–1952), and the earth mysticism of Ludwig Klages (1872–1956), as he expressed it in 'Mensch und Erde' (a possible source for the title of Keyserling's collection), his contribution to *Freideutsche Jugend: Zur Jahrhundertfeier auf dem Hohen Meißner*, [edited by Arthur Kracke] (Jena, 1913), pp. 89–107, reprinted as the first essay in Ludwig Klages, *Mensch und Erde: Zehn Abhandlungen* (Stuttgart, 1956), pp. 1–25 (note the Nietzschean allusions on pp. 22–23). But, as Julian Roberts has argued, it is also possible to read Nietzsche's own philosophy as urging us to heed the call of 'the territorial spirits of our ancestors', advice which Roberts judges to be 'a curiously ineffectual answer to Nietzsche's proclamation of a philosophy of the future' (*German Philosophy: An Introduction* (Cambridge, 1988), p. 234).

personality, which in Jungian vocabulary is called his Shadow – a highly Nietzschean prescription. And sixth, Jung used the image of the snake as a symbol of the 'tierhafte Lebensmasse' ['the animal-like life-mass'], that is to say, 'die Totalität des angeborenen Unbewußten, welches mit dem Bewußtsein vereinigt werden soll' ['the totality of the inherited Unconscious, which is to be united with consciousness'] (GW12 § 184). Indeed, he explictly referred to the episode of the Shepherd and the Snake in 'Vom Gesicht und Rätsel' ['Of the Vision and the Riddle'] from *Zarathustra* (Z III 3 § 2; N2: p. 410). According to Jung, this episode prefigures, as does the episode with the tight-rope walker, the dangerous consequences of confronting Dionysos:

> Das Schlangenerlebnis des Hirten in Nietzsches "*Zarathustra*" wäre demnach ein fatales Omen (übrigens nicht das einzige dieser Art – vergleiche die Prophezeiung beim Tode des Seiltänzers) (GW12 § 184).
>
> [The Shepherd's experience with the Snake in Nietzsche's *Zarathustra* would accordingly be a fatal omen (and not the only one of its kind – cf. the prophecy of the death of the rope-dancer).]

According to Jung's reading, the episode of the Shepherd and the Snake represents a denial of the Unconscious.[9] Echoing his discussion of Schiller and Nietzsche in *Psychologische Typen*, Jung went on to suggest that whereas Schiller had foregrounded the importance of the Unconscious, Nietzsche (as the imagery of *Zarathustra* showed) had refused the Unconscious (embodied in the figure of the Ugliest Man) to the point where consciousness broke down:

> Es ist in der Tat kein bloß individuelles, sondern ein kollektives Problem, indem die in neuerer Zeit merkliche Belebung des Unbewußten, wie dies schon Friedrich Schiller ahnte, Anlaß zu Fragestellungen gibt, welche sich das 19. Jahrhundert nicht träumen ließ. Nietzsche entschied sich im "*Zarathustra*" zur Verwerfung der Schlange und des "häßlichsten Menschen" und damit zu einem heroischen Bewußtseinskrampf, welcher folgerichtigerweise zu dem im "*Zarathustra*" vorausgesagten Zusammenbruch führte (GW12 § 201).
>
> [It is in fact not merely an individual but a collective problem, for the animation of the Unconscious which has become so noticeable in recent times has, as Schiller foresaw, raised questions which the nineteenth century had never dreamed of. Nietzsche in his *Zarathustra* decided to reject the "Snake" and the "Ugliest Man", thus exposing himself to an heroic cramp of consciousness which led, logically enough, to the collapse foretold in the same book.]

What Jung called 'die Abgrundtiefe dionysischen Geheimnisses' ['the abysmal depths of the Dionysian mystery'] are apt to be ignored, he argued, either be-

[9] For an alternative psychoanalytic reading of this episode, see: H. Miles Groth, 'Nietzsche's Ontogenetic Theory of Time: The Riddle of the Laughing Shepherd', *American Imago*, 37 (1980), 351–70.

cause people find it too disturbing, or because they cling to a superficial rationalism (GW12 § 191). However, Jung found the dreams under discussion particularly important inasmuch as they are said to represent an attempt at 'eine Zusammensetzung christlicher und dionysischer religiöser Ideen' ['a combination of Christian and Dionysian religious ideas'] (GW12 § 181). In Jung's view, Modernity is characterized, as the case of Nietzsche also demonstrated, by those efforts on the part of the Unconscious to restore the lost element of Dionysos to the world of religion:

> Das Unbewußte hat aber keine solchen blasphemischen Absichten, sondern versucht einfach, den verlorenen Dionysos, welcher dem modernen Menschen irgendwie fehlt (man denke an Nietzsche!), wieder an die religiöse Welt anzuschließen (GW12 § 181).
>
> [But the Unconscious has no such blasphemous intentions; it is only trying to restore the lost Dionysos who is somehow lacking in modern Man (*pace* Nietzsche!) to the world of religion.]

Only by reinstating Dionysos and thus integrating the Unconscious into consciousness, so Jung's argument ran, could it become possible to create that wholeness which Jung terms the Self. Analogous to the 'Bruderbund' of Nietzsche's Apollo (consciousness) and Dionysos (the Unconscious), Jung is advocating, in the language of alchemy, a psychological *coniunctio oppositorum*. And the *mysterium coniunctionis* is represented in the striking specular image of the union of opposite reflections in a mirror: 'Man könnte [...] den "Mittelpunkt" auch als Schnittpunkt zweier entsprechender, aber im Spiegel umgekehrter Welten betrachten' ['We could regard the centre as the point of intersection of two worlds that correspond but are inverted by reflection'] (GW12 § 225).

This mid-point is what Jung called the 'Self': 'Das Selbst ist per definitionem die Mitte und der Umfang des bewußten und des unbewußten Systems' ['The Self is by definition the centre and the circumference of the conscious and unconscious systems'] (GW12 § 310).[10] Visually represented by the centredness and wholeness of the mandala, the mid-point of the union of opposites is said to be 'unerkennbar' ['unknowable'], and so susceptible only to symbolic representation (GW12 § 327). In *Psychologische Typen*, Jung had argued that only the symbol (Schiller's 'lebende Gestalt' ['living form']) could mediate the opposites and represent their union: 'Nur dem Symbol kann die vermittelnde Stellung zwischen den Gegensätzen zukommen' ['the mediating position between the opposites can be reached only by the symbol'] (GW6 § 169/CW6 § 178).

---

[10] Compare with Jung's reference to the scholastic definition of God: 'Deus est figura intellectualis, cuius centrum est ubique, circumferentia vero nusquam' (GW11 § 92, n. 64, § 229, n. 97) (see Chapter 13, pp. 342–56, for further discussion of the identity of the God-concept and the archetype of the Self).

Both Jung's analysis of the problems of Modernity and his solution have Nietzschean antecedents. First, Nietzsche, too, was concerned with the problem of mediating reason (consciousness) and instinct (the Unconscious), and regarded the extension of consciousness as highly ambivalent. For Nietzsche, too, 'das wachsende Bewußtsein' ['the growth of consciousness'] represented 'eine Gefahr' ['a danger'] (FW/GS § 354; N2: p. 222), and *Die fröhliche Wissenschaft* [*The Gay Science*] (1882) and *Jenseits von Gut und Böse* (1886) in particular present a relentless critique of rationality, showing (as Nietzsche put it in *Menschliches, Allzumenschliches*) 'wie Vernunft kommt – "zur Vernunft"' ['how reason comes "to its senses"'] (MA/HA I 'Unter Freunden'/'Among Friends'; N1: p. 733). Second, the Nietzschean concept of the Superman, exemplified in *Götzen-Dämmerung* [*Twilight of the Idols*] by the figure of Goethe (GD IX § 49; N2: pp. 1024–25), corresponds to Jung's own ideal of 'Totalität'. For Nietzsche, Goethe was a rare example of the unification of 'Vernunft, Sinnlichkeit, Gefühl, Wille' ['reason, sensuality, feeling, will'],[11] an individual who strove against separation, affirmed the whole, and created his own Self. Indeed, Jung marked the conclusion to Nietzsche's encomium with a marginal line in his own copy: 'er löste sich nicht vom Leben ab, er stellte sich hinein' ['he did not sever himself from life, he placed himself within it']. Moreover, according to Nietzsche, a faith in oneself such as Goethe's came, in his later years, to be described by the concept 'Dionysian': 'ein solcher Glaube ist der höchste aller möglichen Glauben: ich habe ihn auf den Namen des *Dionysos* getauft' ['such a faith is the highest of all possible faiths: I have baptized it with the name *Dionysos*']. Correspondingly, Jung's notion of the Self, an integrated wholeness in which the conscious and unconscious aspects of the individual psyche are united, could equally well be regarded in such terms: 'Jedes Leben ist schließlich eine Verwirklichung eines Ganzen, das heißt eines Selbst, weshalb man die Verwirklichung auch als Individuation bezeichnen kann' ['In the last analysis every life is the realization of a whole, that is, of a Self, for which reason this realization can also be called "individuation"'] (GW12 § 330).

The Alchemical Nietzsche

The beginning of Jung's interest in alchemy can be dated to 1928, when the German author, theologian and sinologist Richard Wilhelm (1873–1930) sent Jung a copy of *The Secret of the Golden Flower*, a Taoist alchemical treatise.[12] Jung

[11] These four characteristics corresponding almost exactly to the four Jungian psychic functions: Thinking, Feeling, Sensation and Intuition.

[12] 'Erst durch den Text der "Goldenen Blüte", der zur Chinesischen Alchemie gehört, und den ich 1928 von Richard Wilhelm erhalten hatte, ist mir das Wesen der Alchemie näher gekommen'

discovered in alchemy a rich source of symbolism to which he could apply his ideas, and in his biography he attached immense importance to alchemy:

> Sehr bald hatte ich gesehen, daß die Analytische Psychologie mit der Alchemie merkwürdig übereinstimmt. Die Erfahrungen der Alchemisten waren meine Erfahrungen, und ihre Welt war in gewissem Sinn meine Welt. Das war für mich natürlich eine ideale Entdeckung, denn damit hatte ich das historische Gegenstück zu meiner Psychologie des Unbewußten gefunden. Sie erhielt nun einen geschichtlichen Boden. Die Möglichkeit des Vergleichs mit der Alchemie, sowie die geistige Kontinuität bis zurück zum Gnostizismus gaben ihr die Substanz (ETG: p. 209/MDR: p. 231).
>
> [I had very soon seen that Analytical Psychology coincided in a most curious way with alchemy. The experiences of the alchemists were, in a sense, my experiences, and their world was my world. This was, of course, a momentous discovery: I had stumbled upon the historical counterpart of my psychology of the Unconscious. It now had an historical basis. The possibility of a comparison with alchemy, and the uninterrupted intellectual chain back to Gnosticism, gave substance to my psychology.]

Jung's 'Exerceptbände', the books in which he collected and collated excerpts from the original alchemical texts, provide us with useful insight into his working method, a simultaneous process of analysis and assimilation.[13] Jung was always keen to bring the most disparate topics into contact with each other, and it is therefore not surprising that he should have detected alchemical imagery in Nietzsche. Indeed, his analysis of the 'alchemical Nietzsche' formed part of Jung's presentation of the dramaturgy of the *aurora consurgens*, humanity's coming to consciousness.[14] Furthermore, there was a tradition of a psychoanalytic inter-

---

['Light on the nature of alchemy began to come to me only after I had read the text of the *Golden Flower*, that specimen of Chinese alchemy which Richard Wilhelm sent me in 1928'] (ETG: p. 208/MDR: p. 230).

13 For an account of these notebooks and photographs of selected pages from them, see A. Ribi, 'Zum schöpferischen Prozess bei C. G. Jung: Aus den Excerptbänden zur Alchemie', *Analytische Psychologie*, 13 (1982), 201–21.

14 'Wenn man sich auf die Psychologie des alchemistischen Denkens überhaupt einläßt, so kommen Zusammenhänge in Betracht, welche vom historischen Stoff, rein äußerlich betrachtet, fernab zu liegen scheinen. Wenn wir aber diese Erscheinung von innen, das heißt vom seelischen Standpunkt aus, zu verstehen suchen, so gehen wir von einer Zentralstelle aus, wo äußerlich fernste Dinge in nächster Nachbarschaft zusammenlaufen. Wir begegnen dort jener menschlichen Seele, die, unähnlich dem Bewußtsein, sich auch in vielen Jahrhunderten kaum merklich ändert, und wo eine zweitausend Jahre alte Wahrheit noch die Wahrheit von heute, das heißt noch lebendig und wirksam ist. Dort auch finden wir jene seelischen Grundtatsachen, welche für Jahrtausende dieselben bleiben und auch noch in Jahrtausenden dieselben sein werden. Neuzeit und Gegenwart erscheinen, von dort gesehen, als Episoden eines in grauer Vorzeit begonnenen Dramas, das sich durch alle Jahrhunderte in eine ferne Zukunft erstreckt. Dieses Drama ist eine "aurora consurgens": die *Bewußtwerdung der Menschheit*' ['For the moment we embark upon the psychology of alchemical thought we must take account of connections that seem, on the face of it, very remote from the historical material. But if we try to understand the phenomenon from inside, i.e., from the standpoint of the psyche, we can start from a central position where many lines converge, however far apart they may be in the external world. We are then confronted with the underlying human psyche which, unlike consciousness, hardly changes at all in the course of many centuries. Here, a truth that is two thousand years

est in alchemy. As early as 1914, the Austrian psychoanalyst Herbert Silberer (1881–1923) had provided a psychological interpretation of alchemy,[15] and in 1935 the art historian Rudolf Bernoulli (1880–1948) delivered an Eranos lecture on alchemy.[16]

Nietzsche made use of alchemical imagery and concepts on several occasions. As Richard Perkins has pointed out: 'Beginning in 1882, Nietzsche frequently and fairly insistently poses as an inner alchemist, privately in euphoric notebook entries, confidentially in frantic letters to Franz Overbeck, and publicly in *Also sprach Zarathustra*, a frankly chrysopoetic work culminating in a golden nature won through transmutation'.[17] And more recently, Graham Parkes has also argued that *Zarathustra* is 'a text that contains dozens of images that figure importantly in alchemy – and especially in alchemy understood as a symbol system for psychological transformation – such as chaos; the stone, fire, sun, and moon; the dragon, eagle, lion, serpent, and ouroborus; the child; and of course lead and gold'.[18]

However, Jung was not concerned with reading Nietzsche at such a surface level. Just as he claimed that the events taking place in the alchemical vessel were the objective correlative of psychic transformations, so he tried to understand Nietzsche's concern to transform Mankind in terms analogous to these alchemical/psychological processes. In 'Die Erlösungsvorstellungen in der Alchemie', first delivered in four parts as a lecture to the Eranos Conference from 6 to 14 August 1936 and published in a slightly expanded form in *Psychologie und Alchemie* (GW12 § 332–554),[19] Jung outlined in psychological terms the essential points

---

old is still the truth today – in other words, it is still alive and active. Here too we find those fundamental psychic facts that remain unchanged for thousands of years and will still be unchanged thousands of years hence. From this point of view, the recent past and the present seem like episodes in a drama that began in the grey mists of prehistoric times and continues through the centuries into a remote future. This drama is an "Aurora consurgens" – the dawning of consciousness in Mankind' (P. B.)] (GW12 § 556).

15 Herbert Silberer, *Probleme der Mystik und ihrer Symbolik* (Vienna and Leipzig, 1914).

16 Rudolf Bernoulli, 'Seelische Entwicklung im Spiegel der Alchemie und verwandter Disziplinen', *Eranos-Jahrbuch 1935* (Zurich, 1936), pp. 231–87. Born in Basle, Bernoulli became Professor for Art History at the E. T. H. in Zurich, the institution at which Jung also gave lectures.

17 Richard Perkins, 'Nietzsche's *opus alchymicum*', *Seminar*, 23 (1987), 216–26 (p. 216). Interestingly enough, Nietzsche once spoke of the Revaluation of all Values in terms of alchemical transformation in his letter of 23 May 1888 to Georg Brandes (N3: p. 1295). But in *Morgenröte* (1881), Nietzsche had compared morality to alchemy – he rejected them both (M/D § 103; N1: p. 1077).

18 Graham Parkes, *Composing the Soul: Reaches of Nietzsche's Psychology* (Chicago and London, 1994), p. 166 (cf.pp. 133–34, 141, 158, 418). Parkes continues: 'Since his knowledge of alchemy appears to have been slight, it is likely that these images surfaced spontaneously in Nietzsche's psyche as a result of the upheavals he was undergoing during this period'.

19 'Die Erlösungsvorstellungen in der Alchemie', *Eranos-Jahrbuch*, 4 (1936), pp. 13–111. Although the version in the *Gesammelte Werke* is substantially larger, the text in the passages from which I quote is largely identical with the original, and so I give the paragraph number as usual.

of the alchemical *opus* (GW12 § 333–40): 'Im alchemischen Opus handelt es sich zum größten Teil nicht nur um chemische Experimente allein, sondern auch um etwas wie psychische Vorgänge, die in pseudochemischer Sprache ausgedrückt werden' ['The alchemical *opus* deals in the main not just with chemical experiments as such, but with something resembling psychic processes expressed in pseudochemical language'] (GW12 § 342).

Jung's basic claim is that in the transformation of base matter (the *prima materia*) through the four stages of *nigredo*, *albedo*, *rubedo* and *citrinitas* into the Philosopher's Stone (the *lapis philosophorum*), the alchemist's procedures were projections of the psychological *Individuationsprozeß*.[20] Thus, on Jung's account, both alchemy and Analytical Psychology are concerned with the same problem – coming to terms with the opposites:

> [Nach der Lehre der Alchemisten] enthält jede elementare Seinsform auch ihren inneren Gegensatz, womit sie die moderne psychologische Gegensatzproblematik antizipiert haben [...] Die Identität der Gegensätze ist nun das Charakteristikum jeder psychischen Gegebenheit im unbewußten Zustande (GW12 § 397–98).
>
> [According to the alchemists' teaching every form of life, however elementary, contains its own inner antithesis, thus anticipating the problem of opposites in modern psychology ... identity of opposites is a characteristic feature of every psychic event in the unconscious state.]

According to Jung, the union of the opposites takes place in a middle realm which is neither material nor spiritual but both: that of the symbol (cf. GW12 § 394):

> Der Ort oder das Medium der Verwirklichung ist weder der Stoff noch der Geist, sondern jenes Zwischenreich subtiler Wirklichkeit, die einzig durch das Symbol zureichend ausgedrückt werden kann (GW12 § 400).
>
> [The place or the medium of realization is neither mind nor matter, but that intermediate realm of subtle reality which can only be adequately expressed by the symbol.]

The symbol, already a key category in *Psychologische Typen* and Jung's theory of art, now provides a mediating link between matter and spirit: 'Das Symbol ist weder abstrakt noch konkret, weder rational noch irrational, weder real noch irreal' ['The symbol is neither abstract nor concrete, neither rational nor irrational, neither real nor unreal'] (ibid.).[21] Just as, for the alchemists, the union of

---

[20] For further information on alchemy, see F. Sherwood Taylor, *The Alchemists* (London, 1952); Mircea Éliade, *Forgerons et alchimistes* (Paris, 1956); E. J. Holmyard, *Alchemy* (London, 1957); and Françoise Bonardel, *Philosophie de l'alchimie: Grand Oeuvre et modernité* (Paris, 1993). For a Jungian-inspired, psychological account of alchemy, see Johannes Fabricius, *Alchemy: The Medieval Alchemists and their Royal Art* (Wellingborough, 1989); and for an account which is critical of both Silberer and Jung, see Titus Burckhardt, *Alchemie* (Olten und Freiburg im Breisgau, 1960).

[21] 'Da der psychologische Zustand eines unbewußten Inhaltes eine *potentielle* Wirklichkeit ist (welche durch das Gegensatzpaar Sein-Nichtsein charaktisiert erscheint), so spielt die Vereini-

the opposites was achieved through the agency of Mercurius (the divine winged Hermes, represented by quicksilver), so, analogously, Jung argued that Mercurius himself represented the symbolic union of the opposites: 'Es ist Metall und doch flüssig, Stoff und doch Geist, kalt und doch feurig, Gift und doch Heiltrank, ein *die Gegensätze einigendes Symbol*' ['He is metallic yet liquid, matter yet spirit, cold yet fiery, poison and yet healing draught – a symbol uniting all opposites'] (GW12 § 404). In the post-war years, Jung would devote more time to the psychological significance of Mercurius, whom he associated with Dionysos.[22]

---

gung der Gegensätze im alchemischen Prozeß eine ausschlaggebende Rolle. Dem Resultat kommt daher die Bedeutung eines *vereinigenden Symbols* zu' ['Since the psychological condition of any unconscious content is one of potential reality, characterized by the polar opposites "being" and "not-being", it follows that the union of opposites must play a decisive rôle in the alchemical process. The result is something in the nature of a "uniting symbol"'] (GW12 § 557).

22 Jung's post-war writings on alchemy emphasized the Dionysos motif which he had discussed in his earlier papers on this subject. In 'Der Geist Mercurius' ['The Spirit Mercurius'] (GW13 § 239–303), based on two Eranos lectures delivered in 1942, Jung concentrated on the mythologem of death and rebirth as embodied in the Dionysos-related figure of the alchemical Mercurius. In his paper, Jung claimed to show that Mercurius – 'der vielfach schillernde und ränkevolle Gott' ['this many-hued and wily god'] (GW13 § 239) – was part of a syncretic nexus of mythological imagery, identified with Dionysos, Wotan and Hermes. First, many of the characteristics of Mercurius were said to be associated with the Dionysian. According to Jung, Mercurius is identified with chthonic fire: 'Das Höllenfeuer, die eigentliche Energie des Bösen, erscheint hier als deutliche Gegensatzentsprechung zum Oberen, Geistigen und Guten, gewissermaßen von wesentlich identischer Substanz' ['Hell-fire, the true energic principle of Evil, appears here as the manifest counterpart of the spiritual and the Good, and to a certain extent as identical with it in substance' (P. B.)] (GW13 § 257). For Jung, Mercurius represents that pagan principle which Christianity has diabolized: 'der Mercurius-Lapis [erweist sich] als zweideutig, dunkel, paradox, ja geradezu als heidnisch. Er repräsentiert daher einen Seelenteil, der auf alle Fälle nicht christlich geformt ist' ['Mercurius-Lapis is ambiguous, dark, paradoxical, and thoroughly pagan. It therefore represents a part of the psyche which was certainly not moulded by Christianity'] (GW13 § 289). According to Jung, Mercurius represents those Dionysian forces which Christianity has systematically suppressed, and in this respect, Mercurius is close to the devil, but Jung explicitly rejected Christianity's diabolization of this force: 'Mercurius ist keineswegs der christliche Teufel, welcher weit eher eine "Verteufelung" eines lucifer, eben eines Mercurius, darstellt' ['Mercurius is by no means the Christian devil – the latter could rather be said to be a "diabolization" of Lucifer or of Mercurius'] (GW13 § 300). Second, Jung drew a clear link between Mercurius and Wotan: '[das] heidnische Gott Mercurius [wurde] als mit dem deutschen Nationalgott Wotan identisch empfunden' ['the pagan god, Mercurius, was considered identical with the German national god, Wotan'] (GW13 § 246), and pointed to the Grimms' fairy-tale 'Der Geist im Glas' ['The Spirit in the Bottle'] for evidence of this identification. And third, Mercurius was set alongside Hermes, the phallic god who is often represented, as he was in Jung's early childhood dream, as an ithyphallus (GW13 § 278–81). Nietzsche had emphasized the sensual significance of Dionysos (GD/TI 10 § 4; N2: 1031), and according to Jung, the 'underworldly Hermes' is often culturally associated with pornographica and the representation of repressed desires. Behind this nexus of complex associations referred to as 'Hermes-Mercurius-Wotan-Geist' (GW13 § 250), a set of psycho-mythological representations of one and the same god, stands Dionysos. He is the god whom, in his interpretation of the story 'Der Geist im Glas', Jung described as 'einen heidnischen Gott, welcher unter dem Einfluß des Christentums den Abstieg in die dunkle Unterwelt unternehmen und damit zugleich die moralische Disqualifikation auf sich nehmen mußte' ['a pagan god, forced under the influence of Christian-

During his discussion of a text by the ancient alchemical writer Ostanes, quoted by the third-century writer Zosimos of Panoplis, Jung compared the expulsion of the Mercurial quicksilver, the 'stone which has a spirit', with an overlooked image in *Also sprach Zarathustra*: 'Wenn Nietzsche im "*Zarathustra*" das emphatische Gleichnis "Im Steine schläft mir ein Bild" gebraucht, so sagt er wohl dasselbe, aber in umgekehrter Reihenfolge' ['Nietzsche's metaphor in *Zarathustra*, "an image slumbers for me in the stone", says much the same thing, but the other way round'] (GW12 § 406). The passage to which Jung referred occurs in the chapter entitled 'Auf den glückseligen Inseln' ['On the Blissful Islands']: 'Ach, ihr Menschen, im Steine schläft mir ein Bild, das Bild meiner Bilder! Ach, daß es im härtesten, häßlichsten Steine schlafen muß!' ['Ah, you men, I see an image sleeping in the stone, the image of my visions! Ah, that it must sleep in the hardest, ugliest stone!'] (Z II 2; N2: p. 345). Moreover, in his published revision of 'Zur Empirie des Individuationsprozesses', a lecture first presented to the Eranos conference in 1933 and published in a much revised and expanded form in 1950 (GW9(i) § 525–626),[23] Jung interpreted the picture in the stone, which Zarathustra will release with his hammer, as another way of talking about the philosopher's stone, or the psychological Self.[24] In both texts, Jung draws a parallel between the world of alchemical antiquity and Nietzsche's intuitive imagination: both, he claims, seek to release the spirit from the stone. But, as he noted, it is a reverse parallel, for whereas the alchemists projected spirit onto base matter,[25] Nietzsche wished to snatch the spirit – identified by Jung as the secret of the Superman – from the stone:

---

ity to sink into the dark underworld and be morally disqualified'] (GW13 § 246). For Jung, the return of Dionysos would mean not just de-repression but the recuperation of vital instincts and creative urges which Western civilization had ignored. These energies were to be integrated and the opposites unified in the archetype which Jung called the Self.

[23] 'Zur Empirie des Individuationsprozesses', *Eranos-Jahrbuch*, 1 (1933), pp. 201–14. Although the version in the *Gesammelte Werke* is substantially larger, the text in the passages from which I quote is largely identical with the original, and so I give the paragraph number as usual.

[24] 'Es ist in der Tat das Geheimnis des "Steines", des lapis philosophorum, insofern dieser die materia prima darstellt. Im Steine schläft der Geist Mercurius, der "Kreis des Mondes", der "Runde und Viereckige", der homunculus [...], der Däumling und zugleich der Anthropos, welchen die Alchemie auch als ihren berühmten lapis philosophorum symbolisiert' ['It is, in fact, the secret of the stone, of the *lapis philosophorum*, in so far as this is the *prima materia*. In the stone sleeps the spirit *Mercurius*, the "circle of the moon", the "round and square", the homunculus, Tom Thumb and Anthropos at once, whom the alchemists also symbolized as their famed *lapis philosophorum*'] (GW9(i) § 541).

[25] 'In der Antike wurde die Welt des Stoffes erfüllt von der Projektion eines seelischen Geheimnisses, welches von da an als Geheimnis des Stoffes erschien und in diesem Zustand verharrte bis zum Untergang der Alchemie im 18. Jahrhundert [...] [Die alten Alchemisten] suchten den wundersamen Stein, der ein pneumatisches Wesen enthielt, um daraus jenen Stoff zu gewinnen, der in alle Körper eindringt (weil er ja der "Geist" ist, der in den Stein eingedrungen ist) und alle unedeln Stoffe durch Umfärbung in edle verwandelt. Dieser "Geiststoff" ist wie das Quecksilber, das unsichtbar in den Erzen drin steckt und das zuerst ausgetrieben werden muß, wenn man es "in substantia" gewinnen will. Hat man aber diesen penetrierenden Merkur, so

Die ekstatische Intuition Nietzsches aber möchte das Geheimnis des Übermenschen eben dem Stein entreißen, in welchem es bis dahin geschlafen hat. Er möchte nach diesem Bilde den Übermenschen schaffen, den wir, nach antikem Sprachgebrauch, wohl als den göttlichen Menschen bezeichnen dürfen (GW12 § 406).

[Nietzsche, with his ecstatic intuition, tried to wrest the secret of the Superman from the stone in which it had long been slumbering. It was in the likeness of this slumbering image that he wished to create the Superman, whom, according to ancient usage, we may well call the divine Man. (P. B.)]

Jung suggested that the concept of the Superman was directly analogous to the alchemical Mercury, but emphasized that the former no more represents a moral or spiritual ideal than does the Mercurial spirit. For although the divine tincture can be used as a restorative, it is nonetheless a poison. By emphasizing that the Superman is, so to speak, a dangerous 'solution', Jung voiced his doubts about the moral aspects of Nietzsche's plan to transform Mankind:

Wie Nietzsche reichlich dafür gesorgt hat, daß niemand den Übermenschen etwa für den geistigen und moralischen Idealmenschen halte, so wird auch von der Tinktur oder dem göttlichen Wasser nicht etwa nur die wohltätige Heil- und Veredlungswirkung ausgesagt, sondern es wird auch hervorgehoben, daß das Präparat ein mörderisches Gift sei, das die Körper so durchdringe, wie es den eigenen (das heißt das πνεῦμα seinen Stein) durchdringt (GW12 § 407).

[Just as Nietzsche made absolutely sure that nobody could mistake the Superman for a sort of spiritual or moral ideal, so it is emphasized that the tincture or divine water is far from being merely curative and ennobling in its effects, but that it may also act as a deadly poison as pervasively as the pneuma penetrates its stone.]

---

kann man ihn auf andere Körper "projizieren" und diese aus dem unvollkommenen Zustand in den vollkommenen überführen. Der unvollkommene Zustand ist wie ein Schlafzustand; die Körper sind darin wie "die im Hades Gefesselten und Schlafenden", welche durch die göttliche, aus dem geistesschwangeren Wunderstein gewonnene Tinktur wie vom Tode zu neuem, schönerem Leben auferweckt werden. Es ist hierbei völlig klar, daß die Tendenz dahin geht, das Geheimnis der seelischen Wandlung nicht nur im Stoffe zu sehen, sondern es auch als theoretische Richtschnur zur Hervorbringung chemischer Veränderungen zu benützen' ['In antiquity the material world was filled with the projection of a psychic secret, which from then on appeared as the secret of matter and remained so until the decay of alchemy in the eighteenth century ... The alchemists were looking for the marvellous stone that harboured a pneumatic essence in order to win from it the substance that penetrates all substances – since it is itself the stone-penetrating "spirit" – and transforms all base metals into noble ones by a process of coloration. This "spirit-substance" is like quicksilver, which lurks unseen in the ore and must first be expelled if it is to be recovered *in substantia*. The possessor of this penetrating Mercurius can "project" it into other substances and transform them from the imperfect into the perfect state. The imperfect state is like the sleeping state; substances lie in it like the "sleepers chained in Hades" and are awakened as from death to a new and more beautiful life by the divine tincture extracted from the inspired stone. It is quite clear that we have here a tendency not only to locate the mystery of psychic transformation in matter, but at the same time to use it as a *theoria* for effecting chemical changes'] (GW12 § 406).

For both Nietzsche and Jung, the essential task is the redemption of Mankind. In Nietzsche's view, the Superman represents the higher vision of Man, and in 'Von den Taranteln' ['Of the Tarantulas'], Zarathustra explicitly uses a soteriological vocabulary: 'Denn *daß der Mensch erlöst werde von der Rache*: das ist mir die Brücke zur höchsten Hoffnung und ein Regenbogen nach langen Unwettern' ['For *that Man may be redeemed from the bonds of revenge*: that is the bridge to my highest hope and a rainbow after protracted storms' (P. B.)] (Z II 7; N2: p. 357). But at the same time, Zarathustra declares the impossibility of divine transcendence, so that Man's redemption will be immanent; and this is what Nietzsche meant by 'Selbstüberwindung' ['self-overcoming']. In Jung's view, however, there are two kinds of redemption, expressed in the antinomy between the concepts *ex opere operato* and *ex opere operantis* (GW12 § 414–416, 557).[26] In the first (Christian) view, Man recognizes his need for salvation and attributes the *opus* of redemption to the transcendent divine figure (GW12 § 415). This is said to be the 'ideology' of Christianity, and he placed it in the same category as the myths of Osiris, Orpheus, Heracles and Dionysos:[27]

> Im christlichen Falle sind es das Leben und der Tod des Gottmenschen, die als einmaliges "sacrificium" die Versöhnung des erlösungsbedürftigen, im Stoffe verlorenen Menschen mit Gott herbeiführen [...] Die Ideologie dieses Mysteriums ist antizipiert in den Mythkreisen des Osiris, Orpheus, Dionysos, Herakles und in der messianischen Idee innerhalb der jüdischen Prophetie (GW12 § 415–16).

> [In Christianity it is the life and death of the God-Man which, by a unique sacrifice, bring about the reconciliation of Man, who craves redemption and is sunk in materi-

---

26 'In der kirchlichen Formel des "opus operatum" und "opus operantis" begegnen sich die beiden, in ihren letzten Konsequenzen unversöhnlich gegensätzlichen Standpunkte' ['The two opposed points of view meet in the ecclesiastical formula of the *opus operatum* and the *opus operantis* – but in the last analysis they are irreconcilable'] (GW12 § 557). The term 'opus operatum' was used by the Council of Trent (sess.vii.can.8) to express the nature of the efficacy of the sacraments. When it is said that the sacrament confers grace *ex opere operato*, this means that grace is conferred by virtue of the sacramental act itself instituted by God for this end, and not the merit of the minister or the recipient. See William E. Addis and Thomas Arnold, revised by T. B. Scannell and P. E. Hallett, *A Catholic Dictionary* (London, 1954). 'Opus operantis' means that grace is conferred as result of one's own merit.

27 In a footnote, Jung drew attention to the main points of comparison between these gods: 'die Gottmenschnatur des *Osiris*, der die menschliche Unsterblichkeit garantiert, seine Weizennatur und seine Zerstückelung und Resurrektion; bei *Orpheus* die Triebbezähmung, der Fischer, der gute Hirt, der Weisheitslehrer, die Zerreißung; bei *Dionysos* die Weinnatur, die offenbarende Ekstasis, die Fischsymbolik, die Zerstückelung und die Resurrektion; bei *Herakles* die Erniedrigung unter Eurystheus und Omphale, das schwere Werk (hauptsächlich Erlösung der geplagten Menschheit von Übeln) [...], die Selbstverbrennung und "sublimatio" zum göttlichen Zustand' ['in Osiris, his God-Man nature, which guarantees human immortality, his corn characteristics, his dismemberment and resurrection; in Orpheus, the taming of the passions, the fisherman, the good shepherd, the teacher of wisdom, the dismemberment; in Dionysos, his wine characteristics, the ecstatic revelations, the fish symbolism, the dismemberment and resurrection; in Hercules, his subjection to Eurystheus and Omphale, his labours (mainly to redeem suffering

ality, with God ... The ideology of this *mysterium* is anticipated in the myths of Osiris, Orpheus, Dionysos, and Hercules, and in the conception of the Messiah among the Hebrew prophets.]

And in the second (alchemical) view, Man takes upon himself the work of salvation, so that in this case, it is matter in general which must be redeemed from its suffering (GW12 § 451–52). On this latter view, it is Man himself, as alchemist, who operates the mechanism of salvation: 'da [der Alchemist] nicht der zu Erlösende, sondern ein Gotterlöser ist, liegt ihm in erster Linie daran, die Substanz zu vervollkommnen' ['since the alchemist is the redeemer of God and not the one to be redeemed, he is more concerned to perfect the substance than himself'] (GW12 § 451). Whilst holding that the opposition between these two points of view was irreconcilable (GW12 § 557), there can be no doubt that Jung tended towards the second, immanent concept of redemption. At the end of his paper, Jung placed the irreconcilability of the transcendent and immanent views of redemption in parallel with another, clearly political antinomy, introducing his discussion of Faust and Zarathustra as Supermen: 'Im Grunde handelt es sich um das Gegensatzpaar Kollektivität und Individuum oder Gesellschaft und Persönlichkeit' ['Fundamentally it is a question of polar opposites: the collective or the individual, society or personality'] (GW12 § 557). With an eye on the rise of Fascism in Germany, Jung offered a critique of the political consequences of 'Supermanship'.

Faust and Zarathustra as Supermen

The conflict between collectivity and the individual, the problem which the Dionysian rites underlying tragedy sought to solve, lies at the heart of Jung's critique of the Nietzschean Superman. In the final paragraphs of 'Die Erlösungsvorstellungen in der Alchemie', Jung turned his attention to the figure of the Superman in the light of *Faust II*. Here again, as so often, he tried to read Nietzsche through Goethe on the assumption that *Faust* and *Zarathustra* had world-historical status, and that *Faust* was an alchemical drama through and through:[28]

---

humanity from various evils) ... his self-cremation and *sublimatio* culminating in divinity'] (GW12 § 416, n.36).

[28] For further examples of alchemical/Jungian readings of *Faust*, see Alice Raphael, *Goethe and the Philosophers' Stone: Symbolical Patterns in 'The Parable' and the Second Part of 'Faust'* (New York, 1965) (Jung owned a copy of Raphael's earlier work, *Goethe, the Challenger* (New York, 1932), which contains a detailed comparison between Joseph Conrad's *Victory* (1915) and Goethe's *Faust*, quoting frequently from Jung's works in translation); Ronald D. Gray, *Goethe, the Alchemist: A Study of Alchemical Symbolism in Goethe's Literary and Scientific Works* (Cambridge, 1952) (of which Jung owned a copy); Gottfried Diener, *Fausts Weg zu Helena: Urphänomen und Archetypus* (Stuttgart,

Vor dieser neuesten Veränderung aber erreichte die Alchemie noch eine letzte Höhe und damit den historischen Wendepunkt in Goethes *"Faust"*, der von Anfang bis Ende mit alchemistischen Gedankengängen durchtränkt ist (GW12 § 558).

[Some time previous to this latest development, however, alchemy had reached its final summit, and with it the historical turning-point, in Goethe's *Faust*, which is steeped in alchemical forms of thought from beginning to end.]

For Jung, *Faust* represented a significant advance in the development of alchemical thinking. Whereas alchemy had projected psychic processes onto the chemical transformations in the retort, literature is said to project these processes onto the literary image. According to Jung, this more sophisticated form of projection requires a greater degree of consciousness. For example, in Act I of Part II, Faust, with the help of the Astrologer and in the name of the Mothers, calls up the images of Paris and Helen. The medieval alchemist, Jung claimed, would have understood that the scene of Paris and Helen represented the *mysterium coniunctionis* of the sun (Sol) and the moon (Luna), the alchemical King and Queen in the retort. But modern Man's advance, he continued, is represented by Faust, who recognizes the projection for what it is but nonetheless still identifies with Paris and tries to intervene, thereby bringing the alchemical *coniunctio* into consciousness:[29]

Was im *"Faust"* geschieht, drückt sich wohl am deutlichsten in der Paris-Helena-Szene aus [...] Dadurch, daß sich Faust mit Paris identifiziert, zieht er die "coniunctio" aus der Projektion in die Sphäre persönlich-psychologischen Erlebens und damit in das Bewußtsein. Dieser entscheidende Schritt bedeutet nichts weniger als die Auflösung des alchemistischen Rätsels und damit auch die Erlösung eines bis dahin unbewußten Persönlichkeitsteiles (GW12 § 558–59).

[The essential Faustian drama is expressed most graphically in the scene between Paris and Helen ... By identifying with Paris, Faust brings the *coniunctio* back from its projected state into the sphere of the personal psychological experience and thus into consciousness. This crucial step means nothing less than the solution of the alchemical riddle, and at the same time the redemption of a previously unconscious part of the personality.]

Faust's intervention to wrest Helen from Paris fails, and by breaking the alchemical precept that the adept must not interfere with what happens in the retort,

---

1961); Bettina L. Knapp, 'Faust Revisited' in *Gérard de Nerval: The Mystic's Dilemma* (Alabama, 1980), pp. 78–91); Stephen Abrams, *The Devil You Don't Know*, broadcast on BBC Radio 3 on 24 April 1982; John Fitzell, 'Goethe, Jung: Homunculus and Faust', in *Goethe in the Twentieth Century*, edited by Alexej Ugrinsky (New York, 1987), pp. 107–15; Edward E. Edinger, *Goethe's 'Faust': Notes for a Jungian Commentary* (Inner City Books, 1990); and see also Jeremy Adler, *Eine fast magische Anziehungskraft: Goethes 'Wahlverwandschaften'* (Munich, 1987).

29 Faust cries: 'Was Raub! Bin ich für nichts an dieser Stelle!/[...] Ich rette sie, und sie ist doppelt mein' ['What abduction! Why am I in this place? ... I rescue her, and she is doubly mine'] (*Faust II*, ll.6549, 6557). However, Mephistopheles points out to Faust: 'Machst du's doch selbst, das Fratzengeisterspiel' ['You yourself are responsible for this grotesque ghost-play'] (l.6546).

explodes the vision and brings Act I to an end in darkness and tumult. Traditionally, the alchemical *coniunctio* is followed by the birth of the 'divine child' or *puer aeternus*, a symbolic representation of the *lapis philosophorum*. However, Jung observed that all the rejuvenation figures in *Faust II* meet an unhappy and violent end[30] and that the moment of redemption itself is postponed until after death and projected into the future (i.e. into the Unconscious).[31] Furthermore, in Jung's system, the integration of unconscious process into consciousness poses another danger, that of psychic inflation.[32] In Part I, Faust is mocked by the *Erdgeist* because he is not an 'Übermensch' (l.490), but his conviction that he is the 'Ebenbild der Gottheit' ['image of divinity'] (ll.516, 614) leads him to sign the pact with Mephistopheles.

In the conclusion to 'Die Erlösungsvorstellungen in der Alchemie', Jung devoted an important passage to one of the final scenes in *Faust II*: the murder

---

[30] Jung's claim that Euphorion and other rejuvenation figures (such as the Boy Charioteer and Homunculus) go up in flames and disappear has caused controversy. In an article highly critical of Jung's alchemical reading of *Faust*, Harold Jantz points out that this is not strictly accurate ('Goethe, Faust, Alchemy, and Jung', *The German Quarterly*, 35 (1962), 129–141): the Boy Charioteer retires to rural bliss, Homunculus merges with the life of the sea, and Euphorion, aspiring to fly, falls to his doom. But there is still an important symbolism at work here, since the fates of the Boy Charioteer, Homunculus and Euphorion can be read as referring to three of the four basic alchemical elements, namely earth, water, and air, respectively. Furthermore, there is still a significant use of imagery of fire and flame in the case of both Homunculus and Euphorion. When Homunculus plunges into the waves, Thales observes 'Jetzt flammt es, nun blitzt es, ergießet sich schon' ['Now there are flames, now there is lightning, pouring itself away'] (l.8473), and the Sirens sing: 'Welch feuriges Wunder verklärt uns die Wellen,/[...] Und ringsum ist alles vom Feuer umronnen' ['What fiery wonder transfigures the waves ... and round about everything is licked by flames'] (l.8478). Euphorion sets a girl on fire (literally – '*Sie flammt auf und lodert in die Höhe*' (after l.9807)), and as he falls, his forehead glows ('*sein Haupt strahlt, ein Lichtschweif zieht nach*' (after l.9900)).

[31] Rhetorically, Jung asked whether it was an accident that in the final scene of Part II, the elevation of Faust, the figure of Doctor Marianus (who speaks the lines: 'Hier ist die Aussicht frei,/Der Geist erhoben' ['Here the view is free, the spirit uplifted']) is an apparent reference to a major alchemical writer of the seventh or eighth century, Morenius Romanus, the author of the *Sermo de transmutatione metallica.*

[32] Inflation refers to the identification of the individual Ego with the collective psyche caused by an invasion by unconscious archetypal contents. In a later paragraph, Jung defines inflation as follows: 'Ein aufgeblasenes Bewußtsein ist immer egozentrisch und nur seiner eigenen Gegenwart bewußt. Es ist unfähig, aus der Vergangenheit zu lernen, unfähig, das gegenwärtige Geschehen zu begreifen, und unfähig, richtige Schlüsse auf die Zukunft zu ziehen. Es ist von sich selber hypnotisiert und läßt darum auch nicht mit sich reden. Es ist daher auf Katastrophen angewiesen, die es nötigenfalls totschlagen. Inflation ist paradoxerweise ein Unbewußtwerden des Bewußtseins. Dieser Fall tritt ein, wenn letzteres sich an Inhalten des Unbewußten übernimmt und die Unterscheidungsfähigkeit, diese conditio sine qua non aller Bewußtheit, verliert' ['An inflated consciousness is always egocentric and conscious of nothing but its own existence. It is incapable of learning from the past, incapable of understanding contemporary events, and incapable of drawing right conclusions about the future. It is hypnotized by itself and therefore cannot be argued with. It inevitably dooms itself to calamities that must strike it dead. Paradoxically enough, inflation is a regression of consciousness into unconsciousness. This always hap-

of Philemon and Baucis. This episode is interpreted as showing the consequences of the Faustian drive to be the Superman: 'Faust verursacht in blindem Übermenschendrang den Mord an Philemon und Baucis' ['In his blind urge for superhuman power, Faust brought about the murder of Philemon and Baucis'] (GW12 § 561). Although the figures of Philemon and Baucis, deriving ultimately from the mythic corpus, find their first literary representation in Ovid,[33] Goethe claimed to have distanced himself from his classical source.[34] But in his reading, Jung went back to that classical source. In return for the hospitality which they alone offered the gods (Zeus and Hermes), Ovid's original Philemon and Baucis were rewarded for their generosity by being transformed into immortal beings and united together for all eternity.[35]

As it appears in Jung's lecture, recognition of the gods is the point of this story. He pointed out that even the alchemists located the elements to be transformed outside themselves, and that subsequently, during the Enlightenment, the contents of the psyche were identified exclusively with consciousness. As a result, Jung concluded, the gods who had once been projected outside were introjected into the personal psyche, with the risk that unconscious elements could inflate and invade the Ego: 'So mußten die vordem projizierten Inhalte nunmehr als Besitztümer, das heißt als schemenhafte Phantasiebilder eines Ichbewußtseins erscheinen' ['The contents that were formerly projected were now bound to appear as personal possessions, as chimerical phantasms of the Ego-consciousness'] (GW12 § 562). Thus, according to Jung, the consequences of this inflation are the revenge of the gods on an inhospitable humanity; and the message is that we neglect the gods at our peril:[36]

> Das Feuer erkaltete zu Luft, und die Luft wurde zum Winde des Zarathustra und verursachte eine Inflation des Bewußtseins, welche offenbar nur durch die furchtbarsten Kulturkatastrophen, eben jene Sintflut, welche die Götter der ungastlichen Menschheit sandten, gedämpft werden konnte (GW12 § 562).

> ['The fire chilled to air, and the air became the great wind of Zarathustra and caused an inflation of consciousness which, it seems, can be damped down only by the

---

pens when consciousness takes too many unconscious contents upon itself and loses the faculty of discrimination, the *sine qua non* of consciousness'] (GW12 § 563).

33 Ovid, *Metamorphoses*, Book VIII, ll.628–720.

34 See Goethe's reported remark to Eckermann of 6 June 1831 (J. P. Eckermann, *Gespräche mit Goethe* (Zurich, 1969), pp. 367–68).

35 See Wolfgang Giegerich, 'Hospitality towards the Gods in an Ungodly Age: Philemon-Faust-Jung', *Spring*, 1984, 61–75.

36 It is interesting to note that in the *Bacchae* by Euripides, Dionysos comes disguised as a wandering god to test if his divinity is recognized and whether the people are observing his rites. In his anger at their irreligious behaviour, he causes an earthquake, thereby proving that we neglect the gods, and especially Dionysos, at our peril. For further discussion, see Anne Pippin Burnett, 'Pentheus and Dionysus: Host and Guest', *Classical Philology*, 65 (1970), 15–29.

most terrible catastrophe to civilization, another deluge let loose by the gods upon inhospitable humanity.]

Similarly, in Goethe's text, Baucis specifically refers to Faust's 'godlessness': 'Gottlos ist er, ihn gelüstet/Unsre Hütte, unser Hain' ['He is godless, he craves our little hut, our grove'] (ll.11131–32). Where, in Ovid's original, Philemon and Baucis receive an appropriate reward for respecting the gods, in Goethe's dramatic poem, their fate symbolizes the consequences of Faust's rejection of the divine in his drive to become the Superman.

Jung claimed not only that Faust's 'superhuman' behaviour exemplified the condition of inflation, but that his death in Part II, which postpones the *coniunctio* and subsequent rebirth and transformation until the afterlife, had left the psychic problem of consciousness and the Unconscious unsolved:

> Jeder Zuwachs an Bewußtheit aber birgt die Gefahr der Inflation in sich. Im Übermenschentum Fausts tritt sie uns deutlich entgegen. Faustens Tod ist eine zeitgeschichtlich bedingte Notwendigkeit, aber keine genügende Antwort. Die Geburt und die Wandlung, welche auf die "coniunctio" folgen, sind im Jenseits, das heißt im Unbewußten verlaufen (GW12 § 559).
>
> [But every increase in consciousness harbours the danger of inflation, as is shown very clearly in Faust's superhuman powers. His death, although necessary in his day and generation, is hardly a satisfactory answer. The rebirth and transformation that follow the *coniunctio* take place in the hereafter, i.e., in the Unconscious.]

Jung also added: 'Hier blieb ein Problem hängen, das, wie bekannt, Nietzsche im "*Zarathustra*" wieder aufnahm: nämlich die Wandlung zum Übermenschen' ['This leaves the problem hanging in the air. We all know that Nietzsche took it up again in *Zarathustra*, as the transformation into the Superman'] (GW12 § 559).[37] In other words, Jung thought that the final stage of transformation, which had, in *Faust*, been delayed until the afterlife, was brought closer by Nietzsche in the concept of the Superman, the total individual who unites consciousness and the Unconscious. The unargued assumption informing Jung's discussion of Zarathustra is that we know what the Superman would look like, for, in Jung's view, Zarathustra is himself a Superman.[38] Jung's view of the

[37] See also Jung's letter of 18 June 1958 to Herbert E. Bowman: 'Goethe's *Faust* almost reached the goal of classical alchemy, but unfortunately the ultimate *coniunctio* did not come off, so that Faust and Mephistopheles could not attain their oneness. The second attempt, Nietzsche's *Zarathustra*, remained a meteor that never reached the earth, as the *coniunctio oppositorum* had not and could not have taken place. In the course of my psychiatric and psychological studies I could not help stumbling upon this very obvious fact and I therefore began to speak of the Self again' (L2: p. 453/B3: p. 195).

[38] As Lampert has pointed out, Zarathustra takes on the responsibilities of the Superman in the course of the work. Initially the herald of the Superman, Zarathustra becomes the teacher of the Eternal Recurrence, which is the teaching of the Superman (*Nietzsche's Teaching*, pp. 20–21, 81–82).

Superman was highly negative: he accused Nietzsche of making the Superman too secular ('diesseitig') and disapproved of his anti-christian 'Ressentiment'. Moreover, Jung claimed that Nietzsche's life exemplified that catastrophic destruction of the individual to which the collision between 'eine Hybris des individuellen Bewußtseins' ['the hybris of individual consciousness'] (i.e. inflation) and the 'Kollektivmacht des Christentums' ['the collective power of Christianity'] would inevitably lead (GW12 § 559). Invoking the alchemical formula '*tam ethice quam physice*', glossed as meaning 'sowohl "moralisch" – das heißt psychologisch – wie physisch' ['as much ethical – i.e., psychological – as physical'] (GW12 § 342), Jung identified the 'katastrophale Zerstörung des Individuums' ['catastrophic identification of the individual'] with the fate of Nietzsche: 'Nietzsches Übergriff war die Identifikation mit dem Übermenschen Zarathustra, dem zur Bewußtheit gelangenden Persönlichkeitsteil' ['Nietzsche overreached himself by identifying his Ego with the Superman Zarathustra, the part of the personality that was struggling into consciousness'] (GW12 § 560).

Jung saw Nietzsche's fate as relevant for contemporary society as a whole, and these remarks compensate for the relative absence of any detailed political commentary on the events which were taking place in Germany during the period of his Seminar on *Zarathustra* (1934–1939):

> Und womit antworteten die nachfolgenden Zeiten auf den Individualismus des Nietzscheschen Übermenschen? Sie antworteten mit einem Kollektivismus, einer Kollektivorganisation und einer Anhäufung von Massen "tam ethice quam physice", die alles je Dagewesenen spotten (GW12 § 559).
>
> [And what kind of answer did the next generation give to the individualism of Nietzsche's Superman? It answered with a collectivism, a mass organization, a herding together of the mob, *tam ethice quam physice*, that made everything that went before look like a bad joke.]

The modern age (i.e. the era of totalitarianism) is said to have both stifled the individual personality and left behind an 'ein ohnmächtiges, vielleicht tödlich verwundetes Christentum' ['an impotent, perhaps mortally wounded Christianity' (P. B.)] (GW12 § 559). However, Jung baulked at his own definition of Zarathustra as a mere 'Persönlichkeitsteil' ['part of the personality'] and saw in him an embodiment of 'das Übermenschliche, an dem der Mensch zwar teilhat, das er aber nicht ist' ['something superhuman – something which Man is not, though he has his share in it'] (GW12 § 560). In Jung's view, the concept of the Superman has implications over and above its sociological consequences, and he concluded that Zarathustra in fact represents the repressed element of the divine in Nietzsche:

> Ist der Gott wirklich tot, wenn Nietzsche ihn als verschollen erklärt? Ist er nicht eben in der Verhüllung des "Übermenschlichen" zurückgekehrt? (GW12 § 560).

[Is God really dead, because Nietzsche declared that he had not been heard of for a long time? May he not have, come back in the guise of the Superman?]

On Jung's account, then, Zarathustra/Superman represses the divine into the Unconscious to the point of becoming 'inflated' with the Unconscious, that is to say, to the point of identifying with what has been repressed. But the identity of the deity whom Zarathustra/Superman represses to the point of unconsciously identifying with it remains unclear. Bearing in mind what Jung said elswhere (see above) about the destructive and amoral nature of the Superman, the returning deity has the characteristics, not of the Christian deity, but of an older pagan god. In his Seminar on *Zarathustra* and in his essays on the Second World War, Jung interprets the rise of Fascism as a political phenomenon related to the central concern of Nietzsche and of himself – Dionysos.

According to Jung, both Faust and Nietzsche each committed a major error. Whilst Faust's sin (in the Paris and Helen scene) had been to identify with the transformed and transforming *prima materia* ('Faustens Sünde war die Identifikation mit dem zu Wandelnden und Gewandelten' ['Faust's sin was that he identified with the thing to be transformed and that had been transformed']),[39] Nietzsche's mistake had been to identify with Zarathustra/Superman, i.e. with the component of the personality which the process of transformation had brought to consciousness, 'die Identifikation mit dem Übermenschen Zarathustra' ['identifying with the Superman Zarathustra'] (GW12 § 560). In Jung's view, both mistakes corresponded to an analogous error in alchemy, for neither Faust and Zarathustra nor the alchemists had recognized or given due respect to those contents of the Unconscious not included in the Ego-personality – the gods, or (in Jungian vocabulary) the archetypes: 'die nützlichen und erbaulichen Vorbilder, welche uns Dichter und Philosophen zeigen, Vorbilder oder "archetypi", welche man wohl als Heilmittel für Menschen und Zeiten bezeichnen darf' ['the useful and edifying models held up to us by poets and philosophers – models or *archetypi* that we may well call remedies for both men and the times'] (GW12 § 563). Jung stressed the need to recognize that the archetypes are located neither in matter (as the alchemists had erroneously claimed) nor in the individual Ego (as Faust and Zarathustra had mistakenly believed).

---

39 In his letter to Dr. Paul Schmitt of 5 January 1942 (discussed below), Jung said that Faust had sinned against 'the kiss' and against Baubo, the obscene female deity who, according to myth, made Demeter laugh after the abduction of Persephone by making a lewd gesture: 'Ich gäbe eine Welt darum, zu wissen, ob Goethe wußte, warum er die beiden Alten "Philemon" und "Baucis" nannte. Gegen diese Ureltern (φίλημα und Baubo) hat Faust von Anfang an gesündigt. Man muß ja allerdings fast gestorben sein, bevor man dieses Geheimnis richtig versteht' ['I would give the earth to know whether Goethe himself knew why he called the two old people "Philemon" and "Baucis". Faust sinned from the beginning against these first parents (φίλημα and Baubo). One must have one foot in the grave, though, before one understands this secret properly'] (B1: p. 385/L1: p. 310). The force of Jung's remark seems to lie in a pun on Philemon/'philema' (= the kiss) and Baucis/Baubo.

Philemon and Baucis

According to Jung, the consequences of this fundamental error involved the whole of European society – including himself. There is a highly personal dimension to Jung's discussion of the price of Faust's Superman-like behaviour, the deaths of Philemon and Baucis, and there is a complex nexus of investments and identifications in Jung's work which surrounds this couple. Goethe's *Faust* is mentioned at least eleven times in Jung's autobiography,[40] and on two of those occasions he touches upon the deaths of Philemon and Baucis. First, in the chapter on his student years, the dissatisfaction which Jung expresses with the final scene of Faust (a complaint made also in his 1936 lecture) is accompanied by a reference to the deaths of Philemon and Baucis, which are seen as particularly problematic:

> Trotz meiner Bewunderung kritisierte ich die endgültige Lösung des Faust. Die spielerische Unterschätzung Mephistos kränkte mich persönlich, ebenso Faustens ruchlose Überheblichkeit und vor allem der Mord an Philemon und Baucis (ETG: p. 92/ passage omitted from MDR).

> [Despite my admiration, I was critical of the eventual solution to Faust. The playful underestimation of Mephistopheles wounded me personally, just as did Faust's dastardly arrogance and above all the murder of Philemon and Baucis.]

In a letter of 2 January 1928 (see Chapter 3), Jung's correspondent, Hermann Graf Keyserling, was told that he identified with 'dem ewigschaffenden *ruh- und ruchlosen Gott*' ['the eternally creative, restless and ruthless god'], whereas Jung, by implication, had been able to rid himself of this identification which he also related to Nietzsche. In this letter, the 'small house near the mountains' mentioned is Jung's Tower at Bollingen, the construction of which had begun in 1923. The inscription 'Philemonis Sacrum – Fausti Poenitentia' ('The Shrine of Philemon – the Repentance of Faust') was first placed above the gate of the

[40] In his autobiography, Jung relates that reading *Faust* proved to be a turning-point for him during his school-years. At the suggestion of his mother (!), Jung read and was apparently highly impressed with Goethe's confirmation of the existence of 'das Böse und dessen weltumspannende Macht' ['Evil and its universal power'] and 'die geheimnisvolle Rolle, welche es in der Erlösung der Menschen aus Dunkelheiten und Leiden spielt' ['the mysterious rôle it played in delivering Man from darkness and suffering'] (ETG: p. 66/MDR: p. 78). Jung put the main focus of his thoughts on the rôle of Mephistopheles and his relationship to the mysterious Mothers: 'Das eigentliche Problem sah ich bei Mephisto, dessen Gestalt mir haften blieb und von dem ich unklar eine Beziehung zum Muttermysterium ahnte. Auf alle Fälle blieben mir Mephisto und die große Einweihung am Schluß ein wunderbares und geheimnisvolles Erlebnis am Rande meiner Bewußtseinswelt' ['The real problem, it seemed to me, lay with Mephistopheles, whose whole figure made the deepest impression on me, and who, I vaguely sensed, had a relationship to the mystery of the Mothers. At any rate Mephistopheles and the great initiation at the end remained for me a wonderful and mysterious experience on the fringes of my conscious world'] (ETG: pp. 65–66/MDR: p. 73).

Tower, and when the gate was walled up the inscription was then placed over the entrance to the second tower. I read the 'eternally creative, restless and ruthless god' of Jung's letter to Keyserling as a reference to Dionysos, and Jung's process of 'dis-identification' as part of his coming-to-terms with his sense of identity with Nietzsche and the Dionysian experience of his mental collapse after the break with Freud. Curiously, Jung also called one of the fantasy figures whom he encountered in his confrontation with the Unconscious, Philemon (ETG: pp. 186–88/MDR: pp. 207–09).[41] The second occasion when Jung mentions Philemon and Baucis in his autobiography is in the chapter called 'Der Turm' (which deals with the construction of the Tower in Bollingen), Jung connects the story with the First World War and with his own rôle in the conditions surrounding it:

> Ich konnte ja damals, als ich mit "Faust" bekannt wurde, nicht ahnen, wie sehr Goethes seltsamer Heldenmythus kollektiv war und deutsches Schicksal prophetisch vorausnahm. Deshalb fühlte ich mich persönlich betroffen, und wenn Faust infolge seiner Hybris und Inflation den Mord an Philemon und Baucis veranlaßte, fühlte ich mich schuldig, etwa wie wenn ich in der Vergangenheit am Mord der beiden Alten teilgehabt hätte. Diese sonderbare Idee erschreckte mich, und ich sah es als meine Verantwortung an, diese Schuld zu sühnen, oder ihre Wiederholung zu verhindern (ETG: p. 238/MDR: p. 261).
>
> [In the days when I first read *Faust* I could not remotely guess the extent to which Goethe's strange heroic myth was a collective experience and that it prophetically anticipated the fate of the Germans. Therefore I felt personally implicated, and when Faust, in his hubris and self-inflation, caused the murder of Philemon and Baucis, I felt guilty, quite as if I myself in the past had helped commit the murder of the two old people. This strange idea alarmed me, and I regarded it as my responsibility to atone for this crime, or to prevent its repetition.]

Immediately following this observation, Jung claimed to have seen the archetypal influences which lay behind the catastrophe of the First World War, and in particular, the influence of Dionysos/Wotan: 'Schon pochten die Archetypen Wagners an die Tore, und mit ihnen kam das dionysische Erlebnis Nietzsches, das man besser dem Rauschgott Wotan zuschreibt' ['The archetypes of Wagner

[41] According to F. X. Charet, Goethe's *Faust* was 'probably' the source from which Jung took Philemon's name (*Spiritualism and the Foundations of C. G. Jung's Psychology* (Albany, N. Y., 1993), p. 242), but it is hard to see what the connection, beyond the name, of the two figures is. Charet's interpretation of the significance of Philemon the dream-figure is painted with the broadest of brush-strokes, and cannot be accused of understatement: 'the figure of Philemon [...] is, at least in part, a conflation of the phallus dream, Jung's father, and Freud [...] The importance of the figure of Philemon following Jung's break with Freud can hardly be overstated. In the final analysis Philemon, while being a conflation of Jung's father, Bleuler, Freud, and Flournoy, transcends them all by being a winged creature – a spirit-being. For Jung personally Philemon replaced the father figure of his early life by personifying the spirit. In Jung's psychology Philemon serves as the prototype of the archetype of the Self' (pp. 250, 255).

were already knocking at the gates, and along with them came the Dionysian experience of Nietzsche – which might better be ascribed to the god of ecstasy, Wotan'] (ETG: p. 238/MDR: p. 262). But it is not at all clear why Jung should relate the murder of Philemon and Baucis to the First, instead of the Second World War (which his autobiography does not, in fact, mention directly in detail at all). For, in his Seminar on *Zarathustra* (1934–1939) and in his essays of the late Thirties and early Forties, it is the *Second* (not the First) World War which Jung interprets in terms of a Dionysian irruption; and in 'Nach der Katastrophe' ['After the Catastrophe'] (1945), Jung made an explicit link between the murder of Philemon and Baucis at the behest of Faust and the rise of Fascism which lead to the Second World War:

> An [Faust] sehen wir die aus der inneren Widersprüchlichkeit und Zerrissenheit quellende Sehnsucht der "Hungerleider nach dem Unendlichen", jenen "Eros der Ferne", jene eschatologische Erwartung der großen Erfüllung; an [Faust] erfahren wir jenen höchsten Geistesflug und den Abstieg in Schuld und Finsternis, ja, schlimmer noch, den Fall in hochstaplerischen Schwindel und mörderische Gewalttat, die Auswirkung des Paktes mit dem Bösen (GW10 § 423).

> [In Faust we see the same longing of "hungering for the infinite", born of inner contradiction and dichotomy, that "Eros of distance", that eschatological expectation of great fulfilment; in Faust we experience the loftiest flight of the mind and the descent into the depths of guilt and darkness, and, still worse, a fall so low that Faust sinks to the level of a mountebank and wholesale murderer as the outcome of his pact with the devil (P. B.)].

And although 'Die Erlösungsvorstellungen in der Alchemie' attributes the cause of the First World War to Man's state of unconscious possession, Jung implicitly related his discussion of Faust and Zarathustra to the turbulent politics of the Thirties as well, in such prophetically resonant remarks as the following: 'dieser besessene und unbewußte Zustand geht unentwegt weiter, bis es dem Europäer einmal "vor seiner Gottähnlichkeit bange" wird' ['this state of unconscious possession will continue undeterred until we Europeans become scared of our "god-almightiness"'] (GW12 § 563). Taking into account the comments in his Seminar and published writings of the Thirties and Forties, it seems that the chapter of his autobiography called 'Der Turm' transposes his remarks about the Second World War and his relationship to it on to the First World War instead.[42] Even if Jung were simply confused when he was looking back on this towards the end of his life, such a transposition is a highly significant slip,

[42] Conversely, Jung claimed that his remarks about the blond beast in 'Über das Unbewußte' ['The Rôle of the Unconscious'] (1918) had been a prophecy of the rise of Fascism and the outbreak of the Second World War, even though his remarks would more obviously have applied to the recent calamity of the First World War.

because it displaces Jung's unease regarding his feelings about Dionysos/Wotan onto a less controversial topic.

In a letter to Dr. Paul Schmitt of 5 January 1942, Jung told of how he had suddenly understood the importance for him of Philemon and Baucis (in other words, how he became conscious of the perspective from which he still viewed his relationship to them in *Erinnerungen, Träume, Gedanken*):

> Es ist mir einmal mit Schrecken und urplötzlich klargeworden, daß ich *Faust als Erbschaft übernommen* habe, und zwar als Anwalt und Rächer von Philemon und Baucis, welche, unähnlich Faustens Übermenschentum, die Gastgeber der Götter sind zu einer Zeit der Ruchlosigkeit und Gottvergessenheit (B1: p. 385/L1: pp. 309–10).
>
> [All of a sudden and with terror it became clear to me that I have taken over *Faust as my heritage*, and moreover as the advocate and avenger of Philemon and Baucis, who, unlike Faust the Superman, are the hosts of the gods in a ruthless and godforsaken age.]

And in the same letter, Jung insisted, as he had done in 'Die Erlösungvorstellungen in der Alchemie', that the drama *Faust* posed a question whose solution would have important political consequences:

> Sie haben [...] recht, eine gewissermaßen "goethesche" Welt in mir zu wittern. Eine solche lebt in der Tat in mir, insofern es mir nämlich unumgänglich erscheint, auf den Faust zu *antworten*: man muß doch das furchtbare deutsche Problem, das Europa verheert, weitertragen und ein Stück der faustichen Jenseitsereignisse, z. B. die benigne Tätigkeit des pater profundus, in unser Diesseits herüberziehen (B1: p. 385/L1: p. 310).
>
> [You are right to sense a "Goethean" world in me. Indeed it is there, for it seems to me unavoidable to give an *answer* to Faust: we must continue to bear the terrible German problem that is devastating Europe, and must pull down into our world some of the Faustian happenings in the Beyond, for instance the benign activity of Pater Profundus (P. B.).]

Philemon and Baucis are thus part of a complex nexus of identifications and investments which is inscribed within Jung's life and work as a whole and brings together both his personal struggle with Dionysos, his reception of Nietzsche, his fascination with Faust and the mysterious Mothers, and his attitude towards National Socialism. Jung's feeling in the Twenties of guilt and responsibility for the murder of Philemon and Baucis anticipates his later sense, confirmed by his later admission in 'Nach der Katastrophe', of being implicated, along with the whole of European society, in the events leading up to the Second World War: 'wir sind im allgemeinen viel tiefer in das deutsche Geschehen hineingezogen, als wir es wahrhaben wollen [...] Ich hatte nicht gewußt, bis zu welchem Grade es *mich* angeht' ['We are, on the whole, much more deeply involved in the recent events in Germany than we like to admit ... I had not realized how much I myself was affected'] (GW10 § 402). Thus, behind the abstruse discussion of alchemical union and dissolution there lay matters of real personal and political substance.

In *Erinnerungen, Träume, Gedanken*, Jung concluded his reflections on the importance of alchemy by emphasizing the need to hold onto those precepts which *Faust* teaches us, negatively, by showing us the consequences of ignoring them:

> Später knüpfte ich in meinem Werk bewußt an das an, was Faust übergangen hatte: die Respektierung der ewigen Menschenrechte, die Anerkennung des Alten und die Kontinuität der Kultur und der Geistesgeschichte (ETG: p. 239/MDR: p. 262).
>
> [Later I consciously linked my work to what Faust had passed over: respect for the eternal rights of Man, recognition of "the ancient", and the continuity of culture and intellectual history.]

Similarly, Jung's own behaviour in the late Thirties with regard to National Socialism and the meagre ethical content of his psychology in this respect, stand as an example of and a warning against believing in too much Faustian superpsychology.

Conclusion

Jung's three Eranos lectures of 1933, 1935 and 1936 contain six valuable insights into his developing use of Nietzsche and his understanding of the problem of the Dionysian. First, Dionysos is more clearly defined as instinctual realm of the Unconscious; second, Jung's integrated individual shares the same 'Dionysian faith' as Nietzsche's Goethe; third, Jung brings into relief the often ignored image of the spirit in the stone in *Zarathustra*; fourth, Mercurius as the alchemical parallel to Dionysos begins to take form in Jung's writings; fifth, Nietzsche is used to illustrate the reality of archetypal influences as well as the dangers attendant on any attempt to identify with, rather than assimilate, the archetype; and sixth, Jung's description in the period during and following the Second World War of the psychological dynamics behind the Third Reich in terms of the return of Dionysos/Wotan is prefigured.

Faced with the alleged Nihilism of Modernity, Jung's response was to advocate the cultivation of the needs and instincts of the individual as the only means of constructing a bulwark against the pressures of collectivism, which he characterized by another figure from Nietzsche's *Zarathustra* – the Spirit of Gravity:

> Je weniger wir verstehen, wonach unsere Väter und Vorväter gesucht haben, desto weniger verstehen wir uns selbst, und helfen mit allen Kräften, die Instinkt- und Wurzellosigkeit des Einzelmenschen zu vermehren, so daß er als Massenpartikel nur noch dem "Geist der Schwere" folgt (ETG: p. 240/MDR: p. 263).

> [The less we understand of what our fathers and forefathers sought, the less we understand ourselves, and thus we help with all our might to rob the individual of his roots and his guiding instincts, so that he becomes a particle in the mass, ruled only by what Nietzsche called the Spirit of Gravity.]

In place of Nietzsche's 'Werde der, wer du bist' ['become who you are'], Jung gives his (oracular) psychological equivalent: 'Erkenne dich selbst' ['know yourself/your Self']. Yet Jung's enthusiasm for tradition, not to say the primordial and the archaic, is dangerously close to the reactionary tendencies of such totalitarian movements as National Socialism. Jung's complicity with reactionary politics will be discussed in Chapter 12; but first, in Chapters 9, 10 and 11, I shall examine Jung's verbal remarks about Nietzsche as recorded in the transcripts of his seminars, including the Seminar on *Zarathustra.*

Chapter 9

The Early Seminars (1925–1934)

The Psychologischer Club in Zürich

Following his break with Freud in 1913, Jung had moved quickly to establish an organization, called the *Psychoanalytischer Verein (Verein für analytische Psychologie)*, in Zurich which would support and propagate his own views and beliefs. The first recorded meeting of the *Psychoanalytischer Verein* was held, according to the minutes, on 17 January 1913 in the Restaurant Seidenhof in Zurich. As Friedel Elisabeth Muser has pointed out, Jung's concluding words during the second meeting on 31 January 1913 summarized what he saw as one of the main differences between him and Freud:

> Der Traum gibt die Antwort durch das Symbol, was man verstehen muß. Man darf aber nicht nur die Wünscherfüllung darin sehen – sonst macht der Analytiker einfach die Phantasie des Neurotikers mit. Es müssen die Ziele des Unbewußten aufgedeckt werden, das dem Menschen nie etwas vormacht.[1]

> [The dream provides the answer by means of the symbol, and that must be understood. But you mustn't only see it as wish-fulfilment – otherwise the analyst is merely colluding with the imagination of the neurotic. The point is to uncover the goals of the Unconscious, which can never deceive a person.]

By 30 October 1914, the club had decided to drop any mention of psychoanalysis from its title and to rename itself simply the *Verein für analytische Psychologie.* Feeling the lack of a more permanent residence (or perhaps merely dissatisfied with the Restaurant Seidenhof), the *Verein* moved in 1916 into a magnificent house in Zurich (Löwenstraße 1, which no longer exists), donated by Edith Rockefeller McCormick, one of Jung's American patients. On 26 February 1916, the *Psychologischer Club Zürich* came into being, and in 1918 moved into another house, Gemeindestrasse 25/27 (symbolically located at the intersection between the Minervastrasse and the Neptunstrasse), where the Club's library is still

---

1 Quoted in Friedel Elisabeth Muser, *Zur Geschichte des Psychologischen Clubs Zürich von den Anfängen bis 1928* (Sonderdruck aus dem Jahresbericht des Psychologischen Clubs Zürich) (Zurich, 1984), p. 4. A more recent discussion of the function of the Psychological Club is Andrew Samuels, 'The Professionalization of Carl G. Jung's Analytical Psychology Clubs', *Journal of the History of the Behavioral Sciences*, 30 (April, 1994), 138–47.

housed today. The Club held seminars on Analytical Psychology, often conducted by Jung himself, and organized social events, including a New Year's Eve party in Zuoz at the house of Herr Knabenhans (one of the Club's members) which is recorded to have attained a 'dionysischen Höhepunkt' ['Dionysian climax'].[2] Jung's first proper seminars on Analytical Psychology were, however, given not in Zurich but in England. In 1920, he held a seminar in Sennen Cove in Cornwall on Arthur John Hubbard's *Authentic Dreams of Peter Blobbs and of Certain of his Relatives* (London, 1916). This seminar had been arranged by the analyst Dr. Constance Long and was attended, amongst others, by Esther Harding, Eleanor Bertine and H. G. Baynes, all of whom would later become members of his Seminar on Nietzsche. In 1923, he held another seminar in Cornwall, at Polzeath, this time on 'Human Relationships in Relation to the Process of Individuation'. And from 23 March to 6 July 1925, he held his first set of sixteen seminars on Analytical Psychology to be recorded (by Cary F. de Angulo, who later married the English psychologist H. G. Baynes) and multigraphed.[3] This series of seminars allowed Jung to unfold informally what had now become a more or less coherent system of ideas, which he called 'Analytical Psychology' (as distinct from 'psychoanalysis'). From 1928 to 1930, Jung gave a seminar on dream analysis in Zurich,[4] and from 1930 to 1934 the so-called Visions Seminar took place in Zurich, during which he analyzed the visions of Christiana Morgan, an American woman in her thirties.[5] For his next seminar Jung turned to Nietzsche's *Zarathustra*, and finally, from 1936 to 1941, Jung held a series of seminars in Zurich on children's dreams, this time given in German as many of his Anglo-American followers left Switzerland during the War.[6] There were various other seminars,[7] but those mentioned above are the most important. The seminars held in English have been published in the Bollingen Series at

---

2 Muser, p. 10.

3 *Analytical Psychology: Notes of the Seminar given in 1925 by C. G. Jung*, edited by William McGuire (London, 1990). Cited in the text as AP followed by page reference.

4 *Dream Analysis: Notes of the Seminar given in 1928–1930 by C. G. Jung*, edited by William McGuire (London, 1984). Cited in the text as DA followed by page reference.

5 Excerpts from the Seminar on *Interpretation of Visions*, selected and edited by Jane A. Pratt, appeared in ten installments of *Spring*, 1960–1969. Together with three concluding installments, edited by Patricia Berry, and a postscript by Henry A. Murray, these texts were republished as *The Vision Seminars*, 2 vols (Zurich, 1976). Cited in the text as VS followed by volume number and page reference.

6 C. G. Jung, *Kinderträume*, edited by Lorenz Jung and Maria Meyer-Grass (Olten und Freiburg im Breisgau, 1987).

7 Four lectures of Jung's 'Psychological Commentary on the Kundalini Yoga' (delivered at the Eidgenössische Technische Hochschule, Zurich, in 1932, were published in *Spring*, 1975, pp. 1–32; and excerpts from the lectures on the 'Exercitia Spiritualia of St. Ignatius of Loyola', translated by Barbara Hannah, were published in *Spring*, 1977, pp. 183–200 and *Spring*, 1978, pp. 28–36. For further bibliographical information on the Seminars, see *Collected Works*, volume 19 (*General Bibliography*), pp. 209–15.

Princeton, and the German seminar has appeared as a supplement to the *Gesammelte Werke* entitled *Kinderträume-Seminare.* For Jung, a seminar meant a series of lectures with discussions, and I follow the usage according to which each series of lectures is considered a single seminar.

An account of one of the lectures in Jung's Visions Seminar, published by Elizabeth Shepley Sergeant in *Harper's* of May 1931, captures something of the mood of these events:

> When, on Wednesday morning at eleven, at certain seasons of the Zurich year, Doctor Jung enters the long room at the Psychological Club where his Seminar is held, smiling with a deep friendliness at this or that face, the brown portfolio which he hugs to his side seems to be the repository of this joint account – the collective analytical account of a small international group whose common interest is the psyche. An involuntary hush falls on the room as Jung himself stands quiet and grave for a moment, looking down at his manuscript as a sailor might look at his compass, relating it to the psychological winds and waves whose impact he has felt on his passage from the door. The hush in the assembly means not only reverence but intense expectation.[8]

My discussion of the early seminars in this chapter complements my analysis in Chapter 3 of Jung's remarks about Nietzsche in his autobiography, letters and interviews, together with my detailed chronological analysis in Chapters 4 to 8 of Jung's reception of Nietzsche up to the mid-Thirties. Thus, because their status is not the same as that of Jung's published texts, I am giving his seminars separate consideration, which is not to say that the value of the material in the seminars is any less. Their significance in Jung's intellectual development has been emphasized by William McGuire, who rightly calls them 'an important feature of his working methodology', providing Jung with 'a means of trying out new ideas':[9]

> Jung's seminar colloquies are rich in material that is not to be found, or is only hinted at, in the published writings. For Jung they were germinative: he was often evolving ideas as he talked (DA: p.xvi).[10]

In the remainder of this chapter, I shall survey how Nietzsche is used in the early seminars (1925–1934) – i.e. during that period which I have hitherto considered only from the point of view of Jung's written texts – with special reference to the importance which Jung attached to Dionysos.

---

[8] Elizabeth Shepley Sergeant, 'Doctor Jung: A Portrait in 1931', in: *C. G. Jung Speaking: Interviews and Encounters*, edited by William McGuire and R. F. C. Hull (London, 1978), pp. 50–58 (pp. 52–53).

[9] William McGuire, *Bollingen: An Adventure in Collecting the Past* (Princeton, 1982), pp. 14–15.

[10] As for Jung's style in the seminars, McGuire goes on to characterize it in the following way: 'Altogether, the seminars give us a Jung who was self-confidently relaxed, uncautious and undiplomatic, disrespectful of institutions and exalted personages, often humorous, even ribald, extravagantly learned in reference and allusion, attuned always to the most subtle resonances of the case in hand, and true always to himself and his vocation' (DA: p.xvi).

Seminar on Analytical Psychology (1925)

Jung's extended Seminar on Analytical Psychology contains many passages which relate to topics discussed in the previous chapters. First, it provides useful information on the background to the composition of *Wandlungen und Symbole der Libido* [*Psychology of the Unconscious*] (1911/12) and *Psychologische Typen* [*Psychological Types*] (1921) (AS: pp. 22–25, 27–34 and 38–42). On 13 April 1925, Jung admitted that *Wandlungen und Symbole der Libido* was in essence an exercise in self-analysis: '[*Wandlungen und Symbole der Libido*] can be taken as myself and [...] an analysis of it leads inevitably into an analysis of my own unconscious processes' (AP: p. 27). More specifically, he cited Miss Miller as an example of what he had identified in 1911 as 'fantastic or passive automatic' (as opposed to 'intellectual or directed') thinking, and claimed that he had thereby been able to work through his own problematic relationship with the Unconscious:

> [Miss Miller] stood for that form of thinking in myself. She took over my fantasy and became stage director to it [...] she became an Anima figure, a carrier of an inferior function of which I was very little conscious [...] passive thinking seemed to me such a weak and perverted thing that I could only handle it through a diseased woman [...] in Miss Miller I was analyzing my own fantasy function, which because it was so repressed, like hers, was semi-morbid (AP: pp. 27–28).

Here, Jung is clearly admitting that one of his most important case-histories was in fact carried out in his own interest as much as that of the patient, and constituted an act of self-therapy. Indeed, like Nietzsche's philosophy, which records the individual reactions and responses of the philosopher and his personal struggle with Dionysos, Jung's Seminar on Analytical Psychology bears witness to his 'Auseinandersetzung' with the Dionysian (because dynamic) and Apollonian (because archetypally-structured) Collective Unconscious. Thus, the ultimate source of the fundamental concepts of Analytical Psychology is Jung himself:

> I watched the creation of myths going on, and got an insight into the structure of the Unconscious [...] I drew all my empirical material from my patients, but the solution of the problem I drew from the inside, from my observations of the unconscious processes (AP: p. 34).

Second, on 27 April 1925, he gave a compact account of how he had come to conflate psychological questions with metaphysical issues, abandoning his allegedly Kantian empiricism, as far as the question of the nature of God was concerned, for a stance which moved theological problems into the domain of the psyche.[11] Third, on 4 May 1925, Jung conducted a discussion which focused

[11] 'At that time [i.e. 1912–1916] I was on the Kantian basis that there were things that could never be solved and that therefore should not be speculated about, but it seemed to me [that]

on modern art (AP: pp. 51–57), echoing his earlier essay on psychological aesthetics (1922) and anticipating some of the changes in his later essay (1930). He argued that modern art had a vital psychological rôle to fulfil – to lead us 'away from the too great scattering of the libido on the external object, back to the creative source within us, back to the inner values' (AP: p. 55). Moreover, he characterized the condition of Modernity as the loss of those values whose replacement he saw as precisely the task of modern art: 'the inner unit[y] and quietude gave place to the materialistic urge toward conquest of the outer world. Through science values became exteriorized' (AP: p. 56). And finally, Jung assigned specific literary texts to be studied for their psychological content,[12] anticipating his choice of one major text for analysis in his later Nietzsche Seminar.

In his opening lectures of the Seminar, held on 23 March and 30 March 1925, Jung discussed three of his dominant intellectual sources: Schopenhauer, Eduard von Hartmann and Nietzsche. First, he contrasted Schopenhauer's view of the Will in *Die Welt als Wille und Vorstellung* [*The World as Will and Representation*] (1819) with that in *Über den Willen in der Natur* [*On the Will in Nature*] (1836). On Jung's account, Schopenhauer viewed the will in the first instance as 'a blind urge to existence', whereas later a 'teleological attitude' was added (AP: p. 4). Jung claimed Schopenhauer's later teleological position – i.e. 'that there is direction in the creating will' – for his own, identifying Schopenhauer's Will with his own, post-Freudian concept of the libido. For Jung, both Schopenhauer's Will and his own concept of the libido were an energic stream, manifesting itself in structures (or, in Jungian language, archetypes, corresponding to Schopenhauer's version of the Platonic Ideas): 'My first conception of the libido then was not that it was a formless stream so to speak, but that it was archetypal in character. That is to say, libido never comes up from the Unconscious in a formless state, but always in images' (AP: p. 4). Jung summarized his debt as follows: 'From Schopenhauer I first got the idea of the universal urge of will, and the notion that this might be purposive' (AP: p. 12). He made no mention

---

if I could find such definite ideas about the Anima, it was quite worthwhile to try to formulate a conception of God. But I could arrive at nothing satisfactory and thought for a time that perhaps the Anima figure was the deity. I said to myself that perhaps men had had a female God originally, but, growing tired of being governed by women, they had then overthrown this God. I practically threw the whole metaphysical problem into the Anima, and conceived of it as the dominating spirit of the psyche. In this way I got into a psychological argument with myself about the problem of God' (AP: p. 46). There are more than shades of Johann Jakob Bachofen's notion of matriarchy in this passage, and Jung's attempt to assign feminine gender to the deity and/or the psyche is part of his assimilation of the concept of the Collective Unconscious to the Nietzschean/Dionysian 'Urmutter'.

[12] The texts Jung assigned for analysis were H. Rider Haggard's *She* (London, 1887), Pierre Benoît's *L'Atlantide* (Paris, 1920) and Gustav Meyrink's *Das grüne Gesicht* (Leipzig, 1916) (which was replaced by Marie Hay's *The Evil Vineyard* (New York and London, 1923)).

of Nietzsche's concept of the Will to Power, even though that concept shares more characteristics with the Jungian definition of the libido than does Schopenhauer's concept of the Will to Life. This is characteristic of Jung's reluctance to talk about the Will to Power, a doctrine about which he remained suspicious. For the Will to Power was the doctrine which Jung decisively refused to accept on psychological grounds because of its one-sidedness, as his marginalia make clear (see Chapter 13, pp. 328–29).

Second, Jung interpreted Eduard von Hartmann's *Philosophie des Unbewußten* (1869) as a successor to Schopenhauer's thought: 'Hartmann, having had the advantage of living in a later period than Schopenhauer, formulates the latter's ideas in a more modern way' (AP: p. 5). Whereas Schopenhauer's Will is said to be devoid of 'mind' (intentionality or purposive consciousness), Hartmann's *Weltgrund* is allegedly both unconscious and has 'mind'. Such a position was more sympathetic to Jung who, following Hartmann, holds that 'our Unconscious is not meaningless but contains a mind [...] some thread of purpose running through the Unconscious' (AP: p. 5).

Third, Jung discussed the importance of Nietzsche in the development of his ideas, pointing out that he had first read Nietzsche in 1899, a formative period of his life which, according to Jung, contained 'the origin' of all his ideas. At that time, Jung had embarked on his investigation of the mediumistic séances of his first cousin, and both Nietzsche and Hélène Preiswerk had provided him with remarkable evidence of the autonomy of the unconscious mind or, in other words, the Dionysian propensities of the archetypes. Recalling the first impression which Nietzsche made on him, and emphasizing that Nietzsche had helped him understand his own experiences, Jung testified to the shaping influence which he had had on his thought:

> After this period, which contains the origin of all my ideas, I found Nietzsche. I was twenty-four when I read *Zarathustra*. I could not understand it, but it made a profound impression upon me, and I felt an analogy between it and the girl [i.e. Hélène Preiswerk] in some peculiar way. Later, of course, I found that *Zarathustra* was written from the Unconscious and is a picture of what that man should be [*sic*]. If Zarathustra had come through as a reality for Nietzsche instead of remaining in his "spirit world", the intellectual Nietzsche would have had to go. But this feat of realization, Nietzsche could not accomplish. It was more than his brain could master (AP: p. 7).

Jung's judgment in 1925 confirms what I have suggested in my survey of Jung's writings up to the Thirties. His initial reaction to Nietzsche had been enthusiastic but confused, and was gradually to become more complex. According to his autobiography, Jung had at first identified with Nietzsche (ETG: p. 109/MDR: p. 122–23), and I argued that this identification was tied up with his childhood intuitions of Dionysos and his search for an authority-figure as a substitute for his father. This identification lay at the heart of his initial difficulties with Nietzsche.

After his breakdown of 1916 and his 'confrontation with the Unconscious' – his own Dionysian experience – Jung began to understand Nietzsche in terms of his system of Analytical Psychology, and had even claimed to derive some of his key categories (e.g. Intuition and Sensation) from Nietzsche (GW6 § 223/CW6 § 240).

Jung's later lectures in the 1925 Seminar developed his claim that *Zarathustra* stood in a compensatory (and hence typically Jungian) relation to Nietzsche's Unconscious. But in response to a question from the audience, Jung emphasized that there had also been a creative impulse behind *Zarathustra*, and rejected the suggestion that writing it had simply been an act of compensation for Nietzsche's failure to live up to those ideals which Zarathustra proclaims. Jung claimed that Nietzsche had been moved by the autonomous archetypal forces which structured that text, and hence had experienced an imperative need to materialize the symbolic forms of his Unconscious:

> I believe that [*Zarathustra*] would certainly have been written in any case, because there is a tremendous urge in a creative mind to get the product of the fantasy down in some relatively permanent form in order to hold it [...] Nietzsche felt the need to materialize his symbol (AP: p. 13).

In his later Seminar on *Zarathustra*, Jung would define Nietzsche's tragedy in terms of his inability to constellate successfully the archetype of the Self.

Jung mentioned Nietzsche later on three separate occasions (which I list here in order of importance): on 18 May 1925, with regard to one's psychological attitude to life; on 8 June 1925, in connexion with the archetype of the Wise Old Man in *Zarathustra*; and on 25 May 1925, with reference to the problem of the opposites. With respect to the first question, Jung is still worried by the 'Aesthetism' of *Die Geburt der Tragödie* [*The Birth of Tragedy*] (which Jung had discussed in *Psychologische Typen*). According to Jung, the problem with the aesthetic attitude is that it ignores the practical problems of existence. Taking up the classic problematic of 'Lebensphilosophie', Jung argued that Man's greatest challenge is to combine reflection (discursive understanding) with existence (life); or, in Nietzschean terms, to reconcile Apollo with Dionysos: 'Our effort today should be the double one of consciousness plus a full participation in life' (AP: pp. 67–68).[13] With respect to the second question, on 8 June 1925, Jung

[13] 'When one assumes a perceptional attitude toward one's Unconscious, an attitude often to be observed in certain intuitives, one makes no effort to assimilate the material into the personality. There exists no moral relation then between the observed material and the personality. But if we observe in order to assimilate, it is an attitude that calls for the participation of all our functions. Nietzsche made the aesthetical attitude the foremost attitude of Man, and the intellectual attitude can also be like this, that is, one can simply think about life without ever living. One is not in the process, not even one's own process. For the sake of consciousness we have had to step aside from life and observe; in other words, we have had to dissociate, but necessary as this process is in the evolution of consciousness, it ought not to be used as it is today as a means of keeping us out of life' (AP: pp. 67).

saw the Old Wise Man as being embodied in Goethe's imagination as Faust and in Nietzsche's as Zarathustra:

> The same archetype [i.e. of the Old Wise Man] reappears in Goethe as Faust and as Zarathustra in Nietzsche. Nietzsche has been gripped by the sudden animation of the great wise man. This plays an important role in Man's psychology [...] but unfortunately a less important part than that played by the Anima (AP: p. 94).

This point would be echoed later in his essay on 'Psychologie und Dichtung' (1930) ['Psychology and Literature']; and in his Seminar on *Zarathustra*, Jung would examine in more detail the significance of the archetypes of the Wise Old Man and the Anima in the creation of the work which Jung considered Nietzsche's masterpiece. And with respect to the third question, Jung's comments on Nietzsche in his lecture on 25 May 1925 bring together its moral and metaphysical aspects.

As far as Jung is concerned, the concept of the opposites is an ancient one: 'The idea of the pairs of opposites is as old as the world, and if we treated it properly, we should have to go back to the earliest sources of Chinese philosophy, that is to the *I Ching* oracle' (AP: p. 72). He went on to compare the notions of yin and yang (found in the *I Ching*) with Lao-tse's later conception of the opposites (in his *Tao Te Ching*), in which he also saw a moral complementarity; and he then implied that a similar complementarism was to be found in Nietzsche's philosophy:

> In Lao-tse the idea of the opposites is expressed in this way: High rests upon Low, Great Good and Great Evil, that it to say, nothing exists save by virtue of a balancing opposite. It is the same notion Nietzsche voices when he says the greater the spread of the tree, the deeper the roots (AP: p. 73).

Here, Jung is clearly alluding to Zarathustra's parable of the tree: 'Je mehr er hinauf in die Höhe und Helle will, um so stärker streben seine Wurzeln erdwärts, abwärts, ins Dunkle, Tiefe – ins Böse' ['The more it wants to rise into the heights and the light, the more determindely do its roots strive earthwards, downwards, into the darkness, into the depths – into evil'] (Z I 8; N2: p. 307).[14]

---

[14] Nietzsche made the same point in his notes for *Der Wille zur Macht*: 'Der Mensch ist das *Untier* und *Übertier* [...] Mit jedem Wachstum des Menschen in die Größe und Höhe wächst er auch in das Tiefe und Furchtbare: man soll das eine nicht wollen ohne das andere' ['Man is beast and superbeast ... With every increase of greatness and height in Man, there is also an increase in depth and terribleness; one ought not to desire the one without the other'] (WM/WP 1027 = N3: p. 520). In his foreword to Daisetz Teitaro Suzuki's *Die grosse Befreiung: Einführung in den Zen-Buddhismus* (1949) [*The Great Liberation: Introduction to Zen-Buddhism*] (GW11 § 877–907), Jung traced this image back through the Flemish mystic Jan van Ruysbroek (1294–1381) to the Indian philosophy of the Upanishads. Cf. 'Traumsymbole des Individuationsprozesses' (1935): 'Kein hochgewachsener, edler Baum hat je auf seine dunkeln Wurzeln verzichtet. Er wächst sogar nicht nur nach oben, sondern auch nach unten' (GW2 § 148) ['No noble, well-grown tree ever disowned its dark roots, for it grows not only upward but downward as well'].

Jung then went on to contrast the Chinese conception of the opposites with the Indian one, finding once again a parallel with Nietzsche:

> The philosophical position of India with respect to the opposites is more advanced. There the teaching is, "Be free of the pairs of opposites, don't pay attention to High and Low." The perfect man must be above his virtues as well as above his vices. It is again the same idea that Nietzsche expesses when he says, "Master your virtues as well as your vices." (AP: p. 74).

The passage alluded to here is from *Menschliches, Allzumenschliches* [*Human, All Too Human*]: 'Du solltest Herr über dich werden, Herr auch über die eigenen Tugenden' ['You shall become master over yourself, master also over your virtues'] (MA/HA I Vorrede/Preface § 6; N1: p. 443; cf. WM/WP 911 = N3: p. 850), a passage which Jung had already quoted in 1910 in his 'Randbemerkungen zu Wittels "Die sexuelle Not"' ['Marginal Notes on Wittels, *The Sexual Need*'] (GW18(i) § 930). Thus, this early interest in the implications of Nietzsche's moral ideas reappears in a more developed form in Jung's mature psychology of complementarity and compensation. As Jung put it on 30 March 1925: 'I believe firmly in the rôle that darkness and error play in life' (AP: p. 13), suggesting that the Apollonian clarity of conscious life can be maintained only by accommodating oneself to the Dionysian forces of the Unconscious. What emerges from the 1925 Seminar on Analytical Psychology is Jung's willingness to play and experiment with Nietzschean ideas and his acknowledgement of the formative influence of Nietzsche on his psychology, even though Jung himself might not have fully recognized the nature or extent of that influence.

Dream Analysis: Seminar 1928–1930

In early November 1928, Jung began his extended Seminar on Dream Analysis. As had been the case with the Seminar on Analytical Psychology, most of those attending were either undergoing or had undergone analysis with Jung or one of the other analysts in Zurich (DA: p.x), and many would also attend Jung's Nietzsche Seminar. Both of those extended Seminars were recorded by Mary Foote (1872–1968), who edited the transcript compiled from various participants' notes and then circulated multigraphed copies. Far from being samizdat publications, these notes were presented to Jung for review, but distribution outside analytical circles was forbidden. Unlike the seminars of Jacques Lacan, Jung's were designed to supplement his published texts, not to substitute an oral tradition for the printed word. Nevertheless, the Seminars have been very influential within the Jungian tradition, unfortunately sometimes negatively, setting an example for the oversimplified dogmatism of some of his disciples.

Jung returned to Zarathustra's parable of the tree in his lecture on 13 March 1929 (DA: p. 167), and on 26 February 1930 he pressed his complementaristic point home in a passage which recalls the opening paragraph of the section on Apollo and Dionysos in *Psychologische Typen* (GW6 § 206/CW6 § 223). In this passage, Jung referred to that ambivalence of ancient Greece which Nietzsche had emphasized in *Die Geburt der Tragödie*, pointing out that behind Apollo lurks Dionysos:

> Greece is altogether a puzzle psychologically. Our ideas about Greece have undergone great changes. We used to think of it in terms of pure beauty, wonderful temples gleaming against blue skies, splendid gods, Olympians living a courageous sort of life. Old Greece seemed to be absolutely on the surface in blazing sunshine. But that is all wrong. There is a very dark, tragic, mystical Greece hidden in the past, an entirely different aspect that was discovered in the time of Nietzsche. Before that, people thought only of Attic beauty and paid no attention to the dark side (DA: p. 495).

Jung also discussed what he considered to be the relevance of Goethe and Nietzsche for the present day. Echoing Pope's definition of art as 'what oft was thought, but ne'er so well expressed' and anticipating his own essay on artistic creativity of 1930, Jung suggested that what may be a symbol for the individual might also have a symbolic function in the social realm as well:

> Goethe is, of course, the megaphone of modern times. Every great poet expresses the ideas and feelings common to all, or he would have no audience. He would not be appreciated or understood at all [...] Nietzsche foreshadows our time, as does Goethe in the second part of *Faust*. We can speak of general symbols, common to many people and expressed in many different ways, and we can apply the individual interpretation to the social phenomena of our time (DA: p. 192).

At the same time, Jung brought out the intensely personal significance which Nietzsche had for him: biographically, because they both lived in Basle, and intellectually, because Jung thought he had understood him where others had ignored Nietzsche's message. As we have seen, Jung admitted that Analytical Psychology can be read as a confession of Jung's own therapeutic discoveries, so, by implication, one of the tasks of Analytical Psychology is to express his approach to the philosophy of Nietzsche:

> I have experienced the effect of Nietzsche's ideas when no one else was capable of understanding him. He lived in my own town. His style and thought were peculiar. No one dared to admit that they saw something in Nietzsche, because that would put them outside of the flock. They would have felt outside of their world (DA: p. 192).

What was that 'something', as Jung puts it, in Nietzsche of which everybody was afraid? Although Jung does not say so explicitly, a later comment on the Corybantes and the spirit of Carnival suggests that it was precisely this outburst of unconscious, irrational energy, which the Greeks had embodied in the figure of Dionysos, which was so disturbing to others and to him. Jung pointed to the carnival tradition as a continuation of the ancient Dionysian cults.[15] In ancient Rome, for example, Dionysos-Bacchus was paraded through the streets on a float called the 'carrus navalis' (a possible origin of the word 'carnival').[16] This tradition was still alive when Goethe visited Rome in 1787 and 1788, albeit in a decadent and enfeebled form to judge by his account in the *Italienische Reise* (a detail Jung neglects to mention).[17] On 20 November 1929, Jung lamented the departure of the dancing, laughing god, here presented in his positive aspect as the incarnation of the sheer joy of animality:

> In the cult of Dionysos, the Corybantes were a wild, orgiastic band of dancers. They wore animal skins and goats' horns, to be as much like satyrs as possible, and the girls were nymphs in their lovely nakedness, like maenads, and things really happened. In Athens it was rather obscene; a huge indecent phallus was carried in the parade. Even in Rome as Goethe saw it, during the carnival in the ecclesiastical state, the old Priapus god, in the form of Pulcinello, walked about disturbing women. This was in the eighteenth century, in the very heart of Christendom, and that symbol was intended to suggest animal increase, animal sexuality. It was a survival of the old religious festivals though of course no longer connected with the Church [...] But now only the intoxicating wine is left. In our rituals, even in the Catholic Church, no space is left for orgiastic licence. Now, more than in any other time, Man has no chance whatever in that respect. We need that ceremonial licence (DA: p. 400).

---

15 For Jung's views on Carnival, see his letter to Horst Scharschuch of 1 September 1952: 'Zweifellos drängt in der modernen Kunst das Unbewußte mit seiner Dynamik zur Oberfläche und zerstört damit die dem Bewußtsein eigentümlichen Ordnungen. Dieser Vorgang ist eine Erscheinung, die sich in mehr oder weniger ausgeprägter Form zu allen Zeiten beobachten läßt, so z. B. unter primitiven Umständen, wenn das gewohnte, durch strenge Gesetze geregelte Leben plötzlich durchbrochen wird, entweder durch panikartige, mit wilder Gesetzlosigkeit verknüpfte Zustände bei Sonn- und Mondeklipsen oder in der Form kultischer Lizenz, wie z. B. die dionysischen, kultisch umschriebenen Orgiasmen; bei uns im Mittelalter in den Klöstern mit der Umkehrung der hierarchischen Ordnung und dem heute noch existierenden Karneval. Diese episodischen oder regelmäßigen Durchbrechungen der Ordnung sind als psychohygienische Maßnahmen zu betrachten, indem sie den unterdrückten chaotischen Kräften von Zeit zu Zeit Luft schaffen' ['There can be no doubt that the Unconscious comes to the surface in modern art and with its dynamism destroys the orderliness that is characteristic of consciousness. This process is a phenomenon that can be observed in more or less developed form in all epochs, as for instance under primitive conditions where the habitual way of life, regulated by strict laws, is suddenly disrupted, either by outbreaks of panic coupled with wild lawlessness at solar and lunar eclipses, or in the form of religious licence as in the Dionysian orgies, or during the Middle Ages in the monasteries with the reversal of the hierarchical order, and today at carnival time. These episodic or regular disruptions of the accustomed order should be regarded as psycho-hygienic measures since they give vent from time to time to the suppressed forces of chaos'] (B2: p. 296/L2: p. 81); and 'Zur Psychologie der Trickster-Figur' ['On the Psychology of the Trickster-Figure'] (1954) (GW9(i) § 456–88).

16 See Barbara Swain, *Fools and Folly during the Middle Ages and the Renaissance* (New York, 1932), p. 120; and Martin Vogel, *Apollinisch und Dionysisch* (Regensburg, 1966), p. 51.

17 See Goethe, *Werke* (Hamburger Ausgabe), 14 vols (Munich, 1981), XI, pp. 175 (20 February 1787, Ash Wednesday) and pp. 484–515 ('Das Römische Karnival').

This threnody for the absent Dionysos takes us right back to Jung's letter to Freud of 11 February 1910, when he conceives the project of psychoanalysis in terms of the creation of a new ethical order (FJB: p. 323/FJL: p. 294). Or in other words, once the project of Analytical Psychology had freed itself from Freudian psychoanalysis, it could fulfil its task of creating a new ethical order by taking seriously the moral issues raised by Nietzsche and recognizing the need for Dionysos. Thus, by 1928–1930, the problem of the Dionysian had moved to the foreground of Jung's thinking about a Nietzschean corrective to the shortcomings of Modernity, as he saw them.

The Visions Seminar (1930–1934)

Following the Seminar on Dream Analysis, Jung began another series of lectures dealing with the paintings produced by an American patient in the process of 'active imagination'.[18] The commentary on the visions of Christiana Morgan reads like an extended version of Jung's analysis of the Miller fantasies in *Wandlungen und Symbole der Libido.*[19] The final set of lectures broke off with no conclusion, and, according to Henry A. Murray, the leaking of the identity of the visionary as Christiana Morgan, an American woman in her thirties who was one of Jung's patients, was responsible for the abrupt termination of the Seminar.[20] The two volumes of seminar notes contain several references to Nietzsche, which are here discussed in ascending order of importance.

First, Jung again criticized Nietzsche's emphasis in *Die Geburt der Tragödie* on the aesthetic, thinking in particular of the precept from the 'Versuch einer Selbstkritik' ['Attempt at a Self-Criticism']: 'daß nur als ästhetisches Phänomen das Dasein der Welt *gerechtfertigt* ist' ['that the existence of the world is *justified* only as an aesthetic phenomenon'] (GT/BT Versuch/Attempt § 5; N1: p. 14).[21] As Jung saw it, Nietzsche's main problem lay in his recognition, intellectually,

---

18 'Active imagination' is a technique for bringing archetypal contents to consciousness through artistic form (GW8 § 402–03). For the use of this term in Jung's writings, see R. F. C. Hull, 'Bibliographical Notes on Active Imagination in the Works of C. G. Jung', *Spring*, 1971, 115–20.

19 Jung opened his first lecture of the Visions Seminar as follows: 'Ladies and Gentlemen: I must explain to you that these lectures are about the development, one could say, of the transcendent function out of dreams, and the actual images which ultimately serve in the synthesis of the individual, the reconciliation of the pairs of opposites, and the whole process of symbol formation' (VS:I:p. 1).

20 See Henry A. Murray, 'Postscript: Morsels of Information Regarding the Extraordinary Woman in Whose Psyche the Foregoing Visions Were Begot' (VS:II:pp. 517–21).

21 'Nietzsche said once that the world is merely an aesthetic problem. He said that because without such an attitude he would have suffered so much from the world that his problem would have become insupportable. So he covered up the abyss, and apparently satisfied himself with the polished surface of things' (VS:II:p. 367).

of the dark side of life and his simultaneous inability to apply that knowledge personally and accept the dark side of himself. Although Jung thought that Nietzsche had correctly identified the Dionysian motives behind Greek drama, he also thought that the tragedy of his personal life stemmed from his misrecognition of Dionysos. Despite Nietzsche's dictum (which Jung wrongly attributed to Zarathustra): 'Ihr sollt wieder Freunde von den nächsten Dingen werden' (VS:I:p. 78) – in fact a garbled version of a line from *Menschliches, Allzumenschliches*: 'Wir müssen wieder *gute Nachbarn der nächsten Dinge* werden' ['We must again become *good neighbours to the closest things*'] (MA/HA WS § 16; N1: p. 882) – Jung claimed that Nietzsche had been unable to accept the 'earth' side of his character. In terms of the dramaturgy of *Zarathustra*, this dark side is embodied in the figure of the Ugliest Man whom Jung analysed as follows (in a discussion of the dream symbol of the frog):

> The "Ugliest Man" in *Thus spake Zarathustra* was the thing he could not accept. Like this patient, Nietzsche went back to the Dionysian experience, and the idea of the "Ugliest Man" followed from that; then, after many detours – a serpent-like movement of the symbolism – the book ends with the idea of the Superman. He refused to accept the other side because it was too repulsive, and because it became associated with his phobia. (He suffered from the idea that he had to swallow a frog or a toad, and whenever he saw one he felt a compulsory inclination to swallow it.) This appeared in a dream that he had of a toad sitting on his hand; it referred to his syphilitic infection which he really could not accept. That was where he clashed with the earth, where the earth got him down (VS:I:p. 201).[22]

This excursus is more important than perhaps it at first appears. On the surface, Jung is doing no more than repeating those anecdotes about Nietzsche which he had rehearsed in *Wandlungen und Symbole der Libido* (WSL: p. 48/PU § 58, n.1), blithely associating Nietzsche's apparent obsession on the one hand with his syphilis on the other, without offering any evidence for such a claim. And of course, *Zarathustra* begins, not ends, with the idea of the Superman. However, the two subsequent points are new. First, the recognition of the Ugliest Man is said to follow on from (and hence to be related to) the Dionysian experience; and second, Jung's brief but significant characterisation of the structure of *Zarathustra* indicates an interest in the formal aspects of Nietzsche's work and adumbrates the kind of appreciation that Jung would offer in his Nietzsche Seminar.

On Jung's account, the frog in Christiana Morgan's vision represents 'Man in his chthonic aspect', i.e. Man in his current state is as a frog in terms of psychological evolution compared with the 'superior Man' of the future (cf. VS:I:p. 202). But in the visions, the frog becomes a healing symbol when it

---

22 For an account of this dream related to Clara Thurneysen, see Carl Albrecht Bernoulli, *Franz Overbeck und Friedrich Nietzsche*, 2 vols (Jena, 1908), I, p. 72; and for a different interpretation, see Joachim Köhler, *Zarathustra Geheimnis* (Reinbek bei Hamburg, 1992²), pp. 216–18.

compensates for an identification with the idea of the potential 'beautiful Man', i.e. when a one-sided identification with one part of the personality becomes so strong that there is the risk of 'inflation', as allegedly happened to Nietzsche.[23] This style of reading Nietzsche, whereby his works are seen as the externalization of his own personal psychic drama, anticipates the interpretative methodology of the later Seminar on *Zarathustra*.

Prompted by the material at hand, Jung also dealt explicitly in his Visions Seminar with the significance of Dionysos both in his traditional and in his more modern manifestations. During the first set of lectures (30 October to 5 November 1930), Jung juxtaposed the rational attitude of Socrates with 'the Dionysian element' ('feeling') (VS:I:p. 4). As in *Wandlungen und Symbole der Libido*, Jung treated Dionysos as an important syncretic figure, pointing out that the figure of Christ is assimilated with Orpheus, who, in his incarnation as the Fisher, 'played a great rôle in the Dionysian mysteries' and that in certain ancient inscriptions Christ is 'almost identical' with Bacchus (i.e. Dionysos) (VS:I:pp. 24–25).

Later on, in the second set of lectures (12 November to 9 December 1930), Jung recalled that ancient traditions of Carnival, like the Dionysian festivities and Etruscan ceremonials, lie behind the spring ceremonies of his native town of Basle, which celebrate 'the renewed spirit of Aries [...] the new vegetation power, the new mana for the whole town for the whole year [...] symbolizing the renewed force of nature' (VS:I:p. 57). Continuing to discover archetypal patterns in the visions of Christiana Morgan, Jung reminded his audience that 'the purpose of the Dionysian mysteries' had been 'to bring people back to the animal'; and he clarified this remark by explaining that such a return did not mean an identification with 'what we know as the animal [...] as we understand it' but instead an encounter with 'the animal within' (cf. Zarathustra: 'das innere Vieh' ['the beast within'] (Z IV 13 § 13, Z IV 15; N2: pp. 528, 538)). Jung described Morgan's visionary experiences of the Dionysian mysteries as 'essential', since they formed 'a bridge between herself and the original Man, the primordial Man concealed beneath the historical layers of the past' (VS:I:pp. 62–63). According to Jung, the Dionysian rites re-establish the lost link between Man and Nature, just as Nietzsche had claimed they did in *Die Geburt der Tragödie*, and Jung evaluated this reunion as highly desirable:

> And after that there is a chance that things can come right, be just as they should be, because the original pattern is unveiled, the original law is unfolded again. Then

[23] 'If we, in the form of frogs, identify with the beautiful Prince Charming, we necessarily suffer from inflation; then we are one-sided and unnatural, because we cannot possibly be that superior Man. Nietzsche, who tried to be, overdid it completely, and was threatened with the Ugliest Man. That is the reason why he broke down, and the reason why we break down when we assume a superiority that is not ours' (VS:I:p. 203).

> things take the course they must necessarily take because there is no possibility of loss of connection any more, the break between Man and nature has been abolished, the bridge is there again, and so the possibility of creating dissociated systems in which she could go astray is abolished in principle (VS:I:pp. 63–64).

Although Jung posits an 'original law' (the identification with the animal within and hence reunion with Nature), he tells us no more about it than that it is prior to consciousness, constituting just one step in the dreamer's psychic development: 'that Dionysian cortege was necessary to bring her back to the initial experience of the Unconscious, the identity with the things below, and the experience of being at the origin of things, at the dawn of consciousness; the next move will be forward' (VS:I:p. 65). We should note in this dream interpretation Jung's positive attitude to the Dionysian union of Man and Nature, over which he had previously set a question-mark in *Psychologische Typen.*

In his third set of lectures (13 January to 25 March 1931), Jung treated Lévy-Bruhl's concept of *participation mystique*[24] as a synonym for the state of Dionysian reconciliation, defining both in terms of loss of individuality and individuation:

> [...] through the antique religious experience the individual becomes entirely collective: he becomes a God [...] Thus the effect of *participation mystique* is strengthening. It is really a return to the primitive condition. The Dionysians were seeking that effect – namely, to be like everything else, to feel themselves in everything. The idea was that the blood of Dionysos circulated in every living being, that everything contained a piece of Dionysos. ...This naturally strengthened the *participation mystique*; but, of course, it killed individuality, it offended against it (VS:I:pp. 85–6).

Obviously, this description is very close to Nietzsche's account of the effect of the Dionysian in *Die Geburt der Tragödie.* But Jung went further and tried to understand how the religion of antiquity has passed over into Mithraism and Christianity. The Dionysian attempt to participate in the divine (by discovering the divine within – i.e. the archetypal, intrapsychic divine) is said to have led to the destruction of the divine itself; and this was the reason, Jung argued, why those individuals who had been in power in ancient civilizations had themselves been regarded as divine. Divinity was projected onto the members of the ruling class:

> It was the first appearance in Man of the being that reaches beyond Man, but the shot went too far. They identified with it and they were torn apart. They no longer existed. They were shattered to pieces, so that nothing remained but the remembrance of the divine moment [...] They had no individuality, therefore they had to worship one individual human being (VS:I:p. 86).

---

24 'Participation mystique' is a central concept in the work of the French sociologist Lucien Lévy-Bruhl (1857–1939). See *Les Fonctions mentales dans les sociétés inférieures* (Paris, 1910), a copy of which Jung owned as well as other works by Lévy-Bruhl.

Hence, Jung reasoned, the advent of Christianity had heralded an advance in the psychological development of Man. The loss of individuality in the Dionysian rites with all its consequences (as Jung prudishly puts it: 'Think of all the horrible things they did in the circuses!') had allegedly been superseded by a rite which sacrificed not only the animal side of Man but also the 'human-divine' side (VS:I:p. 85). And by sacrificing his divinity, Jung contended, Man had moved out of his *participation mystique* with God:

> That is why the Christian cult has a great spiritual advantage over the Mithraic cult, for it not only sacrificed the animal part but also the human-divine form of Man, in the shape of the Crucifixus. This meant that not only the things below Man should be sacrificed, but the things above Man, too (VS:I:p. 85).

In other words, it had been necessary for a new form of consciousness to appear, for 'the individual cannot live if individuality is completely denied' (VS:I:p. 86). This historical analysis of the evolution of religion added to his earlier statements in *Wandlungen und Symbole der Libido* (1911/12) and *Die Psychologie der unbewußten Prozesse* (1917) [later translated as *On the Psychology of the Unconscious*] by giving more detail about the shift from Mithraism to Christianity. Furthermore, Jung claimed that precisely such a shift in consciousness – his psychological equivalent of the Nietzschean revaluation of values – was on the point of recurring. For Jung, a new development in consciousness was now indeed possible:

> I put this very strongly, because we are in a time now when old things are beginning to crumble away ... There will have to be a tremendous abolition of old values. I mean if the time is such as it seems almost to be ... (VS:I:p. 86).

These broken remarks, printed in parentheses in the text of the seminar notes, hint at the idea of a profound shift in consciousness and values which Jung would try to work out in more detail in his Seminar on Nietzsche and, after the Second World War, in *Aion* (1951) and *Antwort auf Hiob* [*Answer to Job*] (1952). Jung understood the visions of his female patient to be symptomatic of the general psychological condition of the time just as, in the Nietzsche Seminar, he would assert that Nietzsche had expressed not only the psychic condition of his own age but also, in some way, of ours as well. So far as Jung was concerned, Christiana Morgan's individual, visionary return to Dionysos had a universal, psychological application.[25]

---

[25] 'The religious ideas of the patient seem to be returning in a very interesting fashion to the pre-Christian point of view... It is as if in our late Christian era she reached a point which contained no more life, so that now she has to look for the springs of life, or for roots from which new shoots of life may rise... At the time of the transition to Christianity there were two figures, Dionysos and Christ, representing two different principles. The Dionysian principle was decidedly archaic and Christ was its new opponent... But this woman is not coming forward from

In the sixth set of lectures (16 December 1931 to 10 February 1932), Jung linked this future psychological development with the ancient Greek god Pan who, with his goat's legs and horns, had often been depicted in the Dionysian processions and was hence associated with Dionysos himself. The Death of Pan made its first literary appearance in *De Defectu Oraculorum* by the Greek historian Plutarch (c.45–c.125), who related how the Egyptian sea-farer Thamous announced the news from his ship at the bidding of a mysterious voice.[26] Of course, the Death of Pan is a common topos in world literature, but numerous writers took this theme as their subject during the Victorian and early modern period in particular, including Nietzsche.[27] In Autumn 1870 and early 1871, Nietzsche made some preliminary notes for a dramatic work, provisionally called *Empedokles*. In Nietzsche's draft, the hero Empedocles deposes the oracular god when he refuses to answer his questions, and the sketch for the play concludes with a note for the following scene: 'Bei dem Pantempel. "Der große Pan ist todt"' ['At the temple of Pan. "Great Pan is dead"'],[28] and, in *Die Geburt der Tragödie*, he alluded to Plutarch's story (GT/BT § 11; N1: p. 64). The connection between Nietzsche's interest in Plutarch's account of the death of Pan and his later proclamation of the 'Death of God' is drawn by Cosima Wagner in her correspondence with Houston Stewart Chamberlain.[29]

In the Visions Seminar, Jung argued that *Also sprach Zarathustra* was a modern re-enactment of the Death of Pan, antiquity's version of the 'Death of God'. And according to Jung, the death of the ancient Greek god had signalled the end of one kind of consciousness, as one form of religion declined and another, Christianity, sprang up to take its place:

> There is a very symbolical legend which seems to refer to an actual fact [that in late antiquity a rumour spread throughout the Greek islands that Pan was dead]. Taken as a symptom of the mentality of those days, this would mean that the Unconscious felt the necessity of informing the people that great Pan had died, that that principle had come to an end – and it really was the time when Pan, as the deity of nature, came to an end (VS:I:pp. 207–08).

Dionysos to Christianity... she is trying to develop something new from the Dionysian ideas...' (VS:I:p. 150).

26 See Wilhelm Heinrich Roscher, 'Die Legende vom Tode des großen Pan', *Jahrbücher für classische Philologie*, 145 (1892), pp. 465–77. Jung owned a copy of Roscher's *Ausführliches Lexikon der griechischen und römischen Mythologie*, 11 vols (Leipzig, 1884–1937).

27 See Patricia Merivale, *Pan the Goat-God: His Myth in Modern Times* (Cambridge, Massachusetts, 1969), pp. 103–18.

28 Nietzsche, *Kritische Gesamtausgabe Werke*, edited by G. Colli and M. Montinari, 30 vols (Berlin, 1967 –), III 3, 5 [116], p. 129.

29 'Aus "Pan ist tot" raunt ihm [= Nietzsche] der Teufel ins Ohr: "Gott ist tot"' ['Out of "Pan is dead", the devil whispered in Nietzsche's ear: "God is dead"'] (*Cosima Wagner und Houston Stewart Chamberlain im Briefwechsel 1888–1908*, edited by Paul Pretzsch (Leipzig, 1934), p. 609).

Similarly, Jung diagnosed a similar crisis of consciousness in modern society, believing that it was now the turn of Christianity to be superseded by the next spiritual development in the form of another enantiodromian shift or, in Nietzschean terms, a further Revaluation of Values:

> Now in our time again, after the reign of the spirit, something similar is happening. In *Thus Spake Zarathustra* Nietzsche says: "God is dead." It is the same but now it means that the spiritual God has come to an end. And the Unconscious reacts immediately, bringing up the symbols of Pan once more... (VS:I:p. 208).[30]

The enigmatic category of 'Spirit' becomes a central concept for Jung in his later period, but its greater importance does not bring with it a concomitant increase in clarity as to its meaning. Earlier in the Visions Seminar, Jung had, however, defined 'Spirit' in terms of a mediation through the Dionysian between 'the earth' and 'the spirit' (conceived of here as polar opposites within Nature):

> Instantly when the earth is touched the other phenomenon belonging to nature comes up; the compensating phenomenon is the spirit. Therefore one finds them together in the Dionysian cult...
>
> There is nothing without spirit, for spirit seems to be the inside of things. Dionysos is concerned with the outside of things, with tangible forms, with everything that is made of earth, but inside is the spirit, which is the soul of objects. Whether that is our own psyche or the psyche of the universe we don't know, but if one touches the earth one cannot avoid the spirit. And if one touches it in the friendly way of Dionysos, the spirit of nature will be helpful; if in an unfriendly way, the spirit of nature will oppose one (VS:I:pp. 164–65).

According to Jung, the chthonic qualities of Dionysos are needed to revitalize a spirit which has become too airily Apollonian. In *Die Geburt der Tragödie*, Nietzsche says that, under the spell of Dionysos, the bonds of the *principium individuationis* are broken and the individual is returned to the 'Urmutter' (GT/BT § 16; N1: p. 93), the (pleromatic) plenitude of the womb of Being; and Zarathustra taught: '*Bleibt der Erde treu* [...] An der Erde zu freveln ist jetzt das Furchtbarste und die Eingeweide des Unerforschlichen höher zu achten, als den Sinn der Erde' ['*Remain true to the earth* ... To blaspheme the earth is now the most dreadful offence, and to

[30] In the ninth set of lectures (1 June 1932 to 18 January 1933), subtitled in the notes of the seminar 'The Reappearance of the Dionysian', Jung described in detail what the death of a religious 'truth' meant: 'Now when you throw over all your convictions, your whole *Weltanschauung*, it really means destroying a world [...] The breakdown of a *Weltanschauung* has always produced a general revolution, a time of catastrophe, a complete upheaval, not only of political and social conditions, but also of economic conditions [...] The destruction of a hitherto firmly believed and eternal truth is by no means a simple matter. You may think that it is simple enough to throw away the superstitious belief that there is a God in some way responsible for this world [...] But a psychological change has occurred [...] You call [the all-powerful being] your superstition and refuse to accept it, whereupon you become God yourself, that is, you now function as if you were God [...] And that leads on to the state we are in today; our neuroses are due to that' (VS:II:pp. 313–14).

esteem the bowels of the Inscrutable more highly than the meaning of the earth'] (Z Vorrede/Preface § 3; N2: p. 280). For Jung, 'the earth' symbolized potential sources of psychic vitality, precisely those which he associated with Dionysos.

In the twelfth set of lectures (24 January to 21 March 1934), Jung related the effect of the Dionysian dismemberment to another key category in his psychology, the 'Self'. In his Nietzsche Seminar, Jung would spend much time trying to define this equivocal concept of the Self. So, without going into unnecessary detail at this point about that concept as it is used in his Visions Seminar,[31] we may see that here, the Dionysian seems to be the path to the Self, a means of opening oneself to the powers of the Unconscious and an attempt to integrate consciousness and the Unconscious:

> The breaking up or the dismemberment is part of the ritual of the mystery cults. It is the communion ritual, the breaking of the bread, and the distribution of the mantle, and the tearing asunder of the living flesh in the Dionysian mysteries [...] the dismemberment is part of the ritual, and it is of course as a ritual necessary to the becoming real of the Self. The Self is such an intangible something, almost a magical existence, that it needs ritual to solidify it (VS:II:pp. 469 and 517).

However, Jung also discerned a less spiritual side to Dionysos. In his thirteenth set of lectures (7 to 21 March 1934), shortly before the abrupt conclusion of the Seminar,[32] he questioned the meaning for the modern age of the gods and mythologies of antiquity and, in a penetrating passage, made special mention of the German wanderer-god Wotan as a later manifestation of the Greek god Dionysos. This passage, with its note of despair, reflects Jung's doubt as to the ability of the categories of rational thought to deal with such religious or spiritual (i.e. for Jung, psychological) issues. In Jung's view, Modernity has alienated Man from his most vital (Dionysian) instincts, and just as gods become idols, so these repressed desires threaten to return in hollow and insubstantial form:

> Who among the living is capable of having more than sentiment in an old temple? Yes, it is aesthetic, it is beautiful, but do you understand what an antique god means?

---

[31] In the Visions Seminar, Jung defined the Self as follows: 'One could say the idea of the Self was an equivalent of the concept of God as it is in Eastern philosophy. Atman is the equivalent of God, and Atman is the Self. Thus, as somebody must be responsible for all the Evil in the world, the Self naturally shares the responsibility. Therefore the Self leads not only to all the good and respectable things but also to all the very disreputable things Man is capable of doing. We understand the Self as being the reconciling symbol, the most desired fruit of the transcendent function; but when it is necessary, it is a trouble-maker, its own fool, and that is good too' (VS:II:p. 472). For a more detailed discussion of the Self in Jungian psychology, see Chapter 13.

[32] In addition to the reasons Murray gives for the termination of the Visions Seminar, Jung himself also suggested that there was now an appetite for Nietzsche amongst the members of his seminar in view of the international political situation: 'The discussion of these visions was not continued, because my audience preferred to have a seminar about Nietzsche's *Zarathustra*. The reasons for this new interest was presumably the growing political tension in Europe' (C. G. Jung, 'Postscript to the Visions Seminars', *Spring*, 1977, p. 213).

How is it possible that they came to a conclusion that there was such a thing as Apollo or Ceres? Of course we can be sentimental about it, but it is very rarely experienced. Old Wotan has now been resuscitated but what is Wotan to us? He was experienced once, but now it is only historical sentimentality. Our intellect, our discrimination, has killed all these things. When the Christian missionaries cut down the oaks of Wotan and destroyed the poles or sacred idols, it was their discriminating minds which said it was impossible for a divine presence to be present in such man-made figures, in such clumsy dirty idols smeared with blood or dirt; their mental knife cut them down and they were obliterated, they crumbled away (VS:II:p. 502).

This passage has an unmistakeably elegaic note in its lament for the lost rites and deities of paganism and its sense of irreparable loss. Nevertheless, at the same time, Jung proclaimed the persistence of one of these ancient deities: Wotan lives. The passage above recalls an early train of Jung's thought which first appeared in his letter of 26 May 1923 to Oskar A. H. Schmitz.[33] Here, Jung expressed the same idea in almost identical images:

Wie die Wotanseichen, so wurden die Götter gefällt, und auf die Stümpfe wurde das inkongruente Christentum, entstanden aus einem Monotheismus auf weit höherer Kulturebene, aufgepfropft. Der germanische Mensch leidet an dieser Verkrüppelung. Ich habe gute Gründe zur Annahme, daß jeder Schritt über das Gegenwärtige hinaus dort unten bei den abgehauenen Naturdämonen anzusetzen hat. D.h. es ist ein ganzes Stück Primitivität nachzuholen (B1: p. 61/L1: pp. 39–40).

[Like Wotan's oaks, the gods were felled and a wholly incongruous Christianity, born of monotheism on a much higher cultural level, was grafted upon the stumps. The Germanic Man is still suffering from this mutilation. I have good reasons for thinking that every step beyond the existing situation has to begin down there among the truncated nature-daemons. In other words, there is a whole lot of primitivity in us to be made good.]

---

[33] Jung's letter to Oskar Schmitz of 26 May 1923 was to find a strangely similar echo in the Thirties when, from within the Far Right, the philosopher of National Socialism, Alfred Rosenberg (1893–1946), declared that Christianity had not been able to supplant the pagan cult of Wotan. Discussing the Christianization of German-speaking Europe in *Der Mythus des 20. Jahrhunderts* (1930), Rosenberg wrote: 'Der Wotanglaube war zwar im Sterben, aber die heiligen Haine, in denen "der Wode" verehrt wurde, blieben das Ziel germanischer Wallfahrer. Alle Vernichtung der Wotanseichen und alle Verwünschungen des alten Glaubens halfen nichts. So wurden an die Stelle Wotans christliche Märtyrer und Heilige, wie der heilige Martin, gesetzt' ['Belief in Wotan was waning, but the "sacred groves", in which "Wodan" was revered, remained the destination for Germanic pilgrims. All the destruction of Wotan's oaks and all the curses on the old faith were to no avail. Thus Christian martyrs and saints, like Saint Martin, were put in place of Wotan']. Indeed, Rosenberg proclaimed that the Nordic essence of Wotanism was alive and well: 'Eine Form Odins ist gestorben, d. h. Odin, der oberste der vielen Götter als Verkörperung eines der Natursymbolik noch unbefangen hingegebenen Geschlechts. Aber Odin als das ewige Spiegelbild der seelischen Urkräfte des nordischen Menschen lebt heute wie vor 5000 Jahren' ['One form of Odin has died, i.e. Odin, the highest of the many gods who embodied a race still uninhibitedly devoted to Nature symbolism. But Odin as the eternal reflection of the basic spiritual powers of Nordic Man lives today as it did 5,000 years ago'] (*Der Mythus des 20. Jahrhunderts* (Munich, 1935), pp. 163, 678–790).

This remarkable letter contains in embryo two key theses of Jung's post-war writings. First, Jung maintains a respect for the Dionysian together with a healthy suspicion of it: 'Halten Sie es nicht auch für bedenklich, einen alten Sagenstoff dem metaphysischen Bedürfnis unserer Zeit zu bieten? Was wäre geworden, wenn im ersten Jahrhundert p.Chr.n. man die Dionysoslegende als Stoff und Anlaß der Meditation genommen hätte?' ['Do you not find it also rather suspect to nourish the metaphysical needs of our time with the stuff of old legends? What would have happened in the 1st century of our era if people had taken the Dionysos legend as the material and occasion for meditation?'] (B1: p. 62/L1: pp. 40 – 41). Second, the conflict between the civilized and the barbaric in Man can, according to Jung, find resolution only in an experience of divine transcendence:

> Wir bedürfen zum Teil neuer Fundamente. Daher müssen wir zum Primitiven hinuntergraben, und aus dem Konflikt zwischen dem heutigen Kulturmenschen und dem germanischen Primitiven ergibt sich erst, wessen wir bedürfen, nämlich ein neues Gotteserlebnis (B1: p. 62/L1: p. 40).
>
> [We need some new foundations. We must dig down to the primitive in us, for only our of the conflict between civilized Man and the Germanic barbarian will there come what we need: a new experience of God.]

But what did Jung mean when he claimed that Wotan had been resuscitated? At this point, we need to turn to Jung's Seminar on *Zarathustra* which, taken together with his immediate post-war writings, shows Analytical Psychology beginning to grapple with the consequences of a very different reading of Nietzsche – the National Socialist interpretation. As Fascism took over from the Weimar Republic, turning Germany into a totalitarian dictatorship, and the Second World War loomed, Jung warned that Germany was undergoing an archetypal inflation and saw in National Socialism a dangerous form of Dionysian politics, which he baptised as the Teutonic war-god, Wotan. The problem of the 'political' Dionysos and Jung's tentative solution in the form of a 'spiritual' Dionysos are developed in the *Zarathustra* Seminar, which I shall examine in the next two chapters. Overall, the early seminars confirm the pattern of an increasing complexity in Jung's relationship to Nietzsche, and show Jung's growing confidence in using Nietzsche in that diverse and highly unusual manner which he would display to the full in his Seminar on *Zarathustra*.

Addendum

Subsequent to the completion of the preliminary draft of this book, I gained access to another, still unpublished seminar by Jung called *Modern Psychology*. The first set of lectures bearing this title was delivered at the E. T. H. (Eidgenössische Technische Hochschule) in Zurich between October 1933 and February 1934, i.e. concurrently with the Visions Seminar.[34] In the first four lectures, Jung provided a brief survey of the history of psychology, and discussed the psychological ideas in the writings of a wide range of philosophers.[35] According to Jung, 'these ideas were found, carried further or remained intact, lost, rediscovered, etc.'.[36] In the course of his sixteenth lecture of 23 February 1934, Jung included Nietzsche on an obscure chart, designed to illustrate his theory of practical psychological functioning. The categories on this graph are glossed in the earlier fourteenth lecture of 9 February 1934.[37] Below I reproduce this graph and Jung's commentary on it.

Bearing in mind that the significance of Nietzsche both on the personal and the intellectual was well established with Jung by this stage, it is not surprising that he was dissatisfied with treating Nietzsche merely as one figure amongst many in his Seminar of 1933–1934. On the 2 May 1934, Jung began a seminar on Nietzsche's *Also sprach Zarathustra* which was to last for nearly another 5 years. In the next two chapters, I shall examine that Seminar on *Zarathustra*.

Chart of Nietzsche's Practical Functioning[38]

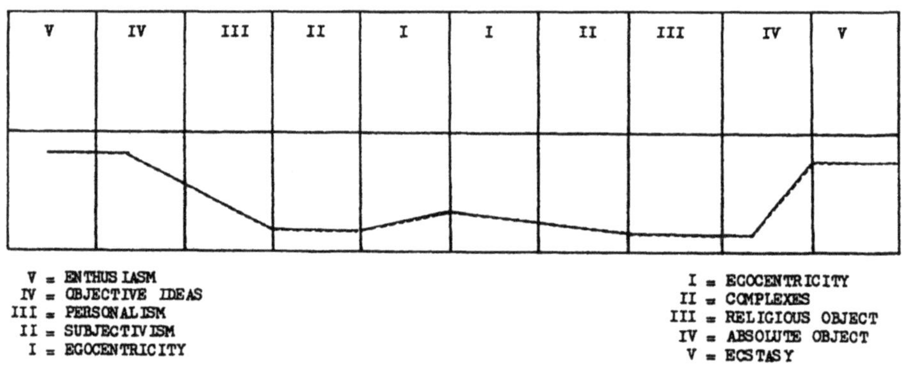

[34] I am grateful to Mrs Eveline Bennet for allowing me to inspect her multigraphed copy of this Seminar. (A second set bearing the same title was delivered from 20 April 1934 to 12 July 1935). For permission to publish this extract from Jung's *Lectures on Modern Psychology*, I am grateful to Dr. Peter Jung. As with all Jung's Seminars, these lectures are based on notes from the Seminar, and therefore have a less authoritative status than Jung's published texts.

[35] Jung mentioned the following thinkers: (Lecture 1) Descartes, Francis Colonna, Leibnitz, C. von Wolff, J. N. Tetens; (Lecture 2) Kant, Hegel, Schelling, Berkeley, Hume, David Hartley, Joseph Priestley, Thomas Reid, Dugald Stewart; (Lecture 3) Julien Offray de Lamettrie, Etienne Bonnot de Condillac, Charles Bonnet; (Lecture 4) J. F. Herbart, Wilhelm Wundt, Gustav Fechner, C. G. Carus, Schopenhauer, Eduard von Hartmann, Maine de Biran, Théodule Ribot, Alfred Binet, Pierre Janet, Ambroise Liébeault and William James.

[36] *Modern Psychology* [I], contents page.

[37] *Modern Psychology* [I], pp. 61–66.

[38] *Modern Psychology* [I], p. 68

Jung's Commentary on the Chart

Before I begin to explain this last chart, I should like to point out that these curves of consciousness do not always remain valid for the person's whole life. Consciousness changes and moves to Right or to Left. In this way we cannot regard Nietzsche's consciousness as static, it was on the contrary in a constant state of change and movement and one can discern three phases in his life which correspond to the high points on his chart.

The first summit appears in Right V and in Right IV, where Nietzsche experienced intense spirituality and powerful ideas; he was capable of an exceptional degree of objectivity.

The second high mark, in Right I, shows his neurotic disposition which was already observable in Right III and Right II, the Ego coming more and more to the fore. The curve is also pretty high in Left I and in part of Left II, for Nietzsche was very much concerned with complexes, he was a forerunner of analytical psychology. Left III is empty, but in Left IV the curve rises again slowly.

The third summit is reached in Left IV and in Left V. In Left IV Nietzsche had his Zarathustra experience and saw this very objectively when he said:

"Da wurde Eins zu Zwei
Und Zarathustra ging an mir vorbei".
(One became two and Zarathustra passed by).

In Left V he had his Dionysian experience which was wholly unorthodox. Nietzsche moved slowly towards the Left, away from the human being and towards Dionysian ecstasy.

In both Goethe and Nietzsche we become aware of the terrible tension between the two poles, which are utterly different. When we look at things from the Right side we see the house or man from the outside and when we look at them from the Left side we see the house or the man from within. It is most important to be able to see both these aspects – and it is a fine art to be able to discern the inside from the outward appearance.[39]

---

[39] *Modern Psychology* [I], pp. 74–75.

Chapter 10

Jung's Seminar on Nietzsche (1934–1939)

Part I: General Analysis

In my earlier chapters, I argued that Jung's reception of Nietzsche puts the problem of the Dionysian at the forefront of Analytical Psychology. Although only a few pages in these two large, gnomic and occasionally rambling volumes are specifically devoted to Dionysos, this problem is nevertheless a key element in the *Zarathustra* Seminar. Consequently, I shall regard Jung's Seminar on *Zarathustra* as providing the link between the pre-war and post-war stages of his Nietzsche reception with particular reference to the following two areas. First, Jung's political reading of Nietzsche in his analysis of the Third Reich and the causes of the Second World War (see Chapter 12); and second, Jung's attempt in his final years to respond to Nietzsche's proclamation of the 'Death of God' with the announcement of the future Dionysian Self (see Chapter 13). At the same time, the Seminar provides additional information on other areas which I have discussed: the importance of Nietzsche for the intellectual climate in Basle during Jung's period as a student, the use of Analytical Psychology to interpret works of art, and the extent to which Jung himself recognized his intellectual affinities with Nietzsche. I shall therefore start by providing an account of the conceptual content of the Seminar, and then go on to consider its two larger themes in Chapter 11.

History of the Seminar

Jung's extended Seminar on Nietzsche (1934–1939) has long enjoyed a somewhat occult status within the Jungian tradition, even though its importance has been noted by various Jung scholars, including his biographer Vincent Brome.[1] Jung forbade the distribution of the notes taken during this Seminar (as during all the others which he gave), and did not lift the ban until 1957. Indeed, until the publication of these Seminar notes in 1989, access to them was usually

---

[1] Vincent Brome, *Jung* (New York, 1978), p. 289.

restricted to readers undergoing Jungian analysis or training! In the case of the Seminar on Nietzsche's *Zarathustra*, Jung was however prepared to make exceptions, for in his letter of 11 November 1948 to Miss Piloo Nanavutty, Jung gave her permission to read but not cite the Nietzsche Seminar. His explanation for this refusal points to the provisional and unrevised status of the notes: 'they should be read with criticism, since they are merely notes taken by members of my audience which I never corrected. They certainly contain quite a number of mistakes' (B3: pp. 136–37/L1: pp. 512–13). Even as late as 1988, a footnote to Peggy Nill's article on Jung and Nietzsche explains that she was given permission to read but not quote from the Seminar, even though it was published in the following year[2] and even though two short excerpts from the notes on the Seminar had appeared in Jungian journals before their publication *in toto*.[3] It is therefore not surprising that the review of the published Seminar by Dr. Thomas Kirsch (whose mother, Hildegard Kirsch, had attended the meetings) opens with the following statement: 'In the lore of analytical psychology Jung's seminar discussions on Nietzsche's *Thus Spake Zarathustra* have long carried a mysterious and numinous quality'.[4] Furthermore, Mary Bancroft, who also attended the Seminar, has written of the 'talisman syndrome' which surrounded not only the warning that the notes were not for circulation, but also some of the other people who attended the Seminar![5]

The Seminar was attended by a large and exceptionally varied group of people.[6] In the words of Mary Bancroft: 'most were doctors, analysts, college professors, or students of esoteric subjects, with only a few being auditors like myself. I was fascinated by those I thought of as the handmaidens or Vestal Virgins, Jung, of course, being the Flame'.[7] William McGuire has pointed out that most of the Seminar members were analysands of either Jung or other analytical psychologists, so that 'the experience had an evident psychotherapeutic

---

[2] Peggy Nill, 'Die Versuchung der Psyche: Selbstwerdung als schöpferisches Prinzip bei Nietzsche und C. G. Jung', *Nietzsche-Studien*, 17 (1988), 250–79 (p. 258).

[3] 'Answer by Dr. Jung to a Question Concerning the Archaic Elements in the Self. Zurich Seminar, June 3, 1936', *Bulletin of the Analytical Psychology Club*, 30, no.5 (May), 14–19; and 'Comments on a Passage from Nietzsche's Zarathustra (1936)', *Spring*, 1972, 149–61. The full text was published as C. G. Jung, *Nietzsche's "Zarathustra": Notes of the Seminar given in 1934–1939*, edited by James Jarrett, 2 volumes (London, 1989). Cited in the text as SNZ with volume number plus a page reference.

[4] Thomas Kirsch, 'Nietzsche's *Zarathustra*: Notes of the Seminar given in 1934–1939' (book review), *Quadrant*, 22, no.2 (1989), 101–02 (p. 101).

[5] Mary Bancroft, 'Jung and his Circle', *Psychological Perspectives*, 6 (1975), 114–27 (p. 117).

[6] See my article 'The Members of Jung's *Zarathustra* Seminar', *Spring* 56 (1994), 92–122.

[7] Mary Bancroft, *Autobiography of a Spy* (New York, 1983), p. 93. 'Those women who were part of the inner circle around Jung from the earliest days of his career [...] were known to the student by several irreverent nicknames: the Vestal Virgins, the Maenads, the Jungfrauen, and the Valkyries' (Maggy Anthony, *The Valkyries: The Women Around Jung* (Shaftesbury, 1990), p. 2).

function' as well.[8] According to Professor Dr. Tadeus Reichstein,[9] attendance at this Seminar was only for the initiated – a category from which he modestly excludes himself. But it seems that there were almost as many curious, albeit enthusiastic onlookers as there were committed Jungians present. Bancroft has related how she obtained permission to attend by writing to Jung himself[10] and has given an example of Jung's seminar style: 'Jung had a marvellous way of cutting through overblown pretentiousness. At one seminar, a woman asked him if he didn't think it basic to remember the second law of thermodynamics. Jung chuckled and replied, "Maybe I would – if I knew what it was!"'.[11]

Bancroft has described the exterior of the *Psychologischer Club* (where the Seminar took place) as 'a dark, ivy-covered villa, surrounded by dense shrubbery that always seemed to be dripping wet'.[12] The interior surroundings in which nearly all the Seminars were given are described by Hildegard Kirsch with a distinct emphasis on the auratic atmosphere:

> Paintings of the Chakras, of the Kundalini Yoga, and paintings from the Unconscious were hanging on the walls. Each chair had the name of its owner [...] Each chair radiated *mana* and nobody else would even want to sit on them. If any of these people did not attend the meeting, the chair remained empty. So a tradition had already developed.[13]

More details on the hierarchical structure of the seating in the room have been provided by Dr. Joseph Wheelwright, who attended the Seminar together with his wife, Jane.[14] According to the Wheelwrights, Jung sat at one end of the room, facing the audience, whilst Linda Fierz-David sat on his left and Toni Wolff on his right, and his wife, Emma Jung, sat opposite him in the front row, where the remaining seats were hotly contested by the other female participants. The ritualistic climate of the Seminar is further emphasized by the recollection of its youngest participant, Cornelia Brunner (then in her mid-twenties), that she was forbidden by Fierz-David to attend the Seminar during her two pregnancies![15] The records of the proceedings of the Seminar (like those of the Seminars on Dream Analysis (1928–1930), on Kundalini Yoga (1932) and the Visions Seminar (1930–1934)) were assembled and written up by Mary Foote, who employed a stenographer, Emily Köppel (an English woman married to a Swiss), to take shorthand notes. Foote subsequently edited her transcript, some-

---

8 William McGuire, *Bollingen: An Adventure in Collecting the Past* (Princeton, 1982), pp. 14–15.
9 Letter from Prof. Dr. T. Reichstein to me, 23 January 1992.
10 Bancroft, 1975, pp. 115–16.
11 Bancroft, 1983, p. 93
12 Bancroft, 1975, p. 116.
13 Hildegard Kirsch, 'Crossing the Ocean: Memoirs of Jung', *Psychological Perspectives*, 6 (1975), 128–34 (p. 131).
14 Letter from Dr. Joseph and Mrs. Jane Wheelwright to me, 26 October 1991.
15 Letter from Cornelia Brunner to me, 16 January 1992.

times in consultation with Jung. Although Foote initially paid for the production and binding of the multigraphed copies which were distributed to the Seminar members and was reimbursed directly by the purchasers, Alice Crowley and Mary Mellon (who both attended the Seminar on Nietzsche) later financed the edition and distribution of the Seminar notes.[16]

According to Cornelia Brunner,[17] the Seminar meetings took place on Wednesdays between 11 a.m. and 1 p.m., with a short pause and an 'Imbiß' at midday (i.e. a quick bite to eat at the hour of the 'großer Glockenschlag'). At the meetings the procedure was as follows. Jung would read out a passage from the text and then invite a response. The competition between the various participants for Jung's attention and approval accounts for the seemingly arcane nature of some of the contributions.[18] But Frau Manuela Jaeger has emphasized how Jung directed the literary material down the interpretative paths he wished to follow,[19] and one has the distinct sense that Jung never lost control over the discussion.

Jung's Wednesday Seminars had been running since 1925, i.e. for over ten years before the subject of Nietzsche was tackled head-on. According to Cornelia Brunner, the suggestion to read *Zarathustra* had come from a member of the Seminar, Frau Martha Sigg, and on 6 May 1936, Jung reminded his audience that it was *they* who wanted to read Nietzsche! However, it is hard to imagine that Jung really held so many individual meetings under protest. Dr. Henderson thinks that Jung had wanted to show 'how Nietzsche both anticipated his understanding of archetypes but became also inflated by this',[20] and, according to the same source, Nietzsche's false understanding of the archetype of the Self was paralleled by 'the collective inflation taking place in Germany under Hitler'. Similarly, Dr. Marie-Louise von Franz has suggested that the study of Nietzsche enabled Jung to analyse the pathological elements in modern culture more generally.[21] The disagreement between the Wheelwrights over the significance of Nietzsche for Jung, with Joseph emphasizing his 'philosophical influence' and Jane referring to Jung's constant recognition of Nietzsche's madness, replicates Jung's own equivocal attitude towards Nietzsche, and there is evidence that Jung's Seminar group as a whole shared that ambivalence. For example, Professor Reichstein has said that he thought Nietzsche to be 'ein besessener, eingebildeter Mensch' ['an obsessed and conceited

---

16 I am indebted to Mr. William McGuire for these details concerning the recording of the Seminars.

17 Brunner, loc. cit.

18 As Joseph Wheelwright has admitted, sometimes the answers were 'rather wild'. William McGuire recounts one round of 'guess the symbolic allusion' in the Seminar (*Bollingen*, p. 14; cf.SNZ: II:p. 1282).

19 Letter from Manuela Jaeger to me, undated, 1991.

20 Letter from Dr. Joseph Henderson to me, undated [1992].

21 Letter from Marie-Louise von Franz to me, 16 May 1991.

man']; Liliane Frey-Rohn's book *Jenseits der Werte seiner Zeit: Nietzsche im Spiegel seiner Werte* (Zurich, 1984) is adamant that Nietzsche's breakdown was an inevitable consequence of his philosophy; and Aniela Jaffé saw in Nietzsche a man who had refused reconciliation with the archetypal.[22]

In general, attendance at the Nietzsche Seminar seems to have confirmed the enthusiasm for Analytical Psychology of many of its members. One of these, Linda Fierz-David, went on to write a psychological commentary on *Hypnerotomachia Poliphili*, published in Venice in the Trecento and attributed to the Dominican monk Francesco Colonna.[23] In his preface to her book there is a curious moment where Jung slips into a rôle which is highly reminiscent of one of Nietzsche's literary-biographical tropes, i.e. his relationship with Cosima Wagner, whom he referred to as Ariadne. In his introduction to Fierz-David's commentary (published in 1947), Jung wrote that her 'verblüffende Lösungen' ['dazzling feats of interpretation'] had succeeded in illuminating 'jene labyrinthisch verschlungenen Irrgänge, in denen sich die Eitelkeiten des männlichen Verstandes ihre eigenen Fallgruben anlegen' ['the tortuous ways of the masculine mind, creating traps for itself with its own vanities'] (GW18(ii) § 1751). As Maggy Anthony has pointed out,[24] Jung, by implying that Fierz-David is Ariadne, attributes to himself the role of Dionysos, thus re-enacting the mythological pairing which Nietzsche had imagined in his fantasy with Cosima and used as an image in his philosophical texts, particularly *Zarathustra*. However, as I shall suggest later on, the significance of Dionysos in the Seminar on Nietzsche is more than merely incidental.

Jung's (Auto)-Biographical Remarks

Some of Jung's remarks substantiate the claim in his autobiography that his interest in Nietzsche went back to his time at Basle (1895–1900). Early on in the Seminar, Jung claimed: 'I know people who knew Nietzsche personally, because he lived in my own town, Basle, so I heard many details' (SNZ:I:p. 16; cf. II:p. 1467). More specifically, on 23 October 1935, Jung claimed that he had been acquainted with the theologian Franz Overbeck (1837–1905), with whom Nietzsche had had a lengthy and revealing correspondence. Although Jung says

---

22 Interview in Zurich with the late Aniela Jaffé, April 1991.

23 Linda Fierz-David, *Der Liebestraum des Poliphilo: Ein Beitrag zur Psychologie der Renaissance und der Moderne* (Zurich, 1947). Fierz-David went on to do research into Dionysian initiation rites, writing a book on the Villa of Mysteries in Pompeii, published in mimeographed form by the Psychological Club as *Psychologische Betrachtungen zu der Freskenfolge der Villa dei Misteri in Pompeii: Ein Versuch* (Zurich, 1957) (translated as *Women's Dionysian Initiation: The Villa of Mysteries in Pompeii* (Dallas, 1988).

24 See Anthony, p. 41.

that he had known Overbeck personally (SNZ:I:p. 635), there is no evidence that this went beyond the extent of his acquaintanceship with Jacob Burckhardt, whom he knew by sight: 'I wish I could show you [...] Burckhardt as I saw him practically every day, walking near the Cathedral coming from the University library' (SNZ:II:p. 862). Nevertheless, Jung made repeated reference to Burckhardt's allegedly negative reaction to *Zarathustra*, whilst admitting that he had learnt about it from second-hand sources: '[Nietzsche's] contemporary Jacob Burckhardt, the famous historian, grew quite afraid when he read *Zarathustra* – as I know from people in Basle who were acquainted with them both' (SNZ:I:p. 29; cf. SNZ:I:p. 274; SNZ:II:pp. 1358, 1454). In saying this, it is also possible that Jung is projecting onto Burckhardt his own fear of Nietzsche which he would discuss in *Erinnerungen, Träume, Gedanken* (see Chapter 3). He also referred to four other mutual acquaintances: Lou Andreas-Salomé (SNZ:I:p. 633); 'a professor of internal medicine [...] whom Nietzsche considered one of his great friends' (SNZ:I:p. 635); 'a rich old lady who contributed to Nietzsche's life when he was writing *Zarathustra*' (SNZ:II:p. 961; cf. SNZ:II:p. 1362) (possibly Malwida von Meysenbug (1816–1903)); and Johann Jakob Bachofen (SNZ:II:p. 1301). And Jung may also have known the student who features in the story which he told twice about Nietzsche's attitude towards other people (SNZ:I:pp. 16–17 and SNZ:II:p. 1361). The student in this anecdote is probably Ludwig von Scheffler, a pupil whom Nietzsche invited to accompany him to Italy in 1876.[25]

It seems as if Jung's anxiety as an adolescent vis-à-vis Nietzsche threatened to return during the reading of certain passages in the Seminar, as evidenced by his very strong personal reaction to 'Vom bleichen Verbrecher' ['Of the Pale Criminal'] on 8 May 1935 (SNZ:I:pp. 457–73) and to certain lines of the chapter 'Das Grablied' ['The Funeral Song'] on 30 June 1937 (SNZ:II:p. 1200). In the margins of his copy of *Zarathustra*, Jung had noted that the Pale Criminal is 'Der, der mit seinem Ich nicht einverstanden ist, weil er daran leidet. Er soll es sterben lassen' ['Someone who is not in accord with his Ego, because he suffers from it. He should let it die'], and on 6 May 1936 he admitted:

> I myself often felt when I was ploughing through the text that it had disagreeable effects upon me. There are passages which I intensely dislike and they really are irritating. But when you plough through your own psychology you also come across certain irritating places. So when I am irritated in those places in *Zarathustra* I say, well, here is a sore spot or an open wound (SNZ: II:p. 895).

Such remarks suggest that certain traces of Jung's earlier identification with Nietzsche were still latent within him. But his stress on how close he was to

---

[25] See *Conversations with Nietzsche: A Life in the Words of his Contemporaries*, edited by Sander L. Gilman and translated by David J. Parent (Oxford and New York, 1987), pp. 73–74.

Nietzsche historically and geographically is actually a cipher for the psychological proximity between them which he felt as a student, as the following statement makes clear:

> I was a boy when [Nietzsche] was a professor at the university [of Basle]. I never saw him, but I saw his friend Jacob Burckhardt very often, and also Bachofen, so we were not separated by cosmic distances. Nietzsche's mind was one of the first spiritual influences I experienced. It was all brand new then, and it was the closest thing to me (SNZ:II:p. 1301).

Even more significant are Jung's frequent reminders that Nietzsche, too, was a parson's son (SNZ:I:pp. 69, 261, 429, 576; SNZ:II:pp. 961, 1095) – 'I know what *that* means' (SNZ:I:p. 31)! These suggestive remarks highlight their common psychological background. Just as Nietzsche's philosophy of self-assertive autolegislation can be read as a response to the early death of his father, so Jung had searched for a substitute authority-figure to replace his father.[26] Similarly, in another autobiographical reminiscence in the Seminar, Jung recalled a theological discussion with his father about the existence of Evil (SNZ:II:p. 1041); and his comments about the relationship between Nietzsche and Nietzsche's father look like projections both of his own experience of the father/son relationship and of his own awareness of the Dionysian:

> I think the fact that [Nietzsche] had a father who was a theologian points rather to another kind of wisdom, a religious wisdom which did not fulfil its promise. It did not enlighten him about the darkness of the soul (SNZ:II:p. 1205).

Furthermore, the 'Wotan dream' of the fifteen-year old Nietzsche, lifted directly from Elisabeth Förster-Nietzsche's biography and interpreted in the Seminar as evidence of Nietzsche's 'archetypal memory', corresponds to Jung's own oneiric encounters at an even younger age (in the dream of the monocular ithyphallus and the scatological vision of God above Basle Cathedral) with the Dionysian 'darkness of the soul'.

Intellectual Tradition

In his reading of *Zarathustra*, Jung related Nietzsche to two intellectual traditions in European thought: the philosophical tradition in Germany and the suppressed mystical tradition of alchemy. These contextualizations were not new. In his book on psychological typology (1921) and his concurrently delivered Eranos lectures of 1933–1936, he had situated Nietzsche within these two

---

[26] Jung's relationship with Freud constituted another search for a patriarchal authority-figure – and an equally unsuccessful one (ETG: pp. 61, 162/MDR: pp. 73, 181–82).

traditions. But Jung's Seminar transmits an even greater sense of his overarching view of intellectual history and hints at an awareness of his own historico-intellectual position.

On 20 June 1934, Jung suggested that Nietzsche had taken up the problem of the opposites as that had been discussed by Schiller and Schopenhauer. According to Jung, 'Schiller discovered [the] problem of the pairs of opposites: the problem that Man, on the one side, is a fairly civilized being, and on the other, quite barbarous' (SNZ:I:p. 118). Schiller's solution, Jung continued, was in the 'vision of beauty' (i.e. the satisfaction of the ludic drive in art), and he again criticized the 'aesthetic solution' for being too superficial (SNZ:I:p. 120). Whereas Jung felt that Schiller had understood the problem of the opposites as purely psychological, he charged Schopenhauer with viewing that split 'as *being*, not psychological, but as a split in the world' (SNZ:I:p. 118). Nevertheless, Jung claimed that Schopenhauer's pessimism had found an identical solution ('he unites the opposites') in the form of the denial of the Will, which presupposes an identity between the individual Will (i.e. the individuated Will) and the universal Will (SNZ:I:p. 119). Having then criticized Schopenhauer's 'heroic attempt' for its excess which 'annuls all existence in order to settle the conflict of Man' (SNZ:I:p. 120), Jung asserted that Nietzsche had taken up this problem in *Zarathustra*, and he linked the conflict of the opposites with the encounter with the Shadow. For Jung, the solution to the problem of the opposites lay in Nietzsche's attempt in *Zarathustra* to arrive at a stable psychic configuration which unites both consciousness and the Unconscious. It is therefore not a conceptual answer for which Jung was looking in *Zarathustra*, but rather a symbolic representation of a solution to the problem of the opposites (SNZ:I:p. 120). Much later on in the Seminar, however, on 8 June 1938, Jung claimed that Nietzsche himself had embodied the solution to the problem of the opposites only negatively, by being unable to accept 'that to everything positive there is a negation', and that he had, in fact, rejected his Shadow (SNZ:II:p. 1292).

On 31 October 1934, Jung suggested a link between Nietzsche and more mystical traditions of Western thought such as medieval alchemistic philosophy, the religious philosopher Meister Eckhart (c.1260–1327?), and Goethe's *Faust*. According to Jung, this tradition emphasized the non-rational convergence of the opposites, as symbolized by certain medieval theological notions like those informing Dante's *La Divina Commedia*:

> The future idea is already appearing when Dante reaches Paradise, for at the very summit of Paradise is the mystical rose in which individuation is indicated. That is the end of the Christian mandala, the highest realization of the time, and the mystical rose is the future. And it is Nietzsche [...] who takes up the eternal thread and carries it further, bringing the idea of the mystical rose down into the being of Man (SNZ:I: p. 204).

In keeping with this occult view, Jung claimed on 15 May 1935 that it had been a mistake for Nietzsche to publish *Zarathustra*, for in it he saw 'a partial revelation of the Unconscious' (SNZ:I:p. 475). Echoing Nietzsche's own view of the composition of *Zarathustra* as described in *Ecce Homo* (EH Z § 3; N2: p. 1131), Jung asserted that 'it is full of inspiration, of the immediate manifestation of the Unconscious' and that it should be read 'with due preparation, with due knowledge of the style and the intentions of the Unconscious' (SNZ:I:p. 475). These remarks imply that Jung wished to operate with a particular interpretative method in his Seminar, and we need to examine the methodological principles which informed his reading.

Methodology

Nietzsche's work itself foregrounds the problematic identity of its main figure. In 'Von der Erlösung' ['Of Redemption'], the crowd asks Zarathustra: '"wer ist uns Zarathustra? Wie soll er uns heißen?"' ['Who is Zarathustra to us? What shall we call him?'] (Z II 20; N2: p. 393). Zarathustra describes himself as: 'Ein Seher, ein Wollender, ein Schaffender, eine Zukunft selber und eine Brücke zur Zukunft – und ach, auch noch gleichsam ein Krüppel an dieser Brücke' ['A seer, a willer, a creator, a future itself and a bridge to the future – and, alas, also like a cripple upon this bridge'] (Z II 20; N2: p. 393), but goes on to problematize his identity yet further (Z II 20; N2: p. 394; cf. Z IV 11; N2: p. 517).

In 1935, the German philosopher Karl Löwith (1897–1973) had insisted on the possibility as well as the necessity of a psychological interpretation of Nietzsche's *Zarathustra*.[27] Löwith had argued that each figure in *Zarathustra* (the Tightrope Walker, the Clown, the Wanderer, the Shadow, the Shepherd, the Magician) represents a fragment of a dialogue conducted with Nietzsche himself.[28] Jung's method is similarly psycho-biographical: he called *Zarathustra* the

[27] 'Die philosophische Auslegung orientiert sich, wie jede sachgebundene Interpretation, vorzüglich an dem, was Nietzsche selber in der Figur des Zarathustra bewußtermaßen sagen und lehren wollte; die psychologische Ausdeutung hält sich vorwiegend an das, was in allem Gesagten ungesagt bleibt und, entgegen der bewußten Absicht des Autors, unwillkürlich mit zur Sprache kommt' ['The philosophical interpretation orientates itself, as does every proper interpretation, best of all around what Nietzsche himself consciously wanted to say and teach in the figure of Zarathustra; the psychological interpretation follows predominantly what remains unsaid in all that is said and which articulates itself contrary to the conscious intention of the author'] (Karl Löwith, *Nietzsches Philosophie der ewigen Wiederkehr des Gleichen*, (Hamburg, 1978³), p. 186). Löwith acknowledged Nietzsche's own rôle in making such a psychological interpretation possible, but restricted himself to a more philosophical reading. The first edition of Löwith's book was published in 1935, one year after the start of Jung's Seminar on *Zarathustra*.

[28] See Löwith, p. 188–89.

'*drame intérieur* of the author himself' (SNZ:I:p. 112) but qualified this description as follows:

> *Thus Spake Zarathustra* is not a series of experiences of the inner world; there are very few of those. The book mainly consists of the thoughts and values Nietzsche develops from them, the experiences themselves being left pretty much in the dark (SNZ:I:p. 219).

The status of the figure of Zarathustra caused Jung much vexation and is the greatest source of confusion in the Seminar. By the eighth lecture, on 27 June 1934, Jung himself had sensed this, and made a spurious reference to Aristotelian logic to justify his assertion, which resembles Löwith's, that Nietzsche was to be identified with each figure of his poetic drama (SNZ:I:pp. 129–31). Although Jung's reference to 'black magic' in order to describe his own methodological procedure is not entirely fanciful, given that he appeals to ancient Greek logic in order to justify having his interpretative cake and eating it, his approach to the text is, in fact, perfectly in keeping with his view as expounded in 1922 and 1930 that a work of art is the product both of the individual artist and at the same time of his archetypal imagination.

Thus, for Jung, *Zarathustra* is on one hand a highly personal work (SNZ:II:p. 1037), an aspect of the unfolding psychological tragedy of an individual, and which marks the start of both Nietzsche's (unresolved) mid-life crisis (SNZ:I:p. 226; SNZ:II:p. 1070) and his mental illness (SNZ:I:p. 695). But on the other hand, Jung argued that *Zarathustra* stands in a dialectical relationship to the age in which it was written, because Nietzsche is both a 'child' of that time and a 'forerunner of times that have come since and of times that are still to come' (SNZ:II:p. 1037). Because Jung saw *Zarathustra* as both an individual and an archetypal work, he attached great importance to the account of its composition which Nietzsche provided in the short poem 'Sils-Maria', one of the 'Lieder des Prinzen Vogelfrei' ['Songs of Prince Vogelfrei'] which were published as an appendix to *Die fröhliche Wissenschaft* [*The Gay Science*] in 1897 (FW/GS Anhang/Appendix; N2: p. 271) and whose title refers to the Swiss location where most of *Zarathustra* was written. In this poem, Jung saw the expression both of a real psychological event and of an authentic archetypal experience: '[Nietzsche] said: "Da wurde eins zu zwei und Zarathustra ging an mir vorbei" ['Then one turned into two – and Zarathustra walked into my view'] [...] meaning that Zarathustra then became manifest as a second personality in himself' (SNZ:I:p. 10).[29]

---

[29] See Nill, p. 263. However, the philosopher of hermeneutics Hans-Georg Gadamer has explicitly warned that to posit a simple 'identity' between Nietzsche and Zarathustra is to renege on the task of interpretation: '[E]s [ist] gewiß nicht richtig, Zarathustra einfach mit Nietzsche und seine Reden mit Nietzsches Philosophie zu identifizieren. Vielmehr ist es eine hermeneutische Aufgabe ersten Ranges, das "Zwischen" von Lehre und Handlung, das hier vorliegt, zu bestimmen, das jedem poetischen Text eigen ist' ['It is certainly not right simply to identify Zarathustra with Nietzsche and his speeches with Nietzsche's philosophy. Rather it is a hermeneutic task

Jung is not alone in giving such a relentlessly literalistic reading to this text. Apart from Löwith,[30] the French literary critic René Girard in *Critiques dans un souterrain* (1976) derived the dynamics of Nietzsche's entire *oeuvre* and life from the mysterious encounter presented in the poem, describing this 'expérience du Double' as 'une véritable épiphanie du désir mimétique'.[31] And as if in substantiation of this claim, Nietzsche had argued in *Die Geburt der Tragödie* [*The Birth of Tragedy*] that the figures in a dramatic literary work are only different projections of the author's subjective self.[32] Thus, Jung's own view of the complex relationship between Nietzsche and Zarathustra is best summarized in his own words as follows: 'Zarathustra speaks to Nietzsche, but Nietzsche speaks out of his time' (SNZ:II:p. 831).

More specifically, in 'Die psychologischen Aspekte des Mutterarchetypus' ['Psychological Aspects of the Mother Archetype'], an Eranos lecture delivered in 1934 – i.e. the same year in which he began his Nietzsche Seminar – Jung identified Zarathustra as the archetype of the Old Wise Man (cf. GW9(i) § 77); and on 2 May 1934, he interpreted the figure of the old man whom Zarathustra meets in the woods (Z Vorrede/Prologue § 2; N2: p. 278) and the old man who gives Zarathustra food and drink (Z Vorrede/Prologue § 8; N2: p. 288) as extensions of this archetypal manifestation (SNZ:I:p. 13). According to Jung, the archetype of the Old Wise Man in the context of *Zarathustra* represented 'the original Christian revelation continued in the idea of the paraclete, the Comforter, withdrawing slowly from the world and becoming a hermit, re-identifying himself again with the natural background from which he came' (SNZ:I:p. 41; cf. GW9(i) § 36). Similarly, Jung's gloss on the following phrase from the chapter 'Von alten und neuen Tafeln' ['Of Old and New Law-Tables'] – '*In uns selber* wohnt er noch, der alte Götzenpriester' ['He still lives on *in us ourselves*, the old idol-priest'] (Z III 12 § 6; N2: p. 447) reads: '[he] doesn't mean this as we would interpret it; he means the old priests who preached a sort of metaphysical reli-

of the highest order to determine the "In-Between" of teaching and action which is present here and which is peculiar to each poetic text'] ('Das Drama Zarathustras', *Nietzsche-Studien*, 15 (1986), 1–15 (p. 5)).

30 'Zarathustra ist Nietzsches bewußter gewollter Vorwurf und zugleich eine aus der Tiefe des Unbewußten geschehende Projektion. Daß in allem bewußten Wollen von Nietzsche-Zarathustra etwas von sich aus geschieht, das nicht gewollt werden kann, bekundet die immer wiederkehrende Frage: "was geschah mir doch?"' ['Zarathustra is Nietzsche's consciously willed reproach and at the same time a projection from the depths of the Unconscious. In all the conscious willing of Nietzsche-Zarathustra something happens of its own accord which cannot be willed, as the constantly recurring question makes clear: "what has happened to me?"'] (Löwith, p. 186).

31 See Girard's discussion of the experience of 'the Double' in *Critiques dans un souterrain* (Paris, 1976), pp. 23 and 93.

32 'Die Bilder des Lyrikers [sind] nichts als *er* selbst und gleichsam nur verschiedene Objektivationen von ihm' ['the images of the *lyrist* are nothing but *his very* self'] (GT/BT § 5; N1: p. 38).

gion, and that we with our belief still support that old prejudice' (SNZ:II:p. 1520). In accordance with Jung's general approach, his claim here is a dual one. First, it assumes that the text signifies in ways of which Nietzsche himself was unaware:[33]

> I try to give both the positive and the negative aspects so that you can see Nietzsche from all sides, a man who received a sort of revelation, yet in a mind which was clouded, an understanding which was not quite competent, so he was unable to realize the meaning of his own words (SNZ:II: p. 1489).

And second, it grants a privileged position to the archetypally-aware reader,[34] thereby evoking what has been called the Modernist sense of a clear distinction between the pre-psychological age and the psychologically-enlightened present.

Zarathustra: Structure and Image

In his Seminar, Jung paid closer attention than hitherto to the formal aspects of *Zarathustra*, though his sense of literary structure lacks a certain sophistication. According to Jung, the underlying psychological dynamic in *Zarathustra* is that of enantiodromia, or the emergence of the unconscious opposite in chronological sequence. Indeed, the structure of *Zarathustra* as a whole is said to enact one great enantiodromic moment: 'The book begins with that great spiritual solitude, and at the end come the Dionysian dithyrambs' (SNZ:II:p. 1492). This view is consonant with the world-historical importance which Jung consistently assigned to this work:

> *Zarathustra* [...] is like a dream in its representation of events. It expresses renewal and self-destruction, the death of a god and the birth of a god, the end of an epoch and the beginning of a new one. When an epoch comes to an end a new epoch begins. The end is a beginning: what has come to an end is reborn in the moment when it ceases to be (SNZ:II:p. 1132).

Moreover, Jung thought that each chapter represented 'a stage in a process of initiation' (into the archetypal Unconscious) and, more specifically, 'a new image in the process of initiation' (SNZ:I:pp. 459, 461). And, convinced that there was 'a secret logic, a sort of Homeric chain' throughout the work (SNZ:I:p. 462), Jung also sought evidence of the enantiodromic structural principle in the links

---

[33] As Peggy Nill has pointed out, Jung's attempt to read *Zarathustra* in terms of the processes of the archetypal Unconscious displays all the hallmarks of a structuralist enterprise: 'die Worte symbolisch hören und zurückübersetzen in die Ur-Sprache der Psyche' ['to listen symbolically to the words and translate them back into the primordial language of the psyche'] (Nill, pp. 266–67).

[34] 'But we belong to a time after Nietzsche. We know of symbols and we have an idea of psychology, and to us it cannot mean the same' (SNZ:I:p. 925).

between various sections of the text, between individual chapters, and even within image clusters: '*Zarathustra* [...] is split up into many chapters very loosely hung together, and the chapters themselves are split up by a multitude of intuitive sparks or hints' (SNZ:II:p. 1133). For example, on 30 June 1937, Jung suggested that the group of three chapters – 'Das Nachtlied' ['The Night Song'], 'Das Tanzlied' ['The Dancing Song'] and 'Das Grablied' – represented the descent into Nietzsche's inferior function (i.e. the unconscious side of his psyche), whilst 'Das Grablied' itself led to 'the precincts of the Unconscious' (SNZ:II:p. 1189). And on 27 May 1936, he maintained that 'if you carefully study the end of a chapter and compare it with the subsequent title, you discover how he arrives at the particular theme of the next chapter', seeing in the dramatic structure of the 'spiral' a similarity with Goethe's *Faust* (SNZ:II:p. 956; cf.pp. 786, 1243).

The annotations and underlinings in Jung's copy of *Zarathustra* show how Jung noted the recurrence of certain images such as the 'Untergang' ['descent'] (SNZ:I:pp. 86–87, 88–89, 243; SNZ:II:pp. 1160, 1492), the dancing star (SNZ:I:pp. 107, 708) and the 'Possenreißer' ['buffoon'] (SNZ:I:pp. 102, 109–12, 141–50, 520; SNZ:II:pp. 1161, 1262, 1387–92). By noting these page references, Jung was able to make connections across the text and reel off one reference after another in his Seminar. This technique became elevated into a methodological principle: 'First, there is generally an allusion to a certain situation, and then the motif goes on and on, returning from time to time in a more definite form, a more definite application', and according to Jung, 'that is absolutely typical of the way in which the Unconscious works' (SNZ:II:p. 1387).

Zarathustra, Archetypes and Animals

The psychological change which is charted by *Zarathustra* manifests itself, according to Jung, in at least five interconnected symbolic motifs. First, there is Zarathustra's inability to accept the Shadow (embodied in the Ugliest Man) (SNZ:II:p. 960) and the subsequent, enantiodromic return of this repressed component of the psyche: 'You will see how the Shadow comes back at Nietzsche with a vengeance: that is the tragedy of *Zarathustra*' (SNZ:II:p. 1114; cf.p. 1504). Second, Jung pointed out the absence from *Zarathustra* (until the end) of an Anima figure: 'It takes the whole development of *Zarathustra* to call Nietzsche's attention to the fact that there is an Anima' (SNZ:I:p. 533; cf.pp. 597, 631).[35] Third, there is Nietzsche's related attempt to deal with the

[35] The Anima archetype has a dual function, representing both the feminine principle (SNZ:II:p. 1492) and the inferior function (SNZ:II:p. 1163).

archetype of the Puer Aeternus, which Jung interpreted as the growth of an ideological attitude: 'a mass movement' with 'a very mystical idea behind it' (SNZ:II:pp. 1108–09), and itself an enantiodromic development, i.e. a moment of violent transition.[36] Fourth, there is the more explicitly political theme of the enantiodromic return of Dionysos in the guise of the Germanic war-god Wotan. Indeed, this aspect of the Seminar parallels external political developments: the rise of National Socialism and the start of the Second World War, which brought the Seminar to a premature end. Finally, there is the more explicitly spiritual or theological theme of the enantiodromic return of God (or the God-archetype) which, I shall argue, anticipates Jung's later writings and takes the form of the hope of a more positive manifestation of Dionysos.

The range of Jung's intellectual sources in the Seminar is typically wide, drawing on Gnosticism, alchemy, international mythology and world literature. To take one example only, one important image cluster which Jung discussed in detail is that of the eagle and the serpent/snake, a symbol which also attracted the critical attention of Martin Heidegger.[37] On 2 May and 7 November 1934, Jung interpreted these animals as a premonitory symbol of the union of spirit (eagle) and body (serpent), i.e. a 'reconciliation of opposites' (SNZ:I:pp. 18–19):

> Zarathustra sees [the eagle and the serpent] together, representing pairs of opposites, because spirit is always supposed to be the irreconcilable opponent of the chthonic, eternally fighting against the earth (SNZ:I:p. 227).

Behind these remarks lies an ancient interpretative tradition which David Thatcher has discussed with reference to Nietzsche.[38] Examination of this tradi-

---

[36] The archetype of the young boy which symbolizes psychological rebirth but in an ambivalent manner; ambivalent, because one-sided: 'The psychology of the *Puer Aeternus* is exclusively masculine' (SNZ:II:p. 1108). This aspect of psychological change is the least-developed motif in the Seminar, and its political context derives anyway from Jung's reading of *Das Reich ohne Raum* (Potsdam, 1919) by Bruno Goetz (1885–1954) (see Chapter 12, p. 310).

[37] Martin Heidegger, 'Wer ist Nietzsches Zarathustra?', in: *Vorträge und Aufsätze* (Pfullingen, 1954), p. 104. See also Karl Löwith's extensive interpretation of the symbol of the snake in *Nietzsches Lehre der ewigen Wiederkehr des Gleichen*, where he also points out that 'die schwarze Schlange des würgenden Nihilismus [wird] zur Schlange der ewigen Wiederkehr' ['the black snake of strangulating Nihilism becomes the black snake of the Eternal Recurrence'] (Löwith, pp. 134–35), and Jung's footnote in *Mysterium Coniunctionis* (1952) (GW14(ii) § 148, n.336/CW14 483, n.328), discussed in Chapter 13, pp. 341–42. Nietzsche's *Nachlaß* contains the following note: 'Und kündet mir doch ihr Thiere: Steht schon die Sonne im Mittag? Ringelt sich schon die Schlange welche Ewigkeit heißt? Blind wird Zarathustra' ['And yet tell me, you animals: does the sun stand at midday? Does the snake which is called eternity already coil up? Zarathustra becomes blind'] (Friedrich Nietzsche, *KGW*, VII, 1, p. 43).

[38] 'Behind this choice [of the eagle and the serpent] lies an authentic and authenticating tradition of mythological, religious and artistic symbolism which virtually guarantees that we will respond to it neither as "arbitrary" nor as superficially decorative' (David S. Thatcher, 'Eagle and Serpent in *Zarathustra*', *Nietzsche-Studien*, 6 (1977), 240–60 (p. 258)); see also Eugen Fink, *Nietzsches Philosophie* (Stuttgart, 1973), p. 70; Laurence Lampert, *Nietzsche's Teaching* (New Haven and London,

tion shows, in a particularly striking manner, the extent to which Jung and Nietzsche shared the same intellectual background. Jung knew, as his Seminar on 2 May 1934 (SNZ:I:pp. 6–7) made clear, that the basic myth of the original Persian Zoroastrianism was the conflict between Good and Evil, represented by Ahura Maszda (or Ormuzd) and Angra Mainyu (or Ahriman). Moreover, Jung had read Friedrich Creuzer's *Symbolik und Mythologie der alten Völker* [*Symbolism and Mythology of the Ancient Peoples*] (1837–41) (FJB: p. 284/FJL: p. 258; WSL: pp. 41, 241, 399, 400/PU § 45, n.33, 369, n.67, 682, n.33 and n.37; ETG: p. 166/ MDR: p. 186), where the symbolic eagle is attributed to Ormuzd. Nietzsche, too, was familiar with Creuzer's work on mythology[39] – indeed, there is even evidence to suggest that Creuzer's view of Dionysos in the above work influenced Nietzsche's *Die Geburt der Tragödie*.[40] Similarly, Nietzsche knew Ludwig Preller's *Griechische Mythologie* (1854), to which Jung referred in 1911/12 (WSL: pp. 41, 270, 399/PU § 44, n.32, 427, n.10, third reference omitted) and a copy of which he also owned. Preller not only mentions the legendary incident of the eagle bringing Zeus nectar (just as Zarathustra's eagle brings him food), but points out that the legend of Zeus had much in common with the cult of Dionysos-Zagreus.[41] One of Nietzsche's colleagues at Basle, Jacob Mähly, wrote a detailed study on the ritual significance of snake symbolism.[42] Finally, Schopenhauer, an even more important common source for Nietzsche and Jung, explicitly associated Ahriman with the snake or dragon, as David Thatcher has

1986), p. 29). Thatcher discusses Jung and lists several common sources with Nietzsche, without explicitly recognizing them as such, but his article is extremely useful.

39 According to documentation provided by Albert Lévy, Nietzsche borrowed volume III of Creuzer's *Symbolik* from Basle University Library on 18 June during the 'Sommersemester' of 1871 and 9 August during the 'Sommersemester' of 1872 (*Stirner et Nietzsche* (Paris, 1904), pp. 100, 104), and later bought the complete work for his library (see *Nietzsches Bibliothek* (Weimar, 1942), p. 10).

40 Martin Vogel, *Apollinisch und Dionysisch* (Regensburg, 1966), pp. 97–98. See also Werner Frizen, "'Von der unbefleckten Erkenntniss": Zu einem Kapitel des *Zarathustra*', *DVJS*, 58 (1984), 428–53, which uses Creuzer to identify mythological motifs in *Also sprach Zarathustra*.

41 For the references to the eagle of Zeus, see Ludwig Preller, *Griechische Mythologie*, 2 vols (Berlin, 1860–61), I, pp. 62, 99, 103, 110 and 392–93. 'Auch von dem Tode des Zeus erzählte man bekanntlich auf Kreta, wie sonst von dem des Dionysos Zagreus, dessen Cultus sich überhaupt mit dem dieses gebornen und verstorbenen Zeus in verschiedenen Punkten berührte' ['It is known that on Crete the death of Zeus was also recounted as was otherwise the death of Dionysos Zagreus, whose cult in general coincided with that of the born and deceased Zeus in various points'] (I, p. 103). There is an important section on Dionysos in I, pp. 519–64. Nietzsche borrowed Preller's *Griechische Mythologie* from Basle University Library on 7 November during the 'Wintersemester' of 1869–1870 and 25 October of 'Wintersemester' 1870–1871, and volume I on 5 April during 'Sommersemester' 1873 and volume III on 21 September during 'Wintersemester' 1875–1876 (Lévy, pp. 94. 98, 105, 109).

42 Jacob Mähly, *Die Schlange im Mythus und Kultus der klassischen Völker* [*The Snake in the Myths and Cult of the Classical Peoples*] (Basle, 1867); Jung referred to Mähly's work twice in 1911/12 (WSL: pp. 343, 350/PU § 582, n.73, 589, n.99).

pointed out.[43] In *Wandlungen und Symbole der Libido* (1911/12), Jung had read Zarathustra's vision as a symbol of psychic renewal through the introversion of the libido (WSL: p. 355/PU § 596). And over 25 years later, in his *Zarathustra*-Seminar, Jung reasserted the idea of an attempted transformation into divinity, interpreting the snake as the '*deus absconditus*, the god concealed in darkness [...] this is the dark god and the god that died, the god that Nietzsche declared to be non-existent' (SNZ:II:p. 1295). In antiquity, the serpent was frequently associated with Dionysos,[44] in particular by means of phallic symbolism.[45] And when, on 8 and 15 June 1938, Jung discussed the episode of the Shepherd and the Snake at the end of the chapter 'Vom Gesicht und Rätsel' ['Of the Vision and the Riddle'] (Z III 2; N2: p. 410), he said that the snake represented the deity in daimonic form: 'the snake is the symbol of the saviour, the *agathodaimon*, the good daimon, the redeemer that forms the bridge between heaven and hell, or between the world and god, between the conscious and the Unconscious' (SNZ:II:p. 1300). In *Zarathustra*, the shepherd is transformed after the decollation of the snake and, consistently interpreting the sun as the deity in accordance with ancient tradition, Jung considered that this episode was saturated in imagery of divine transformation:

> The shepherd got rid of his snake form but then he was 'no longer Man'. So what is he? Either an animal or a god [...] It is the eternal mystery happening before Zarathustra's eyes, but he doesn't realize it; he is only fascinated by that very uncanny laughter [...] He was transfigured, so we can say that Nietzsche hears the laughter of a superhuman being, the laughter of a god that has transformed himself, that has got rid of his snake form and become the sun again (SNZ:II:pp. 1295–96).

Jung further related the laughter that Zarathustra hears in the vision of the Shepherd and the Snake to the laughter in his earlier dream in 'Der Wahrsager' ['The Prophet'] (Z III 19; N2: p. 390), and interpreted both these outbursts of mirth as grim portents of a psychic spasm from which there would be no recovery:[46]

---

[43] Thatcher, p. 243, n.10; see Schopenhauer, *Parerga und Paralipomena*, 2 vols (Leipzig, 1891), II, pp. 392, 395 and 402. Thatcher also draws attention to the fact that the eagle-snake motif was used as a title-page colophon in Carl Albrecht Bernoulli's *Franz Overbeck und Friedrich Nietzsche: Eine Freundschaft* (Jena, 1908), a copy of which Jung had in his personal library.

[44] Mähly, p. 7; Johann Jakob Bachofen, *Versuch über die Gräbersymbolik der Alten* (Basle, 1954), p. 185.

[45] M. Oldfield Howey, *The Encircled Serpent: A Study of Serpent Symbolism in All Countries and Ages* (London, 1926), p. 127; Jung owned a copy of this work. In *Wandlungen und Symbole der Libido*, Jung also associated Dionysos with the phallus.

[46] Another Nietzsche commentator has seen in Nietzsche's prose (in this case Section 288 (N2: pp. 167–68) of *Die fröhliche Wissenschaft*) a symptom of mental instability: 'It is difficult to read this passage without suspecting that the exhilarated euphoric state here described (evidently the manic-depressive temperament, both aspects of which are later fully developed in *Zarathustra*) is an experience upon or around which much of Nietzsche's metaphysics, ethics and metabiology is built up' (F. D. Luke, 'Nietzsche and the Imagery of Height', in: *Nietzsche: Imagery and Thought*, edited by Malcolm Pasley (London, 1978), pp. 108–09).

> The laughter here has to do with the thousand peals of mad laughter when the coffin was split open. The shepherd went mad – that is perfectly clear [...] That is Nietzsche's madness: it explodes his brain-box. Therefore the last part, the transfigured shepherd, is so terribly tragic (SNZ:II:p. 1306–07).

In a similar vein, Nietzsche's madness on Jung's psychological reading was his identification with the Dionysian, as evidenced by his final letters which he signed 'Dionysos-Zagreus' (SNZ:II:p. 1306). Just as Jung tended to regard his own life in mythic terms, so his Seminar on *Zarathustra* mixes mythological allusion with biographical reference to make an interpretative cocktail which it is not always easy to swallow. Although, possibly without knowing it, Jung went back to the same sources of information about antiquity as Nietzsche had used, in the end, one has to ask whether reference-hunting is sufficient to discover the meaning of any text, let alone *Zarathustra*. Nietzsche himself noted with interest that the name 'Zarathustra' meant 'golden star'[47] and declared that one could say that 'die ganze Conception' of his book was rooted in this etymology. But what does this really tell us about 'das eigentliche Höhenluft-Buch' ['the actual book of the mountain air' (P.B.)], Nietzsche's 'Dithyrambus auf die Einsamkeit' ['dithyramb on solitude'] (EH Vorwort/Preface § 4, § 8; N2: pp. 1067 and 1080)? And whilst the Seminar on *Zarathustra* is invaluable as a guide to Jung's thinking about Nietzsche, it has three major shortcomings. First, too much attention is paid to parallels in traditions with which Nietzsche is only loosely connected, if at all. Second, the whole question of his use of rhetoric is almost totally ignored. By attributing responsibility for the text almost entirely to the personal and collective Unconscious, Jung overlooks much of Nietzsche's deliberate play with images and metaphors. And third, unless one subscribes to the basic tenets of Analytical Psychology, many of Jung's assertions remain too questionable to be really enlightening about the text he analyses.

[47] See Nietzsche's letter to Peter Gast of 23 April 1883: 'Heute lernte ich zufällig, *was* "Zarathustra" bedeutet: nämlich "Gold-Stern". Dieser Zufall machte mich glücklich. Man könnte meinen, die ganze Conception meines Büchleins habe in dieser Etymologie ihre Wurzel: aber ich wußte bis heute nichts davon' ['Today I learnt by chance *what* "Zarathustra" means: it means "Gold-Star". This coincidence made me happy. One might think that the whole idea of my little book was rooted in this etymology – but until today I knew nothing about it'] (*Briefwechsel: Kritische Gesamtausgabe*, edited by G. Colli and M. Montinari, 24 vols in 4 sections (Berlin, 1975–1984), III 1, p. 366). Thus he discovered this fact only after he had begun the composition of *Zarathustra*. Cf. Jung: 'Nach einer Vermutung von [Otto] Kern soll Zarathustra "Goldstern" heißen und mit Mithra identisch sein' ['According to a surmise by Kern, Zarathustra may mean "golden-star" and be identical with Mithra'] (WSL: p. 401/PU § 687).

Chapter 11

Jung's Seminar on Nietzsche (1934–1939)

Part II: Later Themes of Jungian Psychology in the Seminar

Jung developed his understanding of Dionysos by relating him to his analysis of two larger concerns: first, his analysis of the rise of Fascism (implicitly and in some cases explicitly referring to the political drama unfolding around Switzerland in Europe), and second, his hope of a spiritual renewal as expressed in his post-war writings. In this context, Jung spoke not just of Dionysos but of the Teutonic war-god Wotan (known to the Scandinavians as Odin and to the Anglo-Saxons as Woden), typically depicted as a wanderer or a horseback rider. Jung sensed a great affinity between the Greek god, his Germanic relation and Nietzsche.

Dionysos and Wotan

In his first lecture on *Zarathustra* of 2 May 1934, Jung inscribed Dionysos within the very heart of the text he proposed to study, characterizing that work as 'the Dionysian experience *par excellence*':

> *Zarathustra* really led [Nietzsche] up to a full realization of the mysteries of the cult of Dionysos: he had already ideas about it, but *Zarathustra* was the experience which made the whole thing real (SNZ:I:p. 10).

In *Ecce Homo*, Nietzsche, too, had characterized *Zarathustra* as a work in the Dionysian style: 'Mein Begriff "dionysisch" wurde hier *höchste Tat*' ['My concept "Dionysian" has here become the *supreme* deed'] (EH Z § 6; N2: p. 1134). Quoting substantial passages of his earlier text, Nietzsche summarized their content as '*der Begriff des Dionysos selbst*' ['the concept of Dionysos himself'] (EH Z § 6; N2: p. 1136); he also foregrounded the dithyrambic, i.e. Dionysian, language and form of 'Das Nachtlied' ['The Night Song']: 'so leidet ein Gott, ein Dionysos' ['thus does a god suffer, a Dionysos'] (EH Z § 8; N2: p. 1138); and finally, he saw the symbol *par excellence* of his '*dionysische* Aufgabe' ['*Dionysian* task'] (EH Z § 8; N2: p. 1140) in the image of the hammer and the stone in the chapter 'Auf den glückseligen Inseln' ['On the Blissful Islands'], a passage commented on by Jung in his writings on psychology and alchemy. And in his lecture on *Zarathustra* of 9 May 1934 (SNZ:I:p. 24), Jung quoted from Nietzsche's account of his *ekstasis* when writing *Zarathustra* (EH Z § 3; N2: pp. 1131–32), i.e. from that very passage which had prompted him to write to Elisabeth Förster-Nietzsche in 1899.

Another passage which Jung considered particularly Dionysian was Zarathustra's dream in 'Der Wahrsager' ['The Prophet'] (Z II 19; N2: p. 389–90), in which he saw several Wotanic motifs. On 4 May 1938, Jung interpreted the 'distorted figures' of that dream as a prefiguration of Nietzsche's future mental collapse and, as such, as the quintessential Wotanic experience:

> It is Wotan who gets him, the old wind god breaking forth, the god of inspiration, of madness, of intoxication and wildness, the god of the Berserkers, those wild people who run amok. It is, of course, the shrieking and whistling of the wind in a storm in a nocturnal wood, the Unconscious. It is the Unconscious itself that breaks forth. This is very beautifully described here: doors fly open and out bursts that wind, bringing a thousand laughters. It is a horrible foreboding of his insanity [...] (SNZ:II:p. 1227; cf.pp. 1228–29).

On 30 June 1937, Jung asserted that Nietzsche had had a Wotanic experience earlier on in his life as a result of which, he argued, Nietzsche had gained privileged access to a form of 'archetypal' knowledge (SNZ:II:pp. 1205–06). And on 15 June 1938, he reminded his audience that, in his madness, Nietzsche had identified with Dionysos. More importantly still, Jung regarded Nietzsche's Wotanic experience and subsequent collapse as a prefiguration of the collective experience of Germany under Hitler's régime.[1] Despite that, however, on 12 February 1936 he agreed with Mrs. Cary Baynes that Nietzsche himself must be exculpated of any proto-Nazi chauvinism (SNZ:II:p. 827).

But there is an even more overtly political dimension to Jung's understanding of the return of Pan/Dionysos which becomes increasingly clear in the course of the lectures. On 22 May 1935, Jung claimed that 'old Pan is again abroad in the woods' (SNZ:I:p. 500), and spoke in this connexion of the 'Wotan experience'. And on 26 February 1936, Jung again referred to what he saw as a revival of Wotanism:

> Yet it is a fact that old Wotan has to a certain extent come to life again [...] the myth is *en marche*, old Wotan is going strong again; you might even include Alberich and those other demons. That thing lives (SNZ:II:p. 868).

---

[1] On 8 February 1939, Jung claimed: 'Perhaps I am the only one who takes the trouble to go so much into the detail of Zarathustra – far too much, some people may think. So nobody actually realizes to what extent [Nietzsche] was connected with the Unconscious and therefore with the fate of Europe in general' (SNZ:II:p. 1518).

Jung's pre- and post-war essays took up this claim in greater detail, but the ideas which form the core of such texts as 'Wotan' (published in March 1936) and 'Nach der Katastrophe' ['After the Catastrophe'] (1945) were developed at the same time as (or first discussed in) his Seminar on *Zarathustra*. To understand the relation between his theory of Fascism and his reading of *Zarathustra*, we need to look at how this theory was developed in the Seminar.

There are two passages in particular which Jung interpreted with reference to Wotanic symbolism. The first passage (which gave rise to the observations just quoted) comes at the end of 'Das Kind mit dem Spiegel' ['The Child with the Mirror'] (Z II 1; N2: p. 343). In his edition of *Zarathustra*, Jung wrote in the margin: 'Wuote's hêr', referring to the medieval Swiss legend which sees storm clouds in the sky as the troops of the Germanic war-god, Wotan. According to Jung, this syncretic deity is closely related to Dionysos, and christianization has dissociated the key characteristics of the pagan deity Dionysos/Pan/Wotan and demonized them.[2] In particular, for Jung, Wotan retains his characteristic relationship with stormy weather (here, a metaphor for political turmoil):

> Just now one hears many complaints of this peculiarly inhuman quality of the spirit of adventure and experience; the thing that is riding through the forests in Germany is by no means human or very compassionate. It is a great wind, passionate, and all things will tremble (SNZ:II: p. 862).

In the lecture of 26 February 1936 from which this passage is taken, Jung compared the chief characteristics of the Teutonic war-god with those of two other mythological deities. Because of his occult and mystical qualities, Wotan is like Hermes,[3] and because of his connexion with the underworld, he is like Osiris.[4] In addition, Wotan is said to have particular relevance to the 1930s,[5] exemplifying what Nietzsche called 'wilde Weisheit' ['wild wisdom']:

> So on account of all his qualities, Wotan expresses the spirit of the time to an extent which is uncanny, and that wisdom or knowledge is really wild – it is Nature's wisdom. Wotan is not the God of civilized beings but a condition of Nature (SNZ:II: p. 869).

---

[2] See Jung's comments on the paragraph 'Wahrlich, einem Sturme gleich kommt mein Glück und meine Freiheit! Aber meine Feinde sollen glauben, *der Böse* rase über ihren Häuptern' ['Truly, my happiness and my freedom come like a storm! But my enemies shall think the *Evil One* is raging over their heads'] (Z II 1; N2: p. 343) (SNZ:II:pp. 867–68).

[3] 'The figure of Wotan [...] is a romantic god as well [...] the god of oracles, of secret knowledge, of sorcery, and he is also the equivalent of Hermes *psychopompos*' (SNZ:II:p. 869).

[4] 'He has, like Osiris, only one eye; the other eye is sacrificed to the underworld' (SNZ:II:p. 869).

[5] 'Therefore, he is an exceedingly apt symbol for our modern world in which the Unconscious really comes to the foreground like a river, and forces us to turn one eye inward upon it, in order that we may be adapted to that side also; we feel now that the greatest enemy is threatening us, not from without but from within' (SNZ:II:p. 869).

Finally, Jung spoke of Wotan in distinctly apocalyptic tones, using a terminology of energic hydraulics. The dynamic of tension and release described in this discussion recalls the moment of enantiodromia which Jung takes throughout his Seminar to be the key structural principle in *Zarathustra*, with Wotan representing the negative aspect of this process. Again, the condition of one-sidedness is said to precede the enantiodromic reversal:

> He is not just an integration, but a disintegration. You see, the storm does not cause integration, but destroys whatever allows itself to be destroyed. It is simply the movement after a long tension or standstill, like waters that break loose after long accumulation. This will happen in different periods of history when things have reached a certain one-sidedness. Then suddenly the whole thing will crash down, in a sort of revolutionary outburst of energy that has been too tightened up, put under too much pressure (SNZ:II: p. 870).

In his lecture of 6 May 1936, Jung went even further and explicitly associated Wotan with Dionysos in two respects. Both deities represented a principle whose assimilability was highly problematic,[6] and both, as vegetation deities, represented an experience which rendered the relationship between consciousness and the Unconscious exceptionally complex.[7]

As far as Jung was concerned, the political and social events of his day were a consequence of cultural and religious (and thus, for Jung, psychological) changes which he was eager to chart. In terms of Jungian psychology, it is impossible to separate sociological and personal psychological change since individual psychological developments both reflect and anticipate developments in the collective social sphere. Jung's various understandings of Dionysos – both as Wotan in the form of National Socialist politics and in a different, more theological sense – subsume diverse areas of interest under one single figure. And as the Seminar moved towards its premature conclusion, so Jung's comments on the political developments in Germany became increasingly dark and ominous, employing sacrificial metaphors which uncannily anticipate the term 'holocaust'.[8]

In what turned out to be the penultimate seminar, on 8 February 1939, Jung made it clear that he regarded the increasing tension in international relations

---

6 'Wotan is also the great sorcerer, and he is a spirit of enthusiasm, of ecstasy; therefore he has very much in common with Dionysos. If you have any knowledge of Greek religion, you know that there was the same difficulty when the Greeks were confronted with the task of integrating that Dionysian spirit [...] So Dionysos could be assimilated while Wotan is an unassimilated element' (SNZ:II:p. 898).

7 'Wotan is a phenomenon like Dionysos who is also a god of vegetation; it means a sort of enthusiastic or ecstatic condition in which those things which are already in the Unconscious reach the daylight' (SNZ:II:pp. 903–04).

8 However, Jung never explicitly discussed the plight of the Jews under National Socialism. For a commentary on the possible reasons for this omission, see Chapter 12, pp. 303–07.

and the internal situation in Germany as a consequence of the return of hitherto absent or repressed archetypal forces. In his commentary on section 6 of 'Von alten und neuen Tafeln' ['Of Old and New Law-Tables'] (Z III 12; N2: p. 447), he declared:

> The state is merely the modern pretence, a shield, a make-belief, a concept. In reality, the ancient war-god holds the sacrificial knife, for it is in war that the sheep are sacrificed [...] So instead of human representatives or a personal divine being, we now have the dark gods of the state – in other words, the dark gods of the Collective Unconscious [...] The old gods are coming to life again in a time when they should have been superseded long ago, and nobody can see it (SNZ:II:pp. 1517–18).

Linking the return of the old to a failure on the part of the new to find 'value' in the Jungian sense of a 'leading idea' (cf.SNZ:I:p. 646), Jung argued that the absence of a guiding principle and the failure of the attempt to find values by relating to the archetypes in a positive, unrepressed way had left a vacuum in society which the Collective Unconscious would fill with archaic (and hence often negative) archetypal forms:

> Wherever we fail in our adaptation, where we have no leading idea, the Collective Unconscious comes in, and in the form of the old gods. There the old gods break into our existence: the old instincts begin to rage again (SNZ:II:p. 1517).

Jung even went so far as to link the constellation of the Wotan-archetype and the rise of National Socialism with the collapse of Christianity, as if the 'death' of the Christian God were the precondition for the return of paganism: 'when we destroyed Christianity [...] the ghost of Christianity was left, and we are now possessed' (SNZ:II:p. 1519). Jung emphasized that the events of his day re-enacted a parallel shift which could be observed in antiquity, and he portrayed political events in terms of a psychic *dénouement*, a doomsday prepared by the Collective Unconscious:

> Whatever has been in a metaphysical heaven is now falling upon us, and so it comes about that the mystery of Christ's sacrificial death, which has been celebrated untold millions of times by the masses, is now coming as a psychological experience to everybody. Then the lamb sacrifice is assimilated in *us*: we are becoming the lambs, and the lambs that are meant for sacrifice. We become gregarious as if we were sheep, and there will surely be a sacrifice (SNZ:II:p. 1520).

Thus, in the Seminar, Wotan is represented as a highly dangerous political manifestation of Dionysos, revealing the cruel and destructive aspect of the ancient, ambiguous god. However, Jung's comments on the psychic phenomenon which he termed *Geist* simultaneously disclose his desire to re-enlist that same Dionysian energy in a creative and positive form. Thus, his notion of *Geist* forms a central part of his discussion of religion in the Seminar.

The Death and Rebirth of God

As Jung observed in his third lecture, on 16 May 1934, Zarathustra's claim that 'God is dead' is central to the work: 'It is, one could say, the exposition of the whole problem of *Zarathustra*' (SNZ:I:p. 43). Nevertheless, Jung believed that the way in which the work unfolded showed that the problem was much more complex and that, as he put it, God was not so much dead as 'somehow lurking in the background' (SNZ:I:p. 72; cf.SNZ:II:p. 843). Claiming that Nietzsche had 'got the essence of his time' (SNZ:I:p. 69) because he was the son of a pastor, 'the representative of a dying system and a dying spirit', Jung insisted that Nietzsche could not help 'yielding at times to his Christian background' (SNZ:II:p. 1000).[9] He also saw in Nietzsche's claims to exclusivity and originality a repetition of the Church's mistake of pretending that Christ was the first resurrected deity, forgetting about the myth of Isis and Osiris (SNZ:II:p. 1385). For Jung, there is of course but one religion and one myth, uniquely embodied in the Dionysian mythologem: the archetype of the born-dying-reborn god.

In the sixth set of lectures of his Visions Seminar (16 December 1931 to February 10 1932), Jung had claimed that *Zarathustra* re-enacted the 'death of Pan',[10] and he returned to this theme at the end of his second Nietzsche lecture,

---

9 Karl Löwith has described both the literary form and content of *Also sprach Zarathustra* as 'ein antichristliches Evangelium und eine umgekehrte Bergpredigt' ['an antichristian Gospel and an inverted Sermon on the Mount']. Claiming that 'Zarathustras Vorrede hat fast Zeile für Zeile einen wesentlichen Bezug auf das Christentum' ['almost every line of Zarathustra's Prologue contains a substantial reference to Christianity'], Löwith has enumerated the parallels between *Zarathustra* and the Bible (Löwith, pp. 189–90). According to Karl Jaspers, 'Nietzsches Kampf gegen das Christentum erwächst aus seiner eigenen Christlichkeit' ['Nietzsche's battle with Christianity grows out of his own Christian nature'] (*Nietzsche und das Christentum* (Hameln, 1938), p. 5), and as early as 1918, Ernst Bertram claimed: 'Nietzsche blieb – trotz jedes Grades von Versüdlichung, von Selbstbefreiung, von Sehnsucht ins Plastische – nordgebundener Musiker, blieb Christ [...] der Antichrist ist eine theologische Streitschrift, wie der Zarathustra eine spätprotestantische Lutherdichtung' ['Nietzsche remained, despite every degree of "southernization", self-liberation, desire for the tangible and visible – a musician bound to the North and remained a Christian ... the Anti-Christ is a theological polemic, just as Zarathustra is a composition of late-protestant Lutheranism'] (*Nietzsche: Versuch einer Mythologie* (Berlin, 1918), p. 126). And the intellectual historian Allan Megill has said of Nietzsche: '[...] this pastor's son tries to save Christianity even as he destroys it, imputing to the Overman those qualities that he is no longer willing to see embodied in the Godhead. He thus remains a secret Christian: like Heidegger, a post-Christian rather than an anti-Christian' (*Prophets of Extremity* (Berkeley, 1985), p. 315).

10 In the Visions Seminar, Jung argued that *Also sprach Zarathustra* was a modern re-enactment of the Death of Pan, antiquity's version of the 'Death of God'. And according to Jung, the death of the ancient Greek god had signalled the end of one kind of consciousness, as one form of religion declined and another, Christianity, sprang up to take its place (C. G. Jung, *The Vision Seminars*, 2 vols (Zurich, 1976), I, pp. 207–08). Similarly, Jung diagnosed a similar crisis of consciousness in modern society, believing that it was now the turn of Christianity to be superseded by the next spiritual development in the form of another enantiodromian shift or, in Nietzschean terms, a further revaluation of values (I, p. 208).

on 9 May 1934, relating this *topos* to the encounter between Zarathustra and the old saint in the forest (Z Vorrede/Prologue § 2; N2: pp. 278–79). Jung emphasized the elements of continuity as well as those of change in the psychological phenomenon of the 'Death of God':

> In this chapter, then, we have watched the way in which the spirit of a whole historical epoch recedes, disappears into nature, and how at the same time it is renewed in a new figure with a new message. Yet [it] is still the same old figure; the same spirit that taught mankind the difference between Good and Evil is now informing us of the fact that there is no difference and that God is dead (SNZ:I:p. 37).

Jung defined the loss of what he termed the 'objectivity' or 'trans-subjectivity' of religious experience not as an event but as a process, which could be traced back to the Reformation:

> More and more people felt that nothing from beyond came to them, that they were safely cut off from beyond, that all things divine were on this side of the river, in the visible church, for instance, in man-made images, ideas, rites, and so on. And they missed the beyond, the trans-subjective fact, without which no religious experience is possible (SNZ:I:p. 292).

To substantiate this, Jung pointed to the experiences of Francis of Assisi, Jakob Böhme, Nikolaus von der Flüe and Angelus Silesius as examples of true religious experience which had evaded the bounds and restrictions of authoritarian dogma. Two years later, on 6 May 1936, Jung traced the shift in the conception of God from the fifteenth century to modern-day Protestantism (SNZ:II:pp. 907–08), a development whose outcome was, in his view, the philosophical rationalism and materialism of the nineteenth century (SNZ:II:p.1248) which Jung presented as the intellectual background to *Zarathustra.*[11] On 28 November 1934, Jung had applied the criterion of 'value' to the age of Nietzsche – the modern age which is also ours – and found it wanting:

> Nietzsche was exceedingly sensitive to the spirit of the time; he felt very clearly that we are living now in a time when new values should be discovered, because the old ones are decaying [...] Nietzsche felt that, and instantly, naturally, the whole symbolic process that had come to an end outside, began in himself (SNZ:I: p. 279).

Thus, what Nietzsche called the 'Umwertung aller Werte' ['the Revaluation of All Values'], the rejection of old values and the search for new ones, is understood by Jung as the culmination of an historical process, which Nietzsche at once consummated and advanced to a new stage.

The passage quoted above also demonstrates the highly important link in Jungian thought between value and the symbol. For Jung, the process of self-

[11] 'Nietzsche's *Zarathustra* is one of the first attempts in modern times to come back to the immediate, individual initiation' (SNZ:I:pp. 460–61).

transformation, i.e. the transformation into the Self, which is in his view the psychological meaning at the heart of religious rites, is accomplished by means of the symbol (SNZ:II:p. 1249). Quoting the tag of a sixteenth-century Hermetic philosopher – '*In habentibus symbolum facilior est transitus*'[12] – Jung argued that, by denying to the God-concept its *symbolic value*, Nietzsche had been unable to deal with or successfully integrate the Unconscious in its archetypal form: 'He wiped out his symbol when he declared that God was dead [...] He had destroyed all the old values, so there was nothing left to defend him' (SNZ:II:p. 1249). In other words, Jung's critique of Nietzsche's attitude to religion is remarkably simple and eminently pragmatic: it doesn't work. As Jung rather bluntly put it: 'Nietzsche cannot convince one of the tremendous advantages of being outside the walls of the church if one is threatened by the madhouse' (SNZ:II:p. 1012). For Jung, then, the negative side of the 'Death of God' is the loss of a psychological possibility, that is to say, the loss of the potential to constellate psychic energy in a particular archetypal configuration.

However, Jung also argues the 'Death of God' experience can have a more positive side to the extent that it triggers a series of psychological reactions, and this side of Jung's analysis of the 'Death of God' experience involves one of his most notoriously difficult categories, that of 'Spirit' or *Geist*. In the first lecture, on 2 May 1934, Jung had interpreted the 'Death of God' as a statement about Spirit: 'when Nietzsche says God is dead, then it naturally means that supreme guiding principle is dead, the spirit, love' (SNZ:I:p. 40). And on 8 May 1935, Jung spoke of the historical background to *Zarathustra* in terms of the consequences of materialism: the eclipse of the Spirit. Referring to Nietzsche's declaration that 'God is dead' (FW/GS § 108, § 125; N2: pp. 115, 126–28; cf. Z Vorrede/Prologue § 2; p. 279), Jung said that this had been the pivotal moment in Nietzsche's psycho-biography: 'The spirit gripped him in that moment when it was completely denied. For it is just then that the spirit cannot be hidden any longer' (SNZ:I:p. 461). But to understand why this is so, the remarks in the Seminar about 'Spirit' need to be placed in the context of Jung's earlier writings.

The term 'libido' – the conceptual rock on which the relationship between Jung and Freud foundered and which had become the corner-stone of Jungian psychology – is curiously absent from the Nietzsche Seminar.[13] It is not mentioned until the seventh lecture (SNZ:I:p. 111), and thereafter in only two other

---

[12] Jung translated this as: 'For those who have a symbol, the passing from one side to the other, the transmutation, is easier' (SNZ:II:p. 1248).

[13] Cf. the Seminar on Analytical Psychology (1925), where the concept of libido is mentioned at least ten times (*Analytical Psychology: Notes of the Seminar given in 1925 by C. G. Jung*, edited by William McGuire (London, 1989)), and the Seminar on Dream Analysis (1928–1930), where the concept is mentioned at least eighteen times (*Dream Analysis: Notes of the Seminar given in 1928–1930 by C. G. Jung*, edited by William McGuire (London, 1984)).

lectures (SNZ:II:pp. 1151, 1299). In contrast, Jung discussed the concept of 'Spirit' on numerous occasions, and from its usage it is clear that the term 'Spirit' has taken over the function of the earlier term 'libido'. For example, in *Wandlungen und Symbole der Libido* [*Psychology of the Unconscious*] (1911/12), Jung had discussed how the libido was transformed into 'Spirit' (or *Geist*),[14] and had noted an etymological link between 'Libido' and 'Liebe' ['love'] (WSL: pp. 131–32, n.31/PU 218, n.29). Furthermore, he had also defined the metaphysical concept of God as the projection of libidinal energy (WSL: p. 71/PU § 111) and explicitly associated the creative potential of libido with the phallic Dionysos (WSL: pp. 127–29/PU § 209–11).

In his Seminar on *Zarathustra*, however, Jung emphasized that his notion of *Geist* is richer in meaning than the concepts of *spiritus* or *pneuma* (SNZ:I:pp. 365, 379), and cited Ludwig Klages and Max Scheler as examples of what he saw as the increasingly impoverished understanding of 'Spirit' (SNZ:I:p. 494). Whereas Scheler's attitude towards *Geist* is said to be ambivalent and Klages's downright hostile, Jung saw Spirit as the purest form of vitality, 'a culmination of life' (SNZ:I:p. 365).[15] Jung attributed to *Geist* the quality of 'eine führende Obervorstellung' ['a guiding key idea'] and characterized it as an 'effervescence', 'a welling up', 'a heightened or exalted condition', 'an objective spontaneous event', 'an intensity, a volcanic outburst' (SNZ:I:pp. 365, 379–80; SNZ:II:p. 1128) which involved a special attitude towards the Unconscious (SNZ:I:p. 380).

Indeed, Jung not only imputed to *Geist* a typically Dionysian mutability and fecundity, but also explicitly associated the experience of Spirit with Dionysos, detecting in the songs of Part IV of *Zarathustra* (later collected and expanded as the *Dionysos-Dithyramben*) a poetic record of Nietzsche's confrontation with Dionysian *Geist*:

> In the latter part of *Zarathustra* there is a beautiful poem where Nietzsche describes how he was digging down into himself, working into his own shaft; there you can

---

[14] '*So wird die Libido auf unmerkliche Weise geistig*'; '*Das Geistige ist die Mutterlibido*' ['Thus the libido becomes *spiritualized in an imperceptible manner*'; 'The *spiritual is the mother-libido*'] (WSL: pp. 223, 337/PU § 342, 571).

[15] Ludwig Klages (1872–1956), author of *Der Geist als Widersacher der Seele* (1929–1932), saw *Geist* as 'eine fremde, eigenständige Macht' ['a strange, autonomous power'] inimical to life. For a further discussion of Klages, see SNZ:II:p. 1128. Max Scheler (1874–1928) took issue with Klages, defining *Geist* as: 'das einzige Sein, das selbst *gegenstandsunfähig* ist – er ist reine, *pure Aktualität*, hat sein Sein nur *im freien Vollzug seiner Akte*' ['the only being which is itself incapable of being an object – it is sheer, *pure actuality*, which only has its being *in the free performance of its acts*'] (*Die Stellung des Menschen im Kosmos* [*The Position of Man in the Cosmos*] (Bonn, 1988), p. 48), but Scheler's conception lacks that transcendent quality which Jung is so keen to impute to *Geist*. Not without just cause, Scheler complained in 1928: 'selten ist mit einem Worte [*Geist*] so viel Unfug getrieben worden – einem Worte, bei dem sich nur wenige etwas Bestimmbares denken' ['seldom has there been so mischief done by one word, *Geist* – a word which makes only a few people think of anything definite'] (p. 38).

> see how intensely he experienced the going into himself, till he suddenly produced the explosion of the most original form of spirit, the Dionysian (SNZ:I: p. 369).

Jung might be referring here to the Magician's Song (Z IV 5; N2: pp. 491–94), later called 'Klage der Ariadne' (DD 7; N2: pp. 1256–59), or perhaps to 'Zwischen Raubvögeln' ['Amid Birds of Prey'] (DD 4; N2: pp. 1249–52) (even though that was never actually part of *Zarathustra*). On 2 June 1937, Jung read the line 'Geist ist das Leben, das selber ins Leben schneidet' ['Spirit is the life that itself strikes into life'] from the chapter 'Von den berühmten Weisen' ['Of the Famous Philosophers'] (Z II 8; N2: p. 361) as a rediscovery of Dionysian *Geist*:

> Nietzsche discovered by the onslaught of the spirit that spirit was life itself, and life which was against life, which could overcome life ['daß das Leben sich immer wieder selber überwinden muß' {'Life must overcome itself again and again'} (Z II 7, 12; N2: pp. 358, 371); cf. 'Libido gegen Libido' {"libido opposes libido'} (WSL: pp. 159, 256, 284/PU § 249, 398, 457)]. And from that experience he rightly concluded that the spirit is a vital power; it is not an empty, dead, ice-cold space, but is warm intense life, even hot life, most dynamic [...] Nietzsche himself had what we would call a definite religious experience, but he called it the experience of Dionysos. It was the experience of the free spirit, the spirit that was against his hitherto prevailing attitude of mind, a spirit that changed his life, that exploded him completely [...] So he himself has an experience at first hand of how the spirit can cut into life (SNZ:II:pp. 1128–29).

In his third lecture, on 16 May 1934, Jung had anticipated his later exegesis by declaring that the 'Death of God' marked a new psychological point of departure whose goal was described as the archetypal process of 'Rebirth':

> When Nietzsche declares that God is dead, instantly he begins to transform [...] He immediately gets into the process of that archetype of rebirth, because those vital powers in us which we call "God" are powers of self-renewal, powers of eternal change (SNZ:I:p. 54).

Jung's explanation of one aspect of the Dionysian in terms of the archetype of Rebirth provides a framework for his interpretations of two other Nietzschean concepts. First, although Jung made little reference to Nietzsche's concept of the Eternal Recurrence, his discussion of the notion on 24 October 1934 interpreted it as a form of Dionysian Rebirth: '[Eternal Recurrence] belongs to the Dionysian stage of his initiation; it is the feeling of rebirth which always accompanies the revelation of Dionysos' (SNZ:I:pp. 191–92). Second, Jung attributed a psychological, quasi-religious significance to Nietzsche's injunction to create the Superman, describing it as 'the most valuable kernel of Nietzsche's teaching' and as 'the message to our time' (SNZ:II:p. 906). Indeed, he argued that the creation of the Superman represented nothing other than his own doctrine of individuation, which, defined by Jung as the gathering of the world to one's self

(GW8 § 432), accomplishes a meaningful (because structured) union of consciousness and the Unconscious (and all other opposites) (SNZ:I:p. 433). According to Jung, the Self as symbolized by the Superman unites two pairs of opposites in particular, that of Good and Evil (SNZ:I:pp. 568; SNZ:II:pp. 1215, 1364); and that of the spirit (in the sense here of intellect or mind, i.e. the conscious faculties) and the body (SNZ:I:pp. 86, 370; SNZ:II:pp. 805, 1359). In taking this stance, Jung was accepting Nietzsche's reinstatement of the body in the sense of an accommodation of the instinctual life within the psychological economy of the individual.[16] But that said, the creation of the Superman involves, in Jung's view, the same risks as the 'Individuationsprozeß' ['process of individuation']: inflation, the secession by the Ego of total control to the Unconscious. Jung also inserted the figure of the Superman into his key Dionysian mythologem of life-death-rebirth, and in this sense he understood the birth of the Superman as the return of God (SNZ:II:p. 925). Thus, from Jung's point of view, the Nietzschean Superman represents a new stage in Western Man's religious development: an extension of Christianity (SNZ:I:p. 448) rather than the radical break which Nietzsche apparently wanted.

The psychological equivalence Jung implied between the return of God and the birth of the Self anticipates the key themes of Jung's post-war writings (see Chapter 13), and the conclusion to Jung's penultimate lecture on 8 February 1939 adumbrates the central question of the last period of Jung's thought. What does the rebirth of God mean in psychological terms? Jung's final peroration, a gloss on Zarathustra's exclamation 'Das eben ist Göttlichkeit, daß es Götter, aber keinen Gott gibt!' ['Precisely this is godliness, that there are gods but no God'] (Z III 12 § 11; N2: p. 449), asserted the persistence of the God-concept and pondered the means of its next manifestation:

> We know that Nietzsche has declared God to be dead, and here it appears as if God were not so dead; that is, as if there were no personal or monotheistic God, but there was divinity [...] Nietzsche thinks here of a peculiar transformation: namely, that through the abolition of Christianity the divine element will leave the dogmatic idea of God and will become incarnated in Man, so there will be *gods*. That is a sort of intuition of an individuation process in Man, which eventually leads to the deification of Man or to the birth of God in Man. Then we are confronted with that dilemma: is it the deification of Man or the birth of God in Man? (SNZ:II:pp. 1526–27).

In the lecture 'Die verschiedenen Aspekte der Wiedergeburt' ['The Various Aspects of Rebirth'] which he gave at the Eranos Conference on 'Die Symbolik

[16] See 'Seele und Erde' ['Mind and Earth'] (1927/1931): 'Die *Archetypen* [...] sind gewissermaßen die in der Tiefe verborgenen Fundamente der bewußten Seele, oder – um ein anderes Gleichnis zu gebrauchen – ihre Wurzeln, die sie nicht nur in die Erde in engerem Sinne, sondern in die Welt überhaupt gesenkt hat' ['the archetypes are as it were the hidden foundations of the

der Wiedergeburt in der religiösen Vorstellung der Zeiten und Völker' ['The Symbolism of Rebirth in the Religious Imagination of Epochs and Peoples'] later on in 1939,[17] Jung followed up his discussion of the archetype of Rebirth which he had conducted during his 1934–1939 Seminar. Here, he emphasized Nietzsche's Dionysianism in the 'Fourth and Final Part' of *Zarathustra*, the part of the book where he thought that God returned. In the final section of this chapter, I shall examine what Jung might have been going to say about the return of the deity, and which deity he might have meant, if the Seminar had not been abandoned because of the outbreak of the Second World War.

The Return of Dionysos

As early as 26 February 1936, when he first discussed Wotan in detail (SNZ:II:pp. 868–70), Jung expressed the hope that the destructive side of Wotan (which had not yet made itself fully apparent) would be superseded by something else: 'I am convinced that behind it something else follows, but it won't be Wotan. It cannot be' (SNZ:II:p. 870). Although the outbreak of the Second World War prevented Jung's Seminar from reaching the end of the book, we can turn to the pencilled comments in Jung's copy of *Zarathustra* to undertake a tentative reconstruction of what he might have said in the light of his earlier remarks. His marginal comments on the later sections of Part III and on Part IV of *Zarathustra* make several references to God, and Jung might have seen in the final sections of *Zarathustra* a return of the deity. But which one? Bearing in mind the hope expressed in Jung's later lectures for a revival of authentically Dionysian *Geist*, I suggest that Jung could have found in *Zarathustra* the sign of a return of the deity: not the Christian God, but Nietzsche's Dionysos.

Laurence Lampert has pointed out that certain key sections of Parts III and IV in *Zarathustra* depict the coming of Dionysos.[18] The chapter 'Von der großen Sehnsucht' ['Of the Great Longing'] (Z III 15; N2: pp. 467–69) prepares for the return of the vintner with a diamond-studded knife, 'der Namenlose – dem zukünftige Gesänge erst Namen finden!' ['the nameless one for whom only future songs will find a name!']. 'Das andere Tanzlied' ['The Second Dance Song'] (Z III 15; N2: pp. 470–73) depicts the epiphany of Dionysos as a mystic dance. And in 'Die sieben Siegel' ['The Seven Seals'] (Z III 16; N2: pp. 473–76),

---

unconscious mind, or, to use another comparison, the roots which the psyche has sunk not only in the earth in the narrower sense but in the world in general'] (GW10 § 53, cf. 103).

[17] *Eranos-Jahrbuch*, 7 (1939), 399–447, later revised and expanded as 'Über Wiedergeburt' (1950) (GW9(i) § 199–258).

[18] Laurence Lampert, *Nietzsche's Teaching: An Interpretation of Thus Spoke Zarathustra* (Yale and London, 1986), pp. 223–44, 298–99.

the marriage of Life and Zarathustra forms a parallel to the nuptials of Ariadne and Dionysos.[19] Lampert's Straussian reading of *Zarathustra* rightly characterizes Nietzsche's Dionysos as follows: 'The god who comes is a god not of being, but of coming and becoming, of rising and dying; he is a god whose nature it is to die, but whose dying presages birth'.[20]

On 27 June 1934, Jung had looked ahead to the chapter 'Das Eselsfest' ['The Ass Festival'] (N2: pp. 548–51) in Part IV of *Zarathustra*, which he described as a 'Dionysian orgy' (SNZ:I:p. 143). And on 6 February 1935 he had claimed that the *Dionysos-Dithyramben* expressed 'the explosion of the most original form of spirit, the Dionysian' (SNZ:I:p. 369). It is unlikely that Jung, who was nothing if not sensitive to symbolism, would have missed the allusions to Dionysos in the latter part of *Zarathustra*. According to Nietzsche's famous words (GD III § 6; N2: p. 961), Kant was a cunning Christian, and, in the margin of his copy, Jung turned this accusation back on Nietzsche, writing 'Tu ipse' against this passage from *Götzen-Dämmerung*. Judging by Jung's comments in his Seminar and from his own marginal annotations, it seems that Jung was a cunning Dionysian.

Jung's marginalia in his German edition of *Zarathustra* reflect this theme of the rebirth of God. Against the paragraph 'Meßbar für den, der Zeit hat, wägbar für einen guten Wäger, erfliegbar für starke Fittiche, erratbar für göttliche Nüsseknacker: also fand mein Traum die Welt' ['Measurable to him who has time, weighable to a good weigher, accessible to strong pinions, divinable to divine nutcrackers: thus did my dream find the world'] which introduces Zarathustra's dream in the chapter entitled 'Von den drei Bösen' ['Of the Three Evil Things'] (Z III 10 § 1; N2: p. 435), Jung wrote in his own German copy: 'hier ist der vermisste Gott' ['here is the missing god']. Against the paragraphs 'Alle Dinge sehnen sich nach dir, dieweil du sieben Tage allein bliebst, – tritt hinaus aus deiner Höhle! Alle Dinge wollen deine Ärzte sein!' ['All things long for you, since you have been alone seven days – step out of your cave! All things want to be your physicians!'] and the paragraph 'Für mich – wie gäbe es ein Außer-mir? Es gibt kein Außen! Aber das vergessen wir bei allen Tönen; wie lieblich ist es, daß wir vergessen!' ['For me – how could there be an outside-of-me? There is no outside! But we forget that, when we hear music; how sweet it is, that we forget!'] in the chapter entitled 'Der Genesende' ['The Convalescent']

---

[19] Nietzsche gestures towards the union of Ariadne and Dionysos on two other occasions. First, at the conclusion of 'Klage der Ariadne' ['Ariadne's Complaint'] in the *Dionysos-Dithyramben*, Dionysos appears to Ariadne to answer her lament with the words: '*Ich bin dein Labyrinth...*' ['*I am thy labyrinth*'] (DD 7; N2: p. 1259). Second, in his sketched notes for a drama (sometimes referred to as 'Naxos'), featuring Theseus, Dionysos and Ariadne, written in the autumn of 1887, Nietzsche concluded his draft with the 'Hochzeit des Dionysos und der Ariadne' ['Marriage of Dionysos and Ariadne'] (*KGW*, VIII 2, 9 [115], p. 66). See Erich F. Podach, *Ein Blick in Notizbücher Nietzsches: Eine schaffensanalytische Studie* (Heidelberg, 1963), pp. 115–28.

[20] Lampert, p. 228.

(Z III 13 § 2; N2: pp. 462–63), Jung wrote in his own copy: 'Gott'. And against the paragraph '– "ach, der Mensch kehrt ewig wieder! Der kleine Mensch kehrt ewig wieder!"' ['"Alas, man recurs eternally! The little man recurs eternally!"'] from the same chapter (Z III 13 § 2; N2: p. 465), Jung wrote a barely legible note: '[...] dann kehrt [...] der Gott wieder' ['then the god returns']. Furthermore, in his German copy against the paragraphs 'das aber ist der Winzer, der mit diamantenem Winzermesser wartet, –/– dein großer Löser, o meine Seele, der Namenlose – dem zukünftige Gesänge erst Namen finden!' ['he, however, is the vintager who waits with diamond-studded vine-knife, your great redeemer, O my soul, the nameless one for whom only future songs will find a name!'] from the chapter entitled 'Von der großen Sehnsucht' (N2: p. 469), Jung wrote: 'ein "Erlöser"!' ['a "redeemer"!']. And in his Eranos lecture 'Die verschiedenen Aspekte der Wiedergeburt' (1939), Jung would interpret the noontide vision in 'Mittags' (Z IV 10; N2: pp. 512–15) as a visionary experience of Dionysos (GW9(i) § 210).

Taken together, both the marginalia and the remarks which Jung made in his Seminar suggest that he may well have been sensitive to the Dionysian allusions of such chapters as 'Von der großen Sehnsucht' and 'Das andere Tanzlied' of Part III and such chapters as 'Mittags' of Part IV. If so, then irrespective of the answer to the question of whether, as Jung put it, the psychological message of *Zarathustra* was the deification of God or the birth of God in Man, it would appear that the god whose return Jung thought that Nietzsche had foreseen was not the Christian God but rather the pagan Dionysos. And this Dionysos, Jung's God, combines Apollo and Dionysos in exactly the way in which, according to Walter Kaufmann, Nietzsche's mature concept of the Dionysian does.[21]

Conclusion

The Seminar on *Zarathustra* shows the extent to which, by the end of the Thirties, Jung was able to relate almost every significant point in Nietzsche's philosophy to a corresponding idea in his Analytical Psychology. As Roderick Peters has pointed out: 'The Superman [...] is to be understood as the Self, and the doctrine preached by Zarathustra is none other than the doctrine of individuation'.[22] In my previous chapters, I have shown how Nietzsche is used by Jung

---

[21] 'The later Dionysos is the synthesis of the two forces represented by Dionysos and Apollo in *The Birth of Tragedy*' (Walter Kaufmann, *Nietzsche: Philosopher, Psychologist, Antichrist* (Princeton, 1968), p. 129).

[22] Roderick Peters, 'C. G. Jung: *Nietzsche's Zarathustra*' [book review], *Journal of Analytical Psychology*, 36 (1991), 125–27 (p. 125).

in different ways as a means to help him move away from Freud and replace psychoanalysis with that set of ideas which he came to call Analytical Psychology. I have also shown how this use of Nietzsche also reflects Jung's interest in the many other intellectual fields which feed into Analytical Psychology. The Seminar on *Zarathustra* both confirms this twofold argument and represents the high-point of Jung's 'Auseinandersetzung' with Nietzsche, relating him as it does to alchemy, medieval theology, atomic physics, Indian mysticism, and, pointing forward to Jung's post-war thinking on Nietzsche, to the politics of Fascism and to modern religious experience. It is to these two topics in the context of Jung's reception of Nietzsche that I shall turn in the next two chapters.

Chapter 12

Jung's Reception of Nietzsche in his Writings 1935–1945: Wotan: The Shadow of Dionysos

In Chapter 5, I touched upon the issue of Jung's position with regard to National Socialism, and the question of the causes of the Third Reich and the Second World War became an explicit theme in Jung's writings shortly before, during and after the War.[1] Although Jung claimed that he had already warned of the rise of German nationalism as far back as 1918, his views about this period need to be seen against the background of the reception of Nietzsche by the Far Right in general and in terms of his own psychological preoccupation with Dionysos in particular. Before looking at Jung's writings and lectures on National Socialism and reading them in their historico-intellectual context, I shall examine two short theoretical works which underpin his statements about the Third Reich.

Jungian Theoretical Background: The Two Halves of Life; The Archetypes and the Instincts

In a lecture of 1930, subsequently published in the *Neue Zürcher Zeitung* (14/16 March 1930) and revised for publication as 'Die Lebenswende' ['The Stages of Life'] in *Seelenprobleme der Gegenwart* (Zurich, 1931), Jung argued that the human life can be divided into two chronological sections. His starting-point was that human existence within the realm of Culture is, in its very essence, problematic (GW8 § 750) because of the dichotomy between 'Kultur' (associated with consciousness) and 'Natur' (associated with instinct). To pose the problem in such a way was in itself reminiscent of Nietzsche's critique of morality, according to which the genesis of moral values was derived from Man's most basic, animal drives. But for Jung, Culture was not just that more complex and beautified form of savagery which it was for Nietzsche. Instead, he suggested that Man's

[1] According to Raynald Valois, the question of the cause of war is the dominant theme of the whole of Jung's work ('C. G. Jung et les racines de la guerre', *Laval théologique et philosophique*, 48, no.2 (June 1992), 263–77 (p. 263)).

difficulties arise because Culture represents, at least in part, the negation of Nature such that the benefits of consciousness ('das Danaergeschenk der Kultur' ['the Danäan gift of Culture']) are highly equivocal:

> Instinkt ist Natur und will Natur. Bewußtsein hingegen kann nur Kultur oder deren Negation wollen, und wo immer es, beflügelt von Rousseauscher Sehnsucht, zurück zur Natur strebt, "kultiviert" es die Natur (GW8 § 750).
>
> [Instinct is Nature and seeks to perpetuate Nature, whereas consciousness can only seek Culture or its denial. Whenever, inspired by a Rousseau-esque longing, it strives to return to Nature, it "cultivates" Nature. (P.B.)]

In Jung's model, consciousness develops when, within the psychic economy of the individual, one particular drive or impulse encounters and conflicts with another drive. Thus, his concept of consciousness is actually founded on the notion of self-alienation brought about by the conflict of two sets of drives (one belonging to the Ego, one outside or beyond the Ego) (GW8 § 757).

Nietzsche's attitude towards consciousness was similarly ambivalent. In *Die fröhliche Wissenschaft* [*The Gay Science*] (1882), he had poured scorn on what he called 'diese lächerliche Überschätzung und Verkennung des Bewußtseins' ['this ridiculous overestimation and misunderstanding of consciousness'] and given priority instead to an increasing awareness of the instincts (FW/GS § 11; N2: p. 44). In another aphorism from the same work, he even went so far as to argue that consciousness was 'eine Krankheit' ['a sickness'] (FW/GS § 354; N2: p. 222) because of its superficiality.[2]

Jung's paper of 1930 related the inner dialectic of consciousness and the Unconscious to a changing but continuous attitude of adaptation to the world, described by Jung using the Goethean terms of 'systole' and 'diastole'. Accordingly, Jung drew an analogy between his two-fold division of life and the daily solar cycle. The morning of life (lasting from puberty until the age of 35–40) is related to the development of the individual with regard to the world of Nature (GW8 § 787). At this point, prevailing values collapse, the 'mid-life crisis' occurs, and a new psychological strategy becomes necessary to meet the demands of new cultural ends (GW8 § 769). Summarizing the implications of this development – and, incidentally, revealing his innate conservatism – Jung remarked that the answer to the problem of the future lay in the past: 'Das Problem wird also gelöst dadurch, daß das durch die Vergangenheit Gegebene an die Möglichkeiten und Forderungen des Kommenden angepaßt wird' ['The dilemma is often solved, therefore, in this way: whatever is given to us by the past is adapted to the possibilities and demands of the future'] (GW8 § 770). What does this mean?

---

[2] However, Nietzsche's theory of the development of consciousness in *Die fröhliche Wissenschaft* was different from Jung's (FW/GS § 354; N2: p. 220).

The theme of regression was an old Jungian idea. Both in his correspondence with Freud and in *Wandlungen und Symbole der Libido* [*Psychology of the Unconscious*] (1911/12), Jung had referred to the astral myth and the Mithras cult, interpreting the image of sunrise and sunset as a metaphor for the regression of the libido. And in this context, he had quoted the conclusion of the chapter 'Von der schenkenden Tugend' ['Of the Bestowing Virtue'] in *Zarathustra* (WSL: p. 362/PU § 615; cf. Z I 22; N2: p. 340).[3] However, the solar imagery in *Zarathustra* also refers back to a passage in an earlier work, the section entitled 'Am Mittag' ['At Noon'] in Volume II of *Menschliches, Allzumenschliches* [*Human, All Too Human*], where Nietzsche had used the very phrase 'den Mittag des Lebens' ['the noontide of life'] to describe a moment of enantiodromian proportions (MA/HA WS § 308; N1: pp. 996–97).[4] Moreover, in the chapter entitled 'Von der Seligkeit wider Willen' ['Of Involuntary Bliss'], Zarathustra apostrophizes the 'Nachmittag' of his life and praises the moment 'mitten in meinem Werke' ['in the midst of my work'] (Z III 3; N2: pp. 411–13). But, as Julian Roberts has pointed out, the solar imagery of *Zarathustra* involves a sombre ambiguity which first makes itself noticeable in the contrast between 'die Untergehenden' [those who go under'] and 'die Hinübergehenden' ['those who go over'] in the *Vorreden*.[5] There, Zarathustra declares: 'Ich liebe den, welcher die Zukünftigen

---

[3] The motif of sunset and sunrise, descent and subsequent ascent recurs frequently throughout *Zarathustra*. Not only does Zarathustra go down from his mountain and return to it again and again, reflecting the motion of the sun (see in particular the opening section, where Zarathustra addresses the sun: 'Ich muß, gleich dir, *untergehen*' ['Like you, I must go *down*'] (Z Vorrede/Prologue § 1; N2: p. 277)), but in the *Vorreden* Zarathustra defines virtue ('Tugend') as the 'Wille zum Untergang' ['will to downfall'] (Z Vorrede/Prologue § 4; N1: p. 282).

[4] Jung may also have found the idea of regression in another passage of *Menschliches, Allzumenschliches*, which he marked in the margin of his edition. In the section called 'Einige Sprossen zurück' ['A Few Steps Back'], Nietzsche wrote of the need, once religion and superstition had been disposed of, to overcome metaphysics by taking a 'retrograde step' ('einige Sprossen rückwärts steigen'): '*Dann* aber ist eine *rückläufige Bewegung* nötig: er muß die historische Berechtigung, ebenso die psychologische in solchen Vorstellungen begreifen, er muß erkennen, wie die größte Förderung der Menschheit von dorther gekommen sei und wie man sich, ohne eine solche rückläufige Bewegung, der besten Ergebnisse der bisherigen Menschheit berauben würde' ['*Then*, however, he needs to take a *retrograde step*: he has to grasp the historical justification that resides in such ideas, likewise the psychological; he has to recognize that they have been most responsible for the advancement of Mankind and that without such a retrograde step he will deprive himself of the best that Mankind has hitherto produced'] (MA/HA I § 20; N1: p. 462). Jung retained the substance of this principle of individual psycho-biography. And in an aphorism entitled 'Die Lebensalter' ['The Ages of Life'], Nietzsche wrote that 'Die Vergleichung der vier Jahreszeiten mit den vier Lebensaltern ist eine ehrwürdige Albernheit' ['The comparison of the four seasons of the year with the four ages of life is a piece of worthy silliness'] (MA/HA WS § 269; N1: pp. 978–79). The classical source of Nietzsche's idea of the seasonal ages of the individual is probably the Athenian statesman and poet Solon (638?–559 B. C.) (see fragment 27 of the Poems). I am grateful to Professor Roger Stephenson for drawing this to my attention.

[5] Julian Roberts, *German Philosophy: An Introduction* (Cambridge, 1988), p. 231. In his Seminar on Nietzsche, Jung concluded his lecture on the final part of 'Von der schenkenden Tugend' ['Of

rechtfertigt und die Vergangenen erlöst: denn er will an den Gegenwärtigen zugrunde gehen' ['I love him who justifies the men of the future and redeems the men of the past: for he wants to perish by the men of the present'] (Z Vorrede/Prologue § 4; N2: p. 282). On the one hand, 'zugrunde gehen' means 'to go to (the) ground (of Being)', and, on the other, 'to perish'. This ambiguity is particularly significant in the context of Jung's essay of 1930, which not only uses solar imagery but also discusses the 'evening of life' before the final 'zugrunde gehen' of death.[6]

In the same essay, Jung also adopted Nietzsche's slogan of the 'Umwertung aller Werte' ['Revaluation of All Values'] and psychologized it into the 'Umkehrung aller Werte und Ideale' ['reversal of all values and ideals'] (GW8 § 778). In *Wandlungen und Symbole der Libido* and 'Die Lebenswende' (1930), Jung had applied the Heraclitean principle of enantiodromia and the Nietzschean 'Revaluation of Values' to individual psycho-biography, and elsewhere he used it as a law of historical development. For example, in *Die Psychologie der unbewußten Prozesse*

---

the Bestowing Virtue'] (12 February 1936) by seeing in the Superman less a return to the Unconscious and more an absorption of the Unconscious into consciousness (inflation) creating the 'super-problem' of superconsciousness (SNZ:II:p. 839). Indeed, this equivocation is located, as Bruce Detwiler has shown, at the heart of what it means to be 'Dionysian': 'In other words in the *Birth* [*of Tragedy*] Dionysian man joins his god by obliterating himself, whereas in the final period Dionysian man experiences his own divinity by obliterating self-consciousness and by going under, reuniting with the primal ground of his being' (*Nietzsche and the Politics of Aristocratic Radicalism* (Chicago, 1990), pp. 162–63). And the philosopher Karl Löwith, concentrating on the enormous significance of the imagery of noontide in Nietzsche's work as a whole, reads the last instance of Nietzsche's use of this imagery in the poem 'Die Sonne sinkt' ['The Sun Sinks'] from the *Dionysos-Dithyramben* (DD 6) as revealing what the real nature of the solution to the Noonday crisis would be: the descent of the sinking sun into night represents the slither into the darkness of insanity (*Nietzsches Philosophie der ewigen Wiederkehr des Gleichen* (Hamburg, 1978), pp. 110–12).

6 Although both Jung and Nietzsche use the same image of the solar cycle, they do so for different reasons. According to Jung: 'Alle mythisierten Naturvorgänge, wie Sommer und Winter, Mondwechsel, Regenzeiten usw., sind nichts weniger als Allegorien eben dieser objektiven Erfahrungen, sondern vielmehr symbolische Ausdrücke für das innere und unbewußte Drama der Seele, welches auf dem Wege der Projektion, das heißt gespiegelt in den Naturereignissen, dem menschlichen Bewußtsein faßbar wird' ['All the mythological processes of nature, such as summer and winter, the phases of the moon, the rainy seasons, and so forth, are in no sense allegories of these objective occurrences; rather they are symbolic expressions of the inner, unconscious drama of the psyche which becomes accessible to Man's consciousness by way of projection – that is, mirrored in the events of nature'] (GW9(i) § 7). Werner Frizen has pointed out the implications of the solar imagery for the structure of *Zarathustra*: 'Die Struktur der Bewegung [...] greift ins Archaische zurück und sagt die Ewige Wiederkehr als Wiederkehr der Selbstüberwindung im Bilde der Sonnenreise aus. Sie münzt das naturmythische Modell des ewigen Kreislaufes um in den Freiheitsakt der sich selbst übersteigenden Vernunft' ['The structure of the movement goes right back to archaic elements and proclaims the Eternal Recurrence as the recurrence of self-overcoming in the image of the solar journey. It replaces the natural-mythical model of the eternal cycle with the act of freedom of reason which goes beyond itself'] ('"Von der unbefleckten Erkenntniss": Zu einem Kapitel des *Zarathustra*', *Deutsche Vierteljahrsschrift*, 58 (1984), 428–53 (p. 432).

[translated as *On the Psychology of the Unconscious*] (1917), his revision of 'Neue Bahnen der Psychologie' ['New Paths in Psychology'] (1912), Jung had written: 'So läuft die rationale Kultureinstellung notwendigerweise in ihr Gegenteil, nämlich in die irrationale Kulturverwüstung' ['Thus the rational attitude of Culture necessarily runs into its opposite, namely the irrational devastation of Culture'] (GW7 § 111).[7] In two further revisions, entitled *Das Unbewußte im normalen und kranken Seelenleben* (1925) and *Über die Psychologie des Unbewußten* (1942), Jung added a footnote which reemphasized the historical relevance of this formulation not just to the First but also to the Second World War:

> Dieser Satz wurde während des Ersten Weltkrieges geschrieben. Ich habe ihn in seiner ursprünglichen Form stehenlassen; denn er enthält eine Wahrheit, die sich noch mehr als einmal im Verlauf der Geschichte bestätigen wird (1925 geschrieben). Wie die gegenwärtigen Ereignisse zeigen, hat die Bestätigung nicht allzu lange auf sich warten lassen. Wer will eigentlich diese blinde Zerstörung?... Aber alle helfen dem Dämon mit letzter Hingabe. O sancta simplicitas! (1942 hinzugefügt) (GW7 § 111, n.13).

> [This sentence was written during the First World War. I have let it stand in its original form because it contains a truth which has been confirmed more than once in the course of history. (Written in 1925). As present events show, the confirmation did not have to wait very long. Who wants this blind destruction? But we all help the daemon to our last gasp. *O sancta simplicitas*! (Written in 1942).]

The deterministic element of Jung's thought at this time is reflected in the title of a lecture delivered in 1936 and published the following year entitled 'Psychologische Determinanten des menschlichen Verhaltens' ['Psychological Factors determining Human Behaviour'] (GW8 § 232–62). In this paper, Jung stressed the importance of 'Instinkte' as what he termed the '*motivierenden Kräfte* des psychischen Geschehens' ['the motivating forces of psychic events']. Of all the various factors which can influence human behaviour, these autonomous complexes of energy, expressed in archetypal form in art and religion, are said to be the most significant (GW8 § 254), and as an important piece of evidence to support his case, Jung cited the example of Nietzsche and the psychological characteristics of Zarathustra. As we saw earlier, the exact nature of the relationship between the author and his archetype had caused Jung much perplexity in

---

7 Not just the idea but also the phrasing of this statement are highly reminiscent of Ludwig Klages's warning in an essay written in 1913: 'Wir täuschten uns nicht, als wir den "Fortschritt" leerer Machtgelüste verdächtig fanden, und wir sehen, daß Methode im Wahnwitz der Zerstörung steckt. Unter den Vorwänden von 'Nutzen', 'wirtschaftlicher Entwicklung', 'Kultur' geht er in Wahrheit auf *Vernichtung des Lebens* aus' ['We were not wrong to be suspicious about the "progress" of empty cravings for power, and we can see that there is method in the madness of destruction. Under the pretext of "profit", "economic development", "culture", Man is in reality intent on the destruction of life'] ('Mensch und Erde', in *Freideutsche Jugend: Zur Jahrhundertfeier auf dem Hohen Meißner*, edited by Arthur Kracke (Jena, 1913), pp. 89–107 (p. 98), reprinted in Ludwig Klages, *Mensch und Erde* (Jena, 1937), p. 25.

his Nietzsche Seminar, and in his 1930 essay both complexes and archetypes are said to have in common an immense power to transform human behaviour, sometimes in alarming ways (GW8 § 254). So whilst arguing that all psychic processes are founded on instincts, Jung also maintained that, *mutatis mutandis*, psychic processes can influence the instincts. Although the goal of Jungian psychology was the creation of an integrated personality, Jung was also forced to concede that the dialectic between consciousness and the Unconscious could run out of control. In Jung's view, one archetypal complex of energy in particular revealed the animal side of Man in its most negative mode: the Dionysian archetype of Wotan.

Jung's Alleged Anti-Semitism

Nietzsche was an important source for right-wing thought and Fascist ideology in the twentieth century, and not just in Germany. Indeed, writing in 1940, Crane Brinton pointed out that there was 'a good deal of material [in Nietzsche] suitable for anti-Semitic use' in particular.[8] Jung's analysis of the rise of National Socialism is distinctive in its exclusive reliance on psychological factors, and could even be said to have similar roots to the occult beliefs and pagan mysticism which, as is well-known, fed into the ideology of the Nazi party.[9] On this account, it could be argued that Jung fell into the same ideological pit as did such writers as Ludwig Klages, Alfred Schuler and Edgar Dacqué, and he has been accused of having sympathies with National Socialism, of racism and of anti-Semitism, most notably by Ernst Bloch.[10] It is impossible to say how many of the large number of pseudo-intellectual circles obsessed with pagan ritual and notions of Nordic purity which were operating before the Second World War Jung may actually have heard of, apart from Hauer's 'Deutsche Glaubensbewegung' (see below). But it is possible that he picked up on some of the images used by these writers. For example, in his Eranos lecture 'Über die Archetypen des kollektiven Unbewußten' ['Archetypes of the Collective Unconscious'] (1934), Jung referred to the Poetic Edda: 'Mit der *Völuspâ* können wir fragen: "Was murmelt noch Wodan mit Mimes Haupte?/ Schon kocht es im Quell"' ['In the words of the *Völuspa* we may ask: "What murmurs Wotan over Mimir's

[8] Crane Brinton, 'The National Socialists' Use of Nietzsche', *Journal of the History of Ideas*, 1 (1940), 131–50 (p. 137).

[9] George L. Mosse, 'The Mystical Origins of National Socialism', *Journal of the History of Ideas*, 22 (1961), 81–96 (p. 96). See also Jochen Kirchoff, *Nietzsche, Hitler und die Deutschen* (Berlin, 1990).

[10] Ernst Bloch, 'Imago als Schein aus der "Tiefe"', in: *Erbschaft dieser Zeit* (Erweiterte Ausgabe) (Frankfurt am Main, 1985), pp. 344–51. This claim against Jung has most recently been restated by Richard Noll in *The Jung Cult: Origins of a Charismatic Movement* (Princeton, 1994).

head?/ Already the spring boils...'] (GW9(i) § 50). How would a member of the Germanic 'ariosophical' lodge called the 'Edda Society' have reacted to such a question?[11] And when, in his post-war writings, Jung talks about the 'Gottmensch', who might not detect an echo here of the 'Gottmenschen' referred to by Hanns Hörbiger (1860–1931), an Austrian engineer who propagated the so-called 'World Ice Theory'?[12]

As mentioned in Chapter 5, Jung has repeatedly been accused of anti-Semitism, and much of the evidence for the case against Jung comes from his paper entitled 'Zur gegenwärtigen Lage der Psychotherapie' ['The State of Psychotherapy Today'] (GW10 § 333–70), first published in the *Zentralblatt für Psychotherapie und ihre Grenzgebiete*, 7, no.1 (Leipzig, 1934), pp. 1–16). Insisting in 1934 as he had in 'Über das Unbewußte' ['The Rôle of the Unconscious'] (1918) that there was an essential difference between Jewish and German psychology, Jung's language came precariously close to the anti-Semitic vocabulary of Werner Sombart (1863–1941) in *Die Juden und das Wirtschaftsleben* (1911) and, even worse, Hitler's *Mein Kampf* (1925/26) (see in particular GW10 § 353–54). Jung went on to attribute a greater potential to the 'Aryan Unconscious' than to the 'Jewish Unconscious', and rejected what he called 'jüdische Kategorien' (a crude stab at Freud's supposedly 'Jewish' psychology) as being inappropriate for understanding the German psyche. Furthermore, he positively boasted of the barbaric components which were supposedly constituent of the 'Aryan psyche' (GW10 § 353–54). Whilst it may be true that Freud was also prepared to differentiate between 'Jewish' and 'Aryan' psychologies,[13] what might have been permissible for Freud as a Jew to say in Austria before 1933 was not permissible for a non-Jew to publish in Germany after 1933, as Tilman Evers has observed.[14]

Various reasons have been suggested for Jung's apparently anti-semitic attitude and his animus against Freud at this stage. The simplest explanation is, of course, that he was simply manoeuvring for personal and political tactical advan-

---

11 For a discussion of these and other Nordic lodges, past and present, see Friedrich-Wilhelm Haack, *Wotans Wiederkehr: Blut-, Boden- und Rasse-Religion* (Munich, 1981). The Eugen Diederichs Verlag flooded the German book-market with cheap editions of Icelandic Edda in the Thirties: 'by making this epic available to the public, Diederichs hoped to spark a spiritual rebirth of the *Volk*, just as the rediscovery of classic Greek texts had sparked the Renaissance in Italy' (Gary D. Stark, *Entrepreneurs of Ideology: Neoconservative Publishers in Germany, 1890–1933* (Chapel Hill, 1981), pp. 191–92

12 See Robert Bowen, *Universal Ice: Science and Ideology in the Nazi State* (London, 1993).

13 Freud himself was sensitive to the racial differences between himself and Jung, as his letter of 3 May 1908 to Karl Abraham shows (Sigmund Freud/Karl Abraham, *Briefe 1907–1926*, edited by Hilda C. Abraham and Ernst L. Freud (Frankfurt am Main, 1965), p. 47). And in a letter of 13 August 1908 to Jung, Freud referred to Jung's ethnic status as enabling him to act as more effective ambassador for psychoanalysis (FJB: p. 186/FJL: p. 167).

14 Tilman Evers, *Mythos und Emanzipation: Eine kritische Annäherung an C. G. Jung* (Hamburg, 1987), p. 141.

tage. But some psychologists, both Jungian and non-Jungian, have argued, at times convincingly, that there was a deeper struggle going on within Jung.[15] Furthermore, Jung would not have been alone in deriving a negative image of the Jews from Nietzsche's writings, and the Nazis made notorious misuse of his remarks in their anti-semitic propaganda campaigns. Bearing in mind Jung's awareness of the divergence between Freud's Jewish background and his own Protestant upbringing, it is likely that he was struck by Nietzsche's many comments on the Jews, several of which invite misunderstanding.[16] For example, there are Nietzsche's notoriously essentialist references to the difference between Germans and Jews, referring to 'die Arier' ['the Aryans'] as 'die Eroberer- und *Herren-Rasse*' ['the conqueror and *master race*'] (GM I § 5; N2: p. 776) and to 'die Juden' ['the Jews'] as 'jenes priesterliche Volk des Ressentiment *par excellence*' ['the priestly nation of *ressentiment par excellence*'] (GM I § 16; N2: p. 795). We know that Jung had read *Zur Genealogie der Moral* [*On the Genealogy of Morals*], where these remarks occur, and in his copy of *Die Geburt der Tragödie* [*The Birth of Tragedy*], he highlighted Nietzsche's following remark: 'Das, was die arische Vorstellung auszeichnet, ist die erhabene Ansicht von der *aktiven Sünde* als der eigentlich prometheischen Tugend' ['What distinguishes the Aryan notion is the sublime view of *active sin* as the characteristically Promethean virtue'] (GT/BT § 9; N1: p. 59). In the same work, Nietzsche had characterized the essence of the Dionysian, in a passage marked by Jung, as 'titanisch-barbarisch' ['titanic-barbaric'] (GT/BT § 4; N1: p. 35), and precisely this barbaric aspect of Dionysos/Wotan is emphasized in Jung's *Aufsätze zur Zeitgeschichte* [*Essays on Contemporary Events*].

In 1935, Jung gave a series of lectures to the Institute of Medical Psychology, known later as the 'Tavistock Lectures'. Here, Jung cited Nietzsche as an example of his notion of the two stages of life, calling him 'a most impressive example of a change of psychology into its opposite at middle age' (CW18 § 61). As he had already noted in *Psychologische Typen* (GW6 § 214/CW6 § 232), Nietzsche had 'burst out in a Dionysian mood which was absolutely the contrary of everything he had written before' in the second half of his life (CW18 § 61). More impor-

---

15 Harry Slochower, 'Freud as Yahweh in Jung's *Answer to Job*', *American Imago*, 38, no.1 (Spring 1981), 3–60 (pp. 8, 38); James Kirsch, 'Jungs sogenannter Antisemitismus', *Analytische Psychologie*, 16 (1985), 40–65 (p. 51); Micha Neumann, 'Die Beziehung zwischen Erich Neumann und C. G. Jung und die Frage des Antisemitismus', *Analytische Psychologie*, 23 (1992), 3–23 (pp. 11–12); Andrew Samuels, 'Nationale Psychologie, Nationalsozialismus und Analytische Psychologie', *Analytische Psychologie*, 23 (1992), 41–94 (p. 57).

16 For a further discussion of this aspect of Nietzsche, see Arnold M. Eisen, 'Nietzsche and the Jews Reconsidered', *Jewish Social Studies*, 48 (1986), 1–14; Michael F. Duffy and Willard Mittelman, 'Nietzsche's Attitude towards the Jews', *Journal of the History of Ideas*, 49 (1988), 301–18; and Gillian Rose, 'Nietzsche's Judaica', in: *Judaism and Modernity: Philosophical Essays* (Oxford, 1993), pp. 89–110.

tantly, the Tavistock Lectures referred to the image of the blond beast, that infamous Nietzschean motif which Jung had first used in 'Über das Unbewußte'. One year before the onset of the Second World War, Jung claimed in his Tavistock Lectures that he had foreseen the oncoming catastrophe, and referred to this earlier paper.[17] In the midst of a lecture on transference, Jung broke out into several astonishing paragraphs, whose intensity is heightened by their frenzied repetitiveness. Here is a sample:

> The archetypal image which the moment requires gets into life, and everybody is seized by it. That is what we see today. I saw it coming, I said in 1918 that the "blond beast" is stirring in its sleep and that something will happen in Germany. No psychologist then understood at all what I meant [...] The archetypes are the great decisive forces, they bring about the real events, and not our personal reasoning and practical intellect [...] Sure enough, the archetypal images decide the fate of man [...] it has nothing to do with rational judgment, it is just history [...] Give an archetype to the people and the whole crowd moves like one man, there is no resisting it (CW18 § 371–72).

The vigour of these pronouncements lies in Jung's unquestioning confidence in his prophetic abilities ('I saw it coming'), his intense fatalism ('it is just history'), and his instant absolution of any personal responsibility on the part of those who are 'seized' or 'gripped' by the archetype. But as well as noting the moral deficiency of these views and objecting to their self-righteous tone, it is important for us to uncover the deeper psychological reasons for Jung's distress at this moment. For apart from communicating what was presumably a genuine despair at what was afoot in Europe, akin to the sense of threat present in the apocalyptic scenarios toward the end of the Nietzsche Seminars (e.g. SNZ:II:pp. 1519–20), Jung's reaction was clearly a highly personal one.

As I have already argued, Jung's original premonition in 'Über das Unbewußte' about an imminent outbreak of the blond beast (the page reference to which Jung noted on the back fly-leaf of Volume 7 of his copy of Nietzsche's *Werke*) forms part of his ongoing 'Auseinandersetzung' with Nietzsche and the Dionysian and, in the Twenties, his response to the Apollonian 'Ästhetismus' of Schiller. As his observations in 1918 were far too gnomic to be taken as a proper warning (and would have been read more naturally as a reference to the First World War), it is not surprising that, as Jung complained in 1935, nobody had understood what he had meant. Bearing in mind the apparently positive tenor

---

[17] Jung repeated this claim on at least four other occasions: in 1936 in 'Psychologie und nationale Probleme' ['Psychology and National Problems'] (GW18(ii) § 1322); in 1937 in *Psychologie und Religion* [*Psychology and Religion*] (GW11 § 44); in 1946 in 'Der Kampf mit dem Schatten' (GW10 § 447); and in 'Nachwort zu "Aufsätze zur Zeitgeschichte"' ['Epilogue to *Essays on Contemporary Events*'] (1946), Jung adduced further apparent warnings, adding: 'Ich will die Zitate nicht häufen' ['I don't want to pile up the quotations'] (GW10 § 472).

of some of Jung's remarks about Hitler and the Nazis, perhaps Aniela Jaffé was right to point out that in a sense Jung *himself* failed to hear his own warning.[18] Because of the Nietzschean allusion to the 'blonde Bestie' of *Zur Genealogie der Moral*, we can read Jung's 'warning' as a reference not just to the political scene but also to his own personal struggle to come to terms with the forces of Dionysos. Indeed, Jung himself provided the Nietzschean context of the image one year later in another separate lecture to the Tavistock Clinic called 'Psychology and National Problems' (1936):

> I saw Nietzsche's "blond beast" looming up, with all that it implies. I felt sure that Christianity would be challenged and that the Jews would be taken to account. I therefore tried to start the discussion in order to forestall the inevitable violence of the unconscious outburst of which I was afraid – though not enough, as subsequent events have unfortunately shown only too clearly (CW18 § 1322).

Jung himself, having undergone his own 'Dionysian experience' in 1913–1919 during his period of intense introversion and confrontation with the Unconscious, was fully aware of both the positive and constructive potential of these drives and energies *and* their negative powers to destroy (as in the case of Nietzsche). After the war, Jung was prepared to admit (even if only in a roundabout way) that he was in some sense personally involved with what had happened in Germany. In 'Nach der Katastrophe' ['After the Catastrophe'] (1945) he wrote:

> Wir sind im allgemeinen viel tiefer in das deutsche Geschehen hineingezogen, als wir es wahrhaben wollen [...] Ich will es dem Leser nicht verheimlichen: noch nie hat ein Aufsatz mir solche moralische, ja menschliche Mühe gekostet. Ich hatte nicht gewußt, bis zu welchem Grade es *mich* angeht (GW10 § 402).
>
> [We are, on the whole, much more deeply involved in the recent events in Germany than we like to admit ... I must confess that no article has ever given me so much trouble, from a moral as well as a human point of view. I had not realized how much I myself was affected.]

Jung's essays on European politics between 1936 and 1945 reflect his own ambitions, fears, hopes; and his awareness of his own responsibility and his feelings of guilt.

Wotan

Jung's essay 'Wotan' was first published in the *Neue Schweizer Rundschau* in March 1936 and was later included in the *Aufsätze zur Zeitgeschichte* (1946). It opens with

[18] Aniela Jaffé, 'C. G. Jung und der Nationalsozialismus', in: *Parapsychologie, Individuation, Nationalsozialismus: Themen bei C. G. Jung* (Zurich, 1985), pp. 141–64 (p. 157).

a quotation from the famous collection of prophecies, the *Centuries astrologiques* (1555), by the celebrated sixteenth-century Provençal astrologer, Michel de Notre-Dame (or Nostradamus) (1503–1566), who ostensibly predicted the return of paganism to Germany (GW10: p. 203/CW10: p. 179). Jung had already quoted this passage on 22 May 1935 in his Seminar on *Zarathustra*, when he compared Nostradamus's prophetic insight with that which he imputed to Nietzsche (SNZ:I:p. 496). Such a reference to paganism at the very beginning of his essay sets the tone for his discussion of National Socialism as a Dionysian phenomenon, a revival of pre-Christian, Wotanic religion. According to Jung, the state of Germany in 1936 was one of 'Ergriffenheit', i.e. possession by an archetype. Not only did Jung think that Hitler had fallen under the sway of *Wotan redivivus*, but he also compared the Dionysian maenads to a bunch of female storm-troopers (GW10 § 386)! The main attributes of Wotan are listed by Jung as follows: 'Er ist ein Sturm- und Brausegott, ein Entfeßler der Leidenschaften und der Kampfbegier, und zudem ein übermächtiger Zauberer und Illusionskünstler, der in alle Geheimnisse okkulter Natur verwoben ist' ['He is the god of storm and frenzy, the unleasher of passions and the lust of battle; moreover he is a superlative magician and artist in illusion who is versed in all secrets of an occult nature'] (GW10 § 375). Moreover, Wotan is also associated with such other ancient gods as Mercury, Pluto, Kronos, Hermes (GW10 § 394), and with the mythologem of the dying and rising god – 'der Christus- und Dionysosfigur' ['the Christ and Dionysos figure'] (GW10 § 373). At the conclusion of his essay, Jung stressed the ambivalence of this archetype (like all others), which in addition to his 'unruhvollen, gewalttätigen und stürmischen Charakter' ['restless, violent, stormy character'] is said to have 'seine ganz andere, ekstatische und mantische Natur' ['quite different ecstatic and mantic qualities'] (GW10 § 399).

Elsewhere, Jung expanded his list of characteristics of Wotan. In his letter of 16 April 1936 to Wilhelm Laiblin, he had associated Wotan with the Great Mother archetype ('Wotans innerer Sinn [...] ist Erda, die Magna Mater' ['Wotan's inner meaning is Erda, the *Magna Mater*'] (B1: p. 273/L1: p. 213)), thus correlating Wotan with two important motifs of his system.[19] Although his essay of 1936 considered Wotan to be a specifically German configuration of Dionysos, by 16 December 1939 in a letter to Erich Neumann, Jung was prepared to extend its application to the whole of the civilized world (at least as far as his interpretation of one of Neumann's dreams was concerned) and attribute to it a more positive meaning: 'Die Wotan-Assoziation weist nicht auf die ger-

[19] In *Wandlungen und Symbole der Libido* (1911/12), Jung had linked Dionysos with the Nietzschean 'Urmutter'; and in 'Seele und Erde' (1927), he had emphasized the importance of being psychologically 'rooted' in the 'dunkeln, mütterlichen, erdhaften Urgrund seines Wesens' ['dark, maternal, earthy ground of his being'] (GW10 § 103).

manische Regression in Deutschland hin, sondern ist ein Symbol für eine die ganze Kulturwelt angehende geistige Bewegung' ['The Wotan association does not point to the Teutonic regression in Germany but symbolizes a spiritual movement affecting the whole civilized world'] (B1: p. 352/L1: p. 280). In a letter of September 1956 to Melvin Lasky, Jung spoke of 'den Zusammenhang des Wotansgeistes mit dem Dämonisch-Chthonischen' ['Wotan's connection with the daemonic and chthonic realm'] and in that same letter, as in his autobiography and elsewhere, he defined Wotan as a traditional European configuration of an archetype which Christianity had consistently striven to repress and diabolize: 'Wotan wurde vom Christentum ins Reich des Teufels verwiesen oder mit diesem identifiziert [...] Erst durch die christlichen Missionare wurde Wotan zum Teufel' ['Wotan was banished by Christianity to the realm of the devil, or identified with him ... It was the Christian missionaries who turned Wotan into the devil' (P. B.)] (B3: pp. 59–60/L2: p. 332, ETG: p. 316/MDR: p. 345; cf. GW8 § 17). In *Erinnerungen, Träume, Gedanken*, he also described a terrifying dream of Wotan which he had experienced in 1923, shortly before the death of his mother; and he unabashedly claimed Wotan for his own as the god of his Alemannic ancestors (ETG: pp. 316, 321/MDR: pp. 345, 350).[20]

Whilst the figure of Wotan remained a central concern in Jung's later thought and continued his preoccupation with the problem of the Dionysian, his essay of 1936 was also more historically conscious, tracing the presence of 'jenes Rauschen im Urwald des Unbewußten' ['rustling in the primeval forest of the Unconscious'] back through contemporary German literature and thought

---

[20] Jung recounts his Wotan dream as follows: 'Ich befand mich in einem dichten, finsteren Wald; phantastische, riesige Felsblöcke lagen zwischen gewaltigen, urwaldartigen Bäumen. Es war eine heroische, urweltliche Landschaft. Mit einem Male hörte ich ein gellendes Pfeifen, das durch das Universum zu hallen schien. Die Knie wurden mir weich vor Schrecken. Da krachte es im Gebüsch, und ein riesiger Wolfshund mit einem furchtbaren Rachen brach heraus. Vor seinem Anblick gerann mir das Blut in den Adern. Er schoß an mir vorbei, und ich wußte: jetzt hat der Wilde Jäger ihm befohlen, einen Menschen zu apportieren' ['I was in a dense, gloomy forest; fantastic, gigantic boulders lay about among huge jungle-like trees. It was a heroic, primeval landscape. Suddenly I heard a piercing whistle that seemed to resound through the whole universe. My knees shook. Then there were crashings in the underbush, and a gigantic wolf-hound with a fearful, gaping maw burst forth. At the sight of it, the blood froze in my veins. It tore past me, and I suddenly knew: the Wild Huntsman had commanded it to carry away a human soul'] (ETG: p. 316/MDR: pp. 344–45). On Jung's interpretation, the dream signified that Wotan, the god of his Alemannic forefathers, had returned to 'gather' his mother to her ancestors: 'In Wahrheit aber war es der Wilde Jäger, der "Grünhütl", der in jener Nacht [...] mit seinen Wölfen jagte. Es war Wotan, der Gott der alemannischen Vorväter, welcher meine Mutter zu ihren Ahnen "versammelte", nämlich negativ zum wilden Heer, positiv aber zu den "sälig Lüt"' ['But to be accurate the dream said that it was the Wild Huntsman, the "*Grünhütl*", or Wearer of the Green Hat, who hunted with his wolves that night ... It was Wotan, the god of my Alemmanic forefathers, who had gathered my mother to her ancestors – negatively to the "wild horde", but positively to that "*sälig Lüt*", the blessed folk'] (ETG: p. 316/MDR: p. 345).

(GW10 § 375). As well as referring more generally to the contemporary revival of Nordic ritual and pagan cult ('die deutschen sonnwendfeiernden Jünglinge' ['the German youths who celebrate the solstice']), Jung mentioned the following eight writers in particular as important sources of what could be called 'Twentieth-Century Wotanism': Martin Ninck (1895–1954),[21] Jacob Wilhelm Hauer (1881–1962),[22] Bruno Goetz (1885–1954),[23] Alfred Schuler (1865–1923),[24] Stefan George (1868–1933) (the members of whose literary circle were avid, not to say rabid readers of Nietzsche),[25] Ludwig Klages (1872–1956) (a popularizer of Nietzsche),[26] Houston Stewart Chamberlain,[27] and, finally, Nietzsche himself. In Schuler, George and Klages in particular, Jung saw 'die Anfänge einer stufenweisen Verwerfung der Wirklichkeit und einer Ablehnung des Lebens, so wie es ist' ['the origin of a gradual rejection of reality and a negation of life as

---

21 Jung possessed a copy of Ninck's *Wodan und germanischer Schicksalsglaube* (1935), which provided him with much of the information for his own account of Wotan.

22 Hauer, an 'Indologe' and professor of religious studies by profession, founded in 1933 and led until 1936 the so-called 'Deutsche Glaubensbewegung' ['German Faith Movement'], a group dedicated to the creation of an 'arteigene Religion' ['race-specific religion']. In 1936, Jung described this movement in highly favourable terms (GW10 § 397), and praised Hauer's book, *Deutsche Gottschau: Grundzüge eines deutschen Glaubens* (1934) (GW10 § 398). Despite his positive comments here about the 'Deutsche Glaubensbewegung', Jung later changed his mind about Hauer: in his Seminar on *Zarathustra* of 5 February 1936, he said that Hauer had become 'the saviour of the fools' (SNZ:II: p. 813), and in his letter to Hauer of 7 June 1937 he distanced himself from his suggested project of a study of 'der Zusammenhang von Rasse und Religion' ['the connection between race and religion'] (B1: p. 296/L1: p. 233).

23 Bruno Goetz was born in 1885 in Riga, studied in Vienna and Munich and then lived as a writer in Berlin and finally Zurich until 1954. Jung claimed that *Das Reich ohne Raum* (first published in 1919 and republished in extended form in 1925) could be read as a 'deutsche Wetterprognose' ['a forecast of the German weather'] (GW10 § 384). Jung also mentioned Goetz's article, published in *Deutsche Dichtung* (1935), which identifies Odin with Wotan (GW10 § 391). In his *Zarathustra* Seminar, Jung identified the impish young boys in *Das Reich ohne Raum* with the child archetype (the archetype of the 'Puer Aeternus'), hailing the novel as the most 'characteristic' example of the psychology of the 'Puer Aeternus' he had ever come across (SNZ:I:p. 634) and recommending it to his Seminar as 'a remarkable anticipation of the political conditions prevailing in Germany' (SNZ:II:p. 1107). His library contains several works by Goetz. Jung's later reservations about Goetz were signalled in a letter of 7 October 1946 (B2: pp. 58–59/L1: p. 445), where 'Herr Z.' is identified in the English version as Bruno Goetz.

24 The Munich writer Alfred Schuler was a member of the Stefan George circle. A follower of Ludwig Klages (see below), believed himself to be the reincarnation of a Roman patrician of the time of Nero. His lyric poetry, published posthumously, attacked the allegedly moribund Judeo-Christian tradition and looked forward to a 'Blutleuchte' to introduce an era of violent ecstasy and Dionysian frenzy.

25 See Heinz Raschel, *Das Nietzsche-Bild im George-Kreis: Ein Beitrag zur Geschichte der deutschen Mythologeme* (Berlin and New York, 1984); and Frank Weber, *Die Bedeutung Nietzsches für Stefan George und seinen Kreis* (Frankfurt am Main, 1989).

26 Jung saw Klages's biocentric metaphysics as expounded in *Vom kosmogonischen Eros* (1922) as the opposition of logos and consciousness to the creativity of preconscious life (GW10 § 375).

27 In *Die Grundlagen des XIX. Jahrhunderts* (Munich, 1899), Chamberlain saw history in terms of a Darwinian struggle amongst nations for survival and supremacy.

it is'], culminating in a false transcendence: 'Dies führt schließlich zu einem Kult der Ekstase, der in der Selbstauflösung des Bewußtseins im Tode gipfelt, welcher ihnen die Überwindung materieller Begrenzungen bedeutet' ['This leads in the end to a cult of ecstasy, culminating in the self-dissolution of consciousness in death, which meant, to them, the conquest of material limitations'] (GW10 § 375, n.3). However, it is the Dionysian/Wotanic elements in the work of Nietzsche which occupy the conceptual heart of his paper, and he emphasized that what could be found in these other writers was uniquely present in Nietzsche: 'Nietzsches Fall ist allerdings besonderer Art' ['Nietzsche's case is certainly a special one'] (GW10 § 376).

Jung's analysis uncovers the presence of Dionysos/Wotan in a series of Nietzsche's texts. Although God is meant to be dead for Nietzsche, Jung argued that the poetic epic *Also sprach Zarathustra* staged a series of encounters between Zarathustra and the supposedly moribund deity (not the Christian God, but the pagan Dionysos), and that even Zarathustra himself was sometimes identifiable with the 'Wahrsager, Zauberer und Sturmwind' ['soothsayer, magician and storm-wind'] (GW10 § 376), i.e. Wotan. In support of this interpretation, Jung referred to two sections from *Zarathustra*, the conclusion of the chapter entitled 'Vom Gesindel' ['Of the Rabble'] and Zarathustra's dream in 'Der Wahrsager' ['The Prophet'].[28] Jung then quoted three poetic texts by Nietzsche, 'Dem unbekannten Gott' ['The Unknown God'] (1864), 'An den Mistral' ['To the Mistral'] (1887) and 'Klage der Ariadne' ['Ariadne's Complaint'] (1885, revised 1888) which, he said, characterized the sought-after deity, the mistral wind and the hunter-god in Dionysian/Wotanic terms respectively. Relating literary text to biography, Jung then went even further and interpreted the image of the hunter-god in these poems as a reflection of an event in Nietzsche's life, based on an account of a dream reproduced in Elisabeth Förster-Nietzsche's *Der werdende Nietzsche* (1924) (GW10 § 382). According to Nietzsche's autobiographical sketch, the dream culminated in the following scene:

> Wir gelangten endlich in ein Tal, rings von wildem Gestrüpp umgeben. Plötzlich setzte unser Begleiter eine Pfeife an den Mund und ließ einen schrillen Ton hören.

[28] Jung offered the same interpretation in his Seminar on *Zarathustra*. On 12 and 19 March 1937, he concluded his reading of 'Vom Gesindel' ['Of the Rabble'] by glossing the phrase 'Wahrlich, ein starker Wind ist Zarathustra allen Niederungen' ['Truly, Zarathustra is a strong wind to all flatlands'] (Z II 6; N2: p. 356) as follows: 'he is Wotan, the wind god – that is perfectly clear [...] Wotan is the wind god *par excellence* and since Nietzsche was expressing himself in a German *milieu*, you can be sure that he got something of Wotan: that is in the German substance as you know' (SNZ:II:pp. 1074–75); and on 4 May 1938, he related Zarathustra's dream in 'Der Wahrsager' ['The Prophet'] (Z II 19) to one of Nietzsche's childhood nightmares (see below) and interpreted the wind as an image of Nietzsche's imminent insanity: 'Now this shrieking here, this whistling and whizzing, is the cry from the lunatic asylum [...] It is, of course, the shrieking and whistling of the wind in a storm in a nocturnal wood, the Unconscious [...] doors

> Wir sahen uns verdutzt an; aber auf einmal wurde es im Wald lebendig, hier und da leuchteten Facklen auf, wild vermummte Menschen umschlossen uns beide im Kreis, die Besinnung verging mir und ich wußte nicht, was mit mir vorging. – (N3: p. 67).[29]

> [At last we reached a valley surrounded on all sides by thick undergrowth. Suddenly our guide put a whistle to his mouth and blew shrilly. Taken aback, we looked at each other; but all at once, everything in the wood came alive. Here and there, torches lit up, and wildly masked people came and surrounded us in a circle. I lost consciousness: I didn't know what was happening to me.]

Although the content of this dream is very similar to Jung's own Wotanic dream of 1923, Jung apparently did not notice the resemblance. And in his autobiography, he surprisingly neglected to make any link between his dream and its collective associations – a possible oversight which looks more like a deliberate repression.

According to Jung, Nietzsche could equally well have identified the deity whom he encountered as Wotan, but decided to call the god Dionysos instead, due to the influence of Wagner: 'War es wirklich nur der Altphilologe in Nietzsche und nicht am Ende auch die fatale Begegnung mit Wagner, daß der Gott Dionysos hieß und nicht Wotan?' ['Was it really only the classical philologist in Nietzsche that led to the god being called Dionysos instead of Wotan – or was it perhaps due to his fateful meeting with Wagner?'] (GW10 § 383). In the following year, in his lectures on psychology and religion (originally delivered in English at Yale University in 1937 and published in translated and revised form in 1940), Jung repeated his conviction not only that Dionysos and Wotan were one and the same, but that this was the god whom Nietzsche had psychologically encountered:

> In Nietzsches Biographie kann man unwiderlegliche Beweise dafür finden, daß der Gott, den er ursprünglich meinte, in Wirklichkeit Wotan war; aber als klassischer Philologe der Siebziger- und Achtzigerjahre des 19. Jahrhunderts nannte er ihn Dionysos (GW11 § 44).

---

fly open and out bursts that wind, bringing a thousand laughters. It is a horrible foreboding of his insanity' (SNZ:II:p. 1227).

[29] Furthermore, according to Förster-Nietzsche's biography, as a child, the young Nietzsche participated in pagan celebrations which invoked Wotan: 'Wir hätten zufällig gehört, daß der Kirchberg eine alte Opferstätte gewesen sei, fanden Steine und Knochen, bauten einen Altar, schichteten Knochen und Holz darauf und zündeten es an. Als der treffliche Pfarrer, durch den sonderbaren Geruch aufmerksam gemacht, zu uns kam, fand er uns feierlich mit brennenden Kienspänen den Altar umschreitend, in seltsamen Tönen eine Art Hymnus singend: "Wotan erhöre uns!"' ['By chance we had heard that the Kirchberg had been an old place of sacrifice; we found rocks and bones, built an altar, piled and wood upon it, and lit them. When the worthy pastor, alerted by the strange aroma, came and found us, we were solemnly marching round the altar, carrying burning pine-shavings, and singing in strange tones a kind of hymn: "Wotan, o hear us!"'] (Elisabeth Förster-Nietzsche, *Der werdende Nietzsche* (Munich, 1924), p. 196). Köhler analyses these events in his psycho-biography of Nietzsche, *Zarathustras Geheimnis: Friedrich Nietzsche und seine verschlüsselte Botschaft* (Reinbek bei Hamburg, 1992), pp. 31–35.

[In Nietzsche's biography you will find irrefutable proof that the god he originally meant was really Wotan, but, being a philologist and living in the seventies and eighties of the nineteenth century, he called him Dionysos.]

If Jung had been familiar with Nietzsche's *Nachlaß*, he might have found other passages which, when read as autobiographical, would further support his reading. For example, in one *Nachlaß* fragment, Nietzsche confessed to a mysterious experience in his early youth: 'Als ich jung war, bin ich einer gefährlichen Gottheit begegnet, und ich möchte niemandem das wiedererzählen, was mir damals über die Seele gelaufen ist' ['When I was young, I encountered a dangerous deity, and I would not want to tell anyone what kind of feeling ran through my soul then'].[30] Other passages from the autobiographical sketches called 'Mein Leben' contain further speculative passages on theological and existential questions, apparently based however on some kind of personal experience, such as this well-known fragment, written in 1863:

> Und so entwächst der Mensch allem, was ihn einst umschlang; er braucht nicht die Fesseln zu sprengen, sondern unvermutet, wenn ein Gott es gebeut, fallen sie ab; und wo ist der Ring, der ihn endlich noch umfaßt? Ist es die Welt? Ist es Gott? – (N3: p. 110).
>
> [Thus Man grows out of everything which once embraced him; he does not need to break the shackles – they fall away, unexpectedly, when a god bids them; and where is the ring which in the end still encircles him? Is it the world? Is it God? –]

Similarly, in his sketches for *Zarathustra*, Nietzsche actually envisaged an encounter with Dionysos, and other fragments exist which evoke the god poetically.[31] Furthermore, there are passages in the quasi-autobiographical *Ecce Homo* which also license Jung's style of reading. There, Nietzsche claimed that his philosophy was based on his psychological experiences in general and his encounters with the Dionysian in particular: 'Ich hatte zu meiner innersten Erfahrung das einzige Gleichnis and Seitenstück, das die Geschichte hat, *entdeckt* – ich hatte ebendamit das wundervolle Phänomen des Dionysischen als der erste begriffen' ['I had *discovered* the only likeness and parallel to my own innermost experience which history possesses – I had therewith become the first to com-

---

[30] Nietzsche, *KGW*, VII 3, 34 [232], p. 218 (= UW I 1237).

[31] Nietzsche, *KGW*, VII 3, 34 [181], p. 202–03; and:

'Ich habe ihn gesehn: seine Augen wenigstens – es sind bald tiefe stille, bald grüne und schlüpfrige Honig-Augen
sein halkyonisches Lächeln,
der Himmel sah blutig und grausam zu'

(*KGW*, VIII 1, 1 [162], p. 43).

['I have seen him: his eyes at least – they are honey-eyes, now deep, still – now green and salacious –
his halcyon smile
the sky looked on bloody and cruel'.]

prehend the wonderful phenomenon of the Dionysian'] (EH GT/BT § 2; N2: p. 1109). Later on in that same work, Nietzsche claimed that *Die Geburt der Tragödie* was a direct transcription of the Dionysian rhythms of his own soul, and, significantly, added that a psychologist would understand this:

> Ein Psychologe dürfte noch hinzufügen, [...] daß wenn ich die dionysische Musik beschrieb, ich *das* beschrieb, was *ich* gehört hatte – daß ich instinktiv alles in den neuen Geist übersetzen und transfigurieren mußte, den ich in mir trug (EH GT/BT § 4; N2: p. 1111).
>
> [A psychologist might add ... that when I described the Dionysian music I described *that* which *I* had heard – that I had instinctively to translate and transfigure into the latest idiom all I bore within me.]

In other words: whilst for Nietzsche (and possibly for Jung, too) the Christian God had passed away, the god Dionysos was still very much alive for Nietzsche – and, so it seems, for Jung as well.

Further on in his essay on Wotan, Jung took the central categories of Nietzsche's *Die Geburt der Tragödie* – i.e. Apollo and Dionysos – and applied them to the political and social sphere to explain the founding of the Third Reich in Germany:

> Deutschland ist ein geistiges Katastrophenland [...] Der Widersacher ist ein Wind, der aus Asiens Unendlichkeit und Anfänglichkeit, in breiter Front von Thrazien bis Germanien, nach Europa hineinbläst [...] ein elementarischer Dionysos, der apollinische Ordnung durchbricht (GW10 § 391).
>
> [Germany is a land of spiritual catastrophes ... The disturber of the peace is a wind that blows into Europe from Asia's vastness, sweeping in on a wide front from Thrace to the Baltic ... an elemental Dionysos breaking into the Apollonian order.]

In terms of Jungian psychology, this Dionysian eruption in the form of Wotan functions in the collective psyche of the German nation as a moment of enantiodromia when regression occurs, when the repressed returns, and when the values are revalued. As such, Jung thought that the return of Wotan was not just a political event, but a potentially spiritual revival. Remember, Wotan has an 'ekstatische und mantische Natur' as well as his 'unruhvollen, gewalttätigen und stürmischen Charakter' (GW10 § 399). So perhaps Jung really did think that, beneath the pagan hocus-pocus of National Socialism, a truly religious transformation was being prepared. Perhaps he really was looking forward in the course of the next few years or decades to what he called 'hintergründige Dinge [...] von denen wir uns jetzt allerdings noch schlecht eine Vorstellung machen können' ['things concealed in the background which we cannot even imagine at present'] (GW10 § 399). In the same way and for similar reasons, Heidegger thought that the rise of Fascism represented a moment of authenticity in the spirit of Being.[32] But if in 1936, Jung was still waiting to find out what Wotan was saying when he murmured over Mimir's head, then by 1945, it was clear, both to Jung and to Heidegger, that above all else what had happened in Germany was a 'Katastrophe'.

The Pale Criminal and the Shadow

Jung's later essays on Nazi Germany extended his 'Wotanist' interpretation of Fascism even further. Just as he had hinted in his 1925 and 1942 revisions of *Die Psychologie der unbewußten Prozesse* (1917) that the outbreak of Dionysos followed an enantiodromian pattern, so his essays of 1945 and 1946 worked out an explanation for the rise of Hitler both in terms of the Nietzschean image of the Pale Criminal and in terms of a psychological concept of his own for which Nietzsche was a source: the Shadow.[33] For example, in a scene which recapitulates the opening dialogue of the second section of Volume Two of *Menschliches, Allzumenschliches*, 'Der Wanderer und sein Schatten', ['The Wanderer and his Shadow'] (MA/HA WS; N1: p. 871), Zarathustra encounters his shadow, described as 'dünn, schwärzlich, hohl und überlebt' ['slight, dark, hollow and spent'], and highly displeasing, in the chapter entitled 'Der Schatten' ['The Shadow'] in Part 4 of *Zarathustra* (Z IV 9; N2: p. 510). It is the Shadow who sings the erotic song 'Die Wüste wächst: weh Dem, der Wüsten birgt!' ['The Desert Grows: Woe to Him Who Harbours Deserts'] (Z IV 16 § 2; N2: pp. 539–44). Elsewhere, Nietzsche also once observed: 'Wenn man eine eigene leibhafte Persönlichkeit haben will, so muß man sich nicht sträuben, auch einen Schatten zu haben' ['If you want to have a lively personality, you must not be reluctant to also have a shadow'].[34] And in *Zur Genealogie der Moral*, Nietzsche compared the philosopher to a shadow: 'Darin ist er wie ein Schatten: je mehr ihm die Sonne sinkt, um so größer wird er' ['In this he is like a shadow: the lower his sun sinks the bigger he becomes'] (GM III 8; N2: p. 852). Nietzsche's investigation of the Dionysian depths parallels Jung's concern with the 'dark side' of the soul.

Whereas in 'Wotan' (1936) Jung had stressed the importance of Dionysos as an archetypal phenomenon affecting the collective German psyche, the post-war essays 'Nach der Katastrophe', first published in the *Neue Schweizer Rundschau* in 1945 (GW10 § 400–443), and 'Der Kampf mit dem Schatten' ['The Fight with the Shadow'], first given as a talk on the BBC's Third Programme broadcast

---

32 Martin Heidegger, *Die Selbstbehauptung der deutschen Universität* (Breslau, 1933).

33 For Jung's definition of the Shadow, see GW11 § 131.

34 Friedrich Nietzsche, *Sämtliche Werke: Kritische Studienausgabe*, edited by Giorgio Colli and Mazzino Montinari (Munich and Berlin, 1980), VIII, p. 511.

in 1946 (GW10 § 444–57), sought to place responsibility for the Second World War on specific agents of Dionysos such as Goethe, Wagner, Ernst Jünger and, above all, Nietzsche.

In 'Nach der Katastrophe', Jung drew attention to an alleged 'inferiority complex' of the Germans ('das deutsche Minderwertigkeitsgefühl'): 'Was haben Goethe, Heine und Nietzsche über ihr eigenes Land gesagt?' ['What did Goethe, Heine, and Nietzsche have to say about their countrymen?'] (GW10 § 417).[35] And 'Der Kampf mit dem Schatten' put forward two slightly different psychological theories to account for the success of Hitler. First, he suggested that the Germans had recognized in Hitler an embodiment of the Will to Power (GW10 § 449). And second, Jung also pursued the idea that National Socialism had represented the Shadow of German society: 'In Hitler hätte jeder Deutsche seinen eigenen Schatten, seine eigene schlimmste Gefahr erkennen müssen' ['In Hitler, every German should have seen his own Shadow, his own worst danger'] (GW10 § 455).

In 'Nach der Katastrophe', Jung suggested that the personality of the German nation as a whole was best characterized in terms of an hysterical Pale Criminal, a highly negative image which he borrowed from *Zarathustra* (GW10 § 455). The Pale Criminal is the subject of the sixth of the *Reden Zarathustras*, the individual who, having conceived and then executed his deed, regrets the memory of his act and condemns himself for it.[36] In his Seminar, Jung had registered a very strong emotional reaction to 'Vom bleichen Verbrecher' ['Of the Pale Criminal']: '[this chapter] is exceedingly disgusting to my feeling [...] Here Nietzsche really becomes an intellectual criminal. That is the disgusting thing – he reaches here one of the pre-stages of his own madness [...] The criminal is only a sort of mirror reflex of the criminal impetus of Nietzsche' (SNZ:I:pp. 459, 468). It is therefore highly significant that Jung should have chosen to invoke an image which he, personally, had found so disturbing in the context of his discussion of Nazi Germany. Unconsciously, Jung is voicing his

---

[35] At one point the text of 'Nach der Katastrophe' gives a clear hint that Jung's personal affinity with the German psyche may have gone deeper than he he thought. For example, Jung declared in its opening paragraphs that he approached the problem of recent German history with a sense of inferiority ('von der Seite [...] der eingestandenen Unterlegenheit' (GW10 § 402)). Just a few pages on, however, he drew attention to an alleged inferiority complex of the Germans ('das deutsche Minderwertigkeitsgefühl') (GW10 § 417).

[36] See Laurence Lampert, *Nietzsche's Teaching: An Interpretation of 'Also sprach Zarathustra'* (New Haven and London, 1986), p. 43. See also *Jenseits von Gut und Böse*: 'Der Verbrecher ist häufig genug seiner Tat nicht gewachsen: er verkleinert und verleumdet sie' ['A criminal is frequently not equal to his deed: he makes it smaller and slanders it'] (JGB/BGE § 109; N2: p. 631). Freud had briefly discussed this Nietzschean figure in his conclusion to 'Einige Charaktertypen aus der psychoanalytischen Arbeit' ['Some Character Types Met with in Psycho-Analytic Work'] (1915) (*Gesammelte Werke*, 18 vols (Frankfurt am Main, 1968–1978), X, p. 391).

horror not just of the Germans, but of the 'shadow-side' of his own personality, and his analysis of the Germans is simultaneously an exercise in self-analysis.

Jung went on to extend the characteristics of the Pale Criminal, which he diagnosed as hysterical, to the whole of the German nation, which he accused of collective hysteria (GW10 § 417).[37] According to Jung, an hysterical condition is brought about by the oppositions and contradictions within the psyche. Whilst the greater distance between the opposites in the Germans' psyche is said to account for their amazing energy drive, it is also held responsible for their supposedly fractured personalities and unhappy lives (GW10 § 423). Both these aspects of the German character, produced by the problem of the opposites, find personified expression for Jung in the figure of Faust. In *Wandlungen und Symbole der Libido* (1911/12), Jung had presented the dilemma of Faust as an impossible choice between 'die *Sehnsucht nach dem Jenseitigen*' ['the longing for the Beyond'] and 'die *Sehnsucht nach der Schönheit des Diesseits*' ['the longing for the beauty of this world'] (WSL: p. 87/PU § 136). Now the Faustian condition is more simply and less technically described as an 'inneren Widersprüchlichkeit und Zerrissenheit' ['inner contradiction and dichotomy'] from which there is said to result his 'Sehnsucht der "Hungerleider nach dem Unendlichen" [...] jenen "Eros der Ferne", jene eschatologische Erwartung der großen Erfüllung' ['the longing of "hungering for the infinite" ... that "Eros of distance", that eschatalogical expectation of great fulfilment' (P. B.)] (GW10 § 423). By 1945, Jung saw more in the qualities of Faust, and in his pact with the devil and the murder of Philemon and Baucis – he saw something quintessentially German:

> Faust erreicht nirgends den Charakter der Wirklichkeit: er ist kein wirklicher Mensch, und kann keiner werden (wenigstens nicht im Diesseits), sondern er bleibt die deutsche Idee vom Menschen, und damit eine, wenn auch etwas übertriebene und verzerrte Spiegelung des deutschen Menschen (GW10 § 423).

> [Faust never attains the character of reality: he is not a real human being and cannot become one (at least not in this world). He remains the German idea of a human being, and therefore an image – somewhat overdone and distorted – of the average German.]

[37] This represents a theoretical U-turn in two respects. First, one of the reasons why he had so strongly condemned the Freudians in 1934 had been their blindness in interpreting the alleged 'unerhörte Spannung und Wucht' of National Socialism as a neurotic symptom. After the War, however, Jung himself rushed to the vocabulary of pathology in order to describe the psychology of the Führer. And second, Jung was now (GW10 § 418) much more uncomplimentary about Hitler than he had been in his interview with Dr. A. Weizsäcker for Berlin Radio on 26 June 1933 (reproduced in Evers, pp. 241–47; and see also 'Diagnosing the Dictators', an interview with the American foreign correspondent H. R. Knickerbocker in *Hearst's International-Cosmopolitan* (January, 1939) (reproduced in: *C. G. Jung Speaking*, edited by William McGuire and R. F. C. Hull (Princeton, 1977), pp. 115–40)).

What Jung had earlier in 'Nach der Katastrophe' described in terms of Nietzsche's Pale Criminal, he now termed in his own vocabulary as the Shadow. And discussing *Faust*, Jung argued that Faust's Shadow is symbolized by Mephistopheles, an autonomous complex who splits off from Faust's main personality and is hypostatized as the Devil (GW10 § 439).

Goethe's *Faust*, Friedrich Nietzsche and the German psyche are the three terms of a triangular nexus of relations to which Jung returned again and again. In *Wandlungen und Symbole der Libido*, Jung had quoted from Jacob Burckhardt's letter of 1855 to Albert Brenner, according to which Faust constitutes 'ein großes urtümliches Bild' ['a great primordial image' (P. B.)] representing in German culture the equivalent of Oedipus in Greek culture (WSL: p. 47, n.48/ PU § 56, n.42). In 'Die Erlösungsvorstellungen in der Alchemie' ['The Idea of Redemption in Alchemy'] (1936), Jung had related the Nietzschean Superman to Goethe's Faust as a possible solution to an as yet unsolved problem, 'nämlich die Wandlung zum Übermenschen' ['namely the transformation into the Superman'] (GW12 § 559). And in 1941, in 'Paracelsus als geistige Erscheinung' ['Paracelsus as a Spiritual Phenomenon'], Jung had drawn a straight line from Goethe's dramatic hero to the person of Friedrich Nietzsche, 'der ein faustischer Mensch war, wie nur je einer' ['who was a Faustian Man if ever there was one'] (GW13 § 154). In 'Nach der Katastrophe', Jung recalled what Burckhardt had said (GW10 § 434) and went on to claim that the madness of Nietzsche had itself been a 'prophetisches Beispiel' ['prophetic example'] of the fate of Germany: 'Nietzsche ist deutsch bis in die letzten Fasern seines Wesens, bis in den abstrusen Symbolismus seines Wahnsinns hinein' ['Nietzsche was German to the marrow of his bones, even to the abstruse symbolism of his madness'] (GW10 § 432).[38]

The chord of Faust, Jung argued, had echoed further in Nietzsche's vision of the Superman, understood here as 'der amoralische Triebmensch, dessen Gott tot ist und der sich selber Gottheit anmaßt, oder vielmehr Dämonie, sein Jenseits von Gut und Böse' ['the amoral man of instinct, whose God is dead and who claims for himself divinity, or rather devilry, beyond good and evil'] (GW10 § 434). Furthermore, Jung related the *Übermensch* to the disappearance of the Feminine in Nietzsche's personality and questioned the meaning of its absence: 'Und wo ist bei Nietzsche das Weibliche, die Seele, hingeraten?' ['And

[38] In the very same year in a lecture given in the United States, Thomas Mann made a similar point in a very similar way. For Mann, there existed a dark and irrational component to the German mind ('eine geheime Verbindung des deutschen Gemütes mit dem Dämonischen' ['a secret union between the German soul and the daemonic']), an aspect best symbolized by the devil, as in the case of Luther, or as in the case of the Goethean figure of Mephistopheles ('Deutschland und die Deutschen', *Gesammelte Werke*, 13 vols (Frankfurt am Main, 1960–1974), XI, pp. 1126–48 (p. 1131)).

where has the feminine side, the soul, disappeared to in Nietzsche?'] (GW10 § 434). In his Seminar on *Zarathustra*, Jung had already touched upon this problem: 'we have no Anima in *Zarathustra* [...] It takes the whole development of *Zarathustra* to call Nietzsche's attention to the fact that there is an Anima' (SNZ:I:p. 533), and argued that it was not until Part IV, in the erotic poem 'Die Wüste wächst: weh dem, der Wüsten birgt' (Z IV 16 § 2), that Zarathustra reached his real 'hour of descent' which was also 'the coming-up of Yin, the feminine substance' (SNZ:II:p. 1492).

In Jungian psychology in general as in this text, Woman represents the chthonic energies and subterranean forces of Dionysos, and Jung drew attention to the traditional function of Woman as a representation of the dark side of life: 'the Female meant darkness and Evil' (SNZ:II:p. 1080). Unlike Derrida, who has identified Woman (albeit in a somewhat different, although not necessarily clearer sense) with Nietzsche's very philosophical technique,[39] Jung saw in Nietzsche's thought the eclipse of the Feminine: 'Helena ist im Hades verschwunden, und Eurydike kehrt nicht mehr zurück' ['Helen has vanished in Hades, and Eurydice will never return'] (GW10 § 434).[40] According to Jung, the return of these lost instincts and psychic potentialities in the form of Dionysos in Nietzsche's life anticipated the advent of the same psychological forces in the shape of Dionysos/Wotan in Germany:

> Schon kündigt sich die schicksalsmäßige Travestie des verleugneten Christus an: der kranke Prophet ist selber der Gekreuzigte, ja, noch weiter zurück, selber der zerrissene Dionysos-Zagreus. Denn in die unterirdisch gewordene Vorzeit weist der rasende Prophet zurück. Sein Berufungserlebnis ist der pfeifende Jäger, der Gott der rauschenden Wälder und des Rausches und aller von Tiergeistern besessenen Berserker (GW10 § 434).
>
> [Already we behold the fateful travesty of the denied Christ: the sick prophet is himself the Crucified, and, going back still further, the dismembered Dionysos-Zagreus. The raving prophet carries us back to the long-forgotten past: he has heard the call of destiny in the shrill whistling of the hunter, the god of the rustling forests, of drunken ecstasy, and of the berserkers who were possessed by the spirits of wild animals.]

---

[39] Jacques Derrida, *Éperons: Les styles de Nietzsche* (Paris, 1978).

[40] In Jung's system, the feminine is identified with Eros and the masculine with Logos (cf. GW9(i) 178). For the most part, Jung's followers – such as Mary Esther Harding in *The Way of All Women* (London and New York, 1933) and *Women's Mysteries* (London and New York, 1955), Florida Scott-Maxwell in *Women and Sometimes Men* (New York, 1957), Karl Stern in *The Flight from Woman* (New York, 1965), Irene Claremont de Castillejo in *Knowing Woman* (New York, 1973) and June Singer in *Androgyny: Toward a New Theory of Sexuality* (New York, 1976) – have accepted this distinction. For feminist critiques of Jung, see: Andrea Dworkin, *Woman Hating* (New York, 1974), pp. 159–62 (particularly critical of Harding as well as Jung), and Mary Daly, *Gyn/Ecology: The Metaethics of Radical Feminism* (Boston, 1990²), pp. 253–54, 280 and 287.

Jung then went on in the same essay to point to two strategies for coping with the return of Dionysos/Wotan and the collapse of Christianity in the spheres of music and literature. First, Jung interpreted Wagner's *Parsifal* as a failed attempt to replace the Body of the Church with the Castle of the Grail, but 'nur der Orgiasmus steckte an und breitete sich aus wie eine Epidemie. Der Rauschgott Wotan hat gesiegt' ['only the orgiastic frenzy caught on and spread like an epidemic. Wotan the storm-god has conquered'] (GW10 § 435). And second, Ernst Jünger's *Auf den Marmorklippen* [*On the Marble Cliffs*] (1939) is said to have been equally unsuccessful as a solution: 'Nirgends in der Welt sprach der europäische Geist vernehmlicher als in Deutschland, und nirgends wurde er tragischer mißverstanden' ['Nowhere did the European spirit speak more plainly than it did in Germany, and nowhere was it more tragically misunderstood'] (GW10 § 435). As a result of this 'misunderstanding', Jung presented an apocalyptic vision of Germany's condition as an amalgam of Faustian, Dionysian and Wotanic fates: a projection of the dangerous psychological forces which had brought about Nietzsche's collapse into madness and dragged Jung close to the brink of insanity as well:

> Nun hat Deutschland den Teufelspakt und dessen unvermeidliche Folgen erlitten, die Geisteskrankheit erfahren, ist zerrissen wie Zagreus, geschändet von den Berserkern seines Wotan, betrogen um Gold und Weltherrschaft, besudelt vom Auswurf des untersten Abgrundes (GW10 § 436).

> [Now Germany has suffered the consequences of the pact with the devil, she has experienced madness and is torn in pieces like Zagreus, she has been ravished by the berserkers of her god Wotan, been cheated of her soul for the sake of gold and world-mastery, and defiled by scum rising from the lowest depths.]

In his post-war essays, Jung presented Nietzsche as a prophetic figure, whose personal fate foretold the political destiny of Germany, and yet also as a psychiatric patient, whose sick fantasies he held responsible for polluting the political imagination of the Germans. 'Nach der Katastrophe' in particular marks a distinct turning away from Jung's favourite philosopher, as considerable antipathy is displayed towards Nietzsche. Thus, despite his own fascination with them, Jung branded Nietzsche's 'pathological' predilection for such concepts as the Superman and the 'blond beast' as 'hysterische Phantasien' ['hysterical fantasies'] (GW10 § 432). At the same time, however, Jung tried to recuperate Nietzsche's reputation by portraying him also as a self-critic who did not spare himself the ruthless exposure of motives to which he submitted others. More clearly than ever, Jung's view of Nietzsche is revealed as an essentially tragic vision: a man who knew that his enemy was Dionysos but could not defeat the god and so succumbed. The fate of Germany was in Jung's eyes therefore equally tragic, inasmuch as it, too, had failed to heed the warning:

> Die verwandte Schwäche des deutschen Wesens erwies sich für derartige hysterische Phantasien als zugänglich, wo doch Nietzsche nicht nur sehr kritisch über den deutschen Philister dachte, sondern selber der Kritik eine breite Angriffsfläche bot. Dadurch hatte der deutsche Geist wiederum eine kostbare Gelegenheit zur Selbsterkenntnis – und hat sie verpaßt (GW10 § 432).
>
> [The weakness of the German character, like Nietzsche's, proved to be fertile soil for hysterical fantasies, though it must be remembered that Nietzsche himself not only criticized the German Philistine very freely but laid himself open to attack on a broad front. Here again the Germans had a priceless opportunity for self-knowledge – and let it slip.]

And yet: Jung's pre- and post-war essays show that he too had not only failed to hear his own warnings but had equally let slip a priceless opportunity for self-knowledge. It seems that Jung never fully understood, and could therefore not acknowledge, his involvement with the Dionysian aspects of National Socialism. What kind of a self-understanding does a psychologist have when he can admit, as, according to Gershom Scholem, Jung did in 1946 to Rabbi Leo Baeck: 'Jawohl, ich bin ausgerutscht' ['Well, I slipped up']?[41] Jung's own investments and internalizations vis-à-vis Nietzsche and Dionysos greatly contribute towards our understanding of why Jung 'slipped up', and why he fell so conspicuously victim to the lies and deception of the political Dionysian – Fascism.

As well as analysing the destructive possibilities of Fascism's mythological radicalism, 'Nach der Katastrophe' also placed the case of Germany in the context of an apparently larger European decline: 'die deutsche Katastrophe [ist] nur eine Krisis der europäischen Krankheit überhaupt' ['The German catastrophe is only one crisis in the general European sickness'] (GW10 § 437). The Dionysian explosion of National Socialism was, Jung thought, symptomatic of a much deeper cultural transformation, which he characterized in Nietzschean terms as the 'Death of God'. The release of those instinctual (Dionysian) forces which had been stabilized by the logocentric (Apollonian) deity of Christianity was, Jung thought, the inevitable consequence of the Death of God. At this point in his writings Jung clearly shifts from political theory to theology, as I shall show in the next chapter. And Jung's post-war writings concentrate on the possibility of a spiritual renewal in the form of the construction of a Dionysian Self.

Jung never dropped his guard, however, against a renewal of Dionysian politics. As late as 14 September 1960, in a letter to the Chilean ambassador in New Delhi, Miguel Serrano, he was warning again of the potential return of Wotan (B3: pp. 341–42/L2: p. 594). But in this letter Jung also indicates that the problem of the Dionysian – 'our ultimate principle of behaviour' – must

---

[41] Gershom Scholem, letter to Aniela Jaffé, in: Jaffé, *Aus Leben und Werkstatt von C. G. Jung* (Zurich, 1968), p. 104.

be solved in terms of a different attitude towards religion and 'a new religious attitude'. And in his writings of the post-war period until his death in 1961, Jung envisaged a 'spiritual Dionysos' which formed the heart of his new Myth for Modern Man.

Chapter 13

The Mystic Dionysos: Nietzsche, Jung, and the Death of God

Introduction

In his Seminars on *Zarathustra* and in the *Aufsätze zur Zeitgeschichte* [*Essays on Contemporary Events*], Jung had argued that the rise of Fascism represented the release of the 'blond beast', those instinctual drives which Nietzsche had called the Dionysian. As Philip Rieff has suggested, Jung himself may have been drawn to Fascism because he detected in it 'the stirrings of the subterranean God against the banality of liberal culture'.[1] But precisely those dark and primal instincts which his psychological system wanted to recuperate had swung out of control. Thus, with the approach of the Second World War, Jung's attitude towards Nietzsche became increasingly negative, as the introductions to each new 'term' of the Seminar on *Zarathustra* and his war-time essays show.[2] And from 1937 onwards, Jung viewed Nietzsche increasingly in the light of his researches into the psychology of religion. Indeed, his later writings are the final working-out of those Neo-Kantian and Vitalist ideas which he had discussed in his student lectures to the Zofingia Club. In this last phase of his thought, the question of Dionysos was subsumed under the debate on the nature of the transcendent itself, as Jung strove to set up a religion of pure immanence.[3] In almost all his essays written in the decade between 'Wotan' (1936) and 'Der Kampf mit dem Schatten' ['The Fight with the Shadow'] (1946), Jung discussed

---

1 Philip Rieff, *The Triumph of the Therapeutic: Uses of Faith after Freud* (New York, 1968), p. 132.

2 See SNZ:II:pp. 893, 1037, 1209, 1339). Yet despite his ambivalent feelings about Nietzsche, Jung devoted part of his Eranos lecture of 1939 to an important interpretation of the chapter 'Mittags' ['At Noontide'] in Part IV of *Zarathustra*.

3 The difficulty of interpreting Jung's later texts has been appositely noted: 'Much of Jung's later work, e.g. his lectures in 1938 on 'The Psychology of Religion', is so mysterious as to be almost indiscussable' (*Brett's History of Psychology*, edited and abridged by R. S. Peters (London, 1953), p. 695). In a recent article, Jef Dehing has revealed a characteristic manoeuvre in Jung's writings on religion, pointing out that 'on the one hand Jung insinuates that the reality of the statement of belief is in fact a psychological one; on the other hand, whilst criticising the hypostasis of the metaphysical statement, he boldly hypostatizes psychic reality' ('Jung and Knowledge: From Gnosis to Praxis', *Journal of Analytical Psychology*, 35 (1990), 377–396 (p. 382).

both Western and Eastern religion in detail;[4] and in his last three major works – *Aion* (1951), *Antwort auf Hiob* [*Answer to Job*] (1952) and *Mysterium Coniunctionis* (1955/56) – he analysed the psychological aspects of Christianity, Gnosticism and alchemy.[5] Because the post-war texts explore the same problems and much of the time even repeat each other, the writings of the last twenty years of Jung's life can be read synchronically without damage to the chronological framework of my analysis.

Jung's critique of religion and its relation to Nietzsche

Much of Nietzsche's work constitutes a critique of religion, and stands at the beginning of a period when theology was being scrutinized by such theologians as Albert Schweitzer (1875–1965), Rudolf Bultmann (1884–1976), Karl Barth (1886–1968), Paul Tillich (1886–1965) and Dietrich Bonhoeffer (1906–1945). Tillich and Bultmann in particular drew on the ideas of Existentialism, which was itself an avowed descendent of Nietzsche.[6] Indeed, 'radical theology', which reached its apogee in America in the Sixties, derived its other name, 'Death of God theology', in part from Nietzsche's parable of the madman.[7] However, the declaration of Nietzsche's 'toller Mensch' is not without its own genealogy:[8] Pascal,[9]

4 For a bibliographical overview of the vast literature on Jung's relevance to theology, see James W. Heisig, 'Jung und die Theologie: eine bibliographische Handlung', *Analytische Psychologie*, 7 (1976), 177–220.

5 See Thomas J. J. Altizer, 'Science and Gnosis in Jung's Psychology', *The Centennial Review of Arts and Science*, 3 (1959), 304–20; and Roman Lesmeister, 'Die Gnosis als unbewältigte esoterische Erbe der Analytischen Psychologie C. G. Jungs', *Analytische Psychologie*, 22 (1991), 191–208.

6 For a further discussion of Existentialist theology, see: John Macquarrie, *Existentialism* (New York, 1972) and *An Existentialist Theology: A Comparison of Heidegger and Bultmann* (Harmondsworth, 1973); and Alistair Kee, *The Way of Transcendence* (Harmondsworth, 1971) (particularly 'Nietzsche and the Godless World', pp. 113–32).

7 For further discussion, see: Eugen Biser, *"Gott ist tot": Nietzsches Destruktion des christlichen Bewußtseins* (Munich, 1962) ; T. J. J. Altizer and William Hamilton, *Radical Theology and the Death of God* (Indianapolis, 1966); and Klaus Rohmann, *Vollendung im Nichts?: Eine Dokumentation der amerikanischen "Gott-ist-tot-Theologie"* (Zurich, 1977).

8 For further discussion, see: *Towards a New Christianity: Readings on the Death of God Theology*, edited by T. J. J. Altizer (New York, 1967); Eric von der Luft, 'Sources of Nietzsche's "God is dead!" and its Meaning for Heidegger', *Journal of the History of Ideas*, 45 (1984), 263–76; and R. H. Roberts, 'Nietzsche and the Cultural Resonance of the "Death of God"', *History of European Ideas*, 11 (1989), 1025–35.

9 Pascal specifically noted Plutarch's proclamation in *De Defectu Oraculorum* [*The Obsolescence of Oracles*] that 'Le grand Pan est mort' and observed elswhere that not only had God disappeared, but Nature too was corrupt (Blaise Pascal, *Pensées et Opuscules*, edited by Léon Brunschvicg (Paris, 1959), nos.695 and 441, pp. 647 and 536.

Schelling[10] and the early Hegel[11] are three major precursors in the history of a motif which Nietzsche made notorious and to which the 'Death of God theology' was a response.[12]

A concern with theological issues was apparent in Jung's earliest intellectual endeavours, as the lectures to the Zofingia Club show, and his autobiography suggests that he was deeply affected by the apparent loss of faith of his father, a Protestant pastor. Jung's annotations in his edition of Nietzsche's *Werke* show that he paid close attention to Nietzsche's comments on religion from *Die Geburt der Tragödie* [*The Birth of Tragedy*] (1872) through to *Der Antichrist* [*The Anti-Christ*] (written 1888), and these annotations point to the main ideas from Nietzsche with which Jung chose to engage.

To begin with, Nietzsche claimed in *Die Geburt der Tragödie* (in a passage which Jung marked in his copy) that the main reason for the decline of religions was their substitution of (dead) dogma for (living) myth:

> Denn dies ist die Art, wie Religionen abzusterben pflegen [...] wenn also das Gefühl für den Mythus abstirbt und an seine Stelle der Anspruch der Religion auf historische Grundlagen tritt (GT/BT § 10; N1: p. 63).
>
> [For this is the way in which religions are wont to die out ... the feeling for myth perishes, and its place is taken by the claim of religion to historical foundations.]

Similarly, Jung recognized that 'das Schicksal der allmählichen Entseelung droht schließlich jedem Dogma' ['the ultimate fate of every dogma is that it gradually becomes soulless'] (GW14(ii) § 153/CW14 § 488) and castigated those whom

---

10 In *Die Weltalter* [*The Ages of the World*] (1811), Schelling discussed the nature of God and the proposition 'Also ist Gott nicht' (F. W. J. von Schelling, *Werke*, 6 vols (Munich, 1958–1959), IV, pp. 573–720). Schelling made an important distinction between the 'Seyn Gottes' and the 'Existenz Gottes' (p. 692), and Jung took this over into his own insistence that he was talking about God not as a metaphysical but as a psychological concept.

11 At the end of *Glauben und Wissen* (Tübingen, 1802) (and with reference to Pascal), Hegel discussed the religious sentiment of his age ('das Gefühl [...], worauf die Religion der neuen Zeit beruht' ['the feeling on which religion of the modern age is founded']) in terms of 'das Gefühl: Gott selbst ist tot' ['the feeling that God himself is dead'] and characterized this as 'das absolute Leiden oder den spekulativen Charfreitag' ['absolute suffering or the speculative Good Friday'] (Hegel, *Werke*, 20 vols (Frankfurt am Main, 1986), II, p. 432); and in the section on religion at the end of *Die Phänomenologie des Geistes* (Bamberg and Würzburg, 1807) he made two references to 'der Schmerz, der sich als das harte Wort ausspricht, daß *Gott gestorben ist*' ['the pain which articulates itself as the hard saying: God is dead'] and 'das schmerzliche Gefühl des unglücklichen Bewußtseins, daß *Gott selbst gestorben* ist' ['the painful feeling of the unhappy consciousness that God himself is dead'] (*Werke*, III, pp. 547, 572). For a discussion of the differences between Pascal's, Hegel's and Nietzsche's view of the Death of God, see Karl Löwith, *Nietzsches Philosophie der ewigen Wiederkehr des Gleichen* (Hamburg, 1978), pp. 42–44.

12 The theme of the Death of God occurs very early in Nietzsche's thought, and indeed he had already proclaimed his anti-faith in one of his notes from the time of *Die Geburt der Tragödie* (i.e. around 1870): 'Ich glaube an das urgermanische Wort: alle Götter müssen sterben' ['I believe in the original Germanic saying: all gods must die'] (Nietzsche, *KGW*, III 3, 5 [115], pp. 128–29 (= UW I 1)).

he called 'seichte Aufklärer und flache Vernünftler' ['shallow enlighteners and superficial rationalists' (P. B.)] (GW14(ii) § 154/CW14 § 489). But unlike Nietzsche, who welcomed the collapse of Christianity, Jung's attitude to its demise was more ambivalent and less intensely hostile. And unlike Nietzsche, who provided an account in *Zur Genealogie der Moral* [*On the Geneology of Morals*] of why Christianity *had* to fail (GM III § 27; N2: pp. 898–99), Jung never explained why the power of some symbols must fade or why the 'charisma of faith' is not granted to all.

In his middle period, Nietzsche's critique of Christianity was fundamentally psychological (see, for example, 'Das religiöse Leben' ['The Religious Life'] in Volume I of *Menschliches, Allzumenschliches* [*Human, All Too Human*]). By showing the psychological genealogy of religious belief, Nietzsche believed he had destroyed that belief itself: 'Mit der Einsicht in diese Verirrung der Vernunft und Phantasie hört man auf, Christ zu sein' ['With the insight into this aberration of reason one ceases to be a Christian'] (MA/HA I § 135; N1: p. 535). His attack continued in *Morgenröte* [*Daybreak*], where he drew a devastating psychological portrait of 'Der erste Christ' ['The first Christian'], the Apostle Paul (M/D § 68; N1: pp. 1055–58).[13] Although the parable of the madman is the most celebrated passage in Nietzsche's writings to announce the Death of God (FW/GS § 125; N2: p. 126–28), this news is actually broken earlier in section 108 of *Die fröhliche Wissenschaft* [*The Gay Science*] and its consequences are discussed in section 343 (N2: pp. 115, 205–06). Oddly enough, Jung never made any specific reference to that parable and his copy of *Die fröhliche Wissenschaft* contains no annotations. Nevertheless, there are repeated references to the Death of God in *Zarathustra*[14] which Jung lined in his edition. Moreover, in paragraph 46 of the third part of *Jenseits von Gut und Böse* [*Beyond Good and Evil*] entitled 'Das religiöse Wesen' ['The religious essence'] (possibly an allusion to Ludwig Feuerbach's *Das Wesen des Christentums* [*The Essence of Christianity*] (1841)), Nietzsche summarized the chief characteristic of Christianity as 'Opferung aller Freiheit, alles Stolzes, aller Selbstgewißheit des Geistes zugleich Verknechtung und Selbst-Verhöhnung, Selbst-Verstümmelung' ['a sacrifice of all freedom, all pride, all self-confidence of the spirit; at the same time, enslavement and self-mockery, self-mutilation'] (N2: p. 610), a passage which Jung underlined. In the same aphorism, Nietzsche sharply criticized the lack of sensitivity of modern believers:

---

13 For a discussion of Nietzsche's attitude towards this saint, see Jörg Salaquarda, 'Dionysos gegen den Gekreuzigten', *Zeitschrift für Religions- und Geistesgeschichte*, 26 (1974), 97–124; and for a discussion of Jung's attitude, see David Cox, *Jung and Saint Paul* (New York, 1959).

14 The news of the 'Death of God' is presented in *Zarathustra* with several elaborations (Z Vorrede/Prologue § 2; N2: p. 279, where we are reminded that God is dead; Z II 4, Z IV 6; N2: pp. 348, 498–99, where God has died because of his pity for Man; Z III 8; N2: p. 431, where a jealous God is laughed to death; and Z IV 7; N2: pp. 502–03, where God has been killed by the Ugliest Man).

> Die modernen Menschen, mit ihrer Abstumpfung gegen alle christliche Nomenklatur, fühlen das Schauerlich-Superlativische nicht mehr nach, das für einen antiken Geschmack in der Paradoxie der Formel "Gott am Kreuze" lag (JGB/BGE § 46; N2: p. 610).
>
> [Modern men, obtuse to all Christian nomenclature, no longer feel the gruesome superlative that struck a classical taste in the paradoxical formula "God on the cross".]

Jung wanted to investigate the symbolism of the Cross and other religious paradoxes in psychological terms, and reinterpreted the Crucifixion in opposition to Nietzsche's understanding of it. For example, in *Aion* (1951), Jung argued that the crucifixion of Christ symbolically represented Man's attainment of knowledge of his Shadow.[15] This account of the meaning of Christianity can be read as a reply to Nietzsche's account of asceticism in Section 8 of the first essay in *Zur Genealogie der Moral* (N2: pp. 780–81).

In section 53 of *Jenseits von Gut und Böse*, where Nietzsche asked: 'Warum heute Atheismus?' ['Why atheism today?'] (N2: p. 615), Jung underlined the following observation: 'daß zwar der religiöse Instinkt mächtig im Wachsen ist' ['the religious instinct is indeed in the process of growing tremendously'], but then failed to underline the conclusion: 'daß er aber gerade die theistische Befriedigung mit tiefem Mißtrauen ablehnt' ['but the theistic satisfaction it refuses with deep suspicion'] (N2: p. 615). Then again, Jung marked Nietzsche's claim in the following section, that all post-Cartesian philosophy was, in the disguise of a critique of the subject-predicate form, in fact an attack on the concept of the soul and ultimately 'ein Attentat auf die Grundvoraussetzung der christlichen Lehre' ['an attempt on the life of the basic presupposition of the Christian doctrine'] (N2: pp. 615–16). And, reacting to the comment in section 58 about the response of the contemporary academy to religion, Jung noted in the margin: 'also ist Nietzsche sehr religiös' ['so Nietzsche is very religious'], sensing in Nietzsche's treatment of religion an underlying fascination and obsession with it.

Nietzsche interpreted religion in the light of the doctrine of the Will to Power, and his teaching is outlined in two important aphorisms in *Jenseits von*

---

15 'Wie Christus zwischen den Schächern gekreuzigt ist, so hat der Mensch allmählich Kenntnis von seinem eigenen Schatten und dessen Dualität bekommen. Letztere nämlich war durch den Doppelsinn des Schlangensymbols antizipiert. Wie die Schlange das Heilende sowohl wie das Verderbliche darstellt, so ist der eine der Schächer nach oben, der andere aber nach unten bestimmt, und so bedeutet auch der "Schatten" einerseits bedauerliche und verwerfliche Schwäche, andererseits gesunde Instinktivität und unerläßliche Bedingung zu höherer Bewußtheit' ['Through the Christ crucified between the two thieves Man gradually attained knowledge of his Shadow and its duality. This duality had been anticipated by the double meaning of the serpent. Just as the serpent stands for the power that heals as well as corrupts, so one of the thieves is destined upwards, the other downwards, and so likewise the Shadow is on one side

Gut und Böse which deal with the psychology of the saint, a topic which he had previously discussed in *Menschliches, Allzumenschliches* (MA/HA I § 143, 144; N1: pp. 543–44). First, in section 47 of *Jenseits*, Nietzsche drew attention to the saint as a subject worthy of psychological enquiry and asked: 'Wie ist Willensverneinung *möglich*? wie ist der Heilige möglich?' ['How is the denial of the Will *possible*? how is the saint possible?'] (N2: p. 611). A page later, in a passage marked by underlining and marginal lines in Jung's copy, Nietzsche asked why throughout the ages the saint has exercised so much fascination, even on philosophers (such as Schopenhauer), and suggested that the answer lay in: 'der unmittelbaren *Aufeinanderfolge von Gegensätzen*, von moralisch entgegengesetzt gewerteten Zuständen der Seele' ['the immediate *succession of opposites* of states of the soul that are judged morally in different ways'] (N2: p. 612). Criticizing psychology for its reticence on this question, Nietzsche ascribed this lack of interest to psychology's adherence to the belief in the opposition between Good and Evil: 'Die bisherige Psychologie litt an dieser Stelle Schiffbruch [...] weil sie sich unter die Herrschaft der Moral gestellt hatte, weil sie an die moralischen Wert-Gegensätze selbst *glaubte*' ['The psychology we have had so far suffered shipwreck at this point ... because it had placed itself under the dominion of morals, because it, too, *believed* in opposite moral values'] (N2: p. 612).[16] Nietzsche returned to this subject in section 51, asking why the most powerful individuals had always bowed before the saint, and he explained the superiority of the saint over the warrior with reference to the Will to Power: 'der "Wille zur Macht" war es, der sie nötigte, vor dem Heiligen stehnzubleiben' ['it was the "Will to Power" that made them stop before the saint'] (N2: p. 614).

Jung accepted Nietzsche's challenge to psychology to investigate the dynamics at work in religion but – and this is an important difference between him and Nietzsche – he rejected the doctrine of the Will to Power in favour of his own psychological critique of Christianity. The doctrine of the Will to Power was unacceptable to Jung because of its psychological one-sidedness, as his marginal notes on section 44 of *Jenseits von Gut und Böse* make clear. Against Nietzsche's attack on 'die *Nivellierer*' ['the *levellers*'] (N2: p. 606) Jung wrote: 'Wille zur Macht – das Grundprinzip' ['Will to Power – the basic principle'], but against the claim that Man's Will to Life must become a Will to Power, he wrote: 'Wo ist das Nicht-Können!! und Alles Schwache und Moralische dazu' ['where

regrettable and reprehensible weakness, on the other side healthy instinctivity and the prerequisite for higher consciousness'] (GW9(ii) § 402).

[16] Jung's work also seeks to deconstruct the opposition between Good and Evil. He relativized Good and Evil by calling them merely subjective judgements about relationships. According to Jung, psychology does not know what good and evil are, it only knows *that* they are (GW9(ii) § 97).

is the lack of ability!! and everything weak and moral that goes with it?'].[17] In Jung's thought, both weakness and strength, regression and progression are inescapably paired. Accordingly, Jung considered Nietzsche's Will to Power to be just as reductive as Freud's sexual theory of the libido.

Finally, there are many underlinings, marginal linings and jottings in Jung's copy of *Der Antichrist*, Nietzsche's exercise in 'historical semiotics' which proposes a 'non-narrative psychology of the redeemer'.[18] For example, Jung's marginal comment against section 9 – 'Grosspapa und Vater!!' ['Grandpa and father!!'] – both emphasizes the biographical background to Nietzsche's declaration: 'Diesem Theologen-Instinkte mache ich den Krieg: ich fand seine Spur überall' ['I make war on this theologian instinct: I have found traces of it everywhere'] (AC § 9; N2: 1170), and implicitly draws attention to his own background as well. In section 16, Jung underlined Nietzsche's remark that Christianity had in effect castrated God – 'die *widernatürliche* Kastration eines Gottes zu einem Gotte bloß des Guten' ['the *anti-natural* castration of a God into a God of the merely good'] (N2: p. 1176); in section 51 he marked Nietzsche's vitriolic attack on the Church (N2: pp. 1216–18); and in sections 40 and 51 he underlined Nietzsche's exposure of 'diese schauerlichste Paradoxie' ['this most terrible paradox'] of the Crucifixion (N2: p. 1201 and 1216–17), an interpretation to which the passage in *Aion* alluded to above is also a response. And in the margin of section 46, where Nietzsche described Jesus as not only the first but also the last Christian, Jung wrote in the margin: 'bist es selbst' ['you yourself are'], echoing his words in his Seminar of 12 May 1937 when he referred to Nietzsche as 'the last real Christian' (SNZ:II:p. 1069).

Nietzsche's notoriety as an anti-Christian thinker makes it easy to forget that he continued an interest in theology at the same time as he developed his reasons for rejecting it. For instance, Nietzsche apparently paid great attention to the Ukrainian philosopher of religion African Spir (1837–1890), whom he mentioned at least four times in his writings;[19] and one does not have to go as

---

[17] That the Will to Power was the doctrine which Jung decisively refused to accept is confirmed by his note against section 23 of *Jenseits von Gut und Böse*, where he rebuffed Nietzsche's definition of psychology as the 'Morphologie und *Entwicklungslehre des Willens zur Macht*' ['morphology and the *doctrine of the development of the Will to Power*'] with a curt wave of the hand (and of the pencil): 'schlechte Interpretation' ['bad interpretation'].

[18] Gary Shapiro, *Nietzschean Narratives* (Bloomington and Indianapolis, 1989), pp. 124, 131.

[19] See N1: p. 459–60 (MA/HA I § 18); N3: p. 400 (*Die Philosophie im tragischen Zeitalter der Griechen/ Philosophy in the Tragic Age of the Greeks*, 15); and Nietzsche, *Gesammelte Werke* (Musarionausgabe), 23 vols (Munich, 1920–1929), VII, p. 29; XVI, pp. 88, 111. According to Spir's sister, Hélène Claparède-Spir, Nietzsche had studied Spir's *Denken und Wirklichkeit* (Leipzig, 1884/85) in great detail, and she corresponded, like Jung, with Elisabeth Förster-Nietzsche to confirm this. She even visited the Nietzsche-Archiv in Weimar to examine the annotations in his copy. Hélène was married to the Swiss psychologist Edouard Claparède, a colleague of Théodore Flournoy (an important influence on Jung's early experimental psychology).

far as Father Frederick Copleston does in defence of the Church to see that the 'nay-saying' of this 'yea-saying philosopher' shows him to be almost completely governed by what he so vociferously repudiates.[20] At the same time, Jung's own religious investments prevented *him* from fully engaging with Nietzsche's arguments against Christianity. In section 50 of *Jenseits von Gut und Böse*, Nietzsche mocked the French Quietist author Madame de Guyon (1648–1717) for what he called her 'frauenhafte Zärtlichkeit und Begehrlichkeit [...], welche schamhaft und unwissend nach einer *unio mystica et physica* drängt' ['womanly tenderness and lust that presses bashfully and ignorantly toward a *unio mystica and physica*'] (N2: p. 614). One wonders how Jung must have read this remark, and whether this ardent dreamer of the *coincidentia oppositorum* understood, even if only for a moment, that one could also in a sense apply this jibe to him and that, had Nietzsche still been alive, he would almost certainly have done so...

The Death of God

Much of Analytical Psychology, especially in the post-war period, can be read as a response to the religious crisis inaugurated by Nietzsche's claim that 'God is dead'. And although he talks a lot about God, Jung, too, is apparently willing to admit that He is in some sense 'dead'. In 'Psychologie und Religion' ['Psychology and Religion'], originally delivered in English as the Terry Lectures at Yale University in 1937 and published in German in revised form in 1940 (GW11 § 1–168), he claimed that psychology had become a necessary substitute for faith:

> Ich wende mich [...] gar nicht an die beati possidentes des Glaubens, sondern an jene vielen, für die das Licht erloschen, das Mysterium versunken, und Gott tot ist [...] Zum Verständnis der religiösen Dinge gibt es heute wohl nur noch den psychologischen Zugang (GW11 § 148).
>
> [I am not addressing myself to the happy possessors of faith, but to those many people for whom the light has gone out, the mystery has faded, and God is dead ... To gain an understanding of religious matters, probably all that is left us today is the psychological approach.]

In his lecture 'Wissenschaft als Beruf' ['Science as a Vocation'], delivered in 1919 in the wake of the Great War in Europe, Max Weber had spoken of the 'Entzauberung der Welt' ['disenchantment of the world'], by which he had meant the withdrawal of value from the objective sphere (of society) into the purely subjective spheres of mysticism or personal relationships:

---

20 Frederick Copleston, *Friedrich Nietzsche: Philosopher of Culture* (London, 1942) (especially p. 142).

Es ist das Schicksal unserer Zeit, mit der ihr eigenen Rationalisierung und Intellektualisierung, vor allem: Entzauberung der Welt, daß gerade die letzten und sublimsten Werte zurückgetreten sind aus der Öffentlichkeit, entweder in das hinterweltliche Reich mystischen Lebens oder in die Brüderlichkeit unmittelbarer Beziehungen der Einzelnen zueinander.[21]

[It is the fate of our age, with its own special rationalization and intellectualization and above all disenchantment of the world, that it is precisely the final and most sublime values which have withdrawn themselves from the public sphere into either the otherworldly realm of mystical life or into the fraternity of immediate connections between individuals.]

For his part, Jung sketched out the historical context for the disappearance of Man's highest value in his numerous lectures on psychology and religion, suggesting that the Death of God could be understood as the culmination of a psychological dynamic which had constituted the development of Western religion. Jung argued that the withdrawal of the deity from the world was nothing new, and indeed that it was a process which had been going on for centuries (GW11 § 141). This neo-Weberian notion of 'the withdrawal of projections', which Peter Homans has correctly identified as one of Jung's most important concepts,[22] was taken up in Jung's post-war essay 'Nach der Katastrophe' ['After the Catastrophe'] (1945), where he placed what had occurred to Germany in the context of an allegedly larger European decline (GW10 § 437) and the complete withdrawal of Spirit from the world of Nature:

Nun ja, wir haben ja auch – zum erstenmal seit der Urzeit – es fertig gebracht, die ganze ursprüngliche Beseeltheit der Natur in uns aufzuschlucken; nicht nur sind die Götter aus ihren himmlischen Planethäusern heruntergestiegen oder vielmehr heruntergeholt worden und haben sich zunächst in chthonische Dämonen verwandelt, sondern auch das Heer letzterer, das sich zur Zeit eines Paracelsus noch fröhlich in Bergen, Wäldern, Gewässern und menschlichen Behausungen tummelte, ist unter dem Einfluß zunehmender wissenschaftlicher Aufklärung bis auf klägliche Reste zusammengeschrumpft und schließlich gar verschwunden. Seit unvordenklichen Zeiten war die Natur immer beseelt gewesen. Jetzt leben wir zum erstenmal in einer entseelten und entgötterten Natur (GW10 § 431).

[For the first time since the dawn of history we have succeeded in swallowing the whole of primitive animism into ourselves, and with it the Spirit that animated Nature. Not only were the gods dragged down from their planetary spheres and transformed into chthonic daemons, but, under the influence of scientific Enlightenment, even this band of daemons, which at the time of Paracelsus still frolicked happily in mountains and woods, in rivers and human dwelling-places, was reduced to a miserable remnant and finally vanished altogether. From time immemorial, Nature was

---

[21] Max Weber, 'Wissenschaft als Beruf' ['Science as a Vocation'] (1919), *Gesammelte Aufsätze zur Wissenschaftslehre* (Tübingen, 1968), p. 612.

[22] Peter Homans, 'C. G. Jung: Christian or Post-Christian Psychologist?' in: *Essays on Jung and the Study of Religion*, edited by Martin and Goss (Lanham, 1985), pp. 26–44 (p. 33).

always filled with Spirit. Now, for the first time, we are living in a lifeless Nature bereft of gods.]

Besides the clear echoes in these lines of such exponents of the lyric German tradition as Schiller[23] and Hölderlin,[24] several of Jung's contemporaries were making an analogous complaint. During the Second World War, the Frankfurt School sociologists Max Horkheimer and Theodor W. Adorno were elaborating a similar view in their *Dialektik der Aufklärung* [*Dialectic of Enlightenment*], where the transition from the religion of Greek antiquity to the modern period of the Renaissance and the Reformation is discussed in terms of a dramatic change in Man's relationship to Nature.[25] And in 1957, Mircea Eliade observed a 'desacralization' of society which also had consequences for Man's attitude towards his natural environment.[26]

Jung also argued that the Death of God represented the collapse of the theocentric medieval world-picture, and that the guarantee of an ordered and providential universe had died with God: 'Das mittelalterliche Weltbild zerfiel, und die dieser Welt übergeordnete metaphysische Autorität schwand dahin, um im Menschen wieder aufzutauchen' ['The medieval picture of the world was breaking up and the metaphysical authority that ruled it was fast disappearing, only to reappear in Man'] (GW10 § 437). In Jung's view, modern Christian theology had been left with a major dilemma: 'wo ist die Autorität des Guten und des Rechtes, welche bisher metaphysisch verankert war, hingeraten?' ['where now is the sanction for goodness and justice, which was anchored in metaphysics?'] (GW10 § 438).

To illustrate the psychological dangers attendant upon the Death of God, Jung cited Nietzsche as his example. In particular, he questioned two famous Nietzschean slogans: 'Jenseits von Gut und Böse' and 'Zerbrich mir die Tafel!' ['Break the law-tablets!']. On the first count, Jung thought that modern Man had reached a psychological turning-point where Good and Evil could be relativized to the point of ethical inefficacy: 'jener Zeitwende, wo Gut und Böse anfangen sich zu relativieren, sich selbst zu bezweifeln, und wo sich ein Ruf

---

23 See Friedrich Schiller, 'Die Götter Griechenlandes' ['The Gods of Greece'], *Sämtliche Werke*, 3 vols (Munich, 1965), I, pp. 169–73 (p. 172).

24 See Friedrich Hölderlin, 'Brod und Wein' ['Bread and Wine'], *Sämtliche Werke*, 8 vols (Stuttgart, 1946–1985), II, pp. 90–95 (p. 93).

25 See Max Horkheimer and Theodor W. Adorno, *Dialektik der Aufklärung: Philosophische Fragmente* [*Dialectic of the Enlightenment: Philosophical Fragments*] (Frankfurt am Main, 1969), p. 38. The parallels between Critical Theory and Jungian cultural criticism are discussed by Tilman Evers in *Mythos und Emanzipation: Eine kritische Annäherung an C. G. Jung* (Hamburg, 1987), pp. 183–96.

26 See Mircea Éliade, *The Sacred and the Profane: The Nature of Religion*, translated by William R. Trask (New York, 1959), pp. 23–24). And, like Jung, Éliade recognized that 'certain traditional images, certain vestiges of the behaviour of archaic man still persist, in the condition of "survivals", even in the most highly industrialized societies' (p. 51).

erhebt nach einem "Jenseits von Gut und Böse"' ['that turning-point where Good and Evil begin to relativize themselves, to doubt themselves and the cry is raised for a morality "beyond Good and Evil"'] (GW11 § 258). But at the same time he declared that to abandon all traditional morality and go 'beyond Good and Evil' would be impossible: 'Wir werden auch auf dem höchsten Gipfel nie jenseits von Gut und Böse sein' ['Even on the highest peak we shall never be beyond Good and Evil'] (GW11 § 267). On the second count, he warned of the consequences of erecting new law tables *à la* Zarathustra: 'Dabei wird es gar nichts nützen, das moralische Kriterium zum alten Eisen zu werfen und "neue Tafeln aufzurichten" (nach bekannten Mustern)' ['It will not help us in the least to throw the moral criterion on the rubbish heap and to "set up new tablets" after known patterns'] (GW11 § 267).

Instead, the answer to the problems caused by the demands of ethics on the one hand and the psychological challenges involved in Death of God on the other would, he hoped, be found instead in the form of a direct intervention of the Unconscious itself as 'Geist':

> In dieser äußersten Unsicherheit bedürfen wir der Erleuchtung aus einem heiligen und ganzmachenden Geiste, der alles andere sein kann, nur nicht gerade unser Verstand (GW11 § 267).
>
> [In this utmost uncertainty we need the illumination of a holy and whole-making spirit – a spirit that can be anything rather than our reason.]

In Jung's view, Nietzsche's proclamation of the Death of God had prefigured the psychological condition of post-war Europe (GW11 § 145), and by recognizing it as such, Jung transformed Nietzsche's formula from a statement of ontological despair into a confession of psychological crisis (GW11 § 144). Moreover, in Jung's view, Nietzsche himself exemplified the full ambiguity of this condition, for although in the form of Zarathustra he had smashed the tables of the old Law, yet Zarathustra had gone on to invent new Law tables, too (GW11 § 142). For Jung, this split in Nietzsche's personality manifested itself in his final identification with the forces of the Unconscious – a paradox which he summarized as follows: 'Nietzsche war kein Atheist, aber sein Gott war tot' ['Nietzsche was no atheist, but his God was dead'] (ibid.). As a result, Jung argued, Nietzsche himself had become dangerously god-like, and therein lay his tragedy: 'Die Tragödie von "*Also sprach Zarathustra*" besteht darin, daß Nietzsche selbst zu einem Gott wurde, weil sein Gott starb; und das geschah so, weil er kein Atheist war' ['The tragedy of *Zarathustra* is that, because his God died, Nietzsche himself became a god; and this happened because he was no atheist'] (ibid.). Although Jung is not explicit here about the identity of the god which Nietzsche became, it is, bearing in mind his earlier claims about Nietzsche's Dionysian fate (GW6 § 214/CW6 § 232), not too difficult to guess which god he had in mind.

Jung's psychological diagnosis of Modernity echoes Heidegger's declaration in his discussion of Hölderlin that the modern epoch is not just bereft of the gods but also full, so to speak, of their absence – a double lack of divinity: 'Es ist die Zeit der entflohenen Götter *und* des kommenden Gottes. Das ist die *dürftige* Zeit, weil sie in einem gedoppelten Mangel und Nicht steht: im Nicht-mehr der entflohenen Götter und im Nochnicht des Kommenden' ['It is the time of the gods that have fled *and* of the god that is coming. It is the time *of need*, because it lies under a double lack and a double Not: the No-More of the gods which have fled and the Not-Yet of the god that is coming'].[27] Both Jung and Hölderlin were waiting for the same god to return, and a clue to his identity is given when Jung makes a comparison between the mid-twentieth century and an earlier but similar metaphysico-theological crisis. In 'Psychologie und Religion' (GW11 § 145), and later in a footnote in *Mysterium Coniunctionis*, Jung made the same point which he had first voiced in his *Visions Seminar* of the early Thirties, seeing Nietzsche's proclamation of the Death of God as a repetition of the announcement in antiquity of death of the ruling god of that period, Pan:

> In der späteren Antike war Pan nicht mehr der groteske Hirtengott, sondern hatte philosophische Bedeutung angenommen. Bei den Naassenern des Hippolytus ist er eine der Formen des [πολύμορφος Ἄττις] und synonym mit Osiris, Sophia, Adam, Korybas, Papa, Bakcheus usw. [...] Die moderne Entsprechung ist Zarathustras Ruf: "Gott ist tot" (GW14(ii) § 174, n.401/CW14, § 510, n.393).
>
> [In late antiquity Pan was no longer a grotesque pastoral deity but had taken on a philosophical significance. The Naassenes of Hippolytus regarded him as one of the forms of the "many-formed Attis" and as synonymous with Osiris, Sophia, Adam, Korybas, Papa, Bakcheus, etc. ... Its modern equivalent is Zarathustra's cry "God is dead!".]

By ranking the Death of (the Christian) God on the same level as the Death of Pan, the nature-god who shared many of the classical characteristics of Dionysos, Jung is implying that there would indeed be a resurrection or return of (a not necessarily Christian) god: Pan joins Christ and the company of dying and resurgent gods whose supreme representative is the archetypal Dionysos.[28]

---

27 Martin Heidegger, 'Hölderlin und das Wesen der Dichtung' ['Hölderlin and the Essence of Poetry'], in: *Erläuterungen zu Hölderlins Dichtung* (Frankfurt am Main, 1951), pp. 31–45 (p. 44).

28 In 'Psychologie und Religion', Jung made it explicitly clear that the figure of Christ fitted into fundamental Dionysian mythologem of the dying and rising god: 'Christus ist selber der Typus des sterbenden und sich wandelnden Gottes' ['Christ himself is the typical dying and self-transforming god'] (GW11 § 146). In fact, Christ is associated with the only ontological certainty in Jung's system, namely the archetype: 'Insofern nun das Christusleben in hohem Maße archetypisch ist, stellt es in ebensolchem Maße das Leben des Archetypus dar [...] was im Christusleben geschieht, ereignet sich immer und überall' ['Since the life of Christ is archetypal to a high degree, it represents to just that degree the life of the archetype ... what happens in the life of Christ happens always and everywhere'] (GW11 § 146). The death and resurrection of Christ was thus for Jung nothing other than the symbolic transformation of Dionysian libido.

At the same time, Jung's transformation of Nietzsche's Death of God into the death of Pan, a god who would arise, like Dionysos, from death and dissolution, is intimately bound up with Jung's project to transform Christ back into Dionysos, the goal of psychoanalysis as he had originally conceived it. This project is visible in Jung's writings of the late Thirties and thereafter in another theologico-psychological transformation which Analytical Psychology seeks to effect: a change in the relationship between God/Self and Man/Ego. In *Die Beziehungen zwischen dem Ich und dem Unbewußten* [*The Relations between the Ego and the Unconscious*] (1928), Jung had written that the archetype of the Self had nothing to do with either 'eine Vergottung des Menschen' ['a deification of Man'] or 'eine Herabsetzung Gottes' ['a dethronement of God'] (GW7 § 400). But by 1939 he was prepared to countenance precisely these possibilities, for his penultimate seminar on *Zarathustra* ended thus: 'We are confronted with that dilemma: is it the deification of Man or the birth of God in Man?' (SNZ:II:p. 1527).

Then again, in his essay 'Versuch einer psychologischen Deutung des Trinitätsdogmas' ['A Psychological Approach to the Dogma of the Trinity'] (1942/1953), first given as an Eranos lecture in 1941,[29] Jung suggested that Man represented a point of transition in the nature of the deity himself, making use of two of the central images in *Zarathustra* to do so. First, Man is represented by Zarathustra as a tight-rope: 'Der Mensch ist ein Seil, geknüpft zwischen Tier und Übermensch – ein Seil über einem Abgrunde' ['Man is a rope, fastened between animal and Superman – a rope over an abyss'] (Z Vorrede/Prologue § 4; N2: p. 281). Similarly, according to Jung, Man stands at the mid-point between two different aspects of the Unconscious: 'Der *Mensch* ist recht eigentlich die Brücke, welche den Abgrund zwischen "dieser Welt", dem Reiche des dunklen Tricephalus und der himmlischen Trinität überspannt' ['Man is, in truth, the bridge spanning the gulf between "this world" – the realm of the dark Tricephalus – and the heavenly Trinity'] (GW11 § 263). Second, Man is, for Zarathustra: 'eine Brücke [...] und kein Zweck' ['a bridge and not a goal'] (Z III 12 § 3; N2: p. 445; cf. GM II § 16; N2: p. 826). In an extension of this image, Jung compared the situation of Man to that of a bridge bestridden by God:

> Der lichte Gott beschreitet die Brücke Mensch von der Tagseite, der Schatten Gottes aber von der Nachtseite. Wer wird entscheiden in diesem furchtbaren Dilemma, das mit nie gekannten Schauern und Trunkenheiten das armselige Gefäß zu zersprengen droht? Es wird wohl die Offenbarung eines Heiligen Geistes aus dem Menschen selber sein (GW11 § 267).

Jung answered Nietzsche's question '– Hat man mich verstanden? – *Dionysos gegen den Gekreuzigten...*' ['– Have I been understood? – *Dionysos against the Crucified...*'] (EH IV § 9; N2: p. 1159) by conflating Dionysos with the Crucified, thereby uniting the symbolic opposites which Nietzsche had set up.

29 'Zur Psychologie der Trinitätsidee', *Eranos-Jahrbuch 1940–41* (Zurich, 1942), pp. 31–64.

[The light God bestrides the bridge – Man – from the day side; God's shadow, from the night side. What will be the outcome of this fearful dilemma, which threatens to shatter the frail human vessel with unknown storms and intoxications? It may well be the revelation of the Holy Ghost out of Man himself.]

But whereas, for Nietzsche, these related images suggested that Man was a point of transition from the beast to the Superman, and *en route* to a form of non-metaphysical transcendence, for Jung, they suggest that Man is an instrument through which divinity itself develops and realizes itself in a series of transitions from God (the Unconscious) and Man (consciousness) to the 'God-Man' (the union of Unconscious and consciousness and hence all other opposites) in a realm of pure (psychological) immanence. Thus the Death of God looks forward to a rebirth of divinity in a new form.

Dionysos, Rebirth and Eternal Recurrence

In a major theoretical text, 'Theoretische Überlegungen zum Wesen des Psychischen' ['On the Nature of the Psyche'] (GW8 § 343–442), the original version of which was delivered as an Eranos lecture in 1946 and then substantially revised in 1954,[30] Jung attempted to provide a philosophical context to the Death of God by considering the way in which the concept of the Unconscious had gradually usurped the place of the concept of God in post-Kantian German Idealism. According to this scheme, Schopenhauer had redefined God as the Will, Carl Gustav Carus had replaced God with the Unconscious, and Hegel had identified the subject with God and equated reason with 'Geist'. In fact, Hegel, the 'psychologist in disguise' as Jung called him, was the main target of his argument, and he accused Hegelian philosophy of projecting subjectivity into the universal:

> Der Sieg Hegels über Kant bedeutete für die Vernunft und die weitere geistige Entwicklung, zunächst des deutschen Menschen, eine schwerste Bedrohung, um so gefährlicher, als Hegel ein verkappter Psychologe war und große Wahrheiten aus dem Bereich des Subjekts in einen selbstgeschaffenen Kosmos hinausprojizierte (GW8 § 358).
>
> [The victory of Hegel over Kant dealt the gravest blow to reason and to the further development of (first of all) the German mind, all the more dangerous as Hegel was a psychologist in disguise who projected great truths out of the subjective sphere into a cosmos he himself had created.]

Moreover, he did not hesitate to draw a straight line from Hegel to Nietzsche: 'Die diese unheilvolle Entwicklung kompensierenden Kräfte personifizieren sich

[30] 'Der Geist der Psychologie', *Eranos-Jahrbuch 1946* (Zurich, 1947), pp. 385–490.

zum Teil im späteren Schelling, zum Teil in Schopenhauer and Carus, während dagegen bei Nietzsche jener hemmungslose "bacchantische Gott", den schon Hegel in der Natur witterte, vollends durchbrach' ['The forces compensating this calamitous development personified themselves partly in the later Schelling, partly in Schopenhauer and Carus, while on the other hand that unbridled "bacchantic God" whom Hegel had already scented in nature finally burst upon us in Nietzsche'] (GW8 § 358). In this last remark, an allusion to a well-known passage in the Preface to Hegel's *Phänomenologie*,[31] Jung was suggesting that the compensatory realization of the Unconscious was connected with the return of Dionysos.

The fundamental importance of Dionysos in Jung's view of Nietzsche was already crystal-clear in a lecture which predated his major discussions of the Death of God. In this lecture, written in 1939 as the Second World War began to engulf Europe,[32] Jung suggested that the Unconscious contained an archetype which, unlike his other archetypes (such as the Great Mother, the Old Wise Man, the Anima/Animus, and the Trickster), was manifested not as a figure or a person but as a process: Rebirth.

From a Jungian perspective, the archetype of Rebirth embodies an enantiodromian moment which is latent in Nietzsche's thought but never performed. For, as both Karl Löwith and Ofelia Schutte have suggested, there is an important twist in Nietzsche's argument concerning Nihilism: 'Der radikal vollendete Nihilismus schlägt um in den "klassischen" Positivismus der dionysischen Philosophie der ewigen Wiederkehr des Gleichen' ['Nihilism taken to its radical completion is transformed into the "classical" positivism of the Dionysian philosophy of the Eternal Recurrence of the Same'].[33] Or in other words, Nihilism involves a fresh task, that of finding what Nietzsche called 'Mein neuer Weg zum "Ja"' ['My new path to a "Yes"'] (WM/WP 1041 = N3: p. 834) – a way of affirmation which stands under the sign of the ancient Greek god:

> Eine solche *Experimental-Philosophie*, wie ich sie lebe, nimmt versuchsweise selbst die Möglichkeiten des grundsätzlichen Nihilismus vorweg: ohne daß damit gesagt wäre, daß sie bei einer Negation, beim Nein, bei einem Willen zum Nein stehen bliebe. Sie will vielmehr bis zum Umgekehrten hindurch – bis zu einem *dionysischen Ja-sagen* zur Welt, wie sie ist, ohne Abzug, Ausnahme und Auswahl –, sie will den ewigen Kreislauf: – dieselben Dinge, dieselbe Logik und Unlogik der Verknotung. Höchster Zustand, den ein Philosoph erreichen kann: dionysisch zum Dasein stehn –: meine Formel dafür ist *amor fati* (WM/WP 1041 = N3: p. 834).

---

31 G. W. F. Hegel, *Werke*, 20 vols (Frankfurt am Main, 1986), III, p. 46.

32 'Die verschiedenen Aspekte der Wiedergeburt', *Eranos-Jahrbuch 1939* (Zurich, 1940), pp. 399–429, revised as 'Über Wiedergeburt' in *Gestaltung des Unbewußten* (Zurich, 1950) (GW9(ii) § 199–258).

33 Karl Löwith (1978), p. 51; Ofelia Schutte, *Beyond Nihilism: Nietzsche without Masks* (Chicago and London, 1984), p. 4.

> [Such an experimental philosophy as I live anticipates experimentally even the possibilities of the most fundamental Nihilism; but this does not mean that it must halt at a negation, a No, a will to negation. It wants rather to cross over to the opposite of this – to a Dionysian affirmation of the world as it is, without subtraction, exception, or selection – it wants the eternal circulation: – the same things, the same logic and illogic of entanglements. The highest state a philosopher can attain: to stand in a Dionysian relationship to existence – my formula for this is *amor fati.*]

Although most fully expounded in his *Nachlaß* (most of which was probably unfamiliar to Jung), Nietzsche's anti-nihilistic, Dionysian affirmation of Life was also formulated in other writings which Jung certainly *had* read. For example, in the section on the 'Genius of the Heart' at the end of *Jenseits von Gut und Böse*, Nietzsche described himself as 'der letzte Jünger und Eingeweihte des Gottes Dionysos' ['the last disciple and initiate of the god Dionysos'] (JGB/BGE § 295; N2: p. 755) and, in the foreword to *Ecce Homo* as 'ein Jünger des Philosophen Dionysos' ['a disciple of the philosopher Dionysos'] (EH Vorwort/Foreword § 2; N2: p. 1065). In the section of *Götzen-Dämmerung* [*Twilight of the Idols*] entitled 'Was ich den Alten verdanke' ['What I Owe to the Ancients'], Nietzsche explained, in a passage which Jung marked in his copy with a marginal line, exactly what Dionysos meant to him:

> Das *ewige* Leben, die ewige Wiederkehr des Lebens; die Zukunft in der Vergangenheit verheißen und geweiht; das triumphierende Ja zum Leben über Tod und Wandel hinaus; das *wahre* Leben als das Gesamt-Fortleben durch die Zeugung, durch die Mysterien der Geschlechtlichkeit. Den Griechen war deshalb das *geschlechtliche* Symbol das ehrwürdige Symbol an sich, der eigentliche Tiefsinn innerhalb der ganzen antiken Frömmigkeit [...] Damit es die ewige Lust des Schaffens gibt, damit der Wille zum Leben sich ewig selbst bejaht, *muß* es auch ewig die "Qual der Gebärerin" geben... Dies alles bedeutet das Wort Dionysos: ich kenne keine höhere Symbolik als diese *griechische* Symbolik, die der Dionysien (GD/TI 10 § 4; N2: pp. 1031–32).

> [*Eternal* life, the eternal recurrence of life; the future promised and consecrated in the past; the triumphant Yes to life beyond death and change; *true* life as collective continuation of life through procreation, through the mysteries of sexuality. It was for this reason that the *sexual* symbol was to the Greeks the symbol venerable as such, the intrinsic profound meaning of all antique piety ... For the eternal joy in creating to exist, for the will to life eternally to affirm itself, the "torment of childbirth" *must* also exist eternally... All this is contained in the word Dionysos: I know of no more exalted symbolism than this *Greek* symbolism, the symbolism of the Dionysian.]

Although Nietzsche had complained in *Der Antichrist* that during two thousand years of Christianity not a single new god had been discovered (AC § 19; N2: p. 1178), *Also sprach Zarathustra* was clearly designed to prepare the way for the return of Dionysos. Indeed, Laurence Lampert has characterized 'the secret heart' of Nietzsche's book for All and for None as nothing less than the advent of 'a god not of being, but of coming and becoming, of rising and dying [...] a god whose nature it is to die, but whose dying presages birth'.[34]

In Jung's system, the possibility of a psychological enantiodromia is envisaged as an archetypal process which he called 'Rebirth': '"Wiedergeburt" ist eine Aussage, die zu den Uraussagen der Menschheit überhaupt gehört. Diese Uraussagen beruhen auf dem, was ich als "Archetypus" bezeichne' ['Rebirth is an affirmation that must be counted among the primordial affirmations of Mankind. These primordial affirmations are based on what I call archetypes'] (GW9(i) § 206–07). By calling this process an archetype, Jung was only making even more explicit that dynamic psychological process of life, death and rebirth of which Analytical Psychology so often and so consistently speaks: the dynamic of Dionysos. For Jung, the 'Mittagsvision' ['midday vision'] in *Also sprach Zarathustra* provided a 'klassisches Beispiel' ['classic example'] of a particular type of Rebirth experience which represented what he called the 'transcendence of life'. Significantly, in view of his emphasis in 'Psychologie und Religion' on the superiority of immediate experience over dogma, Jung placed Zarathustra's Noontide Vision in the sub-category of 'Unmittelbare Erlebnisse' ['Immediate Experiences']: 'Was das Mysteriendrama darstellt und im Zuschauer bewirkt, das kann auch ohne Ritus als spontanes, ekstatisches oder visionäres Erlebnis vorkommen' ['All that the mystery drama represents and brings about in the spectator may also occur in the form of a spontaneous, ecstatic, or visionary experience, without any ritual'] (GW9(i) § 210). Moreover, Jung's observations in his Seminar on Nietzsche concerning the Eternal Recurrence, Rebirth and Dionysos achieved greater clarity in his commentary on 'Mittags', a chapter in *Zarathustra* which his disbanded Seminar was never able to reach. But because his commentary was written as part of a lecture delivered in 1939, i.e. the same year in which his Seminar on Nietzsche came to its premature conclusion, it provides us with a glimpse of how that Seminar might have been concluded.

The Noontide Vision which comes in the chapter entitled 'Mittags' occurs exactly in the middle of Part IV of *Also sprach Zarathustra* and, as both Löwith and Lampert have shown, it is saturated with Dionysian imagery.[35] This chapter also refers back to the Noon of the Great Pan in the short lyrical section 'Am Mittag' ['At Noon'] in Volume II of *Menschliches, Allzumenschliches* (MA/HA WS § 308; N1: pp. 996–97), where Nietzsche had evoked the image of the sleeping Pan as the tranquil prelude to an enantiodromian renewal of energy, an eery scene pervaded by a distinctly mystical atmosphere:

---

[34] Laurence Lampert, *Nietzsche's Teaching: An Interpretation of Thus Spake Zarathustra* (New Haven and London, 1986), p. 228.

[35] See Lampert, p. 228; Löwith (1978), pp. 106–08.

> Auf einer verborgenen Waldwiese sieht er den großen Pan schlafend; alle Dinge der Natur sind mit ihm eingeschlafen, einen Ausdruck von Ewigkeit im Gesichte – so dünkt es ihm. Er will nichts, er sorgt sich um nichts, sein Herz steht still, nur sein Auge lebt, – es ist ein Tod mit wachen Augen. Vieles sieht da der Mensch, was er nie sah, und soweit er sieht, ist alles in ein Lichtnetz eingesponnen und gleichsam darin begraben. Er fühlt sich glücklich dabei, aber es ist ein schweres, schweres Glück (MA/HA WS § 308; N1: p. 996).

> [Upon a concealed woodland meadow he sees great Pan sleeping; all things of nature have fallen asleep with him, an expression of eternity on their faces – that is how it seems to him. He wants nothing, he is troubled by nothing, his heart stands still, only his eyes are alive – it is a death with open eyes. Then the man sees many things he never saw before, and for as far as he can see everything is enmeshed in a net of light and as it were buried in it. He feels happy as he gazes, but it is a heavy, heavy happiness.]

'Mittags' recounts Zarathustra's ecstatic vision at noonday beneath an old gnarled tree encircled by a fully-laden grape-vine. There are several parallels between 'Am Mittag' (in *Menschliches, Allzumenschliches*) and 'Mittags' (in *Zarathustra*): the intense sunlight from directly above, the silence of the hour, and the quiet yet wakeful attitude of the subject. Zarathustra asks his soul if she desires to sing, an invitation which recalls the moment in 'Von der großen Sehnsucht' ['Of the Great Longing'] when Zarathustra exclaims to his soul that '*daß ich dich singen hieß*, siehe, das war mein letztes!' ['*that I bade you sing*, behold, that was the last thing I had to give!'] (Z III 14; N2: p. 469).[36] But whereas Nietzsche did not heed the call to song, Zarathustra does, and in 'Von der großen Sehnsucht', 'Das andere Tanzlied' ['The Second Dancing Song'] and 'Die sieben Siegel' ['The Seven Seals'] goes on to sing of the return of Dionysos and his marriage to Ariadne. For Jung, this return is depicted psychologically in the imagery of 'Mittags'.

Jung interpreted 'Mittags' as an attempt by Nietzsche to substitute the mystery of Christianity with the myth of Dionysos, thereby imputing to Nietzsche a strategy which closely resembles his own psychoanalytic agenda to transform Christ into Dionysos (both dying and resurgent gods): 'Bei [Nietzsche] tritt, wie bekannt, Dionysos-Zagreus, der Zerstückelte und Wiedererstandene, an Stelle des christlichen Mysteriums ("... von der reichen Liebe eines Weinstocks rings umarmt und vor sich selber verborgen ...")' ['Nietzsche, as we know, substitutes for the Christian mystery the myth of Dionysos-Zagreus, who was dismembered and came to life again ("embraced around by the abundant love of a vine and hidden from itself")'] (GW9(i) § 210). For Jung, this episode is no mere syncretic reconstruction of the Dionysian mysteries or the revelation of Pan, but a direct

[36] The 'reden'/'singen' dichotomy can be subsumed under the more general tension continually present within Nietzsche's thought between 'denken' and 'dichten', and his later writings are characterized by the emphasis they place on song instead of speech.

transcription of Nietzsche's own experience: 'So ist sein Erlebnis dionysisch-naturhaft [...] Das Erlebnis geschieht ihm so, wie wenn er einer Mysterienhandlung beigewohnt hätte' ['His experience has the character of a Dionysian nature myth ... It is just as if Nietzsche had been present at a performance of the mysteries'] (GW9(i) § 210). In this way, Jung regards the final part of *Zarathustra* as the outcome of Nietzsche's philosophical project which began with the work on the religious and metaphysical significance of tragedy in *Die Geburt der Tragödie* and the rôle of Dionysos.

Jung also related the archetype of Rebirth to the Nietzschean doctrine of the Eternal Recurrence. In general, Jung paid little attention to the implications of this aspect of Nietzsche's teaching.[37] But in his Seminar on *Zarathustra*, Jung had dealt briefly with the idea of Eternal Recurrence and made three points about this most enigmatic of Nietzsche's doctrines. First, he had presented the Eternal Recurrence as an affect accompanying Dionysian Rebirth:

> Nietzsche had a sort of revelation about the eternal return of things [...] This is the main idea in the idea of the eternal return, which is a peculiar way of talking of rebirth [...] It belongs to the Dionysian stage of his initiation; it is the feeling of rebirth which always accompanies the revelation of Dionysos (SNZ:I: pp. 191–92).

Second, he had claimed that the idea of Eternal Recurrence was related to his own notion (as outlined in 'Die Lebenswende' ['The Stages of Life'] (1930)) that the goal of life is death (SNZ:I:p. 405). And third, whilst admitting that he did not fully comprehend the idea of Eternal Recurrence, Jung understood the symbol of the ring to represent the goal of the individuation process which, in his terminology, culminated in the totality of the Self:

> Nietzsche's idea of the Eternal Recurrence is in a posthumous publication by Horneffer [*Nietzsches Lehre von der Ewigen Wiederkunft*], consisting of fragments from the manuscripts in the Nietzsche archives [...] It belongs with this symbolism of the ring, the ring of rings, the ring of Eternal Recurrence. Now, this ring is the idea of totality and it is the idea of individuation naturally, an individuation symbol (SNZ:II: p. 1044).

Later, in an important footnote in *Mysterium Coniunctionis* (1955), Jung would suggest that pairs of animals symbolized the circularity of time, and pointed to the eagle and the serpent and the shepherd and the snake in *Zarathustra* as examples of this symbolism.[38]

---

[37] Nevertheless, Jung's idea of 'synchronicity' represents an attack on the Kantian forms of intuition (i.e. time and space), and *Antwort auf Hiob* could be seen to elaborate a notion of repetition (GW11 § 629, 648).

[38] 'Der Wurm stellt sozusagen die primitive, archaische Lebensform dar, aus welcher sich dann die definitive oder wenigstens eine gegensätzliche Gestalt entwickelt, nämlich im Gegensatz zum chthonischen Tier ein Vogel. Dieses Gegensatzpaar – Schlange und Vogel – ist klassisch. Adler und Schlange, die beiden Tiere Zarathustras, symbolisieren den Kreis der Zeit, das heißt der ewigen Wiederkunft. "Denn deine Tiere wissen es wohl, oh Zarathustra, wer du bist und

In 'Mittags', Zarathustra/Nietzsche sees a ring in his vision as a representation of the perfection of the world: 'Wie? Ward die Welt nicht eben vollkommen? Rund und reif? O des goldenen runden Reifs [...]' ['What? Has the world not just become perfect? Round and ripe? Oh, the golden round ring']. Jung identified this ring as the 'ring of return' from the chapter entitled 'Die sieben Siegel' (Z III 16; N2: pp. 473–76) and interpreted it as a guarantee of resurrection and new life: 'Selbst der "goldene Reif", der "Ring der Wiederkunft" erscheint ihm hier, Auferstehung des Lebens verheißend' ['Even the "golden ring", the "ring of return", appears to him as a promise of the resurrection of life'] (GW9(i) § 210).

By insisting on the Dionysian implications of this episode, Jung is suggesting that the doctrine of the Eternal Recurrence is a guarantee of new life. Not, however, in the sense of a never-ending repetition of the same, but rather in the sense of the promised return of the deity. But whatever the manner of return (cosmic or psychological), in Nietzsche's view – and in that of Jung as well – the deity who returns is Dionysos.

The Concept of the Self as a Replacement for God

In his foreword to Daisetz Teitaro Suzuki's *Die grosse Befreiung: Einführung in den Zen-Buddhismus* [*The Great Liberation: Introduction to Zen Buddhism* (1949) (GW11 § 877–907), Jung asked: 'Wer weiß von den tiefsten Beweggründen zum "Hauptgeschäft", wie Goethe den *"Faust"* nannte, oder von den Schauern des "Dionysos-Erlebnisses"?' ['What do we know of the deepest motives for Goethe's "main business", as he called his *Faust*, or of the shudders of the "Dionysian experience"?'] (GW11 § 905). And in his autobiography, Jung suggested that Goethe's 'main business' had been his initiation into the archetypal

werden mußt: siehe, du bist der Lehrer der ewigen Widerkunft" [Z III 13 2; N2: p. 466]. Vgl. "Ring der Wiederkunft" [Z III 16 1; N2: p. 473], das "A und O" [Z III 16 6; N2: p. 476]. Auch der Hirt, dem die Schlange in den Schlund kroch, ist verknüpft mit der Idee der Wiederkunft. Er bildet (als Drache) mit der Schlange den Kreis des Uroboros. "Der Kreislauf ist nichts gewordenes, er ist das Urgesetz" (bei Horneffer, *Nietzsches Lehre von der ewigen Wiederkunft*, Nr. 29, p. 78) [UW II 1328]'; ['The worm stands for the most primitive and archaic form of life from which ultimately developed the direct opposite of the earth-bound creature – the bird. This pair of opposites – snake and bird – is classical. The eagle and the serpent, the two animals of Zarathustra, symbolize the cycle of eternal return. "For thine animals know well, O Zarathustra, who thou art and must become: behold, thou art the teacher of the eternal return". Cf. the "ring of return" and "alpha and omega". The shepherd into whose mouth the serpent crawled is also connected with the idea of eternal return. He forms (as dragon) with the snake the circle of the uroboros. "The circle did not evolve: it is the primary law" (Aphorism 29 in Horneffer, *Nietzsches Lehre von der ewigen Wiederkunft*, p. 78)'] (GW14(ii): § 148, n.336/CW14, § 483, n.328).

world, of which *Faust* is the major testimony, an aim with which Jung himself claims to identify:

> Ich selber bin vom gleichen Traum ergriffen und habe ein Hauptwerk, das in meinem elften Jahre angefangen hat. Mein Leben ist durchwirkt und zusammengefaßt durch ein Werk und ein Ziel, nämlich: in das Geheimnis der Persönlichkeit einzudringen. Alles ist aus diesem zentralen Punkt zu erklären, und alle Werke beziehen sich auf dieses Thema (ETG: p. 210/MDR: p. 232).
>
> [I myself am haunted by the same dream, and from my eleventh year I have been launched upon a single enterprise which is my "main business". My life has been permeated and held together by one idea and one goal: namely, to penetrate into the secret of the personality. Everything can be explained from this central point, and all my works relate to this one theme.]

Jung went on to claim that the link between Goethe, Nietzsche and himself was their common quest for wholeness – a difficult and obscure quest which, Jung said, explained numerous misunderstandings of *Faust* and *Zarathustra*. He then added that the attainment of wholeness is a project on which to stake one's whole being, because it is the only goal worth striving for (GW11 § 906). In Nietzsche's epic poem, Zarathustra also advocated a programme of self-creation in the following words: 'Schaffen – das ist die große Erlösung vom Leiden, und des Lebens Leichtwerden' ['Creation – that is the great redemption from suffering, and life's easement'] (Z II 2; N2: p. 345), and for Jung, as for Nietzsche, what must be created is a Self.

Although Jung's concept of the Self, so fundamental to Analytical Psychology, goes back to well before the Second World War, Jung's most complex discussions of this subject were not written until the post-war period, after he had conducted the historical researches necessary to find analogies for his ideas in the mystical traditions of both Western and Eastern religion. And it is only in the later period of his thinking that the full significance of the Self in Jung's project to overcome Nietzsche, resurrect the God-concept and turn Christ back into Dionysos, becomes clear.

As far as I can tell, the concept of the Self (the archetype of order and psychic totality) was first mentioned by Jung in 'La Structure de l'inconscient' ['The Structure of the Unconscious'] (1916).[39] There are preliminary formulations in the first edition of *Psychologische Typen* (1921) and in the Seminar on Analytical Psychology (given in English in 1925), where Jung said that the Self was 'the totality or sum of the conscious and unconscious processes' and that 'this centre of self-regulation' was 'a postulate that is assumed' (AP: p. 120).

---

[39] 'Les éléments personnels inconscients constituent l'individualité (*das Selbst*) ou *moi inconscient ou subconscient*' (C. G. Jung, 'La Structure de l'inconscient', *Archives de Psychologie*, 16, no. 62 (December, 1916), 152–79 (p. 177)).

However, the first detailed definition of the Self – referred to in 'Psychologie und Religion' as: 'die Totalität des Menschen, die Summe seiner bewußten und unbewußten Gegebenheiten' ['the totality of Man, the sum total of his conscious and unconscious contents'] (GW11 § 140) – did not emerge until *Die Beziehungen zwischen dem Ich und dem Unbewußten* (1928), where it was described as the goal of the individuation process:

> Es gibt eine Bestimmung und eine Möglichkeit, über die im ersten Teil [des Buches] behandelten Stufen hinauszugelangen. *Das ist der Weg der Individuation.* Individuation bedeutet: zum Einzelwesen werden, und, insofern wir unter Individualität unsere innerste, letzte und unvergleichbare Einzigartigkeit verstehen, zum *eigenen Selbst werden.* Man könnte "Individuation" darum auch als "Verselbstung" oder als "Selbstverwirklichung" übersetzen [...] So ist das Selbst auch das Ziel des Lebens, denn es ist der völligste Ausdruck der Schicksalskombinationen, die man Individuum nennt (GW7 § 266, 404).

> [There is a destination, a possible goal, beyond the alternative stages dealt with in our last chapter. That is the way of individuation. Individuation means becoming a single, homogeneous being, and, in so far as "individuality" embraces our innermost, last, and incomparable uniqueness, it also implies becoming one's own Self. We could therefore translate individuation as "coming to Selfhood" or "Self-realization" ... The Self is our life's goal, for it is the most complete expression of that fateful combination we call individuality.]

According to this definition, the archetype of the Self is 'eine dem bewußten Ich übergeordnete Größe' ['a quantity that is superordinate to the conscious Ego']: '[das Selbst] umfaßt nicht nur die bewußte, sondern auch die unbewußte Psyche und ist daher sozusagen eine Persönlichkeit, die wir *auch* sind' ['The Self embraces not only the conscious but also the unconscious psyche, and is therefore, so to speak, a personality which we *also* are'] (GW7 § 274). But at the same time, Jung imbued this psychological concept with a more distinctly religious overtone:

> Dieses "Etwas" ist uns fremd und doch so nah, ganz uns selber und uns doch unerkennbar, ein virtueller Mittelpunkt von solch geheimnisvoller Konstitution, daß es alles fordern kann, Verwandtschaft mit Tieren und mit Göttern, mit Kristallen und Sternen, ohne uns in Verwunderung zu versetzen, ja ohne unsere Mißbilligung zu erregen [...] Ich habe diesen Mittelpunkt als das *Selbst* bezeichnet. Intellektuell ist das Selbst nichts als ein psychologischer Begriff, eine Konstruktion, welche eine uns unerkennbare Wesenheit ausdrücken soll, die wir als solche nicht erfassen können, denn sie übersteigt unser Fassungsvermögen, wie schon aus ihrer Definition hervorgeht. Sie könnte ebensowohl als "der Gott in uns" bezeichnet werden (GW7 § 398–99).

> [This "something" is strange to us and yet so near, wholly ourselves and yet unknowable, a virtual centre of so mysterious a constitution that it can claim anything – kinship with beasts and gods, with crystals and with stars – without moving us to wonder, without even exciting our disapprobation ... I have called this centre the

> *Self.* Intellectually the Self is no more than a psychological concept, a construct that serves to express an unknowable essence which we cannot grasp as such, since by definition it transcends our powers of comprehension. It might equally well be called the "God within us".]

In his Seminar on *Zarathustra*, Jung discussed the Self with reference to the totality of the individual, i.e. both his/her mind and body (the instincts). For example, in his lecture of 6 June 1934, Jung stated that Nietzsche saw the 'acceptance of the real concrete man, identical with his body, as the greatest meaning of our time' and as a challenge to come to terms with our own particularity (SNZ:I:p. 86). And in his lecture of 6 February 1935 on 'Von den Verächtern des Leibes' ['On the Despisers of the Body'], Jung claimed that a return to the body could lead to a renewal of spirit: 'We should return to the body in order to create spirit again' (SNZ:I:p. 368). Using the vocabulary of alchemy, Jung further identified the rediscovery of 'Geist' with the experience of Dionysos.[40] Finally, in his lecture of 5 May 1937 on 'Von den Tugendhaften' ['Of the Virtuous'], Jung related the imagery of circumambulation in Nietzsche's chapter to his own doctrine of individuation, i.e. the transition from mere (Cartesian/ Freudian) Ego to the (Jungian) Self (SNZ:II: p. 1045).[41] In his commentary on 'Von den Freuden- und Leidenschaften' ['Of Joys and Passions'], Jung glossed the remark 'Einst hattest du Leidenschaften und nanntest sie böse. Aber jetzt hast du nur noch deine Tugenden: die wuchsen aus deinen Leidenschaften' ['Once you had passions and called them evil. But now you only have virtues: they grew from out your passions'] (Z I 5; N2: p. 302) as follows:

> [Nietzsche] is anticipating modern [i.e. Jungian!] psychology when he sees virtue in connection with passions; he understands that the Self consists of pairs of opposites and that it is in a way a reconciliation of opposites (SNZ:I:p. 433).

And in his interpretation of *Zarathustra*, Jung interpreted the images of the golden ball (Z I 22; N2: p. 336), the dancing star (Z Vorrede/Prologue § 5; N2: p. 284) and the wheel which rolls out of itself (Z I 1; N2: p. 294) as so many various symbols of the Self (SNZ:I:p. 107, 708; II:p. 781).

Clearly, the concept of the Self does not so much reject as replace the notion of divine transcendence with the much less clear notion of psychological transcendence.[42] In other words, as Jung put it at the end of *Die Beziehungen*

---

[40] 'Nietzsche returned to himself, isolated himself from the whole of the world, crept into his own retort and underwent this process. Then suddenly he discovered that he was filled with a new orgiastic enthusiasm which he called his experience of Dionysos' (SNZ:I:pp. 368–69).

[41] 'Es gibt keine lineare Entwicklung, es gibt nur eine Circumambulation des Selbst' ['There is no linear evolution; there is only a circumambulation of the Self'] (ETG: p. 200/MDR: p. 222).

[42] For Jung, the archetype of the Self replaces the concept of God in the psychic economy that his system proposes. The close affinity – indeed, identity – of the God-concept and the concept of the Self is suggested by the transposition of the definition of God attributed by Jung to Alanus de Insulis in 'Das Wandlungssymbol in der Messe' ['Transformation Symbolism in the Mass'] (1952) and in 'Versuch einer psychologischen Deutung des Trinitätsdogmas' ['A

zwischen dem Ich und dem Unbewußten, in a remark which reflects his acute sense of the need to maintain a moral attitude towards existence, God becomes a moral problem: 'Die Auffassung Gottes als eines autonomen, psychischen Inhaltes macht Gott zu einem *moralischen Problem*' ['The conception of God as an autonomous psychic content makes God into a moral problem'] (GW7 § 402). Jung also described the Self as a 'Grenzbegriff' ['borderline concept'] like Kant's 'Ding an sich'.[43] But in fact, the concept functions in Analytical Psychology much more like the regulative principles or 'leitende Vernunftbegriffe', which Kant calls 'Ideen'. And in *Erinnerungen, Träume, Gedanken* [*Memories, Dreams, Reflections*], Jung placed the striving for totality at the heart of both Eastern and Western religion, rescuing the desire for knowledge of God by replacing it with the concept of self-realization:

> Die unbewußte Ganzheit [...] strebt nach totaler Verwirklichung, also totaler Bewußtwerdung im Fall des Menschen. Bewußtwerdung ist Kultur im weitesten Sinne und Selbsterkenntnis daher Essenz und Herz dieses Vorgangs. Der Osten mißt dem Selbst unzweifelhaft "göttliche" Bedeutung bei, und nach altchristlicher Anschauung ist Selbsterkenntnis der Weg zur cognitio Dei (ETG: p. 327/MDR: p. 356).
>
> [Unconscious wholeness ... strives for total realization – which in Man's case signifies the attainment of total consciousness. Attainment of consciousness in culture in the broadest sense, and self-knowledge is therefore the heart and essence of this process. The Oriental attributes unquestionably "divine" significance to the Self, and according to the ancient Christian view self-knowledge is the road to knowledge of God.]

In contrast, much of Nietzsche's work (particularly his notes for *Der Wille zur Macht*) is concerned with the abolition of the subject (WM/WP 370, 371, 481 and 552 = N3: pp. 534, 485, 903 and 540), forming part of his attack on the Kantian 'Ding an sich' (GM I § 13; N2: p. 790) and the 'hangman's metaphysics' of Christianity (GD/TI 6 § 7; N2: p. 977). This is a highly problematic area of Nietzsche's philosophy which cannot be discussed here in detail, but the main difficulty has been well stated by Christopher Janaway:

> Thus, while rejecting as an illusion the notion of a subject distinct from its states, Nietzsche has nevertheless to conceive the self as something more than a flux of

---

Psychological Approach to the Dogma of the Trinity'] (1942), 'Deus est circulus cuius centrum est ubique, circumferentia vero nusquam' ['God is a circle whose centre is everywhere and the circumference nowhere'] (GW11 § 92, 229), to the Self: 'Das Selbst ist nicht nur der Mittelpunkt, sondern auch jener Umfang, der Bewußtsein und Unbewußtes einschließt' ['The Self is not only the centre but also the whole circumference which embraces both conscious and unconscious'] (GW12 § 44).

[43] 'Das "Selbst" [ist] lediglich ein Grenzbegriff, etwas wie bei Kant das "Ding an sich"' ['The "Self" is merely a borderline concept similar to Kant's "thing in itself"' (P. B.)] (GW12 § 247) (cf. Kant, *Die Kritik der reinen Vernunft*, edited by Raymund Schmidt (Hamburg, 1990), p. 305 (B 311): 'Der Begriff eines Noumenon ist also bloß ein *Grenzbegriff*' ['The concept of a noumenon is thus merely a *borderline concept*']).

> many processes, and has to reckon with the question: how does this harnessing, affirming self arise out of the subjectless flow? Even here he remains closer than he might like to think to the ambit of *The World as Will and Representation*. He inherits few of that work's doctrines, but is haunted by echoes of its deepest dilemmas.[44]

Despite that fundamental difficulty, in his lecture of 20 February 1935 in the Seminar on *Zarathustra*, Jung claimed that his concept of the Self derived, at least in part, from Nietzsche:

> Of course I knew that Nietzsche had [the concept of the Self] because I read *Zarathustra* for the first time when I was only twenty-three [...] I was already interested in the concept of the Self, but I was not clear how I should understand it [...] The concept of the Self continued to recommend itself to me nevertheless. I thought Nietzsche meant a sort of thing-in-itself behind the psychological phenomenon (SNZ:I:p. 391).

So what does Jung's notion of the Self have in common with Nietzsche's concept, which Jung alleges is the same?

Throughout his philosophical writings, Nietzsche sought to elaborate a notion of the Self whilst at the same time rejecting the notion of the Cartesian *ego*. In the third of the *Unzeitgemäße Betrachtungen* [*Untimely Meditations*], 'Schopenhauer als Erzieher' ['Schopenhauer as Educator'], he wrote: 'Der Mensch, welcher nicht zur Masse gehören will, braucht nur aufzuhören, gegen sich bequem zu sein; er folge seinem Gewissen, welches ihm zuruft: "sei du selbst! Das bist du alles nicht, was du jetzt tust, meinst, begehrst" ' ['The man who does not wish to belong to the mass needs only to cease taking himself easily; let him follow his conscience, which calls to him: "Be your self! All you are now doing, thinking, desiring, is not you yourself" '] (UB/UM III § 1; N1: pp. 287–88). Later in this essay, Nietzsche referred to a higher agency within the individual which he called 'dein eigentliches Selbst' ['your own true self']: 'dein wahres Wesen liegt nicht tief verborgen in dir, sondern unermeßlich hoch über dir, oder wenigstens über dem, was du gewöhnlich als dein Ich nimmst' ['your true nature lies, not concealed deep within you, but immeasurably high above you, or at least above that which you usually take yourself to be'] (UB/UM III § 1; N1: p. 290). According to Nietzsche, the purpose of true education ('Erziehung'/'Bildung') is to uncover the higher potentiality of the individual ('der wahre Ursinn und Grundstoff deines Wesens' ['the true basic meaning and material of your being']), and the true educator is the liberator of the individual ('deine Erzieher vermögen nichts zu sein als deine Befreier' ['your educators can only be your liberators']). According to Jung's autobiography and letters (ETG: p. 109/MDR: p. 123; B3: p. 371/L2: pp. 621–22), the *Unzeitgemäße Betrachtungen* was the first

[44] Christopher Janaway, 'Nietzsche, the Self, and Schopenhauer', in: *Nietzsche and Modern German Thought*, edited by Keith Ansell-Pearson (London and New York, 1991), pp. 119–42 (p. 138).

work by Nietzsche that Jung ever read. Even though Jung made no annotations in the copy of this work which exists in his library (which he may also have acquired after his first reading), there are important conceptual parallels between what Nietzsche called 'das Grundgesetz des eigentlichen Selbst' ['the fundamental law of your own true self'] and the Jungian 'Individuationsprozeß' ['individuation process'].

Nietzsche picked up the theme of the Self in the aphorism 'Verkehr mit dem höheren Selbst' ['Traffic with One's Higher Self'] in *Menschliches, Allzumenschliches*, where he talked about the rare moments in the life of every individual where he or she discovers his or her own Self: 'Ein jeder hat seinen guten Tag, wo er sein höheres Selbst findet' (MA/HA I § 624; N1: pp. 720–21). There are references in a similar vein elsewhere in Nietzsche's *oeuvre*, apparently alluding to Pindar.[45] For example, in *Die fröbliche Wissenschaft*, he answered his question: '*Was sagt dein Gewissen?*' ['*What does your conscience say?*'] with the same answer as that which Zarathustra would later give: '"Du sollst der werden, der du bist"' ['You shall become the person you are'] (FW/GS § 270; N2: p. 159). In *Ecce Homo*, with its significant subtitle (see below), Nietzsche described this answer and subsequent statements as 'die graniten Sätze [...] mit denen sich ein Schicksal für *alle Zeiten* zum ersten Male in Formeln faßt' ['the granite sentences with which a destiny for *all ages* formulates itself for the first time'] (EH FW/GS; N2: p. 1127). Later on in *Die fröbliche Wissenschaft*, he said that he did not want to be associated with those who worry about 'das ganze moralische Geschwätz' ['all the moral chatter'] but wanted instead: 'Wir aber *wollen die werden, die wir sind* – die Neuen, die Einmaligen, die Unvergleichbaren, die Sich-selber-Gesetzgebenden, die Sich-selber-Schaffenden!' ['We, however, *want to become those we are* – human beings who are new, unique, incomparable, who give themselves laws, who create themselves'] (FW/GS § 335; N2: p. 197).

---

[45] Drawing on statements from Nietzsche's letters to Erwin Rohde of 3 November 1867 and to Lou Andreas-Salomé of 10 June 1882 (N3: pp. 984, 1181), Walter Kaufmann confidently asserts that Nietzsche's injunction to become who one is alludes to Pindar's second Pythian Ode (l.72): γένοι' οἷος ἐσσὶ μαθών, translatable as 'having learnt what sort of man you are, become it' (*Nietzsche: Philosopher, Psychologist, Antichrist* (Princeton, 1974[4]), p. 159, n.1). But as a philologist, Nietzsche would doubtless have been aware of the difficulty in interpreting this line. As far as twentieth-century scholarship is concerned, more traditional scholars take the line in the existential sense of 'having learnt what your true nature is, manifest it in your action' (for further information, see *The Odes of Pindar*, edited by Sir John Sandys [The Loeb Classical Library] (London, 1915), pp. 169, 179; and *The Works of Pindar*, edited by Lewis Richard Farnell (London, 1932), pp. 128–29). Less philosophically, more recent scholarship suggests the line means 'show yourself who you are, having learnt [from the poet?] what you are' (see R. W. B. Burton, *Pindar's Pythian Odes: Essays in Interpretation* (Oxford, 1962; and *Pindar's Victory Songs*, edited and translated by Frank J. Nisetich (Baltimore, 1980), p. 165; but cf. *Pindar: The Olympian and Pythian Odesu*, edited by Basil L. Gildersleeve (London, 1885), p. 264). The complexity of Nietzsche's understanding of the self is thus matched by that of his probable classical allusion.

The most detailed exposition of Nietzsche's idea of the Self comes in the section entitled 'Von den Verächtern des Leibes' ['On the Despisers of the Body'] from 'Die Reden Zarathustras' ['Zarathustra's Discourses'], where Zarathustra briskly dismisses the body and soul dualism of the child in favour of the esoteric declarations of the mysterious 'one who knows' ('der Erwachte, der Wissende') (Z I 4; N2: p. 300). In his commentary on *Zarathustra*, Lampert shows how this section both continues and denies the project of rationalization on which the Cartesian concept of the ego rests,[46] and against the third paragraph of this section Jung noted in the margin of his edition: 'Wirklichkeit des Imaginären?' ['Reality of the Imaginary?']. In the later section called 'Von den Tugendhaften' ['Of the Virtuous'], Zarathustra advocated a Spinozist definition of virtue as self-affirmation:[47]

> Es ist euer liebstes Selbst, eure Tugend. Des Ringes Durst ist in euch; sich selber wieder zu erreichen, dazu ringt und dreht sich jeder Ring.
>
> [...]
>
> Daß eure Tugend euer Selbst sei, und nicht ein Fremdes, eine Haut, eine Bemäntelung: das ist die Wahrheit aus dem Grunde eurer Seele, ihr Tugendhaften!
>
> [...]
>
> Ach, meine Freunde! Daß *euer* Selbst in der Handlung sei, wie die Mutter im Kinde ist: das sei mir *euer* Wort von Tugend! (Z II 5; N2: pp. 352–53).

> [Your virtue is your dearest Self. The ring's desire is in you: to attain itself again – every ring struggles and turns itself to that end.
>
> ...
>
> That your virtue is your Self and not something alien, a skin, a covering: that is the truth from the bottom of your souls, you virtuous!
>
> ...
>
> Ah, my friends! That *your* Self be in your action, as the mother is in the child: let *that* be your maxim of virtue!]

In his own copy, Jung underlined the phrase 'Daß eure Tugend euer Selbst sei und nicht ein Fremdes'. And later, in 'Der Wanderer' ['The Wanderer'], the opening section of Part III, Zarathustra describes the Self as a home-coming, the moment where, in the words of Julian Roberts, 'virtue, having first thrown itself out in a careless venture, recognizes that the world into which it has thrown itself, the disparate world of experiences and contingencies, is in fact its own':[48]

> Es kehrt nur zurück, es kommt mir endlich heim – mein eigen Selbst, und was von ihm lange in der Fremde war und zerstreut unter alle Dinge und Zufälle (Z III 1; N2: p. 403).

[46] Lampert, 1986, pp. 38–40.
[47] See Paul Tillich, *The Courage to Be* (New Haven and London, 1952), pp. 18–31.
[48] Julian Roberts, *German Philosophy: An Introduction* (Cambridge, 1988), p. 233.

[It is returning, at last. It is coming home to me – my own Self and those parts of it that have long been abroad and scattered amongst all things and accidents.]

In his own copy, Jung underlined the phrase: 'man erlebt endlich nur noch sich selber' ['in the final analysis one experiences only oneself'] (cf. MA/HA I 513; N1: p. 697). In 'Von der Erlösung' ['Of Redemption'] and 'Von alten und neuen Tafeln' ['Of Old and New Law-Tables'], Zarathustra describes himself in the following way: 'Und das ist all mein Dichten und Trachten, daß ich in Eins dichte und zusammentrage, was Bruchstück ist und Rätsel und grauser Zufall' ['And it is all my art and aim, to compose into one and bring together what is fragment and riddle and dreadful chance'] (Z II 20; N2: p. 394; cf. Z III 12 § 3; N2: p. 445). In 'Das Honig-Opfer' ['The Honey Offering'], Zarathustra describes himself in the following phrase which, according to Alexander Nehamas, 'leads, if not to the centre, at least through the bulk of Nietzsche's thought':[49] '*Der* nämlich bin ich von Grund und Anbeginn, ziehend, heranziehend, hinaufziehend, aufziehend, ein Zieher, Züchter und Zuchtmeister, der sich nicht umsonst einstmals zusprach: "Werde, der du bist!"' ['For I am *he*, from the heart and from the beginning, drawing, drawing towards me, drawing up to me, raising up, a drawer, trainer, and taskmaster who once bade himself, and not in vain: "Become what you are!"'] (Z IV 1; N2: p. 479). And in 'Das trunkne Lied' ['The Intoxicated Song'], Zarathustra contrasts what Woe says and Joy wants (in Jung's copy, these words are marked with a marginal line): 'Weh spricht: "[...] Ich will Kinder, ich will nicht *mich*"' – /Lust aber [...] will sich selber' ['Woe says: "I want children, I do not want *myself*". Joy however, wants itself'] (Z IV 19 § 9; N2: p. 556).

In his preface to *Zur Genealogie der Moral*, Nietzsche returns to the theme of knowing (or *not* knowing) who one is, and Jung marked the following lines in his copy with a marginal line:

> Wir sind uns unbekannt, wir Erkennenden, wir selbst uns selbst: das hat seinen guten Grund. Wir haben nie nach uns gesucht – wie sollte es geschehn, daß wir eines Tages uns *fänden*? [...] Wir bleiben uns eben notwendig fremd, wir verstehn uns nicht, wir *müssen* uns verwechseln, für uns heißt der Satz in alle Ewigkeit "Jeder ist sich selbst der Fernste" – für uns sind wir keine "Erkennenden"... (GM Vorrede/Preface § 1; N2: p. 763).

> [We are unknown to ourselves, we men of knowledge – and with good reason. We have never sought ourselves – how could it happen that we should ever *find* ourselves? ... So we are necessarily strangers to ourselves, we do not comprehend ourselves, we *have* to misunderstand ourselves, for us the law "Each is furthest from himself" applies to all eternity – we are not "men of knowledge" with respect to ourselves.]

---

[49] Alexander Nehamas, *Nietzsche: Life as Literature* (Cambridge, MA, 1985), p. 172.

Jung also marked with a marginal line the celebrated passage in *Götzen-Dämmerung* where Nietzsche lavished praise on Goethe for having had the discipline to shape himself into a totality and to create *himself*: 'er löste sich nicht vom Leben ab, er stellte sich hinein [...] Was er wollte, das war *Totalität* [...] er disziplinierte sich zur Ganzheit, er *schuf* sich...' ['he did not sever himself from life, he placed himself within it ... What he aspired to was *totality* ... he disciplined himself to a whole, he created himself']. Nietzsche then went on to baptize Goethe's credo as the 'Dionysian' faith: 'ein solcher Glaube ist der höchste aller möglichen Glauben: ich habe ihn auf den Namen des *Dionysos* getauft' ['such a faith is the highest of all possible faiths: I have baptized it with the name *Dionysos*'] (GD/TI 9 § 49; N2: p. 1024)

Nietzsche gave his autobiography the subtitle: 'Wie man wird, was man ist' ['How One Becomes What One Is'], and admitted: 'Daß man wird, was man ist, setzt voraus, daß man nicht im entferntesten ahnt, *was* man ist' ['That one becomes what one is presupposes that one does not have the remotest idea *what* one is'] (EH II § 9; N2: pp. 1095). He went on to talk about an organizing idea from 'the depths' (the Unconscious?) which has the power to synthesize various individual qualities and capacities into a whole, an experience which sounds remarkably close to what Jung meant by the 'Individuationsprozeß':

> Inzwischen wächst und wächst die organisierende, die zur Herrschaft berufne "Idee" in der Tiefe – sie beginnt zu befehlen, sie leitet langsam aus Nebenwegen und Abwegen *zurück*, sie bereitet *einzelne* Qualitäten und Tüchtigkeiten vor, die einmal als Mittel zum Ganzen sich unentbehrlich erweisen werden – sie bildet der Reihe nach alle *dienenden* Vermögen aus, bevor sie irgend etwas von der dominierenden Aufgabe, von "Ziel", "Zweck", "Sinn" verlauten läßt (EH II § 9; N2: p. 1095).
>
> [In the meantime the organizing "idea" destined to rule grows and grows in the depths – it begins to command, it slowly leads *back* from sidepaths and wrong turnings, it prepares *individual* qualities and abilities which will one day prove themselves indispensable as means to achieving the whole – it constructs the *ancillary* capacities one after the other before it gives any hint of the dominating task, of the "goal", "objective", "meaning"].

And in that autobiography, Nietzsche ascribes to Zarathustra precisely that quality which Jung saw as the main characteristic of the Self – the unification of opposites: 'in [Zarathustra] sind alle Gegensätze zu einer neuen Einheit gebunden' ['all opposites are in Zarathustra bound together into a new unity'] (EH Z § 6; N2: p. 1135).[50]

---

[50] A similarly proto-Jungian notion of an existential *coniunctio oppositorum* can also be found in Nietzsche's notes for *Der Wille zur Macht* (e.g. WM/WP 693, 967 = N3: pp. 778, 450). In another note from the *Nachlaß*, Nietzsche wrote: 'Künstler (Schaffender), Heiliger (Liebender) und Philosoph (Erkennender) in *Einer Person* zu werden: – *mein praktisches Ziel!*' ['To become Artist (Creator), Saint (Lover) and Philosopher (Knower) in *one person*: – *my practical goal!*'] (*Nietzsche, KGW*, VII 1, 16 [11], p. 527). Although Jung may not have read these posthumous

The chief characteristic of the Jungian Self is its capacity for creation and self-transformation, a striving for an ever more complete union of the two great opposites, consciousness and the Unconscious. In the process of creating the Self, the libido (conceived by Jung as a stream of psychic energy) descends into the depths of the Collective Unconscious (the great psychic M/Other), dying unto the conscious world as it introverts, to re-emerge stronger, bolder, more creative, born anew: like a god which dies and is reborn. This is the Dionysian Self, and the Self as Jung conceives it is 'dionysisch' in precisely the sense in which Nietzsche had defined the term in his notes for *Der Wille zur Macht*:

> Mit dem Wort "*dionysisch*" ist ausgedrückt: ein Drang zur Einheit, ein Hinausgreifen über Person, Alltag, Gesellschaft, Realität, über den Abgrund des Vergehens: das leidenschaftlich-schmerzliche Überschwellen in dunklere, vollere, schwebendere Zustände; ein verzücktes Jasagen zum Gesamt-Charakter des Lebens, als dem in allem Wechsel Gleichen, Gleich-Mächtigen, Gleich-Seligen; die große pantheistische Mitfreudigkeit und Mitleidigkeit, welche auch die furchtbarsten und fragwürdigsten Eigenschaften des Lebens gutheißt und heiligt; der ewige Wille zur Zeugung, zur Fruchtbarkeit, zur Wiederkehr; das Einheitsgefühl der Notwendigkeit des Schaffens und Vernichtens (WM/WP 1050 = N3: p. 791).

> [The word "*Dionysian*" means: an urge to unity, a reaching up beyond personality, the everyday, society, reality, across the abyss of transitoriness: a passionate-painful overflowing into darker, fuller, more floating states; an ecstatic affirmation of the total character of life as that which remains the same, just as powerful, just as blissful, through all change; the great pantheistic sharing of joy and sorrow that sanctifies and calls good even the most terrible and questionable qualities of life; the eternal will to procreation, to fruitfulness, to recurrence; the feeling of the necessary unity of creation and destruction.]

As Janaway has emphasized: 'The significance of Nietzsche's injunction to "become who you are" is that one creates oneself, progressively over one's life, rather than finding a pre-existing unity that one timelessly is'.[51] But, whereas Nietzsche always talks about *creating* one's self, Jung talks instead about *discovering* the Self (cf. 'The Undiscovered Self', the title of the English translation of 'Gegenwart und Zukunft' (1957)):

> Einesteils ist die Bewußtwerdung, als eine Zusammenführung abgesplitterter Teile, eine bewußte Willensleistung des Ich, anderenteils aber bedeutet sie auch ein spontanes Hervortreten des Selbst, das von jeher war (GW11 § 400).

> [Conscious realization or the bringing together of the scattered parts is in one sense an act of the Ego's will, but in another sense it is a spontaneous manifestation of the Self, which was always there.]

---

texts, they represent an obvious affinity with the concept of the Dionysian Self as he tried to expound it.

[51] Janaway, p. 136. Nehemas separates Nietzsche's idea of the self from Freud's concept for reasons which apply even more strongly in the case of Nietzsche and Jung (p. 173). For further discussion, see: Stanley Corngold, 'The Question of the Self in Nietzsche during the Axial Period

It is almost as if the archetype of the Self were not just something greater than but in fact entirely external to one's Ego personality (for some, perhaps, a comforting thought...).

This difference between discovering (Jung) and creating (Nietzsche) the Dionysian Self points, in turn, to another major difference between the two thinkers in their attitude towards the Dionysian. Although Nietzsche consistently argues against the unity of the self in the middle and later periods of his philosophy, the kind of unity which Jung envisages in respect of the Self is that which Nietzsche described as the effect of the Dionysian in one of his earliest major works, *Die Geburt der Tragödie*, and elsewhere.[52] However, there is an important shift in Nietzsche's understanding of Dionysos. Whereas, in *Die Geburt der Tragödie*, the Dionysian is presented as the objective ground of Being, his later writings tend to speak of the Dionysian in psychological, not ontological terms. As Kurt Hübner writes: 'das Dionysische "degeneriert" nunmehr zu einem bloßen Kennzeichen für eine rein psychologisch-anthropologische Bestimmung, nämlich für die Wesensbestimmung des Menschen als Wille zur Macht' ['From now on the Dionysian "degenerates" to a mere sign for a purely psycho-anthropological classification, namely for the classification of the essence of Man as Will to Power'].[53] Jung reverses this shift in Nietzsche's thought, and reinvests the Dionysian with that 'objectivity' of which the later Nietzsche deprived it.

In 'Das Wandlungssymbol in der Messe' ['Transformation Symbolism in the Mass'] (1942/1954), first delivered as an Eranos lecture in 1941,[54] Jung specifically related the legend of Dionysos to the archetype of the Self, arguing, in a long and complicated passage written entirely in the spirit of Nietzsche's *Die Geburt der Tragödie*, that the unity of the *principium individuationis* must be replaced by a higher unity, symbolized by Dionysos:

(1882–1888)', *Boundary 2*, 9/10 (1981), 55–98; and J. Hillis Miller, 'The Disarticulation of the Self in Nietzsche', *The Monist*, 64 (1981), 247–61.

52 'References to the "Ur-Eine" are not restricted only to his early writings, where he still accepted the Kantian distinction between the noumenal and the phenomenal, and the Schopenhauerian separation of the world as will and idea, primal unity and its objectifications. There are also references to primal Oneness, the "Ur-Eine," in his later works. But, on the whole, Nietzsche's position must be interpreted as a denial of the duality of the empirical and the noumenal will. This is particularly true after 1881, the period during which the concept of the eternal recurrence was developed' (Rose Pfeffer, *Nietzsche: Disciple of Dionysus* (Lewisburg, 1972), p. 152. See Kurt Hübner's remark below.

53 'Der spätere Nietzsche hat schließlich auch das Dionysische in Psychologie aufgelöst und so dem griechischen Mythos jenen "objektiven" Rest geraubt, den er ihm noch in seinem Buch "Die Geburt der Tragödie" zugesprochen hatte' ['The later Nietzsche finally dissolves the Dionysian into psychology, thus depriving the Greek myth of that "subjective" remnant which in *The Birth of Tragedy* he had still imputed to it'] (Kurt Hübner, *Die Wahrheit des Mythos* (Munich, 1985), pp. 58–59).

54 *Eranos-Jahrbuch 1940–1941* (Zurich, 1942), pp. 65–155.

> Der Logos ist recht eigentlich das principium individuationis, denn aus ihm ist alles hervorgegangen, und alles, was ist, existiert in individueller Form vom Kristall bis zum Menschen. In diesen vielfach geteilten und durch unendliche Verschiedenheit differenzierten Erscheinungen drückt sich das Wesen des auctor rerum aus. Dem entspricht einerseits das Selbst mit der Unbestimmtheit und Unbegrenztheit seiner unbewußten Existenz (trotz seiner Einmaligkeit und Einzigartigkeit!) und seinem Schöpferverhältnis zum individuellen Bewußtsein, andererseits der individuelle Mensch als Erscheinungsform des Selbst. Die antike Philosophie hat diesen Gedanken an die Legende vom zerstückelten Dionysos angelehnt, welcher als Schöpfer der ἀμέριστος νοῦς, als Geschöpf aber der μεμερισμένος νοῦς [= 'der nichtgeteilte und geteilte Geist']. Dionysos ist durch die ganze Natur ausgeteilt, und wie Zeus einst das noch zuckende Herz des Gottes verschlang, so zerfleischten auch seine Gläubigen wilde Tiere, um den zerstückelten Geist des Dionysos wieder zu integrieren [...] Dem entspricht psychologisch die Integration des Selbst durch Bewußtmachung abgespaltener Inhalte. Selbstbesinnung ist ein Sich-selber-Sammeln (GW11 § 400).

> [The Logos is the real *principium individuationis*, because everything proceeds from it, and because everything which is, from crystal to Man, exists only in individual form. In the infinite variety and differentiation of the phenomenal world is expressed the essence of the *auctor rerum*. As a correspondence we have, on the one hand, the indefiniteness and unlimited extent of the unconscious Self (despite its individuality and uniqueness), its creative relation to individual consciousness, and, on the other hand, the individual human being as a mode of its manifestation. Ancient philosophy paralleled this idea with the legend of the dismembered Dionysos, who, as creator, is the ἀμέριστος (undivided) νοῦς, and, as the creature, the μεμερισμένος (divided) νοῦς. Dionysos is distributed throughout the whole of nature, and just as Zeus once devoured the throbbing heart of the god, so his worshippers tore wild animals to pieces in order to reintegrate his dismembered spirit ... The psychological equivalent of this is the integration of the Self through conscious assimilation of the split-off contents. Self-recollection is a gathering together of the Self.]

By smashing the *principium individuationis*, the Dionysian experience takes place outside time and space so that we can know nothing of it: the Dionysian moment requires Apollinian form before we can experience it in tragedy. The Jungian concept of the Self is equally unknowable. Indeed, the achievement of the Self is posited as an ideal, unrealizable in the reality of history, society or human existence.

Like Nietzsche's self, Jung's notion is not one of simple stasis but implies great activity, and is best understood in terms of the image which Jung used in 'Zur Psychologie der Schelmenfigur' ['On the Psychology of the Trickster Figure'] (1954)[55] and in *Mysterium Coniunctionis* (1955/56) – the living unity of a waterfall which dynamically mediates between the two symbolic opposites of above and below (GW9(i) § 484 and GW14(ii) § 339, 365/CW14 § 674, 705–06).

---

[55] Originally published as part of *Der göttliche Schelm* (Zurich, 1954) by Paul Radin, with commentaries by Jung and Károly Kerényi.

Jung says that, although we can find 'empirical' evidence of the Self in the symbols of the mandala and witness the effects of the 'transcendent function' in pathology, we cannot 'know' the Self, as indeed we cannot know any archetype. We could only 'be' the Self and, given the impossibility of achieving this union of opposites, Jung is faced in the end with four alternatives. First, he can push the moment of union into a putative afterlife, rather in the same way that he accuses Goethe of transferring the 'coniunctio' at the end of *Faust II* into the 'Jenseits' (GW12 § 559). We can see Jung trying to do this in his autobiography, most obviously in the chapter entitled 'Über das Leben nach dem Tode' ['On Life after Death'], which starts off with the alarming remark: 'Was ich Ihnen über das Jenseits und über ein Leben nach dem Tode erzähle, sind alles Erinnerungen' ['What I have to tell about the hereafter, and about life after death, consists entirely of memories'] (ETG: p. 302/MDR: p. 330)! ('Erinnerungen' as opposed to 'Träume' or 'Gedanken', one supposes...) And, Jung speculated, that afterlife will be, like God and Nature, 'großartig [...] und furchtbar' ['grand and terrible'] (ETG: p. 323/MDR: p. 352). Second, he can admit that his whole project is not just psychological but metaphysical, and return to the ontology which he had laid out amid much mystification in his *VII Sermones ad mortuos* (1916). For example, although *Antwort auf Hiob*, not Jung's last work but arguably the most significant and original of his post-war period, makes no mention at all of Nietzsche, it clearly operates within the dualistic ontology of Nietzsche's *Die Geburt der Tragödie*, which Jung had already taken over in the Gnostic terminology employed in the *VII Sermones ad mortuos*. But Jung still poses ostensibly as a psychologist, not as a metaphysician, although this is patently untrue.[56] Third, Jung can say that he is waiting for an historical moment to arrive when what is impossible now will become possible, just as Nietzsche's Revaluation of all Values became a historical moment which he believed was on the point of occurring.[57] This move is tentatively made in several of his later works and finally becomes explicit in *Antwort auf Hiob*. There he spoke of the Incarnation as an 'historisches Ereignis' ['historical event'] (GW11 § 633) of immense significance in the psychological development of

[56] J. Harley Chapman gives two convincing reasons why Jung resisted any description of Analytical Psychology as in any sense metaphysical: 'First, the tactical reason is that acceptance of metaphysics in the late nineteenth- and early twentieth-century milieu could have jeopardized his scientific undertakings and standing in the scientific community [...] The strategic reason [...] is Jung's understanding of metaphysics as providing empty knowledge, a "news from nowhere"' (*Jung's Three Theories of Religious Experience* (Lewiston, NY, 1988), pp. 135–36).

[57] In his final months of sanity, Nietzsche believed that his final book (to be called *Der Wille zur Macht* or *Umwertung aller Werte*) would bring about a world-historical moment of change. Similarly, in his letter to Peter Gast of 9 December 1888, Nietzsche wrote that *Ecce Homo* would split the history of the world in two: 'es sprengt, wörtlich, die *Geschichte* der Menschheit in zwei Stücke' ['it literally explodes the history of humanity into two'] (N3: p. 1338).

both God and Man: 'im gleichen Maße, in dem Gott Mensch zu werden sich anschickt, [wird] der Mensch in das pleromatische Geschehen eingetaucht' ['in the same measure as God sets out to become Man, Man is immersed in the pleromatic process'] (GW11 § 677). At the end of the book, Jung seemed to hint that he, too, looked forward to another such change, which he obliquely called the 'Christification of many', leading to the possible advent of the 'God-Man':

> Durch die Einwohnung der dritten göttlichen Person im Menschen, nämlich des Heiligen Geistes, entsteht eine Christifikation vieler, und dann erhebt sich das Problem, ob diese vielen lauter totale Gottmenschen seien (GW11 § 758).
>
> [The indwelling of the Holy Ghost, the third Divine Person, in Man, brings about a Christification of many, and the question then arises whether these many are all complete God-Men.]

Fourth, Jung can rescue himself by appealing to the position which Nietzsche adopted in his perspectivism,[58] i.e. an extreme relativism, and argue that Analytical Psychology is just his version of the 'truth', his own personal 'myth'. For Jung's late writings also represent a return to the early Nietzsche in their emphasis on the importance of myth.

Myth

In 'Der Dichter und das Phantasieren' ['Creative Writers and Day-Dreaming'], which was first given as a lecture in Vienna in 1907, Freud had suggested that myths represented collective wish-phantasies,[59] and in the same year Otto Rank had said much the same thing in *Der Künstler: Ansätze zur einer Sexualpsychologie* [*The Artist: Towards a Sexual Psychology*].[60] Ever since *Wandlungen und Symbole der Libido* (1911/12), Jung had taken this idea and run with it as far and as fast as he could. In all his psychological writings, mythology is read for its archetypal content, and any work by Jung contains numerous mythological references. Jung's most explicit statements on the importance of myth are made in his

---

[58] For further discussion of Nietzsche's theory of truth and his perspectivism, see Alan D. Schrift, *Nietzsche and the Question of Interpretation* (New York and London,1990), pp. 144–68; Maudemarie Clark, *Nietzsche on Truth and Philosophy* (Cambridge, 1990); Bruce Detwiler, *Nietzsche and the Politics of Aristocratic Radicalism* (Chicago and London, 1990), pp. 17–27; and Nehamas, pp. 42–73.

[59] 'Die Untersuchung dieser völkerpsychologischen Bildungen ist nun keineswegs abgeschlossen, aber es ist z. B. von den Mythen durchaus wahrscheinlich, daß sie den entstellten Überresten von Wunschphantasien ganzer Nationen, den *Säkularträumen* der jungen Menschheit, entsprechen' ['Investigation into these national psychological forms has in no way been completed, but it is, for example, highly probably that myths correspond to the distorted vestiges of desire fantasies of entire nations, the timeless dreams of young humanity'] (Freud, *Gesammelte Werke*, 18 vols (Frankfurt am Main, 1968–1978), VII, pp. 213–223 (p. 222).

[60] Otto Rank, *Der Künstler: Ansätze zu einer Sexualpsychologie* (Vienna, 1907), p. 36.

autobiography, and to conclude my chronological survey of his writings I shall examine these remarks and compare them with some of Nietzsche's in *Die Geburt der Tragödie.*

In their concern for myth, both Nietzsche and Jung revive a specifically Romantic fascination. For example, in *Das älteste Systemprogramm des deutschen Idealismus* [*The Oldest Systematic Programme of German Idealism*] (1796), Hegel, together with Schelling and Hölderlin, boldly declared: 'die Mythologie muß philosophisch werden und das Volk vernünftig, und die Philosophie muß mythologisch werden, um die Philosophen sinnlich zu machen' ['mythology must become philosophical, the people rational, and philosophy must become mythological, to make the philosophers sensuous'].[61] In *Athenäum* (1798–1800), Friedrich Schlegel defined poetry as mythology, the modern counterpart of religion: 'Der Kern, das Zentrum der Poesie ist in der Mythologie zu finden, und in den Mysterien der Alten. Denn Mythologie und Poesie, beide sind Eins und unzertrennlich' ['The core, the centre of poetry is to be found in mythology, and in the mysteries of the ancients. For both mythology and poetry are one and indivisible'].[62] And in *Die Weltalter* [*The Ages of the World*] (1811), Schelling looked forward to a 'golden age' which would synthesize truth and fable.[63] Because Schlegel and Schelling were so widely read in the middle of the previous century, Martin Vogel is virtually certain that Nietzsche was familiar with their work.[64]

Nietzsche's concern with myth forms both an important part of his early and his late writing[65] and a counterpart to his reflections on the collapse of religion. In *Die Geburt der Tragödie*, Nietzsche had written of the disastrous consequences for modern society of the loss of myths which had brought cohesion, identity and purpose:

> Die Bilder des Mythus müssen die unbemerkt allgegenwärtigen dämonischen Wächter sein, unter deren Hut die junge Seele heranwächst, an deren Zeichen der Mann sich sein Leben und seine Kämpfe deutet: und selbst der Staat kennt keine

---

61 Hegel, I, pp. 234–36 (p. 236).

62 Friedrich Schlegel, *Athenäum* (Berlin, 1798–1800), III, 18, 96).

63 'Es wird Eine Welt seyn, und der Friede des goldnen Zeitalters zuerst in der einträchtigen Verbindung aller Wissenschaften sich verkünden [...] Vielleicht kommt der noch, der das größte Heldengedicht singt, im Geist umfassend, wie von Sehern der Vorzeit gerühmt wird, was war, was ist, und was seyn wird' ['There will be one world, and the peace of the golden age will announce itself first of all in the amicable conjunction of all the sciences. Perhaps he, too, will come, who sings the greatest heroic poem, embracing in spirit, for which he was extolled by the prophets of prehistoric times, what was, what is and what will be'] (Schelling, IV, p. 582).

64 Martin Vogel, *Apollinisch und Dionysisch* (Regensburg, 1966), p. 96. Vogel also points out that the *Nachlaß* material from Nietzsche's early years contains references to Schlegel.

65 For further discussion of Nietzsche's thinking on mythology in general and in *Die Geburt der Tragödie* in particular, see Benjamin Bennett, 'Nietzsche's Idea of Myth: The Birth of Tragedy from the Spirit of Eighteenth-Century Aesthetics', *PMLA*, 94 (1979), 420–33; Hugh Ridley, 'Myth as Illusion or Cognition: Feuerbach, Wagner and Nietzsche', *GLL*, 34 (1980/81), 74–80.

mächtigeren ungeschriebnen Gesetze als das mythische Fundament [...] (GT/BT § 23; N1: p. 125).

[The images of myth have to be the unnoticed omnipresent daemonic guardians, under whose care the young soul grows to maturity and whose signs help the man to interpret his life and struggles. Even the state knows no more powerful unwritten laws than the mythical foundation.]

Furthermore, in the same work, Nietzsche also pointed to the Faustian strivings of 'der moderne Kulturmensch' ['modern cultured Man'] as evidence that he was beginning to discover the limits of the Socratic love of knowledge and to yearn 'aus dem weiten wüsten Wissensmeere nach einer Küste' ['for a coast in the wide waste of the ocean of knowledge'] (GT/BT § 18; N1: p. 100). In the fourth of his *Unzeitgemässe Betrachtungen*, 'Richard Wagner in Bayreuth' (1876), Nietzsche repeated his earlier encomium of Richard Wagner in *Die Geburt der Tragödie*, praising Wagner because of his ability 'den Mythus ins Männliche zurückzuschaffen und die Musik zu entzaubern, zum Reden zu bringen' ['to restore to the myth its manliness, and to take the spell from music and bring it to speech'] (UB/UM IV § 8; N1: 406), and defined Wagner's *Ring*-cycle in terms of its relation to myth (UB/UM IV § 9; N1: p. 413).

Nietzsche later claimed that these remarks on Wagner applied to his own philosophy, too, and presumably so do his references to the importance of myth. Looking back in *Ecce Homo* on his essay from the perspective of over a decade and with madness imminent, he commented: 'an allen psychologisch entscheidenden Stellen ist nur von mir die Rede' ['in all the psychologically decisive passages I am the only person referred to'], adding: 'Das ganze Bild des *dithyrambischen* Künstlers ist das Bild des *präexistenten* Dichters des Zarathustra' ['The entire picture of the *dithyrambic artist* is a picture of the *pre-existent poet* of Zarathustra'] (EH GT/BT § 4; N2: p. 1112). For *Also sprach Zarathustra* is Nietzsche's answer to the need for myth, bringing with it the new mystical doctrine of the Eternal Recurrence. As Giorgio Colli has observed, there is an 'eminent mystische und mysterienhafte Anlage' ['eminently mystical and mysterious conception'] in Nietzsche's philosophy.[66] How the concern to found, in the words of *Das älteste Systemprogramm des deutschen Idealismus*, 'eine neue Mythologie' fits into Nietzsche's project as a whole can be seen from a note in the *Nachlaß* from Autumn 1883:

Um schaffen zu können, müssen wir selber uns größere Freiheit geben als je uns gegeben wurde; dazu Befreiung von der Moral und Erleichterung durch Feste (Ahnungen der Zukunft! die Zukunft feiern, nicht die Vergangenheit! Den Mythus der Zukunft dichten! In der Hoffnung leben!) Selige Augenblicke! Und dann wieder den Vorhang zuhängen und *die Gedanken zu festen, nächsten Zielen* wenden![67]

---

[66] Giorgio Colli, *Nach Nietzsche* (Frankfurt am Main, 1980), p. 19.

[67] Nietzsche, *KGW*, VII 1, 21 [6], p. 638.

[In order to be able to create, we must give ourselves greater freedom than has been given us before; at the same time, liberation from morality and relief through festivals (premonitions of the future! celebrate the future, not the past! compose the myth of the future! live in hope!). Blissful moments! And then cover up the curtain again and turn *our thoughts to fixed, close goals*!]

Jung's concern with myth dates back to his reading of Friedrich Creuzer's *Symbolik und Mythologie der alten Völker* (1810–23), Richard Payne Knight's *A Discourse on the Worship of Priapus* (1865) – and Nietzsche's *Die Geburt der Tragödie*. In his key letter to Freud of 11 February 1910, Jung had rejected Alfred Knapp's idea for an 'Internationaler Orden für Ethik und Kultur' and argued instead that psychoanalysis represented a unique opportunity to return to myth (FJB: pp. 323–34/FJL: p. 294). And as I have argued throughout this book, there can be no doubt about the Dionysian content of the myth to which Jung wished to return:

Eine echte und rechte ethische Entwicklung kann das Christentum nicht lassen, sondern muß in ihm emporwachsen, muß seinen Hymnus der Liebe, den Schmerz und das Entzücken über den sterbenden und wiedererstehenden Gott, die mystische Kraft des Weines und die anthropophagischen Schauer des Abendmahles zur Vollendung führen – nur *diese* ethische Entwicklung macht sich die Lebenskräfte der Religion dienstbar (FJB: p. 324/FJL: p. 294).

[A genuine and proper ethical development cannot abandon Christianity but must grow up within it, must bring to fruition its hymn of love, the agony and ecstasy over the dying and resurgent god, the mystic power of the wine, the awesome anthropophagy of the Last Supper – only *this* ethical development can serve the vital forces of religion.]

In *Wandlungen und Symbole der Libido* (1911/12), Jung claimed that philosophy was 'innerlich' ['internally'] nothing other than a refined and sublimated form of mythology (WSL: p. 397/PU § 681), and even went so far as to suggest that archetypal limitations were inherent in the language of philosophy (WSL: p. 311/ PU § 514). In 'Über die Archetypen des kollektiven Unbewußten' ['Archetypes of the Collective Unconscious'] (1934), Jung argued that one of the roads to the archetypal structures was language: 'Die Singebung bedient sich gewisser sprachlicher Matrizen, die ihrerseits wieder von urtümlichen Bildern abstammen. Wir können diese Frage anfassen, wo wir wollen, überall geraten wir in die Sprach- und Motivgeschichte, die immer stracks in die primitive Wunderwelt zurückführt' ['Interpretations make use of certain linguistic matrices that are themselves derived from primordial images. From whatever side we approach this question, everywhere we find ourselves confronted with the history of language, with images and motifs that lead straight back to the primitive wonderworld'] (GW9(i) § 67). Clearly, this view of language is much closer to that of

Schelling[68] than that of Nietzsche in *Über Wahrheit und Lüge im außermoralischen Sinn* [*On Truth and Lies in a Nonmoral Sense*] (N3: pp. 309–323) and in *Götzen-Dämmerung* (GD/TI 3 § 6; N2: p. 960). And in 'Die psychologischen Aspekten des Mutterarchetypus' ['Psychological Aspects of the Mother Archetype'] (1934), Jung had moved from a Kantian transcendental position which seeks to uncover necessary laws to a relativistic view of *Verstand* and *Vernunft* as arbitrarily determined, sometimes irrational psychic functions (GW9(i) § 150).

Jung's autobiography – treated in my chronological survey as his last major publication – is saturated with references to the importance of myth. In the prologue to *Erinnerungen, Träume, Gedanken*, Jung made it plain that he conceived of his autobiography less as an exercise in documentation and more as an exercise in mythopoiesis: 'Was man der inneren Anschauung nach ist, und was der Mensch sub specie aeternitatis zu sein scheint, kann man nur durch einen Mythus ausdrücken' ['What we are to our inward vision, and what Man appears to be *sub specie aeternitatis*, can only be expressed by way of myth'] (ETG: p. 10/ MDR: p. 17). Like the opening of *Ecce Homo*, where Nietzsche presents himself as the 'Erzähler' of his own life, Jung tells himself the story of his life:

> An diesem vollkommnen Tage, wo alles reift und nicht nur die Traube braun wird, fiel mir eben ein Sonnenblick auf mein Leben [...] Nicht umsonst begrub ich heute mein vierundvierzigstes Jahr, ich *durfte* es begraben [...] *Wie sollte ich nicht meinem ganzen Leben dankbar sein?* – Und so erzähle ich mir mein Leben (EH; N2: p. 1069).
>
> [On this perfect day, when everything has become ripe and not only the grapes are growing brown, a ray of sunlight has fallen onto my life ... Not in vain have I buried my forty-fourth year today, I was *entitled* to bury it ... *How should I not be grateful to my whole life?* – And so I tell myself my life.]
>
> So habe ich es heute, in meinem dreiundachtzigsten Lebensjahr, unternommen, den Mythus meines Lebens zu erzählen (ETG: p. 10/MDR: p. 17).
>
> [Thus it is that I have undertaken, in my eighty-third year, to tell the myth of my life. (P. B.)]

Just as Nietzsche argued that what was necessary for life might not in itself be true (FW/GS § 121; N2: p. 124; cf. JGB/BGE § 4; N2: p. 569; and WM/WP 483 = N3: p. 915) and, admitting that his philosophy consisted of *his* truths (and not necessarily those of other people), embraced perspectivism, so Jung underplayed the significance of the truth-content of one's personal myth and emphasized instead the importance of its existential validity:

---

68 'Die Sprache selbst sey nur die verblichene Mythologie, in ihr sey nur in abstracten und formellen Unterschieden bewahrt, was die Mythologie noch in lebendigen und concreten bewahre' ['Language itself is only faded mythology, in it is retained in abstract and formal differences what mythology retains in living and concrete ones'] (F. W. J. Schelling, *Sämtliche Werke*, Part I, vols.1–10, Part II, vols 1–4 (Stuttgart, 1856–1861), II, 1, p. 152).

> Ich kann jedoch nur unmittelbare Feststellungen machen, nur "Geschichten erzählen". Ob sie wahr sind, ist kein Problem. Die Frage ist nur, ist es *mein* Märchen, *meine* Wahrheit? (ETG: p. 10/MDR: p. 17).
>
> [I can only make direct statements, only "tell stories". Whether or not they are true is not a problem. The only question is whether what I tell is *my* fable, *my* truth. (P.B.)]

Like Nietzsche, Jung considered that the loss of myth had atrophied man's instincts and sensitivities. Agreeing with Kant's view that we are lodged within the phenomenal world of the categories, but nonetheless unable fully to accept that limitation, Jung suggested that myth provides us with the only opportunity to transcend the life of the *principium individuationis*, and acts as a therapy for 'das Gemüt':

> Der mythische Mensch verlangt zwar ein "Darüber-Hinausgehen", aber der wissenschaftlich verantwortliche Mensch kann es nicht zulassen. Für den Verstand ist das "mythologein" eine sterile Spekulation, für das Gemüt aber bedeutet es eine heilende Lebenstätigkeit; sie verleiht dem Dasein einen Glanz, welchen man nicht missen möchte (ETG: p. 303/MDR: p. 331).
>
> [Mythic Man, to be sure, demands a "going beyond", but scientific Man cannot permit this. To the understanding, all mythologizing is futile speculation; to the mind or soul, however, it is a healing activity of life. It gives existence a gleam which we would not like to do without (P. B.).]

However, he also admitted that an excess of myth could be equally dangerous: 'Umgekehrt bedeutet aber die Berücksichtigung der mythischen Ansätze auch eine Gefahr für schwache und suggestible Geister, Ahnungen für Erkenntnisse zu halten und Phantasmata zu hypostasieren' ['too much traffic with these germs of myth is dangerous for weak and suggestible minds, for they are led to mistake vague intimations for substantial knowledge, and to hypostatize mere phantasms'] (ETG: p. 319/MDR: p. 348). But, whereas Nietzsche had argued that the beliefs of the 'Hinterweltler' had ruined this world and devalued the earth, Jung reversed this argument and blamed recent political upheavals and the 'demonisation' of the world on the collapse of the belief in transcendence:

> Die Erscheinung der Diktatoren und all des Elends, das sie gebracht haben, geht darauf zurück, daß dem Menschen durch die Kurzsichtigkeit der Allzuklugen die Jenseitigkeit geraubt wurde. Wie diese ist auch er der Unbewußtheit zum Opfer gefallen (ETG: pp. 328–29/MDR: pp. 357–58).
>
> [The phenomenon of dictators and all the misery they have wrought springs from the fact that Man has been robbed of transcendence by the shortsightedness of the super-intellectuals. Like them, he has fallen a victim to consciousness.]

Recognizing that a myth is dead 'wenn er nicht mehr lebt und sich nicht mehr weiter entwickelt' ['if it no longer lives and grows'], Jung concluded with respect to Christianity that 'unser Mythus ist stumm geworden und gibt keine Antwort' ['our myth has become mute, and gives no answers'] and that 'uns kein Mythus zu Hilfe kommt, dessen wir doch so dringend bedürften' ['no myth will come to our aid although we have such urgent need of one'] (ETG: pp. 334–35/MDR: pp. 364–65). However, by translating theological dogma into psychological statement (ETG: p. 339/MDR: p. 369), Jung felt that he was able to preserve the sense of Christianity whilst at the same time radically transforming it. For he argued that the dualism which placed 'ein ewiger dunkler Widersacher' ['an eternal dark antagonist'] next to 'das allmächtige Gute' ['the omnipotent Goodness'] must give way to a more sophisticated understanding of the God-concept, similar to that anticipated by Nicolas of Cusa (1401–1464) and Jakob Böhme (1575–1624), in the *coniunctio* of the alchemists or the mystic union of the saints. This new version of the God-concept is, of course, the archetype of the Self, which reconciles the major opposites of Jung's psychological project: consciousness and Unconscious; Christ and Dionysos; 'der "hêr Jesus"' and 'sein unterirdischer Gegenspieler'; and – as in this passage – Man and God:

> Wer es erfahren hat, daß "von Natur aus" durch das Symbol Gegensätze sich so einen können, daß sie nicht mehr auseinanderstreben und sich bekämpfen, sondern sich gegenseitig ergänzen und das Leben sinnvoll gestalten, dem wird die Ambivalenz im Bild eines Natur- und Schöpfergottes keine Schwierigkeiten verursachen. Er wird im Gegenteil den Mythus von der notwendigen Menschwerdung Gottes, der essentiellen christlichen Botschaft, als schöpferische Auseinandersetzung des Menschen mit den Gegensätzen und ihre Synthese im Selbst, der Ganzheit seiner Persönlichkeit, verstehen (ETG: pp. 340–41/MDR: p. 370).
>
> [Once it has been experienced that symbols, by their very nature, can so unite the opposites that these no longer diverge or clash, but mutually supplement one another and give meaningful experience to life, then the ambivalence in the image of a nature-god and a creator-god cease to present difficulties. On the contrary, the myth of the necessary incarnation of God, the essence of the Christian message, can then be understood as Man's creative confrontation with the opposites and their synthesis in the Self, the wholeness of his personality (P. B.).]

At the end of *Ecce Homo*, Nietzsche wrote: '– Hat man mich verstanden? – *Dionysos gegen den Gekreuzigten...*' ['– Have I been understood? – *Dionysos against the Crucified...*'] (EH IV § 9; N2: p. 1159). For the late Jung, such an opposition made no sense. The opposites must be united! Thus Man and God (symbolically representing all other pairs of opposites) are brought together in the concept of the Self (indeed a *mysterium coniunctionis*) – and this is Jung's myth, the central myth which underlies the 'religion' of Analytical Psychology in the face of the 'Death of God'. For, as both Jung and Nietzsche knew, myth is the precondition of religion: 'der Mythus, die notwendige Voraussetzung jeder Religion' ['myth, the necessary prerequisite of every religion'] (GT/BT § 18; N1: p. 100–01):

> In der Erfahrung des Selbst wird nicht mehr, wie früher, der Gegensatz "Gott und Mensch" überbrückt, sondern der Gegensatz im Gottesbild [...] Es ist ein erklä-

render Mythus, der langsam im Lauf der Jahrzehnte in mir gewachsen ist (ETG: p. 341).

[In the experience of the Self it is no longer the opposites "God" and "Man" that are reconciled, as it was before, but rather the opposites within the God-image itself … It is an explanatory myth which has slowly taken shape within me in the course of the decades (MDR: pp. 370–71).]

Chapter 14

Conclusion

In *Wandlungen und Symbole der Libido* [*Psychology of the Unconscious*] (1911/12), Jung described 'die Urgewalt [...] das Bedingungslose und Unerbittliche, Ungerechte und Übermenschliche' ['the primitive power ... the unconditional and inexorable, the unjust and the superhuman'] (WSL: p. 72/PU § 111) as 'echte und rechte Attribute der Libido' ['truly and rightly attributes of the libido']. He added: 'Es gibt nichts anderes, als daß der Mensch mit diesem Willen zusammengehe, was uns Nietzsches Zarathustra eindringlich lehrt' ['Nothing remains for Mankind but to work in harmony with this Will. Nietzsche's Zarathustra teaches us this impressively']. In this book, I have argued that Jung's reading of Nietzsche provided him with a means to create the conceptual space in which to develop Analytical Psychology as a form of psychology which was distinct in method, assumptions and intent from Freudian psychoanalysis.[1] This is not to say, however, that the Jungian concept of the libido can be simply equated with Nietzsche's concept of the Will to Power (or, for that matter, with Schopenhauer's Will to Life) (cf. WSL: pp. 130, 139/PU § 212, 223). On the one hand, Jung attributes an essential ambivalence to his concept of libido as 'psychic energy' which perpetually introverts and regresses, to be then reborn, like the dying and rising Dionysos. What, for Jung, is an intra-psychic pattern is, for Nietzsche, the Dionysian view of the world as the Will to Power: 'diese meine *dionysische* Welt des Ewig-sich-selber-Schaffens, des Ewig-sich-selber-Zerstörens [...] ein Meer in sich selber stürmender und flutender Kräfte, ewig sich wandelnd, ewig zurücklaufend, mit ungeheuren Jahren der Wiederkehr' ['this, my

[1] The difference between Freud and Jung on the question of archetypes and the inheritance of archaic material is, however, arguably quite small. A number of passages from Freud sound very Jungian. In 'Eine Kindheitserinnerung des Leonardo da Vinci' ['Leonardo da Vinci and a Memory of his Childhood'] (1910), which Jung acclaimed in his letter to Freud of 17 June 1910 as 'wunderbar' ['wonderful'], Freud brings in numerous literary and mythological references to explain Leonardo's childhood fantasy of the vulture (*Gesammelte Werke*, 18 vols (Frankfurt am Main, 1968–1978), VIII, pp. 127–211). In 'Zeitgemäßes über Krieg und Tod' ['Thoughts for the Times on War and Death'] (1915), Freud used the notion that characteristics of the primitive mind could still manifest themselves (regression) to help explain the First World War (X, pp. 324–55 (p. 337). And in 'Das Ich und das Es' ['The Ego and the Id'] (1923), Freud spoke of an 'archaic inheritance' (XIII, pp. 237–89 (p. 265)).

Dionysian world of the eternally self-creating, the eternally self-destroying ... a sea of forces flowing and rushing together, eternally changing, eternally flooding back, with tremendous years of recurrence'] (WM/WP 1067 = N3: pp. 916–17). On the other hand, this last concept, the Eternal Recurrence, marks the end of the similarities in outlook between Jung and Nietzsche and the first point of a number of important differences.

First, Nietzsche presents the Eternal Recurrence as the ultimate absence of meaning: 'die extremste Form des Nihilismus: das Nichts (das "Sinnlose") ewig!' ['the most extreme form of Nihilism: the nothing (the "meaningless"), eternally!'] (WM/WP 55 = N3: p. 853). In contrast, Jung argues that there *is* meaning, and that it is dependent upon interpretation (GW9(i) § 65–67). Second, any residual meaning within Nietzsche's system is located within the Will to Power itself, in the form of relationships within that disposition to will: 'Aller Sinn ist Wille zur Macht (alle Beziehungs-Sinne lassen sich in ihn auflösen)' ['All meaning is Will to Power (all relative meaning resolves itself into it)'] (WM 590 = N3: p. 503). Indeed, Nietzsche holds that interpretation is a function of the Will to Power ('Der Wille zur Macht *interpretiert*' ['The Will to Power *interprets*'] (WM/WP 643 = N3: p. 489), so that all interpretation (i.e. all Will to Truth) is also a Will to Power (JGB/BGE § 9, 22; N2: pp. 573 and 586). In contrast, Jung believes that by following the pattern of introversion and rebirth into the Dionysian Self (a process mediated by the (archetypal) symbol), we are opened up to those very archetypal structures which are, for him, the source of meaning. Indeed, *Erinnerungen, Träume, Gedanken* [*Memories, Dreams, Reflections*] is saturated with references to the meaning of dreams and psychological disorders and to a putative 'meaning of life' (e.g. ETG: pp. 131–33, 249, 255, 259–60, 280, 320–21, 342–43, 360/MDR: pp. 146–49, 274, 280–81, 284–85, 306, 350–51, 371–73, 391–92). However, as I suggested in Chapter 13, Jung ultimately rejected the doctrine of the Will to Power (to the extent that he understood it), as his marginal annotations in his edition of Nietzsche's *Werke* confirm. And third, Nietzsche sees in the Eternal Recurrence a radical denial of all teleology and 'purpose': 'Die absolute Notwendigkeit *ganz von Zwecken zu befreien* [...] Erst die Unschuld des Werdens gibt uns den *größten Mut* und die *größte Freiheit*!' ['The absolute necessity of a total liberation from ends ... Only the innocence of becoming gives us the *greatest courage* and the *greatest freedom*!'] (WM/WP 787 = N3: p. 891). In contrast, within Jung's system, the pattern of regression and progression of the libido *does* have a (threefold) purpose: 'the daily advance of psychological adaptation', the unification of the opposites and the birth of the Dionysian Self.

This brings us to another area of difference over and above their differing attitudes towards the Will to Power. For Nietzsche, the Self remains something that must be *created* since only self-overcoming can bring about the Superman.

But for Jung, the Self is something to be *discovered*, so that the 'unifying' character of the symbol of totality is held to be universally valid. Moreover, Jung posits a principle of integration in human nature which he misleadingly calls 'Geist' and believes that we can always have recourse to the archetypes of the Collective Unconscious. In contrast, for Nietzsche, there is no such thing as 'human nature' (WM/WP 120 = N3: p. 616), at least not in the conventional sense (GD/TI 9 § 48; N2: p. 1023). For Nietzsche, the 'Death of God' and the advent of Nihilism have unchained the earth from the sun and made 'tolle Menschen' of us all. So it is non-metaphysical transcendence to which the 'komplementärer Mensch, in dem das *übrige* Dasein sich rechtfertigt' ['complementary Man in whom the *rest* of existence is justified'] (JGB/BGE § 207; N2: p. 669) must turn. This divergence is also reflected in the way in which Nietzsche and Jung placed their hopes in myth. Yet here too an important difference separates them.

Whereas Nietzsche both turns back to Greek antiquity and looks forward to the gospel of the future ('*Incipit Zarathustra*'), Jung tends to look back only to the past – or rather, very far back *in* the past. Arguably, Analytical Psychology is more an extension of alchemy, Gnosticism and Christian mysticism than anything radically new, and this is precisely what Jung intended.[2] Indeed, in his autobiography, Jung wrote of his delight at discovering what he thought were his ideas in ancient alchemical texts:

> Sehr bald hatte ich gesehen, daß die Analytische Psychologie mit der Alchemie merkwürdig übereinstimmt. Die Erfahrungen der Alchemisten waren meine Erfahrungen, und ihre Welt war in gewissem Sinne meine Welt. Das war für mich natürlich eine ideale Entdeckung, denn damit hatte ich das historische Gegenstück zu meiner Psychologie des Unbewußten gefunden. Sie erhielt nun einen geschichtlichen Boden. Die Möglichkeit des Vergleichs mit der Alchemie, sowie die geistige Kontinuität bis zurück zum Gnostizismus gaben ihr die Substanz (ETG: p. 209/MDR: p. 231).
>
> [I had very soon seen that Analytical Psychology coincided in a most curious way with alchemy. The experiences of the alchemists were, in a sense, my experiences, and their world was my world. This was, of course, a momentous discovery: I had stumbled upon the historical counterpart of my psychology of the Unconscious. It now had an historical basis. The possibility of a comparison with alchemy, and the uninterrupted intellectual chain back to Gnosticism, gave substance to my psychology.]

Thus, Jung's psychic archaeology is a relatively straightforward matter: the archetypal text can easily be read off from dreams, myths and religious cultic practices. Now, although Nietzsche wished to cultivate 'den *historischen Sinn*' ['the *historical* sense'] (JGB/BGE § 224; N2: p. 686), he also recognized that the 'Grundtext *homo natura*' ['basic text of *homo natura*'] has been distorted and rendered opaque (JGB/BGE § 230; N2: p. 696) so that the genealogical task of tracing the Will

[2] As Leon Surette has recently pointed out: 'Like Creuzer and the theosophists, Jung believed in a single revelation, a single tradition of Gnosis' (*The Birth of Modernism* (Montreal, 1993), p. 198).

to Power is hindered, since each new configuration erases the meaning of the preceding one (GM II § 12; N2: p. 818). The uncertainty of interpretation is another reason why Nietzsche cannot participate in nostalgia for the mythical past, a luxury in which Jung indulges to the utmost.

This difference between the two men in their attitude towards myth, as well as in their general approach to History, is encapsulated in the different ways in which each uses one particular image. This is the image of the root, a pervasive image throughout Jung's later writings. For example, in the Terry lectures on Psychology and Religion, delivered at Yale University in 1937, Jung said:

> Das Symptom ist wie ein Pflanzenschößling über der Erde, die Hauptpflanze ist jedoch ein ausgedehntes unterirdisches Rhizom. Dieser Wurzelstock ist der Inhalt der Neurose; er ist der Mutterboden der Komplexe, der Symptome und der Träume. Wir haben sogar guten Grund, anzunehmen, daß die Träume eben gerade die unterirdischen Prozesse der Psyche spiegeln. Und wenn wir in dieses Rhizom kommen, kommen wir buchstäblich an die "Wurzel" der Krankheit (GW11 § 37).
>
> [The symptom is like the shoot above ground, yet the main plant is an extended rhizome underground. The rhizome represents the content of a neurosis; it is the matrix of complexes, of symptoms, and of dreams. We have every reason to believe that dreams mirror exactly the underground processes of the psyche. And if we get there, we literally get at the "roots" of the disease.]

And in 'Über den Gegensatz Freud und Jung' ['Freud and Jung: Contrasts'] (first published in 1929 and revised for the fifth time in 1950), Jung wrote:

> Ergreifende, sogenannt wahre Ideen haben etwas Sonderliches an sich; sie entstammen einer Zeitlosigkeit, einem Immer-Dagewesensein, einem mütterlichen, seelischen Urgrunde, aus dem der ephemere Geist des einzelnen Menschen emporwächst wie eine Pflanze, die Blüten trägt, Frucht bringt und Samen, dahinwelkt und stirbt (GW4 § 769).
>
> [Impressive ideas which are hailed as truths have something peculiar about them; they originate in something timeless, something which has always been there, a maternal, spiritual source, out of which the ephemeral mind of the single human being grows like a plant that blossoms, bears fruit and seed, and then withers and dies. (P. B.)]

Moreover, in the foreword to the fourth, extensively revised edition of *Wandlungen und Symbole der Libido*, renamed *Symbole der Wandlung* [*Symbols of Transformation*] (1950), he wrote:

> Das individuelle Bewußtsein aber ist nur der saisongemäße Blüten- und Fruchtständer, der aus dem perennierenden unterirdischen Rhizom emporwächst, und dieser befindet sich in besserer Übereinstimmung mit der Wahrheit, wenn er die Existenz des Rhizoms mit in seine Rechnung einbezieht, denn das Wurzelgeflecht ist aller Mutter (GW5: p. 13/CW5: p.xxiv).
>
> [Individual consciousness is only the flower and the fruit of a season, sprung from the perennial rhizome beneath the earth; and it would find itself in better accord

with the truth if it took the existence of the rhizome into its calculations. For the root matter is the mother of all things.]

Finally, Jung used the same image of the root on two occasions in his autobiography. First, in the prologue where he posited an ephemeral and an eternal component to life, Jung wrote:

> Das Leben ist mir immer wie eine Pflanze vorgekommen, die aus ihrem Rhizom lebt. Ihr eigentliches Leben ist nicht sichtbar, es steckt im Rhizom. Das, was über dem Boden sichtbar wird, hält nur einen Sommer. Dann verwelkt es – eine ephemere Erscheinung. Wenn man an das endlose Werden und Vergehen des Lebens und der Kulturen denkt, erhält man den Eindruck absoluter Nichtigkeit; aber ich habe nie das Gefühl verloren für etwas, das unter dem ewigen Wechsel lebt und dauert. Was man sieht, ist die Blüte, und die vergeht. Das Rhizom dauert (ETG: p. 11/MDR: p. 18).

> [Life has always seemed to me like a plant that lives on its rhizome. Its true life is invisible, hidden in the rhizome. The part that appears above ground lasts only a single summer. Then it withers away – an ephemeral apparition. When we think of the unending growth and decay of life and civilizations, we cannot escape the impression of absolute nullity. Yet I have never lost a sense of something that lives and endures underneath the eternal flux. What we see is the blossom, which passes. The rhizome remains.]

And second, in the chapter on his school years, Jung spoke of his earliest memories – such as his phallic dream – as offshoots of a single unconscious root, which even in his old age he could not properly disentangle:

> Es ist mir bis heute, wo ich in meinem dreiundachtzigsten Lebensjahre meine Erinnerungen aufschreibe, nie ganz klar geworden, welchen Zusammenhang meine frühesten Erinnerungen haben: sie sind wie die einzelnen Schosse eines unterirdischen, zusammenhängenden Rhizoms. Sie sind wie die Stationen eines unbewußten Entwicklungsganges (ETG: p. 33/MDR: pp. 42–43).

> [To this day, writing down my memories at the age of eighty-three, I have never fully unwound the tangle of my earliest memories. They are like individual shoots of a single underground rhizome, like stations on a road of unconscious development.]

In contrast, Nietzsche rejected any suggestion that there were two worlds (a transient, phenomenal world and an invisible, noumenal world), even though *Die Geburt der Tragödie* [*The Birth of Tragedy*] worked within the ontological framework of Kantian and Schopenhauerian metaphysics and even though this dualism also hangs uneasily in the background of some of his later philosophy. There is an important passage in *Die Geburt der Tragödie* which tellingly summarizes all of what Nietzsche would have most vehemently rejected about Jung and which reads like a thumbnail sketch of Jung's psychological project to rediscover the world of myth:

> Und nun steht der mythenlose Mensch, ewig hungernd, unter allen Vergangenheiten und sucht grabend und wühlend nach Wurzeln, sei es daß er auch in den entlegen-

sten Altertümern nach ihnen graben müßte. Worauf weist das ungeheure historische Bedürfnis der unbefriedigten modernen Kultur, das Umsichsammeln zahlloser anderer Kulturen, das verzehrende Erkennenwollen, wenn nicht auf den Verlust des Mythus, auf den Verlust der mythischen Heimat, des mythischen Mutterschoßes? (GT/BT § 23; N1: p. 125).

[And now the mythless Man stands eternally hungry, surrounded by all past ages, and digs and grubs for roots, even if he has to dig for them among the remotest antiquities. The tremendous historical need of our unsatisfied modern culture, the assembling around one of countless other cultures, the consuming desire for knowledge – what does all this point to, if not to the loss of myth, the loss of the mythical home, the mythical maternal womb?]

So Nietzsche agrees with Jung that the 'Matrix der mythenbildenden Phantasie' ['matrix of a mythopoeic imagination'] has disappeared from our 'rationalem Zeitalter' ['rational age'] (ETG: p. 192/MDR: p. 213); but, unlike Jung, he insists that a return to the mythopoeic imagination is not possible except in ironic, stylized form.

Whilst acknowledging these differences between Jung and Nietzsche, I have at the same time argued that a fundamentally similar concern lies at the heart of their philosophy and psychology respectively. This central concern is symbolized for them both by an identical mythologem: Dionysos.

Jung and the Tradition: Dionysos

Both Jung and Nietzsche situate themselves within a greater tradition in German literature and thought – the Romantic yearning for the return of Dionysos, 'der kommende Gott' ['the coming god'], who is, according to Hölderlin, 'allzeit froh' ['always glad'].[3] The Romantic philosopher Schelling discussed the significance of the Dionysian in *Die Weltalter* [*The Ages of the World*] (1813) and in his *Philosophie der Offenbarung* [*Philosophy of Revelation*] (1841/42).[4] And in the same Romantic era, 'Das älteste Systemprogramm des deutschen Idealismus' ['The Oldest Systematic Programme of German Idealism'] (c.1796/97), to which

[3] Friedrich Hölderlin, 'Brod und Wein', in: *Sämtliche Werke*, 6 vols (Stuttgart, 1944–1962), II, pp. 94–99.

[4] '*So ist Alles Dionysos*' (Friedrich Wilhelm Joseph Schelling, *Philosophie der Offenbarung 1841/42*, edited by Manfred Frank (Frankfurt am Main, 1977), p. 237; *Die Weltalter*, edited by Manfred Schröter (Munich, 1946), pp. 42–43 (cf. GT/BT 20; N1: p. 113); '[...] ein kommender, ein im Kommen begriffener – denn erst am Ende und Ziel dieses Prozesses hat er sich vollständig verwirklicht' ['one who comes, who is in the process of coming – for only at the end and the goal of this process is his realization complete'] (*Sämtliche Werke*, edited by K. F. A. Schelling, Part I, 10 vols, Part II, 4 vols (Stuttgart, 1856–1861), II/2, p. 254). For a discussion of Nietzsche's indebtedness to Schelling, see Manfred Frank, *Der kommende Gott* (Frankfurt am Main, 1982), pp. 344–47.

Schelling may well have contributed, called for the creation of a 'new mythology': 'wir müssen eine neue Mythologie haben'.[5]

Although the classical scholar Winckelmann had already distinguished between two types of Greek youth and associated them and their respective aesthetic principles with Apollo and Bacchus in his *Geschichte der Kunst des Altertums* [*History of the Art of Antiquity*] (1764),[6] it was Friedrich von Schlegel who first really developed the Apollo/Dionysos dichotomy in *Über das Studium der griechischen Poesie* [*On the Study of Greek Poetry*] (written 1795–97).[7] Through Schlegel, Nietzsche became aware of the Romantic concern with myth in general and the Dionysian in particular.[8] If the Romantics were fascinated with the mythologem of Dionysos, so were their academic successors, the nineteenth-century philologists, with whose works both Nietzsche and Jung were familiar. For example, Friedrich Creuzer (1771–1858), the infamous lover of Karoline von Günderode, wrote a tract on Dionysos in 1808/09.[9] In his major work *Symbolik und Mythologie der alten Völker* [*Symbolism and Mythology of the Ancient People*] (1810/11), he devoted a complete section to various aspects of Dionysos.[10] And in an important book-review of 1817, Creuzer returned once more to the theme of Dionysos.[11] Both Nietzsche and Jung owned a copy of Creuzer's *Symbolik und Mythologie.* Jung had also probably read the chapters on Dionysos in the work on mythology by Ludwig Preller (1809–1861)[12] and the study by Pierre Nicolas

---

[5] 'Das älteste Systemprogramm des deutschen Idealismus', in G. W. F. Hegel, *Werke*, 20 vols (Frankfurt am Main, 1986), I, p. 236. For a further discussion of the authorship of this document and interpretation of it, see Christoph Jamme and Helmut Schneider, *Mythologie der Vernunft: Hegels "Ältestes Systemprogramm des deutschen Idealismus"* (Frankfurt am Main, 1984).

[6] Johann Joachim Winckelmann, 'Das Götterbild als Ideal', in *Geschichte der Kunst des Altertums,* edited by Wilhelm Senff (Weimar, 1964), pp. 136–40.

[7] 'Im Gemüte des Sophokles war die göttliche Trunkenheit des Dionysos, und die tiefe Empfindsamkeit der Athene, und die leise Besonnenheit des Apollo gleichmäßig verschmolzen' ['In the soul of Sophocles the divine intoxication of Dionysos, the deep sensitivity of Athens, and the gentle calm of Apollo were evenly blended'] (Friedrich Schlegel, *Kritische Ausgabe seiner Werken*, edited by Ernst Behler, 18 vols (Munich, 1958–1963), p. 298.

[8] For a further discussion of Nietzsche's indebtedness to Schlegel, see Adrian Del Caro, 'Dionysian Classicism, or Nietzsche's Appropriation of an Aesthetic Norm', *Journal of the History of Ideas,* 50 (1989), 589–605; and Ernst Behler, 'Die Auffassung des Dionysischen durch die Brüder Schlegel und Friedrich Nietzsche', *Nietzsche-Studien*, 12 (1983), 335–54.

[9] Friedrich Creuzer, *Dionysus sive commentationes academicae de rerum Bacchicarum Orphicarumque originibus et caussis* (Heidelberg, 1808/09).

[10] See Creuzer, *Symbolik und Mythologie der alten Völker* (originally published in 2 vols (Darmstadt, 1810/11), 4 vols (Leipzig and Darmstadt, 1837–1842[3]), I, p. 479. For a list of Creuzer's own sources, see his footnote (IV, pp. 5–6).

[11] 'Mythologische Schriften von Schelling, Ouwaroff, Millin und Welker', in: *Heidelburger Jahrbücher der Literatur*, 10 (1817), Nrs.47–52, pp. 737–823 (discusses Schelling's *Über die Gottheiten von Samothrace* (1815), M. Ovaroff's *Essai sur les Mystères d'Eleusis* (1816), A. L. Millin's *Description des Tombeaux de Cunosa* (1816) and the first volume of the *Zeitschrift für Geschichte und Auslegung der alten Kunst* (edited by F. G. Welker) (1817)).

[12] Ludwig Preller, *Griechische Mythologie*, 2 vols (Berlin, 1860) (referred to by Jung in WSL: pp. 41, 270, 399/PU § 44, n.32, 427, n.10, third reference omitted; and GW13 § 91, 275).

Rolle (1770–1855) on the cult of Bacchus,[13] for there are copies of both works in his library.

This long-standing interest in the categories of the Dionysian and Apollonian was taken up by Bachofen, who mediated eighteenth-century Romanticism and nineteenth-century philology to Basle and hence to the city where Nietzsche lectured and Jung would later study. In several of his major works,[14] Bachofen presented a dualistic system in which Dionysos was associated with what he called the telluric sphere, and Apollo with what he called the uranic sphere. Moreover, having defended *Die Geburt der Tragödie* against its poor reception by the Berlin philologist Ulrich von Wilamowitz-Moellendorf (1848–1931), Erwin Rohde (1845–1900), a close personal friend of Nietzsche, took up the category of the Dionysian in his major work *Psyche* (1893).[15] Following closely Nietzsche's account of the Dionysian orgy,[16] Rohde went beyond Nietzsche to argue that primitive immortality cults had developed from the mystical, primordial unity which was experienced in these rituals. The kind of spiritual monism or psychic pantheism which Rohde attributes to the Greeks is very close both to Schelling's notion of the Absolute and Jung's notion of the collective psyche.[17] Jung referred on four occasions to Rohde in *Wandlungen und Symbole der Libido* (WSL: pp. 301, n.11, 323, 342, n.129, 349, n.156/PU § 489, n.6, 539, 582, n.72, 588, n.95) and owned a copy of the fourth edition of *Psyche.*

In 1933, Walter Friedrich Otto published a comprehensive study of the Greek god in *Dionysos: Mythos und Kultus* [*Dionysos: Myth and Cult*] and wrote in detail about his psychological significance.[18] In the following year, the cultural anthropologist Ruth Benedict argued that human cultures could be divided into Apollonian societies (characterized by order and control, e.g. the Zuni Indians) and Dionysian societies (characterized by emotional abandonment, e.g. the Kwakiutl Indians):[19] Jung bought the 1946 edition of her book. In 1941, *Eros*

13 Pierre Nicolas Rolle, *Recherches sur le culte de Bacchus* (Paris, 1824).

14 Johann Jakob Bachofen, *Versuch über die Gräbersymbolik der Alten* [*Study of Tomb Symbolism of the Ancients*] (Basle, 1859); *Das Mutterrecht: Eine Untersuchung über die Gynaikokratie der alten Welt nach ihrer religiösen und rechtlichen Natur* [*Matriliny: An Investigation of Gynaecocracy in Religion and Law of the Ancient World*] (Stuttgart, 1861); and *Die Unsterblichkeit der orphischen Theologie auf den Grabdenkmälern des Altertums* [*Immortality and Orphic Theology on the Grave Memorials of Antiquity*] (Basle, 1867).

15 Erwin Rohde, *Psyche: Seelencult und Unsterblichkeitsglaube der Griechen* [*Psyche: The Cult of Souls and Belief in Immortality among the Greeks*], 2 vols (Freiburg im Breisgau, 1890–1894); quoted here from Erwin Rohde, *Psyche: Seelenkult und Unsterblichkeitsglaube der Griechen*, selected and edited by Hans Eckstein (Leipzig, 1929). See also *Friedrich Nietzsches Briefwechsel mit Erwin Rohde*, edited by Elisabeth Förster-Nietzsche (Berlin, 1902^3).

16 Rohde, p. 156; cf. GT/BT § 1; N1: p. 25.

17 Rohde, pp. 156–57.

18 Walter Friedrich Otto, *Dionysos: Mythos und Kultus* (Frankfurt am Main, 1933); translated as *Dionysus: Myth and Cult* (Dallas, TX, 1981). pp. 180, 140–41, 179 and 143.

19 Ruth Benedict, *Patterns of Culture* (Boston and New York, 1934).

und Religion, a study of the psychology of myth and religion by the German philosopher, Walter Schubart (1897–c.1941), also appeared. His discussion of the cult of the phallus is very similar to Jung's in *Wandlungen und Symbole der Libido*, and Schubart explicitly engaged with Nietzsche's and Rohde's definitions of the Dionysian.[20] Moreover, like Jung, Schubart saw in Goethe's *Faust* a quasi-Jungian message of the greatest relevance for Modernity.[21] Thus, Nietzsche's and Jung's concern with Dionysos forms part of a larger pattern of research and analysis of this particular aspect of Greek culture and civilization.

Jung and the Tradition: Wotan

We can also situate Jung within a long line of references to the Germanic deity Wotan, who is closely related to Dionysos. When he wrote 'Wotan' (1936), Jung was not the first to regard the god of the Berserkers as a symbol of a dangerous potential in the German psyche. In *Zur Geschichte der Religion und Philosophie in Deutschland* [*History of Religion and Philosophy in Germany*] (1834–35), Heine had welcomed the way in which Christianity had subdued 'die dämonischen Kräfte des altgermanischen Pantheismus' ['the daemonic powers of old-Germanic pantheism'], but went on to paint an apocalyptic picture of a revival of the Nordic gods.[22] Jung owned a copy of Heine's *Sämtliche Werke*, and prefaced *Psychologische Typen* (1921) with a quotation from Heine's history of German philosophy (GW6: p. 1/CW6: p. 2). In the realm of literature, we can also find premonitions of a return to Wotanism in the twentieth century. For example, in 'A Letter from Germany' (1924), D. H. Lawrence wrote: 'the moment you are in Germany, you know it. It feels empty and, somehow, menacing', and he imagined apocalyptic scenes of a return to barbarism.[23] In the same year, the expressionist playwright, Ernst Toller (1893–1939), used the image of the Teutonic deity to parody the revival of Nordic cults in his play *Der entfesselte Wotan* [*Wotan Unchained*].[24] It is unlikely that Jung was familiar with these works, and there is no evidence that he had read the Nazi philosopher Alfred Rosenberg (see Chapter 9), although

---

20 Walter Schubart, *Religion und Eros*, edited by Friedrich Seifert (Munich, 1966), pp. 48–51. Schubart's discussion of the cults of Attis and Tamuz (pp. 42–43) even recalls Jung's letter to Freud of 15 November 1909 (FJB: pp. 289–90/FJL: pp. 262–64).

21 Schubart, p. 71.

22 Heinrich Heine, *Sämtliche Werke*, 10 vols (1910–1915), VII, pp. 351–52.

23 D. H. Lawrence, *Phoenix* (London, 1967), pp. 107–110 (p. 108).

24 See Hermann Korte, 'Die Abdankung der "Lichtbringer": Wilhelminisches Ära und literarischer Expressionismus in Ernst Tollers Komödie "Der entfesselte Wotan"', *Germanisch-Romanische Monatsschrift*, 65 (1984), 117–32; and Richard Dove, *He was a German: A Biography of Ernst Toller* (London, 1990), pp. 126–29.

he did read M. H. Göring's review of *Der Mythus des 20. Jahrhunderts*, and wrote to the author to criticize Rosenberg's anti-Semitism (B1: p. 302/L1: p. 238).

However, it is much harder to believe that the French historian of religion, Georges Dumézil (1898–1986), was not in his turn familiar with Jung's work and in particular with his essay. For in *Mythes et Dieux des Germains* (1939), a detailed study of Germanic myth and folklore which concentrated in detail on the Norse god Odin (i.e. Wotan), Dumézil, like Jung, suggested that the primitive god had once more seized control of the Germans. According to Dumézil, twentieth-century Germany had not just seen the revival of mythology, but had actually been 'remythicised', thus attributing to myth equally as strong an influence as Jung had done in 1936.[25] Furthermore, Dumézil specifically cited Wotan, Wagner and pagan mysticism as the real roots of the Third Reich, claiming, just like Jung, that the Germans had embraced National Socialism with a curious spontaneity and enthusiasm which only the similarity between Hitler's political ideology and ancient religious custom could explain.[26] Although Jung owned a copy of Dumézil's *Mythes et Dieux des Germains*, he never referred to it in defence of his own propositions and there is no evidence of any correspondence between him and Dumézil. Conversely, Dumézil's work makes no reference to Jung. However, both men had a common intellectual source in Marcel Mauss, to whom Dumézil pays tribute in his introduction and to whose notion of the 'catégories de l'imagination' Jung repeatedly referred.[27] Furthermore, both had a common source of mythological data in the fourth edition of Jakob Grimm's *Deutsche Mythologie* (1835, 1876–77⁴), to which Dumézil refers in his introduction and a copy of which is to be found in Jung's personal library. Finally, just as Jung has been accused of Nazi sympathies, so Dumézil, too, has been suspected of conniving with Nazi ideology.[28]

During the Second World War, the English psychotherapist and translator/interpreter of Jung, Helton Godwin Baynes (1883–1943), explicitly embraced Jung's theory of *Wotan redivivus* in *Germany Possessed* (1941). Here, he explained the Third Reich and Second World War in terms of a 'Wotan-wind', which was

---

[25] Georges Dumézil, *Mythes et Dieux des Germains* (Paris, 1939), pp. 155–56.

[26] Dumézil, pp. 156–57.

[27] 'Constamment présentes dans le langage, sans qu'elles y soient de tout nécessité explicites, [les catégories] existent d'ordinaire plutôt sous la forme d'habitudes directrices de la conscience, elles-mêmes inconscientes' (H. Hubert and M. Mauss, *Mélanges d'Histoire des religions* (Paris, 1909), p.xxix. Jung interpreted these categories to mean the same as 'archetypes' (GW7 § 220; GW8 § 52, n.42 and n.254; GW 9(i) § 89, 153; GW11 § 89, n.59).

[28] See Carlo Ginzburg's sharp criticism of Dumézil in 'Mitilogia germanica e nazismo: Su un vecchio libro di Georges Dumézil' (*Miti emblemi spie: Morfologia e storia* (Torino, 1986), pp. 210–38). For a defence of Dumézil, see Didier Eribon, *Faut-il brûler Dumézil?* (Paris, 1992); and for further discussion, see Roger Chartier's book-review entitled 'Dumézil innocenté', *Le Monde*, 30 October 1992, p. 28.

allegedly blowing across Europe.[29] His wife, Cary F. Baynes, is known to have attended Jung's Seminar on *Zarathustra* and Baynes himself probably visited some of these lectures, too. Jung's Wotan thesis was also completely accepted by Mary Bancroft, another Jungian who had attended the Seminar on *Zarathustra* and who later worked for the C. I. A. during the Second World War.[30]

Jung's view of Fascism had great influence on one of the foremost spokesmen for German culture, Thomas Mann, whose novel *Doktor Faustus* (1947) propounds a mythological understanding of Nazi Germany which is remarkably similar to Jung's. As T. E. Apter has put it: 'Aesthetics and psychology turned into politics: that is the substance of Mann's analysis of Nazism'.[31] Moreover, both Jung and Mann are ultimately concerned with the problem of Dionysos.[32] Like Jung, Mann conflated 'das Dionysische' ['the Dionysian'] and 'das Dämonische' ['the daemonic'], and the final paragraph of his novel depicts Germany trying to recover from its drunken and dangerous revelry.[33] Indeed, there are numerous examples of the motif of Dionysos in all his various manifestations, not just in Thomas Mann but in twentieth-century literature in general, ranging from writers such as Rilke, Stefan George and Alfred Schuler to André Gide and André Malraux.[34]

In his posthumously-published work *Der Mythus des Staates* [*The Myth of the State*], the German philosopher, Ernst Cassirer (1874–1945), remarked that the most important and disquieting aspect of the radical shift which had brought about the Second World War had been the demonstration of a new political power, that of what he termed 'Mythical Thought'.[35] Later, in the Sixties, the French sociologist and essayist, Roger Caillois (1913–1978), a colleague of

---

29 H. G. Baynes, *Germany Possessed* (London, 1941), pp. 291–92.

30 Mary Bancroft, *Autobiography of a Spy* (New York, 1983), pp. 92, 96–97.

31 T. E. Apter, *Thomas Mann: the Devil's Advocate* (London, 1978), p. 139. See also my articles '"*Literarische Beziehungen haben nie bestanden*"? Thomas Mann and C. G. Jung', *Oxford German Studies*, 23 (1994), 124–72; and '*Jung-Joseph*: Analytical Psychology in Thomas Mann's "Joseph" Tetralogy', *The Modern Language Review*, 91 (1996).

32 T. J. Reed, *Thomas Mann: The Uses of Tradition* (Oxford, 1974), p. 396.

33 Thomas Mann, *Gesammelte Werke*, 13 vols (Frankfurt am Main, 1960–1974), VI, p. 676.

34 Monroe Kirk Spears, *Dionysos and the City: Modernism in Twentieth-Century Poetry* (New York, 1970) (discusses modern English and American poetry); Lillian Feder, *Madness in Literature* (Princeton, 1980), pp. 203–47 (discusses Thomas Mann's *Tod in Venedig* and *Doktor Faustus*, the Performance Group's dramatic version of Euripides' *Bacchae* directed by Richard Schechner called *Dionysus in 69* and the Nigerian playwright Wole Soyinka's *The Bacchae of Euripides*, first performed in London in August 1973); John Burt Foster, jr., *Heirs to Dionysus* Princeton, 1981) (discusses Gide, Lawrence, Malraux and Thomas Mann); and Manfred Frank, *Gott im Exil* (Frankfurt am Main, 1988) (discusses Rilke, George, Schuler and Thomas Mann). For a commentary on the Dionysos/Bacchus motif in (mainly French) literature and art, see Nathalie Mahé, *Le mythe de Bacchus* (Paris, 1992).

35 Ernst Cassirer, *Der Mythus des Staates: Philosophische Grundlagen politischen Verhaltens* (Zurich and Munich, 1978), p. 7.

Georges Dumézil, applied Weber's concept of 'charisma' to Adolf Hitler, drawing attention (as both Jung and Dumézil had done) to the apparent 'traits mythologiques' of the Nazi leader.[36] In the early Eighties, the so-called 'Weltanschauungsexperte', Friedrich-Wilhelm Haack, has labelled the 'Neugermanismus' of the Third Reich as the 'return of Wotan' and documented the persistence of mystical Far Right ideologies in post-war Germany.[37] And more recently still, Jochen Kirchhoff has rejected socio-economic explanations of the rise of Fascism as insufficient and insisted on the archetypal reality of the psychological forces unleashed by the Third Reich.[38] Through such mediators, both Nietzsche's discussion in *Die Geburt der Tragödie* of the importance of myth as the founding-moment of the nation – 'erst ein mit Mythen umstellter Horizont schließt eine ganze Kulturbewegung zur Einheit ab' ['only a horizon defined by myths completes and unifies a whole cultural movement'] (GT/BT § 23; N1: p. 125) – and Jung's ideas about 'national psychology'[39] continue to reverberate in political and cultural historical debate and point to certain key ideas which they had in common.

Post-Jungian Dionysiacs

In the post-Jungian era, classical scholars, psychologists and feminists have continued to debate the significance of this controversial god. Jung's followers in particular have been keen to develop further his interest in Dionysos. For example, Linda Fierz-David, who was analysed by Jung personally, wrote a book on the frescoes at the 'Villa of Mysteries' in Pompeii which she read in terms of a Dionysian initiation rite.[40] And Eleanor Hall, who has written a psychological study of the first generation of female Jungians, has placed considerable emphasis on the significance of Dionysos for 'those women', the first generation of Jungian followers who were mostly female.[41]

As well as writing specifically on the rôle of Dionysos in Jung's writings,[42] the archetypal psychologist, James Hillman, has discussed Heraclitus's conjunc-

---

36 Roger Caillois, *Instincts et société* (Paris, 1964), pp. 152–80 (p. 158).

37 Friedrich-Wilhelm Haack, *Wotans Wiederkehr: Blut-, Boden- und Rasse-Religion* (Munich, 1981).

38 Jochen Kirchhoff, *Nietzsche, Hitler und die Deutschen* (Berlin, 1990), p. 18. Kirchhoff revises Jung's allegedly negative evaluation of the archaic (pp. 30–31).

39 See Andrew Samuels, *The Political Psyche* (London, 1993).

40 Linda Fierz-David, *Psychologische Betrachtungen zu der Freskenfolge der Villa dei Misteri in Pompeii: Ein Versuch* (Zurich [mimeographed], 1957); translated by Gladys Phelan, *Women's Dionysian Initation: The Villa of Mysteries in Pompeii* (Dallas, TX, 1988).

41 Eleanor Hall, *Those Women* (Dallas, TX, 1988), pp. 13–14.

42 James Hillman, 'Dionysus in Jung's Writings', *Spring* (1972), 191–205 (pp. 194, 197 and 200).

tion of Hades and Dionysos in *The Dream and the Underworld*.[43] And the analytical psychologist, Joseph Henderson, who attended Jung's Nietzsche Seminar, has traced the development of mystery initiation rites from Dionysiac rites through the worship of Orpheus to Christianity in his contribution to Jung's *Man and his Symbols*. Like Jung, Henderson goes so far as to posit an identity between Christ and Dionysos which he sees mediated through the figure of Orpheus.[44] In the early Eighties, a Jungian analyst, Lyn Cowan, wrote a study of the pathology of masochism from an analytical psychological perspective. One chapter, entitled 'Dionysus, or The Madness of Masochism', opens with a translation of the Magician's Song from Part IV of *Zarathustra* (Z IV 5; N2: pp. 491–94)[45] and analyses masochistic feelings as a quintessentially Dionysian experience.[46] Cowan also notes that the neo-Freudian analyst Karen Horney (1885–1952) was the first psychologist to argue explicitly for a link between masochistic striving and Dionysian urges.[47] Finally, the classical scholar, Karóly Kerényi (1897–1973), published, during the post-war period, a number of influential studies on the Dionysian, the later ones of which show the clear influence of his collaboration with Jung on the archetypal analysis of mythology. This is particularly clear in his choice of the subtitle 'Das archetypische Bild des unzerstörbaren Lebens' ['Archetypal Image of Indestructible Life'] to describe Dionysos.[48]

However, it has not just been Jungians who have trodden the Dionysian path. For example, in the Freudian tradition, Herbert Marcuse (1898–1979) championed the cause of Dionysos (*and* Orpheus and Narcissus) against that of Prometheus and the 'performance principle' in *Eros and Civilisation* (1956).[49] Also on the cusp of the Sixties, the maverick psychoanalytic writer, psycho-

---

[43] James Hillman, *The Dream and the Underworld* (New York, 1979), pp. 44–45).

[44] Joseph Henderson, 'Ancient Myths and Modern Man', in: C. G. Jung et al, *Man and his Symbols* (London, 1964), pp. 104–57 (pp. 143–45).

[45] Lyn Cowan, *Masochism: A Jungian View* (Dallas, TX, 1982), p. 97.

[46] Cowan, pp. 97, 97–98, 104, 105 and 111.

[47] 'All masochistic strivings are ultimately directed towards satisfaction, namely, toward the goal of oblivion, of getting rid of self with all its conflicts and all its limitations. The masochistic phenomena which we find in neuroses would then represent a pathological modification of the dionysian tendencies which seem to be spread throughout the world' (Karen Horney, *New Ways in Psychoanalysis* (New York, 1939), p. 248). (In a footnote, Horney refers to Nietzsche's *Die Geburt der Tragödie* and Ruth Benedict's *Patterns of Culture* (1934)).

[48] Karl Kerényi, *Dionysos und das Tragische in der Antigone* [Frankfurter Studien zur Religion und Kultur der Antike, Band 13] (Frankfurt am Main, 1935); *Die Herkunft der Dionysosreligion nach dem heutigen Stand der Forschung* [Arbeitsgemeinschaft für Forschung des Landes Nordrhein-Westfalen (Geisteswissenschaften), Heft 58] (Cologne and Opladen, 1956); *Der frühe Dionysos* [Die Eitrem-Vorlesungen, gehalten an der Universität Oslo im September 1960] (Oslo, 1961); and *Dionysos: Archetypal Image of Indestructible Life*, translated Ralph Manheim (London, 1976).

[49] Herbert Marcuse, *Eros and Civilisation: A Philosophical Inquiry into Freud* (London, 1956), pp. 161–62.

cultural historian and campaigner for the abolition of repression, Norman O. Brown (b.1913), who is on record as disliking both 'Jungian *Schwärmerei*' and neo-Freudianism for the same reason,[50] provided a rereading of Freud which brought him back to the Nietzschean antinomy of Apollo and Dionysos. Brown pointed out that there were important similarities between Freud's description of the Id as 'ein Chaos, einen Kessel voll brodelnder Erregungen' ['a chaos, a cauldron of seething excitement'][51] and Nietzsche's description of the Dionysian as 'jener scheußliche Hexentrank aus Wollust und Grausamkeit' ['the horrible "witches' brew" of sensuality and cruelty'] (GT/BT § 2; N1: p. 27). Agreeing with Nietzsche that 'the Apollonian preserves, the Dionysian destroys, self-consciousness', Brown went beyond Nietzsche and Freud to join the dancer Isadora Duncan[52] in arguing that the Apollonian structures of the Ego should be replaced by a more Dionysian entity, going so far as to claim that 'the problem is the construction of a Dionysian Ego'.[53] Subsequently, Richard King has noted the points of similarity and convergence between Brown and Nietzsche,[54] and in doing so has observed that: 'though no Jungian, Brown's efforts were reminiscent of Jung's (and Reich's) attempt to point the way for a new resurgence of spiritual vitality'.[55] Most recently, the notorious American critic and scourge of literary theorists and feminists, Camille Paglia, has taken her central aesthetic category of the chthonian straight out of Nietzsche, as the preface to her book *Sexual Personae* shows.[56]

Not everybody is quite so fond of Dionysos, however. The feminist writer and self-styled Revolting Hag, Mary Daly, has decisively rejected all twentieth-century interpretations of Dionysos and in particular attacked Norman O. Brown's version of 'The Illusion of "Dionysian" Freedom'.[57] Not surprisingly, Daly is also scathing about Jungian psychology. Describing Jung's theories as 'pernicious traps which often stop women in the initial stages of mind-journeying', she concludes: 'Tokenism is embedded in the very fabric of Jung's ideology – in contrast to the more obvious misogynism of Freud's fallacious phallocentrism'.[58] Since, according to Jung and others, Dionysos is a phallic god, it is

---

50 Norman O. Brown, *Life Against Death: The Psychoanalytic Meaning of History* (Middletown, CT, 1959), p. 126.

51 Freud, *Gesammelte Werke*, XV, p. 80.

52 See Isadora Duncan, *My Life* (New York, 1927), p. 105.

53 Brown, pp. 175–76.

54 Richard King, *The Party of Eros: Radical Social Thought and the Realm of Freedom* (Chapel Hill, 1972), pp. 166–67.

55 King, p. 172.

56 Camille Paglia, 'Sex and Violence, or Nature and Art', *Sexual Personae* (New York, 1991), pp. 1–39; see also '*Sexual Personae*: The Cancelled Preface', in: *Sex, Art and American Culture* (New York, 1992), pp. 101–24 (pp. 101–02).

57 Mary Daly, *Gyn/Ecology* (Boston, 1990[2]), 'The Illusion of "Dionysian" Freedom', pp. 64–69.

58 Daly, pp. 253, 280.

not surprising that the followers of this deity cause offence to women who wish to conceive a different future for themselves than being Maenads.

More broadly, both Nietzsche and Jung are part of the struggle between the rational(istic) and the irrational(istic) outlook. By arguing, in *Die Geburt der Tragödie*, that Dionysos must be united with Apollo for the moment of tragic insight to occur and be sustained, Nietzsche suggests that the highest wisdom comes only though a bonding of certain opposites. Similarly, through his self-overcoming, the Superman unites both Apollonian and Dionysian tendencies, and Nietzsche's greatest example for this is Goethe: 'er disziplinierte sich zur Ganzheit, er *schuf* sich...' ['he disciplined himself to a whole, he *created* himself...'] (GD/TI 9 § 49; N2: p. 1024). For Jung, the greatest pair of opposites to be united are consciousness (Apollo) and the Unconscious (Dionysos) to create the Dionysian Self. Yet to assign any rôle at all to the Unconscious in the construction of our identity is a highly precarious business. Proof of this assertion was compellingly provided by Nietzsche, who spent his last ten years in a sanatorium, and by Jung, who virtually turned Analytical Psychology into a substitute religion.

Conclusion

In this book, I have tried to resituate C. G. Jung within the intellectual tradition from which his Analytical Psychology issues, i.e. German Idealism and German Romantic philosophy in general and the works of the apogee of post-Enlightenment thought, Friedrich Nietzsche, in particular. Jung's life and work were, as I have shown, intimately connected with his reading of Nietzsche, and Jung's personal feelings about Nietzsche and the Dionysian stood in a complex but structured relationship to his intellectual response. And as far as both his life and his work are concerned, Jung's dialogue with Nietzsche is more sophisticated than it is allowed to appear in his autobiography, his sense that 'there but for the grace of Dionysos go I' leading him to suppress his ackowledgement of his debt to Nietzsche in certain areas and to exaggerate it in others. From Jung's reception of Nietzsche, we can also begin to understand the (relative) importance of his reading of Kant, Schelling and Schopenhauer. All these writers are concerned in one way or another with the question of the self, and Jung's Dionysian Self articulates his own answer to this question.

For, whatever the deficiencies of his thought, Jung tried to go beyond Freudian psychoanalysis and, had he but known it, Lacanian psychology and Post-Modernism. Whilst accepting the analysis of ontological and existential despair which Nietzsche described as the result of the 'Death of God' (and, concomitantly, the deconstruction of the subject), Jung rejected Nietzsche's solution in the form of the Superman (at a loss, perhaps, to imagine what an 'Übermensch' would look like). But he agreed profoundly with Nietzsche's sense that gods – drives or instincts given structure and purpose by the archetypes of the Collective Unconscious – other than the Christian would come to our aid as 'der rettende Gedanke' ['the saving thought']. The two men are at one in their sense of mission to construct the Dionysian Self, despite the important differences in their respective interpretations of what this implied. It is highly ironic therefore, that Nietzsche should have been so misused by the National Socialists, and that Jung should have risked complicity with that abuse, apparently unable to combat the tenets of reactionary, pagan politics – Dionysos in the Wotanist mode.

I have also shown that, as well as trying to read Jung in the light of Nietzsche, it is equally important to realize how both Jung and Nietzsche were closely bound up with the Romantic project of a new, and Dionysian, mythology. Both derived their learning about classical mythology from the same scholarly sources. Both interpreted the central Dionysian mythologem in the light of a common Romantic and German Idealist framework. And both wrote complex texts which work on at least two levels: Nietzsche's *Die Geburt der Tragödie* is both a theoretical discussion of the origin of tragic drama and the rôle of art and myth in society and also a polemic against his former metaphysical master, Arthur Schopenhauer. Jung's *Wandlungen und Symbole der Libido* is both a theory of how archetypal mythology relates to the psychic economy of the individual and also a polemic against Jung's former psychoanalytic 'father', Freud. This complexity, present in Nietzsche's work to a higher degree than in Jung's, makes it difficult to identify common ground between them which is not at the same time the site of divergence. To study Jung's reception of Nietzsche is not only to throw light on the intellectual sources of Analytical Psychology, it is also to perform a textual *coniunctio oppositorum*, with all the ambiguities, complexities and hope of a miracle which that term implies.

Bibliography

Abrams, M. H., *The Mirror and the Lamp* (Oxford, 1953).

Abrams, Stephen, *The Devil You Don't Know*, broadcast on BBC Radio 3 on 24 April 1982.

Addis, William E. and Arnold, Thomas (revised by Scannell, T. B. and Hallett, P. E.), *A Catholic Dictionary* (London, 1954).

Adler, Jeremy, *Eine fast magische Anziehungskraft: Goethes 'Wahlverwandschaften'* (Munich, 1987).

Aksakow, Alexander Nicolaevic, *Animismus und Spiritismus: Versuch einer kritischen Prüfung der medizinischen Phänomene mit besonderer Berücksichtigung der Hypothesen der Halluzinationen und des Unbewußten* (Leipzig, 1890).

Altizer, Thomas J. J., 'Science and Gnosis in Jung's Psychology', *The Centennial Review of Arts and Science*, 3 (1959), 304–20.

Altizer, Thomas J. J., ed., *Towards a New Christianity: Readings on the Death of God Theology*, (New York, 1967).

Altizer, Thomas J. J. and Hamilton, William, *Radical Theology and the Death of God* (Indianapolis, 1966).

Anderson, Lorin, 'Freud, Nietzsche', *Salmagundi*, No.47–48 (Winter-Spring 1980), 3–29.

Andler, Charles, *Nietzsche und Jakob Burckhardt* (Basle and Strasbourg, n.d.)

Ansell-Pearson, Keith (ed.), *Nietzsche and Modern German Thought* (London and New York, 1991).

Anthony, Maggy, *The Valkyries: The Women Around Jung* (Shaftesbury, 1990).

Apter, Terri Eve, *Thomas Mann: The Devil's Advocate* (London, 1978).

Ascheim, Steven E., *The Nietzsche Legacy in Germany 1890–1990* (Berkeley, 1994).

Assoun, Paul Laurent, *Freud et Nietzsche* (Paris, 1980).

Bachofen, Johann Jakob, *Das Mutterrecht: Eine Untersuchung über die Gynaikokratie der alten Welt nach ihrer religiösen und rechtlichen Natur* (Stuttgart, 1861).

Bachofen, Johann Jakob, *Der Mythus von Orient und Occident*, edited by Manfred Schröter and introduced by Alfred Baeumler (Munich, 1965).

Bachofen, Johann Jakob, *Der Mythus von Orient und Occident: Eine Metaphysik der alten Welt*, edited by Alfred Baeumler (Munich, 1956).

Bachofen, Johann Jakob, *Die Unsterblichkeit der orphischen Theologie auf den Grabdenkmälern des Altertums* (Basle, 1867).

Bachofen, Johann Jakob, *Versuch über die Gräbersymbolik der Alten* (Basle, 1954).

Bär, Eugen, 'Archetypes and Ideas: Jung and Kant', *Philosophy Today*, 20 (1976), 114–23.

Baeumer, Max, 'Nietzsche and the Tradition of the Dionysian', in *Studies in Nietzsche and the Classical Tradition*, edited by James C. O'Flaherty, Timothy F. Sellner, and Robert M. Helm (North Carolina, 1976).

Baeumer, Max L., 'Das moderne Phänomen des Dionysischen und seine "Entdeckung" durch Nietzsche', *Nietzsche-Studien*, 6 (1977), 123–53.

Baeumer, Max L., 'Die romantische Epiphanie des Dionysos', *Monatshefte für deutschen Unterricht, deutsche Sprache und Literatur*, 57 (1965), 225–36.

Baird, James, 'Jungian Psychology in Criticism: Theoretical Problems', in: *Literary Criticism and Psychology*, edited by J. P. Strelka (*Yearbook of Comparative Criticism*, VII) (Pennsylvania University, 1976), pp. 3–30.
Bancroft, Mary, *Autobiography of a Spy* (New York, 1983).
Bancroft, Mary, 'Jung and his Circle', *Psychological Perspectives*, 6 (1975), 114–27.
Barnaby, Karin, 'A Poet's Intuition of C. G. Jung's Psychology in "Über naive und sentimentalische Dichtung"', in *Friedrich von Schiller and the Drama of Human Existence*, edited by Alexander Ugrinsky (New York, 1988), pp. 119–28.
Barnaby, Karin and D'Acierno, Pellegrino (eds.), *C. G. Jung and the Humanities: Towards a Hermeneutics of Culture*, (London, 1990).
Baroni, Christophe, 'Dieu est-il mort? De Nietzsche à Jung', *Synthèses*, 19, no.224 (January 1965), 328–43.
Bauemler, Alfred, *Bachofen und Nietzsche* (Zurich, 1929).
Baynes, Helton Godwin, *Germany Possessed* (London, 1941).
Behler, Ernst, 'Die Auffassung des Dionysischen durch die Brüder Schlegel und Friedrich Nietzsche', *Nietzsche-Studien*, 12 (1983), 335–54.
Benedict, Ruth, *Patterns of Culture* (Boston and New York, 1934).
Bennett, Benjamin, 'Nietzsche's Idea of Myth: The Birth of Tragedy from the Spirit of Eighteenth-Century Aesthetics', *PMLA*, 94 (1979), 420–33.
Benz, Ernst, *Nietzsches Ideen zur Geschichte des Christentums wider der Kirche* (Leiden, 1956).
Bernoulli, Carl Albrecht, *Franz Overbeck und Friedrich Nietzsche: Eine Freundschaft*, 2 vols (Jena, 1908).
Bernoulli, Carl Albrecht, *Johann Jakob Bachofen und das Natursymbol* (Basle, 1924).
Bernoulli, Carl Albrecht, *Nietzsche in der Schweiz* (Leipzig, 1922).
Bernoulli, Rudolf, 'Seelische Entwicklung im Spiegel der Alchemie und verwandter Disziplinen', *Eranos-Jahrbuch*, 3 (1935), 231–87.
Bertram, Ernst, *Nietzsche: Versuch einer Mythologie* (Berlin, 1918).
Biser, Eugen, *"Gott ist tot": Nietzsches Destruktion des christlichen Bewußtseins* (Munich, 1962).
Bishop, John, *Joyce's Book of the Dark: Finnegans Wake* (Madison, 1986).
Bishop, Paul, 'Jung's Annotations of Nietzsche's Works: An Analysis', *Nietzsche-Studien*, 24 (1995), 271–314.
Bishop, Paul, 'The Jung/Förster-Nietzsche Correspondence', *German Life and Letters*, 46 (1993), 319–330.
Bishop, Paul, '*Jung-Joseph*: Analytical Psychology in Thomas Mann's "Joseph" Tetralogy', *The Modern Language Review*, 91 (1996).
Bishop, Paul, '"Literarische Beziehungen haben nie bestanden"? Thomas Mann and C. G. Jung', *Oxford German Studies*, 23 (1994), 124–72.
Bishop, Paul, 'The Members of Jung's Seminar on *Zarathustra*', *Spring*, 56 (1994), 92–122.
Bleuler, Eugen, *Die Psychoide als Prinzip der organischen Entwicklung* (Berlin, 1925).
Bloch, Ernst, *Das Prinzip Hoffnung*, 3 vols (Frankfurt am Main, 1959).
Bloch, Ernst, *Erbschaft dieser Zeit* (Erweiterte Ausgabe) (Frankfurt am Main, 1985).
Bodkin, Maud, *Archetypal Patterns in Poetry: Psychological Studies of Imagination* (Oxford, 1934).
Bodlander, R. C., 'Heraklit und Jung', *Analytische Psychologie*, 21, no.2 (June, 1990), 142–49.
Bonardel, Françoise, *Philosophie de l'alchimie: Grand Oeuvre et modernité* (Paris, 1993).
Bonnette, Lucie, *Le Fondement religieux de la pensée de Jung* (Montreal, 1986).
Brandt, Rudolf J., 'Freud and Nietzsche', *Revue de l'Université d'Ottowa*, 25 (1955).
Braun, Henry Walter, 'C. G. Jung und Schopenhauer', *Schopenhauer-Jahrbuch*, 46 (1965), 76–87.
Brenner, E. M., 'Gnosticism and Psychology: Jung's *Septem Sermones ad Mortuos*', *Journal of Analytical Psychology*, 35 (1990), 397–419.

Brett's History of Psychology, edited and abridged by R. S. Peters (London, 1953).
Brinton, Crane, 'The National Socialists' Use of Nietzsche', *Journal of the History of Ideas*, 1 (1940), 131–50.
Brivic, Sheldon R., *Joyce between Freud and Jung* (New York, 1980).
Brockway, Robert W., 'Religion and "Creative Illness" in Jung's Night Journey into the Psychic Depth', *Journal of Dharma*, 14, no.3 (July–September 1989), 277–86.
Brome, Vincent, *Jung* (London, 1978).
Brooke, Roger, *Jung and Phenomenology* (London and New York, 1991).
Brown, Clifford A., *Jung's Hermeneutic of Doctrine: Its Theological Significance* (Chicago, 1981).
Brown, J. A. C., *Freud and the post-Freudians* (Harmondsworth, 1961).
Brown, Norman O., *Life against Death* (Middletown, 1959).
Burckhardt, Jacob, *Griechische Kulturgeschichte*, 4 vols (Berlin and Stuttgart, 1898–1902).
Burckhardt, Jacob, 'Briefe Jakob Burckhardts an Albert Brenner. Mit Einleitung und Anmerkungen von Hans Brenner', *Basler Jahrbuch 1901* (Basle, 1901), 87–110.
Burckhardt, Titus, *Alchemie* (Olten und Freiburg im Breisgau, 1960).
Burnett, Anne Pippin, 'Pentheus and Dionysus: Host and Guest', *Classical Philology*, 65 (1970), 15–29.
Bygrave, Mike, 'Jung: the Key that's Hidden at 228 Seestrasse', *The Independent*, 28 March 1992, p. 29.
Caillois, Roger, *Instincts et société* (Paris, 1964).
Capra, Fritjof, *The Turning Point: Science, Society, and the Rising Culture* (New York, 1982).
Carlsson, Anni, 'Der Mythos als Maske Friedrich Nietzsches', *Germanisch-romanische Monatsschrift*, 39 (1958), 388–401.
Carotenuto, Aldo, *A Secret Symmetry: Sabina Spielrein between Jung and Freud* (New York, 1982).
Cassirer, Ernst, *Der Mythus des Staates: Philosophische Grundlagen politischen Verhaltens* (Zurich and Munich, 1978).
Chamberlain, Houston Stewart, *Die Grundlagen des XIX. Jahrhunderts* (Munich, 1899).
Chapman, J. Harley, *Jung's Three Theories of Religious Experience* (Lewiston and Queenston, 1988).
Charet, F. X., *Spiritualism and the Foundations of C. G. Jung's Psychology* (New York, 1993).
Clark, Maudemarie, *Nietzsche on Truth and Philosophy* (Cambridge, 1990).
Clarke, John J., *In Search of Jung: Historical and Philosophical Enquiries* (London and New York, 1992).
Clift, Wallace B., *Jung and Christianity: The Challange of Reconciliation* (New York, 1982).
Cocks, Geoffrey, 'C. G. Jung and German Psychotherapy, 1933–1940: A Research Note', *Spring*, 1977, 221–27.
Colli, Giorgi, *Nach Nietzsche* (Frankfurt am Main, 1980).
Copleston, Frederick, *Friedrich Nietzsche: Philosopher of Culture* (London, 1942).
Cornford, F. M., *From Religion to Philosophy* (London, 1912).
Corngold, Stanley, 'The Question of the Self in Nietzsche during the Axial Period (1882–1888)', *Boundary 2*, 9/10 (1981), 55–98.
Cowan, Lyn, *Masochism: A Jungian View* (Dallas, TX, 1982).
Cox, David, *Jung and Saint Paul: A Study of the Doctrine of the Justification by Faith and its Relation to the Concept of Individuation* (New York, 1959).
Crawford, Claudia, 'Nietzsche's Mnemotechnics, the Theory of Ressentiment, and Freud's Topographies of the Psychical Apparatus', *Nietzsche-Studien*, 14 (1985), 281–97.
Creuzer, Friedrich, *Dionysus sive commentationes academicae de rerum Bacchicarum Orphicarumque originibus et caussis* (Heidelberg, 1808/09).

Creuzer, Friedrich, 'Mythologische Schriften von Schelling, Ouwaroff, Millin und Welker', in: *Heidelburger Jahrbücher der Literatur*, 10 (1817), Nrs.47 – 52, pp. 737 – 823.
Creuzer, Friedrich, *Symbolik und Mythologie der alten Völker, besonders der Griechen*, 4 vols (Leipzig and Darmstadt 1810 – 1823, repub. Darmstadt, 1973).
Crookshank, F. G., *Individual Psychology and Nietzsche* (London, 1933).
Cross, F. L. (ed.), *The Oxford Dictionary of the Christian Church*, (Oxford, 1974).
Currie, Robert, 'Christopher Caudwell: Marxist Illusion, Jungian Reality', *The British Journal of Aesthetics*, 18 (1978), 291 – 99.
Daly, Mary, *Gyn/Ecology: The Metaethics of Radical Feminism* (Boston, 1990²).
De Castillejo, Irene Claremont, *Knowing Woman: A Feminine Psychology* (New York, 1973).
De Man, Paul, *Allegories of Reading: Figural Language in Rousseau, Nietzsche, Rilke, and Proust* (New Haven, 1979).
Dehing, Jef, 'Jung and Knowledge: From Gnosis to Praxis', *Journal of Analytical Psychology*, 35 (1990), 377 – 396.
Del Caro, Adrian, 'The Immolation of Zarathustra: A Look at "The Fire Beacon"', *Colloquia Germanica*, 17 (1984), 252 – 56.
Del Caro, Adrian, *Dionysian Aesthetics: The Role of Destruction and Creation as Reflected in the Life and Works of Friedrich Nietzsche* (Frankfurt am Main, 1981).
Del Caro, Adrian, 'Dionysian Classicism, or Nietzsche's Appropriation of an Aesthetic Norm', *Journal of the History of Ideas*, 50 (1989), 589 – 605.
Del Caro, Adrian, *Nietzsche contra Nietzsche: Creativity and the Anti-Romantic* (Baton Rouge and London, 1991).
Derrida, Jacques, *Éperons: Les styles de Nietzsche* (Paris, 1978).
Dervin, Daniel, 'A Crux in the Jung/Freud letters', *Bulletin of the Menninger Clinic*, 41 (1977), 131 – 44.
Detwiler, Bruce, *Nietzsche and the Politics of Aristocratic Radicalism* (Chicago, 1990).
Diener, Gottfried, *Fausts Weg zu Helena: Urphänomen und Archetypus* (Stuttgart, 1961).
Dimitrov, Christo and Jablenski, Assen, 'Nietzsche und Freud', *Zeitschrift für psychosomatische Medizin und Psychoanalyse*, 13 (1967), 282 – 98.
Dixon, Patricia Eileen, *Nietzsche and Jung: Wholeness through the Union of Opposites*, Diss. Ph.D. unpub. (The American University, Washington D. C.), forthcoming in New York.
Dove, Richard, *He was a German: A Biography of Ernst Toller* (London, 1990), pp. 126 – 29.
Driesch, Hans, *Philosophie des Organischen*, 2 vols (Leipzig, 1909).
Duffy, Michael F. and Mittelman, Willard, 'Nietzsche's Attitude towards the Jews', *Journal of the History of Ideas*, 49 (1988), 301 – 18.
Dumézil, Georges, *Mythes et Dieux des Germains* (Paris, 1939).
Duncan, Isadora, *My Life* (New York, 1927).
DuPrel, Baron Karl Ludwig August Friedrich Maximilien Alfred, *Das Rätsel des Menschen* (Leizpig, 1892).
Dworkin, Andrea, *Woman Hating* (New York, 1974).
Eckermann, J. P., *Gespräche mit Goethe* (Zurich, 1969).
Eckman, Barbara, 'Jung, Hegel, and the Subjective Universe', *Spring*, 1986, 88 – 99.
Edinger, Edward F., *Ego and Archetype: Individuation and the Religious Function of the Psyche* (New York, 1972).
Edinger, Edward F., *Goethe's Faust: Notes for a Jungian Commentary* (Toronto, 1990).
Eisen, Arnold M., 'Nietzsche and the Jews Reconsidered', *Jewish Social Studies*, 48 (1986), 1 – 14.
Éliade, Mircea, *Forgerons et alchimistes* (Paris, 1956).

Éliade, Mircea, *The Sacred and the Profane: The Nature of Religion*, translated by William R. Trask (New York, 1959).

Ellenberger, Henri F., *The Discovery of the Unconscious: The History and Evolution of Dynamic Psychiatry* (New York, 1970).

Ellis, Mrs. Havelock Ellis [Edith M. O. Ellis], *Three Modern Seers: Hinton, Nietzsche, Carpenter* (London, 1910).

Evans, Richard I., *Jung on Elementary Psychology: A Discussion between C. G. Jung and Richard I. Evans* (London, 1979).

Evers, Tilman, *Mythos und Emanzipation: Eine kritische Annäherung an C. G. Jung* (Hamburg, 1987).

Evers, Tilman, 'C. G. Jung – Psychologie und Gnosis', in: *Gnosis und Mystik in der Geschichte der Philosophie*, edited by Peter Koslowski (Zurich and Munich, 1988), pp. 329–351.

Fabricius, Johannes, *Alchemy: The Medieval Alchemists and their Royal Art* (Wellingborough, 1989).

Fechner, Gustav Theodor, *Elemente der Psychophysik* (Leipzig, 1860).

Fechner, Gustav Theodor, *Nana oder über das Seelenleben von Pflanzen* (Leipzig, 1848).

Fechner, Gustav Theodor, *Zend-Avesta oder über die Dinge des Himmels und das Jenseits*, 3 vols (Leipzig, 1851).

Fierz-David, Linda, *Der Liebestraum des Poliphilo: Ein Beitrag zur Psychologie der Renaissance und der Moderne* (Zurich, 1947).

Fierz-David, Linda, *Psychologische Betrachtungen zu der Freskenfolge der Villa dei Misteri in Pompeii: Ein Versuch* (Zurich, 1957).

Fink, Eugen, *Nietzsches Philosophie* (Stuttgart, 1973).

Fitzell, John, 'Goethe, Jung: Homunculus and Faust', in: *Goethe in the Twentieth Century*, edited by Alexej Ugrinsky (New York, 1987), pp. 107–15.

Fleischer, Margot, 'Das Spektrum der Nietzsche-Rezeption im geistigen Leben seit der Jahrhundertwende', *Nietzsche-Studien*, 20 (1991), 1–47.

Flournoy, Théodore, 'Quelques faits d'imagination créatrice subconsciente', *Archives de psychologie*, 5 (1906), 36–51.

Fodor, Nancy, 'Jung's Sermons to the Dead', *The Psychoanalytic Review*, 51 (1964), 74–78.

Fordham, Frieda, *An Introduction to Jung's Psychology* (Harmondsworth, 1953).

Förster-Nietzsche, Elisabeth, *Der werdende Nietzsche* (Munich, 1924).

Förster-Nietzsche, Elisabeth, *Das Leben Friedrich Nietzsche's*, 2 vols (Leipzig, 1895–1904).

Foster, John Burt, Jr., *Heirs to Dionysus: A Nietzschean Current in Literary Modernism* (Princeton, 1981).

Foucault, Michel, 'Nietzsche, Freud, Marx', in: *Nietzsche* (Cahiers de Royaumont, Philosophie, no.VI) (Paris, 1967).

Frank, Manfred, *Der kommende Gott: Vorlesungen über die Neue Mythologie, I. Teil* (Frankfurt am Main, 1982).

Frank, Manfred, *Gott im Exil: Vorlesungen über die Neue Mythologie, II. Teil* (Frankfurt am Main, 1988).

Freud, Sigmund and Abraham, Karl, *Briefe 1907–1926*, edited by Hilda Abraham and Ernst Freud (Frankfurt am Main, 1965).

Freud, Sigmund and Jung, C. G., *Briefwechsel*, edited by William McGuire and Wolfgang Sauerländer (Frankfurt am Main, 1974).

Freud, Sigmund and Jung, C. G., *The Freud/Jung Letters: The Correspondence between Sigmund Freud and C. G. Jung*, edited by William McGuire, translated by Ralph Manheim and R. F. C. Hull (Cambridge, MA, 1988).

Freud, Sigmund, *Gesammelte Werke*, 18 vols (Frankfurt am Main, 1968–1978).
Frey-Rohn, Liliane, *Jenseits der Werte seiner Zeit: Friedrich Nietzsche im Spiegel seiner Werke* (Zurich, 1984).
Frey-Rohn, Liliane, *Von Freud zu Jung: eine vergleichende Studie zur Psychologie des Unbewußten* (Zurich, 1980).
Frizen, Werner, '"Von der unbefleckten Erkenntniss": Zu einem Kapitel des *Zarathustra*', *Deutsche Vierteljahrsschrift*, 58 (1984), 428–53.
Frommel, Wolfgang, 'Alfred Schuler: Spuren heidnischer Gnosis', *Castrum Peregrini*, 34 (1985), 5–23.
Frye, Northrop, *An Anatomy of Criticism: Four Essays* (Princeton, 1957).
Gadamer, Hans-Georg, 'Das Drama Zarathustras', *Nietzsche-Studien*, 15 (1986), 1–15.
Giegerich, Wolfgang, 'Hospitality towards the Gods in an Ungodly Age: Philemon-Faust-Jung', *Spring*, 1984, 61–75.
Giegerich, Wolfgang, 'Postscript to Cocks', *Spring*, 1979, 228–31.
Gilliard, Charles, *La Société de Zofingue 1819–1919* (Lausanne, 1919).
Gilman, Sander L., and Reichenbach, Ingeborg, *Begegnungen mit Nietzsche* (Bonn, 1981).
Gilman, Sander L. (ed.), *Conversations with Nietzsche: A Life in the Words of His Contemporaries*, translated by David J. Parent (New York and Oxford), 1991.
Ginsberg, Mitchell, 'Nietzschean Psychiatry', in: *Nietzsche: A Collection of Critical Essays*, edited by Robert C. Solomon (University of Notre Dame, 1973), pp. 293–315.
Ginzburg, Carlo, *Miti emblemi spie: Morfologia e storia* (Torino, 1986).
Girard, René, *Critiques dans un souterrain* (Paris, 1976).
Glover, Edward, *Freud or Jung* (London, 1950).
Goethe, Johann Wolfgang von, *Werke (Hamburger Ausgabe)*, 14 vols (Munich, 1981).
Goetz, Bruno, *Das Reich ohne Raum* (Potsdam, 1919).
Goldenberg, Naomi R., *Returning Words to Flesh: Feminism, Psychoanalysis and the Resurrection of the Body* (Boston, 1990).
Golomb, Jacob, *Nietzsche's Enticing Psychology of Power* (Ames and Jerusalem, 1989).
Golomb, Jacob, 'Freudian Uses and Misuses of Nietzsche', *American Imago*, 37 (1980), 371–85.
Goodheart, William B., 'C. G. Jung's First "Patient": On the Seminal Emergence of Jung's Thought', *Journal of Analytical Psychology*, 29 (1984), 1–34.
Gossman, Lionel, 'Antimodernism in Nineteenth-Century Basle: Franz Overbeck's Antitheology and J. J. Bachofen's Antiphilology', *Interpretation*, 16 (1989), 359–89
Gossman, Lionel, 'Basle, Bachofen and the Critique of Modernity in the Second Half of the Nineteenth Century', *Journal of the Warburg and Courtauld Institutes*, 47 (1984), 136–85.
Gossman, Lionel, *Orpheus philologus: Bachofen versus Mommsen on the Study of Antiquity* (Philadelphia, 1983 [*Transactions of the American Philosophical Society*, vol. 73, pt.5]).
Granier, Jean, *Le Problème de la vérité dans la philosophie de Nietzsche* (Paris, 1966).
Granier, Jean, 'Le Statut de la philosophie selon Nietzsche et Freud', *Nietzsche-Studien*, 8 (1979), 210–24.
Gray, Ronald D., *Goethe, the Alchemist: A Study of Alchemical Symbolism in Goethe's Literary and Scientific Works* (Cambridge, 1952).
Green, Martin, *Mountain of Truth: The Counterculture begins: Ascona, 1900–1920* (Hanover, NH, 1986).
Grimm, Reinhold, 'Embracing Two Horses: Tragedy, Humor, and Inwardness; or, Nietzsche, Vischer, and Julius Bahnsen', *Nietzsche-Studien*, 18 (1989), 203–20.
Gronicka, André von, '"Myth plus Psychology": A Style Analysis of *Death in Venice*', *Germanic Review*, 31 (1956), 191–205.

Grossman, S., 'C. G. Jung and National Socialism', *Journal of European Studies*, 9 (1979), 231–59.
Groth, H. Miles, 'Nietzsche's Ontogenetic Theory of Time: The Riddle of the Laughing Shepherd', *American Imago*, 37 (1980), 351–70.
Guzzoni, Alfredo (ed.), *90 Jahre philosophische Nietzsche-Rezeption* (Königstein im Taunus, 1979).
Haack, Friedrich-Wilhelm, *Wotans Wiederkehr: Blut-, Boden-und Rasse-Religion* (Munich, 1981).
Habermas, Jürgen, 'Der Eintritt in die Postmoderne', *Merkur*, 37 (1983), 752–61.
Hall, Eleanor, *Those Women* (Dallas, TX, 1988).
Hannah, Barbara, *Jung: His Life and Work* (London, 1976).
Harding, Mary Esther, *The Way of All Women: A Psychological Interpretation* (London and New York, 1933).
Harding, Mary Esther, *Women's Mysteries, Ancient and Modern* (London and New York, 1955).
Harms, Ernest, 'Carl Gustav Jung – Defender of Freud and the Jews', *The Psychiatric Quarterly*, 20 (1946), 199–230.
Harrison, Jane, *Prolegomena to the Study of Greek Religion* (London, 1935).
Hartmann, Eduard von, *Die deutsche Ästhetik seit Kant* (Leipzig, 1886).
Hartmann, Eduard von, *Die moderne Psychologie* (Leipzig, 1901).
Hartmann, Eduard von, *Die Philosophie des Unbewußten* (Leipzig, 1923[12]).
Hartmann, Eduard von, *Die Weltanschauung der modernen Physik* (Baad Sachse, 1909).
Haym, Rudolf, *Hegel und seine Zeit: Vorlesungen über Entstehung und Entwicklung, Wesen und Werth der Hegel'schen Philosophie* (Berlin, 1857).
Haymond, Robert, 'On Carl Gustav Jung: Psycho-Social Basis of Morality During the Nazi Era', *Journal of Psychology and Judaism*, 6, no.2 (Spring/Summer 1982), 81–112.
Hegel, G. W. F., *Werke*, 20 vols (Frankfurt am Main, 1986).
Heidegger, Martin, *Die Selbstbehauptung der deutschen Universität* (Breslau, 1933).
Heidegger, Martin, *Erläuterungen zu Hölderlins Dichtung* (Frankfurt am Main, 1951).
Heidegger, Martin, *Vorträge und Aufsätze* (Pfullingen, 1954).
Heine, Heinrich, *Sämtliche Werke*, 10 vols (Leipzig, 1910–1920).
Heisig, James W., *Imago Dei: A Study of C. G. Jung's Psychology* (Lewisburg, 1979).
Heisig, James W., 'Jung und die Theologie: eine bibliographische Handlung', *Analytische Psychologie*, 7 (1976), 177–220.
Heisig, James W., 'The *VII Sermones*: Play and Theory', *Spring*, 1972, 206–18.
Heller, Erich, 'Burckhardt and Nietzsche', in: *The Disinherited Mind* (London, 1952), pp. 59–77.
Helmholtz, Hermann von, *Handbuch der physiologischen Optik* (Leipzig, 1856–1866).
Henderson, Joseph, 'Ancient Myths and Modern Man', in: C. G. Jung et al, *Man and his Symbols* (London, 1964), pp. 104–57.
Henrichs, Albert, 'Between Country and City: Cultic Dimensions of Dionysus in Athens and Attica', in: *Cabinet of the Muses: Essays on Classical and Comparative Literature in Honour of Thomas G. Rosenmeyer*, edited by Mark Griffith and Donald Mastronarde (Atlanta, GA, 1990), pp. 257–77.
Henrichs, Albert, '"He Has a God in Him": Human and Divine in the Modern Perception of Dionysus', in: *Masks of Dionysus*, edited by Thomas H. Carpenter and Christopher A. Faraone (Ithaca and London, 1993), pp. 13–43.
Henrichs, Albert, 'Loss of Self, Suffering, Violence: The Modern View of Dionysus from Nietzsche to Girard', *Harvard Studies in Classical Philology*, 88 (1984), 205–40.

Hershbell, Jackson P. and Nimis, Stephen A., 'Nietzsche and Heraclitus', *Nietzsche-Studien*, 8 (1979), 17–38.
Herter, Hans, *De Priapo* (Giessen, 1932).
Herter, Hans, *Vom dionysischen Tanz zum komischen Spiel: Die Anfänge der attischen Komödie* (Iserlohn, 1947).
Higgins, Kathleen, 'The Night Song's Answer', *International Studies in Philosophy*, 17/II (1985), 33–50.
Hillebrand, Bruno (ed.), *Nietzsche-Rezeption und die deutsche Literatur: I. Texte zur Nietzsche-Rezeption 1873–1963)*, 2 vols (Tübingen, 1978).
Hillman, James, 'Dionysus in Jung's Writings', *Spring*, 1972, 191–205.
Hillmann, James, *The Dream and the Underworld* (New York, 1979).
Hillman, James, 'First Adam, then Eve', *Eranos-Jahrbuch*, 38 (1969), 349–403.
Hillman, James, 'Some Early Background to Jung's Ideas: Notes on *C. G. Jung's Medium* by Stefanie Zumstein-Preiswerk', *Spring*, 1976, 123–36.
Hoeller, Stephen A., *The Gnostic Jung and the Seven Sermons to the Dead* (Wheaton, 1982).
Hogenson, George B., *Jung's Struggle with Freud* (Notre Dame and London, 1983).
Hölderlin, Friedrich, *Sämtliche Werke*, 6 vols (Stuttgart, 1944–1962).
Hollingdale, R. J. (ed.), *A Nietzsche Reader* (Harmondsworth, 1977).
Holmyard, E. J., *Alchemy* (London, 1957).
Homans, Peter, *Jung in Context: Modernity and the Making of a Psychology* (Chicago, 1979).
Horkheimer, Max and Adorno, Theodor W., *Dialektik der Aufklärung: Philosophische Fragmente* (Frankfurt am Main, 1969).
Horneffer, Ernst, *Nietzsches Lehre von der ewigen Wiederkunft und deren bisherige Veröffentlichung* (Leipzig, 1900).
Horney, Karen, *New Ways in Psychoanalysis* (New York, 1939).
Hostie, Raymond, *Religion and the Psychology of Jung* (New York, 1957).
Houdebine, Jean-Louis, 'Jung et Joyce', *Tel Quel*, 81 (Autumn 1979), 63–65.
Houdebine, Jean-Louis, 'Jung et Picasso: le déni de l'exception', *Tel Quel*, 90 (Winter 1981), 45–55.
Howey, M. Oldfield, *The Encircled Serpent: A Study of Serpent Symbolism in All Countries and Ages* (London, 1926)
Howey, Richard Lowell, *Heidegger and Jaspers on Nietzsche* (The Hague, 1973).
Hubert, H. and Mauss, M., *Mélanges d'Histoire des religions* (Paris, 1909).
Hübner, Kurt, *Die Wahrheit des Mythos* (Munich, 1985).
Hubback, Judith, 'VII Sermones ad mortuos', *Journal of Analytical Psychology*, 11 (1986), 95–112.
Innamorati, Marco, 'La presenza dello Zarathustra di Nietzsche nelle opere di Jung', *Giornale storico di psicologia dinimica*, 29 (1991), 73–93.
Jacobi, Jolande, *Komplex/Archetypus/Symbol in der Psychologie C. G. Jungs* (Zurich and Stuttgart, 1957).
Jaffé, Aniela, *Aus Leben und Werkstatt von C. G. Jung* (Zurich, 1968).
Jaffé, Aniela, *Parapsychologie, Individuation, Nationalsozialismus: Themen bei C. G. Jung* (Zurich, 1985).
Jamme, Christoph and Schneider, Helmut, *Mythologie der Vernunft: Hegels "Ältestes Systemprogramm des deutschen Idealismus"* (Frankfurt am Main, 1984).
Jantz, Harold, 'Goethe, Faust, Alchemy, and Jung', *The German Quarterly*, 35 (1962), 129–141.
Jarrett, James L., 'Jung and Nietzsche', *Harvest*, 36 (1990), 130–54.
Jarrett, James L., 'Schopenhauer and Jung', *Spring*, 1981, 193–204.

Jaspers, Karl, *Nietzsche und das Christentum* (Hameln, 1938).
Jaspers, Karl, *Nietzsche: Einführung in das Verständnis seines Philosophierens* (Berlin and Leipzig, 1936).
Jung, C. G., *Analytical Psychology: Notes of the Seminar given in 1925*, edited by William McGuire (London, 1990).
Jung, C. G., *Briefe 1906–1961*, edited by Aniela Jaffé, 3 vols (Olten und Freiburg im Breisgau, 1972–1973).
Jung, C. G., *Collected Works*, edited by Sir Herbert Read, Michael Fordham, Gerhard Adler and William McGuire, 20 vols (London, 1953–1983).
Jung, C. G., *Dream Analysis: Notes of the Seminar given in 1928–1930*, edited by William McGuire (London, 1984).
Jung. C. G., *Erinnerungen, Träume, Gedanken von C. G. Jung*, recorded and edited by Aniela Jaffé (Zurich and Stuttgart, 1983).
Jung, C. G., *Gesammelte Werke*, edited by Lilly Jung-Merker, Elisabeth Ruf and Leonie Zander, 20 vols (Olten und Freiburg im Breisgau, 1960–1983).
Jung, C. G, *Letters*, edited by Gerhard Adler and Aniela Jaffé, 2 vols (London, 1973–1975).
Jung, C. G., *Memories, Dreams, Reflections*, recorded and edited by Aniela Jaffé, translated by Richard and Clara Winston (London, 1983).
Jung, C. G., *Nietzsche's "Zarathustra": Notes of the Seminar given in 1934–1939*, edited by James L. Jarrett, 2 vols (London, 1989).
Jung, C. G., *Psychology of the Unconscious: A Study of the Tranformations and Symbolisms of the Libido: A Contribution to the History of the Evolution of Thought*, translated by Beatrice M. Hinkle, introduced by William McGuire (London, 1991).
Jung, C. G., *The Visions Seminars*, selected and edited by Jane A. Pratt and Patricia Berry, 2 vols (Zurich, 1976)
Jung, C. G., *Wandlungen und Symbole der Libido: Beiträge zur Entwicklungsgeschichte des Denkens* (Munich, 1991).
Jung, C. G., *The Zofingia Lectures*, translated by Jan van Heurck (London, 1983).
C. G. Jung Speaking: Interviews and Encounters, edited by William McGuire and R. F. C. Hull (Princeton, 1977).
C. G. Jung-Bibliothek-Katalog (Küsnacht-Zürich, 1967).
Kaegi, Werner, *Jacob Burckhardt: Eine Biographie*, 7 vols (Basle and Stuttgart, 1947–1982).
Kant, Immanuel, *Vorlesungen über Psychologie mit einer Einleitung, Kants mystische Weltanschaaung*, edited by Carl DuPrel (Leipzig, 1889).
Kant, Immanuel, *Kritik der reinen Vernunft*, edited by Raymund Schmidt (Hamburg, 1990).
Kant, Immanuel, *Träume eines Geistersehers, erläutert durch Träume der Metaphysik* (1766) (Erlangen, 1988).
Karier, Clarence J., 'The Ethics of a Therapeutic Man: C. G. Jung', *Psychoanalytic Review*, 63 (1976), 115–46.
Kast, Verena, *Kreativität in der Psychologie von C. G. Jung*, Diss. Ph.D. unpub. (University of Zurich, 1974).
Kaufmann, Walter, *Discovering the Mind*, 3 vols (New York, 1980), III, *Freud versus Adler and Jung*.
Kaufmann, Walter, *Nietzsche: Philosopher, Psychologist, Antichrist* (Princeton, 1968).
Kaufmann, Walter, 'Nietzsche als der erste große Psychologe', *Nietzsche-Studien*, 7 (1978), 261–75
Kee, Alistair, *The Way of Transcendence: Christian Faith without Belief in God* (Harmondsworth, 1971).

Keilson-Lauritz, Marita, 'Stefan George, Alfred Schuler und die 'Kosmische Runde', *Castrum Peregrini*, 34 (1985), 24–41.

Kerényi, Károly, *Die Herkunft der Dionysosreligion* (Cologne, 1956).

Kerényi, Károly, *Dionysos und das Tragische in der Antigone* (Frankfurt am Main, 1935).

Kerényi, Károly, *Dionysos: Archetypal Image of the Indestructible Life*, translated by Ralph Manheim (Princeton, 1976).

Kerényi, Károly, 'Nietzsche und Ariadne: Gedanken über die Zukunft des Humanismus', *Neue Schweizer Rundschau*, 7, November 1944, 402–12.

Kerr, John, *A Most Dangerous Method: The Story of Jung, Freud, and Sabina Spielrein* (London, 1994).

Keyserling, Hermann Graf (ed.), *Mensch und Erde* (Darmstadt, 1927).

King, Richard, *The Party of Eros: Radical Social Thought and the Realm of Freedom* (Chapel Hill, 1972).

Kirchhoff, Jochen, *Nietzsche, Hitler und die Deutschen: Die Perversion des Neuen Zeitalters: Vom unerlösten Schatten des Dritten Reiches* (Berlin, 1990).

Kirsch, Hildegard, 'Crossing the Ocean: Memoirs of Jung', *Psychological Perspectives*, 6 (1975), 128–34.

Kirsch, James, 'Carl Gustav Jung and the Jews: The Real Story', *Journal of Psychology and Judaism*, 6 no.2 (Spring/Summer 1982), 113–43.

Kirsch, James, 'Jungs sogenannter Antisemitismus', *Analytische Psychologie*, 16 (1985), 40–65.

Kirsch, Thomas, 'Nietzsche's *Zarathustra*: Notes of the Seminar given in 1934–1939' (book review), *Quadrant*, 22, no.2 (1989), 101–02.

Klages, Ludwig, *Mensch und Erde: Zehn Abhandlungen* (Stuttgart, 1956).

Knapp, Bettina L., *Gérard de Nerval: The Mystic's Dilemma* (Alabama, 1980).

Knight, Richard Payne, *A Discourse on the Worship of Priapus and its Connection with the Mystic Theology of the Ancients* (London, 1786).

Köhler, Joachim, *Zarathustras Geheimnis: Friedrich Nietzsche und seine verschlüsselte Botschaft: Eine Biographie* (Reinbek bei Hamburg, 1992).

Kofman, Sarah, 'Nietzsche and the Obscurity of Heraclitus', *Diacritics*, 17, no.3 (Fall 1987), 39–55.

Körner, Stephan, *Kant* (Harmondsworth, 1955).

Korte, Hermann, 'Die Abdankung der "Lichtbringer": Wilhelminisches Ära und literarischer Expressionismus in Ernst Tollers Komödie "Der entfesselte Wotan"', *Germanisch-Romanische Monatsschrift*, 65 (1984), 117–32.

Krackel, Arthur (ed.), *Freideutsche Jugend: Zur Jahrhundertfeier auf dem Hohen Meißner* (Jena, 1913).

Kuhn, Helmut, 'Das Gute', in: *Handbuch philosophischer Grundbegriffe*, edited by Hermann Krings et al. (Munich, 1973), p. 672.

Kundert, Werner, *Abriß der Geschichte des schweizerischen Zofingervereins* (Lausanne, 1961).

Kushner, Eva, *Le Mythe d'Orphée dans la littérature française contemporaine* (Paris, 1961).

Lampert, Laurence, *Nietzsche's Teaching: An Interpretation of Thus Spoke Zarathustra* (New Haven and London, 1986).

Landsberg, Hans, *Friedrich Nietzsche und die deutsche Literatur* (Leipzig, 1902).

Lange, Friedrich Albert, *Geschichte des Materialismus und Kritik seiner Bedeutung in der Gegenwart*, edited by Alfred Schmidt, 2 vols (Frankfurt am Main, 1974).

Lawrence, D. H., *Phoenix* (London, 1967).

Lehmann, Herbert, 'Jung contra Freud/Nietzsche contra Wagner', *International Review of Psycho-Analysis*, 13 (1986), 201–09.

Lesmeister, Roman, 'Die Gnosis als unbewältigte esoterische Erbe der Analytischen Psychologie', *Analytische Psychologie*, 22 (1991), 191–208.

Lévy, Albert, *Stirner et Nietzsche* (Paris, 1904).

Livingstone, Angela, *Lou Andreas-Salomé* (London, 1984).

Lotze, R. H., *System der Philosophie*, 2 vols (Leipzig, 1874–1879).

Löwith, Karl, *Kierkegaard and Nietzsche* (Frankfurt am Main, 1933).

Löwith, Karl, *Nietzsches Philosophie der ewigen Wiederkehr des Gleichen* (Hamburg, 1978).

Luke, F. D., 'Nietzsche and the Imagery of Height', in: *Nietzsche: Imagery and Thought*, edited by Malcolm Pasley (London, 1978).

Macintyre, Ben, *Forgotten Fatherland: The Search for Elisabeth Nietzsche* (London, 1992).

Macquarrie, John, *An Existentialist Theology: A Comparison of Heidegger and Bultmann* (Harmondsworth, 1973).

Macquarrie, John, *Existentialism: An Introduction, Guide and Assessment* (New York, 1972).

Mähly, Jacob, *Die Schlange im Mythus und Kultus der klassischen Völker* (Basle, 1867).

Maidenbaum, Aryeh and Martin, Stephen A. (eds.), *Lingering Shadows: Jungians, Freudians, and Anti-Semitism* (Boston and London, 1991).

Maillard, Christine, *Les Sept sermons aux morts de Carl Gustav Jung* (Nancy, 1993).

Mann, Thomas, *Gesammelte Werke*, 13 vols (Frankfurt am Main, 1960–1974).

Marcuse, Herbert, *Eros and Civilization* (London, 1956).

Martens, Gunter, 'Hölderlin-Rezeption in der Nachfolge Nietzsches – Stationen der Aneignung eines Dichters', *Hölderlin-Jahrbuch*, 23 (1982/83), 54–78.

Martin, Luther H. and Goss, James, (eds.), *Essays on Jung and the Study of Religion* (Lanham, 1985).

Martin, P. W., *Experiment in Depth: A Study of the Work of Jung, Eliot and Toynbee* (London, 1955).

May, Rollo, 'Nietzsches Beiträge zur Psychologie', *Jahrbuch für Verstehende Tiefenpsychologie und Kulturanalyse*, 1 (1981), 11–22.

Mazlish, Bruce, 'Freud and Nietzsche', *The Psychoanalytic Review*, 55 (1968), 360–75.

McDougall, William, 'The Present Chaos in Psychology and the Way Out', *Journal of Philosophical Studies*, 5, no. 19 (July 1930), 353–63.

McGahey, Robert, *The Orphic Moment: Shaman to Poet-Thinker in Plato, Nietzsche and Mallarmé* (New York, 1994).

McGuire, William, *Bollingen: An Adventure in Collecting the Past* (Princeton, 1982).

Megill, Allan, *Prophets of Extremity* (Berkeley, 1985).

Mette, Alexander, *Die psychologischen Wurzeln des Dionysischen und Apollinischen: Ein neuer Versuch* (Berlin, 1940).

Mette, Alexander, *Die tiefenpsychologischen Grundlagen des Tragischen, Apollinschen und Dionysischen* (Berlin, 1934).

Mette, Alexander, 'Nietzsches "Geburt der Tragödie" in psychoanalytischer Beleuchtung', *Imago*, 18 (1932), 67–80.

Meyer, Richard M., *Nietzsche: Sein Leben und seine Werke* (Munich, 1913)

Miller, David L., 'Nietzsche's Horse and other Tracings of the Gods', *Stanford Italian Review*, 6 (1986), 159–170.

Miller, J. Hillis, 'The Disarticulation of the Self in Nietzsche', *The Monist*, 64 (1981), 247–61.

Möbius, Paul Julius, *Über das Pathologische bei Nietzsche* (Wiesbaden, 1902).

Moreno, Antonio, *Jung, Gods and Modern Man* (London, 1974).

Mosse, George L., 'The Mystical Origins of National Socialism', *Journal of the History of Ideas*, 22 (1961), 81–96.

Nagy, Marilyn, *Philosophical Issues in the Psychology of C. G. Jung* (New York, 1991).
Nagy, Marilyn, 'Self and Freedom in Jung's Lecture on Ritschl', *Journal of Analytical Psychology*, 35 (1990), 443–57.
Nehamas, Alexander, *Nietzsche: Life as Literature* (Cambridge, MA, 1986).
Neumann, Micha, 'Die Beziehungen zwischen Erich Neumann und C. G. Jung und die Frage des Antisemitismus', *Analytische Psychologie*, 23 (1992), 3–23.
Nicholls, R. A., 'Beginnings of the Nietzsche Vogue in Germany', *Modern Philology*, 56 (1958/59), 24–37.
Nietzsche, Friedrich, *Basic Writings of Nietzsche*, translated by Walter Kaufmann (New York, 1968).
Nietzsche, Friedrich, *Briefwechsel: Kritische Gesamtausgabe*, edited by Giorgio Colli and Mazzino Montinari, 24 vols in 4 sections (Berlin, 1975–1984).
Nietzsche, Friedrich, *Daybreak*, translated by R. J. Hollingdale (Cambridge, 1982).
Nietzsche, Friedrich, *Dithyrambs of Dionysos*, translated by R. J. Hollingdale (London, 1984).
Nietzsche, Friedrich, *Ecce Homo*, translated by R. J. Hollingdale (Harmondsworth, 1979).
Nietzsche, Friedrich, *The Gay Science*, translated By Walter Kaufmann (New York, 1974).
Nietzsche, Friedrich, *Human, All Too Human*, translated by R. J. Hollingdale (Cambridge, 1986).
Nietzsche, Friedrich, *Thus spake Zarathustra*, translated by R. J. Hollingdale (Harmondsworth, 1961).
Nietzsche, Friedrich, *Twilight of the Idols/The Anti-Christ*, translated by R. J. Hollingdale (Harmondsworth, 1968).
Nietzsche, Friedrich, *Die Unschuld des Werdens: Der Nachlaß*, edited by Alfred Baeumler, 2 vols (Stuttgart, 1978).
Nietzsche, Friedrich, *Untimely Meditations*, translated by R. J. Hollingdale (Cambridge, 1983).
Nietzsche, Friedrich, *Werke in drei Bänden*, edited by Karl Schlechta (Munich, 1966).
Nietzsche, Friedrich, *Werke: Kritische Gesamtausgabe*, edited by Giorgio Colli and Mazzino Montinari, 30 vols (Berlin and New York, 1967 –).
Nietzsche, Friedrich, *The Will to Power*, translated by Walter Kaufmann and R. J. Hollingdale (New York, 1968).
Nietzsche, Friedrich, *Der Wille zur Macht: Versuch einer Umwertung aller Werte*, edited by Peter Gast and Elisabeth Förster-Nietzsche (Stuttgart, 1964).
Nietzsches Bibliothek (Weimar, 1942).
Nill, Peggy, 'Die Versuchung der Psyche: Selbstwerdung als schöpferisches Prinzip bei Nietzsche und C. G. Jung', *Nietzsche-Studien*, 17 (1988), 250–79.
Nilsson, Martin Persson, *Geschichte der griechischen Religion* (*Handbuch der Altertumswissenschaft*, 5. Abteilung, 2. Teil), 2 vols (Munich, 1941–1950).
Nishitani, Keiji, *The Self-Overcoming of Nihilism*, translated Graham Parkes and Setsuko Aihara (Albany, 1990).
Noel, Daniel C., 'Veiled Kabir: C. G. Jung's Phallic Self-Image', *Spring* 1974, 224–42.
Noll, Richard, *The Jung Cult: Origins of a Charismatic Movement* (Princeton, 1994).
Noorden, Hans von, 'Das Rätsel des Hellsehens: Probleme von Kant bis C. G. Jung', *Schopenhauer-Jahrbuch*, 52 (1971), 19–39.
Oeri, Albert, 'Ein paar Erinnerungen', in: *Die kulturelle Bedeutung der komplexen Psychologie* (Berlin, 1935).
Oesterreich, Traugott, *Die deutsche Philosophie des XIX. Jahrhunderts und der Gegenwart: IV. Teil von Friedrich Überwegs Grundriß der Geschichte der Philosophie* (Berlin, 1916[11]).

Oldfield, Helen, 'The Professor who found True Bliss', *The Guardian*, 16 August 1990.
Otto, Walter Friedrich, *Dionysos: Mythos und Kultus* (Frankfurt am Main, 1933).
Owen, Alex, *The Darkened Room: Women, Power and Spiritualism in Late Nineteenth Century England* (London, 1989).
O'Brien, Edward J., *Son of the Morning: A Portrait of Friedrich Nietzsche* (London, 1932).
Paglia, Camille, *Sex, Art and American Culture* (New York, 1992).
Paglia, Camille, *Sexual Personae: Art and Decadence from Nefertiti to Emily Dickinson* (Yale, 1990).
Pannwitz, Rudolf, 'C. G. Jung's Wissenschaft der Seele', *Merkur*, 63 (1953), 418–38.
Papadopoulos, Renos K. and Saayman Graham (eds.), *Jung in Modern Perspective* (Hounslow, 1984).
Parkes, Graham, *Composing the Soul: Reaches of Nietzsche's Psychology* (Chicago and London), 1994.
Pascal, Blaise, *Pensées et Opuscules*, edited by Léon Brunschvicg (Paris, 1959).
Pauck, Wilhelm and Marjon, *Paul Tillich: Sein Leben und Denken*, 2 vols (Stuttgart and Frankfurt am Main, 1977).
Perkins, Richard, 'Nietzsche's *opus alchymicum*', *Seminar*, 23 (1987), 216–26.
Peters, H. F., *Zarathustra's Sister: The Case of Elisabeth and Friedrich Nietzsche* (New York, 1977).
Peters, Roderick, 'C. G. Jung: *Nietzsche's Zarathustra*' [book review], *Journal of Analytical Psychology*, 36 (1991), 125–27.
Pfeffer, Rose, *Nietzsche: Disciple of Dionysus* (Lewisburg, 1972).
Pfotenhauer, Helmut, 'Dionysos: Heinse – Hölderlin – Nietzsche', *Hölderlin-Jahrbuch*, 26 (1988/89), 38–59.
Philipson, Morris H., *An Outline of Jungian Aesthetics* (Boston, 1994^2).
Podach, Erich F., *Ein Blick in Notizbücher Nietzsches: Eine schaffensanalytische Studie* (Heidelberg, 1963).
Preller, Ludwig, *Griechische Mythologie*, 2 vols (Berlin, 1860).
Prinzhorn, Hans, *Nietzsche und das 20. Jahrhundert* (Heidelberg, 1928).
Prinzhorn, Hans, 'Der Kampf um Friedrich Nietzsche', *Deutsche Rundschau*, 58 (1932), 117–124.
Prinzhorn, Hans, 'Nietzsches psychologische Errungenschaften', *Zeitschrift für Menschenkunde*, 2 (1926), 51–58;
Protokolle der Wiener Psychoanalytische Vereinigung, edited by Herman Nunberg and Ernst Federn, 4 vols (Frankfurt am Main, 1976–1981).
Pugmire, David, 'Understanding the Psyche: Some Philosophical Roots and Affinities of Analytical Psychology', *Harvest*, 27 (1981), 90–102.
Radin, Paul, *Der göttliche Schelm* (Zurich, 1954).
Rank, Otto, *Der Künstler: Ansätze zu einer Sexualpsychologie* (Vienna, 1907).
Raphael, Alice, *Goethe and the Philosophers' Stone: Symbolical Patterns in 'The Parable' and the Second Part of 'Faust'* (New York, 1965).
Raphael, Alice, *Goethe, the Challenger* (New York, 1932).
Raschel, Heinz, *Das Nietzsche-Bild im George-Kreis: Ein Beitrag zur Geschichte der deutschen Mythologeme* (Berlin and New York, 1984).
Rattner, Josef, *Klassiker der Tiefenpsychologie* (Munich, 1990).
Reinhardt, Karl, *Nietzsches Klage der Ariadne* (Frankfurt am Main, 1936).
Reichert, Herbert W. and Schlechta, Karl, *International Nietzsche Bibliography* (North Carolina U. P., 1968^2).
Ribi, A., 'Zum schöpferischen Prozess bei C. G. Jung: Aus den Excerptbänden zur Alchemie', *Analytische Psychologie*, 13 (1982), 201–21.

Ridley, Hugh, 'Myth as Illusion or Cognition: Feuerbach, Wagner and Nietzsche', *German Life and Letters*, 34 (1980/81), 74–80.
Rieff, Philip, *The Triumph of the Therapeutic: Uses of Faith after Freud* (London, 1966).
Roazen, Paul, *Freud and His Followers* (London, 1976).
Roberts, Julian, *German Philosophy: An Introduction* (Cambridge, 1988).
Roberts, R. H., 'Nietzsche and the Cultural Resonance of the "Death of God"', *History of European Ideas*, 11 (1989), 1025–35.
Rohde, Erwin, *Psyche: Seelencult und Unsterblichkeit der Griechen* (Tübingen, 1907[4]).
Rohmann, Klaus, *Vollendung im Nichts?: Eine Dokumentation der amerikanischen "Gott-ist-tot-Theologie"* (Zurich, 1977).
Rolle, Pierre Nicolas, *Recherches sur le culte de Bacchus, symbole de la force reproductive de la nature*, 2 vols (Paris, 1824).
Rose, Gillian, *The Broken Middle* (Oxford, 1992).
Rose, Gillian, *Judaism and Modernity: Philosophical Essays* (Oxford, 1993).
Roth, Robin Alice, 'Answer to "The Night Song's Answer"', *International Studies in Philosophy*, 17/II (1985), 51–54.
Rudolph, Arthur William, *Superhistorical Individuality in Nietzsche's Thought*, Diss. Ph. D. unpub. (University of Southern California, 1963).
Rudolph, Arthur William, 'Jung and Zarathustra', *Philosophy Today*, 18 (Winter 1974), 312–18.
Rudolph, Arthur, 'Jung and Zarathustra', *Philosophy Today*, 18 (Winter 1974), 312–18.
Salaquarda, Jörg, 'Dionysos gegen den Gekreuzigten: Nietzsches Verständnis des Apostels Paulus', *Zeitschrift für Religions- und Geistesgeschichte*, 26 (1974), 97–124.
Salaquarda, Jörg, 'Nietzsche und Lange', *Nietzsche-Studien*, 7 (1978), 236–53.
Salin, Edgar, *Jakob Burckhardt und Nietzsche* (Basle, 1938).
Samuels, Andrew, *Jung and the Post-Jungians* (London and New York, 1985).
Samuels, Andrew, Foreword to C. G. Jung's *Essays on Contemporary Events: Reflections on Nazi Germany*, trans. R. F. C. Hull (London, 1988), pp.vii–xiii.
Samuels, Andrew, 'Nationale Psychologie, Nationalsozialismus und Analytische Psychologie', *Analytische Psychologie*, 23 (1992), 41–94.
Samuels, Andrew, 'The Professionalization of Carl G. Jung's Analytical Psychology Clubs', *Journal of the History of the Behavioral Sciences*, 30 (April, 1994), 138–47.
Samuels, Andrew, *The Political Psyche* (London, 1993).
Schacht, Wilhelm, *Nietzsche: Eine psychiatrisch-philosophische Untersuchung* (Berne, 1901).
Scheler, Max, *Die Stellung des Menschen im Kosmos* (Bonn, 1988).
Schelling, F. W. J. von, *Ausgewählte Werke*, 10 vols (Darmstadt, 1975–1976).
Schelling, F. W. J. von, *Philosophie der Offenbarung 1841/42*, edited by Manfred Frank (Frankfurt am Main, 1977).
Schelling, F. W. J. von, *Über die Gottheiten von Samothrace* (Stuttgart, 1815).
Schelling, F. W. J. von, *Werke*, 6 vols (Munich, 1958–1959).
Schiller, Friedrich, *On the Aesthetic Education of Man in a Series of Letters*, edited and translated by Elizabeth M. Wilkinson and L. A. Willoughby (Oxford, 1967).
Schiller, Friedrich, *Werke in drei Bänden*, edited by Herbert G. Göpfert and Gerhard Fricke (Munich, 1966).
Schlegel, Friedrich, *Kritische Ausgabe seiner Werken*, edited by Ernst Behler, 18 vols (Munich, 1958–1963).
Schmitt, Richard, 'Nietzsche's Psychological Theory', *Journal of Existential Psychiatry*, 2 (1961), 71–92.
Schnädelbach, Herbert, *Philosophie in Deutschland 1831–1933* (Frankfurt am Main, 1983).

Schrift, Alan D., *Nietzsche and the Question of Interpretation: Between Hermeneutics and Deconstruction* (New York and London, 1990).

Schubart, Walter, *Religion und Eros*, edited by Friedrich Seifert (Munich, 1966), pp. 48–51.

Schuler, Karl-Heinz, 'Alfred Schuler: Familiengeschichte und Jugend', *Castrum Peregrini*, 34 (1985), 42–58.

Schutte, Ofelia, *Beyond Nihilism: Nietzsche without Masks* (Chicago and London, 1984).

Scott-Maxwell, Florida, *Women and Sometimes Men* (New York, 1957).

Seifert, Friedrich, *Seele und Bewußtsein: Betrachtungen zum Problem der psychischen Realität* (Munich and Basle, 1962).

Shaer, Hans, *Religion and the Cure of Souls in Jung's Psychology* (New York, 1957).

Shamdasani, Sonu, 'A Woman Called Frank', *Spring*, 50 (1990), 26–56.

Shapiro, Gary, *Nietzschean Narratives* (Bloomington and Indianapolis, 1989), pp. 16–21.

Shelburne, Walter A., *Mythos and Logos in the Thought of Carl Jung: The Theory of the Collective Unconscious in Scientific Perspective* (New York, 1988).

Sherry, Jay, 'Jung, the Jews, and Hitler', *Spring*, 1986, 163–75.

Silberer, Herbert, *Probleme der Mystik und ihrer Symbolik* (Vienna and Leipzig, 1914).

Silk, M. S. and Stern, J. P., *Nietzsche on Tragedy* (Cambridge, 1981).

Singer, June, *Androgyny: Toward a New Theory of Sexuality* (New York, 1976).

Slochower, Harry, 'Freud as Yahweh in Jung's *Answer to Job*', *American Imago*, 38, no.1 (Spring 1981), 3–60.

Smith, Evans Lansing, 'Descent to the Underworld: Jung and His Brothers', in *C. G. Jung and the Humanities: Towards a Hermeneutics of Culture*, edited by Karin Barnaby and Pellegrino d'Acierno (London, 1990), pp. 250–64.

Spielrein, Sabina, *Sämtliche Schriften* (Freiburg, 1988).

Spies, Dieter, *Philosophische Aspekte der Psychologie C. G. Jungs*, Diss. Ph.D. unpub. (University of Munich, 1975).

Steele, Robert S., *Freud and Jung; Conflicts of Interpretation* (London, 1982).

Stern, Karl, *The Flight from Woman* (New York, 1965).

Stern, Paul J., *C. G. Jung: The Haunted Prophet* (New York, 1976).

Stevens, Anthony, *On Jung* (London, 1990).

Storr, Anthony, *The Dynamics of Creation* (London, 1972).

Storr, Anthony, *Jung* (London, 1973).

Storr, Anthony (ed.), *Jung: Selected Writings* (London, 1983).

Storr, Anthony, *Freud* (Oxford, 1989).

Strauss, Walter A., *Descent and Return: The Orphic Theme in Modern Literature* (Cambridge, MA, 1971).

Surette, Leon, *The Birth of Modernism* (Montreal, 1993).

Szasz, Thomas, *Heresies* (New York, 1976).

Taylor, F. Sherwood, *The Alchemists* (London, 1952).

Taylor, Seth, *Left-Wing Nietzscheans: The Politics of German Expressionism 1910–1920* (Berlin and New York, 1990).

Thatcher, David, 'Eagle and Serpent in *Zarathustra*', *Nietzsche-Studien*, 6 (1977), 240–60.

Thomas, Richard Hinton, *Nietzsche in German Politics and Society 1890–1918* (Manchester, 1983).

Thomas, Richard Hinton, 'Nietzsche in Weimar Germany – and the Case of Ludwig Klages', in: *The Weimar Dilemma: Intellectuals in the Weimar Republic*, edited by Anthony Phelan (Manchester, 1985), pp. 71–91.

Tilander, Ake, 'C. G. Jung's Autobiography: An Evaluation of C. G. Jung's Autobiography as a Source of Information on his Psychohistory', *Journal of Personality and Clinical Studies*, 6 (1990), 25–34.

Tillich, Hannah, *From Time to Time* (New York, 1973).
Tillich, Paul, *The Courage to Be* (New Haven), 1952).
Tourney, Garfield, 'Empedocles and Freud, Heraclitus and Jung', *Bulletin of the History of Medicine*, 30 (1956), 109–23.
Tramer, Friedrich, 'Friedrich Nietzsche und Sigmund Freud', *Jahrbuch für Psychologie, Psychotherapie und Anthropologie*, 7 (1960), 325–50.
Ulanov, Ann and Barry, *Religion and the Unconscious* (Philadelphia, 1975).
Unger, Franz, *Friedrich Nietzsches Träumen und Sterben* (Munich, 1900).
Valois, Raynald, 'C. G. Jung et les racines de la guerre', *Laval théologique et philosophique*, 48, no.2 (June 1992), 263–77.
Van der Leeuw, P. J., 'The Impact of the Freud-Jung Correspondence on the History of Ideas', *International Review of Psycho-Analysis*, 4 (1977), 349–62.
Van der Post, Laurens, *Jung and the Story of our Time* (London, 1976).
Van Meurs, Jos, *Jungian Literary Criticism, 1920–1980: An Annotated, Critical Bibliography of Works in English* (Metuchen, NJ, 1988).
Vernon, P. E. (ed.), *Creativity* (Harmondsworth, 1972).
Vogel, Martin, *Apollinisch und Dionysisch: Geschichte eines genialen Irrtums* (Studien zur Musikgeschichte des 19. Jahrhunderts, vol. 6) (Regensburg, 1966).
Volz, Pia Daniela, *Nietzsche im Labyrinth seiner Krankheit: Eine medizinisch-biographische Untersuchung* (Würzburg, 1990).
Von der Luft, Eric, 'Sources of Nietzsche's "God is dead!" and its Meaning for Heidegger', *Journal of the History of Ideas*, 45 (1984), 263–76.
Von Martin, Alfred, *Nietzsche und Burckhardt* (Munich, 1942).
Voogd, Stephanie de, 'C. G. Jung: Psychologist of the Future, 'Philosopher' of the Past', *Spring*, 1977, 175–82.
Voogd, Stephanie de, 'Fantasy versus Fiction: Jung's Kantianism Appraised', in: *Jung in Modern Perspective*, edited by Renos K. Papadopoulos and Graham S. Saayman (Hounslow, 1984), pp. 204–28.
Die Vorsokratiker, translated and edited by Jaap Mansfeld, 2 vols (Stuttgart, 1983).
Wallace, Edwin R., 'A commentary on the Freud-Jung letters', *Psychoanalytic Review*, 67 (1980), 111–37.
Waugamann, Richard, 'The Intellectual Relationship between Nietzsche and Freud', *Psychiatry*, 36 (1973), 458–67.
Weber, Frank, *Die Bedeutung Nietzsches für Stefan George und seinen Kreis* (Frankfurt am Main, 1989).
Weber, Max, *Gesammelte Aufsätze zur Wissenschaftslehre* (Tübingen, 1968).
Wehr, Gerhard, *An Illustrated Biography of C. G. Jung*, translated by Michael Kohn (Boston, 1989).
Wehr, Gerhard, *Carl Gustav Jung: Leben, Werk, Wirkung* (Munich, 1985).
Wehr, Gerhard, *Friedrich Nietzsche als Tiefenpyschologe* (Oberwil bei Zug, 1987).
Wesche, Ulrich, 'The Spirits' Chorus in *Faust*: A Jungian Reading', *Germanic Notes*, 14, no.4 (1983), 49–51.
Whyte, Lancelot L., *The Unconscious before Freud* (London, 1960).
Willeford, William, 'Jung's Polaristic Thought in its Historical Setting', *Analytische Psychologie*, 6 (1975), 218–39.
Willey, Thomas E., *Back to Kant: The Revival of Kantianism in German Social and Historical Thought, 1860–1914* (Detroit, 1978).
Wilson, Colin, *Lord of the Underworld* (Wellingborough, 1984).
Winckelmann, Johann Joachim, *Geschichte der Kunst des Altertums*, edited by Wilhelm Senff (Weimar, 1964).

Winnicott, Donald, *Memories, Dreams, Reflections:* By C. G. Jung [book-review], *International Journal of Psychoanalysis*, 45 (1964), 450–55.

Wolff-Windegg, Philipp, 'C. G. Jung – Bachofen, Burckhardt, and Basel', *Spring*, 1976, pp. 137–47.

Wollheim, Richard, 'Freud and the Understanding of Art', in *On Art and the Mind* (London, 1973), pp. 202–19.

Woodman, Ross, 'Nietzsche's Madness as Soul-Making: A View Contra Jung's', *Spring*, 1986, 101–18.

Wright, Thomas, *The Worship of the Generative Powers During the Middle Ages of Western Europe* (London, 1866).

Wundt, Wilhelm, *Grundriß der Psychologie* (Leipzig, 1896).

Wundt, Wilhelm, *Grundzüge der physiologischen Psychologie* (Leipzig, 1911[6]).

Wyly, James, 'Jung and Picasso', *Quadrant*, 19 (1986), 7–21.

Zöllner, Johann Karl Friedrich, *Wissenschaftliche Abhandlungen*, 3 vols (Leipzig, 1878–1879).

Zumstein-Preiswerk, Stefanie, *C. G. Jungs Medium: Die Geschichte der Helly Preiswerk* (Munich, 1975).

Index

Absolute 39*n*, 371
Adler, Alfred 9, 10, 60, 74, 80, 124, 130, 138
Adorno, Theodor W. *see* Horkheimer, Max
aesthetic and rational types 141–2
Aesthetism 146–7, 150, 152, 249, 306
Africa 77, 79
Ahriman 280
Ahura Maszda (Ormuzd) 280
Aksakov, Alexander 31
alchemy 42, 73, 77, 212, 221, 222–30, 272, 273, 279, 297, 324, 345, 362, 366
allegory of reading 16
Allgemeine Ärztliche Gesellschaft für Psychotherapie 130–1*n*
Allgemeine Deutsche Frauenverein 114*n*
Analytical Psychology 7, 13, 39, 73, 75, 81, 123, 190*n*, 270, 335, 339
  and alchemy 223
  and concept of Self 343, 346
  and Hegel 11
  language of 73, 165
  in literary and aesthetic interpretation 177–80, 185, 266
  and myth 157, 356, 362
  Nietzsche's philosophy related to 4, 20, 44, 180, 187–8, 192, 249, 252, 296–7, 364
  phallic vision and 51
  and psychoanalysis 197, 244, 254, 364
  roots of 366, 379
  as substitute religion 378
  and Unconscious 72
analytic–reductive method 16
Anderson, Lorin 195–6
Andreas-Salomé, Lou 24–5, 44*n*, 60, 195, 201, 271, 348*n*
  Friedrich Nietzsche in seinen Werken 26
  In der Schule bei Freud 24–6
Angelus Silesius 289
Angra Mainyu (Ahriman) 280
Angulo, Cary F. de *see* Baynes, Cary F.
Angulo, Ximena de 44
Anima 193, 198, 200–4, 205, 208, 209, 250
  absent in Nietzsche 278, 318–19
  and spirit ('Geist') 198–204
  as temptress and witch 182, 202–4
  see also archetypes
Anima/Animus 337
Anthony, Maggy 270
anti-Semitism 129*n*, 130–1, 303–7, 373
Apollonian societies 371
Apollo–Dionysos polarity 9, 12, 18–19, 55, 62–3, 75, 80, 120, 123, 124–6, 127–8, 134, 137, 139–42, 144, 146–51, 154, 157, 218, 221, 246, 249, 251, 252, 260, 296, 321, 354, 370, 371, 377, 378
Apter, T.E. 374
Aquinas, Thomas 5*n*, 53
archetypes 6, 19, 54, 86–7, 98, 102, 107, 117, 181, 198, 199, 200, 207, 248, 339
  archetypal criticism 2
  in art 163–6, 185–6
  as categories 373*n*
  of father 22
  of life and meaning 204–5
  of Old Wise Man 169, 193, 198, 208–10, 249, 250, 276–7
  and Schopenhauer's Platonic Ideas 247
  and Second World War 306
  Trickster 337
  Wotan/Dionysos 161, 167
  see also Anima; Mother figure; Puer Aeternus; Rebirth; Self
Ariadne 201, 270
Aristotle 5*n*, 139–40, 275
  De anima 187
art
  artistic inspiration 17
  Jung's views of 156–67
  medical vocabulary in discussion of 178*n*
  psychological and visionary modes 168
  theory of 156–86, 247, 253*n*
Aschheim, Steven E. 12–13, 42
Ascona, Casa Gabriella 211
Aston, Luise 115*n*
astral myth 98, 102, 300
astrology 65
atomic physics 297
Augustine, St 3
authenticity 5, 170, 314–15
autonomy 162, 174
  of art 160, 163

Bachofen, Johann Jakob 10, 23, 24, 100*n*, 247*n*, 271, 272, 371
  Gräbersymbolik 24
  Das Mutterrecht 12
  Der Mythus von Orient und Occident 24
Baeck, Rabbi Leo 321
Baeumer, Max 18
Bahadurji, Dr. Piroja 45*n*
Bancroft, Mary 267–8, 374
  Autobiography of a Spy 44
barbarism 126–34, 142, 151, 154
  and one-sidedness 132–3, 166, 169, 175
Barnaby, Karin, and d'Acierno, Pellegrino 14–16
Baroni, Christophe 12
Barrès, Maurice 219*n*
Barth, Karl 324
Basle 252, 270–1
  Cathedral 51, 56, 272
  Gymnasium 52–5
  St Alban's church 52
  spring ceremonies 256
  University 22–3, 24, 27, 46, 47, 55, 272
Baubo 236*n*
Baynes, Cary F. (de Angulo) 244, 284
Baynes, Helton Godwin 244, 373–4
  Germany Possessed 373–4
BBC, Third Programme 315
Behaviourism 9
Benedict, Ruth 371
Benn, Gottfried, 'Turin' 56*n*
Benz, Ernst 211
Berdyaev, Nikolai 8
Bernoulli, Carl Albrecht 19
  Franz Overbeck und Friedrich Nietzsche: Eine Freundschaft 281*n*
Bernoulli, Rudolf 224
Bertine, Eleanor 244
Bertram, Ernst 288*n*
Binswanger, Ludwig 21
Binswanger, Otto 21
Bismarck, Otto Prince 27
Bleuler, Eugen 33*n*, 238*n*
Bloch, Ernst 303
  Das Prinzip Hoffnung 12
blond beast 127–9, 133, 174, 175, 239*n*, 306, 307, 320, 323
Bodkin, Maud 2
Böhme, Jakob 37, 41, 289, 363
Bollingen, Jung's Tower at 75–6, 237–8
Bonhoeffer, Dietrich 324
Bowman, Dr. Herbert E. 45*n*, 80
Brandes, Georg 23
Bremi, Dr. Willi 45*n*
Brenner, Albert 169, 318
bridge, image of 335–6
Brinton, Crane 303
Broch, Hermann, *Der Tod des Vergil* 176
Brome, Vincent 3, 93, 266–70
Brooke, Roger 77
Brown, James 2
Brown, Norman O. 19, 377
Bruderbund 221
Brunner, Cornelia 268, 269
Bruno, Giordano 39*n*
Buber, Martin 211
Büchner, Ludwig, *Kraft und Stoff* 188
Buddha 14*n*
Bultmann, Rudolf 324
Burckhardt, Jacob 22–3, 44, 52, 55, 79, 108, 110, 169, 271, 272, 318
Burghölzli clinic 21, 59, 60

C.I.A. 374
Caillois, Roger 374–5
Campbell, Joseph 14*n*
Capri 110
Carlsson, Anni 9
Carnival tradition 252–3, 256
Carus, Carl Gustav 336, 337
Cassirer, Ernst, *Der Mythus des Staates* 374
castration complex 88
categorical imperative 34–5
causality, category of 34–7
Chamberlain, Houston Stewart 259, 310
chaos 205–6, 253*n*
Chapman, J. Harley 14, 355*n*
Charakter (journal) 193
Charet, F. X. 238*n*
charisma 375
Christ 41, 50, 51, 63, 81, 98, 101, 120, 122*n*, 256, 361–2
  as resurrected deity 288, 334*n*
  see also Dionysos, and Christ
Christianity 22*n*, 39, 40, 41, 51, 63, 64, 72, 93, 105–6, 114, 115, 116, 128–9, 135, 226*n*, 229, 235, 257–9, 276, 287, 288, 293, 309, 324
  and mysticism 366
  Nietzsche's critique of 326–30, 346
chthonic qualities 255, 260, 309
  see also earth
circumambulation, imagery of 345
Claparède, Edouard 329*n*
Claparède-Spir, Hélène 329*n*
Clarke, John J. 7, 8
coincidentia oppositorum 330
Coleridge, Samuel Taylor 160*n*
collective hysteria 317

Collective Unconscious 15, 45*n*, 48, 73, 77, 99*n*, 107*n*, 108, 117, 142*n*, 163–4, 168–9, 175, 181, 186, 198–9, 246, 287, 352, 366, 379
Colli, Giorgio 358
Colonna, Francesco 172, 270
Common, Thomas 16*n*
compensation 168
complementarism 192
coniunctio oppositorum 81, 221, 232, 234, 355, 362, 379
Conrad, Joseph, *Heart of Darkness* 175–6
consciousness, Jung's concept of 299
Copenhagen, University of 23
Copleston, Father Frederick 330
Corti, Walter Robert 45*n*, 78
Corybantes 252–3
cosmos 205–6
Cowan, Lyn 376
Creative Person 15
creativity 11, 13, 19, 20
Creatura 117
Creuzer, Friedrich, *Symbolik und Mythologie der alten Völker* 61, 91, 105, 113, 280, 359, 366*n*, 370
Crookes, William 31
Crookshank, F.G. 9
Crowley, Alice 269
Crucifixion, symbolism and paradox of 327, 329
cryptomnesia 83–4, 86–7
culture
  collective and individual 135–6
  and nature 298–9
  and religion, theory of 103–13

d'Acierno, Pellegrino *see* Barnaby, Karin
Dacqué, Edgar 303
Daly, Mary 377
Dante, *La Divina Commedia* 139, 273
dark (and light) 219–20, 252, 255, 315, 319
Darwin, Charles 36
Death of God theology 325–6
  see also God, death of
Dehing, Jef 323*n*
Del Caro, Adrian 8
depth-psychology 9
Derrida, Jacques 319
desacralization of society 332
Descartes, René 31, 345, 347, 349
descent, visions and myths of 70–1, 112–13, 117, 170, 175–7, 181–3, 198, 216, 218, 278
Detwiler, Bruce 301*n*
Deutsche Glaubensbewegung 303, 310*n*
Devil 95, 309, 318
Diederichs, Eugen, Verlag 304*n*
Dilthey, Wilhelm 12
'Ding an sich' 33, 36–8, 40, 54, 72*n*, 112*n*, 189, 346, 347
Dionysian Self 17
Dionysos 6, 8, 9, 12, 13, 15, 17–20, 24, 33, 39, 42, 46, 47, 49–51, 54–5, 60–8, 109, 125, 131, 229
  and Ariadne 201, 295
  as both victim and murderer 174–5
  and Christ 98, 101, 256, 335, 340
  cult 97, 253, 283
  Dionysian societies 371
  Dionysos–Zagreus (dismembered) 111, 120, 122, 181, 215, 280, 282, 319, 340, 354
    see also enantiodromia
  identified by Jung with himself 270
  identified with Hermes/Mercurius 226*n*
  and Jung's breakdown 68
  Jung's solution to problem of 80–2
  mysteries of 212–13, 216–22, 256–7, 261, 341, 376
  Nietzsche's description of 110–11
  as phallic god 51, 91, 96–103, 291, 377
  as psychological type 17
  return of 294–7
  and Romantic literature 94, 369–72
  symbolic significance 19
  and theory of art 156–86
  and water 199*n*
  see also Apollo–Dionysos polarity; Wotan–Dionysos archetype
divinity 257–8
Dixon, Patricia Eileen 13
dogma 325
Double, the 276
drama, Greek 255
dreams 15, 50–1, 56, 68, 97, 107–8, 238*n*, 272, 367, 368
  and ecstasy 125, 140
  interpretation in terms of individuation process 212–17, 365
  Jung's seminars on 244–5, 251–4, 254–63
Driesch, Hans 33
dualism 37–8, 42, 90, 162, 168, 174, 181, 327*n*, 362, 371
  of body and soul 349
  see also opposites, theory of
Dumézil, Georges 375
  Mythes et Dieux des Germains 373
Duncan, Isadora 377
DuPrel, Baron Karl 31

eagle and serpent, image of 8, 279–81, 341
earth, image of 218–19, 255, 260, 279
Ecclesiasticus, book of 38
Eckhart, Meister 53, 273

Edda Society 304
Edinger, Edward F. 2, 70
Ego 17, 19, 20, 88, 117, 214, 218, 232*n*, 233, 236, 293, 299, 345, 346, 349, 352–3
Elgon, Mount 77
Éliade, Mircea 211, 332
Eliot, T.S., *The Waste Land* 176
Ellenberger, Henri 10, 195
empathy and abstraction 125
Empedocles 38, 53
enantiodromia 122, 138, 260, 277–9, 286, 300, 301–2, 314, 315, 337, 339
Engadine 77
Enlightenment 53, 54, 190
entelechy 32–3
Entwicklung 12
Epicurus 71
Eranos Conferences, Ascona 17, 73, 151*n*, 211–12, 293–4
  see also Jung, C.G., WORKS, Eranos Lectures
Eranos-Jahrbuch 1934 198
Erda 308
  see also Mother figure
Ermatinger, Emil, *Philosophie der Literaturwissenschaft* 157
Eros
  cult of 182*n*
  and Thanatos 90, 216
Eternal Recurrence 18, 26*n*, 46–7, 77, 206, 234*n*, 292, 296, 301*n*, 337, 338, 339, 341–2, 358, 365
  and denial of purpose 365
  Nietzsche's and Jung's view of 365
'Ethos' 13
Euripides, *Bacchae* 233*n*
Europäische Revue 177
Evans, Richard 44
Evers, Tilman 11, 304
Evil, problem of 39, 42, 53, 63, 272, 328
Existentialism 324
Expressionism 7

Fascism 131, 212, 230, 236, 239, 263, 283, 297, 314, 321, 374
Fechner, Gustav Theodor 31, 189
feminism 319*n*, 375, 377–8
Ferdinand, Archduke 68
Feuerbach, Ludwig, *Das Wesen des Christentums* 326
Fichte, Johann Gottlieb 10, 34, 35, 38*n*
Fierz-David, Hans 75
Fierz-David, Linda 75, 268, 270, 375
finalism 7, 163
First World War 69, 131, 155, 238, 306, 364*n*
Flournoy, Théodore 85*n*, 94, 238*n*, 329*n*
Flüe, Nikolaus von der 289
Foote, Mary 251, 268–9
Fordham, Frieda 2
Förster-Nietzsche, Elisabeth 21, 26*n*, 27, 46, 84–5, 130, 284, 329
  'Die Entstehung von „Also sprach Zarathustra"' 85
  Das Leben Friedrich Nietzsche's 84–5, 272
  Der werdende Nietzsche 311, 312*n*
Foster, John Burt, Jr 18
Foucault, Michel 195
fragmentation 181–2, 184, 261
Francis of Assisi 289
Frank, Manfred 19
Franz, Marie-Louise von 35, 36
Freud, Sigmund 4, 5*n*, 8*n*, 31*n*, 56*n*, 59–68, 80, 107*n*, 110, 138, 238*n*, 254
  art criticism 157–8, 164, 167
  Brown on 377
  and concept of symbol 159
  denial of knowledge of Nietzsche's work 130, 195–6
  and Ego 345
  'Jewish' psychology 130, 304–5
  Jung's final break with 68, 87–93, 109, 117, 124*n*, 184, 187, 243, 290, 297
  and Lou Andreas-Salomé 24–6
  relationship with Nietzsche 9, 10, 193–8
  and 'shadow side' 120–1
  WORKS
    Diagnostic Association Studies 59
    'Der Dichter und das Phantasieren' 107–8, 356
    'Das Ich und das Es' 364*n*
    'Eine Kindheitserinnerung des Leonardo da Vinci' 364*n*
    'Selbstdarstellung' 195
    Das Unbehagen in der Kultur 91, 196, 216
    'Zeitgemäßes über Krieg und Tod' 364*n*
    'Zur Geschichte der psychoanalytischen Bewegung' 195
  see also Jung, C.G., letters to Freud; relationship with Freud
Frey-Rohn, Liliane 4
  Jenseits der Werte seiner Zeit: Nietzsche im Spiegel seiner Werte 270
Fries, Jakob Friedrich, *Neue Kritik der Vernunft* 188
Frizen, Werner 301*n*
Fröbe-Kapteyn, Olga 211
Frobenius, Leo 98
  Das Zeitalter des Sonnengottes 70
frog, symbol of 255–6
Fromm, Erich 48
Frye, Northrop 2

Gadamer, Hans-Georg 275*n*
Gast, Peter 355*n*
Gawain and the Green Knight 14*n*
Gedo, John 67–8
'Geist' (spirit) 16, 188, 197–8, 198–204, 260, 279, 287, 290, 292, 294, 333, 336, 345, 366
George, Stefan 11, 310, 374
Germany 269, 284, 287–8
  'Germanic soul' 8, 169
  Jung's theories on 315–22, 331–2
  philosophical tradition 272–4
  political events preceding Second World War 214, 306–7, 308
  see also Idealism; Romantic movement
Gesellschaft für freie Philosophie 219*n*
Gide, André 374
Girard, René, *Critiques dans un souterrain* 276
Glover, Edward 4
Gnosticism 11, 42, 53, 66, 72–3, 116–17, 140, 182, 199, 279, 324, 355, 366
God 85, 95
  castration of 329
  death of (proclaimed by Nietzsche) 17, 28, 115, 116–17, 145, 172–3, 235–6, 259–60, 266, 281, 287, 288–94, 311, 314, 321, 324–5, 326, 330–6, 362, 366, 378
  definitions of 221*n*, 336, 362
  'Gottmensch' (God-Man) 304, 336, 356
  Jung's scatological vision of 51, 56, 272
  as moral problem 346
  as 'Other' 50, 52
  as projection of libidinal energy 291
  rebirth/return of 279, 292–4, 334*n*, 336–42, 352
  Self as replacement for 342–56
Goethe, Johann Wolfgang von 2, 3, 71, 77, 79, 80, 138, 140, 162, 179, 223, 265, 299, 316, 351
  Jung's supposed kinship with 66
  in Rome 253
  WORKS
    Faust 38, 57, 58, 73, 75–6, 80, 116, 139, 161, 169, 172, 178, 182, 201, 230–41, 250, 252, 273, 278, 317–18, 342–3, 372
Mothers scene 65–6, 70–1, 92, 99–101, 111–12, 149–50, 170–1, 183, 240
see also Mother figure
    Die Geheimnisse (projected poem) 194*n*
    Italienische Reise 253
Goetz, Bruno 310
  Das Reich ohne Raum 310*n*
Golden Chain 73
Good and Evil 5, 96, 280, 293, 332
  see also Evil, problem of
Göring, M.H. 373
Göttingen, Convention of Natural Scientists 188
Grail legend 139
Granier, Jean 206
Gravity, Spirit of 241–2
Greece
  ancient culture 24, 97, 108, 110, 128, 136, 143, 146, 150, 252, 255
  war with Turkey (1897) 28
Grimm, Jakob, *Deutsche Mythologie* 373
Grimm, Jakob and Wilhelm, 'Der Geist im Glas' 226*n*
Gross, Otto 7, 44*n*, 124
Grossman, S. 129*n*
Günderode, Karoline von 370
Guyon, Madame de 330

Haack, Friedrich-Wilhelm 375
Haar, Michel 7
Hades, descent to 70–1
  see also descent, visions and myths of
Hall, Eleanor 375
Hanhart, Prof. Ernst 45*n*, 80
Hannah, Barbara 3
Harding, Esther 244
Harlequin 182, 183–4
Harper's 245
Hartmann, Eduard von 28, 29, 34, 36, 37, 40, 45, 247
  Philosophie des Unbewußten 29, 34, 248
Hauer, Jacob Wilhelm 303, 310
Hauptmann, Gerhart 164
Hegel, Friedrich 5*n*, 11, 34, 45, 53, 79, 132*n*, 153, 162, 325, 336–7
  Das älteste Systemprogramm des deutschen Idealismus [attr.] 357, 358, 369–70
  Phänomenologie 337
Heidegger, Martin 5*n*, 12, 79, 279, 288*n*, 314–15, 334
Heine, Heinrich 316
  Zur Geschichte der Religion und Philosophie in Deutschland 139–40, 372
Helmholtz, Hermann von 35
Henderson, Dr. Joseph 269, 376
Henrichs, Albert 18
Heracles (Hercules) 229–30
Heraclitus 53, 122, 198, 208*n*, 301, 375–6
hermeneutics 15
Hermes (Mercurius) 15, 80, 96, 226, 228, 241, 285
Hermes Trismegistus 73
Hermeticism 290
hero-motif 90
Herodotus 61
Higgins, Kathleen 201
Hillebrand, Bruno 2

Hillman, James 6, 19
The Dream and the Underworld 375–6
Hitler, Adolf 129*n*, 269, 284, 307, 308, 315, 316, 317*n*, 373, 375
Mein Kampf 304
Hölderlin, Friedrich 2, 69, 94, 99, 100–1, 178, 179, 332, 334, 357
'Empedokles', 'Achill' and 'Der Mensch' 101
'Patmos' 100–1
Hollingdale, R.J. 206
Homans, Peter 4–5, 93, 331
Homer, *The Odyssey* 176
homosexuality 58
Hörbiger, Hanns 304
Horkheimer, Max, and Adorno, Theodor W., *Dialektik der Aufklärung* 332
Horneffer, Ernst, *Nietzsches Lehre der ewigen Wiederkunft...* 84, 341
Horney, Karen 376
Howey, Richard Lowell 207–8*n*
Hubbard, Arthur John, *Authentic Dreams of Peter Blobbs and of Certain of his Relatives* 244
Hübner, Kurt 353
Hume, David 39*n*
hunter-god image 311–12
Husserl, Edmund 11
Hypnerotomachia Poliphili (attr. Colonna) 172, 270

I Ching 250
Idealism, German 10, 34, 40, 138, 378, 379
'Identitätsphilosophie' 39
imagery 2, 8, 119–20, 160, 203, 218–19, 220, 223–03?, 255, 260, 278, 279, 279–81, 300, 301, 327*n*, 335–6, 341, 345, 367–9
alchemical 223–4
incest theories, incest taboo 61, 62*n*, 65, 67, 87, 89, 91–3, 103, 104, 109
India, mysticism of 250–1, 297
individuation process (*Individuationsprozeß*) 8, 11, 111, 140–1, 212, 214, 225, 257, 273, 292–3, 296, 341, 344, 345, 348, 351
and individuality 257–8, 344
as self-realization 344
inferiority, types of 124
inflation, psychic 232–3, 256, 269, 293
Innamorati, Marco 7
instinct(s) 36, 42, 198, 216, 299, 302–3
alienation from 217–19
and reason 222
Institute of Medical Psychology 305
Insulis, Alanus de 345*n*
integration 6, 303, 354, 366
see also Unconscious, integration into individual psyche
internalization of man 129
International Psychoanalytic Association 68
Internationale Orden für Ethik und Kultur 62
introversion 73, 74, 93–4, 98, 100, 102–3, 115, 122, 365
introverted and extraverted types 124–5, 138, 140–1, 143, 152, 154, 158, 160, 162, 163, 168
intuition 78, 79, 142, 152–3, 341*n*
and sensation 152, 249
Isis 288

Jacobi, Jolande 2
Jaeger, Manuela 269
Jaffé, Aniela 43, 48, 66*n*, 129, 211*n*, 270, 307
Jahrbuch für psychoanalytische und psychopathologische Forschungen 92
James, William 124–5
Janaway, Christopher 346, 352
Jarrett, James 5–6
Jaspers, Karl 5*n*, 12, 19, 288*n*
Jena, University of 21
Jesus Christ *see* Christ; Christianity
Jews 130–1, 286*n*, 304–5, 307
see also anti-Semitism
Joyce, James 156
Ulysses 177–80
Joyce, Lucia 177
Jung, C.G.
alleged anti-Semitism 129*n*, 130–1, 303–7
annotations to Nietzsche's *Werke* 16, 47, 96–7, 110, 119, 129, 190–1, 192, 202, 204, 209, 222, 248, 271, 278, 294, 295–6, 300*n*, 306, 325, 326, 328, 329, 338, 349–51, 365
at Basle Gymnasium 52–5
at Basle University 55–9
biographical connections with Nietzsche 21–7
'Black Book' ('Schwarzes Buch') 115–16
confrontation with Unconscious 68–74, 79, 115, 183–4, 238, 249
correspondence *see* letters
and death of father 272
dreams and visions, early 15, 50–2, 56, 68, 155, 272, 309, 312, 368
dual personality, belief in 57–8
early feelings about Nietzsche 271–2
'Excerptbände' 223
feminist critiques of 319*n*
final break with Freud *see* Freud, Sigmund
flaws in thinking on Nietzsche 282
followers 375–8
influences on and by 372–5
interest in Nietzsche, previous research on 2–16
interviews 43–4, 317*n*

and Kant 28–41
see also Kant, Immanuel
on laughter of Nietzsche 78
letters 14*n*, 43, 44–7, 76, 78–9, 80–1, 84, 236*n*, 237–8, 240, 253*n*, 262–3, 267, 308–9, 321–2
to Freud 44–5, 49, 59–68, 81, 87–8, 96, 97*n*, 196, 254, 359, 364*n*
library 22–3, 26, 34, 36*n*, 84, 213*n*, 280, 281*n*, 310*n*, 348, 371, 372
mental breakdown 17, 68–74, 79, 115, 249
personal character 245
psychiatric practice 2, 49
reactionary tendencies 242, 321
see also alleged anti-Semitism
'Red Book' ('Rotes Buch') 72*n*, 115–16
relationship with Freud 4, 5*n*, 41, 48, 59–68, 72, 74, 104, 107*n*, 123, 124, 193–8, 209, 272*n*, 304–5, 317*n*, 329, 379
see also Freud, Sigmund
'secret' in early life 56
self-knowledge, failure in 321
SEMINARS 17, 43, 168
on Analytical Psychology 244, 246–51, 343
Berlin (1933) 3, 14
on children's dreams 244
Cornwall 245
on Dream Analysis 251–4, 268
'Human Relationships in Relation to the Process of Individuation' 244
on Kundalini Yoga 268
Modern Psychology 263–4
on Nietzsche 266–87
see also WORKS, *Nietzsche's „Zarathustra": Notes of the Seminar given in 1934–1939*
Visions Seminar 244, 245, 254–63, 264, 268, 288, 334
similarities and differences between Nietzsche and 365–9
transposition of First and Second World Wars 239–40
travel round world 77
WORKS
Aion 201–2, 258, 324, 327, 329
'Analytische Psychologie und Weltanschauung' 193
Antwort auf Hiob 117, 258, 324, 341, 355
'Approaching the Unconscious' 83
Aufsätze zur Zeitgeschichte 305, 307, 323
Die Beziehungen zwischen dem Ich und dem Unbewußtem 335, 344
'Diagnosing the Dictators' 317*n*
Eranos Lectures 211–42, 272–3
'Die Erlösungsvorstellungen in der Alchemie' 212, 224–40, 318
'Die psychologischen Aspekte des Mutterarchetypus' 191, 276, 360
'Theoretische Überlegungen zum Wesen des Psychischen' 336
'Traumsymbole des Individuationsprozesses' 212–22
'Über die Archetypen des kollektiven Unbewußten' 303
'Die verschiedenen Aspekte der Wiedergeburt' 293–4, 296, 337
'Versuch einer psychologischen Deutung des Trinitätsdogmas' 335–6
'Das Wandlungssymbol in der Messe' 345*n*, 353
'Zur Empirie des Individuationsprozesses' 212, 227–8
Erinnerungen, Träume, Gedanken 14*n*, 23, 28, 43, 47, 48–50, 60, 66*n*, 69–70, 71–2, 81, 117, 192, 240, 241, 248, 271, 309, 346, 347–8, 355, 360–1, 365
'Der Gegensatz Freud und Jung' 187
'Gegenwart und Zukunft' 352
'Der Geist Mercurius' 226*n*
'Geist und Leben' 198
Gesammelte Werke 14, 46, 48, 49
'Der Kampf mit dem Schatten' 129, 315–16, 323
Kinder-Seminare 245
'Kryptomnesie' 83, 86, 161, 162
'Die Lebenswende' 298, 301, 341
Mysterium Coniunctionis 39, 334, 341, 354
'Nach der Katastrophe' 82, 178*n*, 239, 240, 285, 307, 315–16, 320–1, 331–2
'Neue Bahnen der Psychology' 106, 113–15, 118, 302
Nietzsche's "Zarathustra": Notes of the Seminar given in 1934–1939 16, 17, 18, 44, 49, 55, 59, 74, 83, 118, 121, 154, 156, 162, 163, 167, 183*n*, 186, 196, 209, 212, 235–6, 242, 244, 247, 258, 264, 303, 306, 374, 376
and Anima 250, 319
and archetypes 181
commentators on 3, 5, 10, 13
on Eternal Recurrence, Rebirth and Dionysos 339–42
and Goethe's *Faust* 183*n*
on Nostradamus 308
and Old Wise Man 169
on rise of Fascism 236, 239, 263, 323
on Self 180, 261, 345, 347
on structure 255–6

On the Psychology and Pathology of So-called Occult Phenomena (doctoral dissertation) 83–7
'Paracelsus als geistige Erscheinung' 318
'Picasso' 177, 181–4
Die Psychologie der unbewußten Prozesse 115, 118, 120, 122–3, 129, 134, 149, 258, 302
Psychologie und Alchemie 212, 224
'Psychologie und Dichtung' 157, 167–75, 177, 181, 199, 250
'Psychologie und Religion' (Terry Lectures, Yale University) 312, 323*n*, 334, 339, 344, 367
'Psychologische Determinanten des menschlichen Verhaltens' 302
Psychologische Typen 12, 74–5, 120, 123, 124–55, 156–7, 159, 160, 163, 166, 167, 170–5, 184, 215, 220, 221, 225, 246, 249, 252, 257, 272, 305, 343, 372
'Randbemerkungen zu Wittels „Die sexuelle Not"' 251
'The Reappearance of the Dionysian' 260*n*
'Seele und Erde' ('Die Erdbedingtheit der Pysche') 219*n*, 308*n*
Seelenprobleme der Gegenwart 298
VII Sermones ad mortuos 14*n*, 39, 72–3, 115–18, 355
'Sigmund Freud: Ein Nachruf' 195–8
'Sigmund Freud als kulturhistorische Erscheinung' 193–4
'La Structure de l'inconscient' 343
Symbole der Wandlung 367–8
'Symbolik' 88
Tavistock Lectures 129, 305–7
'Psychology and National Problems' 307
'Theoretische Überlegungen zum Wesen des Psychischen' 32–3
Die transzendente Funktion 118, 120, 145
Über das Unbewußte 124, 128–9, 130, 133, 174, 239, 304, 306
'Über den Gegensatz Freud und Jung' 367
'Über die Archetypen des kollektiven Unbewußten' 198, 202, 208–9, 359
Über die Beziehungen der analytischen Psychologie zum dichterischen Kunstwerk 156–67, 181
'Über die Energetik der Seele' 32–3, 159
Über die Psychologie der Dementia praecox 59
Über die Psychologie des Unbewußten 113, 302
'"Ulysses": Ein Monolog' 177–80
Das Unbewußte im normalen und kranken Seelenleben 302
'Versuch einer psychologischen Deutung des Trinitätsdogmas' 346*n*
'Von den Freuden und Leidenschaften' 345
Wandlungen und Symbole der Libido 60, 67, 68, 88, 92, 93–4, 118, 124*n*, 129, 196, 212, 254, 255, 256, 258, 308*n*, 356, 359, 367, 371, 379
and *Faust* 317, 318
and *Die Geburt der Tragödie* 109–15, 123
and hero motif 90
on libido 65, 93–4, 176, 281, 291, 364
on phallic symbolism 51, 96, 372
as self-analysis 246
and solar myth 70, 300, 301
'Wotan' 49, 82, 200, 285, 307–8, 315, 323, 372–5
The Zofingia Lectures 17, 27–42, 55, 188, 323, 325
'The Border Zones of Exact Science' 28, 30
'Inaugural Address Upon Assuming the Chairmanship of the Zofingia Club' 28–9
'Some Thoughts on Psychology' 28, 30
'Thoughts on the Interpretation of Christianity with Reference to the Theory of Albrecht Ritschl' 29, 40–2, 111
'Thoughts on the Nature and Value of Speculative Inquiry' 29, 33–9
'Zur Frage der Psychologischen Typen' 124–6
'Zur gegenwärtigen Lage der Psychotherapie' 304
'Zur Psychologie der Schelmenfigure' 354
Jung, Emilie (née Preiswerk) 21
Jung, Emma 268
Jung, Johann Paul Achilles 21–2, 28, 238*n*, 248, 272, 325
Jünger, Ernst 316
Auf den Marmorklippen 320

Kant, Immanuel 1*n*, 11, 28–41, 45, 53, 54, 55, 72*n*, 117, 134, 151*n*, 187–9, 191, 210, 246, 295, 336, 341*n*, 353*n*, 360, 368, 378
doctrine of categories 34–5, 191*n*, 361
WORKS
Allgemeine Naturgeschichte und Theorie des Himmels 29, 38
Kritik der reinen Vernunft 29, 33, 35, 106–7, 141, 191
Kritik der Urteilskraft (Third Critique) 36*n*, 37
Träume eines Geistersehers, erläutert durch Träume der Metaphysik 28, 30, 31
Vorlesungen über Psychologie 28
see also 'Ding an sich'
katabasis 66–7, 98

Kaufmann, Walter 7, 8, 41, 296, 348*n*
Discovering the Mind 8
Kerényi, Károly 18, 211, 376
Kerner, Justinus, *Blätter aus Prevorst* 10, 21, 83–4, 86
Kerr, John 93, 113–15*n*
Keyserling, Hermann Graf 44*n*, 45, 76, 78, 219*n*, 237–8
Das Spektrum Europas 78
King, Richard 377
Kirchhoff, Jochen 375
Kirsch, Hildegard 267, 268
Kirsch, Dr. Thomas 267
Klages, Ludwig 12, 291, 302*n*, 303, 310
Der Geist als Widersacher der Seele 197*n*
'Mensch und Erde' 219*n*
Knabenhans, Herr 244
Knapp, Alfred 62, 359
Knickerbocker, H.R. 317*n*
Knight, Richard Payne, *A Discourse on the Worship of Priapus* 61, 97*n*, 359
Kölnische Zeitung 187
Köppel, Emily 268
Kranefeldt, W. M., *Die Psychoanalyse: Psychoanalytische Psychologie*, Jung's preface to 190, 193
Künzli, Arnold 45*n*, 79
Kwakiutl Indians 371

Lacan, Jacques 251, 378
Laiblin, Wilhelm 308
Lampert, Laurence 18, 294–5, 338–9, 349
Lange, Friedrich Albert 32*n*, 189, 190
language, Jung's view of 165, 359–60
Lao-tse, *Tao Te Ching* 250
Lasky, Melvin 309
Lawrence, D.H., ' A Letter from Germany' 372
Lebensphilosophie 11
Lehmann, Herbert 59–60
Leibniz/Geulincz problem 30*n*
Leonardo da Vinci 364*n*
Lévy-Bruhl, Lucien 257
libido 12, 17, 20, 62*n*, 88–113, 125
and Creatura 117
descent and ascent 150, 170
genetic theory of 94
as psychic energy 81, 247–8, 352, 364
sexual interpretation of 61, 65, 92–3, 109, 196, 329
and spirit 290–1
transformation of 94–5, 207, 352
Liebmann, Otto, *Kant und die Epigonen* 34
life force 32
lion motif 119–20
Long, Dr. Constance 244
Lotze, Rudolf Hermann, *Medizinische Psychologie* and *System der Philosophie* 189
Löwith, Karl 18, 211, 274–5, 276, 288*n*, 301*n*, 337, 339
ludic drive *see Spieltrieb*
Lull, Raymond 138
Luther, Martin 116, 318*n*

McCormick, Edith Rockefeller 243
McDougall, William 9
McGuire, William 245, 267–8
madman, Nietzsche's parable of 324, 326
Mähly, Jacob 280
Mallarmé, Stéphane 176
Malraux, André 374
Man and his Symbols 83
Man, Paul de 16
mandala 116, 221, 273, 355
Manichaeism 39
Mann, Thomas 318*n*
Doktor Faustus 374
Joseph und seine Brüder 176
Tod in Venedig 176
Marcuse, Herbert 137
Eros and Civilisation 376
Martin, P.W. 2
Marx, Karl 5*n*
masochism 376
materialism 30, 31, 42, 197, 290
and spiritualism 187–9
'Materialismusstreit' 188
Maurras, Charles 219*n*
Mauss, Marcel 373
Maya 125, 144, 146, 172
Mayer, Robert 92
meaning, problem of 197–8, 204–7
Medical Society of Individual Psychology 9
Megill, Allan 288*n*
Mellon, Mary 269
Mephistopheles 237, 318, 318*n*
Mercury *see* Hermes (Mercurius)
Messiah 230
metaphor 2, 104
organic 160
metaphysics 30, 40*n*, 41, 42, 107, 117, 355, 368
Meysenbug, Malwida von 271
mid-life crisis 299
Miller, Miss Frank 94, 201, 212, 246, 254
Mithras, Mithraism 88, 89–90, 105, 110*n*, 114, 257, 258, 282*n*, 300
Modernism 18, 156, 175–7, 178–9, 277
Modernity 222, 241, 247, 261, 334
Moleschott, Jacob, *Der Kreislauf des Lebens* 188
monism, psychic and volitionary 207, 210, 371
Montaigne, Michel de 71

morality 30–1, 82, 114–15, 133–4
Morenius Romanus 232*n*
Moreno, Antonio 4, 5
Morgan, Christiana 244, 254–8
Mother figure 75*n*, 92, 98–100, 101, 103, 108, 110, 112, 170–1, 183*n*, 191, 201–2, 260, 308, 337
  see also Goethe, Johann Wolfgang von, WORKS, *Faust*, Mothers scene
Munich, Fourth International Psychoanalytic Congress (1913) 26, 124
Murray, Henry A. 254, 261*n*
Muser, Friedel Elisabeth 243
mysterium coniunctionis 221, 231, 363
mysticism 11, 40, 41, 73
myth, mythology 1*n*, 9, 17, 19, 24, 54, 60–2, 87, 111, 123, 229, 279, 356–63, 366, 368–9, 379
  and dogma 325
  Freud's view of 356
  Orphic 176
  Persian 87, 88
  as precondition of religion 362–3
  solar 70, 90, 91
  see also astral myth; descent, visions and myths of; Orpheus myth
'Mythical Thought' 374

Nagy, Marilyn 22, 28, 35, 36
Nairobi 77*n*
naive and sentimental 124, 140, 143, 157, 160–3
Nanavutty, Piloo 45*n*, 267
Narcissus 376
National Socialism 7, 8, 17, 129–31, 167, 175, 178*n*, 240, 242, 262*n*, 263, 279, 286*n*, 287, 298, 303, 307, 308, 314, 316, 321, 372–5, 379
Naturphilosophie 7
Nehamas, Alexander 116, 350
Neo-Kantianism 323
Nerval, Gérard de, *Aurélia* 176
Neue Bahnen 113–15*n*
Neue Schweizer Rundschau 307, 315
Neue Zürcher Zeitung 181, 298
Neumann, Erich 308–9
Neumann, Micha 130
neurotics and schizophrenics 181
'new nobility' 7
Newton, Isaac 31, 38*n*
Nicholls, R. A. 41
Nicolas of Cusa 362
Nietzsche, Friedrich
  on barbarism *see* barbarism
  dream of Wotan 272, 311–12
  exculpated by Jung of proto-Fascism 284
  interest in Jews 130–1
  interest in theology 329–30
  Jung on lack of awareness of 277
  letters 348*n*, 355*n*
  mental breakdown 21, 44, 74, 78–9, 123, 158, 186, 215, 269–70, 275, 282, 285, 318, 320
  practical functioning (chart) 264–5
  as predecessor of Analytical Psychology 192–3
  publications on 26 (Fig. 1), 26, 77
  syphilitic infection 195*n*, 255
  WORKS
    Also sprach Zarathustra 16, 21, 45*n*, 46–7, 57–9, 64–5, 69, 73, 74, 76, 83–7, 94, 102, 109, 116–17, 118–22, 144, 150, 151–4, 158, 161–3, 178, 180, 181, 190, 192, 196, 198, 213–14, 227–30, 239, 248, 300
      and alchemy 77, 212, 224
      and Anima 204
      as archetype 208–10, 249–51, 302–3
      commentators on 3, 7, 8*n*, 9, 10
      and concept of Will 95
      on Death of God 235–6, 326, 333
      Germanic nature of 169
      imagery of 131, 220, 227, 250–1, 335–6, 345
      and Jung's relationship with Freud 67
      and Kerner 83–4
      and masochism 376
      misunderstandings of 343
      and myth 358
      Noontime Vision 339–40
      on Pale Criminal 271, 316–17
      and return of Dionysos 201, 338–42
      and Self 80
      sketches for 313
      style of 172
      and Ugliest Man 145
      'Von den Tugendhaften' 345, 349
      'Von den Verächtern des Leibes' 214, 345
      Vorreden 60, 184
      Zarathustra (as character) 45*n*, 50, 81, 91
      see also Jung, C.G., WORKS, *Nietzsche's "Zarathustra": Notes of the Seminar given in 1934–1939*
    Der Antichrist 325, 329, 338
    'Dionysos gegen den Gekreuzigten' 64
    Dionysos-Dithyramben 102–3, 109, 113, 277, 291, 295, 301*n*
    Ecce Homo 75*n*, 77, 84–5, 161, 178, 274, 283, 313–14, 338, 348, 351, 355, 358, 360, 362
    Empedokles (projected work) 259

Die fröhliche Wissenschaft 137–8, 161–2, 205–6, 222, 273, 299, 326, 348
Die Geburt der Tragödie 12, 24, 60, 71–2, 77, 109, 114, 116, 117, 123, 125, 138, 147, 151, 152, 154–5, 157, 161, 165–6, 166, 170–3, 186, 215, 252, 259, 276, 280, 305, 325, 353, 355, 357–8, 368
and Aesthetism 249, 254
defence of 371
levels of meaning in 379
and Mother figure 92, 100, 108, 170–1, 260
and myth 112–13, 357–8, 359
and union of Dionysos with Apollo 55, 62, 81, 124, 126, 127–8, 134, 144, 147, 256–7, 314, 378
on Wagner 358
Götzen-Dämmerung 96–7, 222, 295, 338, 351
Jenseits von Gut und Böse (*Beyond Good and Evil*) 19, 91, 131, 133–4, 190–1, 192, 199, 214, 222, 326, 327–8, 330, 338
'Klage der Ariadne' 311
'Die Lebensalter' 300*n*
'Lieder des Prinzen Vogelfrei' 161–2, 275
'Mein Leben' 313
Menschliches, Allzumenschliches 29, 71, 78, 107, 108, 109, 126, 179, 202, 214, 222, 251, 255, 300, 315, 326, 328, 339, 340, 348
'An den Mistral' 311
Morgenröte 126, 326
Nachlaß 313, 338, 358–9
'Sils-Maria' 161–2, 275
Über Wahrheit und Lüge im außermoralischen Sinn 360
'Dem unbekannten Gott' 311
Unzeitgemäße Betrachtungen 29, 40, 47, 91
'Richard Wagner in Bayreuth' 358
'Schopenhauer als Erzieher' 40, 53, 347
'Versuch einer Selbstkritik' 151
'Der Wanderer' 137
Werke 7, 47
Der Wille zur Macht 4*n*, 47, 54, 126–7, 206–7, 214, 346, 352
Zur Genealogie der Moral 19, 47, 64, 91, 94, 106, 114, 128, 129, 131, 133, 179, 196, 305, 307, 315, 327, 350–1
Nhilism 5, 15, 18, 197, 206, 241, 337, 338, 365, 366
Nill, Peggy 13, 267
Ninck, Martin 310
Noll, Richard 7
Nominalism and Realism 140
Nostradamus (Michel de Notre-Dame), *Centuries astrologiques* 308
noumenal and phenomenal 72*n*, 117, 353*n*, 368
Novalis (F. von Hardenberg), *Hymnen an die Nacht* 176

objectivity 289
occultism 65, 85, 86
Odin 373
see also Wotan
Odysseus 70, 71
Oedipus 110
complex 93
Oehler, Pastor 84*n*
Oeri, Albert 23, 70, 176
Old Testament 77
Old Wise Man *see* archetypes
Oldfield, Helen 14*n*
one-sidedness 132–3, 166, 169, 175, 248, 256*n*, 286, 328
opposites, theory of 207, 226, 250, 273, 293, 317, 345, 351–2, 362–3, 365, 378
Chinese and Indian conceptions of 250–1
see also coniunctio oppositorum; dualism
Origen 140
Ormuzd 280
Orpheus myth 176, 229–30, 256
Orphic mysteries 61, 376
Osiris 61, 229–30, 285, 288
Ostanes 227
Ostwald, Wilhelm 124
Otto, Rudolf 211
Otto, Walter Friedrich 18, 211
Dionysos: Mythos und Kultus 371
Otto-Peters, Louise 114–15*n*
Overbeck, Franz 224, 270–1
Ovid 233, 234

Paglia, Camille 377
Pale Criminal (as symbol of German nation) 271, 315, 316–18
Pan 259–60, 284–5, 288, 339, 341
death of 334–5
Pannwitz, Rudolf 11
Parkes, Graham 9, 224
Parmenides 39*n*, 208*n*
participation mystique 175, 257–8
Pascal, Blaise 71, 324–5
Paul, St. 120, 138, 326
Perkins, Richard 224
perspectivism (relativism) 154
pessimism 39
Peters, Roderick 296
Pfeffer, Rose 8, 18, 72*n*, 112*n*
Phales 96
phallic gods 15, 50–1, 56, 61, 96, 97, 226*n*, 253, 291, 377–8

phallus
cult of 372
dreams of 15, 50–1, 56, 68, 97, 368
as symbol 94–103, 281
phantasy activity 148–9, 156–7
Philemon and Baucis 233–4, 237–41, 317
Philemon (dream-figure) 238*n*
philosopher's stone 227–8, 228*n*, 232, 241
Picasso, Pablo 156, 177, 181–4
Blue Period 181–2
Pindar 348
Plachte, Dr. Kurt 73
Plato 5*n*, 45, 53, 71, 72*n*, 139–40
Platonic Ideas 247
Pleroma 39, 42, 73, 117, 199, 356
see also Collective Unconscious
Plutarch, *De defectu oraculorum* 259, 324*n*
The Poetic Edda 200, 204, 303–4
'Poiesis' 13
polarity 38, 42
see also Apollo–Dionysos polarity; introverted and extraverted types
Pompeii 375
Pope, Alexander 252
positivism 18
post-Jungians 375–8
Post-Modernism 378
The Power of Myth (television series) 14*n*
Pre-conscious 95
Preiswerk, Hélène (Helly) 85–6, 201, 248
Preiswerk, Samuel 85–6
Preller, Ludwig, *Griechische Mythologie* 280, 370
primal unity 353*n*, 371
primordial experience 170–5, 181–4, 186, 215
Princeton University Press 14*n*
principium individuationis 35, 72*n*, 125, 126, 140–1, 172, 182, 199, 260, 353–4, 361
Logos as 354
Prinzhorn, Hans 19
Progoff, Ira 44
Prometheus 110, 127, 376
Protestantism 289
psyche 22, 32–3, 42, 189, 190, 223*n*
Freud and Jung on nature of 197*n*
Jung's model of 209–10
self-regulating 118–22
see also Anima; soul
psychic energy 81, 352, 364
psychoanalysis 24, 59, 62, 63–4, 66, 72, 87, 190*n*, 193–8, 359, 378
and Analytical Psychology 244, 254, 297, 364
Psychoanalytischer Verein (later *Psychologischer Club*), Zurich 243
psychobiology 190*n*
psychological types 17, 74–5
see also Jung, C.G., WORKS, *Psychologische Typen*
psychologism 188, 189
psychologists, as Jungians 376–7
psychology 187–93
psychological complex 162
'Psychologie ohne Seele' 189
rational and empirical 31–2
in relation to philosophy 187, 192, 264
and religion 199
see also Analytical Psychology
psychophysics 189
Pueblo Indians 77, 80
Puer Aeternus 279, 310*n*
Pythagoras 53

Rank, Otto
Der Künstler: Ansätze zu einer Sexualpsychologie 356
Der Mythus von der Geburt des Helden 98
Rattner, Josef 2
Reading Society of the German Students of Vienna 195
reason, antinomy of 30
Rebirth, archetype of 292, 337, 339–42, 341, 365
see also God, rebirth/return of
redemption 229, 230, 232
reductionism 157–8, 167, 185, 329
Rée, Paul 24
regression 217, 300, 314, 364*n*
Reich, Wilhelm 377
Reichert, Herbert W. and Schlechta, Karl 25, 77
Reichstein, Dr. Tadeus 268, 269–70
relativism 154
religion 4, 15, 17, 28, 42, 46, 63, 64–5, 86, 95, 146, 148–51, 155, 174, 195, 199, 287
evolution of 258–60, 293
Jung's critique of 324–30
modern experience of 297
psychology of 323
see also Christianity; culture and religion, theory of
repression/sublimation 216
ressentiment 8, 115, 194, 235, 305
'Revaluation of All Values' 301, 355
Rieff, Philip 15, 48, 51, 323
Rilke, Rainer Maria 374
Rimbaud, Arthur, *Une Saison en enfer* 176
ring, symbol of 341–2
Ritschl, Albrecht 40–1, 111
Roazen, Paul 2
Roberts, Julian 219*n*, 300, 349

Rohde, Erwin 348*n*
Psyche 371
Rolle, Pierre Nicolas 370–1
romantic and classical 124
Romantic movement 7, 108, 111, 160*n*, 357, 367–9, 378–9
literature, German 18, 94, 138
Rome, ancient and modern 253
root, image of 367–9
Rosegger, Peter, *Die neue Bahn* 114*n*
Rosenberg, Alfred, *Der Mythus des 20. Jahrhunderts* 262*n*, 373
Roth, Robin Alice 201
Rousseau, Jean-Jacques 71, 136, 299
Rudolph, Rev. Arthur W. 13, 45*n*, 80
Runge, Friedlieb Ferdinand 38
Ruysbroek, Jan van 250*n*
Rychlak, Joseph F. 45, 45*n*

Sachsen-Weimar, Carl August Duke of 27
saints 328
Samuels, Andrew 129
Sartre, Jean-Paul 204
satyr 215
Scharschuch, Horst 253*n*
Scheffler, Ludwig von 271
Scheler, Max 12, 291
Schelling, F.W.J. von 10, 29, 34, 36, 38, 39, 95, 113, 140*n*, 325, 337, 357, 360, 371, 378
Philosophie der Offenbarung 96*n*, 369
Die Weltalter 99–100, 357, 369
Schiller, Friedrich 2, 118*n*, 124, 125, 138, 140–50, 153, 161, 162, 174, 220, 221, 306, 332
'An die Freude' 141
and problem of opposites 273
'Der Taucher' 144
Über die ästhetische Erziehung des Menschen... 134–7, 143, 154
Über naive und sentimentale Dichtung 157, 160–1
Schlechta, Paul *see* Reichert, Herbert W. and Schlechta, Karl
Schlegel, Friedrich von
Athenäum 357
Über das Studium der griechischen Poesie 370
Schmitt, Dr. Paul 236*n*, 240
Schmitz, Oskar A.H. 262
Schnädelbach, Herbert 32*n*
Scholem, Gershom 211, 321
Schopenhauer, Artur 1*n*, 3–4, 5*n*, 10, 28, 32, 34, 36, 37, 38*n*, 45, 53–4, 55, 71, 78, 95–6, 99, 113, 125, 126, 138, 144, 150, 151, 153, 205, 247–8, 280, 328, 336, 337, 353*n*, 368, 378
and problem of opposites 273
WORKS
On the Fourfold Root of the Principle of Sufficient Reason 35
Parerga und Paralipomena 28
Über den Willen in der Natur 247
Die Welt als Wille und Vorstellung 28, 29, 39, 126, 247, 347
Schubart, Walter, *Eros und Religion* 371–2
Schuler, Alfred 303, 310, 374
Schutte, Ofelia 7, 207, 337
Schweitzer, Albert 324
Schweizerische Psychiaterversammlung 87
Schweizerland: Monatshefte für Schweizer Art und Kunst 128
Second World War 17, 54, 212, 236, 239–41, 258, 266, 279, 294, 298, 303, 306, 316, 323, 332, 373, 374
The Secret of the Golden Flower 222–3
Selbstüberwindung 8
Self 20, 80, 82, 116, 117, 214, 221, 222, 227*n*, 238*n*, 249, 261, 269, 290, 335, 339
as borderline concept 346
creation of 343, 352–3, 365
discovery of 348, 352–3, 366
integration of 354
as reconciliation of opposites 345
as replacement for God 342–56
self-alienation 299
self-becoming 13
self-therapy 246
Sennen Cove, Cornwall 244
Sergeant, Elizabeth Shepley 245
Serrano, Miguel 321
sexuality 4
conflict within 89
morality of 114–15
self-destructiveness of 88, 90, 98–9
Shadow, concept of 7, 120–1, 130*n*, 145, 220, 273, 278, 315–16, 327
shepherd and snake, vision of 281, 341
Sigg, Martha 269
Silberer, Herbert 224
Silk, M.S. and Stern, J.P. 18
Simmel, Georg 12
Sittler, Margaret 45*n*
Smith, Evans Lansing 175
snake, image of 203, 220, 327*n*
see also eagle and serpent; shepherd and snake
Socrates 5*n*, 256
solar imagery 70, 90, 300, 301
Solon 300*n*
Sombart, Werner, *Die Juden und das Wirtschaftsleben* 304
Sonntagsblatt der Basler Nachrichten 195

soul
  concept of 32–4, 42, 72, 190, 327
  struggle for 188
  see also Anima; psyche
Sphinx 110
Spielrein, Sabina 60, 68, 201
Spieltrieb (ludic drive) 137, 148, 273
Spinoza, Baruch 39*n*, 71, 349
Spir, African 329
spirit *see* 'Geist'
spiritism 4
spiritualism 31
  and materialism 187–9
Spitteler, Karl Friedrich Georg, *Prometheus* 172
Steele, Robert 4
Stephenson, Roger 300*n*
Stern, J.P. *see* Silk, M.S. and Stern, J.P.
Stevens, Anthony 3, 15, 22, 51
Stockholm, fire (1756) 30
Stofftrieb and *Formtrieb* 136–7, 148
Stoicism 114
Storr, Anthony 3–4, 13, 115
Strauss, David Friedrich 40
Strauss, Leo 18
Strauss, Walter 176
Sudan 77
Superman 7, 121, 127, 173, 192, 206, 222, 227, 234, 236, 255, 292–3, 296, 301*n*, 318, 320, 336, 365, 378, 379
  Faust and Zarathustra as 229–6
Surette, Leon 366*n*
Suso, Heinrich 41
Suzuki, Daisetz Teitaro 211
  Die grosse Befreiung: Einführung in den Zen-Buddhismus (foreword by Jung) 342
Swedenborg, Emanuel 30, 31, 138
symbol, symbolism 1*n*, 24, 81, 88, 149–50, 155, 175, 180, 225–6, 290, 327, 329, 365
  and art 156–7, 159, 163
  of dreams 212–17
  see also imagery
symbol-making process 104–5, 156–7
synchronicity 7, 30*n*, 69, 341*n*
synthetic–constructive method 16
systole and diastole 140, 141, 299
Szasz, Thomas 130*n*

Taoism 222–3
Taylor, Seth 27
teleology 33, 36
tender- and tough-mindedness 125
Tertullian 140
Thammuz 61
Thamous 259
Thatcher, David 8–9, 279–80
theology 321, 329
  medieval 273, 289, 297
  modern dilemma of 332
  radical 324–5
  systematic 40–1
thinking, feeling and sensation 140–1
Third Reich 12, 266, 298, 314, 373, 375
  see also National Socialism
Thomas, R. Hinton 27, 42
tight-rope, image of 335
Tillich, Hannah 69*n*
Tillich, Paul 8, 69, 324
Tishtriya, Song of 89
Toller, Ernst, *Der entfesselte Wotan* 372
Tönnies, Ferdinand 7
tragedy 215
tragic, Nietzsche's conception of 18
  see also Nietzsche, Friedrich, WORKS, *Die Geburt der Tragödie*
trans-subjectivity 289
Transcendent Function 149, 159
Transcendental Aesthetic 35
transcendental subjectivity 33, 36–7, 42
Turin 56*n*
typology 124–6

Ugliest Man 118, 145, 220, 255, 278, 326*n*
ugliness and beauty 144–5
Unconscious 10, 17, 34, 37, 48, 65, 81, 86–7, 90, 98, 112, 123, 142*n*, 159, 168, 193, 200, 216, 222, 248, 251, 253, 259, 274, 277–8, 293, 299, 351
  integration into individual psyche 217, 221, 232–3, 261, 273, 290
  Nietzsche's self-identification with 333
  and return of Dionysos 337
  see also Collective Unconscious; Jung, C.G., confrontation with Unconscious
underworld, descent to *see* descent, myths and visions of
Universal Spirit 162
unus mundus 39, 42
Upanishads 250*n*
'Ur-Eine' 72*n*
Urmutter 260, 308*n*
  see also Mother figure
uroboros 342*n*
'Urvision', 'Urerlebnis' *see* primordial experience

value judgments 41, 122–3
Verein für analytische Psychologie (later *Psychologischer Club*), Zurich 243
Vienna Psychoanalytic Society 195, 196
Vischer, Friedrich Theodor, *Auch Einer* 56*n*
vitalism 31, 32, 323

Vogel, Martin 18–19, 100*n*, 357
Völuspâ 200, 204, 303–4

Wagner, Cosima 201, 259, 270
Wagner, Richard 54, 55, 60, 80, 108, 109, 120, 138–9, 150, 182, 238–9, 312, 316, 358, 373
  Parsifal 135, 136, 138–9, 150, 320
  Ring cycle 138, 358
  Tristan 138–9
water, world of 198–90
  see also Collective Unconscious
Weber, Max 375
  'Wissenschaft als Beruf' 330–1
Wehr, Gerhard 12, 70
Weimar, Third International Psychoanalytic Congress (1911) 26
Weizsäcker, Dr. A. 317*n*
Weltgrund 248
Wheelwright, Dr. Joseph 268, 269
Wheelwright, Jane 268, 269
wholeness 6
Whyte, Lancelot 10
Wilamowitz-Moellendorf, Ulrich von 371
Wilhelm I, Kaiser 54, 55
Wilhelm, Richard 222
Will (to Life or Power) 32, 37, 54, 81, 89, 95–6, 99, 106, 111, 151, 206–7, 208*n*, 210, 218, 247–8, 273, 316, 327, 328, 329*n*, 338, 353, 364, 365, 366–7
Wilson, Colin 3
Winckelmann, Johann Joachim, *Geschichte der Kunst des Altertums* 370
Winnicott, Donald 48
withdrawal of projections 331
Wolff, Toni 268
women, and Jungian psychology 319, 375, 377–8
  see also Anima; Mother figure
Woodman, Ross 5
World Ice Theory 304
Worringer, Wilhelm 125
Wotan 17, 46, 54, 55, 80, 114, 121, 226*n*, 263, 279, 294, 307–15, 372–5
  Jung's dream of 309, 312
  Nietzsche's dream of 272
  related to other deities 285, 308
  as wind god 311–12, 373–4
  Wotan/Dionysos archetype 17, 161, 167, 175, 200, 210, 238, 240, 241, 261–2, 283–7, 303, 311–13, 320, 379
Wundt, Wilhelm 32*n*, 38, 40, 85*n*, 189–90
Wyly, James 184

Yale University 312
yin and yang 250, 319

Zentralblatt für Psychotherapie und ihre Grenzgebiete 304
Zofingiaverein 27
Zöllner, Johann 31
Zoroastrianism 280
Zosimos of Panoplis 227
Zumstein-Preiswerk, Stefanie 85–6
Zuni Indians 371
Zurich
  Eidgenössische Technische Hochschule 263
  Kunsthaus 177
  Lake 70
  Psychologischer Club 194–5, 243–5, 268
  University 68, 83

Bei Fragen zur Produktsicherheit wenden Sie sich bitte an:
If you have any questions regarding product safety,
please contact:

Walter de Gruyter GmbH
Genthiner Straße 13
10785 Berlin
productsafety@degruyterbrill.com